advanced history core texts

THE EARLY TUDORS

ENGLAND 1485–1558

David Rogerson
Samantha Ellsmore
David Hudson

Series Editor: Ian Dawson

Hodder Murray

A MEMBER OF THE HODDER HEADLINE GROUP

In the same series

The Reign of Elizabeth: England 1558–1603	Barbara Mervyn	ISBN 0 7195 7486 2
Britain 1790–1851	Charlotte Evers and Dave Welbourne	ISBN 0 7195 7482 X
Communist Russia under Lenin and Stalin	Terry Fiehn and Chris Corin	ISBN 0 7195 7488 9
Fascist Italy	John Hite and Chris Hinton	ISBN 0 7195 7341 6
Weimar and Nazi Germany	John Hite with Chris Hinton	ISBN 0 7195 7343 2

The Schools History Project

The Project was set up in 1972, with the aim of improving the study of history for students aged 13–16. This involved a reconsideration of the ways in which history contributes to the educational needs of young people. The Project devised new objectives, new criteria for planning and developing courses, and the materials to support them. New examinations, requiring new methods of assessment, also had to be developed. These have continued to be popular. The advent of GCSE in 1987 led to the expansion of Project approaches into other syllabuses.

The Schools History Project has been based at Trinity and All Saints College, Leeds, since 1978, from where it supports teachers through a biennial Bulletin, regular INSET, an annual conference and a website (www.tasc.ac.uk/shp).

Since the National Curriculum was drawn up in 1991, the Project has continued to expand its publications, bringing its ideas to courses for Key Stage 3 as well as a range of GCSE and A level specifications.

To
Kathryn, Rowan, Jem,
John, Florence, Jonathan, Shannon,
Polly, Harry, Maeve, Michael,
and
David Wybron

First published in 2001
by John Murray (Publishers) Ltd a member of the Hodder Headline Group
338 Euston Road
London NW1 3BH

Reprinted 2003, 2004, 2005, 2006, 2007

Layouts by Janet McCallum
Artwork by Oxford Illustrators Ltd
Typeset in 10/12pt Berthold Walbaum by Wearset Ltd, Boldon, Tyne and Wear
Printed and bound in Great Britain by Martins the Printers, Berwick-upon-Tweed

A catalogue entry for this title is available from the British Library

ISBN-10: 0 7195 7484 6
ISBN-13: 978 0 7195 7484 9

Contents

Photo credits

COVER *main picture* Mary Evans; *inset* The Royal Collection © 2001, Her Majesty Queen Elizabeth II; **p.9** *t* V&A Picture Library; **p.9***b* **& 71** By courtesy of the National Portrait Gallery, London; **p.19** By permission of the Master and Fellows of St John's College, Cambridge; **p.23** By courtesy of the National Portrait Gallery, London; **p.24** By courtesy of the National Portrait Gallery, London; **p.26** Christies Images/Bridgeman Art Library, London; **p.54** The Royal Collection © 2001, Her Majesty Queen Elizabeth II; **p.70** Public Record Office; **p.73 & p.84** Copyright: Dean and Chapter of Westminster; **p.85** By courtesy of the National Portrait Gallery, London; **p.87** The Royal Collection © 2001, Her Majesty Queen Elizabeth II; **p.88** English Heritage/ Jonathan Bailey; **p.89** © Ashmolean Museum, Oxford; **p.91** By courtesy of the College of Arms, from the Westminster Tournament Roll; **p.93** *t& b* By courtesy of the National Portrait Gallery, London; **p.94** Fotomas Index; **pp.99–110** By courtesy of the National Portrait Gallery, London; **p.119** Mary Evans Picture Library; **p.120** English Heritage; **p.130** By courtesy of the National Portrait Gallery, London; **pp.132–159** The Royal Collection © 2001, Her Majesty Queen Elizabeth II; **p.160** Public Record Office (E30 1110); **p.163** © National Gallery, London; **p.168** Private Collection/Bridgeman Art Library, London; **p.169** *t* By courtesy of the National Portrait Gallery, London, *bl* photo RMN/Hervé Lewandowski, *br* AKG Berlin/Erich Lessing; **p.170** By courtesy of the National Portrait Gallery, London; **p.183** By courtesy of the Master and Fellows of Trinity College, Cambridge; **pp.184–185** © The British Museum; **p.187** By courtesy of the National Portrait Gallery, London; **p.189** The Royal Collection © 2001, Her Majesty Queen Elizabeth II; **p.196 & p.219** *t* Reproduced by permission of the Marquess of Bath, Longleat house, Warminster, Wiltshire, Great Britain (photo: Photographic Survey, Courtauld Institute of Art); **p.197 & p.219** *b* Reproduced by kind permission of Viscount De L'Isle, from his private collection; **p.204** The British Library (Cotton MS Nero C. X., f.113); **p.211** Fotomas Index; **pp.216–7** By courtesy of the National Portrait Gallery, London; **p.218** By courtesy of the National Portrait Gallery, London; **p.220** By permission of the Church Commissioners (photo: Photographic Survey, Courtauld Institute of Art); **p.221** *t & b* By courtesy of the National Portrait Gallery, London; **p.245** By courtesy of the National Portrait Gallery, London; **p.248** Museo del Prado, Madrid; **p.249** photo RMN/J.G. Berizzi; **p.258** Victoria & Albert Museum, London/ Bridgeman Art Library, London; **p.260 & p.270** Fotomas Index; **p.271** By courtesy of the National Portrait Gallery, London; **p.283** By kind permission of the Marquess of Tavistock and the Trustees of the Bedford Estate; **p.285** By courtesy of the National Portrait Gallery, London; **p.293** Institut Amatller d'Art Hispànic; **pp.294-5** Mansell/Timepix/Rex Features; **pp.306–319** Fotomas Index.

t = top, *b* = bottom, *l* = left, *r* = right, *c* = centre.

*Every effort has been made to contact copyright holders, and the publishers apologise for any omissions which they will be pleased to rectify at the earliest opportunity.

Using this book

This is an in-depth study of the Early Tudors: Henry VII, Henry VIII, Edward VI and Mary I. It contains everything you need for examination success and more. It provides all the content you would expect, as well as many features to help both independent and class-based learners. So, before you wade in, make sure you understand the purpose of each of the features.

Focus route

On every topic throughout the book, this feature guides you to produce the written material needed for understanding what you read and, later, for revising the topic (e.g. pages 86, 264). These focus routes are particularly useful for you if you are an independent learner working through this material on your own, but they can also be used for class-based learning.

Activities

The activities offer a range of exercises to enhance your understanding of what you read and to prepare you for examinations. They vary in style and purpose. There are:

- a variety of essays, both AS exam-style structured essays (e.g. page 24) and more discursive A level essays (e.g. page 84)
- source investigations (e.g. page 111)
- examination of historical interpretations, which is central to A level history (e.g. pages 123–26)
- decision-making and role play exercises which help you to see events from the viewpoint of people at the time (e.g. pages 40–45, 265)
- exercises to develop Key Skills such as communication (e.g. page 22).

These activities help you to analyse and understand what you are reading. They address the content through the key questions that the examiner will expect you to have investigated.

Overviews, summaries and key points

In such a large book on such a massive topic, you need to keep referring to the big picture. Each section and chapter begin with an overview and each chapter ends with a review that includes a key-points summary of the most important content of the chapter.

Learning trouble spots

Experience shows that time and again some topics cause confusion for students. This feature identifies such topics and helps students to avoid common misunderstandings (e.g. page 105). In particular, this feature addresses some of the general problems encountered when studying history, such as assessing sources (e.g. page 10); planning essays (e.g. page 114) and assessing historians' views (e.g. page 141).

Charts

The charts are our attempts to summarise important information in note, map or diagrammatic form (e.g. pages 230–31). There are also several grid charts that present a lot of information in a structured way (e.g. pages 61–62). However, everyone learns differently and the best charts are the ones you draw yourself! Drawing your own charts in your own way to summarise important content can really help understanding (e.g. page 144) as can completing assessment grids (e.g. page 130).

Glossary boxes

We have tried to write in an accessible way but occasionally we have used general historical terms as well as some that are specific to the study of the Early Tudors. Some of these may be new to you. These words are explained in glossary boxes in the margin. The first time a glossary word appears in the text it is in SMALL CAPITALS like this.

Talking points

These are asides from the normal pattern of written exercises. They are discussion questions that invite you to be more reflective and to consider the relevance of this history to your own life. They might ask you to voice your personal judgement (e.g. pages 129, 276); to make links between the past and present (e.g. page 313); or to highlight aspects of the process of studying history (e.g. page 64).

The Early Tudors is among the most popular AS and A2 history topics. Throughout this book you will be problem solving, working with others, and trying to improve your own performance as you engage with deep and complex historical issues. Our hope is that by using this book you will become actively involved in your study of history and that you will see history as a challenging set of skills and ideas to be mastered, rather than as an inert body of factual material to be learned.

Introduction

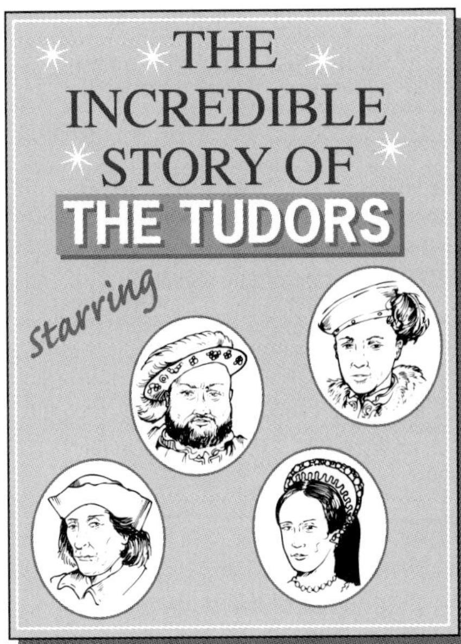

Making a movie

If you were to start writing a script for the latest blockbuster movie, what are the main elements that such a film would have to include? Perhaps you would have:

1. personal tragedy as a family is torn apart
2. conflict between lovers
3. mesmerising, riveting characters
4. violence and destruction
5. improbable twists of fate
6. incredible, against-the-odds stories
7. acts of cruelty
8. a titanic clash of one man's principle versus power
9. moments of amazing drama and tension
10. ridiculous but nearly successful impersonations
11. a family held together, but ripped apart by the one thing they share.

Well, those ideas would probably give you a reasonable chance of a great script! In fact, these are all examples of what you will uncover as you study the fascinating dynasty of the Tudors.

See if you can match the following events to the dramatic situations listed above.

a Henry VII returning to England and winning the battle of Bosworth
b the burning of heretics in the reign of 'Bloody' Mary
c Lambert Simnel impersonating the Earl of Warwick and forcing battle with Henry VII
d Sir Thomas More's crisis of conscience
e the dissolution of every monastery in England
f the tempestuous relationship of Henry VIII and Anne Boleyn
g Edward VI's sudden illness as the boy-king was about to begin ruling in his own right
h the Tudor dynasty
i the unpredictable and irresistible personality of Henry VIII
j Mary never again seeing her mother, Catherine of Aragon, after Henry banished her
k the feared invasion by the two mightiest powers in Europe.

■ **Learning trouble spot**

The Tudors

When we refer to 'the Tudors' in this book, we are referring only to the early Tudors – Henry VII, Henry VIII, Edward VII and Mary I. Elizabeth I is dealt with in a separate book because so much happened in her reign.

What to look for in this book

All essays and books should have an analytical line or an argument that holds them together. The following are the 'golden threads' around which this book is constructed. You should have formed some answers to these questions by the time you have finished this book.

All reigns	How secure and stable was the dynasty?	How important was England in Europe?	What image did contemporaries and historians have of the monarch?
Henry VII	Who threatened his reign and how did he deal with the threats?	Was foreign policy useful for Henry?	How have views of Henry changed?
Henry VIII	Was Henry ever under serious threat?	Was Henry as important in Europe as he wanted to be?	How has history viewed Henry?
Edward VI	Could a minor be secure?	Was England an irrelevance to the rest of Europe?	Was he controlled by others?
Mary I	Why and how were the Tudors still under threat?	Was England a pawn under Spanish control?	Did everything take second place to religion?
Overall question: Were the Tudors a success?			

Were the Tudors a success? This is the central question of the book and you should keep it in mind as you read and work through the activities. It generates lots of sub-questions. What do we mean by success? How do we judge success? What should we compare it against? What evidence should we use to decide? We will return to this question in 'The Verdict' chapters at the end of each section.

The process of writing history

You will almost certainly have studied the Tudors already, so you will have some knowledge about them. Prepare to reject some of this knowledge very quickly! The deeper you go into history, the more you discover that what you learned before was wrong. This is not because your teachers were lying; it is because history has to be simplified and summarised, and when you do this, you obviously lose some of the complexity of the truth.

Here is an interview with Dr Steven Gunn, one of the leading historians on the Tudors. It is intended to shed light on the work of professional historians, on which your study of history is based.

Q: Why are you interested in the Tudors?
A: I have been fascinated by the Tudors since I studied them for history A level. I enjoyed other periods I studied at university, from the Anglo-Saxons to the twentieth century, but I kept coming back to the Tudors and their continental contemporaries. As a researcher, I like the fact that enough documents survive from Tudor England that one can keep finding new things, but not so many that one can't have a good sense of the archival record across a fairly broad chronological and thematic range. As a teacher, I like the fact that students are interested in the Tudors, too!

Q: What is your favourite aspect of the Tudors?
A: I like the idea of trying to fit together aspects that are often kept in separate compartments, seeing how political, cultural, social, economic and religious history all affect one another. I also like the way in which Tudor England was so closely linked to her continental neighbours, in trade, culture, war and religion; that makes it very interesting to study both how the connections worked and what comparing England with her neighbours highlights about England.

ACTIVITY

Read Source 2.2 and answer the following questions.

1 How would Henry's character have been shaped by his upbringing? Think about his attitude to others, his levels of trust, his approach to problems, his view of kingship, etc.
2 Why does C.S.L. Davies argue that Henry had 'the most useful training of any king in English history'? Do you agree with this statement?
3 Henry's support came from three main quarters:
   a) long-standing supporters of the House of Lancaster (e.g. the Earl of Oxford)
   b) relatives and their followers (e.g. Jasper Tudor and Margaret Beaufort)
   c) former Yorkists who had opposed Richard's usurpation.
   How useful would each of these groups of supporters be in helping Henry to govern, if he succeeded in usurping Richard?
4 When he became king in 1485, Henry was very isolated. What were the advantages and disadvantages for him of *not* having
   a) many relatives
   b) many loyal supporters
   c) many links with the nobility in England?

SOURCE 2.3 Lady Margaret Beaufort, at prayer

Margaret Beaufort

- Lady Margaret Beaufort, Countess of Richmond and Derby, was a remarkable character who appears to have made a deep impression on many of her contemporaries and, most significantly, on her son. Her role and importance have recently been reappraised (see M. Jones and M. Underwood, *The King's Mother, Lady Margaret Beaufort*) and it is clear from this biography that she played a central and influential role in the government of Henry VII.
- She gave birth to Henry when she was fourteen. They were separated five years later and, although they kept in contact throughout the 'wilderness' years, they were not able to see each other until he became king (apart from when Henry VI was briefly restored to the throne between 1470 and 1471).
- She married three times and was a significant force herself on the dynastic scene. Her marriage to Lord Stanley was crucial in gaining the support of the Stanleys in 1485, which proved decisive in Henry's victory at Bosworth.
- She was a deeply religious, intelligent and strong-willed woman. Her piety increased in her later years; she dressed in a hair shirt and the black and white attire of a nun, and she became celibate. She was prepared to fight tooth and nail to defend the political interests of her son.
- She was important because she played a key part in the conspiracies against Richard III and was instrumental in getting Henry VII to power; she was a direct route to the King's ear (of crucial importance in an age of personal monarchy); and she had a close working and personal relationship with her son. Jones and Underwood conclude that 'their partnership was for the most part a harmonious one and the degree of influence Margaret enjoyed with her son gave her a dominating position within the realm' (*The King's Mother, Lady Margaret Beaufort*).

FOCUS ROUTE

Read the biographies given here of Margaret Beaufort and Jasper Tudor. Make notes on the ways in which each of these people was important to the development of Henry's character and his performance as king.

Jasper Tudor

Jasper Tudor, Henry's uncle and the Earl of Pembroke, was an important and influential member of the court of the Lancastrian Henry VI. So Henry Tudor was born into a well-known family, heavily involved in national affairs. Jasper was the *only* constant figure in Henry's formative years. Henry was born in Jasper's castle, fled with him to Brittany (after Jasper had been stripped of his earldom and after the defeat of the Lancastrians at Tewkesbury), stayed with him throughout the years of exile and had Jasper in his army at Bosworth. Henry was aware of the debt he owed his uncle and rewarded him by making him Duke of Bedford (a dukedom is the most senior noble title and it was the only one that Henry granted in the whole of his reign, apart from those to his own children). Recent research has emphasised the central role that Jasper Tudor played in Henry's life, giving him stability, loyalty and a political role-model.

D Should Henry have won the battle of Bosworth?

FOCUS ROUTE

To understand the likelihood of Henry Tudor winning at Bosworth, make detailed notes on the following:

a) the strengths and weaknesses of Henry's preparations
b) the strengths and weaknesses of Richard III's preparations
c) the importance of the actions and decisions of the leading nobility.

Henry Tudor's victory over Richard III at the battle of Bosworth on 22 August 1485 gave him the crown (which was allegedly found in a hawthorn bush on the battlefield). Although we know that Henry *was* victorious at Bosworth, we must avoid being drawn towards the conclusion that he was *always* going to win the battle. What really was the likelihood of a victory by this pretender?

■ 2F Areas of England controlled by major nobility

Both Henry and Richard knew that the allegiance of the Duke of Norfolk, the Earl of Northumberland and the Stanleys would probably be the decisive factor in the battle of Bosworth.

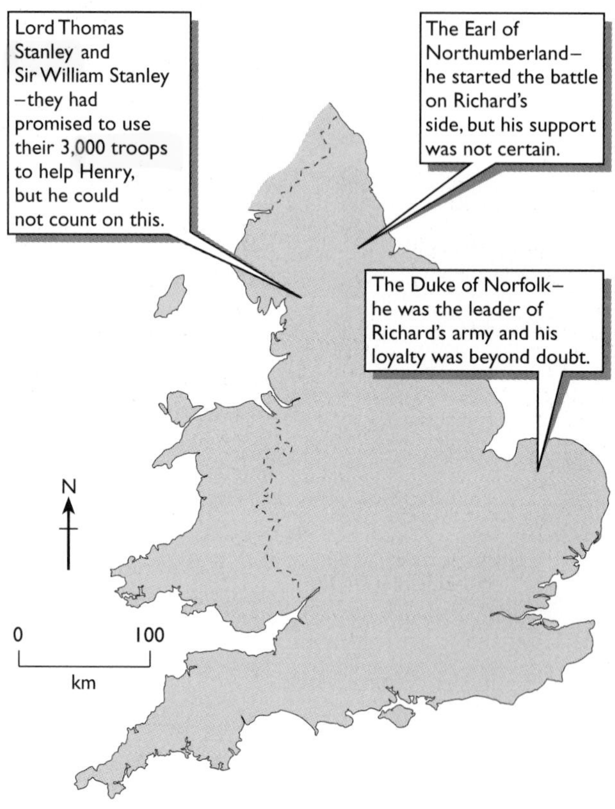
Lord Thomas Stanley and Sir William Stanley –they had promised to use their 3,000 troops to help Henry, but he could not count on this.
The Earl of Northumberland– he started the battle on Richard's side, but his support was not certain.
The Duke of Norfolk– he was the leader of Richard's army and his loyalty was beyond doubt.
N
0
100
km

ACTIVITY

Who is going to win the battle of Bosworth?

1 If you had been Ralph the Bookmaker back in 1485, what odds would you have given on Richard and Henry? Use your historical judgement about the strengths of their relative positions, based on the information opposite, to decide on the odds you are going to give them. If you think the sides are strong, give them short odds (e.g. 3 to 1) or, if you feel certain that only one party can win, make the bets odds-on (e.g. 8 to 1 on).
2 You should compare your odds with those of the other students (and the teacher) in the class and explain your judgement on the basis of the historical knowledge that you have acquired so far.

■ 2G Ralph the Bookmaker

MEETING: 8.30 a.m. BOSWORTH USURPERS' HANDICAP

GOING: GOOD TO FIRM, VERY SOFT IN THE MARSH AT THE BOTTOM OF THE HILL!

COURSE: UNDULATING, HIGH GROUND TAKEN BY RICHARD III.

RUNNERS

1 RICHARD III, experienced competitor, but question marks over the support he'll receive

2 HENRY TUDOR, novice in battle, lacks strength in depth

3 EARL OF NORTHUMBERLAND, wearing blinkers, difficult to get out of the start box

4 DUKE OF NORFOLK, a consistent performer over the flat for Richard

5 JASPER TUDOR, a solid, reliable stablemate for Henry

6 SIR WILLIAM STANLEY, a powerful finisher but allegiance uncertain

7 LORD STANLEY, handicapped by Richard taking his foal (Lord Strange) hostage

■ 2H Henry Tudor's march to Bosworth Field

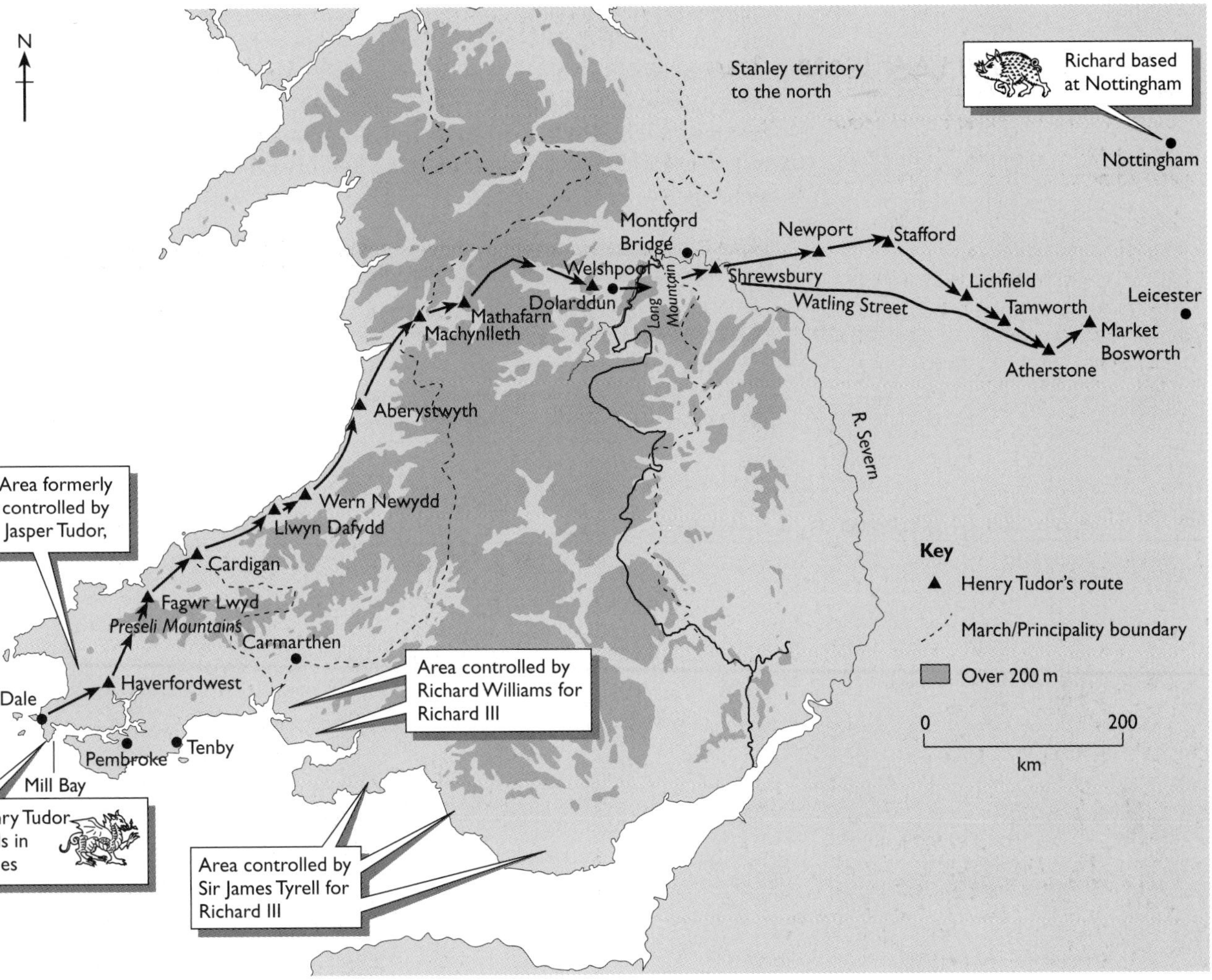

N

Stanley territory to the north

Richard based at Nottingham

Nottingham

Montford Bridge

Newport

Stafford

Welshpool

Shrewsbury

Lichfield

Dolarddun

Long Mountain

Watling Street

Tamworth

Leicester

Mathafarn

Machynlleth

Market Bosworth

Atherstone

Aberystwyth

R. Severn

Area formerly controlled by Jasper Tudor,

Wern Newydd

Llwyn Dafydd

Cardigan

Fagwr Lwyd

Preseli Mountains

Carmarthen

Haverfordwest

Dale

Pembroke

Tenby

Mill Bay

Henry Tudor lands in Wales

Area controlled by Richard Williams for Richard III

Area controlled by Sir James Tyrell for Richard III

Key

▲ Henry Tudor's route

March/Principality boundary

Over 200 m

0 — 200 km

FORM GUIDE by RALPH THE BOOKIE

Richard III

(10,000–15,000 runners) An examination of the position of Richard in 1485 shows how rash it would be to assume that Henry was always going to win.

- In 1483 there had been a rebellion led by the Duke of Buckingham. It had been suppressed and its leader executed. In the same year, Henry Tudor's invasion attempt had been easily repelled.
- Foreign powers treated him with respect: 'Indeed on the continent the general view seems to have been that he had attained a position of strength unprecedented in recent English history' (M. Bennett, *The Battle of Bosworth*).
- He had a reputation for generosity and of being a warrior-king.
- He had very nearly succeeded in getting Henry Tudor extradited from Brittany.
- He had made his peace with one of his most influential enemies, Elizabeth Wydeville (widow of the late Edward IV).
- He had at his disposal the immense resources of England (e.g. the ability to raise troops through the commission of array).

However, the fundamental weakness of Richard was his inability to make a political peace with the nobility (both Yorkist and Lancastrian), whom he had alienated by his usurpation, by his murder of the two princes and by his harsh treatment of opponents. In addition, his dynastic position was seriously damaged by the death of his son, Edward, in April 1484 and by the death of his wife in March 1485. (Again there were rumours that he had poisoned her in order to marry his niece, Elizabeth of York, whom Henry Tudor had already pledged to wed.) It was, though, the uncertainty of the support among the nobility that was Richard's biggest headache.

Henry Tudor

(5,000 runners)
Henry's position was far from strong.

- He was inexperienced both militarily and in English political life.
- His support base in Brittany was narrow. He had loyal support only from his uncle, Jasper, Earl of Pembroke, the Earl of Oxford and a small but impressive group of knights (including many Yorkists alienated by Richard's reign).
- When he returned to Britain, Henry was banking on the support of Lord Stanley (his mother's husband) and his brother Sir William Stanley. The Stanleys dominated the north-west and could provide substantial military support. However, Henry did not know if their promises would materialise into actual support.
- He was the political pawn first of Brittany and then of France. He was dependent on them for support and resources if he were to launch an invasion, but he could not be certain of the support they would provide.

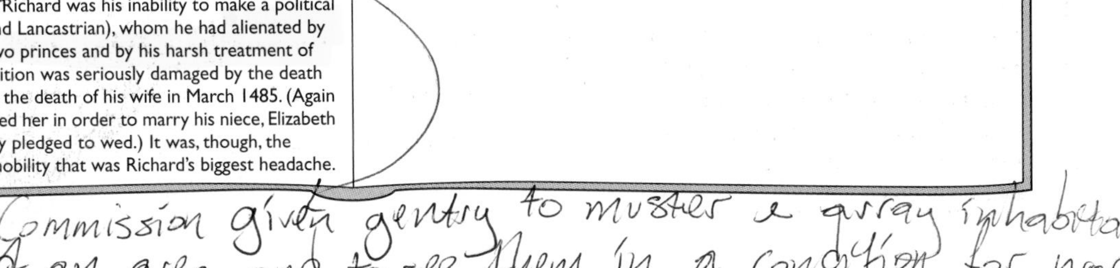

Commission given gentry to muster & array inhabitants
of an area and to see them in a condition for war.

Before the battle

Richard apparently slept uneasily the night before the battle, being haunted by apparitions and demons. In the morning his camp was in chaos. There was no bread to go with the wine for his chaplain to say Mass, and the King, on the day he defended his throne, did not receive any breakfast. He had, though, the largest army in living memory (10,000–15,000 men) and had established the best position on the battlefield on top of Ambien Hill. Henry's army probably numbered only 5,000 and he (having had breakfast!) took up position behind a marsh.

ACTIVITY

1 Write a rousing speech to deliver to your supporters just before the battle commences. You should justify your claim, outline your strengths, describe your background and explain why they should support you. Some of you should write from the point of view of Henry, others as if they were Richard.
2 Deliver your speeches and vote on which was the most convincing.

■ 21 The battle of Bosworth, 22 August 1485

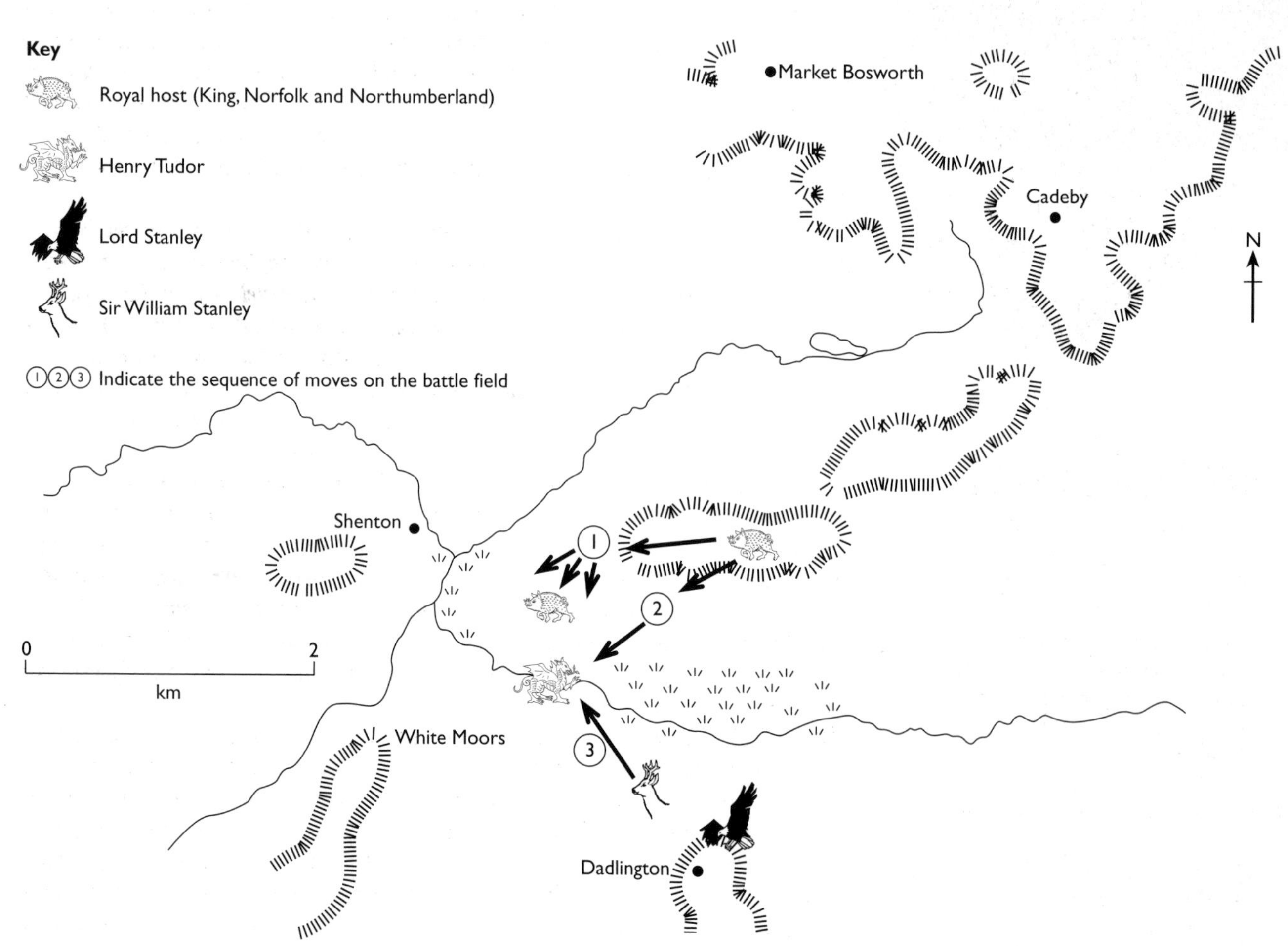

During the battle, Richard and Norfolk's attacks lost them the high ground. Henry was in personal danger for a time, but Sir William Stanley's intervention proved crucial in winning the day for Henry. Neither Lord Stanley nor the Earl of Northumberland committed his forces.

What happened at Bosworth?

The fullest and most useful useful account of the battle of Bosworth comes from Polydore Vergil's *Anglica Historia* (English History). Vergil was an Italian scholar of European renown. He wrote his history at Henry VII's request, working c. 1503–13. He was able to talk to many people who had been at Bosworth including some, like the Earl of Surrey, who had fought for Richard III.

SOURCE 2.5 Richard III

SOURCE 2.4 Polydore Vergil, *Anglica Historia*, c. 1513

The day after King Richard ... drew his whole army out of their encampments, and arrayed his battle-line, extended at such a wonderful length, and composed of footmen and horsemen packed together in such a way that the mass of armed men struck terror in the hearts of the distant onlookers. In the front he placed the archers, ... appointing as their leader John, duke of Norfolk. To the rear of this long battle-line followed the king himself, with a select force of soldiers.

Meanwhile, ... early in the morning [Henry Tudor] commanded his soldiery to set to arms, and at the same time sent to Thomas Stanley, who now approached the place of the fight, midway between the two armies, to come in with his forces ... He answered that ... he would be at hand with his army in proper array. Since this reply was ... contrary to what was expected, ... Henry became rather anxious and began to lose heart. Nevertheless, without delay he arranged his men ... in this fashion. He drew up a simple battle-line on account of the fewness of his men. In front of the line he placed archers, putting the earl of Oxford in command; to defend it on the right wing he positioned Gilbert Talbot, and on the left wing in truth he placed John Savage. He himself, relying on the aid of Thomas Stanley, followed with one company of horsemen and a few foot-soldiers. For all in all the number of soldiers was scarcely 5,000, not counting the Stanleyites of whom about 3,000 were in the battle under the leadership of William Stanley. The king's forces were at least twice as many.

... As soon as the two armies came within sight of each other, the soldiers donned their helms and prepared for the battle, waiting for the signal to attack... There was a marsh between them, which Henry deliberately left on his right side, to serve his men as a defensive wall. In doing this he simultaneously put the sun behind him. The king, as soon as he saw the enemy advance past the marsh, ordered his men to charge. Suddenly raising a great shout they attacked first with arrows, and their opponents, ... returned the fire fiercely. When it came to close quarters, however, the fighting was done with swords.

In the meantime the earl of Oxford, afraid that ... his men would be surrounded by the evening ... ordered that no soldier should go more than ten feet from the standards. When in response ... all the men massed together and drew back a little from the fray, their opponents, suspecting a trick, took fright and broke off from fighting for a while. In truth many, who wished the king damned rather than saved, were not reluctant to do so, and for that reason fought less stoutly. Then the earl of Oxford in the one part, with tightly grouped units, attacked the enemy afresh ...

While the battle ... raged, ... Richard learnt, first from spies, that Henry was some way off with a few armed men as his retinue, and then, as the latter drew nearer, recognised him more certainly from his standards. Inflamed with anger, he spurred his horse, and rode against him ... Henry saw Richard come upon him, and since all hope of safety lay in arms, he eagerly offered himself for the contest. In the first charge Richard killed several men; toppled Henry's standard, along with the standard-bearer William Brandon; contended with John Cheney, a man of surpassing bravery, who stood in his way, and thrust him to the ground with great force; and made a path for himself through the press of steel.

Nevertheless Henry held out against the attack longer than his troops, who now almost despaired of victory, had thought likely. Then, behold, William Stanley came in support with 3,000 men ... At this point ... with ... his men taking to their heels, Richard was slain fighting in the thickest press of his

ACTIVITY

1 What, according to Vergil, were
   a) the key stages of the battle
   b) the main reasons why Henry Tudor won?
2 Can you identify any sections of his account that suggest that Vergil's informants fought in the battle?
3 How does Vergil portray
   a) Richard III
   b) Henry VII?
4 How valuable do you think this account is for
   a) Richard's character and actions
   b) Henry's actions at Bosworth
   c) the reasons why Henry won?
5 'Vergil was writing for Henry VII. Therefore his account of Henry's success at Bosworth can be of no value for historians.' Explain why you agree or disagree with this statement.

enemies. Meanwhile the earl of Oxford put to flight the remainder of the [enemy] troops ... a great number of whom were killed in the rout ...Many more, who supported Richard out of fear and not of their own will, purposely held off from the battle, and departed unharmed, as men who desired not the safety but the destruction of the prince whom they detested. About 1,000 men were slain, including from the nobility John duke of Norfolk, Walter Lord Ferrers, Robert Brackenbury, Richard Radcliffe and several others. Two days after at Leicester, William Catesby, lawyer, with a few associates, was executed ... Francis Lord Lovell, Humphrey and Thomas Stafford ... and many companions, fled into ... sanctuary ... near Colchester ... There was a huge number of captives, for when Richard was killed, all men threw down their weapons, and freely submitted themselves to Henry's obedience, which the majority would have done at the outset if they had not been prevented by Richard's scouts rushing back and forth ... Amongst them the chief were Henry earl of Northumberland and Thomas earl of Surrey. The latter was put in prison, where he remained for a long time, the former was received in favour as a friend at heart. Henry lost in the battle scarcely a hundred soldiers, amongst whom ... was William Brandon, who bore Henry's battle standard...

The report is that Richard could have saved himself by flight. His companions, seeing from the very outset ... that the soldiers were wielding their arms feebly and sluggishly, and that some were secretly deserting, suspected treason, and urged him to fly. When his cause obviously began to falter, they brought him a swift horse. Yet he, who knew that the people hated him, setting aside hope of all future success, allegedly replied, such was the great fierceness and force of his mind, that that very day he would make an end either of war or life ... He went into battle wearing the royal crown, so that he might thereby make either a beginning or an end of his reign. Thus the miserable man ... had such an end as customarily befalls them that for justice, divine law and virtue substitute wilfulness, impiety and depravity...

Immediately after gaining victory, Henry gave thanks to Almighty God with many prayers. Then filled with unbelievable happiness, he took himself to the nearest hill, where after he had congratulated his soldiers and ordered them to care for the wounded and to bury the slain, he gave eternal thanks to his captains, promising that he would remember their good services. In the mean time, the soldiers saluted him as king with a great shout, applauding him with most willing hearts. Seeing this, Thomas Stanley immediately placed Richard's crown, found among the spoil, on his head, as though he had become king by command of the people, acclaimed in the ancestral manner.

After the battle

SOURCE 2.6 In April 1486 an unknown historian, writing at the abbey of Crowland, completed his history of the Yorkist dynasty with the following lines, which contain one of the earliest references to a war between two roses:

In the year 1485 on the 22 day of August the tusks of the boar [Richard] were blunted and the red rose [Henry], the avenger of the white [the Yorkists], shines upon us.

In Source 2.6 the anonymous author is explaining how Henry the Lancastrian has gained revenge over the unpopular Richard and has brought to an end the horrors of the Wars of the Roses. He has achieved this through his union with the Yorkists (by marrying Elizabeth of York and by receiving the support of Yorkists at Bosworth). However, as we will discover in later chapters, this vision was to be a false dawn.

ACTIVITY

Describe how Henry VII was able to take the throne in 1485. In your answer take into consideration:

- his upbringing and his experience in Brittany
- the reign of Richard III
- the legacy of the Wars of the Roses
- the invasion, march and battle
- the support of the nobility.

E Review: The invasion of '85 – how did Henry VII become king?

Henry VII's victory at the battle of Bosworth did *not* show that Henry was supported by the nation. The actions of many nobles had merely shown how unacceptable Richard III was to them. The neutrality of both the Earl of Northumberland and Lord Stanley had been very significant, but more decisive had been the intervention by Sir William Stanley on Henry's behalf.

The victory did *not* make Henry secure and indeed the unlikely success of *this* pretender only served to encourage others, as the affairs of Warbeck and Simnel later showed. If one obscure nobleman who had lived in exile for most of his life could gather a small band of diehards together and take the throne, why couldn't others? It is for this reason that we should not see the battle of Bosworth as a major watershed in English history. It did *not* cure the ills of the Wars of the Roses and in many senses just protracted the problems that arose from having a monarch with contentious legitimacy on the throne.

Bosworth should not be seen as a new beginning or even as the beginning of the end. The subsequent chapters will demonstrate that Henry was to remain insecure for virtually all of his reign. Henry was certainly going to have his work cut out to retain the lofty status to which he had so spectacularly and rapidly risen.

There was an outbreak of sweating sickness after Henry's victory in 1485, and contemporaries in that superstitious age saw this as an ill omen for the coming reign. Their predictions said the sickness foretold a harsh regime in which the King would have to rule by the sweat of his brow. You will discover how right they were.

KEY POINTS FROM CHAPTER 2: The invasion of '85 – how did Henry VII become king?

1. From 1459 the country had been split by the Wars of the Roses, a civil war fought between the noble families of York and Lancaster over who was going to be king.
2. The civil war caused more disruption to the lives of the nobility than to the ordinary people.
3. The Wars of the Roses made the monarchy unstable. The Crown changed hands five times in less than 25 years.
4. Following the accession of Edward IV in 1471, Henry Tudor fled abroad and lived in Brittany until his successful invasion in August 1485.
5. Henry Tudor had a weak claim to the throne.
6. His experiences in the Breton and French courts prepared him well for kingship.
7. Henry Tudor's victory at Bosworth was dependent on the support of the Stanleys.
8. The unpopularity of Richard III (1483–85) is a crucial part of the explanation of why Henry Tudor became king.
9. On becoming king, Henry faced the considerable problem of consolidating his control and preventing a usurpation.

3

The monarch's manifesto – what were Henry's concerns on his accession?

CHAPTER OVERVIEW Whenever a new leader, be it king, queen or politician, takes up their new role, the initial sense of euphoria soon gives way to the practicalities and concerns of the actual job. Such was the case for Henry VII. Victory at Bosworth was only the beginning of a lifelong quest for Henry to be recognised as king at home and abroad: in other words, to secure his position and that of his heirs.

In this chapter, we will be investigating three key questions about how Henry tackled these issues and the context in which he was to operate:

A What were Henry's short-term priorities?

FOCUS ROUTE

As you read pages 26–29, identify and explain Henry's short-term priorities. Organise your notes under the following headings:

- gaining recognition of his position
- dealing with possible threats
- securing the succession.

SOURCE 3.1 This portrait shows an apprehensive Henry VII. He had good reason to be apprehensive, as he had usurped the throne after 24 years of Yorkist rule. As you learn more about the new king, consider whether he ever felt secure as the reign progressed.

Unfortunately, we do not know the date of the painting, or the name of the artist, but it looks like an older likeness of Henry. Does it suggest that he was still apprehensive after having been king for a long while?

ACTIVITY

You are Henry VII. The date is 23 August 1485, the day after the battle of Bosworth and the death of Richard III. What are your immediate priorities?

Study the decisions (below) that Henry had to make, and decide the following:

a) In which order should you do these things?
b) What will the effects be (e.g. make people realise that you are king, placate the Yorkists)?

Present your answer in a table like the one below. An example has been done for you.

Decision	Action	Effect
1 C	Date the reign from before the battle of Bosworth	Opponents can be punished as traitors
2		

A Bring Elizabeth of York out of imprisonment and move her in with your mother, Lady Margaret Beaufort. You wish to keep an eye on this woman, who could be a focus for Yorkist opposition. What better place could there be than under your trustworthy mother's watchful eye? 4

B Place Princess Cecily of York (heiress apparent, after Elizabeth of York, to the House of York), in your mother's household. You don't want Cecily being a focal point for the Yorkists either. 10

C Decide that your reign actually started on 21 August 1485, one day before the battle of Bosworth. If you do this, you can say that anyone who fought against you was a traitor. 1

D Marry Elizabeth of York, which you had promised to do in 1483, in order to get the Yorkist opponents of Richard III on your side. This would build bridges with your opponents and mean that Elizabeth would not be queen in her own right, but only because you are king. Therefore you would feel more secure. 6 18/01/1486

E Begin a progress (a journey through the kingdom). This might feel risky, but it would show the people that you are king and not afraid, especially if you go to the north, where Richard III had been very popular. 9 March 1486

F Get the backing of the Pope because the last thing you want is for the Church not to recognise you as king. 12

G Be crowned king. This solemn occasion is very important as a visible acknowledgement of your reign, and it affords good propaganda opportunities for you as well. 2 30/10/1485

H Call Parliament, so that it can acknowledge that you are king. This will encourage others to do the same. 3 07/11/1485

I Have children, preferably sons, because you want to secure the succession with your direct heirs, rather than having a controversial succession, such as your own. 11 Arthur: 19/09/1486

J Decide how to treat your opponents at Bosworth (e.g. prison, execution, or freedom). If you treat them too leniently, they might cause further problems by rebelling against you later on. If you treat them too harshly, this might cause even more resentment. 5

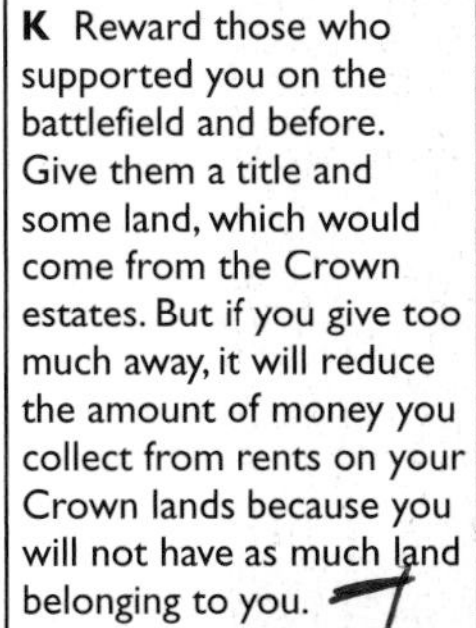

K Reward those who supported you on the battlefield and before. Give them a title and some land, which would come from the Crown estates. But if you give too much away, it will reduce the amount of money you collect from rents on your Crown lands because you will not have as much land belonging to you. 7

L Decide how to treat other claimants to the throne, the Earls of Warwick and Lincoln. You probably don't want them at large in the country because they could gather support from at home and abroad, and threaten your throne. 8

What did Henry do?

You probably decided to do all of the things in the previous activity, in an attempt to bolster your precarious position.

What did Henry actually do? He did predate his reign to 21 August 1485, and in so doing he could treat his opponents as traitors and deal with them accordingly. (For further information about this, see below and also Chapter 5, on how Henry dealt with the nobility.) His marriage to Elizabeth of York on 18 January 1486 would have gone some way to placate the Yorkists. Note, however,

SOURCE 3.2 Parliament recognises Henry as king

[It is] ordained, established and enacted, by the authority of the present Parliament, that the inheritance of the Crowns of the realms of England and of France, with all the pre-eminence and dignity royal to the same pertaining ... be, rest, remain and abide in the most royal person of our sovereign lord King Harry the VIIth, and in the heirs of his body lawfully coming, perpetually with the grace of God so to endure, and in none others.

that Henry was careful to have had himself crowned king already on 30 October 1485, to show that he claimed the throne in his own right and not through Elizabeth. This might seem unnecessary in a time when women were submissive to their husbands, but Henry was probably worried that his subjects might have been confused about his claim if he had married Elizabeth before his coronation. Such was Henry's determination to stake his individual claim to the throne that he delayed the coronation of Elizabeth until 25 November 1487, some two years after his own. No doubt he was also mindful of Elizabeth's four sisters, Cecily, Anne, Catherine and Bridget, who would undoubtedly have children if they married. This might result in threatening claims to the throne. It must therefore have been a great relief to Henry when Prince Arthur was born on 19 September 1486, followed by Margaret in 1488, Henry in 1491 and Mary in 1496.

Henry's coronation was a golden opportunity for him to create a powerful image. No expense was spared; indeed, the aim was to surpass the festivities that accompanied Richard III's coronation. The preparations were supervised by Bishop Courtney and the Earls of Oxford, Pembroke and Nottingham. An exorbitant £8 a yard was paid for gold cloth, purple velvet for the King's robes cost 40 shillings per yard, and crimson satin cost 16 shillings. (One shilling or 12d = 5p. An ordinary soldier earned 6d or $2\frac{1}{2}$p per day.)

It is interesting to note that, while Henry understood the need to look and act like a king, he also realised the need to have some personal protection at a time when there was no standing army or police force in the country. He also wanted to match the royal bodyguard that he had seen at the French court. Henry therefore developed his own personal protection squad – the Yeomen of the Guard. By the end of his reign, their number had increased to some 200.

On 7 November 1485, Henry called the first parliament of his reign. As only the monarch could call Parliament, this was a demonstration of Henry's kingship. He also needed their recognition of his position. Parliament duly obliged by recognising Henry's title to the throne.

Henry had to decide what to do with his opponents at Bosworth. It was like walking a tightrope because to be too draconian in his actions might sow the seeds of discontent among already disgruntled Ricardians – the supporters of the late king, Richard III. On the other hand, if Henry were to appear too lenient, it might damage his standing as king and make him look weak. Luckily for him, less than a quarter of England's TEMPORAL peers fought against him on 22 August 1485, and, of those who did, many had been killed or captured. Moreover, not all Yorkists were staunch supporters of Richard, as the Duke of Buckingham's rebellion against him in October 1483 had shown. Henry was not a vengeful man and so, if former Yorkists were prepared to accept him, they could expect to be treated with dignity and consideration. His aim was to use loyalty to enhance his security.

TEMPORAL

Temporal lords are not members of the Church. This group includes earls, dukes, etc.

Spiritual lords are members of the Church. This group includes archbishops and bishops.

■ 3A How did Henry deal with the key threats?

Person	Action
Earl of Warwick, the ten-year-old nephew of Richard III	He was sent to the Tower, but lived in relative comfort.
John de la Pole, Earl of Lincoln, another nephew of Richard III, who also was named as his heir	He professed his loyalty to Henry VII and was later invited to join the Council.
Duke of Suffolk, father of Lincoln	He also professed loyalty to the new king.
Earl of Surrey, who fought for Richard at Bosworth, where his father was killed	He was kept in prison until 1489 when Henry was satisfied with his intentions.
Earl of Northumberland, who was with Richard at Bosworth, but did not fight for him	He was released from prison at the end of 1485, being given control of the north of England and the opportunity to prove his loyalty.

■ 3B How did Henry reward his supporters?

Person	Action
Jasper Tudor, Henry's uncle	He became Duke of Bedford (one of the few people to be elevated to the peerage), also Chief Justice of Wales, Constable of all the royal castles in the Welsh marches, and Lord Lieutenant of Ireland. As Jasper Tudor was 55 in 1485 and had little chance of having any children, Henry could thus grant him a title in the knowledge that there would be no threats to his position from Jasper Tudor's heirs.
Thomas, Lord Stanley, Henry's stepfather	He was created Earl of Derby.
Sir Thomas Lovell, who had rebelled against Richard in 1483	In 1485 he was made Chancellor of the Exchequer, Treasurer of the Household and Speaker of the House of Commons.
Giles Daubeney, formerly of the household of Edward IV, who rebelled against Richard in 1483	He was created Lord Daubeney and Lieutenant of Calais in 1486. He became Chamberlain of the Household in 1495 after Sir William Stanley's execution.
Bishop Richard Fox, a lawyer who served Edward IV and was with Henry in exile	He was Keeper of the Privy Seal, 1487–1516, often at Council and a frequent ambassador.
John Morton, Bishop of Ely, who resisted Richard's usurpation in 1483	He was appointed Chancellor and Archbishop of Canterbury in 1486.
Sir Reginald Bray, who was originally in the service of Margaret Beaufort and acted as a go-between in the 1483 plot	He became Chancellor of the Duchy of Lancaster and was Henry's chief financial and property administrator after 1485.
Sir William Stanley, who sided with Henry at Bosworth	He was made Lord Chamberlain.

SOURCE 3.3 The city of York, which had previously given support to Richard III, prepared a pageant to welcome Henry in April 1486. The details are recorded in the city's records

At the entry to the city shall be built a place in the manner of heaven, of great joy and angelic harmony. Under the heaven shall be a desolate world, full of trees and flowers into which shall spring up a royal rich red rose conveyed by a device. Unto this rose shall appear another rich white rose unto whom, being together, all other flowers shall bow and give sovereignty, showing the rose to be the principal of all flowers.

Nowadays, if politicians want to publicise themselves, they give an interview on television or create a website on the Internet. Henry did the Tudor equivalent – in March 1486, he began a progress through the kingdom. This enabled him not only to be the visible king to his subjects, but also to use propaganda as a means to glorify his position.

How difficult was Henry's task?

On the evidence you have read so far, you might be thinking that Henry faced a very difficult task as a new king in a country he barely knew. You might be full of admiration for him. Many historians have traditionally praised his approach to the beginning of his reign. However, the revisionist historian Christine Carpenter has questioned how difficult Henry's task of achieving security at the beginning of his reign really was. In fact, Carpenter makes it sound easy.

SOURCE 3.4 C. Carpenter, *The Wars of the Roses: Politics and the Constitution in England c. 1437–1509*, 1997, pp. 221–22

Henry VII became king under better circumstances than any other usurper in late-medieval England. Like Henry IV, he had the enormous advantage of replacing a king who had been widely disliked, although the lingering affection for Richard III in the north might prove a problem. Unlike both Henry IV and Edward IV, he started with the advantage that his predecessor was already dead. Unlike both, he had no powerful kingmaker to contend with; the noble house that gained most from Henry's accession was that of the Stanleys, the family into which Henry's mother, Margaret Beaufort, had married, and it was improbable that the head of the family, Lord Stanley, would lead a rebellion against his own stepson.

Stage is set for period of stability / monarchical success.

ACTIVITY

1. Re-read pages 26–29 on Henry's short-term priorities.
2. Write down reasons why you agree or disagree with Carpenter's views.
3. Discuss your reasons with your fellow students.
4. What else do you need to know about Henry in order to debate this more convincingly?

B How did the government of the country work?

You have already seen examples of the complex decisions that Henry had to make as king. Even though he had more power to make decisions than our monarchy has today, he could not rule the country on his own. The systems that Henry had at his disposal are shown in Charts 3C and 3D.

FOCUS ROUTE

Study pages 30–31 on the government of the country under Henry VII. Draw a spider diagram that covers all the different aspects of government.

3C Layout of the household apartments

Access to the monarchy was strictly controlled. Those who had access to the monarch in the Prescence Chamber or, particularly, in the Privy Chamber had the greatest opportunity to influence the monarch.

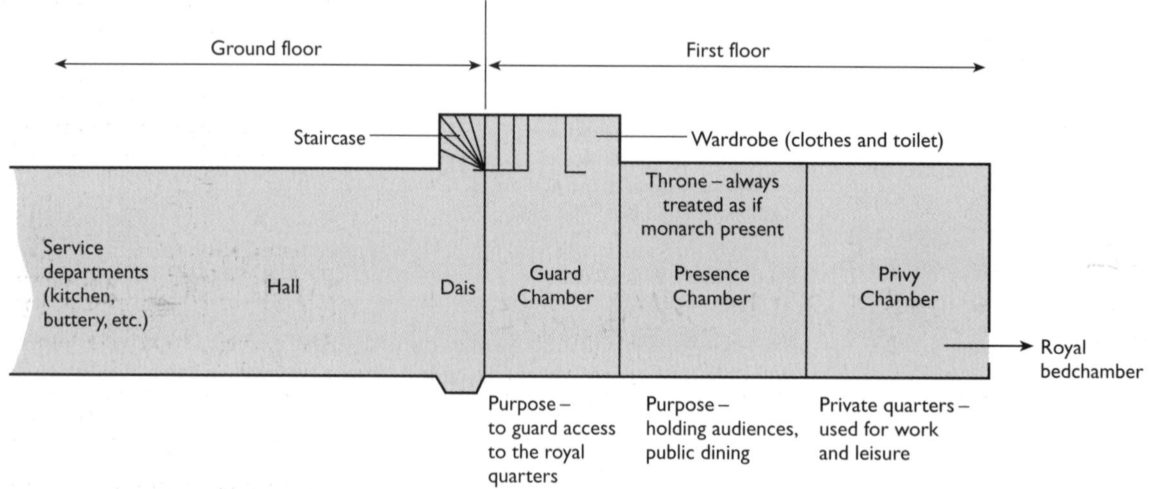

TALKING POINT

When we are looking at Tudor government, notice how some of it is formal, such as Parliament, while some aspects are informal, such as the Privy Chamber. What impact do you think this had on how the King made decisions?

ACTIVITY

1 Study Charts 3C and 3D. Work out which parts of government machinery were likely to **help** Henry restore law and order, and thereby increase his security, and which aspects were likely to **hinder** him. Note that so far we have not identified the financial aspects of Henry's government. Financial administration will be considered in Chapter 5.
2 To what extent would Henry's personal attitude to government affect how it helped his security?

■ 3D How did Henry's government work – who did what?

The King

The King ruled the country and made all decisions relating to its security, when to go to war, who should advise him, and when Parliament should meet.

The Royal Household

These were the people who looked after the domestic needs of the King, rather like servants. They travelled with him wherever he went. All of them were also members of the Court.

Justices of the Peace

Justices of the Peace were responsible for keeping law and order in the localities. You can find out more about them on p. 34.

Parliament

Under Henry VII, Parliament was called to meet by the monarch for specific reasons, usually because the King needed to raise extra money through taxation, especially in times of war.

The Privy Chamber

The Privy Chamber, as you can see from Chart 3C, was at the heart of the household apartments. It may have been set up during the 1490s. The gentlemen of the Privy Chamber, chosen by the King, had the closest access to him and therefore the greatest opportunity to influence him, although probably Henry's Privy Chamber servants were of low status and therefore not very politically influential.

The Court

Like the Household, the Court was a group of people who moved from place to place with the King. A place at court was a sought-after position. The Court's function was to entertain the King and offer whatever company he wished, and to be a good advertisement for him, especially when foreign guests were visiting. People at court often wished to have influence with the King, and, when this coincided with the views of other like-minded courtiers, they formed factions or small interest groups. Such groups were fluid – as soon as a particular issue had been resolved, the factions would usually dissolve, only to build up again when another matter galvanised different views.

The Privy Council

This was a group of advisers, chosen by the King. They were usually from the nobility and the Church, plus lawyers and royal household officers. They gave the King advice, they were a central administrative body and they acted as a court, dealing with grievances from individuals that required the direct judgement of the King. The Council could consist of as many as 40 or 50 people, but attendance at meetings was often much lower.

The Groom of the Stool

This was the person who was in charge of the Privy Chamber. Stool was the medieval word for toilet, so clearly this person knew the King intimately!

Hugh Denys.

C How did Henry approach kingship in the long term?

FOCUS ROUTE

Read pages 32–36 on how Henry approached kingship in the long term. Then copy and complete this table on how Henry's dealings with the Privy Council, Parliament, the Church, local government and the 1489 and 1497 rebellions helped and/or hindered his security.

	Helped security	Hindered security
Privy Council		
Parliament		
Church		
Local government		
1489 and 1497 rebellions		

When you have completed the table, write down a list of points that describe Henry's methods of governing the country. Here are two to get you thinking:

- Henry wanted control over all parts of government.
- Henry chose councillors who would help him to run the country effectively.

All Tudor monarchs encountered similar challenges as their reigns progressed. In Chapter 4 you will learn about the foreign policy decisions that Henry faced, as well as the threats to remove him from the throne. These were issues of the gravest importance. In Chapter 5 you will be introduced to his treatment of the nobles and to his use of finance, both of which served as means of maintaining his position as king.

Here we are going to examine the other ways in which Henry sought to maintain and strengthen his position, namely through:

- the Privy Council
- Parliament
- the Church
- local government
- his response to the rebellions of 1489 (Yorkshire) and 1497 (South-Western; this is often referred to as the Cornish rebellion, but there was also a lot of involvement from Somerset).

The Privy Council

The Privy Council existed to advise the King over matters of state, to administer law and order, and to act in a judicial capacity. Henry was rarely present at meetings. On paper, Henry VII's Council numbered over 240 people, but in reality only six or seven people were in regular attendance at meetings, including the clerics Morton and Fox, the household peer Daubeney, Lovell, a knight, the common lawyer Dudley (see page 33), and Bray, an administrator. It was important for Henry to include people with a legal background, as they could insist on the King's rights.

For Henry, loyalty and service were the most important attributes in a councillor. Henry had taken the throne by force and he was therefore a usurper, who needed his position as king reinforced by servants on whom he could rely. Henry probably only ever really trusted the four people closest to him – his uncle, Jasper Tudor, Duke of Bedford; his friend the Earl of Oxford; his stepfather, Lord Stanley, Earl of Derby; and of course, his mother, Lady Margaret Beaufort.

Henry's Council was divided into different subcommittees, the most famous being the Council Learned in the Law, mostly referred to as the Council

Learned. It was set up in 1495 to defend the King's position as a feudal landlord: that is, to protect his interests as the owner of all the Crown lands, ensuring that he received all the feudal dues that were owed to him (for more on this, see Chapter 5). The Council Learned operated without a jury, and Henry used it to supervise the collection of the financial agreements known as bonds and recognisances, which were used to control the nobility (again, see Chapter 5 for a fuller explanation). The Council Learned became detested when it was controlled by Empson and Dudley because of their harsh enforcement of penalties and because they fabricated cases in which people owed money to the King, when in fact they did not.

Parliament

ATTAINDER
An attainder was a parliamentary Act confiscating lands for treason.

Parliament met seven times during Henry's 24-year reign, mostly during the first part of it. It recognised his title to the throne, passed ATTAINDERS and voted on taxes, although in 1504 it agreed only to £40,000 instead of the £90,000 Henry had asked for. Requests from the King for subsidies were seldom made, however, as Henry was not in constant need of money for war (for more details on Henry's financial situation, see Chapter 5). Acts of Parliament were passed concerning the responsibilities of Justices of the Peace and social discipline. An Act of 1504 forbade corporations from making regulations unless they first had the approval of the King. This is a good example of Henry's purpose in using Parliament – it emphasised that all power derived from the Crown and that there was only one ruler in England. It could be argued that Henry's use of Parliament to strengthen his position as king was as important as the actual legislation that it passed. In this respect, Henry was no different from other Tudor monarchs; parliaments served the interests of the monarch and the greater subjects, not the nation as a whole.

Although Henry did not use Parliament as a consultative body, that does not mean that he did not consult on major issues. He summoned five Great Councils between 1487 and 1502. These comprised nobles, councillors and burgesses – representatives of the whole country.

The Church

In the main, Henry's relationship with the Church was positive. He had Archbishop Morton to thank for this, as it was he who had visited Rome to secure papal support for Henry before Bosworth. This in turn paved the way for papal dispensation (permission) for Henry to marry Elizabeth of York. Henry himself, although not interested in theology, was personally pious.

As with other aspects of his rule, Henry's policies towards the Church embodied his deep-seated desire for security. In 1486, the privilege of ecclesiastical sanctuary was attacked. Sanctuary was usually a church where fugitives from justice could be given refuge – Perkin Warbeck availed himself of this privilege at Beaulieu Abbey in 1497. Henry's judges ruled that only the King could grant sanctuary for treason.

Henry appointed more bishops who were lawyers (sixteen) than bishops who were theologians (six). Most of the latter were administrators too. Henry required bishops to serve the state as well as the Church. In fact, if anything, service to the state came first, as was demonstrated by the case of the bishop of Lincoln. He was refused permission to leave the marches of Wales (the borders between England and Wales), in order to undertake his pastoral work as a bishop.

Perhaps the most important aspect of Henry's dealings with the Church was on the issue of ecclesiastical jurisdiction. At this time, the Church had a separate legal system to that of the state, and the King did not have any influence over the operation of Church courts. Henry must have felt this like a thorn in his side, especially when his position was so tenuous. Henry's legal advisers therefore promoted attacks on the Church courts. Henry was determined that the authority of the Pope in the Church courts should not prejudice his rights and interests as king. The penalty for an individual found guilty of *praemunire* (placing the authority of a foreign power above that of the King) was life imprisonment and the loss of their property to the Crown.

Local government

It was in Henry's interests to have subjects who obeyed the law and kept order throughout the kingdom. The problem was that the nobility and gentry, who should have been helping to maintain law and order, were in danger of becoming too powerful themselves. Henry had continually to balance sustaining and controlling the authority of the nobility in order to survive (see Chapter 5).

Henry realised that Justices of the Peace (JPs) were the key to his success in this area. JPs were chief local government officers who were responsible for maintaining public order and implementing any laws concerning social and economic matters. There were on average eighteen JPs per county, appointed annually from among the local landowners. Although JPs were not paid, it was in their interests as local landowners to do their job properly.

As well as appointing JPs who were the largest landowners, as was customary, Henry began to appoint lesser landowners, so as to weaken the large landowners' power. He also widened the responsibilities of JPs as follows:

- From 1485 they could arrest and question poachers or hunters who were in disguise, as this could be a cover for murder or rebellion.
- From 1487 they could grant bail to those awaiting trial.
- From 1495 they could replace members of juries whom they suspected of having been bribed.

Essentially, Henry was trying to make the JPs more accountable to him in the hope that they would reinforce his position. While the system was only as good as the individual JPs, most fulfilled their role in accordance with the King's wishes, since social disgrace among their peers was the alternative.

Henry also improved the administration of the borders – the areas furthest away from London, notably Wales and the north. The Council of Wales was run by Henry's uncle, Jasper Tudor, and the Council of the North by the Earl of Surrey. Henry himself kept a close watch on the councils to make sure that these areas did not present any challenge to his security.

The 1489 and 1497 rebellions

In addition to the Simnel and Warbeck risings, which you will read about in Chapter 4, Henry VII also faced other, less serious, rebellions – in Yorkshire in 1489, and in Cornwall in 1497. The 1489 rebellion was sparked by a parliamentary tax, voted to finance Henry's aid to Brittany. Not only had Yorkshire suffered from a particularly bad harvest, but there was also resentment that counties further north did not have to pay the tax, as they were expected to undertake the defence of the country against the Scots.

The Earl of Northumberland, having put the case of the northern counties to the King, returned north and was murdered, probably by Sir John Egremont, a leader of the rebellion and an illegitimate member of the Percy family. The rebels were subsequently defeated outside York by the Earl of Surrey, whom Henry then appointed as his lieutenant in the area – the new Earl of Northumberland was a minor and in the WARDSHIP of the King. Egremont escaped to Flanders and Henry pardoned most of the other rebels. However, he did not receive any more of the tax. The total collected nationally was £27,000, far short of the £100,000 originally voted by Parliament.

> **WARDSHIP**
> **If the heir to an estate was still a minor on the death of the father, the monarch had the right to collect revenue from the land until the child came of age.**

Rebellion in Cornwall in 1497 was also triggered by a demand for money, this time to pay for a campaign to resist a projected invasion by James IV of Scotland and Perkin Warbeck. The Cornish refused to pay because they considered that any invasion threat in the north of the kingdom would have little relevance to them. On 16 June, the rebels marched to Blackheath, near London, where they were met by the King's forces under the command of Lord Daubeney. It is estimated that 1,000 rebels were killed in the battle of Blackheath. Three of the main leaders of the rebellion were executed.

The Cornish rebellion was potentially more problematic for Henry than the Yorkshire rebellion because of the threat posed by James IV and Warbeck, and by the rebels who, by marching directly on the capital, posed a threat to the centre of government.

> **TALKING POINT**
> What do these rebellions reveal about Henry's tactics when threatened?

3E The major events of Henry VII's reign

1485	
August	Battle of Bosworth
September	Henry enters London
30 October	Henry's coronation
7 November	First Parliament opens
1486	
18 January	Henry marries Elizabeth of York
4 March	Henry begins first progress throughout the kingdom
Easter	First Parliament dissolves
July	Conspiracy of Lovell and the Staffords; Lovell escapes to France, Humphrey Stafford executed
19 September	Birth of Prince Arthur
1487	
24 May	Lambert Simnel crowned king in Dublin
16 June	Battle of Stoke, Simnel defeated and Lincoln executed
9 November	Second Parliament opens
25 November	Coronation of Queen Elizabeth
1488	
23 February	Second Parliament dissolves
1489	Rebellion in Yorkshire
13 January	Third Parliament opens
17 March	Treaty of Medina del Campo between England and Spain agrees marriage between Prince Arthur and Catherine of Aragon
28 April	Earl of Northumberland murdered
29 November	Birth of Princess Margaret
	Arthur proclaimed Prince of Wales and Earl of Chester
1490	
27 February	Third Parliament dissolves
1491	
28 June	Birth of Prince Henry at Greenwich
17 October	Fourth Parliament opens
November	Perkin Warbeck appears in Ireland
1492	
5 March	Fourth Parliament dissolves
November	Warbeck in France and Burgundy
1493	
November	Warbeck with Maximilian in Vienna
1494	Conspiracies involving the King's Chamberlain, Sir William Stanley
1495	
16 February	Execution of Sir William Stanley
23 July–3 August	Warbeck's failure at Deal, Kent
14 October	Fifth Parliament opens
November	Warbeck arrives in Scotland, accepted as Richard IV by the Scottish court
1496	
18 March	Birth of Princess Mary
September	Invasion of Scots led by James IV and Warbeck
1 October	Treaty for the marriage of Prince Arthur and Catherine of Aragon
21 December	Fifth Parliament dissolves
1497	
16 January	Sixth Parliament opens
13 March	Sixth Parliament dissolves
May	Cornish rebellion
17 July	Cornish rebels defeated at battle of Blackheath
July	Warbeck leaves Scotland
7 September	Warbeck lands in Cornwall
5 October	Warbeck surrenders; Henry seems to accept Warbeck's confession that he is not Richard, Duke of York, and accepts him at Court
December	Henry's palace at Sheen destroyed by fire
1498	Warbeck flees the Court
8 June	Warbeck recaptured and put in the Tower
1499	
21 or 22 February	Birth of Prince Edmund
May	First proxy marriage of Arthur and Catherine of Aragon
	Edmund de la Pole, Earl of Suffolk, flees to Calais
16 November	Warbeck hanged
29 November	Warwick beheaded
1500	
19 June	Death of Prince Edmund
15 September	Death of Cardinal Morton
	Henry begins rebuilding Sheen palace as Richmond Palace
1501	
July	Second flight of Edmund, Earl of Suffolk
14 November	Marriage of Arthur and Catherine at St Paul's Cathedral
1502	
2 April	Death of Arthur at Ludlow Castle, Shropshire
6 May	Execution of Sir James Tyrell for plotting against the King with other Yorkist sympathisers, including Edmund and William de la Pole
26 December	Edmund de la Pole, Earl of Suffolk, proclaimed an outlaw
1503	Work starts on Henry VII chapel in Westminster Abbey
11 February	Death of Queen Elizabeth in childbirth with Princess Catherine
23 June	Betrothal of Prince Henry to Catherine of Aragon
8 August	Marriage of Princess Margaret to James IV of Scotland
1504	
25 January	Seventh Parliament opens
18 February	Prince Henry declared Prince of Wales and Earl of Chester
30 March	Seventh Parliament dissolves
1505	
25 June	Prince Henry protests against proposed marriage with Catherine of Aragon, despite papal dispensation
1506	
24 April	Edmund de la Pole, Earl of Suffolk, imprisoned in the Tower of London
1507	
24 December	George Neville, Lord Abergavenny, fined heavily for raising a large private army and instigating a riot in Kent in 1503
1508	
March	Henry seriously ill
17 December	Proxy marriage of Princess Mary to future Charles V
1509	
21 April	Death of Henry VII at Richmond Palace
23 April	Henry's death announced
24 April	Imprisonment of Edmund Dudley and Richard Empson
11 May	Funeral of Henry VII
29 June	Death of Lady Margaret Beaufort

ACTIVITY

Study Chart 3E, showing the main events of Henry VII's reign. Copy and complete the following table.

Security issues	Family events	Foreign policy events	Parliament	Other

TALKING POINT

Was Henry's reign ever problem-free? Were some periods more difficult than others? Why was this? What do these events tell you about Henry's approach to kingship?

ACTIVITY

Either
As Henry VII, write a king's speech outlining the priorities for your reign.

or
Compose a mission statement for your reign to circulate to your advisers.

KEY POINTS FROM CHAPTER 3: The monarch's manifesto – what were Henry's concerns on his accession?

1 On his accession, Henry secured his position by various means, including dating his reign from before the Battle of Bosworth, gaining Parliamentary approval and marrying Elizabeth of York.
2 His main priorities were to be recognised as king – this meant dealing with threats and securing the succession for his heirs.
3 He rewarded those who had served him before and at Bosworth, some of whom had worked for Edward IV.
4 There is now a debate about how difficult Henry's initial task really was, thanks to the work of Christine Carpenter who believes that the difficulties have been exaggerated.
5 Henry developed the role of JPs to help him to govern the localities.
6 In the long term, Henry had to decide how he would run his Privy Council, Parliament and local government, and what his relations with the Church would be.
7 He had to deal with rebellions in Yorkshire in 1489 and in Cornwall in 1497, in addition to the threats from Simnel and Warbeck (see Chapter 4).

4

Foreign policy – help or hindrance?

CHAPTER OVERVIEW

Henry VII knew that foreign policy could make or break his reign. The pressure was on right from the beginning, when he was weakest and most vulnerable. And although the foreign problems may have become less intense in his later years, they never ceased – England's force and influence always remained at the weaker end of the European power spectrum. In Henry's reign, foreign policy and internal security were inextricably linked, particularly with regard to the PRETENDERS Lambert Simnel, Perkin Warbeck and Edmund de la Pole. Henry's decisions and actions were also to a large extent determined and shaped by events on the Continent.

PRETENDER
The title 'pretender' means that the person made a claim to the throne, not that they were impersonating someone.

In this chapter, we will study foreign policy events in the light of the following key issues:

A How vulnerable was England in late fifteenth-century Europe?

■ 4A Europe in 1485

Ireland – beyond the Pale?
By 1461 English rule in Ireland was limited to the Pale, a strip of land about 32 kilometres deep which stretched along the east coast for 80 kilometres. The rest of Ireland was governed by independent chiefs, the greatest of whom were the Fitzgeralds of Kildare. Ireland was a central concern in English foreign policy:

- It provided an ideal springboard for invasion attempts.
- It had deeply held Yorkist sympathies.
- The area beyond the Pale was not under English control.

Scotland – a thorn in the side
Scotland was a nation of about 400,000 people (about the size of Bristol today) with an annual Crown income of only £8,000. The King of Scotland was utterly reliant on the co-operation of the nobility and was vulnerable to violent usurpations. Despite these weaknesses, Scotland remained a considerable thorn in England's side:

- Its vast and rugged countryside made conquest impossible and invasions difficult.
- The traditional alliance between the Scots and the French could expose England on two flanks simultaneously.
- The threat of border raids necessitated two financially draining, permanent garrisons in Berwick and Carlisle.

England – minor league player?
Internally riven by the Wars of the Roses, England had seen little active involvement in European affairs since the end of the Hundred Years War in 1453. Although an island, England had limited military forces at its disposal and so was vulnerable to attack from foreign powers, especially France. English concerns and interests were as follows:

- Calais and its hinterland were still controlled by England and remained a highly valued English foothold on the Continent.
- The Netherlands, especially Antwerp, were an essential centre of the cloth industry and it was important for England that they remained accessible.
- Yorkist pretenders were likely to generate foreign-backed invasion attempts.

BURGUNDY
The territory ruled by the Dukes of Burgundy may be referred to as Burgundy, the Netherlands or the Low Countries.

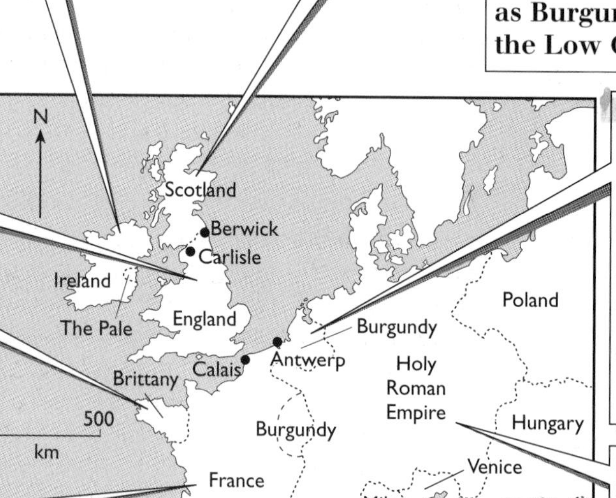

Burgundy – a serious powerbroker
BURGUNDY was a peculiar collection of towns and states that had been rapidly created by three generations of dynastic matchmaking, diplomacy and war. Burgundy was an important territory:

- It was the principal trade and cloth-finishing centre for England.
- Edward IV's sister, Margaret of Burgundy, could act against England.

Brittany – Henry's protector during his exile
Brittany was an independent duchy in the north-west of France ruled by Francis II. After fleeing Britain in 1471, Henry VII had remained in Brittany for most of his exile, so he owed the Duke a debt of gratitude.

France – Europe's greatest power
On becoming king in 1483, Charles VIII inherited a France that had increased quickly in size and power during the fifteenth century. France was strong because of its resources:

- It had the largest and most professional army in Europe.
- It was financially strong – the state had considerable powers in the collection of taxes.
- It had the largest population in Europe at about 15 million.

This 'rejuvenated' France (J. D. Mackie, *The Earlier Tudors, 1485–1558*) could now look to secure Brittany and to pursue its claims to Milan and Naples.

Holy Roman Empire – a ramshackle collection of states
The Holy Roman Empire stretched over much of central Europe and comprised about 20 million inhabitants and a myriad of different states. The Emperor (Frederick III, 1448–93, then Maximilian, 1493–1519) was a force to be reckoned with. The Empire was a central concern in Europe:

- It was large and strong.
- It had claims and ambitions in Italy.
- It had acquired Burgundy when Maximilian had married Mary of Burgundy in 1477.

Spain – a newly unified force
Ferdinand of Aragon and Isabella of Castile had become joint monarchs in 1479. Their marriage gave Spain an 'international existence' (J. H. Elliot, *Imperial Spain*) and its armies were soon to command Europe-wide respect. The priorities of Ferdinand and Isabella were as follows:

- They wanted to drive the Moors (the Muslims) out of Granada in the south of Spain. They had started the reconquest in 1482.
- They wanted to secure their northern border by retaking the territories of Cerdagne and Roussillon (seized by France in 1462) and by capturing the French-supported territory of Navarre.
- Ferdinand also had an inherited claim to Naples.

All three of these foreign policy objectives created the possibility of conflict with France, but not with England.

Italy – the big prize
'Italy' did not exist as a country in early modern Europe. What did exist were a number of wealthy and competing states, the principal ones being Milan, Venice, Florence, Naples and the Papal States. Italy was the crucial political target in the late fifteenth century:

- It was weak and divided into different states.
- It was geographically and commercially at the 'crossroads' of Europe.
- It was hugely wealthy and was experiencing a cultural revolution – the Renaissance.
- France and the Habsburg Empire had dynastic claims in Italy that they wished to pursue.

■ 4B The power of France

France was undoubtedly the greatest power in Europe, and the other kingdoms swung around it in wary orbit. The rising star was the Habsburg dynasty, which controlled the Holy Roman Empire and Burgundy. The storm of conflict between France and the Habsburgs was to break first over Italy in the Italian Wars (1494–1516). At this time, Italy was not one country, but made up of a number of independent states. England was merely a small, distant planet.

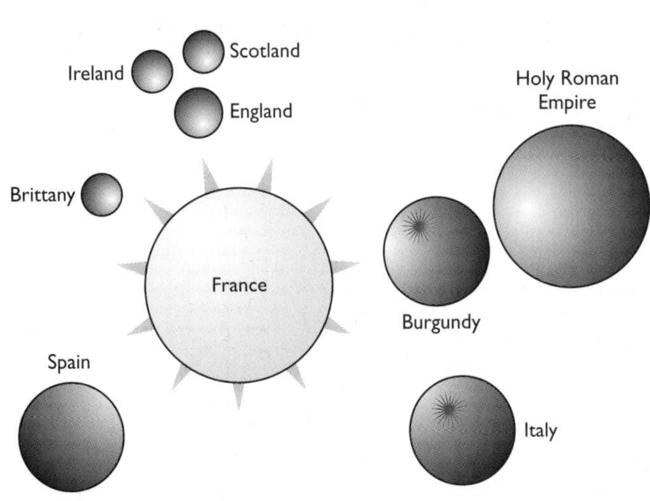

ACTIVITY

In 1485, England had four permanent garrisons: Calais, Carlisle, Berwick and Ireland. The King had around 700 full-time professional soldiers to station at these garrisons.

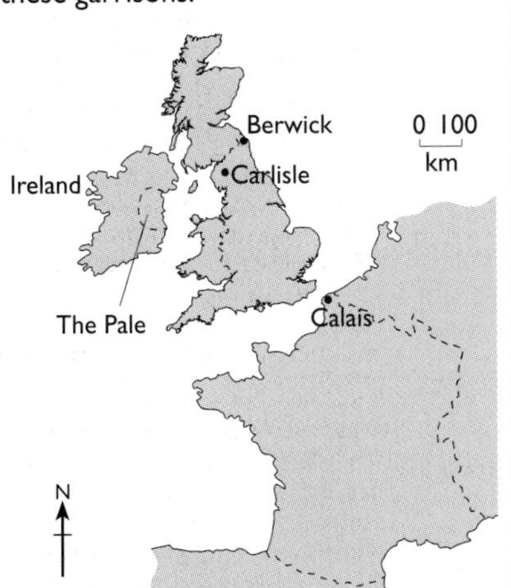

Read Chart 4A and recommend how the soldiers should be divided among the four garrisons. Base your decision on the threats posed by the neighbouring countries and the foreign policy interests of England. Explain your reasons.

SOURCE 4.1 R. B. Wernham, *Before the Armada*, 1966, p. 22

For all of these reasons, then – strategic, dynastic, commercial, religious – Tudor England was never able to cut loose from continental entanglements and relapse into a merely passive insularity. Yet her comparative weakness always made such entanglements dangerous. It called for the highest skill and circumspection in her rulers whenever they had to join in the political rivalries of the continent.

SOURCE 4.2 G. Mattingly, *Renaissance Diplomacy*, 1955, p. 122

It has been fashionable among English historians to say that England, at almost any time from 1485 to 1588, was 'a little country', 'scarcely more than a third-rate power', 'about on a level with Portugal and Denmark'. This is one form of Anglo-Saxon understatement.

It is true that in wealth and population England counted fourth among the Western powers, though it counted ahead of all but its three big rivals by a respectable margin ... At the same time, by the loss of its dependencies, England had gained freedom of diplomatic manoeuvre. Secure behind its seas, England could now take as much or as little of any war as it liked. No commitment was more than tentative, no alliance irrevocable, and at each new shuffle in the diplomatic game the other players had to bid afresh for England's friendship or neutrality.

ACTIVITY

Read the text boxes on Chart 4A and the two interpretations of England's position in Sources 4.1 and 4.2. Which of the two interpretations do you most agree with? Explain your decision.

B How well did Henry respond to the events of his reign?

FOCUS ROUTE

As you work through pages 40–45, complete your own copy of the table below, summarising the main events of Henry's foreign policy.

Event	Problem	Henry's solution
Brittany Crisis (1487–92)		
Italian Wars (1494–1509)		
Castilian Succession Crisis (1504–06)		
Scotland (1485–1509)		

This section attempts to recreate the situations and problems that Henry faced in foreign affairs during his reign. You can do the activities individually by working through the dilemmas and deciding your answers before checking the actual answers at the back of the book. Alternatively, you can form groups and solve the dilemmas individually before awarding points to those in the group who get correct answers.

The Brittany Crisis (1487–92)

When the minor Charles VIII came to the throne of France, his sister, Anne of Beaujeu, acting as regent, set France's sights on recovering the largest remaining semi-independent duchy – Brittany. The time seemed right to do this in 1487. The Duke of Brittany, Francis II, desperately wanted to preserve Breton independence, but he was old and did not have long to live. He had no male heir, only two young daughters, Anne, aged twelve, and Isabel. Anne of Beaujeu therefore sought to marry Charles VIII to Anne of Brittany.

This proposal set alarm bells ringing across the courts of Europe. The absorption of Brittany into the French fold would significantly enhance the power and strategic capabilities of this already mighty country. Ferdinand of Spain and the Habsburg Maximilian both attempted to intervene to prevent the French taking control. The French responded by sending troops into Brittany in May 1487. In reply, troops were sent by Maximilian (1,500), by Spain (1,000) and by Alain d'Albret (4,000), a French nobleman who, like Maximilian, hoped to acquire Brittany for himself by marrying Anne.

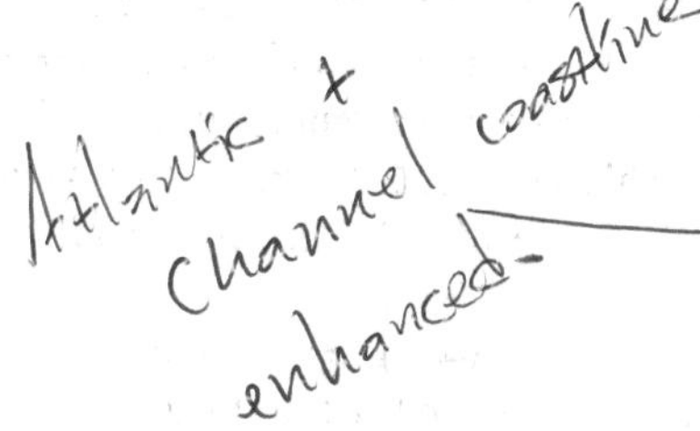

Dilemma 1: How should Henry respond?

Henry was pulled in different directions. Military intervention seemed necessary for several reasons:

- He was very alarmed by the increase in French power that the acquisition of Brittany would bring.
- French control of Brittany would greatly increase their potential to invade England and harry English trading ships. This is because it would leave France with control of almost the entire southern shore of the Channel and with possession of Brittany's excellent ports and considerable maritime resources.
- Henry owed a debt of gratitude to Francis II of Brittany for sheltering him and providing for him through all his years of exile and so should support him in maintaining Breton independence.

On the other hand, he did not want war with France:

- He had been a guest of France during the final period of his exile and he had received substantial French assistance for his own successful invasion attempt.
- Henry was wary of antagonising France so early in his reign.
- Full-scale war would seriously strain his precarious finances.

ACTIVITY

Dilemma 1

Henry's options were:

a) send troops to help to expel the French
b) continue to rely on diplomacy
c) allow unofficial intervention by English soldiers
d) a combination of the above.

Choose one of the options and explain and defend that choice.

Answers to this activity are given on page 321.

The crisis deepened considerably when the French defeated the Breton and allied forces at St Aubin du Corbier (28 July 1488). On 9 September, Francis died and Anne of Beaujeu took over the wardship of Anne of Brittany. French control was almost complete.

The other European powers were concerned, but too deeply engaged elsewhere to be able to divert resources. They did, however, wish to pursue diplomatic solutions and looked to England to help to deal with the crisis.

Dilemma 2: What should Henry do?

This would be Henry's last opportunity to preserve Breton independence and so protect England's trade and security. He needed to consider the following:

- He would need allies if he was going to take on France, but how reliable would Maximilian and Ferdinand and Isabella be?
- Sending a large army over to Brittany might give Henry an opportunity to reclaim English lands (Normandy, Aquitaine and Guyenne) lost during the Hundred Years War.
- He would lose face in England if he failed to act.
- He needed to be sure that he could raise money for the venture.

Now tackle Dilemma 2 in the Activity box.

> **ACTIVITY**
>
> **Dilemma 2**
>
> Henry's options were:
>
> **a)** form alliances with Spain and Burgundy for a joint assault on France
> **b)** launch an immediate unilateral attack
> **c)** accept French control of Brittany.
>
> Choose one of the options and explain and defend that choice.
>
> Answers to this activity are given on page 321.

- Creates anti-French alliances during winter of 1488-9, with Brittany, Spain & Burgundy.

Under the Treaty of Redon (February 1489) with Brittany, Henry agreed to send 6,000 troops to defend Breton independence. In return, Anne pledged to pay for the English troops and not to marry or form alliances without Henry's consent. Henry sent over 3,000 soldiers. Henry is normally regarded as offering a limited proposal so that France would not be too alarmed by the return of English soldiers to French soil. Recent research has, though, suggested that Henry's ambitions stretched to the reconquest of former territories (Normandy and Guyenne) and that it was the Bretons who put the upper limit on the number of troops to be involved.

Under the Treaty of Dordrecht (February 1489) with Maximilian, heir to the Holy Roman Empire, Henry agreed to send 3,000 troops to help Maximilian to relieve a garrison of Maximilian's that was under siege from Flemish and French forces. Maximilian did not honour his side of the bargain to provide troops to help to save Brittany's independence. In July, Maximilian made peace with Charles VIII of France.

Under the Treaty of Medina del Campo (March 1489), Henry and Spain agreed to go to war against France in order to recover lost territories (Normandy and Aquitaine) for England. The alliance was cemented by the arrangement to marry Henry's son Arthur to Catherine of Aragon when they came of age. However, Ferdinand and Isabella were preparing for a final assault on the Moors in Granada and withdrew the forces they had sent to Brittany.

In January 1491 Maximilian married Anne of Brittany by proxy. The situation deteriorated further when the French attacked again and Anne of Brittany was forced to marry Charles VIII of France in December 1491.

Dilemma 3: Should Henry continue the conflict?

Henry was now facing a major crisis:

- He had raised a large amount of money and he would anger his subjects if it was not spent on the war against France. (Parliamentary grants in 1489 and 1491 and a BENEVOLENCE in 1490 had raised £181,500.)
- Henry had invested a great deal of prestige in the war (promising to go in person) and campaigns against France were the traditional sport of English kings. If Henry admitted defeat now, he would lose much-needed credibility.
- Charles VIII's attention seemed increasingly drawn to Italy, so French control of Brittany would be less of a threat.
- James IV of Scotland dropped plans for a Franco-Scottish marriage and was opening negotiations for an English one. This meant that Henry's northern border would be more secure.

> **BENEVOLENCE**
> A benevolence was a forced loan.

ACTIVITY

Dilemma 3

Henry's options were:

a) wage war with France
b) attempt to find a negotiated settlement
c) delay until one of the allies offered firm support
d) a combination of the above.

Choose one of the options and explain and defend that choice.

Answers to this activity are given on page 321.

On the other hand:

- A long war against France would be enormously draining and would almost certainly end in defeat.
- Henry was worried about exposing himself to usurpation by Yorkists. War with France would encourage the French to back challenges to his throne (just as they had successfully sponsored him in 1485). This danger was very real, since the pretender Perkin Warbeck (see pages 48–49) had landed in Ireland in the autumn of 1491.
- Henry was unlikely to receive support from Spain, Maximilian or many Bretons.

Now tackle Dilemma 3 in the activity box.

Under the Treaty of Etaples (November 1492), France agreed to give substantial financial compensation (£159,000 pension) in return for England removing all its troops from French soil (except Calais). A speedy and pain-free reconciliation had been achieved. Although Brittany had been lost, France was now closed to the Yorkists and this was a more tangible benefit for Henry.

The Italian Wars (1494–1509)

The whole focus of European attention shifted decisively south with France's invasion of Italy in 1494. From being at the fulcrum of European politics Henry VII now found himself very firmly at the edge.

Dilemma 4: Should Henry get involved in the Italian Wars?

Henry needed to consider the following:

- England's main foreign policy concern of the 1490s was the threat from Perkin Warbeck. Without the distraction of the Italian Wars, Henry's rivals might devote dangerous time and resources to the Yorkist pretender, so it was in Henry's interests for the war to continue.
- Spain and the Holy Roman Emperor urged Henry to join the alliances against France. Any attack on France would be very costly.
- If England attacked France, the danger posed by French retaliation would be enormous.

Now tackle Dilemma 4 in the activity box.

ACTIVITY

Dilemma 4

Henry's options were:

a) form alliances with Spain and the Holy Roman Emperor
b) attack France
c) remain neutral
d) a combination of the above.

Choose one of the options and explain and defend that choice.

Answers to this activity are given on page 321.

France's invasions of Italy (in 1494 and 1498) had kept the focus of the other European countries away from England and Henry's aloofness had given him room for manoeuvre. Conflict in Italy continued up to the end of Henry's reign.

The Castilian Succession Crisis 1504–06

Henry's foreign policy had been linked to Spain since the betrothal of his son Arthur and Catherine of Aragon in 1489. The roof fell in on Henry's policy, however, with the Castilian Succession Crisis, which broke in November 1504 on the death of Isabella of Castile.

The anti-French alliance of the Netherlands, Spain and England was transformed into a self-destructive feud by Isabella's death. Ferdinand was king only in Aragon and Isabella's will stipulated that it was their eldest daughter, Joanna, who would inherit the larger and more important territory of Castile, with Ferdinand returning to Aragon. In 1496 Joanna had married Archduke Philip, ruler of Burgundy and heir to the Holy Roman Empire. So, in an unexpected twist, Castile was to be absorbed into the vast Habsburg Empire. Ferdinand, one of the wiliest operators on the diplomatic scene, was not willing to abandon the reins of the country that he had come to see as his own to the hands of his bitterest enemy, Philip. A confrontation was clearly brewing.

Dilemma 5: With whom should Henry ally?

Henry was caught in a trap. He had to choose between his alliance with Philip and his alliance with Ferdinand. A repudiation of either was bound to have serious repercussions on England's position. Henry had to consider the following:

- If Ferdinand were king only of insignificant Aragon, Henry would not want to commit his son, Prince Henry, to an embarrassing and valueless marriage to Catherine of Aragon (Arthur had died in 1502).

- Henry *must* maintain the commercial links with Burgundy (controlled by Philip), upon which the cloth trade depended.
- Philip was much younger and more vigorous than Ferdinand.
- There was a possibility of a marriage between Philip's daughter, Eleanor, and Prince Henry.
- Maximilian was sheltering the leading Yorkist pretender, Edmund de la Pole, Earl of Suffolk, and an alliance with Philip (Maximilian's son) would probably enable Henry to regain custody of him.
- Henry VII believed that he had nearly been duped by Ferdinand into marrying the penniless Queen of Naples. (Henry's wife, Elizabeth, had died in 1503.)

Now tackle Dilemma 5 in the activity box.

ACTIVITY

Dilemma 5
Henry's options were:

a) retain the alliance with Ferdinand
b) retain the alliance with Philip
c) attempt to preserve a neutral position between Philip and Ferdinand
d) abandon both Ferdinand and Philip and negotiate an alliance with France.

Choose one of the options and explain and defend that choice.

Answers to this activity are given on page 321.

Ferdinand knew that he had lost his Habsburg alliance (Philip and Maximilian) and that his English alliance was slipping away from him. He feared isolation and so turned to his old enemy, France. Louis XII, perturbed by the expansion of the Habsburg dynasty, agreed to an alliance and signed the Treaty of Blois (October 1505). Ferdinand married Louis' niece, Germaine de Foix.

The race was on for the Castilian crown. With French support, Ferdinand would have been able to force the Castilian nobility to accept him. Philip responded to the urgency of the situation and set sail for Castile with a large fleet in the middle of winter (January 1506). His ships were scattered by a sudden storm and Philip was driven on to the English coast.

Dilemma 6: How should Henry treat his unexpected guest?

Ferdinand's alliance with the French had made an Anglo-Burgundian alliance a necessity. Henry could, though, use the unexpected arrival of the Archduke to force a more profitable treaty. Henry had to consider the following:

- Philip was taking an ambitious political risk in attempting to wrest Castile from Ferdinand's grasp. Should Henry tie himself closely into this gamble by sending troops or money?
- The collapse of the Aragon marriage and the deaths of Henry's eldest son, Arthur, and Henry's wife had left the Tudors dynastically insecure. Should Henry push for marriages for himself, his son Henry and his daughter Mary with the Habsburgs?
- Trade with Burgundy was vital to English merchants. Should Henry take advantage of Philip's temporarily weak position to improve the trading terms agreed under the *Intercursus Magnus* (1496) (see page 52)?
- Philip was now holding the Yorkist pretender Edmund de la Pole, Earl of Suffolk, whom Henry wanted back.

Now tackle Dilemma 6 in the activity box.

ACTIVITY

Dilemma 6
Henry's options were:

a) maintain a distance from Philip
b) give maximum support to Philip
c) concentrate on extracting terms favourable to England
d) a combination of the above.

Choose one of the options and explain and defend that choice.

Answers to this activity are given on page 321.

In mid-April 1506, Philip and Joanna arrived in Castile to a rapturous welcome. Failing to gain any effective French support, Ferdinand retired to Aragon. Balance and security seemed to be restored to western Europe. However, in September 1506 Philip died, shattering once again the unstable network of European alliances. Ferdinand quickly resumed control of Castile and Maximilian assumed the regency of Burgundy for his young grandson, Charles. Philip's widow, Joanna, suffered a mental breakdown, refusing to let anyone bury the body of her husband.

Dilemma 7: How can Henry rescue the situation?

Philip's sudden and unexpected death left Henry isolated and exposed in Europe. Once again his foreign policy had been shown to be entirely at the mercy of the shifting sands of continental events and decisions. To salvage England's position, Henry had to consider the following:

- Secure in his French alliance, Ferdinand no longer needed England's friendship and was bitter about the way Henry had abandoned him for Philip.
- Henry desperately needed some marriage alliances for himself and his family. Should he look for Spanish matches? It was England, after all, that had broken off the marriage to Catherine of Aragon and Joanna was now available for remarriage.

ACTIVITY

Dilemma 7
Henry's options were:

a) restore relations with Ferdinand
b) arrange marriage alliances with Maximilian's family
c) construct alliances with a number of European countries.

Choose one of the options and explain and defend that choice.

Answers to this activity are given on page 321.

- Alliances and marriages could also be sought with Maximilian's family (Henry VII to Margaret of Austria, Prince Henry to Eleanor of Burgundy, and Princess Mary to Charles of Burgundy).
- Marriage alliance with France was a possibility via Prince Henry and Louis' niece, Margaret of Angoulême.

Now tackle Dilemma 7 in the activity box on page 43.

The storms of European events, which had buffeted England and ultimately decided English policy throughout Henry's reign, blew favourable winds in 1508. Once again it was ambition in Italy that brought temporary security to England. Louis XII, Maximilian and Ferdinand formed the League of Cambrai to attack Venice. England was notably excluded from the agreement, but the ailing Henry was probably grateful for the respite that it brought.

Scotland – a constant dilemma (1485–1509)

Dilemma 8: What policy should Henry adopt towards Scotland?

All English kings had difficulties in their dealings with their northern neighbour (see Chart 4A), but Henry came to the throne at a time of particular difficulty. He had to consider the following:

- Edward IV had taken the border towns of Berwick and Dunbar, which the Scots were determined to win back.
- The Scots' traditional alliance with France meant that Scotland always posed a particular danger to England.
- Scottish hostility towards England created the ever-present problem of border raids and invasions, which were especially likely during the time of instability following Bosworth. Henry was therefore anxious to establish peace with the Scots.
- The Yorkist rebels received shelter in Scotland.
- Leniency towards Scotland would not be well received by Henry's subjects.

Now tackle Dilemma 8 in the activity box.

ACTIVITY

Dilemma 8

Henry's options were:

a) restore Berwick or Dunbar to Scotland to win Scottish friendship
b) attempt to reach a diplomatic settlement
c) give no concessions and strengthen his border forces
d) a combination of the above.

Choose one of the options and explain and defend that choice.

Answers to this activity are given on page 321.

Dilemma 9: How should Henry deal with a hostile Scotland?

England's relations with Scotland under James III were improving, but in June 1488, after the battle of Sauchieburn, James III was killed by rebellious Scottish nobles. Henry had to return to the drawing board to create a new policy that would deal with the new challenges that had been thrown up. He had to consider the following:

- James IV was a minor and his regency was dominated by anti-English nobles.
- There were Anglophile Scottish nobility with whom Henry could do business. The leading member of this group was the Earl of Angus.
- Ousted Scottish rebels were sheltering in England and were looking for an opportunity to re-establish themselves.
- Henry's daughter Margaret had been born in November 1489 and was an obvious match for the young James IV.
- Scotland was drawing tighter links with France at the time that Henry was engaged in a war with France over Brittany.
- Henry was fearful that Perkin Warbeck would receive support in Scotland.

Now tackle Dilemma 9 in the activity box.

ACTIVITY

Dilemma 9

Henry's options were:

a) continue to attempt a negotiated settlement
b) pre-empt Scottish action in support of France or Warbeck by launching an attack
c) support the pro-English and rebellious Scottish nobles.

Choose one of the options and explain and defend that choice.

Answers to this activity are given on page 321.

The situation improved markedly in 1492 when the pro-English Earl of Angus re-established control and a nine-year-long truce was signed in 1493. However, the remorseless twists of foreign policy threw Anglo-Scottish relations into confusion again in 1495; in that year the glory-hungry James IV came of age and Perkin Warbeck arrived in Scotland (July 1495). Warbeck was given a royal welcome, a marriage to James' cousin (Lady Catherine Gordon), military support for an invasion in September 1496 and shelter for two years.

Dilemma 10: Should Henry resort to war?

Henry was now facing outright defiance and aggression from his northern neighbour. He had to consider the following points.

> **ACTIVITY**
>
> **Dilemma 10**
>
> Henry's options were:
>
> **a)** launch a full-scale invasion
> **b)** use military preparations as a threat to force the real objective of a negotiated settlement
> **c)** attempt a diplomatic resolution.
>
> Choose one of the options and explain and defend that choice.
>
> Answers to this activity are given on page 322.

- Warbeck had been at large since 1491, and active Scottish support considerably strengthened the threat he posed.
- Warbeck's invasion attempt in September 1496 had been a fiasco because very few Scottish nobles had supported it and the small force (1,400 men) had been easily driven back across the border.
- Parliamentary approval and funding for a war against the Scots, following Warbeck's aborted invasion attempt, would probably be forthcoming.
- In 1496–97 England was free of any other foreign entanglements.
- The successful prosecution of a Scottish campaign could force James IV to the negotiating table.
- The marriage of Margaret to James IV remained an important objective.

Now tackle Dilemma 10 in the activity box.

Again, Henry's plans were foiled. The south-west rose in rebellion in May 1497 (see page 34) and Henry needed to divert forces to suppress the rising. Skirmishes continued in Scotland, but the south-west rose again when Warbeck landed in the autumn of 1497 and called on his 'subjects' to join him.

James IV was himself coming under pressure to cease hostilities and Warbeck's departure (July 1497) made possible the Truce of Ayton (September). This brought to a close the conflicts that Steven Gunn has described as 'perhaps the greatest crisis of his reign' ('Henry VII, 1457–1509' in *The New Dictionary of National Biography*).

Anglo-Scottish relations continued to improve and in 1502 the 'Treaty of Perpetual Peace' was signed. Under this agreement the truce was extended and the marriage of Margaret and James was finalised (it took place in August 1503).

The treaty was less successful than its name suggests. Border raids, the continued Franco-Scottish alliance and James' expansion of his navy led to strained relations between the two countries in the final years of Henry's reign. Crucially, Henry had only stabilised and not secured his northern border. His son was going to have to pick up the pieces.

How well did Henry respond to events?

> **ACTIVITY**
>
> Make a copy of the diagram in Chart 4C. Mark the main events of England's foreign policy across the timeline at the correct points.

At no time was Henry directing foreign policy in Europe. He spent his reign responding to crises as they arose – the Breton and Castilian succession crises, the Italian Wars, the movements of the pretenders and the actions of the Scots. A foreign policy dependent for its effectiveness on distractions elsewhere was always going to be fragile and short term. However, Henry successfully dealt with all these events through a combination of nimble-footed diplomacy and threats of war and peace – at no point was Henry ever dragged into a major conflict. The Milanese ambassador observed, 'In the midst of this, his Majesty can stand like one at the top of the tower looking on at what is passing in the plain.'

■ 4C Foreign policy in the reign of Henry VII

Foreign policy during Henry VII's reign was almost entirely shaped by the activities of France, the dominant European power, and by the Habsburg family. England's foreign policy was a series of cross-currents to the main flow of events on the Continent.

ENGLAND'S FOREIGN POLICY

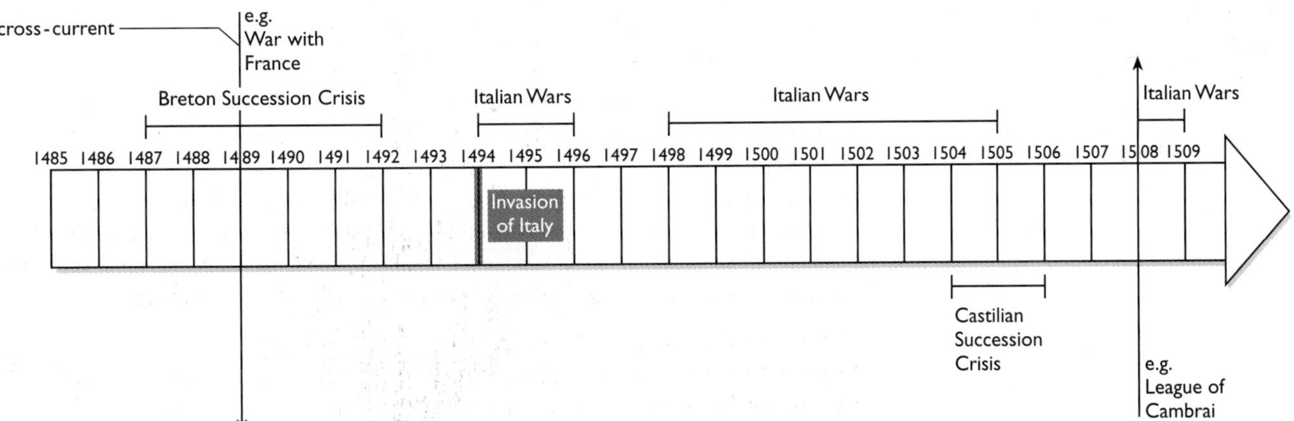

What threat did the pretenders pose to the throne?

Throughout the changing kaleidoscope of diplomatic events, the guiding light of Henry's foreign policy remained security, to be achieved at all costs and by whatever means were necessary. In particular, he was anxious to protect his dynasty from pretenders. Unfortunately for Henry, he had little respite throughout his 24-year reign from challengers to the throne, many of whom received foreign backing.

FOCUS ROUTE

Copy this table and as you read through the text fill in the 'Fate' column to record what happened to the principal challengers to the Tudor dynasty.

Enemy	Position	Fate
Richard, Duke of York	Younger son of Edward IV	Had he been killed in the Tower by Richard III?
Edward V	Elder son of Edward IV	Had he been killed in the Tower by Richard III?
Edward, Earl of Warwick	Son of George, Duke of Clarence (brother of Edward IV)	
Margaret, Dowager Duchess of Burgundy	Sister of Yorkist Edward IV	
Francis, Viscount Lovell	Friend and Chamberlain of Richard III	
John de la Pole, Earl of Lincoln	Son of Richard III's sister and nominated by Richard III as his heir	
Edmund de la Pole, Earl of Suffolk	Younger brother of John de la Pole	

After the battle of Bosworth, Henry did not enjoy any honeymoon period of rest and stability. England was awash with rumours of imminent dangers and prophecies predicting the demise of the new king. Henry showed his sense of vulnerability by issuing proclamations against the publication of books of prophecy and by threatening that all tale-tellers would be pilloried. Henry also established a permanent bodyguard of 50 archers.

■ 4D Threats to Henry's security in 1486

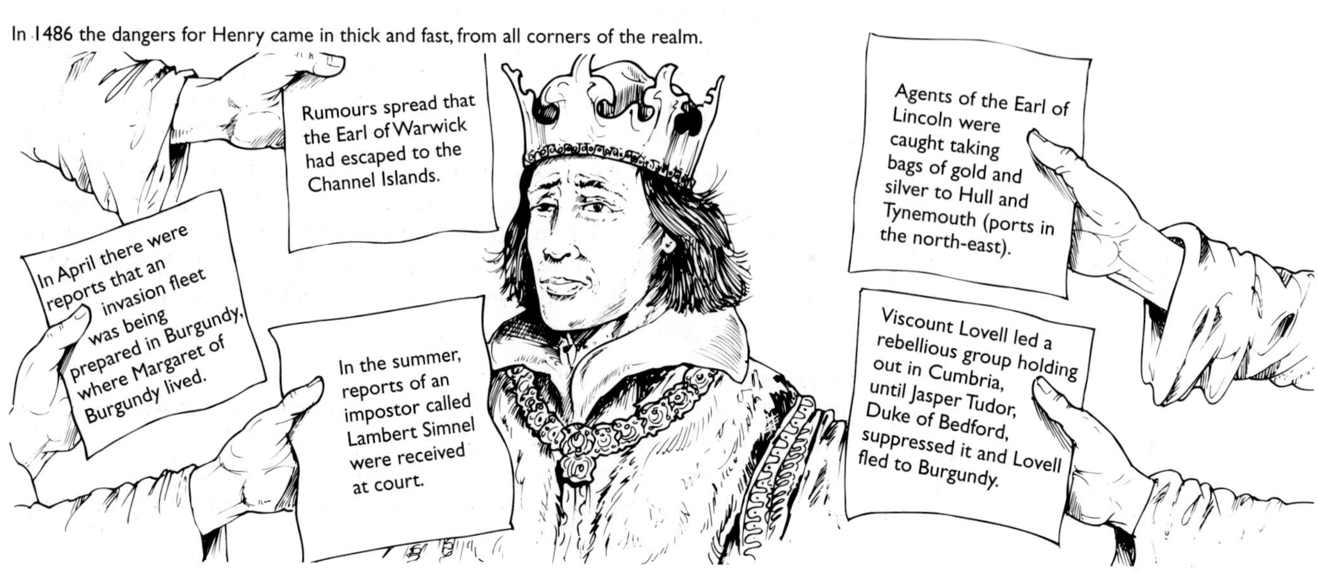

In 1486 the dangers for Henry came in thick and fast, from all corners of the realm.
Rumours spread that the Earl of Warwick had escaped to the Channel Islands.
In April there were reports that an invasion fleet was being prepared in Burgundy, where Margaret of Burgundy lived.
In the summer, reports of an impostor called Lambert Simnel were received at court.
Agents of the Earl of Lincoln were caught taking bags of gold and silver to Hull and Tynemouth (ports in the north-east).
Viscount Lovell led a rebellious group holding out in Cumbria, until Jasper Tudor, Duke of Bedford, suppressed it and Lovell fled to Burgundy.

Lambert Simnel (1486–87)

Among the threats to Henry in 1486, that of Lambert Simnel might initially have seemed the least important, but the Simnel affair was to dominate the Government of Henry VII from mid-February to mid-June in 1487. It is the remarkable story of a young boy from Oxford who was raised from obscurity and presented to Europe as the Yorkist pretender to the throne, Edward, Earl of Warwick. The culmination of the crisis was the battle of Stoke.

How did the Lambert Simnel affair begin?

The traditional version of the affair alleges that it was the creation of Richard Symonds, a 28-year-old clerical resident of Oxford. Symonds had certainly tutored the eleven- or twelve-year-old Simnel who, despite his lowly origins, had sophisticated manners. However, it stretches credibility to believe that the invention of the plot was simply the work of an ambitious priest. Henry VII was probably correct in his guess that John de la Pole, Earl of Lincoln, was behind the scheme.

The Earl of Lincoln was the natural leader of the Yorkist party, being the nephew of the two Yorkist kings (Edward IV and Richard III) and the chosen successor of Richard. Lincoln had initially made his peace with Henry after he had fought against him at Bosworth, but during 1486 he had begun to conspire against Henry. Lincoln had probably been put in contact with Symonds by Bishop Stillington of Bath and Wells, also a resident of Oxford and a known Yorkist.

So why impersonate the Earl of Warwick?

Edward, Earl of Warwick, was the leading Yorkist claimant to the throne, being the son of George, Duke of Clarence (see the family tree on page 17). He had been arrested by Henry after Bosworth and by late 1486 it is possible that the Yorkists feared that he had been murdered in the Tower, like his two cousins before him, since no one had seen him for over a year. In fact he was alive and during the crisis Henry had him paraded through the streets of London in an attempt to prove that Simnel was an impostor.

Who supported the plot?

Margaret of Burgundy, widow of Charles the Bold and sister of the Yorkist kings, was central to this plot and to most of the later attempts to overthrow Henry Tudor. A number of personal and political factors were woven together in the person of Margaret of Burgundy to make her such a doggedly persistent enemy of Henry. On a personal level, Margaret was outraged by the usurpation of her brother, Richard III, and by Henry VII's removal of a number of her own very lucrative trading rights, which had been granted to her by Edward IV. On the political front, Burgundy had enjoyed good relations with the Yorkists and the ruler of Burgundy, Maximilian, was alarmed by Henry's accession. This alarm was heightened by the fact that Henry's successful bid for the throne had been sponsored by France, Burgundy's main rival.

What happened during the plot?

Margaret gave shelter to Viscount Lovell and the Earl of Lincoln, acknowledged Simnel as her nephew and raised 2,000 mercenaries under the command of Martin Schwartz before they set sail for Ireland in April 1487. Meanwhile, in January 1487, Simnel, Symonds and some of Lincoln's retainers had landed at Dublin. Ireland's Yorkist sympathies (see Chart 4A) led many of the leading Irish magnates to welcome and accept Simnel as the Earl of Warwick. Most important of these was Gerald Fitzgerald, Earl of Kildare. Kildare had held the office of Lord Deputy since 1479 and through his extensive family ties was the most powerful and influential man in Ireland. On 24 May 1487, Simnel was solemnly crowned as Edward VI in Dublin Cathedral.

What was Henry's response?

During this time Henry had not been idle. In December 1486 he had summoned a Great Council (it met the following February), which took action against potential conspirators still in England. When he heard that the forces of 'Edward VI' had landed in Lancashire (4 June 1487), Henry set out with his troops.

ACTIVITY

Decide which of the following would have been likely to join the rebels:

a) a northern lord relegated from power
b) a gentleman in the north-west who owed allegiance to the Stanleys (supporters of Henry at Bosworth)
c) a northern lord originally loyal to Richard, but retained in power by Henry VII
d) the Earl of Northumberland (who was on Richard's side at Bosworth, but did not fight and had been allowed to rule the north since Henry's accession)
e) an uncommitted gentleman basing his decision on who was most likely to be the victor.

Explain your decisions.

How was the rebellion ended?

The rebels marched quickly east through Cumbria and north Yorkshire. They hoped to gain support in this area, which retained considerable loyalty to Richard III, but must have been disappointed by the poor response. This failure to swell their numbers may be explained by the speed of their march, which gave little opportunity for troops to be raised (compare this with Henry's slow advance to Bosworth). By 16 June 1487 the rebel army of 8,000 men had confronted Henry's forces of 12,000 men in a field near East Stoke in Nottinghamshire. In what is now regarded as the last conflict of the Wars of the Roses, Henry's forces inflicted a heavy defeat on the rebels.

What happened after the Lambert Simnel affair?

- The Earl of Lincoln was killed during the fighting and Viscount Lovell died soon after.
- Lambert Simnel was captured and went on to enjoy a career first as a turnspit in the royal kitchens and later as the king's falconer.
- Henry, still uneasy, spent the rest of the year until October moving through areas of possible disaffection. He received oaths of loyalty and punished offenders (with fines, rarely with executions) as he went.
- Only 28 men were attainted so Henry had less land available with which to reward supporters. This stands in stark contrast to Richard III's massive transfer of land after the suppression of the 1483 southern rising.
- The parliament called in November 1487 spent more time dealing with those who thought themselves above the law (mainly Henry's supporters) than with Henry's enemies.
- Henry was forced to retain Kildare as the Lord Deputy of Ireland despite his prominent involvement in the plot.

ACTIVITY

1 Why might Henry have been so lenient after Stoke?
2 'The King was walking a political tightrope.' Do the Lambert Simnel affair and its aftermath support this statement?

Perkin Warbeck – an international problem (1491–99)

Perkin Warbeck was a young Flemish boy who, with Yorkist backing, impersonated Richard, the younger son of Edward IV. Improbably, he became the major foreign policy concern of Henry VII for much of the 1490s. Although the concept of high-level political impersonation might seem fanciful to us today, it was used as a very effective weapon against Henry VII. Henry VII's own historian, Polydore Vergil, asserted that Warbeck's story was 'not merely believed by the common people, but . . . many important men . . . considered the matter genuine'.

Whether or not the rulers of Europe believed that the impersonation was genuine is not directly relevant. The support and credence they gave to Warbeck's attempts to usurp Henry are, though, of vital importance in gaining an understanding of England's foreign policy during the 1490s.

ACTIVITY

Study the strip cartoon on the next page, outlining the activities of Perkin Warbeck.

1 Use a map to chart Warbeck's movements and the support he received.
2 Make a list of the occasions when Henry had to act because of the threat posed by Warbeck.
3 Compare the Simnel and Warbeck affairs. What similarities and differences are there between the two challenges to Henry's position?
4 Does the fact that Warbeck received more international support and was 'at large' for longer mean that he was the greater threat to Henry?

■ 4E The activities of Perkin Warbeck

Perkin Warbeck was born in Tournai in the Netherlands in 1475. He became a servant for a Yorkist, Sir Edward Brampton, in 1485 and developed a consuming interest in the Yorkist court.

In 1490 he became a model for a prosperous clothier. He impressed everyone with his handsome appearance and princely bearing. The following year, his employer took him to Ireland with another Yorkist, John Taylor, to impersonate Richard, Edward IV's younger son.

Most Irish lords, including, crucially, Kildare, refused to give Warbeck their backing. Henry dispatched troops to Ireland, so ...

Warbeck travelled to France in 1492, where Charles VIII received him as a prince.

Henry and Charles signed the Treaty of Etaples in November 1492 agreeing not to shelter rebels, so ...

In 1493 Warbeck was forced to go to the court of Margaret of Burgundy. She tutored him in the ways of the Yorkist court.

In 1493 Archduke Philip assumed control of Burgundy. Henry protested to him about the harbouring of Warbeck. When Philip ignored the protest, Henry imposed a trade ban.

Warbeck is welcomed at the court of the new Holy Roman Emperor, Maximilian. Warbeck promised that if he died before becoming king, his 'claim' would fall to Maximilian.

In 1494 Henry's spies uncovered English conspirators among the Government. The most prominent one was Sir William Stanley, who was executed in February 1495.

In July 1495, Warbeck failed in his attempt to land at Deal. He fled to Ireland and enlisted the support of the Earl of Desmond. He was driven out by Sir Edward Poynings, so ...

Warbeck fled to Scotland in 1495 and was given a royal welcome by James IV. He married James's cousin, Lady Catherine Gordon. James supported an unsuccessful invasion of England in September.

James IV signed the Truce of Ayton with Henry VII, so Warbeck had to move again, this time to Ireland. The Irish rejected him in July 1497, so ...

Warbeck landed in Cornwall to profit from the antagonism felt towards Henry following the Cornish rebellion (1497), but he received little support and was arrested.

In 1498 Warbeck was transferred to the Tower.

Warbeck and the Earl of Warwick were said to be involved in an escape attempt and both were executed.

The Earl of Suffolk (1499–1506)

Edmund de la Pole, Earl of Suffolk, was the nephew of the Yorkist kings. His elder brother, John de la Pole, Earl of Lincoln, had been active against Henry early in the reign and had been killed at the battle of Stoke. Edmund was punished for his brother's part in the rebellion by being forced to pay £5,000 to inherit only some of his father's land. He was also not allowed to inherit his father's ducal title. In the intensely ceremonial world of aristocratic politics, this meant that his parliamentary robes bore only three ermine stripes (dukes had four). For a nobleman, precedence was all and Suffolk's grudge may well have derived in part from the slights that Henry's punishment had made him endure.

In 1499 Suffolk killed a man due to appear before the King's court. Suffolk was humiliatingly summoned to appear before an ordinary court and not before his peers. He fled to Burgundy in July 1499. Henry immediately issued emergency orders for the arrest of Suffolk's associates, and envoys were sent to negotiate his return. They proved successful and Suffolk returned later in the same year.

However, in the summer of 1501 he fled again, this time with his brother, Richard. He sought the help of Maximilian and began referring to himself as the 'White Rose', making it clear that he was presenting himself as the Yorkist pretender. All suspected confederates were arrested: Sir William Courtenay (himself of royal blood) remained in the Tower until 1509; William de la Pole (Suffolk's brother) languished in the Tower until his death 38 years later; Sir James Tyrell, Governor of Guisnes Castle in Calais, was executed along with Sir John Wyndham.

Maximilian promised always to help the Yorkist heirs of Edward IV and the two de la Pole brothers settled at Aachen until plans for an invasion could be formulated. Henry, in desperate diplomatic manoeuvres, gave Maximilian £10,000 (supposedly towards the Emperor's campaign against the Ottomans, which never took place), but despite promises Maximilian made no move to expel the de la Poles. The Habsburgs were able to continue their international extortion racket against Henry. They received from the English king over £250,000 in the form of 'loans' that were never repaid. Archduke Philip of Burgundy (Maximilian's son) also used Henry's insecurity about Suffolk to force trade concessions from England. But in January 1505, Henry responded by suspending all trade between the two countries.

The crisis for Henry was only brought to an end by the unexpected death of Isabella of Castile and the freak storm that fortuitously (for Henry) blew Philip on to the English coast as he sailed south to claim the Spanish throne. To pay for his expedition to claim the throne, Philip extracted a further £138,000 from Henry, and in return he surrendered Suffolk to the English commander at Calais on 16 March 1506. Suffolk was paraded through the streets of London and imprisoned in the Tower. Henry acceded to Philip's demand that Suffolk's life should be spared, but Henry VIII finally ordered his execution in 1513.

Henry's responses show that he did not regard Suffolk as an irrelevant and insubstantial threat. Suffolk was, after all, a genuine claimant (something which Henry knew neither Simnel nor Warbeck was) and Suffolk could easily have ventured round to Ireland or Scotland to receive dangerous assistance. More importantly, he could, if events had turned out differently, have received the backing of a European power. Henry was fortunate indeed that events in Italy were again occupying the attention of Europe.

ACTIVITY

1 To understand the extent of Henry's alarm over Suffolk it is vital to understand the wider historical context. Use the 'Deaths' column in Chart 4F on page 54 to explain why Henry was so worried about Suffolk during the period 1501–06.
2 List the ways in which England was badly affected by foreign support for the Earl of Suffolk.
3 During how many years of his reign was Henry challenged by a Yorkist pretender?
4 What can you learn about Henry's treatment of the nobility from the case of the Earl of Suffolk?
5 Use the following Richter scale of unrest to assess the danger posed by the pretenders. First decide whether each of the three rebellions studied in this chapter is a type A or a type B rebellion. Then decide where the rebellions should go on the scale according to how dangerous they were.

- Type A: Attempts by political leaders to seize the throne.
- Type B: Mass demonstrations to draw attention to grievances and to force changes.

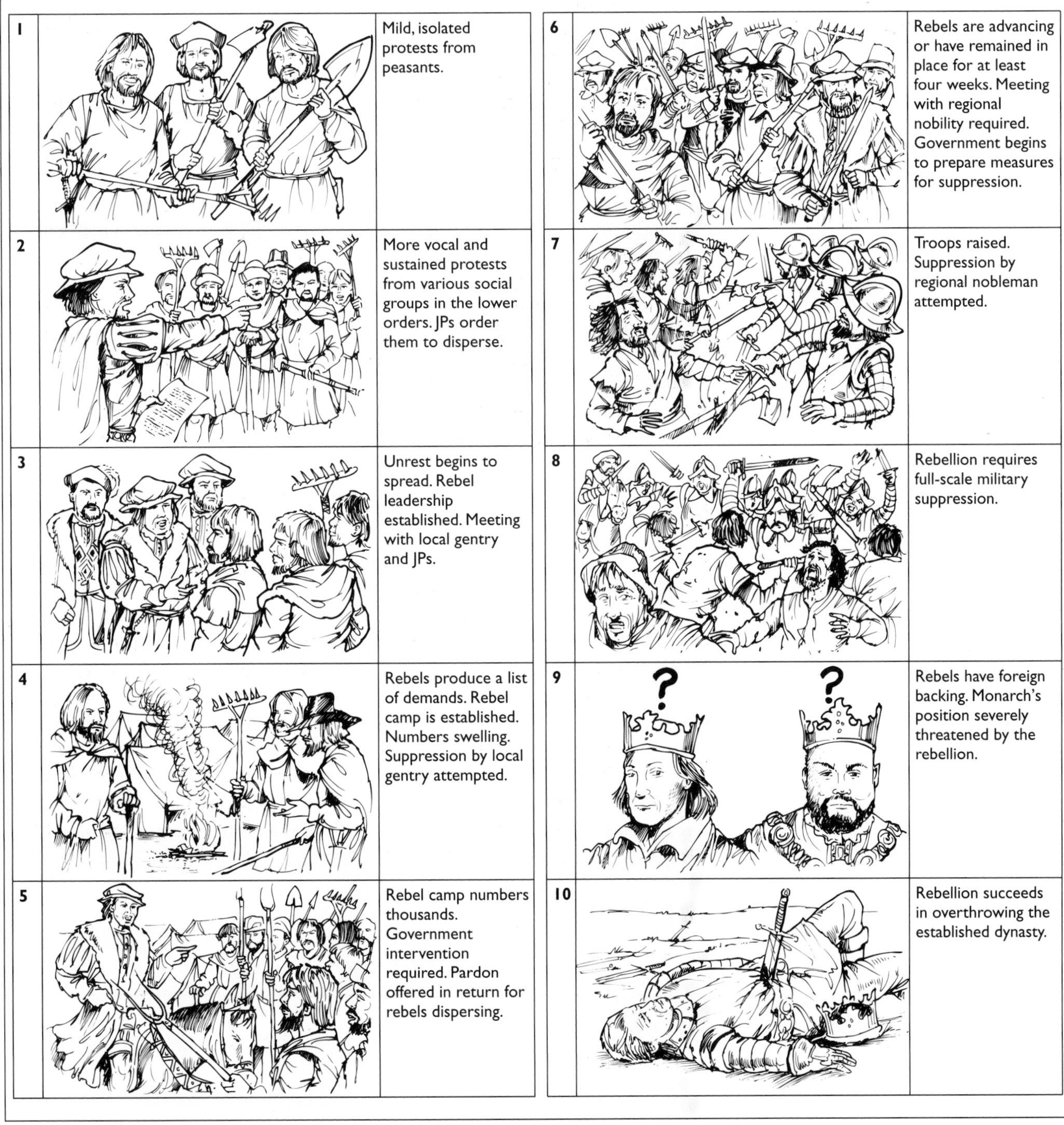

1	Mild, isolated protests from peasants.
2	More vocal and sustained protests from various social groups in the lower orders. JPs order them to disperse.
3	Unrest begins to spread. Rebel leadership established. Meeting with local gentry and JPs.
4	Rebels produce a list of demands. Rebel camp is established. Numbers swelling. Suppression by local gentry attempted.
5	Rebel camp numbers thousands. Government intervention required. Pardon offered in return for rebels dispersing.
6	Rebels are advancing or have remained in place for at least four weeks. Meeting with regional nobility required. Government begins to prepare measures for suppression.
7	Troops raised. Suppression by regional nobleman attempted.
8	Rebellion requires full-scale military suppression.
9	Rebels have foreign backing. Monarch's position severely threatened by the rebellion.
10	Rebellion succeeds in overthrowing the established dynasty.

How did trade and dynastic considerations influence foreign policy?

To be successful in the field of foreign policy, Henry had to consider the particular importance of trade and dynastic interests.

FOCUS ROUTE

1 Study pages 52–53 on Henry's trading agreements. Make notes about the importance of the following factors in influencing trade. Include examples.
 a) Limiting the rights of foreign traders
 b) Establishing equal trading conditions
 c) Dealing with the threat posed by pretenders.
2 Identify the most significant trading agreement that Henry achieved with each country or trading group. Write down the reasons for your choices.

Trade

With France

- 1485: Navigation Act (one which stipulated that goods to the mother country must only be carried in ships from that country) forbade transportation of Gascony wine to England in anything other than English ships.
- 1486: Treaty removing the trade restrictions that had been imposed by France before Henry's reign.
- 1487: France reimposed restrictions because of English support for Breton independence.
- 1489: Navigation Act on Toulouse woad which now had to be transported in English ships.
- 1492: Treaty of Etaples reduced trade restrictions.
- 1495: Restrictions removed by France in return for English neutrality in the Italian Wars.
- 1497: Trading privileges of English merchants restored.

With Spain

- 1489: Treaty of Medina del Campo allowed equal trading rights for merchants from both countries and fixed customs duties at a rate that proved favourable to English traders.
- 1494: Navigation Act imposed by Spain had a damaging effect on English trade with Spain.

With Burgundy

The wool trade was the most important trade for England, and Antwerp in Burgundy was the most important cloth-trading centre in Europe. Therefore commercial relations with Burgundy were of vital importance to the health of England's economy.

- 1487: Commercial agreement (for one year) with Burgundy.
- 1493: Ban on English traders using Burgundy because of Maximilian's support for the Yorkist pretender Perkin Warbeck. Merchants had to use the trading base at Calais and not Antwerp.
- 1496: *Intercursus Magnus* – in the historian Wernham's words, 'the Magna Carta of the English traders' – (*Before the Armada*) signed with Archduke Philip when he had withdrawn support for Warbeck. Under the treaty, English merchants could trade freely in all parts of Burgundy except Flanders.
- 1496–1506: Despite the *Intercursus Magnus*, trading disagreements still arose between England and Burgundy.
- 1506: *Intercursus Malus* – a trade treaty so unfair to Burgundians that it was never implemented.

With the Hanseatic League

The Hanseatic League (or Hansa) was a powerful trading coalition of German cities which had carved out for itself substantial trading privileges in many parts of Europe. In England, the League had enjoyed near-monopolistic rights over some goods since the completion of the Treaty of Utrecht in 1474. Henry VII gradually chipped away at its privileges during his reign.

- 1486: Henry confirmed the rights of the Hansa.
- 1487: Henry banned the export of unfinished cloth by alien merchants.
- 1489: Prohibition on the Hansa's exportation of bullion.
- 1493: Henry paid minimal compensation when the Hansa's London headquarters were attacked by a mob angry at the League's privileges.
- 1504: Henry supported an Act restoring all the Hansa's privileges. This was at a time when he was desperately trying to gain custody of the Yorkist claimant, the Earl of Suffolk, who was a fugitive in Germany.

With other European countries

- 1486: Commercial agreement with Brittany.
- 1489: Commercial friendship treaty with Portugal.
- 1489: Trading rights established with Denmark.
- 1490: Trade agreement with Florence creating an English staple (a trading base) in Pisa. This angered the Venetians, who responded with prohibitions.
- 1492: Henry imposed tariffs on Venetian wine.

How important was trade to Henry?

In the field of trade, as in foreign policy generally, England was not in a position to make the running. Henry did give serious consideration to the effect that his foreign policy would have on commerce, but his approach to trade was by necessity piecemeal and occasioned by other events. According to R. B. Wernham, 'The pattern seems again to have been built up by a series of coherent responses to external opportunities and challenges' (*Before the Armada*).

England's share in the principal trading relationship with Burgundy seems to have remained largely static during Henry's reign, despite his best attempts to reach favourable trading terms for England's merchants, most notably with the *Intercursus Magnus*. However, there were some other trade-related achievements:

- Customs duties were increased by 20 per cent from £33,000 in 1485 to over £40,000 in 1509 (assisted by the new Book of Rates in 1507).
- Henry was responsible for the creation of a small Royal Navy and Europe's first dry-dock at Portsmouth.
- Henry sponsored the transatlantic voyages of John and Sebastian Cabot.

Dynastic considerations

The ultimate objective of a monarch is to ensure the safe succession of the family after his or her death. Therefore, births, deaths and marriages assume a great importance. The significance of dynastic security was heightened for monarchs such as Henry VII, who had experienced the lows of being an 'outsider'. Henry lavished money on displays and ceremonials to celebrate the births and marriages, and to mourn the deaths, of members of his family.

For the first fifteen years of his reign, Henry had much to celebrate.

- His heir, Arthur, was born in September 1486.
- His daughter Margaret was born in November 1489.
- His son Henry was born in June 1491.
- His daughter Mary was born in March 1496.
- His son Edmund was born in February 1499.
- Prestigious marriage plans with the Spanish royal family were finalised in July 1499.

But then Henry's dynastic house of cards began to collapse.

SOURCE 4.3 Arthur, Prince of Wales, painted by an unknown English artist

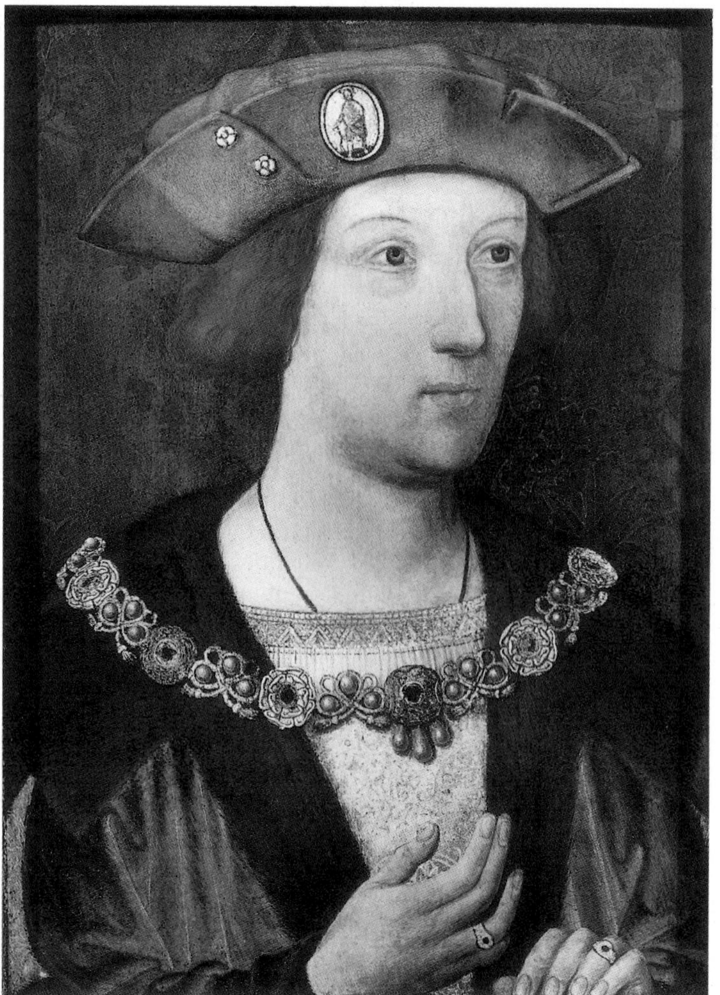

ACTIVITY

1 Study Chart 4F. How might the deaths shown in the chart have affected Henry's sense of security *and* his policies?
2 How significant were Henry's achievements in the field of marriage diplomacy?
3 Can any periods of crisis be identified from the chart?

4F Births, deaths and marriages, 1500–09

Year	Births	Deaths	Marriages proposed	Marriages completed
1500		Edmund (Henry's youngest son) Cardinal Morton (a loyal minister)		
1501		Lord Dinham (a long-standing minister)		Prince Arthur to Catherine of Aragon
1502		Arthur (Henry's eldest son) Lord Willoughby de Broke (a loyal servant)	Princess Margaret to James IV of Scotland	
1503	Catherine	Elizabeth (Henry's wife) Baby Catherine Sir Reginald Bray (one of Henry's most senior ministers)	Henry VII to Catherine of Aragon Prince Henry to Catherine of Aragon	Princess Margaret to James IV of Scotland
1504				
1505			Henry VII to Queen of Naples Henry VII to Margaret of Austria Prince Henry to Eleanor of Burgundy Henry VII or Prince Henry to Margaret of Angoulême	
1506			Princess Mary to Charles of Burgundy (confirmed in 1507 and 1508) Henry VII to Joanna of Castile	
1507				
1508				
1509		Henry VII		Henry VIII to Catherine of Aragon

E How well did Henry manage foreign policy?

ACTIVITY

1 How successful was Henry in achieving his foreign policy objectives?
2 How successfully did Henry deal with the following major foreign issues of his reign? Give him marks out of 10 and explain your scores. Think about whether he emerged stronger or weaker from each issue.
  a) The Simnel Rising and the battle of Stoke, 1486–87
  b) The Brittany Crisis, 1487–92
  c) The pretender Perkin Warbeck, 1491–97
  d) The Castilian Succession Crisis, 1504–06
  e) Scotland, 1485–1509

Henry took measures domestically to secure his position, but he was aware that the real threat to his dynasty would come from abroad. The foreign assistance that swept him to power could easily be raised again for another challenger. To prevent this he set out a number of foreign policy objectives:

- avoid conflict with France
- marry his heir to a powerful country that would seek to support him and his successors
- eliminate claimants to the throne
- maintain trade, especially with Burgundy.

SOURCE 4.4 B. Thompson (ed.), *The Reign of Henry VII*, 1995, p. 8

The avoidance of war was equally no panacea for a new monarchy, since war was more popular than not, and was therefore backed by money and manpower, especially when successful. Even Henry's foreign policy, though astute, was more problematic than it needs to have been as a result of his own need for dynastic security, which was in return prolonged by his inadequate internal governance. In his quarter-century of instability and uncertainty, Henry never secured the loyalty of the realm through stable and representative rule, and therefore never escaped from the consequences of being a usurper. The consequences for the realm were constant disorder and insecurity, which must have maintained the sense of temporariness throughout the reign and always made a Yorkist revanche [revenge] conceivable.

SOURCE 4.5 G. Mattingly, *Renaissance Diplomacy*, 1955, p. 151

Henry VII was akin to Ferdinand of Aragon in temperament and methods. He was better furnished with funds than Maximilian, and he had a more flexible foreign policy (and much less military might) than the French. He understood diplomacy and conducted throughout his reign a series of shrewdly planned negotiations for political and commercial advantages. But his ends were strictly limited. Alone among his contemporaries, he coveted no foreign kingdoms, and valued safety (and gold) above glory. He did not feel the pull of Italy or any interest there beyond solicitude [concern] for the extension of English commerce. Nor was he the man to undertake avoidable expenses.

ACTIVITY

1 Explain in a diagram the vicious circle that Benjamin Thompson (Source 4.4) argues was created by Henry's approach to foreign policy.
2 Explain the link that Thompson draws between Henry's domestic government, his insecurity and his foreign policy.
3 Why does Mattingly (Source 4.5) praise Henry's foreign policy?
4 From the treaties and agreements Henry reached, can you give examples to support Mattingly's claim that Henry 'shrewdly planned negotiations'?
5 Draw up a table like the one below to show the ways in which you and other historians think that Henry's foreign policy was a help or a hindrance. Give examples to support each of your points.

Help	Hindrance
The marriage of Margaret to James IV of Scotland helped to reduce the threat of invasion along Henry's northern border.	Support given to pretenders by foreign powers meant that Henry had to make damaging policy decisions, e.g. he banned trade with Burgundy in 1493 because of Maximilian's support of Warbeck.

F Review: Foreign policy – help or hindrance?

The over-arching policy of Henry's reign was not foreign policy but *security*. Henry's diplomatic manoeuvres and international ventures were all designed as pillars to support this greater concern. It was because of the importance of achieving security for himself, his dynasty and his country that his foreign policy was by necessity defensive and reactive. It was a policy led by international events and domestic interests. The subordination of foreign policy to other concerns meant that Henry was at the mercy of other countries, the flow of events and chance. For instance, he was swung helplessly by the realignment of alliances following the death of Isabella of Castille. He was never in a position to cut loose from the events on the Continent, nor could he set the agenda in Europe. For example, he had to endure the indignities of being toyed with as his rivals picked up and dropped the various pretenders as it suited them.

However, if to some extent he was trapped in an international web, Henry was resourceful and astute enough to ensure that he was never caught. He was also immensely fortunate in the fact that the centre of the European web, for the majority of his reign, was Italy. The remorseless dissection of that peninsula's states spared England the same experience. Henry's foreign adventures suggest that he was a realist, aware of England's limited resources, power and influence. His invasion of France in 1492, for example, was deliberately too late in the year to be able to escalate into a damaging conflict. The lucrative pay-off he received from the French for evacuating the country rewarded his caution. Henry VII's astute handling of foreign affairs meant that most situations were turned to his advantage and so helped his reign.

KEY POINTS FROM CHAPTER 4: Foreign policy – help or hindrance?

1. Henry's foreign policy was inextricably linked with his attempts to achieve internal security.
2. Most of Henry's foreign policy was concerned with limiting the threat posed by the pretenders Lambert Simnel, Perkin Warbeck and Edmund de la Pole.
3. The most important alliance of his reign was with Spain (from 1489 to 1504).
4. Maintaining the cloth trade with Burgundy remained a high priority, and the most significant step he made towards this was the *Intercursus Magnus* agreement (1496).
5. Marriage was a highly valued method of cementing relations between countries for Henry. The most notable matches of the reign were Arthur to Catherine of Aragon and Margaret to James IV of Scotland.
6. The deaths of Henry's family members after 1500 provoked a desperate search for foreign matches.
7. Scotland posed problems for Henry throughout the reign and his largest preparations for war were for the invasion of Scotland in 1496–97.
8. A key aim and achievement of Henry was the avoidance of war, particularly with Europe's strongest power, France.
9. England was dragged into difficulties because of events in Europe, particularly the Brittany Crisis (1487–92) and the Castilian Succession Crisis (1504–06).
10. Henry made effective use of treaties, such as Medina del Campo (1489) and Etaples (1492), to promote trade, protect against pretenders and improve relations with foreign countries.

5

Hanging by a thread – was Henry ever secure?

CHAPTER OVERVIEW

As you have seen in Chapters 2 and 3, Henry's key concern on his accession was his need to achieve security, not only for himself but also for the new Tudor dynasty and for the country. The whole hierarchy of society rested on his efficiency: in defending the realm, administering justice and preserving law and order. If Henry was to be successful in his aim of achieving security, he would have to be strong, well-respected and above all efficient. Weakness in any area would usher in doubts, which would lead to plots against him. The question for Henry was how to sustain, but at the same time control, noble power. If he got this balance wrong, his days were numbered. For Henry to feel secure, he knew that it was essential not only to control the nobility but also to maximise his financial situation. Consequently, Henry paid very close attention to his finances and, in particular, was diligent in trying to spend less than his income.

In this chapter, we will examine how successful Henry was in managing both the nobility and his finances. We will consider the following issues:

A How great a threat was posed by the nobility?

Henry's relations towards the nobility were conditioned by two principal factors. First and foremost, Henry realised that he himself was a usurper. If he could take the throne by force, what was stopping anybody else from doing exactly the same thing? Second, the Wars of the Roses had rumbled on and off for nearly 30 years and the vast majority of people were sick and tired of the uncertainties that such instability brought. Henry knew that, if he was to survive, he had to play the part of a king successfully and bring stability to England.

Henry VI's problems in the 1450s and 1460s had resulted largely from his personal inadequacies as king. Confidence in Henry's ability to rule had been destroyed and the nobility had looked to take power into their own hands. While Edward IV had restored much of the monarchy's strength, his death (in 1483) had revealed that this strength was still tied to the person of the king. As the turbulent years of Richard III show, when the man was weak or disliked, so was the monarchy (see Chapter 2, p.16).

FOCUS ROUTE

As you read pages 58–62, make notes on the following:

1 What threat did the nobility pose?
2 In what ways did Henry control the nobility:
   a) by offering inducements (rewards in return for action)
   b) by issuing threats?

■ 5A Noble power blocs pre-1483

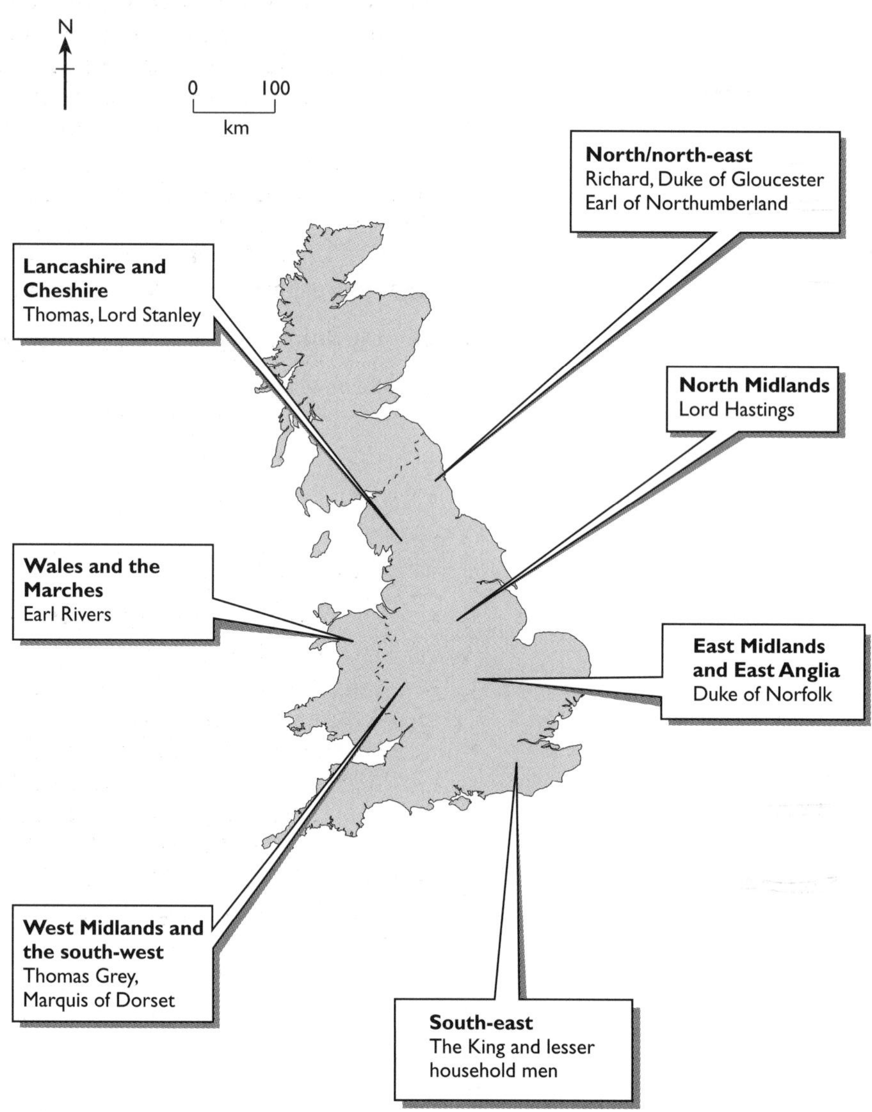

TALKING POINT

You have already seen (page 29) that revisionist historians are suggesting that Henry VII's situation in 1485 was far less difficult and dangerous than has been traditionally thought. Recently, historians have also emphasised that the nobility was not a pack of power-hungry individuals eager for rebellion but that nobles were eager for a stable, secure monarchy. How does this changing view of the nobility affect our view of Henry VII's situation in 1485?

As the nobility's feudal lord, Henry had, therefore, to be sure of securing their loyalty or at least their submission. Without this, he could never be secure. Admittedly, the nobility had been at the heart of many of the century's political upheavals, but, as J. R. Lander makes clear in *Government and Community*, the idea of suppressing or ruling without the support of the nobility was seen by contemporaries as 'wildly eccentric'. Fifteenth-century society saw government as a co-operative effort between king and nobles. Because of the latter's wealth and territorial power, no king could govern effectively without them.

During the reigns of Edward IV and Richard III, the nobility had undoubtedly gained in power. This was due in no small part to Edward's use of the nobility as a means of controlling large areas of England. In *The Wars of the Roses*, A. J. Pollard describes Edward's government as a regime 'founded on regional authority delegated to his most trusted lieutenants'. Chart 5A on page 58 gives some indication of the sorts of power bloc that existed pre-1483.

In contrast, until relatively recently, historians took the line that Henry VII did not have much of a nobility to deal with. This argument largely followed the work of Thomas More, William Tyndale and Sir Thomas Craig, all writing in the sixteenth century. They said that the Wars of the Roses had more or less wiped out the ancient nobility: 'there was not one left to piss against the wall', in Craig's graphic phrase.

The work of K. B. McFarlane in the 1970s, however, changed this interpretation radically. In *The Nobility of Later Medieval England*, he explains that during the fourteenth and fifteenth centuries it was normal for the nobility to lose a number of families from its ranks (a loss of about 25 per cent every 25 years). But the key point is that these families were quickly replaced by wealthy families previously excluded from the peerage.

So, it seems that the nobility did retain its position of importance in society. As C. S. L. Davies has pointed out, 'the King's relations with his nobility were of first importance' (*Peace, Print and Protestantism*). At the same time, changes within the nobility did occur to Henry's advantage. Look at Chart 5B, based on figures produced by Alexander Grant.

5B The reduction in number of nobles

	No. of peers		No. of major peers*	
	Start of reign	**End of reign**	**Start of reign**	**End of reign**
Edward IV	42	46	7	12
Henry VII	50	35	16	10

*Dukes, marquises and earls.

It is clear from the table that a slight alteration is necessary to McFarlane's interpretation. This is a nobility that remained largely intact, but was subtly reduced in power. Most significant, perhaps, is the reduction of 'overmighty' magnates or what Grant (*Henry VII*) calls 'super-nobles', i.e. nobles who combined the lands and inheritances of several major families. Although such nobles did still exist (e.g. the Stafford Dukes of Buckingham and the Percy Earls of Northumberland), there was no one to compare with the Dukes of Clarence and Gloucester under Edward IV. In this Henry was fortunate. Nevertheless, as a feudal lord, it was vital for Henry both to sustain and to control the nobility's authority if he was to survive. What, then, did Henry do in his dealings with the nobility?

TALKING POINT

Which policies of the *present* government can you identify as being carrot and/or stick?

B How did Henry deal with the nobility?

Fundamental to Henry's approach was a 'carrot and stick' policy. Henry had a range of incentives and sanctions at his disposal (see Charts 5C and 5D).

■ 5C Henry's 'carrot and stick' policy: *the carrots*

Form of inducement	Explanation	Evidence
Patronage	If Henry was to remain secure, he had to be able to win over nobles to his cause. Patronage (the giving of positions of power, titles, land, etc.) was only one way, traditionally used by medieval kings, of buying loyalty. Henry VII, however, turned this relationship around by making it clear that patronage came *as a result of* (and not in the hope of) good and loyal service. Just as important was the fact that this form of meritocracy applied to nobility and gentry alike.	First to be rewarded were those who had given Henry loyal support at and before the battle of Bosworth: • The Earl of Oxford (John de Vere) became the major landowner in East Anglia. • Jasper Tudor was made Duke of Bedford, and was restored to his Welsh estates and rewarded with extra land. • Thomas Lord Stanley, Earl of Derby, retained control of Lancashire and Cheshire. • Robert, Lord Willoughby de Broke, received a number of rewards (see pages 63–64). Others were rewarded on the basis of good service: • George Talbot, Earl of Shrewsbury, was one of Henry's closest councillors. • Giles, Lord Daubeney, was promoted to the peerage after showing his value in leading the royal forces against the Cornish rebels in 1497. • Sir Reginald Bray was helped to accumulate land throughout eighteen counties, worth well over £1,000 per annum by the time he died. • Edmund Dudley was a lawyer who became one of Henry's right-hand men and in his own words 'used his title of King's councillor as proudly as any peerage'. Clearly this was a society in which patronage was truly valued because such reward was not bestowed lightly.
Order of the Garter	This was a significant honour reserved for the King's closest servants.	• Henry created 37 Knights of the Garter. More than half of these were his closest associates in war and government. Examples are the Earl of Oxford, Giles Daubeney, Robert Willoughby and Reginald Bray. • S. B. Chrimes comments: 'it seems clear that the Garter rather than anything that could be called a "peerage" was the ultimate mark of honour favoured by Henry VII' *(Henry VII)*. • It was effective for Henry because it gave the recipient prestige but not power or land.
King's Council	A position as king's councillor was a sign of the King's confidence. The emphasis was on loyalty to trusted servants.	• Two Chancellors retained their positions for long periods: John Morton (1486–1500) and William Warham (1504–09). • The position of Treasurer was occupied first by Lord Dinham (1486–1501) and then by the Earl of Surrey (1501–22). • Richard Fox became Keeper of the Privy Seal in 1487, a position he was to retain until 1516. • Henry's five key councillors had all aligned themselves with Henry before Bosworth. They were Reginald Bray, Giles Daubeney and Richard Guildford (all of whom had been involved in the Buckingham conspiracy), and Thomas Lovell and John Riselly (who had joined Henry when he was in exile).
Great Council	These *magna consilia* were meetings of noblemen, called together by the King to discuss high matters of state, usually in moments of emergency when the calling of Parliament would have taken too long. They were also a useful form of control for the King, as they were a way of gaining the agreement and support of his most important subjects for any potentially controversial policy. Put another way, if the nobles had been included in, and had agreed to, a major decision, they could hardly then turn around and criticise Henry for the policy.	There were five meetings of the Great Council: • 1485: for the calling of Parliament and the announcement of Henry's marriage • 1487: in response to Lambert Simnel's threat • 1488: to authorise a subsidy for the campaign in Brittany • 1491: to authorise war against France • 1496: to grant a loan of £120,000 for war in Scotland.

■ 5D Henry's 'carrot and stick' policy: *the sticks*

Form of sanction	Explanation	Evidence
Acts of Attainder	These were nothing new. They dated back to the fourteenth century and were acts that led to a family losing the right to possess its land. Such an 'attainted' family would also lose any right to inherit its land. The loss of such land spelt economic and social ruin for any family. Importantly, however, attainders were reversible and were thus used by Henry VII as 'a sanction for good behaviour' (J. R. Lander, *Government and Community*). In this way, attainders could be both stick *and* carrot – an Act was passed first as a punishment, but good behaviour could then lead to a reversal of the attainder.	The classic example of this 'cat-and-mouse policy' (C. S. L. Davies, *Peace, Print and Protestantism*) is Thomas Howard, the Earl of Surrey. He and his father (John Howard, Duke of Norfolk) had fought for Richard III at Bosworth. However, rather than execute Surrey (his father was killed in action), Henry attainted his lands and imprisoned him. March 1486 – Howard imprisoned and attainted. 1487 – Refused to escape from the Tower during Simnel plot. January 1489 – Released after taking an oath of allegiance; process of reversal of attainder started; restored to title of Earl of Surrey. April 1489 – Put in charge of law and order in the north; quelled Yorkshire rising for Henry; rewarded by Henry (return of the nucleus of the Howard estates). Spring 1491 – Put down second rising in Yorkshire (Ackworth). 1492 – Return of the remainder of attainted Howard estates. However, in spite of Surrey's return to favour, Henry never reinstated him as Duke of Norfolk (this was left to Henry VIII after the battle of Flodden in 1513). Attainders were a traditional form of control but the severity with which Henry used them *was* new. Number of attainders: Passed / Reversed Edward IV: 140 / 42 Henry VII: 138 / 46 It would appear from these figures that Henry was more ready to reverse attainders than Edward IV. When details of the terms of these reversals are looked at, however, we get a different picture: • Nine attainders were passed against nobles; five were reversed, but four of these reversals had special features attached. • Harsh terms were imposed on men of less than noble rank. Payment for reversal was particularly common, e.g. Thomas Tyrell had to pay £1,738 for the reversal of his and his father's attainders. The severity of Henry's policy becomes clear when it is compared with that of Edward IV, in which only one reversal of an Act of Attainder had special terms attached. Henry's policy also increased in severity as his reign progressed. Number of attainders passed: 1485–86: 28 1487: 28 1489–90: 8 1495: 24 1497–1500: 0 1504–09: 51
Bonds and recognisances	Henry was keen to use other traditional 'sticks' as a means of guaranteeing good behaviour. • Bonds were written agreements in which people promised to pay a sum of money if they failed to carry out their promise. • Recognisances were a formal acknowledgement of a debt or an obligation that already existed, with the understanding to pay money if this obligation was not met. Such promises or obligations normally centred around issues such as good behaviour and keeping the peace towards fellow subjects.	• Thomas Grey, Marquis of Dorset, had never been trusted by Henry since his apparent support for Richard in 1485 (when he defected from Henry's camp in France). Thus, in 1492 he was required to transfer all of his land except two manors to trustees, give a recognisance for £1,000 and find others who would give recognisances worth £10,000 on his behalf. By 1499 Dorset had proved his loyalty to Henry (by, for example, helping to put down the Cornish Rebellion) and these agreements were cancelled. The bonds and recognisances had served their purpose. Such evidence points to 'a terrifying system of suspended penalties' (J. R. Lander, *Government and Community*) and one which, like Henry's use of attainders, became more severe as his reign went on. Between 1485 and 1509, 36 out of 62 noble families gave bonds and/or recognisances to Henry. This compares to only one peer during Yorkist rule.

■ 5D Henry's 'carrot and stick' policy: *the sticks* (contd.)

Widowed Duchess, dynastic concern?

21

Form of sanction	Explanation	Evidence
Feudal dues	Henry was keen to emphasise his own power as king by asserting his feudal rights over the nobility. He thus sent out numerous commissions of inquiry to re-establish his rights in the following areas: • Wardship: where the King took control of the estates of minors (those who were too young to be held responsible for their inheritance) until they became of age. In the meantime, the King would take most of the profits from their estates. • Marriage: where the King could profit from the arranged marriages of heirs and heiresses. • Livery: where the King was paid in order for someone to recover land from wardship. • Relief: where the King received money as land was inherited – a form of inheritance tax. • Escheats: payments made when land reverted to the Crown.	• Katherine, Dowager Duchess of Buckingham, was fined around £7,000 in 1496 for marrying without the King's licence. • Her son, Edward, Duke of Buckingham, was fined about £7,000 for entering his inheritance in 1498 without licence before he was 21. • The extent of Henry's increased control can be seen in the increase in proceeds from wardship and marriage: from £350 in 1487 to £6,000 in 1507.
Retaining	Retaining was the long-held noble practice of recruiting gentry followers. The latter were used for general administrative purposes, but also, importantly for Henry, as local fighting forces. They had played an important role in the noble skirmishes of the Wars of the Roses and were thus viewed by Henry as a threat to his own power as feudal lord and king. While Henry took clear steps to limit retaining, however, it is evident that he never intended to do away with retaining altogether.	Henry tried to tackle retaining on two main occasions: 1485 and 1504. • The Lords and Commons had to swear in the 1485 parliament that they would not retain illegally. • In 1504 proclamations ensured that nobles had to obtain special 'placards' or licences to retain. These had to be obtained from the King in person and are another indication of how Henry's policies relied on his personal input. This system was again supported by the threat of financial ruin: • The 1504 Act had a penalty of £5 per month per illegal retainer. This was applied in 1506 to Lord Burgavenny with a fine of £70,550. Although this fine was divided among 26 others and was ultimately scaled down, it nevertheless cast a deep shadow of potential ruin. • A less extreme example is that of the Earl of Devon, who gave a recognisance not to retain illegally in 1494. When he broke that promise in 1506, he was forced to pay part of the sum due. So, while Henry did not stamp out illegal retaining, it seems clear that the nobility was at least much more cagey about the practice. The fact that no written records exist of illegal retaining by nobles seems evidence enough of the nobility's desire to keep any such practice away from Henry's piercing gaze.
Crown lands	Perhaps a more subtle 'stick' was Henry's determined policy to bring back as much land as possible into the hands of the Crown. As we have seen, land in fifteenth-century society equalled power: the more land Henry possessed, the more power he was seen to wield.	• S. J. Gunn (*Early Tudor Government, 1485–1558*) estimates that the amount of Crown land was five times larger by the later years of Henry VII than in Henry VI's reign (1450s). • The lands formerly held by Warwick 'the kingmaker' and by the Dukes of Clarence and Gloucester were almost all retained by Henry throughout his reign. • In 1486 Parliament passed the Act of Resumption, which recovered for the Crown all properties granted away since 1455 (before the Wars of the Roses). • Where possible, Henry rewarded loyal supporters with land not from Crown estates, but from the forfeited lands of opponents. Often people whose land had been forfeited under Acts of Attainder found that they had to fight to get back such lands from royal appointees.

TALKING POINT

Was Henry right to use Acts of Attainder against opponents from Bosworth? They had, after all, only been showing loyalty to the man whom they saw as their rightful king. The Crowland Chronicler at the time deplored Henry's attainting of those loyal to Richard III:

> 'Oh God! What assurance from this time forth are our Kings to have that in the day of battle they will not be deprived of the assistance of even their own subjects when summoned at the dread mandate of the sovereign?'

In a modern context, are we right to pursue in the courts those people who have followed the policies of dictators?

FOCUS ROUTE

Make notes on how the history of the Willoughby de Broke family shows:
a) Henry's loyalty to those who had fought with him in 1485
b) Henry's policy towards those new to power.

Case study: The Willoughby de Broke family

The following case study is adapted from the article 'The rise and fall of a noble dynasty: Henry VII and the Lords Willoughby de Broke' by Dominic Luckett, which appeared in *Historical Research* (October 1996).

Over the years leading up to the battle of Bosworth, the Willoughby de Broke family accumulated substantial estates in the south-west of England. The story of the family's subsequent history reveals much about Henry VII and his relationship with his nobility.

Robert Willoughby

Robert Willoughby de Broke was the first baron of the family. The following is a history of his service from 1470 to 1502.

1452 Born.
1470 Commissioned by Edward IV to raise troops against the Dukes of Clarence and Warwick.
1472 Commissioned by Edward IV to raise troops against France.
1478 Appointed sheriff of Cornwall.
1480 Appointed sheriff of Devon.
1483 One of the key leaders of Buckingham's revolt against Richard III. Fled to Brittany with his brother William to join Henry Tudor.
1484 Richard III passed an Act of Attainder against him (and others). His lands were taken away from him and distributed among Richard's supporters. Followed Henry Tudor to France.
1485 Joined in Henry's invasion of England, fighting at Bosworth.
August: Entrusted with the arrest of the Earl of Warwick.
August–October: Gained a seat in the King's Council; took his seat in the House of Lords; became JP for Devon, Cornwall, Dorset and Wiltshire.
Became steward of the Crown's gold/silver mines in Devon and Cornwall.
Became steward of the Duchess of York's Wiltshire possessions.
1486 Accompanied Henry in his tour round England.
Part of the King's household.
1493 Became steward of the Warwick and Salisbury lands in Wiltshire.
1494 Became steward of the Duchy of Lancaster manors.
1502 Died.

ACTIVITY

1 What evidence is there of Robert Willoughby de Broke's political loyalties from 1470 to 1483?
2 Put forward possible reasons why Robert may have decided to resist Richard III.
3 What evidence is there of his loyalty to Henry VII?
4 What conclusions can you reach about how Henry treated Robert from August 1485 to 1494?
5 Complete this sentence: 'Robert died on 28 September 1502. His career exemplifies [shows]...'

Check your own answers against extracts from the Luckett article which are reproduced on page 322.

Robert Willoughby II

The case of Robert Willoughby demonstrates that in the late fifteenth century opportunities existed for rapid personal promotion. However, the subsequent history of the Willoughby family only serves to indicate that, for so long as Henry VII was king, sustaining such advances was a lot more difficult. Why?

Much of the answer lies in how Henry's personality developed in the years after 1485. Throughout his life, Henry retained a special place in his affections for those who had joined his cause during the dark days of Richard III's rule. Many of these men were entrusted with key positions at the centre of his government and Henry was said to be extremely reluctant to believe ill of them. The downside of this was that, after 1485, he was reluctant to admit new men to his fullest confidence, even after his original intimates began to die off.

This lack of trust was even more marked by events in the later 1490s. William Stanley's treason of 1495 and the south-western revolt of 1497, in particular, shook Henry's faith in his subjects' loyalty. Henry's growing fear of his subjects around this time was reflected in his retreat from the court into the newly constituted Privy Chamber, admission to which was carefully restricted to a small number of professional body-servants.

Such a level of distrust did not bode well for Robert Willoughby II. Indeed, the very wealth and position that he inherited from his father made him an obvious focus of Crown scrutiny. As Polydore Vergil noted, in his later years Henry 'began to treat his people with more harshness and severity . . . in order (as he himself asserted) to ensure they remained more thoroughly and entirely in obedience to him'. The main weapon that Henry employed in his new, harsher policy was finance. As the Spanish ambassador Pedro Ayala reported, the King had openly admitted that he wished to keep his subjects poor 'because riches would only make them haughty'.

So, how did Robert II, lacking any close personal bond with the King, fare?

1502 Took over many of his father's possessions (especially in Devon and Cornwall).
Forced to pay very large fines, e.g. £400 for livery of his lands, £600 to acquire some of his local offices.

1504 Lost land that his father had gained through the previous attainder of Henry Bodrugan. This land was returned to the Crown (to the Crown's profit of £47 19s 10d).
Forced to give a bond of £500 on condition that he keep the peace (probably because he had used excessive force to resolve a dispute).

1505 Brought before a court to prove his title to a manor in Cornwall.
Brought before the Council Learned in the Law in order to prove his claim to some manors in Jersey which the King also claimed.
Robert II lost both of these actions.

1508 Paid £320 to repossess the former possessions of Henry Bodrugan.
So severely short of cash that he was forced to take a loan of £2,000 from the Crown. A condition of this loan was that the Crown could recall it at two months' notice.

Having driven Robert into a position of near-bankruptcy, the Crown now had him at its financial mercy. Any suggestion of disloyalty or unacceptable behaviour would immediately place him in financial jeopardy, without the Crown having to trouble itself with proving anything in a court of law.

At the same time, however, the Crown could still rely on Robert II to exert political control in the name of the Crown in the south-west. This was particularly true as Robert was allowed to serve as a JP (in Cornwall, Devon, Dorset and Wiltshire) and was appointed to several commissions in the area.

TALKING POINT

How valuable is the history of one family to a historian? What are the pluses and minuses?

ACTIVITY

1 Whom did Henry VII trust most and why?
2 Did Henry VII's sense of security increase or decrease as his reign went on? Why?
3 How did Henry VII control Robert II?
4 How was Robert II useful to Henry VII?
5 What lessons can be learned from the history of this one family? Think about:
   - personal advancement
   - personal links to the King
   - the King's control of the nobles.

Check your answer to question 5 by looking at Luckett's own conclusion, which is reproduced on page 322.

ACTIVITY

This is your opportunity to see how you would have fared had you been in Henry VII's position in 1485. How would you have dealt with the important nobles in England on coming to the throne? The activity is a group role-play:

- one student should be chosen as Henry VII
- other students take on the roles of the nobles listed below
- any students left over play the roles of Henry's councillors.

Each of the nobles presents himself before the King to outline his recent history and to pledge loyalty. He can be questioned by the King.

When all of the nobles have appeared, it is the job of the councillors and Henry to place them in order of loyalty. They should also decide what action, if any, should be taken against them. Should they, for example, be imprisoned or given a place on Henry's Council?

Once decisions have been made, you can see how accurate you were by comparing them with the policies that the real Henry VII actually put into practice. Would your decisions have been better than Henry's? For Henry's decisions turn to pages 322–23.

John de la Pole, Earl of Lincoln
- Age: 24.
- Eldest son of Edward IV's sister Elizabeth and John de la Pole, Duke of Suffolk.
- Nephew of Richard III.
- Received a major grant of land for good service to Richard against the Buckingham rebellion.
- Made President of the Council of the North by Richard III in 1484.
- Seen by many as Richard's III's successor.

Thomas Grey, Marquis of Dorset
- Eldest son of Queen Elizabeth by her first marriage.
- Gave help to the Duke of Buckingham in Yorkshire in 1483.
- Denounced by Richard III in October 1483.
- Attainted by Richard III in February 1484.
- Included in Richard III's proclamation against Henry Tudor on 7 December 1484.
- 23 June 1485: His name was dropped from a proclamation by Richard III almost identical to that of 7 December 1484.
- Went into exile with Henry Tudor in France after the Buckingham rising (autumn 1483).
- Deserted Henry's cause in summer 1485, fleeing to Flanders only to be brought back to Henry's camp by Henry's followers.
- At the time of Henry's invasion, he was left behind in Paris as security against a loan from the French King.

Henry Percy, Earl of Northumberland
- Became an earl in 1461.
- Had been Richard III's retainer since 1474.
- Profited from Richard III's grants of land.
- By 1483 was seen to be the greatest magnate north of the River Trent.
- Summoned to the battle of Bosworth by Richard III, but did not take part in the fighting.

Francis, Viscount Lovell
- Age: 29.
- Knighted in 1480 by Richard, Duke of Gloucester, for service in Scotland.
- Created a viscount by Edward IV in January 1483.
- Created a Knight of the Garter in 1483 by Richard III.
- Helped to put down the Buckingham rebellion in October 1483.
- A personal friend of Richard III.
- Fought against Henry Tudor at Bosworth.

Edward Plantagenet, Earl of Warwick
- Age: 10.
- Son of George, Duke of Clarence (Edward IV's brother).
- Seen as heir to the house of York.
- Nephew of Richard III.

Thomas Howard, Earl of Surrey
- Age: 42.
- Son of John Howard, Duke of Norfolk, who was killed in action at Bosworth fighting for Richard III.
- Had fought for Edward IV at the battle of Barnet.
- Steward of the Household for Richard III, 1483–84.
- Wounded at Bosworth and at first reported dead.

Edward Stafford, Duke of Buckingham
- Age: 8.
- Son of Henry Stafford, former Duke of Buckingham, who had rebelled against Richard III in 1483.
- All of his lands were taken into the Crown's possession after the Act of Attainder was passed against his father.

John de Vere, Earl of Oxford
- Fled from England to France in 1485 and had to escape from Calais to join Henry.
- Provided important military support for Henry at the battle of Bosworth.

SOURCE 5.1 Francis Bacon, *History of the Reign of Henry VII*, 1622

[Henry's policy towards the nobility] made for his absoluteness, but not for his safety . . . for his nobles, although they were loyal and obedient, yet did co-operate with him, but let every man go his own way.

SOURCE 5.2 C. S. L. Davies, *Peace, Print and Protestantism*, 1995, pp. 113–14

It is usually assumed that harsh measures against nobles were both justified (because nobles are inherently assumed to be rebellious and given to oppression of the people at large), and politic. The former is debatable; the latter is only true given the right circumstances. Henry VII's actions in his last years . . . are uncomfortably reminiscent of the reign of king John . . . whether he could have gone on much longer with the harsh policy inaugurated in 1502 had he lived (he was only 52 when he died in 1509) is not at all certain.

SOURCE 5.4 J. R. Lander, *Government and Community*, 1980, p. 360

The whole system sounds revolting. Indeed it was! But how else, perhaps, other than by fear, could Edward IV and Henry VII have controlled such a mob of aloof, self-interested magnates? After all, the entire justification for the presence of the nobility lay in its potential fidelity and its governing capacity. If its loyalty were not willingly given there could be no alternative to coercion.

SOURCE 5.5 C. Carpenter, 'Henry VII and the English polity', in B. Thompson (ed.), *The Reign of Henry VII*, 1995, p. 20.

[The nobility] needed his [the King's] power, and needed to make it work to protect their own land, an easily damaged commodity, on which their wealth and their power depended . . . they were unlikely to attack or undermine a system that made them what they were. The King had neither to force nor to buy their loyalty; he had it automatically by virtue of being King. Only a usurper, whose continued tenure of the throne was uncertain, needed to use threats or blandishments.

Henry and the gentry

Much of the focus of this section has been on the nobility. Increasingly, however, historians have recognised Henry's reliance on the gentry for his security. Nowhere is this more clear than in his policy towards the Crown lands. A consequence of taking more land under Crown control was the necessity of finding trusted local gentry who would run the King's affairs efficiently. In turn, these officials would be linked more directly to the Crown and not to the dominating local noble. Because such gentry figures were relatively free from direct Crown control, it meant that 'the power of the Crown and the local dominance of the gentry went hand in hand' (S. J. Gunn, *Early Tudor Government, 1485–1558*).

SOURCE 5.3 S. J. Gunn, *Early Tudor Government, 1485–1558*, 1995, p. 26

The royal demesne [Crown lands] provided men to do the King's bidding, or more immediately the bidding of the knights, esquires and gentlemen who acted as the King's stewards, bailiffs and receivers. Such country gentry were in turn bound into the King's service rather than that of some locally predominant magnate.

A subtle change in power thus happened [illegible] VII. The traditional region[illegible]d by a new kind of region[illegible]iles, Lord Daubeney, in Som[illegible]arches did not rely for their p[illegible] came predominantly from th[illegible]r area. Nevertheless, it shoul[illegible]nd was different from re[illegible]rity of all land held, while g[illegible]ould still dominate.

Inter[illegible]he nobility have varied o[illegible]e.

SOURC[illegible]

The king[illegible] through fear, and he consi[illegible]actuated by their great we[illegible] when found guilty of whate[illegible] especially deprives of their f[illegible]scendants, to make the popul[illegible] undertake any upheaval and to discourage at the same time all offences.

ACTIVITY

Hypothesis: 'Henry had nothing to fear from the nobility.'

Look at the statements in the table below. Make a copy of the table. Then use the evidence from this chapter to evaluate each statement and come to a conclusion about the hypothesis.

	Yes/no	Evidence
Henry had no 'overmighty subjects' to contend with.		
Most nobles were keen for stability.		
Henry gave out land to keep the nobility happy.		
Henry showed loyalty to those nobles who were loyal to him.		
No nobles joined conspiracies against Henry.		
Henry became more suspicious of his nobility as his reign continued.		
Henry's policy towards the nobility was fair and just.		
Henry felt secure enough to include nobles in decision making.		
Henry was quick to punish nobles who showed disloyalty.		
Henry relied more on the gentry than on the nobility for the preservation of law and order.		

C What was the state of royal finances in 1485?

■ **Learning trouble spot**

What was the Chamber?

The Chamber was part of the King's innermost household apartments. Its original function was to take care of the King's private expenditure, but by the late 1490s it had become the centre of most royal finance collections and accounting. Unfortunately, the Chamber accounts do not record revenue from all sources, nor do they record all of Henry's expenditure. This makes our job of trying to work out the state of his finances accurately all the more difficult.

FOCUS ROUTE

Read pages 67–70 and make notes under the following headings:

1 Henry VII's use of the Exchequer and the Chamber

2 Souces of revenue
   a) Ordinary revenue
   b) Extraordinary revenue

3 Henry's main sources of revenue

The Exchequer and the Chamber

At first, Henry used the Exchequer system (see Chart 5E). In the first year of his reign, he received a mere £11,700 from his lands, whereas Richard is estimated to have gathered £25,000 in one year. The following examples show that this system was inadequate for Henry:

- He had to get loans to pay for his coronation and his marriage, and to pay for his progresses to the north to suppress rebellion.
- In 1487, when the feast of St George was to be celebrated at Windsor, there was not enough money to pay for it!

Henry learned the lesson that he needed to keep a close eye on the finances in order to make the most of his land revenues. Gradually, he began to use the Chamber system favoured by the Yorkists.

■ 5E How did Henry collect revenue?

	The Exchequer	The Chamber – favoured by HVII
When?	Carried on beyond the reign of Edward IV.	Developed by Edward IV and also used by Richard III.
Purpose?	To collect revenue from royal property (but there were few Crown lands apart from the Duchy of Lancaster) and, more important, taxes and customs.	Same function as Exchequer.
How?	Had its own officials.	Direct supervision of the King himself.
Advantages	Accurate and subjects knew where they were with it.	Used receivers and officials to get the most profit from estates. Part of the royal household. King had direct control over land revenues and a ready supply of cash if needed. Faster than Exchequer.
Disadvantages	Slow and often dealt not with cash but with finances recorded on paper.	

■ 5F How much was money worth in Tudor times?

	Fifteenth century	Nowadays
A day's wage	6d ($2\frac{1}{2}$p)	£28 (minimum wage, 7 hours' work)
A chicken	4d ($1\frac{1}{2}$p)	£4.50

Ordinary and extraordinary revenue

Tudor kings had two types of revenue, ordinary and extraordinary.

- Ordinary revenue was money that was collected regularly, without the need to obtain the permission of Parliament (see Chart 5G).
- Extraordinary revenue was really for emergencies only, such as war. Parliamentary approval was needed to raise it, but it also came from other sources as well, as you can see in Chart 5H on page 69.

■ 5G Ordinary revenue

Type of revenue	Reason/purpose	How much?
Crown lands	Lands held by the King by inheritance or confiscation from traitors. Henry VII greatly increased the amount of land he had as a result of attainders, the Act of Resumption (1486) and forfeitures. During his reign, there were 138 attainders, although 46 were reversed. In 1495, an Act of Parliament confirmed to Henry VII all the land of Richard III.	Under Edward IV, about £15,000 per annum. In the early part of Henry VII's reign, about £3,000 per annum. It is estimated that the amount of Crown land was five times larger by the end of Henry VII's reign than in the 1450s.
Feudal obligations*	Paid by tenants-in-chief for various reasons: • **Wardship** – the King had the right to look after the heir and their land if the heir was a minor. • **Livery** – a fine paid to recover lands from wardship. • **Relief** – money paid to the King as land was inherited. • **Escheats** – payments made when land reverted to the Crown. • **Marriage dues** for heiresses.	In 1487, under £350 per annum. In 1494, over £1,500 per annum. In 1507, over £6,000 per annum (including marriage dues). In 1502, Robert Willoughby de Broke paid £400 for livery of his lands.
Bonds and recognisances	Bonds were written agreements whereby a person promised to pay a sum of money if they failed to keep their promise. A recognisance was a formal acknowledgement of a debt or an obligation that already existed, with the understanding to pay money if this obligation were not met.	In 1491, friends of the Marquis of Dorset (stepson of Edward IV) signed bonds totalling £10,000 as a promise of his good behaviour.
Customs duties	To pay for English defences, notably the Calais garrison. Two types: • **Prerogative duties** on exports of wool, woolfells, leather and cloth and on some imports. • Import and export duties of **tunnage** (on wine) and **poundage** (on certain other goods), and a **subsidy** on wool exports. These were granted for life in the 1485 parliament.	£70,000 per annum in the last twenty years of Edward IV's reign. £30,000 per annum under Henry VI, probably due to the decline in the export of wool. £40,000 per annum under Henry VII. Increased by a new Book of Rates in 1507 which set new rates that took inflation into account.
Profits of justice	Fees paid for royal writs and letters – no court action could start without them. Fines levied by the courts. Henry VII had a policy of punishing by fine, even in some treasonable cases that should have had the death penalty.	Varied year by year. Difficult to know how much, because they were not usually collected in cash.

*These could also be included in Chart 5H, 'Extraordinary revenue', because they were irregular.

■ 5H Extraordinary revenue

Type of revenue	Reason/purpose	How much?
Parliamentary grants	To help the King when the national interest was threatened. Basic tax = **fifteenth** and **tenth**, theoretically one-fifteenth of the value of goods in rural areas and one-tenth in urban areas.	In 1487, request to pay for the battle of Stoke. In 1489, to go to war against the French. In 1496, for defence against the Scots and Warbeck. Amounts collected based on out-of-date estimates of wealth. Usually £30,000 was agreed.
Loans	From richer subjects in times of emergency. Henry appears to have repaid them.	Estimated £203,000 gained throughout the reign.
Benevolences	A type of forced loan with no repayment.	In 1491 Henry raised £48,500 to take his army to France.
Clerical taxes	'Above board'	In 1489 the Convocations (Archdioceses of Canterbury and York) voted £25,000 towards the cost of the French war.
	Simony – the selling of Church appointments.	Charged £300 for Archdeaconry of Buckingham.
	Vacant bishoprics – on the death of a bishop, his post would be kept vacant for a time and the King would protect the revenue in the meantime.	Later in the reign, a lot of bishops died, so Henry received over £6,000 per annum.
Feudal obligations*	Feudal aid – a due levied on special occasions, e.g. the knighting of Prince Arthur in 1504 and a collection of money on the marriage of Henry's daughter, Margaret.	£30,000 was levied on the knighting of Prince Arthur.
The French pension	Part of the Treaty of Etaples (1492) by which a pension was paid by the King of France, really as a bribe to remove English armies from French soil.	£159,000 to be paid in annual amounts of £5,000.

*In addition to those already mentioned in Chart 5G.

TALKING POINT

Look carefully at Charts 5G and 5H. Why is it difficult for historians to work out precisely what Henry VII's annual income was?

Henry VII annual income - £113,000 (1509)

vs.

Louis XII (1498-1515) - £800,000

Maximilian I (1493-1519) - £1,100,00

TALKING POINT

Look at Source 5.7.

1 What does this page from the book of receipts suggest about Henry's grip on finance?
2 What can we deduce about the amount of money being collected?
3 Does this show that Henry was hard working, or just that this was a task that could be done quite quickly?

SOURCE 5.7 This shows that the King himself examined the accounts of the Treasurer of the Chamber – his monograph appears against every entry of receipt. Until 27 August 1492, this required several strokes. Later it was written in one continuous movement. From April 1503, Henry only initialled every page once.

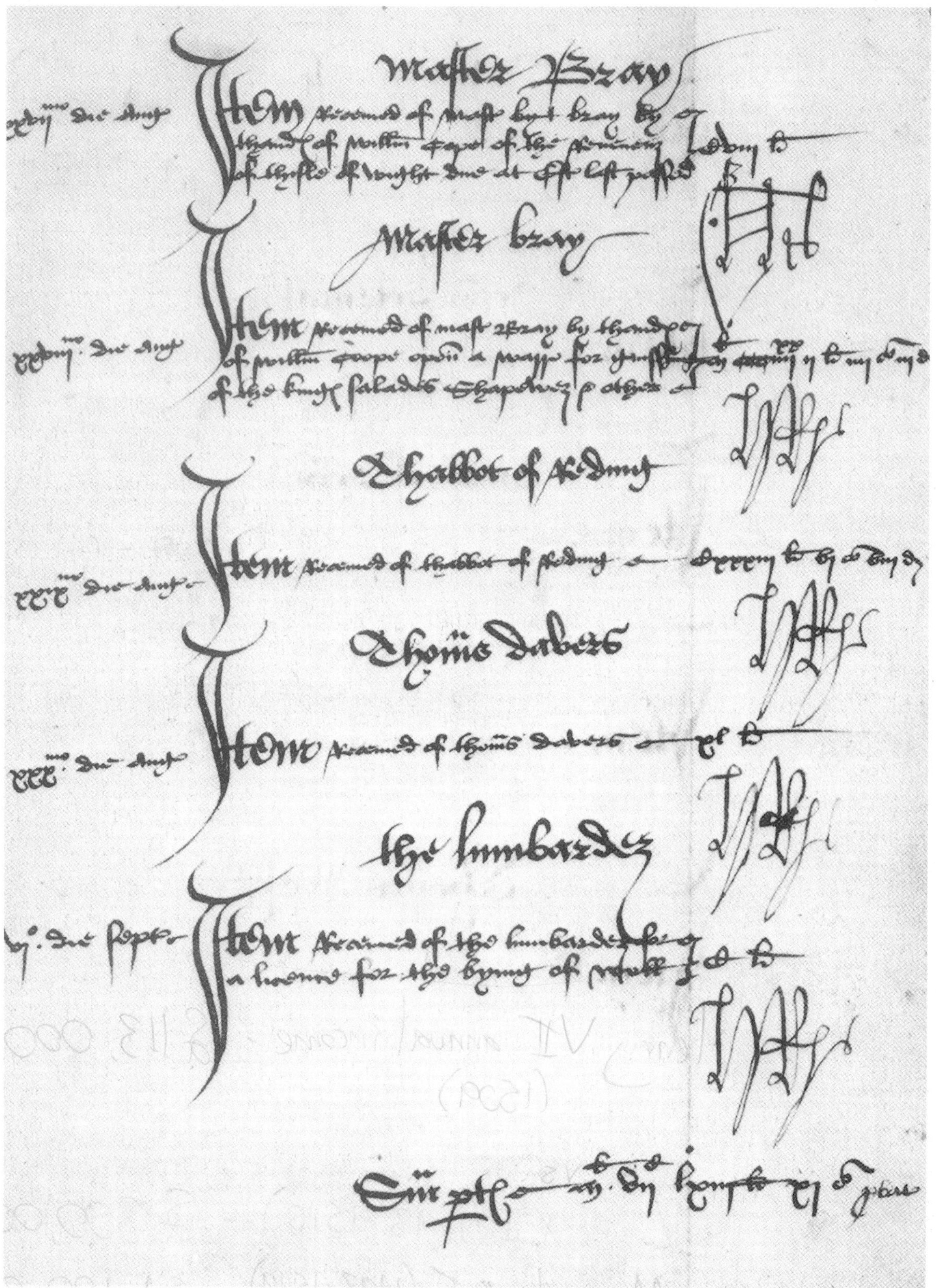

SOURCE 5.8 This portrait of Henry VII was painted in 1505. Notice the grasping hands, which could be interpreted as indicative of Henry's desire to get his hands on as much money as possible. However, he did not always succeed. His customs revenues were less than he might have hoped: for instance, because collection in some ports was difficult. Smuggling occurred especially in the more distant ports, where underpaid customs officers also joined in

D How did Henry use finance to his advantage?

FOCUS ROUTE

Read pages 72–74 and make notes about the following:

1. The different ways in which Henry used money to try to increase his security on the throne.
2. How successful you think this was? Mention any negative aspects, which might actually have been counterproductive.

Crown lands

Land was the key to regular revenue for Tudor kings, so it is no surprise that one of Henry's first priorities was to ensure that his Crown lands were as extensive as possible. The Act of Resumption in 1486 enabled the King to recover for the Crown all lands, offices and revenues that had been lost since 1455. A second Act followed in 1487. However, these gains were mitigated because he had to restore lands to his mother, Margaret Beaufort, the Earl of Oxford and others whose attainders by Edward and Richard were annulled. On the other hand, Henry was perhaps fortunate in that he did not have many male blood relatives to whom he had to give land. His uncle Jasper, Duke of Bedford, was rewarded for his support with commissions in Ireland and Wales, but as he left no heir, his lands reverted to the Crown on his death in 1495. In addition, Henry's land revenues fortuitously received a boost in later years owing to the death of his eldest son Arthur in 1502, his queen Elizabeth in 1503, and her grandmother the Duchess of York.

Additional lands were also gained by attainting Richard III and his followers at Bosworth. If a landowner was attainted, it meant that he and his heirs were deprived of their land by the king, if convicted of treason or a felony. The law that enabled this to happen was called an Act of Attainder. A total of 138 persons were attainted in Parliament during Henry's reign, although 46 attainders were reversed. Even so, the Crown benefited from seizures of estates from notables such as Sir William Stanley and the Earl of Suffolk.

Not only was the *amount* of land important to maximise revenue, but also critical was how *effectively* it was managed. Henry was particularly successful from 1487 onwards in adopting methods used by Edward IV and Richard III. Instead of lands being under the control of the Exchequer, which farmed them out at fixed rents, Henry transferred their control to surveyors, receivers and auditors who specialised in maximising income. The receiver, who accounted personally to the King's Chamber, was responsible for collecting rents, making new leases, expelling bad tenants and authorising repairs.

Unfortunately, it is impossible to determine the extent to which the increased land revenues in Henry's reign were the result of the increased *amount* of Crown lands or the better *management* of them. However, we do have some figures that compare the annual income that Henry VII obtained from Crown lands as compared to other monarchs. These are shown in Chart 5I.

■ 5I Estimated net annual income from Crown lands*

Reign	Annual income from Crown lands
Henry VI	£8,000
Richard III	£22–25,000
Henry VII	£40,000
Henry VIII (beginning of reign)	£25,000
Henry VIII (late 1530s–1540s)	£86,000
Mary I	£83,000

*To the nearest £1,000, not including the Duchy of Lancaster, sales of land or monastic goods.
Source: Adapted from S. J. Gunn, *Early Tudor Government, 1485–1558*, 1995, p.114

TALKING POINT

Finance directed to political ends is a fact of life that we are familiar with nowadays, but was this the case for Henry VII? Re-read Polydore Vergil's comment in Source 5.6 on page 66. What does it tell us about Henry's financial tactics?

Bonds and recognisances

Another important method Henry used to increase revenue was through bonds and recognisances. You have already read about how he did this, but review the examples given on page 61 and look again at Chart 5G (page 68) to remind yourself about how much money was raised in this way.

Expenditure

As well as obtaining as much money as possible in order to bolster his security, Henry also had to spend some. In the absence of a standing army and police force, it was essential for Henry to look and act the part of a powerful monarch. This was important for his image both at home and abroad. Whereas the Holy Roman Emperor enjoyed £1,100,000, and the King of France £800,000 per annum, Henry's total by the end of the reign has been estimated to be in the region of £113,000. This made the *appearance* of being rich all the more necessary.

Henry certainly seems to have impressed the Venetian ambassador, who described being received 'in a small hall, hung with handsome tapestry. [The king was dressed in] a violet-coloured gown, lined with a cloth of gold, and a collar of many jewels, and on his cap was a large diamond and a most beautiful pearl. [Henry leaned against] a tall gilt chair, covered with a cloth of gold.'

Henry spent shamelessly on images to promote himself and his dynasty. All monarchs used flags, banners and badges to heighten their prestige, but Henry VII changed this by making the badges *personal.* The symbols of the Tudor Rose, the Beaufort portcullis, the Richmond greyhound, the Hawthorn bush and the Cadwaladr dragon appeared on everything: ceilings, stained-glass windows, stonework, horses' harnesses and even chamber pots! In 1503 work began on his chapel at Westminster Abbey and no other church building is so emblazoned with the personal imprint of its founder.

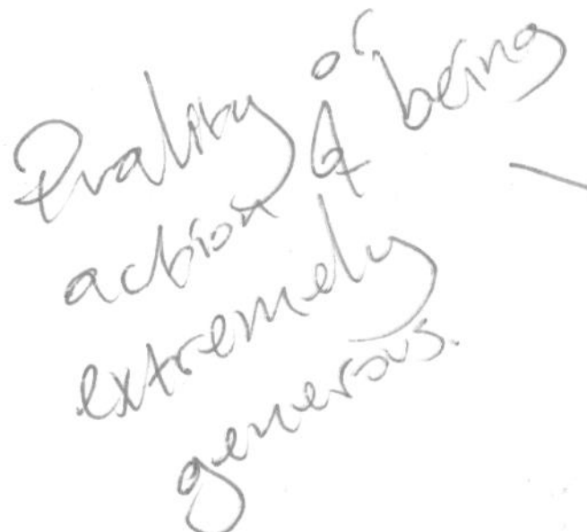

Munificence, then, was an important tool for Henry's security; so were the financial requirements of diplomacy. In 1505, for instance, Henry lent £138,000 to Philip of Burgundy to finance his voyage to Spain. He also lent between £226,000 and £342,000 to Emperor Maximilian between 1505 and 1509. Neither of these loans was ever repaid, but the money was spent in a good cause: the security of the country.

SOURCE 5.9 Henry VII's chapel at Westminster Abbey. This vastly expensive architectural monument is covered with Henry's badges

E Did finance help Henry's security?

FOCUS ROUTE

Using the information in Sources 5.10–5.16 make detailed notes on:

1 the criteria by which we judge how successful Henry VII's financial policies were
2 the differences in the ways in which historians have viewed Henry's financial success.

Use the information in the text as well as the sources to help you.

SOURCE 5.10 R. L. Storey, *The Reign of Henry VII*, 1968, pp. 109 and 115

Thanks to the early success of his diplomacy, Henry had to spend only £45,700 on military and naval expenses. It cost him a further £13,155 to deal with the Cornish Revolt and Perkin Warbeck, but this outlay was more than recovered by the £14,700 paid in fines by the rebels ... The revenues of the crown had without doubt been greatly augmented, enabling the king to maintain his estate with splendour and free his government of the crippling dangers of poverty. His credit balance, however, was not very great.

SOURCE 5.11 G. R. Elton, *England Under the Tudors*, 2nd edn, 1974, p. 54

The reserve [surplus left at the end of Henry's reign] itself was of course gratifying, but it may be doubted whether it really merits all the admiration which it has excited. After all, it took only two years of by no means extravagant war [Henry VIII's First French War 1512–14] in the next reign to wipe it out.

SOURCE 5.12 R. Lockyer and R. Thrush, *Henry VII*, 1983, p. 31

The most reliable estimates seem to be that during the period 1485–1509 the income from royal lands went up by 45%, from £29,000 to £42,000, while the customs revenue increased by just over 20%, from £33,000 to £40,000. By the end of the reign, the chamber was handling a little over £91,000 a year, on the average, while the exchequer received about £12,500. If a further £10,000 is added for other sources of income, this gives a total revenue of something over £113,000 a year.

SOURCE 5.13 C. Coleman and D. Starkey, *Revolution Reassessed*, 1986, p. 203

Louis was rich on paper, and that impresses historians; Henry was rich in cash, and that impressed contemporaries.

SOURCE 5.14 J. Guy, *Tudor England*, 1988, p. 70

By European standards Henry VII's income was comparatively small ... Doubtless it was the glint of gold in the coffers of his chamber that started the rumour of Henry's hoard.

SOURCE 5.15 C. Carpenter, 'Henry VII and the English polity', in B. Thompson (ed.), *The Reign of Henry VII*, 1995, p. 27

Henry's increasingly intensive exploitation of the crown lands and of all the financial powers these put at his disposal raised his revenues from these sources from about £3,000 a year in the early part of the reign to about £40,000 towards the end ... It must be seriously doubted whether the slight benefits of this degree of solvency outweighed the enormous political backlash caused by such exploitation.

SOURCE 5.16 B. Thompson (ed.), *The Reign of Henry VII*, 1995, p. 8

A full treasury was often acquired by rapacity and so proved the downfall of kings rather than their security; what mattered more than the balance of cash was the credit-worthiness of the king, which depended on the quality of his rule in the eyes of his subjects.

TALKING POINT

Christine Carpenter has suggested that 'it must be seriously doubted whether the slight benefits of [Henry's] degree of solvency outweighed the enormous political backlash caused by such exploitation.' Looking at the evidence in this chapter on Henry's dealings with the nobility and finance, how far do you agree with this statement?

ACTIVITY

Using the information on pages 67–74 and Sources 5.10–5.16, answer the following questions:

1 Was Henry financially successful? (You will need to decide his criteria for success.)
2 To what extent did finance help Henry's security?

Henry's use of finance – an assessment

On the whole, Henry exploited the financial system to his advantage, or did he? He certainly had to tread a fine line. To maximise his potential revenue, he had to exploit all the opportunities available to him. This in itself increased the potential for rebellion, the very thing that he was trying to avoid.

On the other hand, as we have seen, Henry's revenue enabled him to build palaces and live like a king. Far from being frivolous, this strengthened his image, and therefore his position, both at home and in the eyes of the all-important foreign ambassadors. Overall, as a result of his financial dealings, he was not 'hanging by a thread', although whether Henry *himself* felt that he was is a different matter entirely.

F Review: Hanging by a thread – was Henry ever secure?

■ 5J Henry's insecure security

- Criteria for establishment of monarchical authority.

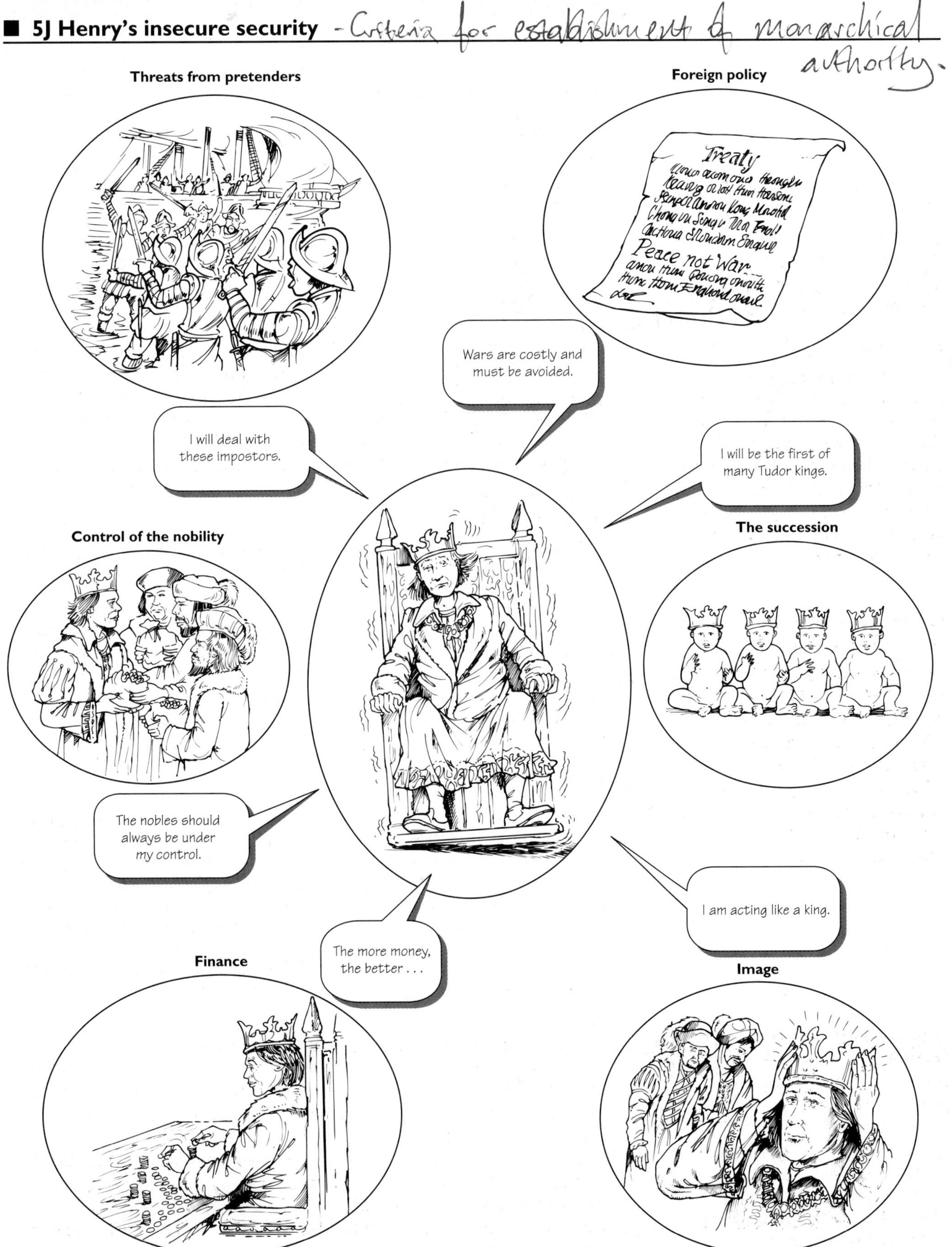

FOCUS ROUTE

1 Using the information on pages 58–74, write detailed notes to explain how Henry VII tried to bolster his security in terms of each of the following:
   a) the nobility
   b) finance.
2 Read Sources 5.17, 5.18 and 5.19. Make notes on the extent to which Chrimes, Guy and Carpenter agree/disagree about how secure Henry was.

TALKING POINT

What does this activity reveal about Henry's security throughout the reign?

What did Henry believe?

Hindsight can cause us, as historians, to make misleading judgements. We know that Henry died of natural causes and that the throne passed to his son, Prince Henry, in 1509. But did Henry VII believe that this would happen, particularly in the final years of the reign, having lost his eldest son Arthur in 1502, and his wife Elizabeth in 1503? If we view the reign of Henry as 'one long usurpation crisis', Henry's security was never certain.

ACTIVITY

1 Make your own copy of the table below.
2 Fill columns 2 and 3 with events from the timeline on page 35.
3 In column 4, give reasons why some events could go into both 'Helped' and 'Hindered' columns.

Year	Helped security	Hindered security	Reason
1485–92			
1492–1503			
1503–09			

The latter years of Henry's reign were still characterised by nagging doubts about his position as king, and that of his son, Prince Henry. We know that Henry was very perturbed by reports of a conversation in Calais, in 1503 or 1504. Several prominent men there had predicted that the King would die, or be assassinated by the end of 1507, before Prince Henry would be old enough to rule in his own right. According to the report, there was talk of the possible accession of the Duke of Buckingham or the Earl of Suffolk. It was probably this that prompted Henry to increase his personal bodyguard, the Yeomen of the Guard, to 200 men by 1508.

Certainly we have examples of Henry extracting more finance from his subjects during this period. For instance, in October 1504 he demanded £2,000 from the counties of Anglesey, Merioneth and Carmarthenshire, in return for a special charter of their liberties that they had requested. In 1507 he insisted on a further £2,300 to confirm the 1504 charter.

What do historians say about the security of the Tudor dynasty?

SOURCE 5.17 S. B. Chrimes, *Henry VII*, 1972, p. 320

If the penury of his earlier years contributed, along with reasons of state, to his becoming sufficiently over-zealous in the accumulation of wealth as to incur a reputation for avariciousness, even miserliness, in his later years, this was a fault which gave an unwonted strength to a Crown weakened for generations by improvident kings. If over-preoccupation in his later years with the problem of security, which had inevitably loomed large during the earlier years, became something of an obsession and led him into arbitrary and unjust actions, at least he left a Crown more secure than it had been since the best days of Edward III. It was unfortunate, perhaps, that his fears for security have taken on the colour of additional avarice. Yet to seek to control his subjects by getting at their purse-strings was better than the more violent forms of terrorism that had not been uncommon in the past and were to reappear in magnified form in the times of his successors.

SOURCE 5.18 J. Guy, *Tudor England*, 1988, p. 79

Henry's diplomacy and security measures guaranteed his dynasty's survival. The turbulence of the fifteenth century was quelled: the way was cleared for Wolsey and Thomas Cromwell.

SOURCE 5.19 C. Carpenter, *The Wars of the Roses: Politics and the Constitution in England c. 1437–1509*, 1997, p. 258

The Tudor dynasty remained for long as insecure as it seemed to its founder, especially once the survival of a male heir to Henry VIII was in doubt. In the 1530s the Wars of the Roses were still going on in the mind of the king, as the last descendants of rival claimants were murdered by his orders…

ACTIVITY

1 a) Study Sources 5.17–5.19, then go back through the chapter to find evidence that supports each view.

b) Which view do you most agree with, and why?

2 a) Study the following list of possible reasons why Henry VII managed to maintain security throughout his reign:

- Henry was decisive.
- There were not many royal males, so there was less political tension.
- Henry was prudent with the finances.
- Henry had a defensive foreign policy (consult Chapter 4 again).
- Henry tried to rule consensually, by summoning five Great Councils.
- Henry used bonds and recognisances.
- Henry disabled the nobility.
- Henry tried to placate the Yorkists.

b) See if you can add any others.

c) Rank the reasons and justify your choices, then discuss them with other people in your class and see if they agree.

KEY POINTS FROM CHAPTER 5: Hanging by a thread – was Henry ever secure?

1 Henry was very loyal to those nobles who had stayed loyal to him when he was in exile and in 1485. He was more watchful of those nobles who were new to him.

2 The extent of the nobility's power in the localities was a threat to Henry's position as king. This was especially true because of Henry's position as an outsider and because several big noble families had fought against him at Bosworth.

3 However, there was a reduction in the number of noble families with extensive landholdings – the 'overmighty magnates'.

4 Henry controlled the nobility by using inducements:

- patronage
- the Order of the Garter
- a position on the King's Council
- meetings of the nobility called 'Great Councils'.

5 Henry also controlled the nobility by using threats:

- Acts of Attainder
- bonds and recognisances
- feudal dues
- Acts against illegal retaining
- the retention of Crown lands in his own hands.

6 Henry made greater use of the Chamber to collect revenue and brought finance under his own personal control.

7 Henry exploited all forms of ordinary and extraordinary revenue to increase his wealth, although he made himself unpopular in the process.

8 Henry was willing to spend lavishly to promote his image.

9 Henry's use of finance was crucial for his security but, even with all of these measures, Henry himself probably never felt totally secure.

6

Henry VII – the verdict

CHAPTER OVERVIEW

In this chapter, we will be trying to reach some conclusions about Henry VII. We will be considering the following issues:

FOCUS ROUTE

As you read pages 78–80:

1 **a)** Make notes on the factors that helped Henry to survive.
  b) Put the factors in order of importance.

2 Draw two spider diagrams to show the positive and negative aspects of Henry's reign.

A What factors played a role in Henry's survival?

ACTIVITY

Draw this diagram in the centre of a piece of A4 paper. Before you read any more text, add your own examples that illustrate these factors.

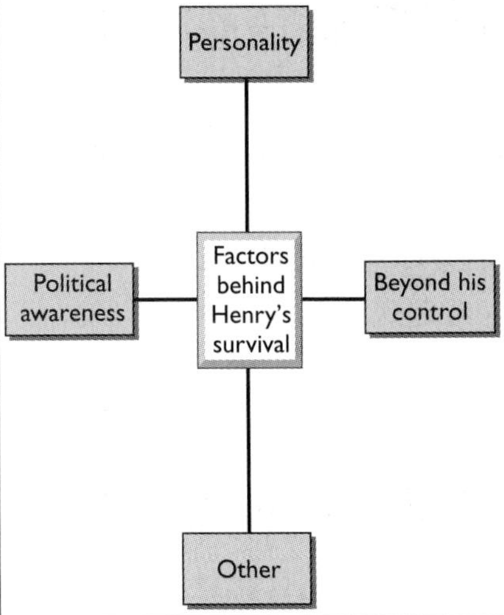

Personality

Political awareness

Factors behind Henry's survival

Beyond his control

Other

You will know from what you have read so far that Henry's position as king was precarious to say the least. How is it that a virtual outsider to the English political scene could not only secure himself as king but also lay the foundations of perhaps the most famous of all English dynasties?

Political awareness

At the heart of Henry's survival was his uncanny ability to make good decisions, particularly in the early days of his reign.

In the short term

- His own marriage to Elizabeth of York provided a clear sign, to Lancastrians and Yorkists alike, of his credentials as a compromise candidate.
- He avoided involvement in expensive foreign wars and was able to focus his energies on establishing himself as king.
- He was able to make a nice judgement as to whom he should execute, punish severely or include in his Government. He made few mistakes of judgement (the Earl of Lincoln being one) and was consequently faced with few problems of his own making.
- His use of Parliament in 1485 to legitimise his claim to the throne was a clever way of wrong-footing his opponents.

However, Henry's desire to rely on his close allies could also pose problems. Dominic Luckett's research has shown that Henry's patronage could be seen as favouritism. In 'Patronage, violence and revolt in the reign of Henry VII' (in R.E. Archer (ed.), *Crown, Government and People in the Fifteenth Century*) he argues that in 1497 the Cornish rebels were not stopped by the local gentry because the latter were unhappy with Henry's reliance on so-called favourites such as Giles Daubeney and Robert Willoughby de Broke.

In the medium to long term

- His diplomatic manoeuvres reinforced the idea of a dynasty that was here to stay: first, the recognition of the legitimacy of his regime by the Pope in 1485, and then the vital acceptance of the Tudors by Ferdinand and Isabella of Spain. The marriage of first Arthur and then Henry to Catherine of Aragon marked the acceptance on the European stage not merely of Henry VII but also of the Tudor dynasty.
- He was able to establish a sense of economic order in the kingdom. At its most basic level, this meant that Henry was forced to resort to demanding taxation from Parliament on no more than three occasions (1489, 1491 and 1497). This reduced the potential for rebellion against his rule.

Personality

Henry VII ruled at a time when the personal quality of the monarch was the key to the quality of his rule. It is clear that he was blessed with the qualities fundamental to survival.

- His own experience in Brittany and France made him uniquely able to recognise plots early and take positive action to minimise their chances of success.
- He possessed a skill in battle that his son, for all of his show, could never match. Two great victories at Bosworth and Stoke marked him out as a king with real authority.
- While he did create enemies, he engendered a real depth of loyalty from his supporters. This loyalty, from men such as Daubeney, Morton and Fox, meant that Henry was able to rely on a hub of men who were rock solid in their support.
- His own efficiency and thoroughness are legendary. He set the tone for a government geared to Henry's own will.

Beyond his control

Luck is a factor sometimes overlooked by historians. Too often rulers such as Henry can be seen as the masters and not the servants of events. The reality is that Henry, like any ruler at any time in history, survived partly through his own ability but also through a range of factors that were completely beyond his control.

- On his accession there was a lack of opponents with an obviously better claim to the throne; nor was there a rival 'kingmaker' in, say, the mould of Richard Neville, Earl of Warwick, during the Wars of the Roses.
- He came to power at a time when the nation was ready for the role of a consolidator. Richard III had undermined the stability that Edward IV had re-established following the disorder of Henry VI's reign. The nobility, in particular, was keen to get back to a situation in which the King would implement royal authority with certainty. It was not in the nobles' interests to have a weak monarch as this would increase the likelihood of disputes between them – disputes that could lead to loss of land, power and influence.
- It has been said by some historians (such as R. L. Storey in *The Reign of Henry VII*) that Henry was lucky to die when he did. By the end of his reign, the severity of his financial penalties was such that some form of rebellion against his rule was, perhaps, merely a matter of time. The sense of crisis at Henry's death, with the unusual delaying of the news of it by 36 hours, shows the gravity of the situation. Henry VII was again fortunate that his son was, first, old enough to accede as an adult, and second, wise enough to distance himself immediately from his father's policies.

ACTIVITY

1 Put the factors outlined on pages 79–80 into rank order of importance. Write a speech that justifies your first choice.
2 Organise a debate on the motion: 'This House believes that Henry VII survived more by luck than by judgement.'

B How significant were Henry's achievements?

The reign of Henry VII used to be seen as a major turning point in English history – the fulcrum of change between the medieval and early modern periods. For many years, Francis Bacon's study of Henry VII cast a long shadow over his reign. According to Bacon, Henry's main achievements were to put both England's finances and a troublesome nobility in order, thus laying the foundations for future Tudor glories.

Clearly these images of Henry's reign have been challenged. No longer is the idea of a 'new' form of monarchy taken seriously, while a range of recent historians have peeled away the superficial image of Henry as the hardworking but faceless bureaucrat to reveal a more colourful and complex character.

It is evident that Henry's main achievement is his foundation of a new dynasty. However, as Christine Carpenter has argued, is this the only achievement for which Henry should be remembered? Has the significance of this achievement actually made dramatic what was, in reality, a reign full of missed opportunities and little achievement of any note? There is a balance to be struck in assessing Henry's reign, and *your* opinion, as long as it is supported by concrete evidence, can stand up against those of professional historians. A study of the points below and of Sources 6.1–6.6 should help you to come to your own conclusion.

Henry's achievements

Positive

- Henry left the Crown solvent, providing stability and a sound base for Henry VIII.
- Henry created a stable diplomatic environment for England, especially during the first fifteen years of his reign. The Spanish alliance was of particular benefit.
- He re-established order after the uncertainties of the reign of Richard III.
- He managed to quell any threat that the nobility might have posed.
- The very fact that he stayed in power and passed his throne on to his son peacefully is impressive given the context of the fifteenth century and the fact that he was a usurper.

Negative

- Can the issue of solvency be seen as so significant? No other Tudor monarch died solvent and yet this has not diminished their reputations.
- England was left largely isolated by 1509. The lack of a glorious foreign campaign did nothing for England's chivalric image.

- While the Crown was solvent, much of its wealth, especially in the final years, was amassed by illegal or at least highly unpopular means.
- Henry overstated the threat posed by the nobility. Had he worked more on the basis of consensus rather than control, he would have had more opportunity to reform local government and keep better control in the localities.
- Henry never established a sense of security. He was a king never sure of his own position, ruling over a country never sure of who its next king would be.
- Henry used patronage excessively, being over-reliant on those men whom he had known in exile.
- Although Henry did pass on his throne peacefully, it was by the skin of his teeth. He was, by 1509, deeply unpopular.

Historians' interpretations

SOURCE 6.1 R. L. Storey, *The Reign of Henry VII*, 1968, p. 216

The reign of Henry VII must still be regarded as one of the great landmarks in England's political development . . . It is the watershed between the old and new pattern of political life; it divides those centuries when the principal and most constant cause of major disorder had been the aspirations and suspicions of the baronial class from a period which saw the emergence of parties making their stand on issues of religion and constitutional principle.

SOURCE 6.2 M. M. Condon, 'Ruling elites in the reign of Henry VII', in C. Ross (ed.), *Patronage, Pedigree and Power*, 1979, p. 124

[There was] a certain superficiality of achievement despite all the auguries of change: an impermanence, a fragility caused in part by the tensions which Henry himself created.

SOURCE 6.3 S. B. Chrimes, *Henry VII*, 1972, pp. 321–22

His steady purposefulness saved England from mediocrity. It was not the union of the Roses that mattered, symbolic enough though that was. What mattered most in the long run was the spadework without which the springs of national genius would not be freed. In the ultimate analysis, the quality of Henry VII was not that of a creator, but rather of a stabilizer for lack of whom the ships of state are apt to founder. For that quality, he stands out pre-eminent among British monarchs.

SOURCE 6.4 J. Guy, *Tudor England*, 1988, pp. 78–79

Henry VII's reign was distinguished by sober statesmanship. Bosworth's victor was a stabilizer: he could be ruthless and severe, but was neither bloodthirsty nor egoistical . . . In 1492 he personally led his 'army royal' to France in the knowledge that the nobility (and Parliament) exalted kings who defended their honour . . . Henry also attempted to centralize English politics. The Tudor Court began to exercise magnetic influence, and, if much territorial power still lay in the hands of regional magnates, faction was tamed by recognizance and the exaction of royal prerogative rights by the Council Learned.

SOURCE 6.5 C. Carpenter, 'Henry VII and the English polity', in B. Thompson (ed.), *The Reign of Henry VII*, 1995, p. 30

Yes, he did manage to pass on the throne to his son and, notoriously, Edward IV did not. It seems almost that this is the only achievement which remains intact, certainly the only one that confirms the two kings in the accepted hierarchy: the king who was not quite up to the demands of the modern world and the one who was. But even here we must pause . . . Henry was extraordinarily lucky in the age of his son, in his son's ability to see immediately what was needed, and in the moment of his death.

SOURCE 6.6 Alexander Grant, *Henry VII*, 1985, p. 50

[As] Henry VII's achievement depended largely on his own incessant personal direction of government, is it possible to suggest that his true successors were not the monarchs who followed him but their great ministers who, like Henry VII, kept close personal control on all the strands of government? . . . And whether or not that idea is acceptable, the debt which the Tudor regime owed to Henry VII is clear. The most important revolution of the period was surely the restoration of a high degree of peace and stability throughout most of the country, and its architect was King Henry VII. For this reason, his victory over Richard III in August 1485 deserves to be re-established as a major turning-point in English history.

ACTIVITY

Read Sources 6.1–6.6.

1. Pick out the positive and negative interpretations of Henry VII's reign.
2. 'Henry VII's sole achievement was to pass on his throne peacefully to his son.' To what extent is this a fair assessment of Henry's reign?

ACTIVITY

Was Henry VII seen as a success by his contemporaries? On your own, or in pairs, take on the role of one of the characters listed below. Your task is to assess the nature and success of Henry VII's reign. Naturally, your assessment must come from the angle of your particular character, with all of his prejudice, bias and vested interest.

Characters

Ferdinand of Spain
The Earl of Surrey
Robert Willoughby de Broke II
Giles Daubeney
A member of the Cornish gentry
The Venetian ambassador
The French ambassador
A London merchant
Henry VIII

1 Prepare a short speech (lasting about 3–4 minutes) to deliver to the rest of the characters. Centre your assessment on the following areas (although your character will probably have a particular interest in certain issues):

- defence of the country
- relations with other countries
- upholding justice
- securing the dynasty
- raising money
- law and order
- trade
- image (of the King and of the country)
- legacy at the end of his reign.

2 You could all then contribute to a debate on the motion: 'The reign of Henry VII has brought only limited advantages to England.'

Review: Henry VII – the verdict

In spite of recent attempts to downgrade Henry VII's achievements as King of England, the case against him has still to be proven. When the odds against him are studied, his role in bringing stability to England surely remains impressive. He was never the obvious choice as king in 1485 and the fact that he carved out such a position of strength is testament to his ability, ruthlessness and perseverance. Admittedly, not all of his dealings with the nobility were exactly moral, but we are on thin ice if we start to judge kings on their moral authority alone. The truth is that Henry did fulfil his main aim of bringing back stability to the English monarchy.

Even if we accept that his main achievement was this right of peaceful succession, given the context of the fifteenth century this is no mean achievement. Henry did have his fair share of luck, but then this is probably true of most successful leaders at any time in history. No, Henry was not simply a lucky survivor and deserves to be recognised as a statesman of real political cunning.

KEY POINTS FROM CHAPTER 6: Henry VII – the verdict

1 Henry survived through a combination of luck and good judgement. The latter outweighed the former.
2 Henry's main achievement was to act as stabiliser – to establish firm foundations for his successor.
3 Henry was successful in exerting personal control over government. The success of his reign is largely attributable to his own qualities as king.

Section 1 Review: Henry VII

Let's recap on what we now know about Henry VII. In Chapter 1, pages 8–10, we explored our first impressions of Henry VII in terms of his appearance and character. We saw that Henry's character and approach to kingship meant that he was more likely to make a success of it than not. We then went on to look at the circumstances in which he became king, in Chapter 2, pages 11–25. We found that, in some respects, England was a stable country prior to Henry VII becoming king, although it was not stable in a political sense. Henry usurped the throne in 1485 by defeating Richard III at the battle of Bosworth on 22 August 1485. Chapter 3, pages 26–36, then dealt with Henry's concerns on his accession, and the steps that Henry took to secure his throne in the short and longer term. In Chapter 4, pages 37–56, we saw that Henry's foreign policy was in the context of England being a weaker country than France and the Holy Roman Empire. Henry also had to be vigilant as to any help that foreign countries might offer to Simnel and Warbeck. Chapter 5, pages 57–77, considered the extent to which Henry was 'hanging by a thread' in terms of his treatment of the nobility and his dealings with finance. Henry needed the co-operation of the nobles to help his security, but he did not want them to have too much power. He tried to control the power of the nobles by using a 'carrot and stick' approach. He also tried to maximise his financial situation as a means of bolstering his security. Finally, we attempted to judge how successful Henry VII was, considering the extent of his achievements in Chapter 6, pages 78–82. An overall assessment of Henry VII's reign is that he was successful, but this view is now being challenged by revisionist historians.

ACTIVITY

How close was Henry VII to being toppled?

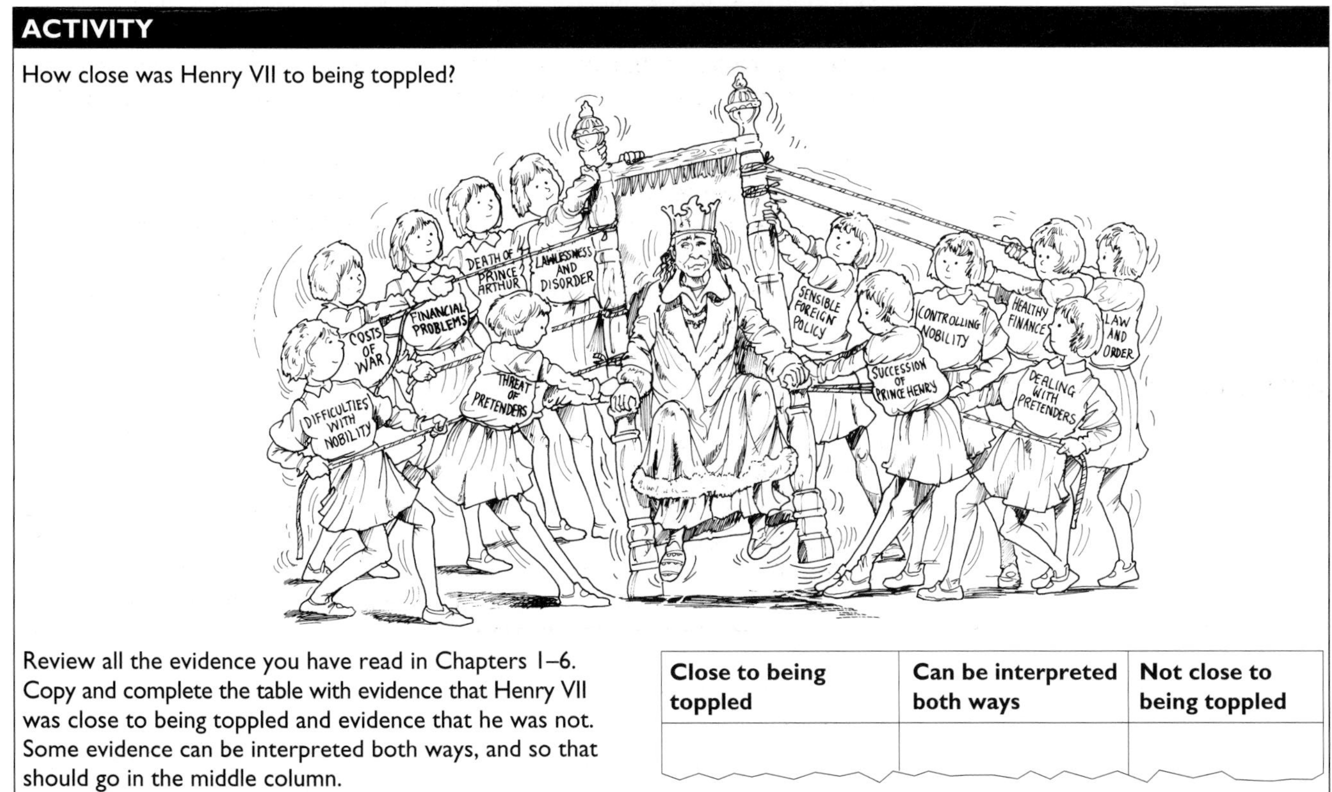

Review all the evidence you have read in Chapters 1–6. Copy and complete the table with evidence that Henry VII was close to being toppled and evidence that he was not. Some evidence can be interpreted both ways, and so that should go in the middle column.

Close to being toppled	Can be interpreted both ways	Not close to being toppled

Funeral effigy of Henry VII

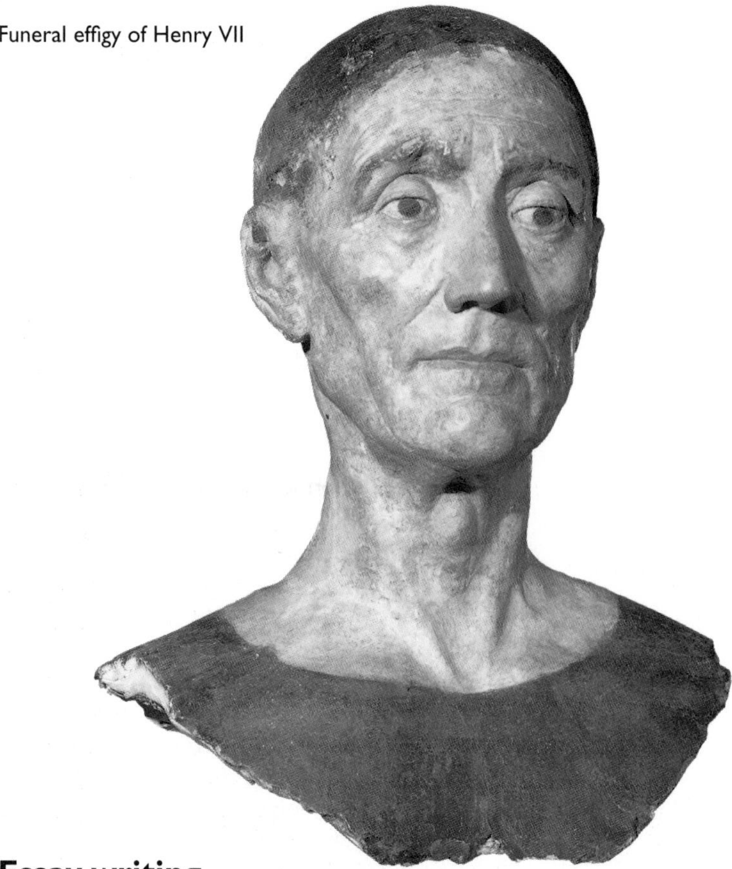

Essay writing

When you write an essay, there is always a lot of thinking and planning to be done first. If you take short cuts, your essay will run the risk of not answering the question asked, which is a common criticism from examiners. There is nothing more soul-destroying than writing a long essay, only to be told that you have not answered the question.

Here are eight tips for essay-writing success:

1 Identify the key word(s) in the title.
2 Brainstorm before you start writing. Brainstorming means writing ideas as they come into your head. Then review your notes to make sure that you have not missed any key topics.
3 Re-order the brainstorm items to form a logical sequence in your essay.
4 Make sure you include a balance of views.
5 Think hard about your introduction and your conclusion. The introduction should show that you understand what the question is asking and identify the main issues that you will be looking at. The conclusion should answer the original question asked. It should not introduce new information or spring any surprises – your final views must be consistent with the general line of your essay.
6 Construct each paragraph carefully.
7 Include evidence and historians' views.
8 Use essay-style language. An essay should be written fairly formally. For example:
'It has been argued that…'
'Historian X has suggested that…'
'One interpretation of… is…'
'This policy can be interpreted as…'
'The debate centres on whether…'
'…is a matter of great debate among historians.'

FOCUS ROUTE

Write a concluding essay: 'Henry VII was never secure.' How accurate is this judgement on his reign?

Having found out about Henry VII, the first of the Tudors, the problems he faced and how he dealt with them, we are now ready to find out whether his son and successor, Henry VIII, had a similar approach to kingship, and what his successes and failures were.

section 2

Henry VIII

Henry VIII, with Henry VII in the background, by Hans Holbein the Younger, c. 1536–37

This image of Henry VIII was drawn in 1537 by Hans Holbein. It was the preparation study for a wall painting in Whitehall Palace. Everything about it shouts out power, dominance, virility, strength, wealth and authority. From shoulder pads to codpiece, this is the picture of a king confident of his heritage and secure in his own legacy. Henry's father, Henry VII, is very much in the background, eclipsed by his son's majesty. The Tudor line, it seems, has gone from strength to strength.

The key question that will pervade this section is: to what extent is this strong image of Henry VIII as a successful king justified?

There is no doubt that Henry is one of the most famous kings of British and world history. But is his fame more rightly described as notoriety? When we peel away the fine clothes and marital history of Henry, what is left? Was Henry himself actually little more than an attention-seeker, desperate to grab the limelight in whatever field he operated?

Or is there something deeper at work? Should we see a deeply religious man, driven by a deep-rooted conscience to further the interests of his nation? Can he be seen as a skilful politician using the talents of others to the best advantage of the country?

Ultimately, the apparently simplistic question 'Was Henry VIII a successful king?' is perhaps the most effective tool to use in guiding you through a fascinating, complicated and often contradictory reign.

7

'So great a prince' – was Henry VIII likely to be a good king?

CHAPTER OVERVIEW

In this chapter, we will learn about the background to Henry VIII's reign. We will examine Henry's upbringing and personality, the legacy of his father and something of Henry VIII's attitude towards kingship. This will then help us to understand events and why Henry dealt with them in the way that he did.

A What was the legacy of Henry VII?

On 21 April 1509, Henry VII died at Richmond. The new king, Henry VIII, was only seventeen years old. He married Catherine of Aragon on 11 June, and their coronation followed on 24 June 1509 at Westminster Abbey.

SOURCE 7.1 The general rejoicing at Henry VIII's accession was encapsulated in a poem written by Sir Thomas More for the coronation. Here is an extract

This day is the end of our slavery, the fount of our liberty; the end of sadness, the beginning of joy.

How had Henry VII left the realm for the young king to take over? Certainly we can assume that Henry VIII was used to a Crown with a lot of surplus money. This money had been used in the past to help fund the magnificence that supported his father's reign, as evidenced by the Henry VII funeral chapel at Westminster Abbey and the Garter Chapel at Windsor.

SOURCE 7.2 J. J. Scarisbrick, *Henry VIII*, 1968, p. 11

[Henry VIII] ascended the throne which his father had made remarkably secure, he inherited a fortune which probably no English king had ever been bequeathed, he came to a kingdom which was the best governed and most obedient in Christendom.

Unlike his father, Henry VIII did not usurp the throne, but did this necessarily mean that he had a more secure start to his reign? The young king did inherit a financial surplus, albeit a small one. One reason for this was his father's avoidance of war, but another was the extent of bonds and recognisances imposed on the nobility, which were vigorously pursued by Empson and Dudley. To get rid of these men would gain the new king a lot of points in the popularity stakes. The nobility had been controlled, but almost at too high a price. As far as Europe was concerned, other countries had clearly accepted the Tudor dynasty, as illustrated by the marriage of Prince Arthur to Catherine of Aragon.

FOCUS ROUTE

Read this page. Make notes to summarise the situation that Henry VIII inherited in 1509, using the headings 'Helpful aspects' and 'Problematic aspects'.

TALKING POINT

Why is it important to check the date of Source 7.2 before accepting the author's conclusions about the situation c.1509?

ACTIVITY

You probably think that Henry VIII's position in 1509 was easier than that of his father in 1485. Let's see if this was the case.

You are attending a Privy Council meeting that is due to report to the new king on the state of the country in mid-1509. Each person, or pair/small group, has a responsibility for the following information:

- foreign policy
- law and order
- finance
- government
- religion.

Refer to the information you have learned about Henry VII, particularly Chapter 6, pages 78–82. Present a short report to the new king about the situation he has inherited.

B Would Henry VIII make a good king?

FOCUS ROUTE

As you read the text and sources on pages 87–90, use the information to complete your copy of this table. In order to do this exercise, you will need to remind yourself about what being a good king meant in Tudor times (see page 6).

Positive characteristics of Henry VIII	Negative characteristics of Henry VIII

SOURCE 7.3 Lord Mountjoy writing on the accession of Henry VIII. Lord Mountjoy was a noble who, under Henry VII, had had to give 23 recognisances. No doubt he looked forward to a more lenient king in Henry VIII

Oh, my Erasmus, if you could see how all the world is rejoicing in the possession of so great a prince.

Lord Mountjoy must have been very optimistic about the new king when he wrote the words in Source 7.3. Erasmus was a very respected humanist scholar in Europe. The epithet 'great' might never have been uttered at all because Prince Henry, as the second son of Henry VII and Elizabeth of York, was 'the spare, not the heir'. Born at Greenwich on 28 June 1491, he was the younger brother of Prince Arthur, the heir apparent. His early upbringing was therefore not one in which he was either expected or apprenticed to become the future king. Henry VIII's early childhood was spent with his sisters Margaret and Mary at Eltham Palace, under the supervision of his mother. His grandmother, Lady Margaret Beaufort, also had an overview. He was surrounded by women and separated from his brother, Prince Arthur, who was brought up 240 kilometres (150 miles) away in the Welsh borders. Nevertheless, Henry played a leading role in the wedding of Arthur to Catherine of Aragon in 1501.

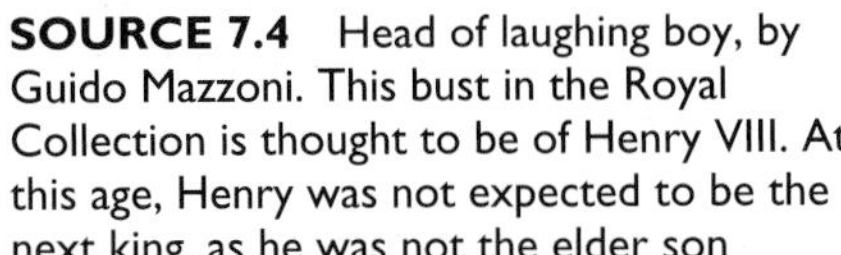

SOURCE 7.4 Head of laughing boy, by Guido Mazzoni. This bust in the Royal Collection is thought to be of Henry VIII. At this age, Henry was not expected to be the next king, as he was not the elder son

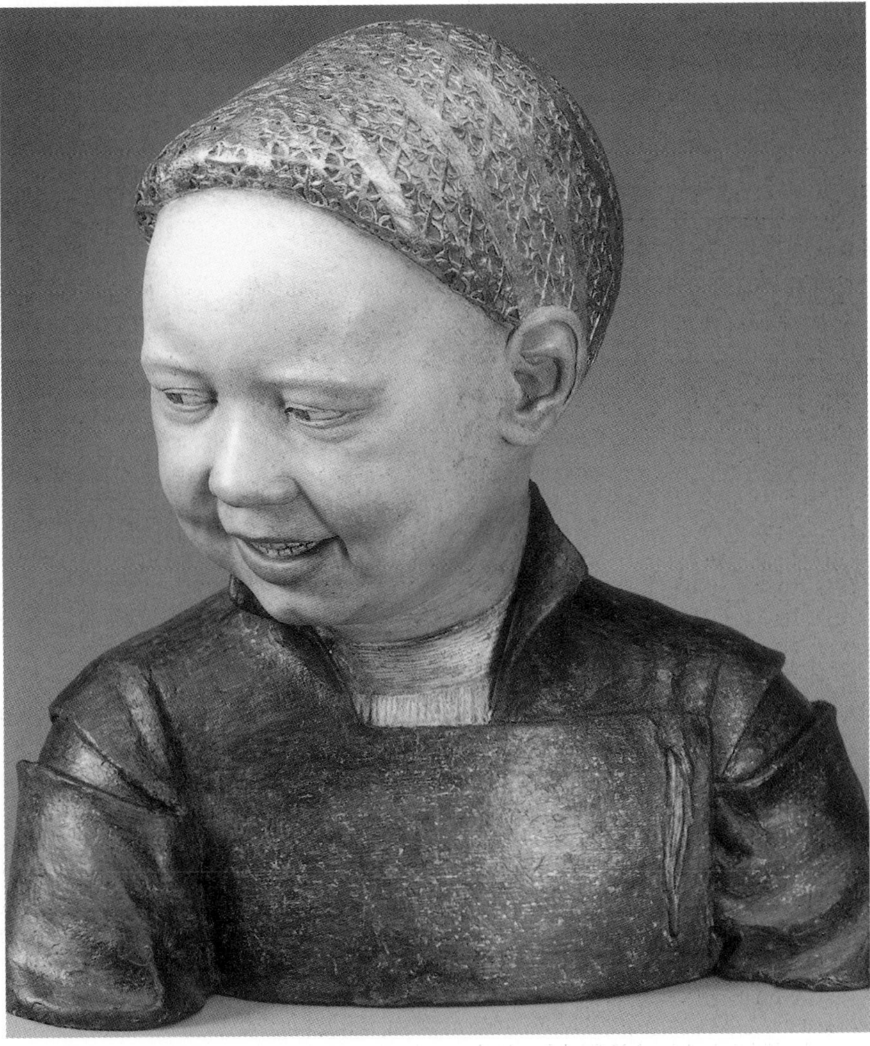

Henry – the Prince

From about the age of five, Henry's education began in earnest. The poet John Skelton was one of his tutors. Henry seems to have been a bright boy – he studied English, French, Latin, arithmetic and astronomy, and he read a lot of history. He was a particularly good musician, playing the lute, organ and virginals, sight reading easily, and singing. Hawking and falconry were sports he learned, as well as jousting and archery.

Henry's life changed when, in the wet spring of 1502, after only six months of marriage, Prince Arthur died, probably from plague or pneumonia. Henry was eleven years old. He was not proclaimed heir, however, until it was confirmed that Catherine, his sister-in-law, was not pregnant. Henry's life was further shattered by the death of his beloved mother in 1503, and the departure of his sister, Margaret, to become Queen of Scotland in the same year.

From Eltham, Henry went upriver to join his father's court at Richmond. There is some debate about the conditions in which young Henry lived there, and the extent to which his new lifestyle prepared him to be king. According to the Spanish envoy, Fuensalida, his life was very restricted. He could go out only through a private door that led to the park, and he could be approached only by specially appointed persons. However, this report is probably misleading, either because Fuensalida did not fully understand how the English court worked or because Henry had been instructed to stay away from him, as Fuensalida's mission was to negotiate the terms by which the widowed Catherine of Aragon might marry Henry himself. Henry had his own suite of rooms next to his father's, and 100 servants. While this undoubtedly enabled him to witness some affairs of state, Henry VII never gave his second son any responsibility for them during his lifetime. Was this because he was over-protective, having already lost one son, or was it because he doubted the abilities of the new heir?

The historian J. J. Scarisbrick, who wrote the famous biography *Henry VIII*, was of the opinion that 'Henry ascended the throne of England – so it seems – unseasoned and untrained in the exacting art of kingship'. This may have been the case, but David Starkey, in his 1998 television programme *Henry VIII*,

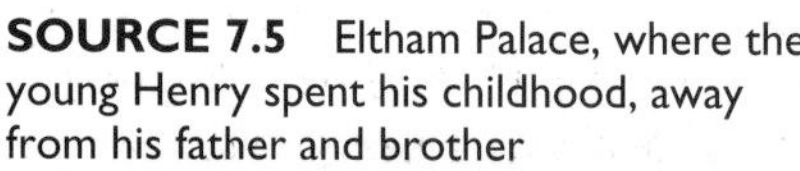

SOURCE 7.5 Eltham Palace, where the young Henry spent his childhood, away from his father and brother

pondered whether one of Henry's surviving school textbooks influenced his thinking. It was written for him by Skelton, his tutor, and was entitled *Speculum Principis* or *The Mirror for a Prince*. In its opening address to Henry, it told him that he could never rest easy with his status, and that he should remember how many of his ancestors had met a terrible fate. He was told the importance of doing the job himself, rather than trusting councillors, who were lazy creatures. We will see whether this advice later rubbed off on Henry as king.

Henry – the man behind the King

Some knowledge of Henry's personality and character is essential if we are to gain any insight into his approach to kingship and why he made some of the decisions he did. Sources 7.7–7.10 will help you to shed some light on this most complex person.

TALKING POINT

How realistic do you think Source 7.7 is as evidence about Henry VIII?

SOURCE 7.7 A description given by the Venetian diplomat Pasqualigo in a dispatch of 1515

His majesty is the handsomest potentate I ever set eyes on; above the usual height, with an extremely fine calf to his leg, his complexion very fair and bright, with auburn hair combed straight and short in the French fashion, and a round face so very beautiful, that it would become a pretty woman, his throat being rather long and thick ... He speaks French, English and Latin, and a little Italian, plays well on the lute and harpsichord, sings songs from book at sight, draws the bow with greater strength than any man in England, and jousts marvellously. Believe me, he is in every respect a most accomplished Prince...

SOURCE 7.8 L. B. Smith, *Henry VIII: The Mask of Royalty*, 1971, pp. 101–2

Emotional imbalance may have been intensified by the opportunities for self-indulgence inherent in kingship, but the real responsibility lay less in the office than in the man, for Henry invariably over-reacted to any stimulus. He sealed his senses against bad news and exulted at good ... Word of Catherine of Aragon's death was celebrated with a masque, banquet and ball where Henry, cross-gartered in yellow hose, danced the night away with Anne Boleyn ... Unfortunately the English King rarely looked before he leaped, and never saw the dark consequences for the pleasure of immediate relief.

SOURCE 7.6 A detail from a sketch of Richmond Palace by Wyngaerde, 1562. Henry moved here on the death of his brother in 1502. His carefree life had changed for ever

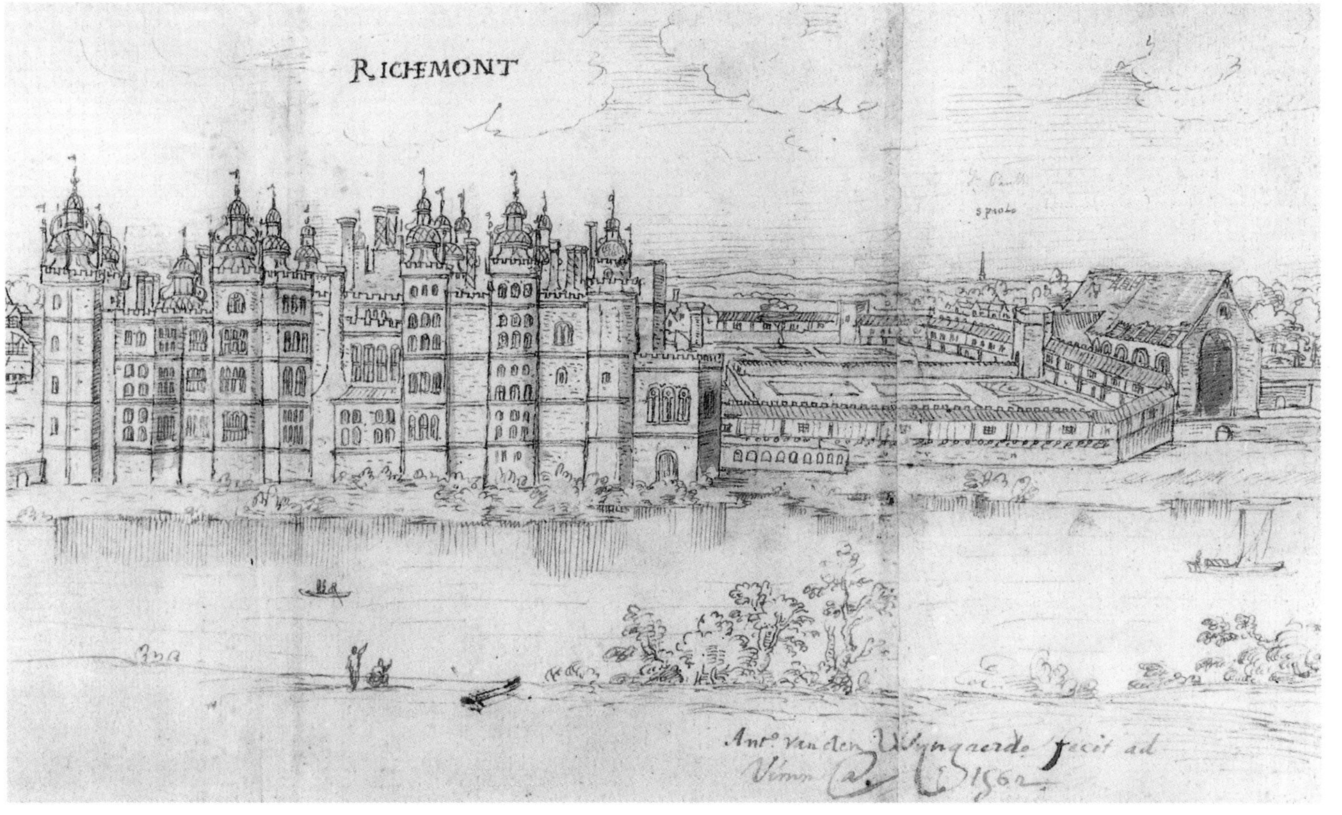

ACTIVITY

1. Summarise Henry's main characteristics according to the information in Sources 7.7–7.10.
2. Do these descriptions of Henry VIII necessarily mean that he would be a bad king?
3. How could Henry's personality help him as king?
4. What do the sources reveal about the difficulties that family members, councillors and courtiers would have encountered in their dealings with the King?

SOURCE 7.9 J. J. Scarisbrick, *Henry VIII*, 1997, p. 17

He was a formidable, captivating man who wore regality with splendid conviction. But easily and predictably his great charm could turn into anger and shouting. When (as alleged) he hit Thomas Cromwell round the head and swore at him, or addressed a Lord Chancellor (Wriothesley) as 'my pig', his mood may have been amicable enough, but More knew that the master who put his arm lovingly round his neck would have his head if it 'could win him a castle in France'. He was highly-strung and unstable; hypochondriac and possessed of a strong streak of cruelty. Possibly he had an Oedipus complex: and possibly from this derived a desire for, yet horror of, incest, which may have shaped some of his sexual life.

SOURCE 7.10 J. Guy, *Tudor England*, 1988, p. 81

Henry's character was fascinating, threatening, and sometimes morbid. His egoism, self-righteousness, and capacity to brood sprang from the fusion of an able but second-rate mind with what looks suspiciously like an inferiority complex ... As his reign unfolded, Henry VIII added 'imperial' concepts of kingship to existing feudal ones; he sought to give the words rex imperator *a meaning unseen since the days of the Roman Empire. He was eager, too, to conquer, to emulate the glorious victories of the Black Prince and Henry V, to quest after the golden fleece that was the French Crown.*

7A The marriages of Henry VIII

Date	Wife	Children	Fate
11 June 1509	Catherine of Aragon	Henry, born 1 January 1511, died February 1511. Mary, born 18 February 1516.	In April 1533, told no longer Queen. In May 1534, placed under house arrest. On 7 January 1536, died at Kimbolton, Cambs.
25 January 1533 (in secret)	Anne Boleyn	Elizabeth, born 7 September 1533.	On 19 May 1536, beheaded.
30 May 1536	Jane Seymour	Edward, born 12 October 1537.	On 24 October 1537, died.
6 January 1540	Anne of Cleves	None	On 12 July 1540, marriage annulled.
28 July 1540	Catherine Howard	None	On 14 November 1541, beheaded.
12 July 1543	Catherine Parr	None	Outlived Henry, died in 1548.

C What was Henry VIII's attitude to kingship?

FOCUS ROUTE

Read pages 90–91. Make notes to explain Henry VIII's attitude to kingship using the following headings:

- Henry's role model
- war and glory in battle
- imperial kingship.

Like his father before him, Henry VIII had a responsibility to maintain the Tudor line of succession. As you can see from Chart 7A, he went to great lengths to achieve this. Also, as king, he had the responsibility of defending England against attack. But Henry VIII wanted more. He wanted to be a *warrior-king*.

Having spent much of his youth in the tiltyard and tournament field playing at war, Henry rejected his father's defensive foreign policy in favour of a more traditional (and costly) interventionist policy. His European counterparts in the early part of his reign were Louis XII of France and the Emperor Maximilian, both of whom spent much of their lives absorbed in war. Henry spoke of his rightful inheritance to the French Crown, and was aware that it was a mere 80 years since Henry VI had been crowned King of France. Henry VIII longed for the glory of Henry V at Agincourt and commissioned a translation of a book about Henry V's early life.

SOURCE 7.11 Henry VIII jousting while Catherine of Aragon looks on

As well as being a warrior-king, Henry also wanted to be an imperial king. The idea of imperial kingship dated back to the Roman Empire and essentially placed the king next to God in importance on Earth. Henry reinforced imperial kingship at various times throughout his reign. For instance, at a tournament in 1511, the imperial crown was to be found as a motif on his gold and purple pavilion. In 1533 the Act in Restraint of Appeals was passed, ordering appeals to be heard in English Church courts rather than in Rome. In its preamble, it asserted Henry's imperial kingship. It referred to England as 'an Empire', governed by 'one supreme head and king'.

SOURCE 7.12 In 1528 William Tyndale, Reformation publicist and translator of the Bible into English, published a work entitled the *Obedience of a Christian Man*. His concept of kingship would certainly have appealed to Henry

God hath made the king in every realm judge overall, and over him there is no judge. He that judgeth the king judgeth God; and he that layeth hands on the king layeth hands on God; and he that resisteth the king resisteth God, and damneth God's law and ordinance.

ACTIVITY

Answer the following questions:

1 How were Henry VIII's priorities as king different from those of his father?
2 Why do you think they were different?
3 Would Henry's attitude to kingship be likely to help or hinder his reign?
4 Was Henry VIII likely to be a great king?

KEY POINTS FROM CHAPTER 7: 'So great a prince' – was Henry VIII likely to be a good king?

1 In 1509 England was in a better condition than it had been when Henry VII became king in 1485.
2 Henry's character was complex, and this would undoubtedly affect his success as king.
3 Henry was not expected to be king in his early life, but when he acceded to the throne he had some firm ideas about what kind of king he wanted to be.
4 Henry was intelligent, attractive and an academically and physically talented man.
5 Henry's main ambitions were to be a warrior and an imperial king.

8

Part-time monarch? Henry VIII and his government, 1509–47

CHAPTER OVERVIEW

We have already seen that Henry's VIII's father took his role in actively governing the country very seriously. He was not a monarch who sat back and just let things happen. He tried to be proactive and made many policy decisions, even if he relied on able administrators to carry them out. We can therefore say that Henry VII not only *reigned*, but also *ruled* the country.

The question of whether Henry VIII actually ruled as well as reigned is fascinating. The image of Henry as someone who enjoyed the good life in the joust, in hunting and through musical entertainment can lull us into thinking that here was a monarch who lacked the gravitas of his father, and who considered the government of the country to be a tedious diversion from what he would rather have been doing. For about 25 years of his 38-year reign, his able servants Wolsey and Cromwell were only too keen to help to run the country. But does this necessarily mean that he was not making the key decisions? Hopefully we can shed some light on this matter as we progress through the chapter. To help unravel the complexities of Henrician government, we must ask ourselves three questions:

ACTIVITY

1. What impression do Sources 8.1 and 8.2 give of Henry VIII – someone who is formidable, not easily crossed and in charge, or someone who is a little unsure of himself, and malleable?
2. As you study the information in this chapter, consider whether either or both of these interpretations of Henry are accurate. Did he change over time, having gained more experience as a monarch?

SOURCE 8.1 A portrait of Henry VIII painted in 1520 by an unknown artist

SOURCE 8.2 A portrait of Henry VIII by an unknown artist, 1536

A How did Henry VIII's government work?

FOCUS ROUTE

Read through pages 94–96. Make notes under the following headings:

- structure of government
- faction and patronage
- similarities and differences compared to the government of Henry VII (refer back to Chapter 3).

We learned about the basic structure of Tudor government when we looked at Henry VII in Chapter 3. During Henry VIII's reign, some interesting developments took place, which are illustrated in Chart 8A.

However, Chart 8A is a simplification of how the government worked. First, it suggests that all three aspects of government were of equal importance, when this was probably not the case. You might expect the councillors to have played the most important role, but David Starkey has argued that during Henry's reign the importance of the Privy Chamber grew, and particularly the influence of the Groom of the Stool, who was responsible for the stool, or Tudor lavatory ('Court and government' in J. Guy (ed.), *The Tudor Monarchy*). Note also that the key personnel are just some of the people who served Henry at different times.

Second, the diagram suggests that the Court, the Council and the Privy Chamber were separate entities, but this was not the case because people could belong to more than one of them. For example, the Gentlemen of the Privy Chamber would be members of the Court by the sheer fact that they were constantly at the beck and call of Henry, and therefore needed to be wherever he was. Henry actually had over 30 houses of his own, mostly within 30 kilometres (18 miles) of London. He used to travel frequently, and in July and August would journey further afield. For instance, in 1526 Henry made a progress to Surrey, Sussex, Hampshire, Wiltshire, Berkshire, Buckinghamshire and Bedfordshire. In that year, 113 nights were spent outside royal palaces.

The Privy Council, which had about twenty members, handled the routine matters of state. Although Henry himself drew up its agendas, he never attended its meetings. The Lord Chancellor or Sir William Paget, the Comptroller of the King's Household, would seek the King's approval on the various matters under discussion.

TALKING POINT

Henry was a king who liked to be on the move. Did this help or hinder the workings of the government, do you think?

SOURCE 8.3 Henry dining in the Privy Chamber, by Hans Holbein. Note the opportunities for influence!

8A The government of Henry VIII

The King

The Court

All persons who were in attendance on the King on any given day. The Court moved from place to place with the King.

Key personnel
Wolsey
Cromwell
Duke of Norfolk

The Privy Council

People appointed by the King to give advice on affairs of state.

Key personnel
Wolsey
Cromwell

The Privy Chamber

Part of the Household. It had its own staff, outside the jurisdiction of the Lord Chamberlain, who looked after the rest of the Household. The head of the Privy Chamber was the **Groom of the Stool**. There were also Gentlemen of the Privy Chamber, who attended to the King's most intimate requirements.

Key personnel
William Compton
Henry Norris

Use of the dry stamp

In the last years of his reign, Henry, not one for the routine tasks of government, allowed various Gentlemen of the Chamber the use of the 'dry stamp' on official documents. This was a 'forged' King's signature that was only ever given to three men at any one time. An impression of the King's signature was pressed on to a document, and the indentation was outlined in ink while the other two men looked on. Men who had access to the dry stamp included Anthony Denny, William Herbert, William Paget and John Gate. A safeguard was built in whereby each document signed had to be listed in a book, of which Henry initialled each page monthly.

Faction

A faction was a group of people who sought to advance shared interests, either positive or negative. Positive interests might include gaining or keeping privileges, grants or jobs for themselves or their associates; negative interests included denying such things to their rivals. However, it is important not to see factions as set groups who existed without change throughout Henry's reign. The most longstanding faction during the reign was the Aragonese faction, who supported the rights and position of the humiliated Queen Catherine of Aragon. Other examples were:

- the Boleyn faction, who orchestrated Wolsey's demise because he would not or could not obtain a divorce for Henry and Catherine of Aragon, to enable Henry to marry Anne Boleyn
- the conservatives under Norfolk and Gardiner, who tried to dispense with Archbishop Cranmer in 1543, and who tried to have Catherine Parr arrested for being a heretic in 1546.

For more information on faction in the Privy Council in the 1540s, see Chart 8C on page 101.

Patronage

By 1547, it has been calculated that there were some 200 posts at court that it was worth a gentleman having, in addition to those in the household. Who decided who was to get those posts? The King and, to a lesser extent, Wolsey and Cromwell. The mechanics of faction and patronage were often inextricably linked, as the case of Sir Ralph Egerton of Ridley shows. Egerton was someone elevated by patronage and humbled by faction, or in the words of the historian Eric Ives, an 'example of what success at court could mean, how it could be won and how it could be lost' ('Patronage at the Court of Henry VIII: the case of Sir Ralph Egerton of Ridley' in the *Bulletin of the John Rylands Library*, Vol. 52, no. 2).

Originating from Cheshire, Egerton first entered court circles in the service of Arthur, Prince of Wales, in 1501. He attended Henry VIII's coronation, and impressed the young king in the joust. He was Henry's standard bearer in the 1513 invasion of France and was made a knight later that year. Between 1514 and 1524, Egerton, by now a leading courtier, amassed different positions as a result of being in favour with the King. These included:

- an annuity of £100 per annum for life in the office of standard bearer
- going with Henry to the Field of Cloth of Gold (see page 154–55)
- appointment to a commission on Ireland
- appointment to Princess Mary's council.

By 1525 Egerton held fifteen Crown offices, three valuable leases and annuities. In 1520 it was observed that he had more than £400 in cash set aside – a great deal of money at that time. Herein lay the seeds of Egerton's downfall, for his wealth became the subject of comment and envy among others at court. His ambition to leave all the offices to his son was thwarted because the latter was still a minor. After he had fallen from the King's favour, therefore, the offices reverted to the Crown, to the benefit of new courtiers and royal servants. Egerton is a prime example of the courtiers who profited and fell on the whim of the King.

ACTIVITY

1. Does the information about Egerton's rise and fall point directly to the influence of faction and patronage on his life? Could there be other explanations for what happened to him?
2. What does Egerton's case tell us about the way in which Henry operated his court?
3. What insight into court life do we get from this case?

B Who dealt with government and politics at home?

FOCUS ROUTE

1 Use the information on pages 97–101 to complete your own copy of the following table.

Period	Key people	Policies	Attitude of King
1509–14 1514–29 1530–40 1540–47			

2 Make notes to explain whether Henry's role and approach to government changed over time.

A sensible way of examining government and politics under Henry VIII is to divide his reign into four periods:

- 1509–14: the early years
- 1514–29: the ascendancy of Wolsey
- 1530–40: the ascendancy of Cromwell
- 1540–47: the end of the reign.

1509–14: the early years

Henry VIII was not yet eighteen when he became king in the summer of 1509. His father had put in place arrangements to govern the country while the young Henry was finding his feet as monarch. Henry VIII therefore inherited a Council chosen by his father, which comprised of most of his father's old councillors: Sir Thomas Lovell; Archbishop Warham; Bishop John Fisher; Thomas Howard, Earl of Surrey, the Lord Treasurer; Sir John Heron, Treasurer of the Chamber; and Bishop Richard Fox, the Lord Privy Seal. It was the latter who used Wolsey's administrative skills and paved the way for Wolsey's acceptance into the Council in 1510.

Although the majority of personnel in the Council provided continuity with the previous reign, the Council's early policies did not. This might say something about the impact that the young Henry VIII had on the Council, even at this early stage. The arrests of the hated Empson and Dudley on the second day after Henry VII's death, and their eventual execution sixteen months later, signalled that Henry VIII was courting popularity and distancing himself from the previous reign. However, the execution of Edmund de la Pole, nephew of Edward IV, in 1513 sent out a clear message about how perceived threats to the throne would be dealt with (de la Pole's brother, Richard, had taken up arms with the French, against whom Henry was about to wage war). Some bonds of Henry VII were cancelled as a gesture of goodwill, but the majority, which did not expire until the 1520s, were maintained.

Perhaps the clearest example of the young king asserting his authority was on the issue of war. Predictably, the old guard on the Council were against an aggressive foreign policy, citing financial and security considerations. But Henry himself was undeterred, and he was supported by other nobles, young and old, who saw war as a golden opportunity, some having been denied such pursuits under the old king. You can read more about the French campaign of 1512–14 in Chapter 11 on page 151.

1514–29: the ascendancy of Wolsey

Chart 8B compares the domestic policies of Henry's reign during the ascendancy of Cardinal Wolsey and that of Thomas Cromwell.

■ 8B Henry VIII's domestic policies under Wolsey and Cromwell

Wolsey	Cromwell
The law **The Court of Star Chamber** Increased in importance. From 1516 onwards, Wolsey wanted it to dispense cheap and impartial justice – corruption was to be rooted out. Wolsey also used it to challenge the power of the nobility. **The Court of Chancery** • Wolsey made decisions here that created legal precedents. • Cases were dealt with in property, wills and contracts. • Wolsey established a permanent judicial committee to deal with cases brought by the poor. • The court was in huge demand as a result of Wolsey's actions and because he got distracted by foreign policy. **Finance** **Act of Resumption 1515** Wolsey wanted to increase revenue from Crown lands, but many had been granted away at the beginning of Henry VIII's reign. Income had decreased to £25,000 per annum. This Act returned some of the lands to the Crown. **The subsidy** • Wolsey wanted the subsidy to replace the fifteenths and tenths tax.The subsidy was a more realistic tax because it was based on more accurate valuations of the taxpayers' wealth. **The 'Amicable Grant'** This was an additional tax that Wolsey demanded in 1525 to fund Henry's expedition to France. It caused rebellion in East Anglia and widespread non-payment as it followed forced loans in 1522 and 1523, which had not been repaid, and the subsidy of 1523, which was still being collected. **Balance sheet** Wolsey raised £322,099 in subsidies, £240,000 in clerical taxation and £260,000 in forced loans. But government expenditure between 1509 and 1520 was £1.7 million. Wolsey's gains in income could not finance war. **Administration** **Eltham Ordinances 1526** • Wolsey tried to reform the royal household to ensure his political supremacy. • The ordinances were an attempt to do this, but they came to nothing as Wolsey found other ways of maintaining his power. **The Church** • Wolsey, as papal legate, had precedence over the Archbishop of Canterbury. • Wolsey showed some reforming intentions that came to little. • He dissolved 30 religious houses and used the proceeds to build colleges at Oxford and Ipswich. • The Church became more centralised under his control – churchmen became used to orders from the Crown. **Enclosures** (see also page 138) • Wolsey was concerned less about the effects of enclosure on the poor than about acting against the landowners. • An inquiry in 1517 identified enclosed land and demolition of buildings. • Legal proceedings were begun against 264 landowners; 222 came to court with 188 clear verdicts (one involved Sir Thomas More). • Enclosure continued and vagrancy was not reduced. • Wolsey stirred up further hatred from the landowners.	**Law and order** In 1540 an Act abolished **sanctuary** (the use of religious buildings to shield criminals). **Finance** • In 1536 the **Court of Augmentations** was established to deal with income from the dissolution of the monasteries. Receivers in the regions dealt with dissolved estates and reported to a central staff. • Crown income increased from £150,000 to £300,000. **Administration** • Elton's 'revolution in government' thesis (*The Tudor Revolution in Government*) suggested that the business of government became less centred on the household – carried out in rooms near the King and by his household staff – and more independent and bureaucratic. • The probability is that administration was a combination of both styles. **The Privy Council** • About 70 people served as Privy Councillors, but by 1536 a smaller group of about 20 seemed to conduct the business of government in its daily workings. • It is debatable whether the importance of the Privy Council increased under Cromwell. **Wales and the north** • In the **Act of Union 1536**, Wales became incorporated into the English legal and administrative system. • An Act of 1543 divided Wales into three shires, each with JPs appointed by the King. Wales was to send 24 MPs to Parliament in London, and English common law was to be the law of the land. English became the language of documentation and officials had to use it. • From 1536 the authority of the **Council of the North** increased after the Pilgrimage of Grace. • The Council was to be responsible for law and order north of the River Trent, nominating and overseeing JPs and dealing with more serious crimes including treason. • The King's authority was felt more directly and rapidly as a result.

Cardinal Wolsey

Born in 1472, Thomas Wolsey was the son of an Ipswich butcher. He graduated from Magdalen College, Oxford, and was ordained into the priesthood in 1498. He became an almoner in the court of Henry VII, and royal chaplain in 1507. The ascent of the new king coincided with Wolsey's further rise to prominence, joining the Council in 1510. It was he who provided the new king with an army and the strategy to beat the French at the battle of the Spurs in 1513. In 1514, he became the Archbishop of York, but it was a disappointment to him that he never held the see of Canterbury, although he did become a papal legate in 1518. The real zenith of his power was reached when he was appointed Cardinal and Lord Chancellor in 1515. He was thereafter effectively Henry's chief minister until his fall from grace in 1529.

Distributor of alms

TALKING POINT

In your wider reading, note that Wolsey and Cromwell are often referred to as Henry VIII's Chief Ministers. This was neither an office nor a term that the Tudors themselves were familiar with.

Why have historians labelled Wolsey and Cromwell as Chief Ministers? Does such labelling help or hinder our understanding of Henry's role in government?

Who was in control of policy, the King or Wolsey? The semblance that Wolsey was directing affairs is misleading according to the historian Eric Ives, who has asserted that Wolsey 'could effectively propose a policy but he was always careful to ensure that Henry owned it' ('Henry VIII: the political perspective' in D. MacCulloch (ed.), *The Reign of Henry VIII: Politics, Policy and Piety*). Certainly Henry was astute enough to realise that Wolsey was not perfect, but he maintained to Wolsey that 'your faults acknowledged, there shall remain in me no spark of displeasure'. Sources 8.4–8.7 demonstrate the difficulty of reaching an unbiased, objective view of Wolsey. (See Chapter 11, pages 165–66, for an assessment of whether Wolsey or Henry controlled foreign policy.)

SOURCE 8.4 S. J. Gunn and P. G. Lindley (eds), *Cardinal Wolsey: Church, State and Art*, 1991, p. 2

His authority as Henry's chief minister was so great, and his apparent responsibility for all areas of government policy so sweeping, that politicians and political commentators alike had to be either entirely for Wolsey or entirely against him ... Once he had fallen from power, on the other hand, it was convenient never to have been his friend.

SOURCE 8.5 Extracts from John Skelton's 'Why come ye nat to courte?' (1522) offer a negative view of the Cardinal

He is set so hye
In his ierarchy
Of frantycke frenesy
And folysshe fantasy
That in the Chambre of Sterres
All maters there he marres
Clappying his rod on the borde.
No man dare speke a worde,
For he hath all the sayenge
Without any renayenge…

Set up a wretche on hye,
In a trone triumphantlye,
Make him a great astate,
And he wyll play checke mate
With ryall majeste
Count himselfe as good as he.

TALKING POINT

Sources 8.5 and 8.6 are prejudiced about Wolsey. Does this affect their value for historians?

SOURCE 8.6 George Cavendish, *Life of Wolsey*, written 1554–58. As Wolsey's gentleman usher, Cavendish writes admiringly of his master, who had fallen from grace as a result of faction in the Council, as Cavendish saw it

All his endeavour was only to satisfy the king's mind, knowing right well that it was in the very vein and right course to bring him to high promotion … [He] took upon him to disburden the king of so weighty a charge and troublesome business, putting the king in comfort that he shall not need to spare any time of his pleasure for any business that should necessary happen in the council as long as he being there, having the king's authority and commandment doubted not to see all things sufficiently furnished and perfected, the which would first make the king privy of all such matters (as should pass through their hands) before he would proceed to the finishing and determination of the same, whose mind and pleasure he would fulfil and follow to the uttermost wherewith the king was wonderfully pleased.

SOURCE 8.7 J. Guy, 'Wolsey, Cromwell and the reform of government', in D. MacCulloch (ed.), *The Reign of Henry VIII: Politics, Policy and Piety*, 1995, p. 36

It is true that Wolsey enjoyed exceptional favour and for a while his position was different. Between 1515 and 1525 it can be argued that Henry treated him more as a partner than a servant. Wolsey enjoyed a uniquely privileged access to the king. They walked arm-in-arm together and were intimate confidantes to the exclusion of others.

Thomas Cromwell

Like Wolsey, Cromwell rose to power from unlikely origins. The son of a Putney cloth worker, he was born around 1475. Though he had no formal education, he travelled abroad widely. In Italy he served as a soldier or a page for the defeated French at the battle of the Garigliano in 1503. Through his employment with Florentine bankers and Venetian and English merchants, he learned about trade and accountancy. Despite his lack of legal training, he built up a successful legal practice and by 1524 was working for Wolsey, initially as his solicitor, then as a commissioner appointed to enquire into the smaller monasteries. Cromwell became an MP in 1523, and later in the 1520s became the Cardinal's secretary, whilst also acting independently as a lawyer, arbitrator, merchant and moneylender.

Sometime during 1529, he was instrumental in persuading Henry VIII to make himself head of the church. Cromwell became a member of the Privy Council in 1531, and Master of the Court of Wards and Master of the Jewel House in 1532, by which time he was effectively the king's Chief Minister, until his demise in 1540.

Research has revealed Cromwell's Protestant leanings. For example, he personally paid for a vernacular Bible to be published.

SOURCE 8.8 E. Ives, 'Henry VIII: the political perspective', in D. MacCulloch (ed.), *The Reign of Henry VIII: Politics, Policy and Piety*, 1995, p. 27

Cromwell … was not Wolsey in lay garb, and not merely because of his lower profile … First, the shift of power back to the court, the immediacy of the king's matrimonial problem and its knock-on effects on foreign policy and finance meant that Henry, willy-nilly, was much nearer to decisions on detail than he had been. Second, the 1530s required a minister who would be pro-active not reactive. Thirdly, Cromwell was in a different league from the Cardinal when it came to political originality. He needed to be. He did not have the advantages of age, European recognition and 'magnificence' which helped Wolsey to impress the king for so long. What is more, the greater involvement of the king meant that Cromwell's arrival did not marginalise the council attendant in the way Wolsey's had done. It was not enough, therefore, to mediate joint royal and ministerial directions to a team of councillors; Cromwell had also to manage an inner ring whose members saw the king more regularly than he did. Nor did Cromwell escape inheriting the problem of the courtiers.

1530–40: the ascendancy of Cromwell

It is widely agreed that Cromwell did not enjoy the same latitude that Wolsey had done at the height of his ascendancy. Source 8.8 provides a comparison of the two chief ministers.

ACTIVITY

Re-read Source 8.8 and the information on pages 98–101 on Wolsey and Cromwell. Explain how and why their roles in Henry VIII's government were similar, and how and why they were different.

1540–47: the end of the reign

The last years of Henry's reign should not be underestimated in terms of the King's grip on power. True, he increasingly suffered from ill health, probably as a result of scurvy (rather than syphilis), his increasing bulk and painful, even life-threatening, leg ulcers. But in these twilight years there was more intrigue to be played out. For instance, in 1540 Henry elevated Cromwell to the earldom of Essex and made him Great Chamberlain, but within two months Cromwell was accused of treason and executed. Henry was to marry three more times in the space of as many years.

As Henry no longer wished to have a chief minister, the government of the country was in the hands of Henry when he felt moved enough to be involved, particularly on religious and foreign policy matters. The Privy Council was riven by faction, as shown in Chart 8C.

■ 8C Privy Council factions in the 1540s

	The conservatives	The reformers
Names	Duke of Norfolk Bishop Gardiner Sir Thomas Wriothesley Lord Russell Earl of Surrey (Norfolk's son)	Earl of Hertford John Dudley (Viscount Lisle) Sir Anthony Denny Sir William Paget Archbishop Cranmer
Aims	A Counter-Reformation, Catholicism and personal gain	Protestant reform and personal gain
Tactics	Engineered the Catherine Howard marriage, 1540 (she was Norfolk's niece). She was executed for treason in 1541. Attempted unsuccessfully to oust Catherine Parr and Cranmer from power, but Henry intervened to save them.	Achieved the Catherine Parr marriage, 1543. Denny obtained use of the dry stamp (see page 96) in 1546 and it was used to alter Henry's will after his death. Two clauses were added, which helped Hertford to establish himself as Protector in the minority of Edward VI. Norfolk and Surrey were accused of treason for Surrey's use of badges which suggested he had a claim to the throne.

So, was Henry in control? As ever when looking at factions, it is difficult to know just how much they influenced the King. Certainly Henry realised that Edward would have to have a regency council. He intended it to have sixteen members, with an equal balance of Protestants and Catholics (see page 198).

C How involved was Henry VIII in government, and did this change?

FOCUS ROUTE

Read the two case studies on this page. Find information/evidence to comment on the following statements and make detailed notes explaining whether each statement is accurate or inaccurate:

- Henry VIII made all key policy decisions.
- Henry VIII was not interested in the day-to-day workings of government.
- Henry VIII did not know what was going on in government on a day-to-day basis.
- Henry VIII gave his ministers a wide latitude.

Case study 1: The Amicable Grant, 1525

After Charles V's success over France at the battle of Pavia in 1525, Henry wished to invade France, but there was no money with which to pay for such an invasion. Wolsey set about raising funds for the war chest by attempting to levy a tax, without the approval of Parliament. Both the clergy and laity were expected to pay this so-called Amicable Grant, but money that had been 'loaned' in 1522–3 had still not been repaid, and a subsidy of 1523 was still being collected. Not surprisingly, there was widespread dissent and the commissioners who were trying to collect the money met resistance. People in Kent, for instance, remarked wryly that it was not as if the King had actually won any land in France, which was quite true. Full-scale revolt erupted in Suffolk and spread to the borders of Essex and Cambridgeshire. Happily for Wolsey and the King, the Dukes of Norfolk and Suffolk, having mustered the East Anglian gentry, negotiated the surrender of 10,000 rebels at Lavenham.

Was the Amicable Grant Henry's idea or, as with other state matters, was it a case of Henry deciding on the broad outline of policy – that is, needing to fund an invasion of France – and Wolsey attending to the fine detail? The information we have is frustratingly sparse. According to Scarisbrick's account in *Henry VIII*, when Henry realised what was going on, he claimed that he 'never knew of the demand', and then converted it into a benevolence. This seems hard to swallow – perhaps he did not know of the precise rate being demanded, but surely such an attempted collection of money cannot have escaped his knowledge completely? Wolsey said that the plan was devised by the Council without the King knowing the full details. Of course, if Wolsey took the blame and the King publicly forgave him, everyone was in the clear.

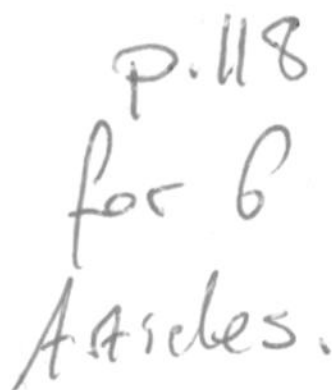

Case study 2: The Act of Six Articles, 1539

As you will see in Chapter 9, the Act of Six Articles was a statement of doctrine that was passed by Parliament in 1539. Put simply, throughout the 1530s, Protestant beliefs were becoming more prevalent, and the Act of 1539 was designed to move people back towards Catholicism by, among other things, reaffirming the 'real presence': that is, the Catholic belief that at Communion the bread and wine actually become the body and blood of Christ. According to the Act of Six Articles, the charge for failure to believe in this doctrine was treason.

As with the Amicable Grant, there is considerable debate about how far the Act of Six Articles resulted from Henry's personal involvement. The Council was certainly divided on religious matters, with Cranmer and Cromwell urging a more Protestant line, and Norfolk and Gardiner advocating a more Catholic one. Was Henry swayed by the more persuasive faction? Or was the Act of Six Articles a statement of doctrine that reflected Henry's own personal religious views? Certainly he had acknowledged three of the Articles in a letter to German envoys in 1538, and there is evidence that he was concerned about what he considered to be the new heresies from abroad that were spreading to England. Was he motivated by a possible invasion threat after 1538 because of the ten-year truce between Francis I and the Emperor Charles V? Henry himself made corrections to the draft bill before it went through Parliament (the bill had to be double-spaced to allow for the King's annotations). So, as the historian Glyn Redworth has argued ('A study in the formulation of policy: the genesis and evolution of the Act of Six Articles', *Journal of Ecclesiastical History*, no. 37), the Act can be interpreted as being the result of any or all of the following: faction, misunderstandings, foreign affairs and the King's own beliefs.

ACTIVITY

1 From what you know of Henry VIII, would he have allowed taxes to be collected and laws to be passed without *any* input at all from him?
2 Do the case studies provide sufficient evidence that Henry's involvement in government changed during his reign? Explain your answer.

FOCUS ROUTE

Using the information in this chapter, write a paragraph on each of the following:

a) How did Henry VIII's government work?
b) Who dealt with government and politics at home?
c) How involved was Henry VIII in government, and did this change?

KEY POINTS FROM CHAPTER 8: Part-time monarch? Henry VIII and his government, 1509–47

1 The King exercised several direct responsibilities in government and had a strong understanding of what was happening at all times.
2 Government and politics were focused on where Henry was; the court always followed him.
3 The Privy Chamber, and especially the Groom of the Stool, increased in influence in Henry VIII's reign.
4 Factions were endemic throughout Henry's reign.
5 The extent to which factions influenced the decisions that Henry made is debatable.
6 Henry relied on Wolsey and Cromwell to exercise affairs of government, but this does not mean that Henry was not in overall charge.
7 When anyone failed the King – wife, minister, friend – they were disposed of.

9

Divorce, doctrine or dosh? The reasons for the break with Rome and the origins of the Reformation

CHAPTER OVERVIEW

The events of the 1530s mark a fundamental turning point in the history of religious change in England. For centuries the English Church had been part of the Catholic Church under the power of the Pope. In 1534 Henry VIII broke away from the Pope's power. If Henry VIII had not performed this radical act, England might now be a predominantly Catholic country. The look of England might have been entirely different, with huge numbers of monasteries and colourful churches still in existence. The national character might have been closer to those of Catholic countries such as Italy, France or Spain. In short, the Reformation, which started in England in the 1530s, has had a massive impact on the history and culture of British society. The world in which you live has been moulded by the beliefs of generations reacting to these vital events.

The key theme of this chapter is: what pushed Henry into this decision? Was it his desire to divorce Catherine of Aragon? Was it his wish to cleanse the Church of corruption? Or was it purely and simply a rush to get his hands on the Church's wealth? There is no real consensus among historians as to the answers to these questions. This gives you the opportunity to come to your own interpretation of events, based on the evidence.

We will be looking at the following issues:

A What were the causes of England's break with Rome?

By the end of 1534, Henry VIII had broken away from the power of the Pope. His Act of Supremacy meant that Henry had complete power over the Church in England. Why had this change come about? Each of the factors in Chart 9A played some part in Henry VIII's decision to break with Rome. Your role as a historian is to analyse each factor in turn and then weigh up its relative importance. You should keep these factors in mind as you study this chapter.

■ 9A Causes of the break with Rome

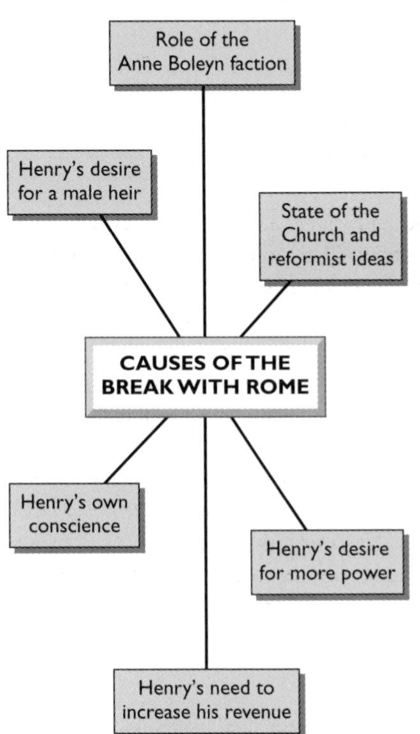

■ Learning trouble spot

The words used to describe changes during this period are often complicated and sometimes not entirely clear. Historians often use single words or phrases as a shorthand for ideas of great depth and complexity. The following are central to a sound understanding.

Reformation

This describes the movement that began in Europe at the start of the sixteenth century under the influence of reformers such as Luther, Zwingli and Calvin. It aimed at reforming the abuses of the Roman Catholic Church and ended in the establishment of separate 'reformed' or Protestant churches free from the control of the Pope. Historians generally see the Reformation as a movement that took many years to achieve its objective. It is not a single event that happened overnight.

However, historians disagree about the speed of the Reformation in England. Some, such as A. G. Dickens in *The English Reformation*, see the Reformation as coming quickly, being provoked by a general public dissatisfaction with the Church. Others, such as Christopher Haigh in *English Reformations: Religion, Politics and Society Under the Tudors*), see it as a slow movement that was not complete until the 1580s, and that was controlled and directed by the actions of kings and queens. (Other interpretations are studied later in this chapter on pages 123–26.)

Given these subtleties of meaning, it is important that you use the term 'Reformation' precisely. It is not interchangeable with the two terms below.

Break with Rome

This phrase should be used only for the technical and legal change in the status of the English Church brought about through the legislation of the 'Reformation Parliament' (1529–36). While this legislation removed the power of the Pope in England, it did not lead to the end of Catholicism in the country. Many Catholic practices remained and many people's beliefs were not changed from Catholicism to Protestantism – this included Henry VIII himself! So you should not assume that the break with Rome led inevitably to a full Reformation in England.

Divorce

This is often used to describe the end of Henry's marriage to Catherine of Aragon. Although many historians use this term, we should more accurately describe the event as an *annulment*, as divorce is not allowed (even today) in the Catholic Church. An annulment states that the marriage was never valid in the first place, and only the Pope has the right to grant such an annulment. It is also important to recognise the difference between the divorce and the break with Rome. They were two separate, though linked processes. Henry's desire for a divorce did not necessarily mean that he wanted to break with Rome. You should be careful not to say 'divorce' when you mean 'break with Rome' and vice versa.

ACTIVITY

Read Chart 9B.

1 Which motives for action seem to be most obvious from this chart:
   a) Henry wanted to end a marriage that went against God's will
   b) Henry wanted a male heir
   c) Henry had fallen in love with Anne Boleyn?

2 Can you identify a turning point after which Henry was committed to:
   a) annulling his marriage to Catherine
   b) marrying Anne?

The origins of the break with Rome are to be found in the 1520s. By 1527 it had become clear that Henry wanted to annul his marriage to Catherine of Aragon. The key question is: why did he want to end a marriage that had already lasted for eighteen years? There are three possible answers:

- He wanted to end a marriage that he believed to be against God's will.
- He wanted a new wife who would provide him with a legitimate male heir.
- He had fallen in love with Anne Boleyn.

The timeline of events shown in Chart 9B was constructed by Eric Ives in his biography, *Anne Boleyn.* Although it is partly speculation, it does give us some clues about Henry's motives.

Historians have disagreed about whether Henry fell in love with Anne Boleyn and *then* grew tired of Catherine, or vice versa. The two leading historians in this debate are Eric Ives and J. J. Scarisbrick (see Sources 9.1 and 9.2).

■ 9B The deteriorating relationship of Henry and Catherine

Date	Event	Explanation
1524	Henry stopped sleeping with Catherine (now aged 39).	Catherine had had several miscarriages and two stillborn babies. There was thus little chance of the birth of a male heir. Her last pregnancy had been in 1518.
1525	Henry Fitzroy was made Duke of Richmond.	Evidence of Henry promoting his illegitimate son as his future heir. This decision was made in the wake of Charles V's rejection of a proposed marriage to Henry's daughter, Mary.
1526	Henry began to woo Anne Boleyn.	Henry had no plans for marriage at this stage.
1526–27	Henry decided on an annulment.	It is possible that Henry's conscience had been pricked by French enquiries as to the legitimacy of Henry's daughter Mary. Henry was trying to arrange Mary's marriage to Francis I, but the French questioning of Henry's marriage to Catherine may well have started a train of thought in Henry's own mind.
1527		
Easter	Henry pressed Anne to become his mistress.	Henry did not want to marry Anne at this stage. He did seem happy to have her as his acknowledged mistress.
May	Secret proceedings started for the annulment.	Not even Catherine knew about this development.
May	Charles V sacked Rome.	Charles' mercenary troops went on the rampage in Rome. The Pope was taken prisoner, which severely limited his ability to negotiate a settlement with Henry, because Charles was Catherine's nephew.
June	Henry told Catherine of his plans.	
July	Henry and Anne agreed to marry after the annulment was granted.	All of these moves suggest that Henry saw no real problems in gaining his annulment.
September	Henry applied to the Pope for a dispensation to marry Anne.	
December	Negotiations in Rome for the annulment.	
1528		
September	Anne was sent to Hever Castle.	This was done to get her out of the way.
October	Cardinal Campeggio arrived in England.	Campeggio was appointed by the Pope to act as judge (with Wolsey) in the hearing of Henry's case. He was originally a popular choice with Henry but this popularity was, however, soon to wane.
December	Anne returned to court.	This is evidence of her influence over Henry.
1529		
May	Proceedings for hearing the case for Henry's annulment started at Blackfriars.	
June	Catherine made her single appearance before the hearing.	Her heartfelt plea for Henry to remain loyal is clear evidence of her own commitment to the marriage.
July	A summer recess was called and the case was recalled to Rome by the Pope.	It has to be remembered that at this stage the Pope was under the complete control of Charles V after the latter's victory at the battle of Landriano (see page 161).

ACTIVITY

What is the key difference between the interpretations of Ives and Scarisbrick in Sources 9.1 and 9.2?

■ Learning trouble spot

Changes in religious and domestic policy were often closely linked to foreign affairs. See pages 161 and 164 for a detailed explanation of how Henry's efforts to gain an annulment were hampered by events abroad.

SOURCE 9.1 Eric Ives, *Anne Boleyn*, 1986, p. 102

The probabilities are … in favour of a relationship which became serious only after the decision to divorce Katherine. In the first place it is clear that Wolsey … was not aware how committed Henry was to Anne Boleyn until the autumn of 1527. In the second, no hint of Anne's involvement with the King has been discovered in any records before that date – an unlikely thing if the affair was already two years old … The normally hawk-eyed Venetians did not become aware of Anne until February 1528.

SOURCE 9.2 J. J. Scarisbrick, *Henry VIII*, 1968, p. 149

By 1525–6 what had probably hitherto been a light dalliance with an 18- or 19-year-old girl had begun to grow into something deeper and more dangerous … Anne refused to become his [Henry's] mistress … and the more she resisted, the more, apparently, did Henry prize her … The King, then, had tired of his wife and fallen in love with one who would give herself entirely to him only if he would give himself entirely to her.

Date	Event	Explanation
1529 (cont)		
October	Wolsey was accused of *praemunire*, forced to surrender the Great Seal and replaced as Lord Chancellor by Thomas More.	*Praemunire* is the offence of recognising or responding to a foreign authority (in this case, the Pope) instead of the King. It is important to note that Henry chooses a layman rather than a man of the Church at this vital time in the annulment process.
November	The 'Reformation Parliament' was assembled.	
1530 January	Anne's brother led a mission to the Pope and Charles V in Bologna to gain support for Henry's case. This failed.	This marked the moment when Henry was pushed into a more radical solution – the rejection of papal authority.
May	Cambridge and Oxford universities found in favour of Henry.	
September	Edward Foxe and Thomas Cranmer presented Henry with their book *Collectanea Satis Copiosa* ('The Sufficiently Abundant Collections').	This justified Henry's annulment on legal grounds, based on historical principles. The authors argued that the English Church had always been under the authority of the monarchy. Henry could therefore claim control over his own matrimonial affairs perfectly legally without reference to the Pope. 'It was the work of the *Collectanea* that was to fuel the extraordinary self-confidence of the King's break with Rome' (D. MacCulloch, *Thomas Cranmer*).
1531 February	The Convocation of Canterbury recognised Henry as 'Supreme Head of the Church so far as the law of Christ allows'.	This brought Henry into direct opposition to the power of the Pope.
1532 May	Submission of the Clergy – the clergy accepted the King and not the Pope as their lawmaker.	This confirmed the strength of Henry's power within the Church.
December	Anne became pregnant.	Anne's reluctance to have sex with Henry had evidently been overcome! The stakes for Henry could not now be any higher.
1533 January	Henry and Anne married in secret.	The ceremony was carried out by Cranmer, who was then made Archbishop of Canterbury (in February).
April	Cranmer ruled that Henry's marriage to Catherine was invalid, whereas his marriage to Anne was legal.	
May	Anne was crowned as Queen of England.	Anne was the only one of Henry's wives (other than Catherine of Aragon) to receive such an honour.

Catherine of Aragon

Catherine remained an important figure throughout her life because she was popular across the country and was supported by powerful nobles in England and by Charles V abroad. She always saw herself as subordinate to her husband, except in the case of the annulment where she took a determined and principled stance.

Henry left Catherine in 1531 and she never saw her husband or daughter again.

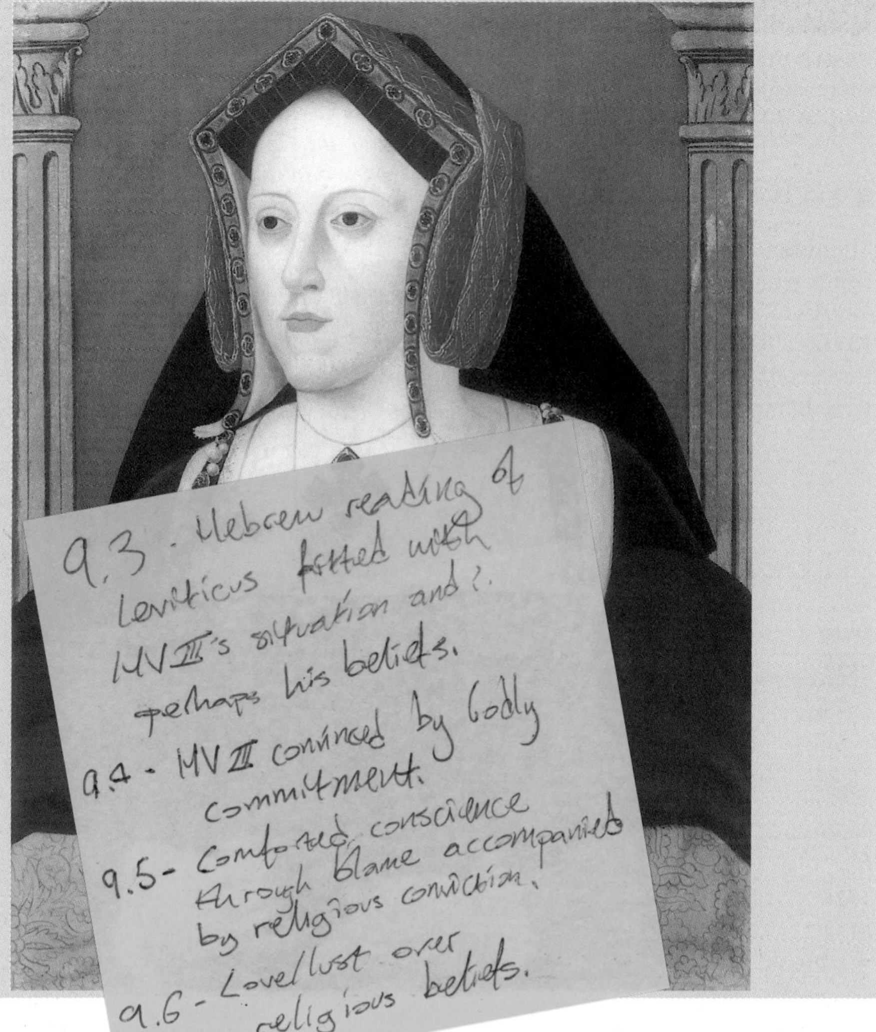

Catherine of Aragon, by an unknown artist, c. 1530

Matter of conscience

It seems clear that by the end of 1527 Henry was convinced of the need to annul his marriage to Catherine of Aragon. It is highly probable, however, that his decision to end the marriage did not necessarily mean that he would actually marry Anne Boleyn. Henry had had several mistresses previously and his willingness to legitimise his bastard son, Henry Fitzroy, is evidence enough of his lack of embarrassment. So, love for Anne Boleyn is not reason enough in itself to explain why Henry felt it necessary to end the marriage to Catherine. Clearly Henry wanted a male heir, but even this cannot completely explain his rejection of Catherine of Aragon – again, Henry Fitzroy seemed to fit the bill to Henry's satisfaction.

So what made such a difference? Most recently, Virginia Murphy has confirmed the work of L. B. Smith (in *Henry VIII: The Mask of Royalty*) in asserting Henry's growing obsession with the fact that his marriage to Catherine was, and always had been, against God's law (see Source 9.3). Central to her argument is Henry's insistence that the words of the Bible in Leviticus 20:21 represented God's own judgement on his marriage to Catherine of Aragon.

In Latin translation, Leviticus says 'If a man shall take his brother's wife, it is an unclean thing . . . they shall be without children.' Clearly, Henry had married the wife of Arthur, his brother. However, they did have one child, Mary, born in 1516. This did not follow Leviticus in the Latin translation, so Henry turned to the Hebrew original, which specified sons rather than children. It was clear to Henry that a male heir to carry forward the Tudor dynasty was hugely important. Even more important, however, was the fact that this heir should be the offspring of a legitimate marriage – a marriage that did not offend God.

ACTIVITY

Read Sources 9.3–9.6.

1 Summarise the arguments of these historians, using about 20 words for each.
2 Which historian is the odd one out? Explain how their interpretations agree/disagree.

SOURCE 9.3 V. Murphy 'The literature and propaganda of Henry VIII's first divorce', in D. MacCulloch (ed.), *The Reign of Henry VIII: Politics, Policy and Piety*, 1995, p. 139

By substituting the Hebrew for the Latin, Leviticus was thus cleverly made to fit Henry's situation exactly; he had married in contravention of Leviticus and as a result had incurred the punishment threatened there, as the loss of all his sons proved. This narrow understanding of Leviticus is important for it allowed Henry to reconcile Leviticus with his own circumstances. How deeply Henry believed the views expressed in the address, especially the rewording of Leviticus, is impossible to say, although it is probable that they reflected a genuine and strongly held conviction. Certainly the connection between the king's failure to have produced a surviving son and Leviticus would become a central theme of the treatises produced in his name.

SOURCE 9.4 E. Ives, *Anne Boleyn*, 1986, p. 101

God had spoken directly to his condition; Henry had no option as a devout Christian but to obey, to contract a legal (indeed his first) marriage, and a son would be the reward. Post-Freudian scepticism may smile, but the vital historical point is that Henry believed. Armed with his certainty he consulted Wolsey and his lawyers, and on 17 May 1527 took the first and secret steps to divorce his wife.

SOURCE 9.5 L. B. Smith, *Henry VIII: The Mask of Royalty*, 1971, p. 111

If there is anything approaching a complete explanation of Henry's actions it lies in an amalgam of his compulsive need to wall out doubt by keeping conscience clear and placing blame on others and his absolute conviction that events are determined by a bargain struck between God and man ... Ultimately the King rested his case on 'the discharge of our conscience'.

SOURCE 9.6 P. Gwyn, *The King's Cardinal: The Rise and Fall of Thomas Wolsey*, 1990, pp. 512–13

The one argument for the divorce that Henry never made in public was that he had fallen in love with Anne, for to have done so would have been tactically foolish. Yet in February 1529 Campeggio was to say that Henry's love was 'something amazing, and in fact he sees nothing and thinks nothing but Anne. He cannot stay away from her for an hour; it is really quite pitiable, and on it depends his life, and indeed the destruction or survival of this kingdom.' Surely Campeggio had got to the heart of the matter, for without the intensity of that love, or perhaps it should be called infatuation, it is difficult to see how Henry could have sustained the campaign for the five and a half years that were needed, or that he would have jeopardized so much in order to do so ... What was at stake was not a 'scruple' but lust, and lust was not something that the Vicar of Christ should encourage, especially when the legal arguments for doing so were not very strong.

■ 9C Henry's motives

Most recent research suggests that Henry was brought into conflict with the Pope at an early stage in the 1520s. The logic of Henry's thinking went as follows:

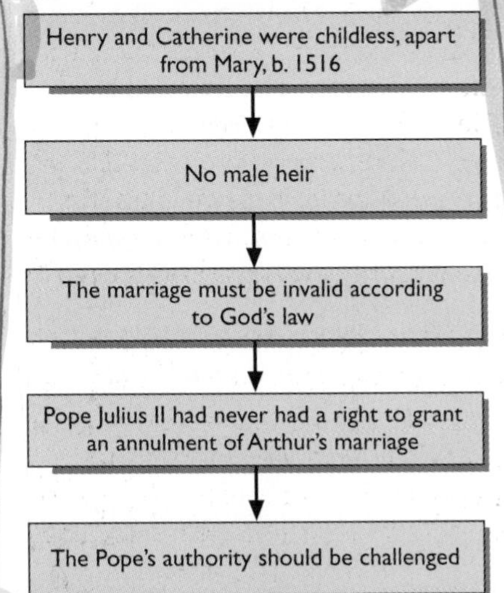

Henry and Catherine were childless, apart from Mary, b. 1516
No male heir
The marriage must be invalid according to God's law
Pope Julius II had never had a right to grant an annulment of Arthur's marriage
The Pope's authority should be challenged

This points to the fact that *from the outset* Henry questioned the Pope's authority to rule over his marriage to Catherine. It supports the argument that Henry's actions were motivated by a genuine sense of conscience, which led him to reject his first marriage and, ultimately, papal authority itself.

The role of Anne Boleyn

Although Henry had found that his marriage to Catherine of Aragon offended his own conscience and God's law, there is no doubt that lurking in the background lay a more earthly temptation, Anne Boleyn. Her tantalising presence at court gave Henry a greater desire to bring an end to his marriage to Catherine of Aragon. The big question, however, is whether Henry's desire for Anne Boleyn pushed him into a separation that would not otherwise have happened.

At the age of 36 and despite hating writing letters, Henry wrote Anne a series of passionate love letters. The letters are fascinating evidence, in that they give us a sense of Henry's growing infatuation with Anne Boleyn at exactly the time that he had decided on annulling his marriage to Catherine of Aragon. Three stages can be identified in Henry's correspondence, as shown in Sources 9.7–9.9 on page 110.

Anne Boleyn
The daughter of Sir Thomas Boleyn, Anne had spent her formative years in France only to return to England in 1522. Here she attracted the attentions of several notable figures at court, including Sir Thomas Wyatt, the poet, and Henry Percy, son of the Earl of Northumberland. When Henry met her, however, he fell head over heels in love with her, ordering Wolsey to stamp on Percy's interest in her.

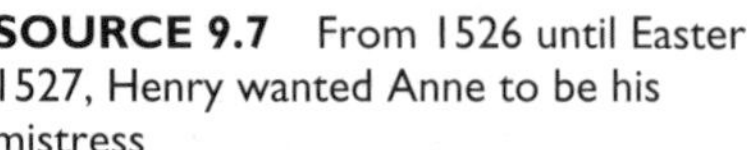

SOURCE 9.7 From 1526 until Easter 1527, Henry wanted Anne to be his mistress

Debating with myself the contents of your letter, I have put myself in great distress, not knowing how to interpret them . . . For of necessity I must assure me of this answer having been now above one whole year struck with the dart of love . . .

If it shall please you to do me the office of a true, loyal mistress . . . I promise you that not only shall the name be given you, but that also I will take you for my only mistress, rejecting from thought and affection all others save yourself, to serve you only.

SOURCE 9.8 From Easter to summer 1527, Henry complained of silence from Anne

Since I parted with you I have been advised that the opinion in which I left you is now altogether changed, and that you will not come to court . . . the which report being true I cannot enough marvel at, seeing that I am well assured I have never since that time committed fault.

TALKING POINT

What parallels might a historian make between Henry's love life and that of the British royal family at the turn of the twentieth century? Are such parallels part of the proper work of a historian?

SOURCE 9.9 In the summer of 1527, Henry wanted Anne to be his wife, not his mistress. When Anne sent Henry a trinket of a ship with a woman on board, he responded with the following letter

The proofs of your affection are such, the fine poesies of the letters so warmly couched, that they constrain me ever truly to honour, love and serve you, praying that you will continue in this same firm and constant purpose . . .

Henceforth, my heart shall be dedicate to you alone, greatly desirous that so my body could be as well, as God can bring to pass if it pleaseth Him, whom I entreat once each day for the accomplishment thereof . . .

Written with the hand of that secretary who in heart, body and will is

Your loyal and most ensured servant
Henry aultre A B ne cherse R.
[Translation: Henry looks for no other]

If Eric Ives' timeline of events (see Chart 9B on page 106–07) is accurate, Henry had already decided to end his marriage to Catherine of Aragon before being smitten by Anne Boleyn's 'dart of love'. This is not to say that Anne Boleyn played an insignificant role in the break with Rome. As we shall see, she and her followers had a significant impact on Henry's thinking (see page 115). We should, however, question the simplistic model that suggests that Henry fell in love with Anne, fell out of love with Catherine, therefore wanted a divorce and then broke with Rome as a result.

B What was the nature of the English Church on the eve of the break with Rome?

FOCUS ROUTE

Using the information on pages 111–115, make notes to answer these questions:

1 What is ANTICLERICALISM and how extensive was it in the period up to 1533?
2 To what extent was Henry influenced by anticlericalism in his decision to break with Rome?

So far we have looked closely at the issue of Henry's break with Rome and not at the Reformation, arguing that they were two separate processes. As we have also seen, however, some historians have argued that the break with Rome was possible only as part of a much bigger process. In this view, Henry was like some sort of sixteenth-century surfer, riding, being carried along by, but never quite being in control of, the wave that was the Reformation. According to historians such as A. G. Dickens (*The English Reformation*), Henry was carried along by PROTESTANTISM and a popular resistance to the Catholic Church. It was this push for reform that led to Henry's break with Rome.

Two key questions are central:

- What evidence is there for a groundswell of opposition to the Church?
- Was Henry pushed by these influences into the break with Rome?

ANTICLERICALISM

This is a term used to describe opposition to the Church, particularly at the end of the fifteenth century, leading through to the Reformation. However, it is important to recognise that this one movement was composed of a huge range of opinions and standpoints. In *The Reformation and the English People*, J. J. Scarisbrick has identified four main strands of anticlericalism:

- **'a negative, destructive anticlericalism' – a widespread feeling of dissatisfaction with the Church at a local level (e.g. resentment against a local parson or the ecclesiastical court). This strand was not motivated by great and deep theological principles.**
- **'a positive and idealistic, though secular, anticlericalism' – a desire from laymen (such as Thomas Cromwell) to reform the English Church, to rid it of the foreign authority of the Pope, to redirect its great wealth and to bring its courts within the state's judicial framework.**
- **'a positive, idealistic and religious anticlericalism' – a theologically based programme of reform to bring fundamental change to Christian life in England.**
- **'the anticlericalism of heresy', i.e. Lollardy. There was a wide range of views within the Lollard movement. Founded by John Wycliffe in the fourteenth century, its main thrust was an emphasis on personal piety and use of scripture. (Devout Protestants believed all actions should be guided by the word of God as it was written in the Bible.) It also opposed the emphasis in traditional religion on the sacraments and cults (e.g. of saints).**

It seems that Lollardy had survived into the sixteenth century, especially in the south-east of England. The dean of St Paul's, for example, wrote in 1511: 'we are ... nowadays grieved of heretics, men mad with marvellous foolishness'. Furthermore, the bishop of London in 1515 complained that Londoners were 'maliciously set in favour of heretical wickedness'.

Overall, however, numbers of Lollards were small. The main pockets were usually in towns (including Bristol, Coventry, Colchester and Maidstone) with artisans providing most support. There is very little evidence of any significant Lollard activity in the north and west.

PROTESTANTISM

The other strand of dissent linked inextricably to anticlericalism was Protestantism. This form of questioning of traditional religion had originated in Germany and Switzerland from about 1517. The main emphasis of writers such as Luther and Zwingli was on personal devotion and Bible study. The other radical element was the doctrine of justification by faith alone. This emphasised an individual's inner faith not their external acts.

Such ideas had clearly reached England by 1530. The bishop of Norwich, for example, noted the conversion of 'merchants and such that hath their abiding not far from the sea'. It is clear that where new Protestant ideas spread to England it was from the Continent via ports such as Bristol and, of course, London. Ports further north and to the west tended to trade with Catholic countries like Ireland, France and Spain; their exposure to Protestant literature and ideas was thus insignificant, which helps to explain the geographical divide in the acceptance of reformist ideas.

A groundswell of opposition?

Robert Whiting (in *The Reign of Henry VIII: Politics, Policy and Piety*, edited by D. MacCulloch) has made an extremely useful audit of the state of the Church on the eve of the Reformation. Looking at the various strands that made up the late medieval church, he assessed just how popular the Church was. His assessment is summarised in Chart 9D.

■ 9D The Church on the eve of the Reformation

Aspect of Church life	Verdict
The Papacy	Most people accepted the Pope's power. Dissent did exist, but it was limited to small groups, especially in the south-east. But there was no great adherence or loyalty to the Pope – especially after 1534 when 'the great majority of people appear to have acquiesced in the removal of Roman authority'.
Religious orders (monks, nuns, etc.)	Support for religious orders clearly survived, but there is evidence of a slight decline in respect and enthusiasm, e.g. a fall in the number of new abbeys, priories and friaries built.
Secular clergy (priests)	The clergy were generally respected, although elements of hostility were evident in the south-east (especially in London). 'In general it seems probable that relationships between priests and people was less frequently characterised by discord than by harmony.'
Parish churches and chapels	'The evidence ... suggests that support for parish churches in general remained high', e.g. • large numbers of churches and chapels were built between 1490 and 1529 with significant donations provided by the public • significant sums were left in parishioners' wills for the purpose of furnishing parish churches.
Religious guilds (lay organisations, often dedicated to a particular saint, which organised prayers and Masses on behalf of their deceased)	'In several areas ... these appear to have remained not only numerous but also active, prosperous and locally supported', e.g. they were left money in wills by a large percentage of people (57 per cent in Devon and Cornwall between1520 and 1529). There was, however, less enthusiastic support in the south-east.
SACRAMENTS and rituals (e.g. processions with the Host)	These remained largely popular, e.g. the high levels of attendance at Mass. The extensive amount of expensive equipment required for celebration of Mass implies support for the ceremonies. Limited opposition was confined to the south-east.
Intercession (prayers and Masses for the dead)	These 'unquestionably continued to attract substantial support', e.g. the continued foundation of CHANTRIES to provide prayers and Masses for the souls of the dead in their passage through PURGATORY.
Images	'Until the 1530s, three-dimensional representations of God or the saints continued to be widely utilised as aids to prayer.' Nevertheless, some criticism of pilgrimages and the apparent readiness of most local communities to accept iconoclasm suggests a lack of enthusiasm for images.

SACRAMENT
A sacrament is a ceremony which has fixed actions and words which bestow God's grace on its participants. Catholics believe in seven sacraments: baptism, the eucharist, confirmation, penance, marriage, ordination and the last rites.

CHANTRY
A chapel or altar in a church where Masses are sung for the souls of the dead.

PURGATORY
This is believed to be the place where the souls of the dead undergo a limited amount of suffering in order to achieve a state of purity before entering heaven.

ACTIVITY

Study Chart 9D carefully. Using this information, write a conclusion to the key question: was there a groundswell of opposition to the Church in England on the eve of the Reformation? When you have written your conclusion, compare it to Robert Whiting's own conclusion given on page 323.

Robert Whiting's conclusion is one of the latest interpretations of the state of the Church. It comes in the wake of a huge historical controversy involving a number of historians, as Sources 9.10–9.14 demonstrate.

SOURCE 9.10 A. G. Dickens, 'The Reformation in England', in J. Hurstfield (ed.), *The Reformation Crisis*, 1965, p. 85

Anticlericalism ... had reached a new virulence by the early years of the sixteenth century ... monasticism was lukewarm and insular, commanding little veneration outside the cloister ... Altogether, the English Church during the period 1500–1530 stood poorly equipped to weather the storms of the new age. It was a grandiose but unseaworthy hulk, its timbers rotted and barnacled, its superstructure riddled by the fire of its enemies, its crew grudging, divided, in some cases mutinous.

SOURCE 9.11 J. J. Scarisbrick, *Henry VIII*, 1968, p. 242.

Despite what has sometimes been said or implied, it is probable that the English Church was in no worse condition, spiritually speaking, in 1529 than it had been fifty, a hundred, or a hundred and fifty years before. The picture of a slow, steady decline into Nemesis is suspect.

SOURCE 9.12 G. R. Elton, *Reform and Reformation: England 1509–1558*, 1977, p. 187

All was not well with the Church in England ... the clergy themselves attracted more dislike than love. The state of the Church was widely believed to be rotten. Popular anticlericalism thrived on tales of gluttonous monks, lecherous friars, ignorant and dishonest parish priests ... Satirists unquestionably exaggerated the evils in the Church, but they had enough reality to draw on to carry widespread conviction. The Church was showing all the signs of an institution in danger but unaware of its peril.

SOURCE 9.13 C. Haigh, '*The continuity of Catholicism in the English Reformation*', in C. Haigh (ed.), *The English Reformation Revised*, 1987, p. 58

Relations between priests and parishioners were usually harmonious, and the laity complained astonishingly infrequently against their priests. There were local tensions, certainly, but they were individual rather than institutionalised, occasional rather than endemic. In a frantic search for the causes of Reformation, we must not wrench isolated cases of discord from their local contexts, and pile them together to show a growing chorus of dissatisfaction: we must not construct a false polarisation between Church and people ... The English people had not turned against their Church, and there was no widespread yearning for reform. The long-term causes of the Reformation – the corruption of the Church and the hostility of the laity – appear to have been historical illusions.

SOURCE 9.14 E. Duffy, *The Stripping of the Altars*, 1992, p. 4

Late medieval Catholicism exerted an enormously strong, diverse, and vigorous hold over the imagination and the loyalty of the people up to the very moment of Reformation. Traditional religion had about it no particular marks of exhaustion or decay, and indeed in a whole host of ways, from the multiplication of vernacular religious books to adaptations within the national and regional cult of the saints, was showing itself well able to meet new needs and new conditions.

ACTIVITY

Read Sources 9.10–9.14.

1 a) Outline each historian's argument in about fifteen words.
b) Which historians agree with each other?
2 Identify the two main lines of argument put forward by the two schools of historians.
3 Write a paragraph that sums up the work of all these historians in relation to the question of whether the state of the Church contributed to the Reformation.

■ Learning trouble spot

Quite often it is hard to know exactly how to start and finish an essay. Both introductions and conclusions are vital, however, because they are the first and last things that the reader (especially the examiner!) reads.

Introductions
The following table is a useful guide.

Context	If the question specifies dates, it is important to make a *brief* reference to what had come before.
Key words	In your planning, you should underline key words in the question. The introduction is an opportunity to focus on *your* definition of such words.
Argument	This is the most important section of the introduction. It is hugely important that you outline the key elements of your argument. You are providing the big signposts for the direction you want your reader to take. Do not go into detail – think about big blue motorway signposts, rather than small white B road signposts! If you get your signposts right, these will be the themes for your paragraphs. Good planning will lead to clear signs and a clearly argued essay.

Conclusions
By the time you come to write your conclusion, you will probably be desperate to finish off your essay as quickly as possible! It has to be said that the reader is also quite keen to come to an end, but a good conclusion *can* make a difference to your final mark.

Key points to consider:

- Keep it short and to the point.
- It is your opportunity to answer the question. Think of the essay title being asked to you orally. What would your answer be? This should form the basis of your conclusion.
- If it is a 'To what extent…' type of essay, be sure to weigh up the arguments for and against and come up with your view of the extent. It might help to think in percentage terms: for example, if it was 75 per cent factor A and 25 per cent other factors, you might say 'To a large extent, factor A can be seen as the main cause…'
- If you have a short and appropriate quotation, this is a good opportunity to use it. Do, however, finish with your own words. After all, it is *your* essay.
- Avoid starting with clichés such as 'Thus we can see that…' or 'So, in conclusion it is clear that…'. Simply say what you want to say; don't feel the need to 'ease your way' into it.

To what extent was Henry VIII influenced by the state of the Church to break from Rome?

What becomes clear from the debate on the influence of anticlericalism is that however strong anticlericalism was, there was undoubtedly a mood in the country for change on some level. Even a historian like J. J. Scarisbrick, who rejects the idea of a corrupt Church ripe for reform, concedes that 'hostility to churchmen was widespread and often bitter, and the conviction intense that something must be done' (*The Reformation and the English People,* 1984).

It seems certain that Henry caught this mood and was influenced by it, probably in 1529. Three events in the autumn of this year are significant:

- He dismissed Cardinal Wolsey, perhaps the epitome of clerical abuses.
- He took the highly unusual step of replacing Wolsey with a layman, Thomas More. The latter was a high-profile reformer, connected closely with the work of Erasmus and a man who had written a shocking critique of English society in his book *Utopia.*
- He summoned Parliament, a body guaranteed to voice anticlerical concerns.

It is clear that Henry was at least influenced by the anticlerical movement. What is not so apparent, however, is that Henry was pushed into the idea of the break with Rome by such concerns. Anticlericalism should not be seen as a vital cause, but rather as an important contributory cause of the break with Rome – it created an environment in which a break from the power of the Pope was at least conceivable.

Henry was influenced by Anne Boleyn's acquaintance with a group of reformist writers. He began to discover that many of their ideas suited his own purposes very well. Three reformers were particularly useful:

- William Tyndale's *Obedience of the Christian Man* used evidence from the Old Testament and early Christian history to defend the power and authority of kings in their own countries. Kings' subjects, argued Tyndale, should owe allegiance only to their king – this clearly excluded allegiance to such 'foreign' authorities as the Pope. Tyndale's book was given to Henry by Anne Boleyn. It seems that he was impressed: 'This is a book for me and for all kings to read,' he said.
- Simon Fish's *A Supplication for the Beggars* was addressed to the King and fiercely criticised greedy and over-fed clerics. Again it seems likely that it was passed his way by Anne Boleyn.
- Christopher St Germain emphasised the role of the state in controlling the Church. Using the evidence of scripture, he acknowledged Henry VIII's right to govern the Church. Furthermore, he attacked the Church for its abuses and alleged racketeering.

In addition, Anne Boleyn was in regular contact with a group of Cambridge academics who included Hugh and William Latimer, Matthew Parker and, most prominently, Thomas Cranmer. The latter has been described by D. MacCulloch as 'the most exalted specimen of Anne's religious patronage'. The ideas of such reformers confirmed Henry in his view that he was well within his rights to reject the authority of the Pope in what was a domestic affair. The seeds of the concept of the Royal Supremacy are there for all to see.

ACTIVITY

For the period 1527–33, which factors pushed or pulled Henry into his break with Rome? Use the information below to help you to decide.

Push factors are what forced Henry into annulling his marriage to Catherine of Aragon and then to breaking with Rome.
Pull factors are what attracted him to the annulment and subsequent break with Rome.

List of factors
- Henry's conscience
- Henry's desire for a male heir
- Henry's love for Anne Boleyn
- Henry's need to increase his revenue
- Henry's desire for power
- Catherine's miscarriages and three stillborn babies
- Charles V's rejection in June 1525 of Henry's proposal that Charles marry Princess Mary
- France's questioning of Princess Mary's legitimacy in 1526–27
- Anne Boleyn's refusal to be Henry's mistress
- the Pope being taken prisoner by Charles V in May 1527
- Wolsey's position as *legate a latere* (Special Representative of the Pope)
- the replacement of Wolsey by Thomas More as Lord Chancellor in October 1529
- the death of William Warham, Archbishop of Canterbury; replaced by Thomas Cranmer
- Foxe and Cranmer's *Collectanea Satis Copiosa* in 1530
- the ideas of Tyndale, Fish and St Germain
- Anne Boleyn's becoming pregnant in December 1532

ACTIVITY

Use the advice in the Learning trouble spot on page 114 to answer the following essay question:

- Describe the reasons why the break with Rome took place.

C What religious changes took place in England between 1530 and 1547?

FOCUS ROUTE

As you read pages 116–19 write down:

a) the key Acts that led to religious change from 1533 to 1538
b) the key Acts that helped to reverse previous changes from 1538 to 1547.

■ 9E Religious events in England, 1530–47

Date	Event	Description
1530 May	William Tyndale's vernacular Bible burnt	An attack on heresy against Catholicism.
December	Clergy as a whole accused of *praemunire*	This attacked the power of the Catholic Church to exercise power through ecclesiastical courts in England.
1531 February	Clergy pardoned of *praemunire* charge	Henry was paid a fine of £119,000 in return for his pardon.
	Convocation of Canterbury recognised Henry as Head of the Church 'so far as the law of Christ allows'.	This marked how far the Church was willing to go in allowing Henry more power. Henry had wanted to be known as 'protector and only supreme head of the English Church'.
1532	First Act of ANNATES	This banned the payment of annates to Rome. It also threatened that bishops could be consecrated by English authorities. Thus, the chief source of papal revenue in England was removed and one of the Pope's main functions as leader of the Church was challenged.
March	Supplication of the Ordinaries	• Clergy were to enact no Church law without royal permission. • Existing Church law was to be examined by a royal commission. • Henry complained that the clergy only gave him 50 per cent loyalty, since they also owed allegiance to the Pope.
May	Submission of the Clergy	The clergy accepted the King and not the Pope as their lawmaker. Thomas More resigned the following day.
1533 February	Act in Restraint of Appeals to Rome	Based on the *Collectanea Satis Copiosa*, this began the work of transferring papal powers to the King: • The King was now supreme head of the Church in England. • Rome had no power to rule over matrimonial cases. Cranmer declared Henry's marriage with Catherine null and void. Henry's marriage to Anne was declared valid.
1534 January	Second Act of Annates	• This confirmed the First Act of Annates. • Abbots and bishops were in future to be appointed by the King, not the Pope.
	Act to Stop Peter's Pence	This abolished the payment of taxation to Rome.
March	Act for the Submission of the Clergy	Appeals in ecclesiastical matters were now to be handled by the King's Court of Chancery and not by the Archbishop's court.
	First Act of Succession	This registered Henry's marriage to Catherine as invalid and replaced it with his marriage to Anne. The Crown was now to pass to Henry and Anne's children. The nation was to take an oath upholding their marriage. It was a treasonable offence to attack or deny the marriage.
April	Execution of Elizabeth Barton ('Holy Maid of Kent'). See p. 132	This is evidence of Henry's lack of toleration of religious diversity.

ANNATES
The payment of their first year's revenue by newly appointed bishops to the Pope.

Date	Event	Description
November	Act of Supremacy (with oath of supremacy administered to all religious houses)	Henry 'justly and rightfully is . . . Supreme Head of the Church of England'. He is also given the right to carry out visitations of the monasteries.
December	Treason Act	• This listed key treasonable crimes, e.g. calling the King or Queen a heretic. • Treason could now be defined as intent expressed in word as well in deed – in other words, what you said could land you in as much trouble as what you did.
	Act for First Fruits and Tenths	These clerical taxes were now to go to the King, not the Pope.
1535 January	Cromwell made Vice-gerent in Spirituals	This is evidence of the swing to reformist influence over Henry.
	Valor Ecclesiasticus	Cromwell commissioned this survey into the wealth and condition of the Church.
	Execution of Carthusian monks, Bishop Fisher (June) and Sir Thomas More (July)	Opposition to break with Rome quashed.
1536 February	Act for Dissolution of Lesser Monasteries	The smaller monasteries (those worth under £200) were closed down.
May	Anne Boleyn beheaded; Henry married Jane Seymour the following day	
July	Act of Ten Articles	The 'Seven Sacraments' of Catholic doctrine were rejected, leaving a belief in only three (baptism, the Eucharist and penance). A clear move towards Protestantism.
August	Royal Injunctions to the clergy issued by Cromwell	These ordered the clergy to: • defend the Royal Supremacy in sermons • abandon pilgrimages • give money for educational purposes to teach children the Lord's Prayer, the Ten Commandments and other scripture.
1537 July	*The Institution of a Christian Man*, also known as the Bishops' Book	The four 'lost' sacraments were rediscovered, though stated to be of lesser value. Other evidence of a drift towards Protestantism includes: • there was no discussion of TRANSUBSTANTIATION • Mass was glossed over • the special status of priests was understated • purgatory was present only by implication.
August	Thomas Matthew published the 'Matthew Bible'	This was a distinctly Protestant version that had the King's permission.
1538 July	Truce of Nice signed by Charles V and Francis I	This brought a temporary halt to the Habsburg–Valois War and created the real possibility of a joint invasion of England by the Catholic powers. This threat lasted until 1540, and prompted Henry to move back to Catholicism in the Act of Six Articles.
September	Royal Injunctions to the clergy issued by Cromwell	• The English Bible was to be placed in all parishes within two years. • All births, marriages and deaths were to be registered in every parish. • People were to be actively discouraged from pilgrimages (e.g. Thomas Becket's shrine at Canterbury Cathedral was destroyed). • Relics were to be removed from churches (confirming a rejection of purgatory).
November	Trial and execution of John Lambert for his rejection of transubstantiation	This was a clear symbol of Henry's commitment to the Catholic belief in Christ's real presence in the Eucharist.
December	Henry excommunicated by Paul III	

(Continues on page 118.)

TRANSUBSTANTIATION

The Catholic belief that at Mass the bread and wine actually change into the substance of the body and blood of Christ.

Date	Event	Description
1539		
April	Publication of the 'Great Bible'	
June	Act of Six Articles	This Act marked a radical shift in doctrine. It confirmed: • transubstantiation • private Masses • the hearing of confession by priests. It banned: • marriage of priests • the marriage of anybody who had taken the vow of chastity • the taking of communion in both kinds (i.e. bread and wine) by lay people. There were severe penalties for those who went against the Act (e.g. the denial of transubstantiation led to automatic burning with no possibility of recantation).
June	Act for the Dissolution of the Greater Monasteries	All monasteries were closed and their land passed to the Crown.
1540		
January	Henry married Anne of Cleves	She was the sister of the Protestant Duke of Cleves.
June	Cromwell arrested	
July	Cromwell executed	
July	Cleves marriage annulled; Henry married Catherine Howard	She was the daughter of the Catholic Duke of Norfolk.
1542		
February	Catherine Howard executed	
1543		
April	Cranmer protected by Henry against the Catholic faction	
May	Act for the Advancement of True Religion	This restricted access to the English Bible to upper-class men and noblewomen in private (not to subjects 'of the lower sort').
	The Necessary Doctrine and Erudition of a Christian Man (The King's Book)	This revised the Bishop's Book, defending transubstantiation and the Six Articles. It also encouraged preaching and attacked the use of images. It was written by Henry himself.
July	Henry married Catherine Parr	
1544		
May	English LITANY introduced into churches	This replaced the Catholic use of a Latin litany, although priests did not *have* to use it.
July	Sir John Cheke appointed tutor to Prince Edward (aged six)	Cheke was a Protestant humanist.
1545		
December	Chantries Act passed (though not enforced)	This allowed for dissolution of chantries.
1546		
July	Anne Askew burned for denying transubstantiation	This was evidence of Henry's continued commitment to parts of Catholicism.
	Henry named heavily Protestant Council of Regency for his heir	This ensured a Protestant-influenced inheritance for Prince Edward.

LITANY

The part of a church service where the priest and congregation make requests to God, according to a set formula.

ACTIVITY

1 a) For the period 1530–35, analyse each event in Chart 9E to see which motives were prominent in Henry's actions. You should think of four key factors:

- power
- doctrine
- finance
- divorce.

You might find it useful to make your own copy of the chart and colour-code it.

b) What does this analysis suggest about the causes of Henry's break with Rome?

2 Construct a graph with the following axes:

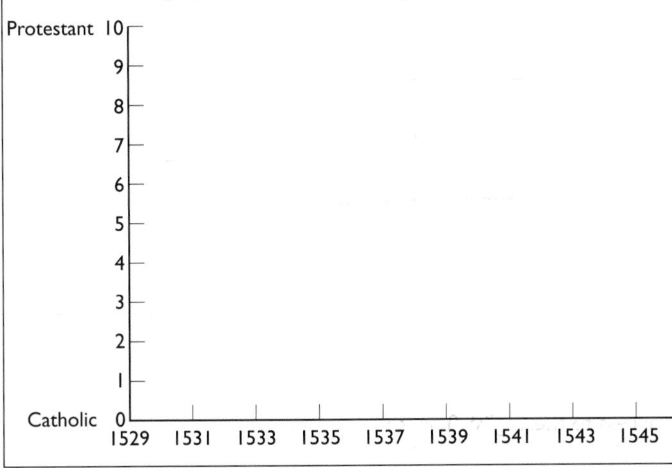

Mark in the most important events along the horizontal axis.

Now, in order to judge to what extent each event was Catholic or Protestant, give each event a score out of 10:

0 = out-and-out Catholic
5 = a balance of Catholicism and Protestantism
10 = out-and-out Protestantism.

To help you make up your mind, think about:

- the position of the Pope
- the number of sacraments
- the role of the bishops
- the availability of the Bible – in Latin or English?
- the religious role of monasteries
- the look of churches (e.g. the use of images)
- influential figures within the Church
- belief in transubstantiation and purgatory
- the role of preaching.

Plot these scores on to the graph and connect the points together. Then answer the following questions:

a) When are the high points of Protestant reform?
b) Is there a consistent trend in religious policy?
c) What turning points can you discern?
d) Is there any point at which the Reformation can be seen to be irreversible?

SOURCE 9.15 The Great Bible, first published in 1539, was the first authorised English-language Bible. All parish churches were ordered to purchase a copy, although many did not do so until fines were threatened in 1541. The title page was commissioned from Holbein's apprentices by Thomas Cromwell

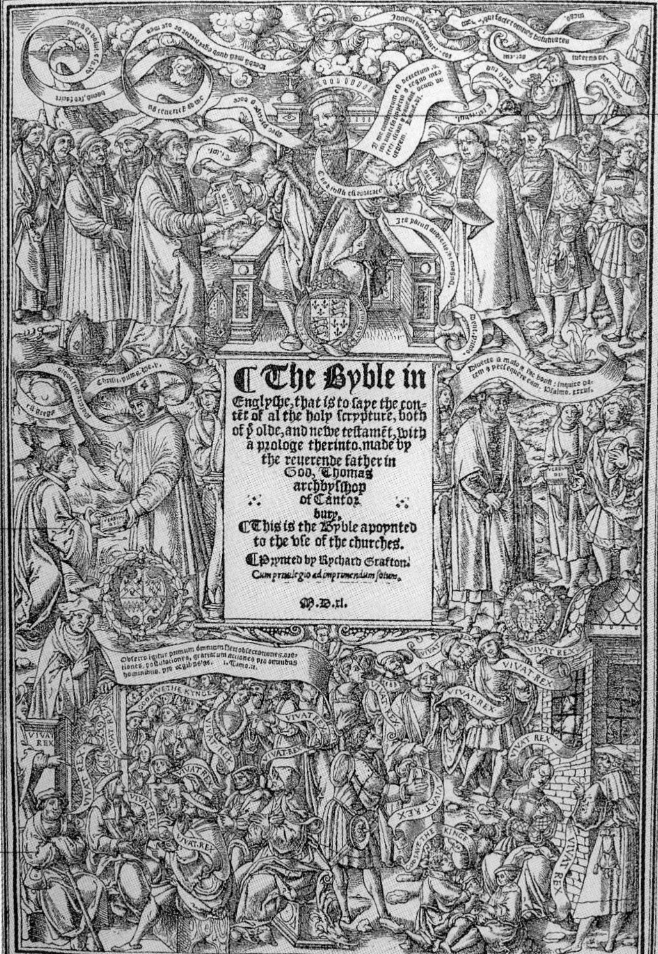

Henry presents the Bible to Cranmer and Cromwell.

Henry kneels to receive the word of God from Christ.

The ordinary people who hear the Bible being read from the pulpit cry, 'God save the King'

D What were the causes and consequences of the dissolution of the monasteries?

FOCUS ROUTE

Using the information on pages 120–22, explain when, why and how the monasteries were dissolved.

On the eve of the Reformation, England was a land of abbeys. Numbering over 800 in England and more than 100 in Scotland, these abbeys or monasteries were central to the life of people both rich and poor. Their main function was as a place where monks said prayers or Masses for the souls of the dead in an attempt to ease their path through purgatory – Henry VII had 10,000 Masses said for his soul in the month after his death and it was monks who performed this service. On top of this, however, monasteries were among the largest landowners in the realm, providing employment on farms. They were also centres of the arts and learning: the buildings themselves towered majestically over the countryside, and monks produced exquisite illuminated manuscripts as well as carvings, paintings and music. There were several monastic orders:

- the Benedictines: the largest single order of monks and nuns and probably the richest
- the Cistercians: a breakaway movement from the Benedictines, aiming at a simpler and more austere life; they were famous for their sheep farming
- the Carthusians: the strictest of all orders; their houses being known as Charterhouses
- the Carmelites or White Friars
- the Dominicans or Black Friars
- the Franciscans or Grey Friars.

In spite of their importance, by 1540 the vast majority of monasteries had been reduced, quite literally, to shells. Over a 4-year period (1536–40), their lead roofs were removed, their windows smashed and their contents ripped out. In many places, all that remain today are walls and empty windows.

SOURCE 9.16 Whitby Abbey

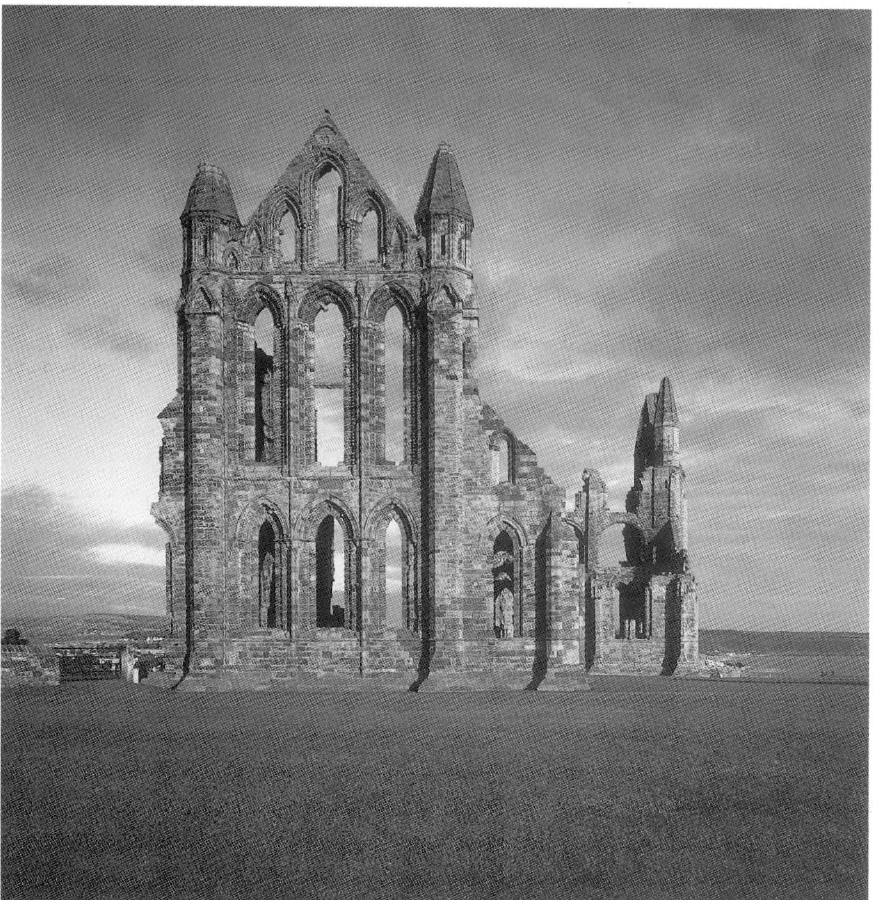

Three key questions arise from this stunning turn of events:

- How did this destruction take place?
- Why did Henry pursue such a policy?
- What were the consequences, both long and short term?

■ 9F The events of the dissolution

Year	Event
1533	While the Act in Restraint of Appeals to Rome was before Parliament, Henry announced his intention to unite to the Crown 'the lands which the Clergy of his dominions held thereof, which lands and property his predecessors on the throne could not alienate to his prejudice'. The clear goal was to increase Crown revenue by taking over Church lands.
1534	Nothing came of the 1533 statement, but its intention was confirmed by an anonymous proposal suggesting the confiscation of all ecclesiastical lands. Out of the proceeds of these lands, the Crown was to support the clergy with annual salaries. The plan was headed: 'Things to be moved for the king's for an increase and augmentation to be had for maintenance of his most royal estate, and for the defence of the realm'. Although we cannot be sure that this proposal received the King's explicit blessing, here lie the seeds of Cromwell's scheme to make the Crown financially self-sufficient. The wealth of the Church could help Henry avoid having to impose taxation and in so doing preserve his own position on the throne. Henry VII would have been delighted by such a proposition!
1535	Cromwell's aim of enhancing the King's finances became evident in *Valor Ecclesiasticus*. Literally meaning 'the value of the Church', *Valor* was a census of the Church to assess its wealth. Cromwell also sent out inspectors to the monasteries to look at the spiritual health of the Church. These visits were known as visitations. He therefore had two very clear aims: • to gauge the true extent of the Church's wealth in order to see how the Crown could increase its income • to cast monasteries in the worst possible light in order to persuade Parliament that they should be dissolved as quickly as possible. Cromwell's agents in this task were six 'visitors' who carried out a lightning tour of religious houses starting in September 1535. Knowing Cromwell's purpose, these visitors produced a mass of evidence confirming the corruption of religious life in England. Sadly, it seems certain that much of this evidence was either fabricated or grossly exaggerated, but it was exactly what Cromwell wanted.
1536	Using the evidence supplied by the visitations, Henry passed the first Act of Dissolution of the Monasteries. Its main provisions were as follows: • All houses worth under £200 a year were dissolved. These were only the smaller monasteries and the minority of all religious houses. • Heads of houses were offered a pension in return for their retirement. Monks were transferred to surviving larger houses, or became secular priests. • The larger monasteries were actually praised. The Act's preamble argued that it was an attempt to strengthen the greater monasteries. • Henry had the power to exempt any house he wanted from the Act.
	The Act was thus presented as a reforming, rather than a destructive, measure. The whole focus rested on the issue of the standards of monastic life; it was not an attack on the institution of monasticism itself. Whether Henry, or indeed Cromwell, had in mind the complete suppression of all monasteries at this stage is open to question. It may be that the conservatism of the Act suggests not: reform is the keynote. At the same time, however, Richard Hoyle has recently argued that Henry's power of exemption was simply a recognition that he could not procure immediately the country's acceptance of a complete dissolution ('War and public finance', in D. MacCulloch (ed.), *The Reign of Henry VIII: Politics, Policy and Piety*). Gradualism was therefore the key, which explains the delay in dissolving the larger monasteries. This delay may also be explained by the Pilgrimage of Grace of 1536. Detailed study of this protest against the King and Cromwell can be found in Chapter 10. For present purposes, however, the origins of the Pilgrimage can be seen in a reaction to the initial dissolutions. Henry may well have been shocked by the strength of this response, although it did not stop him from seizing a handful of religious houses that had taken part in the rebellion. At the same time, Henry perversely refounded a handful of monasteries (e.g. at Stixwould and Bisham).
1537	A number of individual so-called voluntary surrenders of larger houses took place in the summer of 1537. In fact, such surrenders were forced on houses through the pressure exerted by royal commissioners. The crucial moment came in December when the great priory of Lewes in Sussex was persuaded to surrender to the King, with its property passing to Cromwell. The process of dissolution had reached a watershed. It was now clear that all monasteries, large and small, were under attack. The writing was on the wall for all remaining houses.
1538	Cromwell and his agents embarked on the dissolution of the remaining large monasteries. Within sixteen months, 202 houses had surrendered.
1539	The second Act of Dissolution of the Monasteries was passed. This simply legitimised the 'voluntary' surrenders that had already happened, giving parliamentary sanction to the work of Cromwell and his agents. All of the property of the greater houses was now transferred to the Crown. As J. J. Scarisbrick has concluded in *The Dissolution of the Monasteries*, the Act 'ratified a *fait accompli*'.
1540	The final nail was driven into the coffin of monasticism with the surrender of Waltham Abbey in March 1540. David Starkey sees this process as 'the greatest act of nationalisation in English history between the Norman Conquest of 1066 and the Labour Government of 1945'(*Henry VIII*, Channel 4, 1998). In all, 563 houses had been dissolved and 8,000 monks pensioned off; Crown income doubled from £120,000 p.a. to £250,000 p.a., with the resale value of monastic land standing at £1.3 million.

Pensions must have extended beyond heads of houses?

9G The causes of the dissolution

CAUSES OF THE DISSOLUTION

An end to opponents of the break with Rome
Some of the most vociferous opponents of Henry's recent legislation had come from monastic houses, especially the Franciscans and Carthusians.

The 'imperial' idea
The idea of monasteries owing an allegiance to parent institutions outside England became unacceptable to Henry, especially after the Act in Restraint of Appeals to Rome and the Act of Supremacy.
It is evidence of Henry's growing sense of xenophobia.

Financial motives
The financial resources of the Church were huge. While the Crown's finances were healthy enough, there was a clear concern about the possibility of a Catholic crusade (especially in view of the Pope's excommunication of Henry, calling on Francis I and Charles V to attack England in the name of the Catholic Church). A massive building programme of fortifications was undertaken and monastic wealth helped to pay for it.
Money from the Church also gave Cromwell the chance to free Henry from the need to impose taxation again. As A. G. Dickens has commented in *The English Reformation*, Cromwell's chief aim was to 'endow the Crown in perpetuity'. It was a lesson well learned from Henry VII: a stable economy equals a stable monarchy.

Patronage and greed
Following the 1536 Act in particular, the laity gained an increasing appetite for land. Even Catholics such as Norfolk were quick to cash in on sales of monastic land. This, in turn, served a useful political purpose for Henry by pacifying potential critics of his break with Rome. Many may have been unhappy with the turn of religious events, but the pill, though bitter, was easier to swallow with the wealth that dissolution brought.

Continental influence
Religious houses were being dissolved in Germany and Scandinavia, giving a model of what was possible in England. The ideas of Erasmus, Tyndale and Fish, criticising monastic life, were also gaining currency.

9H The consequences of the dissolution

Monastic buildings	Henry has been charged with cultural vandalism as a result of the wholesale destruction of magnificent Gothic church buildings, along with the loss of books (illuminated manuscripts), images and reliquaries. This is undoubtedly true, although, in Henry's defence, he did invest some of his newly found wealth in the cause of education. For example, new cathedral grammar schools were set up at Canterbury, Carlisle, Ely, Bristol and Chester, while Christ Church, Oxford, and Trinity College, Cambridge, were established.
Monks and friars	The majority of monks and friars found alternative paid employment within the Church. About 6,500 out of 8,000 moved on, having been supplied with their pensions. This said, a significant minority were left in hardship.
Nuns	Nuns were less well off. The 2,000 nuns were allowed neither to marry nor to become priests.
The poor	Monasteries had been a traditional source of help for the poor. The dissolution undoubtedly had a detrimental effect on the poor. However, it is likely that this only aggravated an already worsening problem. In *The English Reformation,* A. G. Dickens concludes, 'the theory that the suppression of the monasteries was a major cause of urban poverty has nothing to commend it.'
Profit	Henry has been charged with squandering the wealth acquired through the sale of monastic lands. To some extent this is true: from May 1543 there was a rush to sell land, with most of the profits being used to finance the wars with Scotland and then France (1542–46). Few gains of any long-term significance were made as a result of this major outlay of money (around £2 million). In defence of Henry, however, just over half of monastic lands remained in his possession in 1547, suggesting that he had not been completely reckless. Moreover, by 1547 the Crown had made about £800,000 from the sales, mostly in cash, which meant that Henry's subjects were spared even harsher taxation.
Social change	The sale of monastic lands meant that there was a transfer of power into the hands of the laity at local level. As a result, the powers of patronage now lay with squires, JPs and the chief landowners, not the Church. There is also some limited evidence to suggest that land ownership was extended down the social ladder – to some lawyers, but particularly to younger sons of landowning families who would otherwise have missed out on a landed inheritance. To say that there was some sort of social revolution heralding the 'rise of the gentry', however, would be wrong. It seems clear from local studies (such as that of Joyce Youings in Devon, *The Dissolution of the Monasteries*) that land was transferred into the hands of men who were already established in the countryside. What had happened was simply that more men had bought their way into local politics. G. R. Elton sees neither a decline of the aristocracy nor a rise in the gentry, but rather a move away from 'the predominance of the few to a general power vested in larger numbers' (*Reform and Reformation: England 1509–1558*).

ACTIVITY

1 Using the information in Chart 9H, divide the consequences of the dissolution of the monasteries into two lists: long-term and short-term consequences.
2 Write either a justification or a denunciation of the dissolution: argue either that it was a positive process or that it was a negative process.

Review: Divorce, doctrine or dosh? The reasons for the break with Rome and the origins of the Reformation

FOCUS ROUTE

Look back to Chart 9A on page 105 to remind yourself of the key factors behind the break with Rome. Write a short report to explain which factors were the most important and why.

This section aims to bring together the main themes of the chapter and to answer the main question.

As we stated at the beginning of this chapter, historians have been unable to come to any real consensus over this issue. Interpretations have changed over time and have reflected the different approaches that historians have taken towards the study of history. Outlined below are the interpretations of the historians who have most influenced the arguments.

A. F. Pollard (1869–1948)

Context

Pollard wrote the biography *Henry VIII* in 1902. He attempted to develop a more scientific approach to the writing of history than his predecessors. His aim was to analyse the existing evidence as objectively as possible in order to explain how and why the Reformation occurred. This was a significant departure from previous historians, who had been primarily concerned with the morality of the Reformation – that is, whether it was a good or bad thing. This said, Pollard based much of his analysis on the printed *Letters and Papers of Henry VIII*, which inevitably emphasised official policy to the neglect of other factors.

Interpretation

For Pollard, there was no doubt as to the architect of the break with Rome and thus the Reformation – an all-powerful Henry VIII. The Reformation was an act of Henry's own will and, what is more, the English people were right behind him. They trusted him as a Tudor to bring peace and stability, for 'England in the sixteenth century put its trust in its princes far more than it did in its parliaments, it invested them with attributes almost divine.'

Pollard introduces his argument thus: '"If a lion knew his strength," said Sir Thomas More of his master to Thomas Cromwell, "it were hard for any man to rule him." Henry VIII had the strength of a lion; it remains to be seen how soon he learnt it, and what use he made of that strength when he discovered the secret.' So, in Pollard's eyes, it was simply a question not of whether Henry would break with Rome, but of when and how. The key issue was one of power. The Church would not allow Henry to annul his marriage to Catherine of Aragon and this gave him the opportunity to rid himself of the Church's constraining influence: 'the divorce, in fact, was the occasion and not the cause of the Reformation.' The cause was Henry's determination to exercise supreme power in England. Ultimately, 'the wonder is, not that the breach took place when it did, but that it was deferred for so long.'

The success of Henry's mission was, for Pollard, confirmed by a rising tide of nationalism felt by the English people and voiced by Parliament. The allegiance owed to the Pope could no longer be accepted. The Church *in* England had to become the Church *of* England. The lion was truly master of his own jungle.

G. R. Elton (1921–94)

Context

Elton started to develop his work in the late 1940s and early 1950s. He based his interpretation on a very close study of the documents of central government and administration. His research is characterised by a desire to examine the detail of government policy. He was keen to shed new light on the reign of Henry VIII and, in particular, to highlight the role of Thomas Cromwell. Most famously, his interpretations are found in *The Tudor Revolution in Government* (first published in 1953) and *England under the Tudors* (first published in 1955).

Interpretation

Elton challenges Pollard's proposition that Henry was in complete control of the break with Rome. Elton's Henry VIII is 'a nimble opportunist', keen to leave the detail of government to his councillors: 'in the day to day business of governing England, Henry VIII was not so much incapable as uninterested and feckless'. This analysis leads Elton to conclude that the changes in policies throughout Henry's reign are explained not by the King, but by his advisers. 'Each section of the reign differed from the rest in a manner which can only rationally derive from changes in the men who directed affairs . . . The King was always there . . . the differences lay in the men he employed.'

Elton argues that 'it is doubtful if he [Henry] was the architect of anything, least of all the English Reformation'. So, if not Henry, then who? Clearly Elton's architect or puppet master was Thomas Cromwell. It was Cromwell who gave Henry a solution to the problem of being unable to gain an annulment of his marriage to Catherine of Aragon. This solution came in the form of the Act in Restraint of Appeals to Rome, crafted by Cromwell and signalling the break with Rome. '[Cromwell] offered to make a reality out of Henry's vague claims to supremacy by evicting the pope from England. To the king this meant a chance of getting his divorce, and a chance of wealth; to Cromwell it meant the chance of reconstructing the body politic.'

According to Elton, Cromwell had his own agenda. His was not a religious but rather a political motivation. His aim was to set up a limited constitutional monarchy in which King and Parliament acted together. Even though Elton recognised Cromwell's dislike of Catholicism, he still saw the Reformation as a political act. 'It was Cromwell's purpose to remake and renew the body politic of England, a purpose which because of the comprehensiveness of his intentions amounted to a revolution.'

A. G. Dickens (b. 1910)

Context

Dickens wrote his masterpiece *The English Reformation* in 1964 (and revised and updated it in 1989). He aimed to bring religion to the forefront of his interpretation of the period. Both Pollard and Elton had analysed events from an almost exclusively political perspective. For the first time Dickens looked to get 'behind the scenes' – in other words, he attempted to understand the motivations of 'the people'. In particular, he was interested in people's religious motivation, a previously, and rather curiously, neglected aspect of the Reformation.

Interpretation

For Dickens, the Church as it was in 1530 could not possibly have remained unreformed. The state of the Catholic Church in England was so bad that Henry would have been unable to leave it unreformed. Reformist ideas from a range of sources, emphasising the corruption of the Church, were thus vital in pushing Henry towards a reformed Church. Dickens follows Elton in promoting the role of Thomas Cromwell. It was the latter who pushed Henry into far deeper religious waters than he had ever envisaged. Cromwell's solution to Henry's divorce dilemma marked the point of no return: 'From this stage we cannot understand Crown policy if we continue to envisage Thomas Cromwell as merely a smart lawyer who made his fortune by solving the king's matrimonial problem. For good or ill, he is a figure of far greater significance in our history.'

While Pollard and Elton gave centre stage to Henry and Cromwell, Dickens marked out new ground by looking at other factors. He studied the state of popular religion and how this affected a demand for change, emphasising, in particular, the role of the Lollards in preparing the way for the Reformation. First, Lollard ideas provoked a conservative and negative reaction from English bishops that 'helped to exclude the possibility of Catholic reforms' and thus made the chances of radical anti-Catholic reform more likely. Second, the Lollards 'provided a spring-board of critical dissent from which the Protestant Reformation could overleap the walls of orthodoxy. The Lollards were the allies and in some measure the begetters of the anticlerical forces which made possible the Henrician revolution.' And third, the Lollards cultivated an atmosphere in certain parts of the country that made the reception of continental Protestant ideas possible.

For Dickens, therefore, it was forces from below – the Lollards, William Tyndale, people motivated by a passion for religious reform – who deserve the real credit for pushing Henry into his break with Rome and consequently for the Reformation.

J. J. Scarisbrick (b. 1928)

Context

Scarisbrick's authoritative biography *Henry VIII* (first published in 1968) was concerned to put the key political players back on centre stage. In something of a return to Pollard, we see Henry as the driving force behind policy.

Interpretation

Scarisbrick emphasises Henry's dominant role in government throughout his reign. If there was a sense of uncertainty about the process, it was precisely because the process was Henry's and Henry himself was full of uncertainties and contradictions. 'The Henrician Reformation was a movement of inexplicable halts and starts, sudden hesitation and zig-zagging . . . But this is not to deny the overall purposiveness of these years. They were as was Henry himself – belligerent and outwardly confident, yet nervous and uncertain; and they were thus precisely because he dominated them.'

In spite of Henry's contradictions, Scarisbrick is clear that the King worked consistently toward asserting Royal Supremacy. While gaining his divorce was an important part of the process, 'Henry never had . . . a one-track mind'. He claimed a pastoral role in the Church as early as 1529, claimed power over the national Church by 1531 and finally excluded the primacy of the Pope with his attack on clerical privileges in 1532.

What of Cromwell's role in all of this? Scarisbrick acknowledges the central role that Cromwell played. 'That the 1530s were a decisive decade in English history was due largely to his energy and vision. He was immediately responsible for the vast legislative programme of the later sessions of the Reformation Parliament.' However, Scarisbrick is at pains to point out that it was always Henry who handed Cromwell the blueprint of action required: 'as far as the central event of the 1530s is concerned, namely the establishment of the Royal Supremacy, he was the executant of the king's designs. He may have determined timing and sequence . . . But he neither worked alone nor was the true initiator of these royal undertakings.'

Christopher Haigh

Context

Christopher Haigh led a group of revisionist historians who looked to 'revise' interpretations of why the Reformation came about. In particular, he aimed to challenge Dickens' assertion that the Catholic Church was 'ripe for reform'. He has been supported in his work by historians such as J. J. Scarisbrick (*The Reformation and the English People*, 1984) and, more recently, Eamon Duffy (*The Stripping of the Altars*, 1992). Haigh's own views are put forward in *The English Reformation Revised* (1987) and *English Reformations: Religion, Politics and Society under the Tudors* (1993).

Interpretation

The title of Haigh's most recent work indicates how he sees religious change in England to have been a series of Reformations. This is a significant move away from the idea of the Reformation as a single event that happened in the reign of Henry VIII. 'The religious changes of sixteenth century England were far too complex to be bound together as "the Reformation", too complex even to be "a Reformation".' So, for Haigh, the study of religious change must be pursued beyond the reign of Henry VIII, with the changes that we know as the Reformation being in any way complete only half way through the reign of Elizabeth I.

ACTIVITY

1 Look at the cartoons below. Match them up to each of the historians' interpretations on pages 123–26.
2 Compare your own interpretation with those of the historians. To whom are you closest and why? Has reading their views changed your mind? Is it possible to 'mix and match' interpretations?

To complicate the picture further, Haigh outlines Reformations happening on two different levels: political and evangelical. In other words, what made people Protestant was a combination of legislation and preaching. What is vital for Haigh in all of this is that historians have to study Reformation 'as it actually happened' – *did* people really follow the diktats of their politicians? If this question is to be answered at all satisfactorily, local variations have to be taken into account. Historians must accept that some of their beloved generalisations may not always be accurate enough.

Thus Haigh concludes that 'England had blundering Reformations, which most did not understand, which few wanted, and which no one knew had come to stay.' He rejects the 'master-plan' approach to explaining Reformation, preferring to study each event as it happened and trying to gauge how people at the time would have experienced changes.

Conclusion

Having looked at all of the various aspects of Henry VIII's religious policies, it should have become abundantly clear that nothing is clear or simple about Henry and religion. Nevertheless, as historians we must try to make sense of the apparently senseless.

Divorce, doctrine or dosh? These were the three alternatives given at the start of this chapter. Apart from their alliterative quality, do they give us a lead into explaining Henry's motives in religion?

- **Divorce:** This was hugely important in planting in Henry's mind the question of who should exert control over the Church in England. Importantly, however, Henry's questioning of papal authority came with his denial of Julius II's right to dispense Arthur's marriage to Catherine of Aragon. Once Henry felt that his own marriage to Catherine of Aragon was against God's law (because the marriage was childless), he then questioned the role of the Pope. Nevertheless, the fact that Henry went to great lengths to find a solution that included the Pope suggests that he was not completely against the Pope's authority.
- **Doctrine:** At no point in the legislation of the Reformation Parliament does doctrine feature strongly, if at all. The initial impetus towards change is thus not doctrinal. Of course, this changed once Cromwell became more influential in 1536–38 and again in the 1540s as Henry reasserted his own very personal doctrinal interpretation. Nevertheless, it is noticeable that it was Cromwell and Henry who were the driving force behind religious change and not, as one might expect, the Archbishop of Canterbury, Thomas Cranmer. D. MacCulloch has argued in *Thomas Cranmer* that, 'the woeful number of loose ends in the Supremacy, exposed by the events of 1534, led to a stage-by-stage rethink, which in the end would leave the Archbishop much more clearly the junior partner to the vice-gerent in spirituals [Cromwell]'. The break with Rome was, therefore, predominantly a political process and Cranmer was marginalised. Cranmer 'had shown himself a popular and successful politician and an exceptional researcher and deviser of texts for a complex and difficult problem, but he was no politician. He lacked the political ruthlessness or deviousness to outface even clerical politicians like Stokesley and Gardiner, let alone the hardfaced noblemen on the King's Council. That was best left to Cromwell.'
- **Dosh:** Again, the legislation of the Reformation Parliament suggests that Henry did have at least one eye on the revenue that could come his way rather than going into papal coffers. It would appear, however, that this was more of a fringe benefit than a major motivating factor. It was not until the dissolution of the monasteries that the urgent need for money became apparent.

So all three factors were involved. But fundamental in all of this discussion is the role of Henry himself. As you will see elsewhere in this section, ultimately Henry was in full control of the policies carried out in his name. His religious policies were exactly that – his. As such, they reflect the ego, contradictions, passions and convictions of an extraordinarily complex character. As Erasmus said of Henry, he did not 'desire gold or gems or precious metals but virtue, glory and immortality' (*Epistles*, I). This gets to the heart of the question. Henry was desperate to make his own mark in history and was unwilling to let anybody – the Pope, Wolsey, More or Cromwell – get in his way. The origins of the break with Rome and the subsequent Reformation are thus to be found in Henry's own intensely personal drive towards immortality.

KEY POINTS FROM CHAPTER 9: Divorce, doctrine or dosh? The reasons for the break with Rome and the origins of the Reformation

1. Henry made the decision to seek an annulment of his marriage to Catherine of Aragon in 1527. This was before he decided to break with Rome. Thus, the divorce and the break with Rome are two separate processes.
2. Henry used Leviticus to justify his annulment. It said that Henry should never have married his brother Arthur's wife. This was probably a genuine belief on Henry's part.
3. Henry fell head over heels in love with Anne Boleyn. As a reformist, she was an important factor in pushing him towards religious change.
4. Although it is difficult to generalise, the Catholic Church was supported by the majority of the population. Most opposition that did exist was in the south-east of England.
5. Henry was influenced by reformist writers, particularly Cranmer, Fish, Foxe, St Germain and Tyndale. They helped to justify his rejection of the Pope's authority.
6. Key changes that led to a more Protestant Church up until 1538 were:
   - February 1533: Act in Restraint of Appeals
   - March 1534: First Act of Succession
   - November 1534: Act of Supremacy
   - July 1536: Ten Articles
   - July 1537: Bishops' Book
   - August 1537: Bible in English with King's consent
   - September 1538: first set of Royal Injunctions.
7. Key changes that reversed some Protestant reform were:
   - June 1539: Act of Six Articles
   - May 1543: Act for the Advancement of True Religion
   - May 1543: King's Book.
8. The smaller monasteries were dissolved in 1536. The larger monasteries had all been dissolved by 1540.
9. Monasteries were dissolved for a range of motives (see Chart 9G on page 122). Henry's desire to raise money for foreign policy concerns was uppermost.
10. There is a range of interpretations of the causes of Henry's break with Rome and subsequent Reformation. Henry VIII himself stands as the central factor in explaining religious change.

10

Why wasn't there an early Tudor crisis? How serious was the opposition to the Reformation?

CHAPTER OVERVIEW

The work of the historian is in some ways similar to that of the bird spotter; they both have to search hard to identify particular 'types' or species and they are often in unofficial competition with others in the same field. Historians most often behave with the frantic, nervous energy of 'twitchers' when they are trying to identify moments of 'crisis', such as the alleged mid-Tudor crisis in the reigns of Edward and Mary.

The reign of Henry VIII, however, conceals the rarer 'early Tudor crisis' – a crisis that should have happened, but never did. Within the 1530s there lies a mystery: how could all the changes and events of that decade have been forced through without provoking a crisis of opposition? Nothing short of a religious, political, legal and economic transformation was carried out during the 1530s, yet Henry VIII emerged from the decade with his power undiminished. During the 1530s:

- the Reformation technically ripped the nation from its age-old adherence to Catholicism and thrust new and alien customs and ceremonies into its religious life
- the King, in an unprecedented move, became the country's spiritual leader – the head of the Church of England
- the north erupted into the largest single revolt in English history – the Pilgrimage of Grace
- the law and the constitution underwent the most wide-ranging reforms of the entire sixteenth century
- the dissolution of all the country's monasteries brought a cherished tradition to an abrupt end, and precipitated the greatest transfer of land since the Norman Conquest.

Few in the country would have remained untouched by these sweeping reforms.

The following hypothesis will form the central premise of this chapter:
The Reformation should have provoked more opposition than it did.

The chapter will seek to uncover the nature and extent of the opposition to the Reformation by examining the following issues:

TALKING POINT

What possible reasons are there why the changes of the 1530s did not create more opposition? Make a note of your ideas and compare them with your conclusions when you have finished the chapter.

A Who opposed the Reformation? How did they oppose it and why?

FOCUS ROUTE

1 Who opposed the Reformation? How and why? And how serious was their opposition? As you study this chapter, complete your own copy of the following table. You will not always be able to identify the opponent by name, so if necessary enter 'Unknown' in the first column. Judge the seriousness of the opposition on a scale of 1–5 with 5 being the most serious.

Opponent	Why they opposed	How they opposed	Seriousness of opposition (1–5)

2 Make notes on which methods of opposition were the most
   a) threatening
   b) difficult to deal with.
3 Make notes on the most common reasons for opposing the Reformation.

Who opposed the Reformation?

Sir Thomas More

This portrait of More, painted in 1527 by an unknown artist, vividly brings the character of the man to life; the sharply intelligent eyes, the face set firm in a calm, unshakeable determination. More's devotion to the Catholic faith and his resolve may also be deduced from the picture, when you realise that under his velvet doublet he was wearing a hair shirt that would have painfully chafed his skin. More's principled stance against Henry's Royal Supremacy and his complex personality have fascinated historians over the years.

Henry VIII was aware of More's opposition to his plans to divorce Catherine of Aragon, but he still appointed him Lord Chancellor on the fall of Cardinal Wolsey in 1529. More became increasingly uncomfortable with the King's divorce proceedings and resigned his post in 1532 following the Submission of the Clergy. He retired from public life, but the crunch came when he was called on to swear the Oath of Succession. He refused to swear the oath, but would not give any reasons. His silence rang loudly in Henry's ears and some historians regard the King as vengefully hounding More to his death. Recent research by John Guy suggests that More was more of a politician than a principled saint. He argues in *Tudor England* that More engaged in a dangerous game of opposition, even publishing his view and reasons for opposing the King.

More was imprisoned in the Tower and interrogated three times by Cromwell, but his continued silence baffled the Government and meant that no charge could be brought under the newly introduced Treason Act (see page 144). More was then visited by the Solicitor General, Richard Riche, who engaged him in conversation about the supremacy (see Source 10.4). What More was alleged to have said was used to convict him in the trial that followed. He was executed in July 1535.

SOURCE 10.1 G. R. Elton, *Policy and Police: The Enforcement of the Reformation in the Age of Thomas Cromwell*, 1972, p.44

Any thought that the political and doctrinal changes were simply and silently absorbed by the people must be forgotten ... There was a real problem facing the King and his advisers, a real problem of disaffection, disobedience and disturbance. No doubt the problem can now in retrospect be seen to have been far from enormous, but at the time only its reality could be taken for granted, not its size.

SOURCE 10.2 P. Ackroyd, *The Life of Thomas More*, 1998, p.354

He had rejected the oath and was therefore to be charged with 'misprision [concealment] of treason'. But he had refused to give his reasons for his fatal decision and, at this moment, he entered silence. Or, rather, silence entered him. In a sense it was no longer his own choice; he ceased to be aware of himself, and at this level of conscience or knowledge he became part of the larger world of faith and spirit. He had always followed the imperatives of duty and service, but now that duty had turned irrevocably from his society to his God.

The range of people who opposed the Reformation was huge – from martyrs to monks, and from rebels to refugees. Historians have probably concentrated too much on the headline-grabbing opponents like Sir Thomas More, Bishop John Fisher and Elizabeth Barton. However, there were simply too few principled, public opponents for them to have posed any real problem to the Government.

Much more widespread were the nameless people who accepted the superiority of the King's authority, but who remained Catholic in their beliefs. It is impossible for historians to assess how many ordinary people opposed the Reformation, but the very fact that they remained silent and obscure helped to ensure that the speculative early Tudor crisis did not occur.

SOURCE 10.3 From the official record of the trial of Thomas More (this document is only partially complete and crucial parts are missing)

Richard Riche: *Ask ... you this case if it were enacted by Parliament that I should be King ... and whosoever said nay ...*
Thomas More: *... put another higher case which was this Sir I put case ... by Parliament that God were not God ...*
Richard Riche: *... that act was not possible to be made to make God ungod but sir by cause your case is ... you agree that you were bound so to affirm and accept me to be King ...*
Thomas More: *... the cases were not like by cause that a king ... although the King were accepted in England yet most outer parts do not affirm the same.*

SOURCE 10.4 Thomas More speaking at his treason trial after he had been found guilty

Thomas More: *Seeing that I see you are determined to condemn me (God knows how) I will now in discharge of my conscience speak my mind plainly and freely touching my Indictment and your Statute. For as, my Lord, this Indictment is grounded upon an Act of Parliament directly repugnant to the laws of God and his Holy Church, the supreme government of which, or of any part where of, may no temporal prince presume by any law to take upon him, as rightfully belonging to the See of Rome, a spiritual pre-eminence by the mouth of our Saviour himself, personally present upon the earth, only to St Peter and his successors, Bishops of the same See, by special prerogative granted; It is therefore in law amongst Christian men insufficient to charge any Christian man ... No more might this realm of England refuse obedience to the See of Rome than might a child refuse obedience to his own natural father.*

ACTIVITY

1. Study Source 10.3. Can you spot the slip that More made in his conversation with Riche which led to the guilty verdict against him? (It has to do with More's comment on Henry's authority as Supreme Head.)
2. Peter Ackroyd suggests that the phrases 'put case' and 'ask you this case' were the conventional procedural phrases used by lawyers in the sixteenth century to say 'Imagine if ...'. Knowing that More and Riche both had legal backgrounds, how might More have interpreted the conversation?
3. Study Source 10.4. Does the fact that Thomas More revealed his inner thoughts only *after* the guilty verdict mean that he was not taking a truly principled stance during the trial?
4. What do Source 10.2 and Source 10.4 suggest More's reasons were for taking the stand that he did?
5. Study Source 10.4. What does More say were his reasons for not taking the Oath of Succession?
6. Use the sources and your own knowledge to complete the following statement. More was executed because:
   - **a** he refused to confirm Henry's Royal Supremacy (he equally declined to affirm Papal Supremacy)
   - **b** he made a treasonable comment to Riche about Parliament not being able to make a king Supreme Head
   - **c** Henry could not tolerate any opposition
   - **d** More's character meant that he would not back down in his confrontation with Henry.

John Fisher, Bishop of Rochester

By the time of the break with Rome, Fisher was in his sixties and was respected across Europe for his piety and scholarship. He stood steadfastly by Catherine and his belief that the powers of the Pope were God-given. This principle led him into direct conflict with Henry, as he argued that any denial of Papal Supremacy was sinful. He belonged to the circle that was in contact with Emperor Charles V's active ambassador, Chapuys, and had himself been in direct correspondence with the Emperor, urging him to use armed intervention. Fisher was imprisoned and threatened by the Government when he refused to swear the Oath of Succession in April 1534. His execution in June 1535 seems to have been precipitated by the Pope's decision to make him a cardinal.

Cardinal Fisher, Bishop of Rochester, by Hans Holbein the Younger

Carthusian and Observant Franciscan monks

One of the most principled and determined stands against Henry's break with Rome came from these two strict religious orders. Both orders were suppressed and many of their members were imprisoned, where they were executed or died as a result of the appalling conditions.

Elizabeth Barton, The Holy Maid of Kent

This unknown 16-year-old girl was rocketed to national fame in 1525 by a vision of the Virgin Mary that she had while suffering from a mental illness. Her visions continued and she rapidly came under the spiritual guidance of Dr Edward Bocking. Her later prophecies were chiefly exhortations against the King's marriage to Anne Boleyn. She even railed against the King in person when he visited Canterbury. She remained important until 1533 when her claim that the King would cease to be on the throne in a month and Bocking's plans to publish a collection of her prophecies forced Cromwell into action. In April 1534 her execution (along with five of her followers) was considered a political necessity.

Why did people oppose the Reformation?

The Reformation embraced a host of political, religious, legal and constitutional changes, all of which would affect different people in different ways. Therefore, to look for a simple rejection or acceptance of the Reformation as a whole would be to oversimplify this enormous event. Historians must regard it instead as a series of individual events to which people reacted either for or against. A crisis would have occurred only if the opposition of a vast number of people had come together on one issue. As it was, people tended to pick and choose what they would oppose. Some of the main bones of contention are shown in Chart 10A (opposite).

10A The rocky road to Reformation

- **Fundamental religious opposition.** The Reformation posed a threat to the country's traditional faith and many saw in it the onset of Protestantism.
- **Opposition to the Royal Supremacy.** Few had the courage to question openly Henry's claim that he was the Supreme Head of the Church, but those who did paid the ultimate price. Fifty martyrs died, including Sir Thomas More, John Fisher and monks drawn from the eight religious houses of strict observance.
- **Opposition to the dissolution of the monasteries.** The opposition to the dissolution was on both social and religious grounds: social in that the monasteries played a key role in the life of local communities; religious in that they represented one of the strongest bastions of Catholicism.
- **Defence of traditional practices.** There was a strong feeling in many local communities that their Church was under attack. The Ten Articles and the injunctions enforcing them, the visitations and the dissolution provoked a popular religious reaction against the perceived attacks on the Church. The loss of saints' days appears to have been a cause of particular disquiet, as in Kirkby Stephen in 1536, when the priest's failure to announce St Luke's Day sparked the first unrest of the Pilgrimage of Grace in Westmorland.

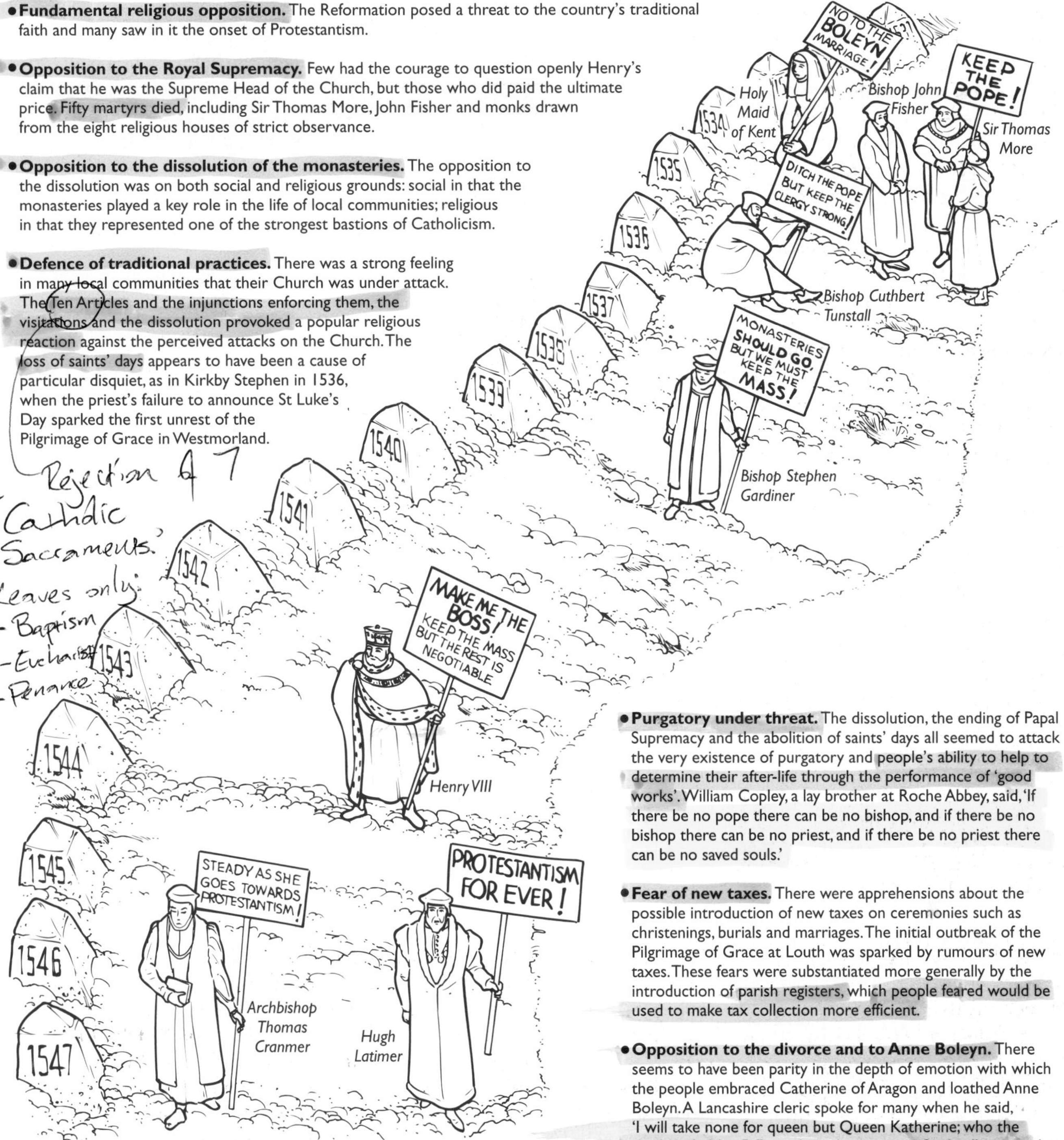

- **Purgatory under threat.** The dissolution, the ending of Papal Supremacy and the abolition of saints' days all seemed to attack the very existence of purgatory and people's ability to help to determine their after-life through the performance of 'good works'. William Copley, a lay brother at Roche Abbey, said, 'If there be no pope there can be no bishop, and if there be no bishop there can be no priest, and if there be no priest there can be no saved souls.'
- **Fear of new taxes.** There were apprehensions about the possible introduction of new taxes on ceremonies such as christenings, burials and marriages. The initial outbreak of the Pilgrimage of Grace at Louth was sparked by rumours of new taxes. These fears were substantiated more generally by the introduction of parish registers, which people feared would be used to make tax collection more efficient.
- **Opposition to the divorce and to Anne Boleyn.** There seems to have been parity in the depth of emotion with which the people embraced Catherine of Aragon and loathed Anne Boleyn. A Lancashire cleric spoke for many when he said, 'I will take none for queen but Queen Katherine; who the devil made Nan Boleyn, that whore, queen, for I will never take her for queen!'

ACTIVITY

With the other students in your class, take on the viewpoint of one of the characters below and explain whether you would have been for or against the following events. Think about what effect the events would have on your daily life and whether the events would affect your beliefs.

Characters

- An ordinary parish priest
- A gentleman with reformist tendencies
- A commoner with little understanding of doctrine
- An urban merchant

Events

1 Henry's marriage to Anne Boleyn (1533)
2 The rejection of papal authority (1534)
3 Higher taxes on churchmen (1535)
4 The dissolution of the monasteries (1536–40)
5 The Ten Articles (1536)
6 The Great Bible (1539)
7 The Act of Six Articles (1539)

How did people oppose the Reformation?

How people decided to oppose the Reformation was probably the most important factor in determining whether a crisis was going to emerge. The intransigence of individuals like More and Fisher and the hostility of the Pilgrims of Grace (see pages 135–41) brought them into open conflict with the Crown. However, more people expressed their opposition in small actions, such as refusing to erase the Pope's name from their church books. Although small-scale protest was difficult to counter, the Government could survive it.

■ 10B The nature of protests against the Reformation

Type of protest	Description
Open challenge	A few brave individuals (e.g. More and Fisher) openly criticised the King from within England, while others (e.g. Cardinal Reginald Pole) attacked his reforms from abroad. The Pilgrims of Grace used open rebellion as their method of expression.
Private opposition	'I will pray for [the Pope] as the chief head of Christ's Church, and so I will advise all men to do secretly. But we may say nothing openly, for the knaves hath our heads under their girdle' (London priest, 1536).
Remaining loyal to Catholicism	Ronald Hutton's studies of churchwardens' accounts ('The local impact of the Tudor Reformations', in C. Haigh (ed.) *The English Reformation Revised*) have shown that most of the traditional habits of the 1520s (the washing of saints, replacement of banners, veils, etc.) continued well into Henry VIII's reign. His research into the 1550s has revealed the vitality of Catholicism at the local level in Mary's reign. Altars, images, crucifixes and candlesticks were quickly restored to the churches and there was a rise in the number of men training to be priests.
Refusal to act until forced to do so	Studies of churchwardens' accounts have revealed that many of the traditional Catholic practices continued until the Government could enforce compliance. Six months after the 1538 Injunctions, 80 per cent of churches in three Lincoln deaneries had not bought the new English bibles and diocesan officials were doing nothing to enforce them. However, a proclamation and the threat of a £2 fine in 1541 encouraged their use. By 1545 most churches had them.
Opposition from the inside	Some people believed that the best method of preventing the spread of Protestantism was to attack it discreetly from within. Bishop Longland of Lincoln, for example, continued preaching Catholic doctrine in his diocese.

Conclusion

The Reformation was opposed by many different people, in many different ways and for many different reasons. It was this diversity that probably helped to prevent a major crisis from developing. There was no single, obvious issue around which opposition forces could muster. Nor was there an obvious moment (apart from the Pilgrimage of Grace) when opposition could coalesce. The dates of the religious changes are clear enough, but it is much less clear when these began to have effect in the localities and when people realised the full significance of what they were living through.

Revisionist historians would go further in arguing that the individuals involved in the Reformation responded to individual events without necessarily seeing the full, broad sweep of change. Did the people of England know that they were living through a Reformation? If they did not, this goes a long way towards explaining why opposition did not materialise on a major scale.

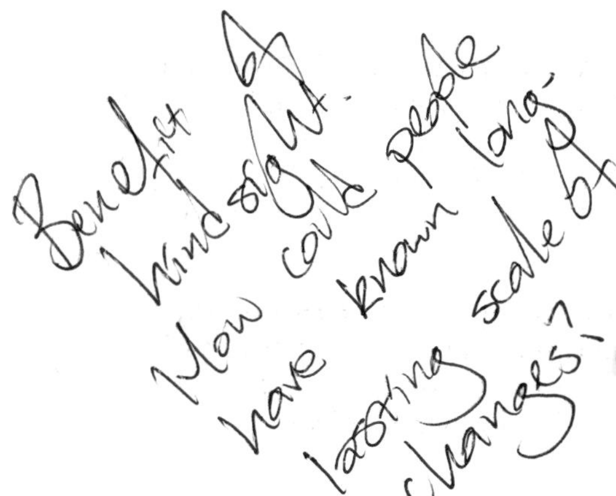

Benefit of hindsight.
How could people have known long lasting scale of changes?

B Why did the north rebel in the Pilgrimage of Grace?

FOCUS ROUTE

Read pages 135–41 on the Pilgrimage of Grace and write down your answers to the following questions:

1. What were the main reasons for the rebellion?
2. How different were the motivations of the gentry, nobility, clergy and commons (the ordinary people)?
3. How seriously was the Government threatened by the Pilgrimage of Grace?
4. What are the main historiographic controversies surrounding the Pilgrimage?
5. Which of the historians' explanations do you find the most convincing and why?

Opposition to the Reformation was nationwide. But there was a massive variation in the regional reaction to the changes that Henry imposed. The north erupted in major rebellion, while the south was disturbed only by the ravings of one butcher! (See Chart 10D on page 136.)

The rebellion in the north in 1536–37 was made up of three separate, but related, uprisings:

- the Lincolnshire rising, 1–11 October 1536
- the Pilgrimage of Grace, 8 October–8 December 1536
- Sir Francis Bigod's revolt and the Cumberland rising, 16 January–10 February 1537.

The Lincolnshire rising

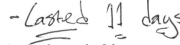

Beginnings

Tensions had been raised in the region by the work of three government commissions operating in the county. They were working on dissolving the smaller monasteries, collecting the subsidy, inspecting the quality of the clergy and enforcing new religious laws. However, wild rumours ran rife that they were after gold, jewels, plate and extra taxes.

Progress of the rising

The rising began at Louth on 1 October 1536, moving across the county before gathering with the parallel Horncastle rising at Lincoln. Anger and violence erupted as the people of Horncastle set upon the chancellor of the Bishop of Lincoln and murdered him in a frenzy. Initially led by a local shoemaker, Nicholas Melton (who called himself Captain Cobbler), the rising's leadership soon devolved on to the gentry, priests and even armed monks who joined the rebels. At least 10,000 people assembled at Lincoln and several lists of articles, combining grievances of the gentry and the commons, were drawn up.

The end of the rebellion

The collaboration between the gentry and the commons evaporated as the Duke of Suffolk's army drew near. The gentry ran for cover and sought forgiveness, and the commons collapsed into confusion. The few rebels who remained were sent home when the Government's herald arrived on 11 October.

The Pilgrimage of Grace

Beginnings

News of the Lincolnshire rising spread quickly and reached the ears of Robert Aske, a Yorkshire lawyer, on 4 October 1536. He dispatched letters across the county calling on men to maintain the Holy Church. Recent local research, notably by M. L. Bush, has led to the Pilgrimage being seen as a series of interconnected regional revolts, as opposed to one large, fluid movement. In *The Pilgrimage of Grace: A Study of Rebel Armies of October 1536* Bush identified nine 'host' armies that had their own separate origins, but most of which joined with the main rebel army (see Chart 10D).

Progress of the rising

By 10 October, Aske had become chief captain of an army of 30,000 men. The rebels made their headquarters in York before moving down to Pontefract on 21 October, where Lord Darcy handed over Pontefract Castle, the most important fortress in the north. Aske provided disciplined leadership for the Pilgrimage, ensuring that all goods were paid for and that no murders were committed.

The Government's response

The Government was caught off guard and soon the Pilgrims held sway over virtually the whole of the north. Faced with a force far larger than he himself could muster, Henry wisely played for time, sending a delegation led by the Duke of Norfolk to meet the rebels. The rebels presented their five articles (see

■ 10C Actors in the events

Lord Hussey	By the time of the rebellion he was an elderly man of dwindling authority in the north. He was linked to the Aragon faction at court, but stayed on the sidelines during the uprising.
Lord Darcy	The keeper of Pontefract Castle, the most important fortress in the north. He initially tried or pretended to be on the King's side, but he surrendered the castle with indecent haste to the rebels.
Lord Dacre	The most senior nobleman in the north. Astutely, he remained aloof from the proceedings, but his two sons became involved on the rebels' side.
Earl of Northumberland	An ailing, childless nobleman who was being pressured to leave his lands to the Crown.
Duke of Norfolk	The King's loyal commander, but an opponent of Protestantism and a rival to Thomas Cromwell.
Robert Aske	A one-eyed, younger son of a Yorkshire gentleman who had been trained as a lawyer in London. He became an inspirational leader of the Pilgrimage, giving an atmosphere of spirituality and honour to the protest.

Source 10.5 opposite). A truce was signed on 27 October, under which Sir Ralph Ellerker and Robert Bowes were to meet with the King. In the meantime, the Pilgrims kept their forces and their chain of command in place. At the meeting with Bowes and Ellerker, Henry offered no concessions, except that he would pardon all but ten ringleaders.

The end of the rebellion

The representatives of the host armies met again at Pontefract between 2 and 4 December to finalise their demands in the 24 articles (see Source 10.6 opposite). These were presented at a meeting between Norfolk and Aske. Henry had given Norfolk permission to grant a general pardon, a prolonged truce and the promise of a parliament to discuss most of the issues that the rebels had raised. Aske agreed, but insisted that the monasteries must not be suppressed before the parliament met. The agreement reached was reluctantly accepted by the commons, who began to disperse after the Lancaster Herald read the King's pardon on 8 December.

■ 10D The Pilgrimage of Grace

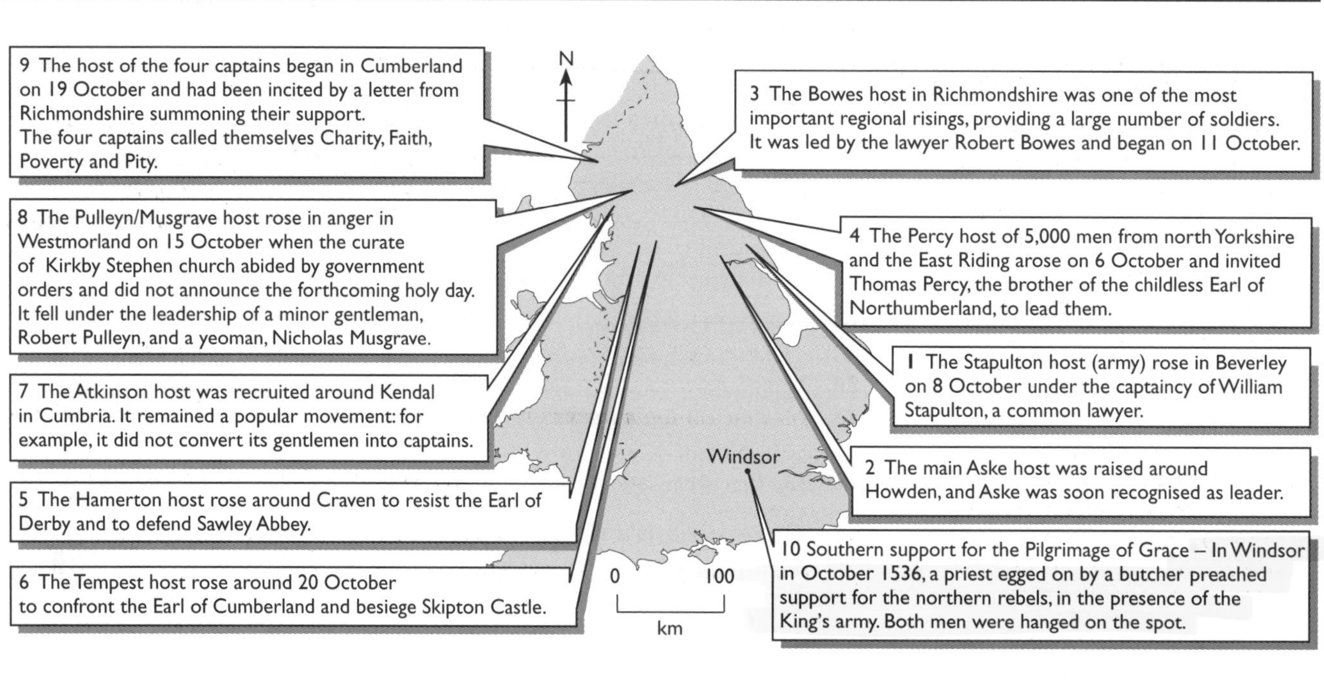

9 The host of the four captains began in Cumberland on 19 October and had been incited by a letter from Richmondshire summoning their support. The four captains called themselves Charity, Faith, Poverty and Pity.
8 The Pulleyn/Musgrave host rose in anger in Westmorland on 15 October when the curate of Kirkby Stephen church abided by government orders and did not announce the forthcoming holy day. It fell under the leadership of a minor gentleman, Robert Pulleyn, and a yeoman, Nicholas Musgrave.
7 The Atkinson host was recruited around Kendal in Cumbria. It remained a popular movement: for example, it did not convert its gentlemen into captains.
5 The Hamerton host rose around Craven to resist the Earl of Derby and to defend Sawley Abbey.
6 The Tempest host rose around 20 October to confront the Earl of Cumberland and besiege Skipton Castle.
N
3 The Bowes host in Richmondshire was one of the most important regional risings, providing a large number of soldiers. It was led by the lawyer Robert Bowes and began on 11 October.
4 The Percy host of 5,000 men from north Yorkshire and the East Riding arose on 6 October and invited Thomas Percy, the brother of the childless Earl of Northumberland, to lead them.
1 The Stapulton host (army) rose in Beverley on 8 October under the captaincy of William Stapulton, a common lawyer.
2 The main Aske host was raised around Howden, and Aske was soon recognised as leader.
Windsor
10 Southern support for the Pilgrimage of Grace – In Windsor in October 1536, a priest egged on by a butcher preached support for the northern rebels, in the presence of the King's army. Both men were hanged on the spot.
0
100
km

10E The Five Wounds of Christ

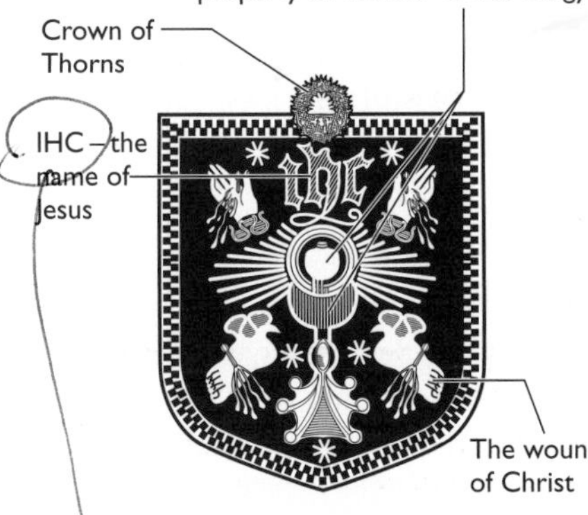

Religious imagery was very important to the rebels. They wore badges of the Wounds of Christ, called themselves Christ's soldiers and took oaths to the movement.

Greek Christogram, iota - eta - sigma, ΙΗΣ.

SOURCE 10.5 The York Articles. These grievances were written up by Aske and sent to the mayor of York on 15 October 1536

1 *The suppression of so many religious houses . . . whereby the service of God is not well [maintained] but also the [commons] of your realm be unrelieved, the which as we think is a great hurt to the common wealth . . .*

2 *that the act of uses may be suppressed because we think by the said act we your true subjects be clearly restrained of our liberties in the declaration of our wills concerning our lands, as well as for payment of our debts . . .*

3 *[A tax on sheep and cattle] which would be an importunate charge to them considering the poverty that they be in all ready and loss which they have sustained these two years past.*

4 *your grace takes of your counsel and being about you such persons as be of low birth and small reputation which hath procured the profits most especially for their own advantage, the which we suspect to be the lord Cromwell and Sir Richard Riche . . .*

5 *[We are] grieved that there be diverse bishops of England of your Graces late promotion that have . . . the faith of Christ, as we think, which are the bishops of Canterbury, the bishop of Rochester, the bishop of Worcester, the bishop of Salisbury, the bishop of Saint Davids, and the bishop of Dublin, and especially we think the beginnings of all the trouble of that . . . and the vexation that has been . . . of your subjects the bishop of Lincoln.*

SOURCE 10.6 The Pontefract Articles. These demands were drawn up on 2–4 December 1536

1 *. . . to have the heresies . . . within this realm to be annulled and destroyed.*

2 *. . . to have the supreme head of the church . . . restored unto the see of Rome . . .*

3 *. . . that the Lady Mary be made legitimate . . .*

4 *To have the abbeys suppressed to be restored . . .*

5 *To have the tenth and first fruits and tenths clearly discharged.*

6 *To have the Observant Friars restored to their houses again.*

7 *To have the heretics . . . [have] punishment by fire . . .*

8 *To have the lord Cromwell, the Lord Chancellor, and Sir Richard Riche . . . [receive] punishment.*

9 *That the lands . . . may be tenant right, and the lord to have at every change two years gressom [entry fine] and no more . . .*

10 *The statutes of handguns and crossbows to be repelled . . .*

11 *That doctor Ligh and doctor Layton . . . [receive] punishment for their extortions in their time of visitations.*

12 *Reformation for the election of knights of shire and burgesses . . .*

13 *Statute for enclosures and intacks to be put into execution . . .*

14 *To be discharged of the quindine [a form of tax] and taxes now granted . . .*

15 *To have the parliament in a convenient place at Nottingham or York . . .*

16 *The statute of the declaration of the crown by will . . . be repealed.*

17 *. . . that all the recognisances, statutes, penalties new forfeited during this time of commotion may be pardoned . . .*

18 *The privileges and rights of the church to be confirmed . . .*

19 *The liberties of the church to have their old customs . . .*

20 *To have the statute that no man shall will his lands to be repealed.*

21 *That the statutes of treasons by for words . . . [be] repealed.*

22 *That the common laws may have place as was used in the beginning of your grace's reign . . .*

23 *That no man upon subpoena [court writ] is from Trent north appear but at York . . .*

24 *A remedy against escheators [officers who collect land that reverts to the Crown] for finding of false offices and extortions fees . . .*

ACTIVITY

1 Which of the Pontefract Articles could the rebels realistically expect Henry to accept?
2 What do the Pontefract Articles suggest was the most important grievance of the rebels?
3 Study each of the York Articles. Identify which articles are representing the interests of:
   a) the nobility and gentry
   b) the commons
   c) all social groups.
4 How useful are the York and Pontefract Articles for historians attempting to uncover the real motivation behind the rebellion?

ENCLOSURE

To enclose is to fence or hedge around a piece of ground that has previously been open. Enclosure could take place on any type of land – arable fields (tillage), meadows or pasture land (often wooded) – and was done to increase the productivity and profitability of the land. Enclosure occurred throughout the early modern period and often passed unnoticed. However, it could be a cause of great hostility, particularly in times of shortage or if the landowner rode roughshod over the rights of others. It was often most strongly opposed because it removed people's right to graze their animals on common land. The common people had a highly developed sense of what rights had been established over time and would defend them vigorously, sometimes by raising a 'common purse' to pay for legal action against the encloser, but more often by throwing down the offending hedges and fences.

In the sixteenth century, there was a growing awareness of some of the effects of enclosure on the economy. The Government was especially concerned with enclosure that converted the use of land, particularly from arable to pasture, as it was seen to be a cause of depopulation and unemployment.

Modern historical thinking suggests that enclosure was more of a symptom than a cause of economic distress. But it was held up as a symbol of greed and selfishness in a time of need and want. In the mid-Tudor period, a group of liberal humanist thinkers labelled the 'Commonwealth men' criticised enclosure and attributed the woes of the time to 'Men without a conscience. Men utterly void of God's fear. Yea, men that live as though there were no God at all!' This was obviously hyperbole, but it found a receptive audience.

Sir Francis Bigod's revolt and the Cumberland rising

While Aske toured the north trying to sell the deal that he had made to the gentry, a disaffected rebel, Sir Francis Bigod, remained unconvinced of the Government's sincerity. He planned to capture Hull and Scarborough and force the Duke of Norfolk to act as a go-between. This hare-brained scheme went into operation on 16 January 1537, but it was doomed to failure and collapsed in a few days. Bigod fled and was eventually arrested in Cumberland, where the frustrated commons had launched their own unsuccessful attack on Carlisle in early February.

The aftermath

The north expected the King's confirmation of the terms agreed, but Henry had no intention of honouring the deal. Bigod's rising provided Henry with the evidence he needed of the rebels' bad faith. Retribution began. Commons, gentry and nobility were rounded up and executed. The final death toll of 178 included Aske, Lord Darcy and Bigod. The Percy family was destroyed as the Earl of Northumberland agreed to hand over his lands to the Crown and his brother Sir Thomas Percy was beheaded. Greater royal control of the north was ensured through the reorganisation of the Council of the North.

What caused the rebellions?

Dissolution of the monasteries

The dissolution was claimed by Aske to be the 'greatest cause' of the rising. The rebels demanded (and in some cases took the initiative in) the restoration of the monasteries. Religious houses played an important secular and spiritual role in the life of the north: they provided food, clothing and shelter to travellers and the poor; they acted as safe houses for goods; and they provided tenancies for farmers. The closure of the monasteries, therefore, cast a looming shadow over the welfare – spiritual, social and economic – of the north.

Defence of the Faith

The imagery, oaths, songs and propaganda of the Pilgrims gave the rebellion a deliberately cultivated religious resonance. This religious aura gave the rebellion a justification and motivation that helped to sustain it. The rebels demanded the rooting out of heresy. They called for an end to the draining of the churches' wealth, the renunciation of Henry's Royal Supremacy and the rehabilitation of the Catholic Princess Mary.

Food shortages and agrarian issues

There had been poor harvests in 1535 and 1536. In addition, many other agricultural issues seem to have motivated the rebels, including renewal of tenancies, border tenures (granting of land in return for military service), ENCLOSURES and rack-renting (raising of rents). In most areas, these issues were put on the back-boiler when the commons and gentry joined together.

Taxation

Opposition to the King's demands for taxes was a consistent theme in the rebels' articles. There was particular hostility to Cromwell's initiative of taxing in time of peace, introduced in the 1534 Subsidy Act. There was also opposition to the Statute of Uses, which was effectively a feudal tax on aristocratic landed inheritances.

Opposition to Cromwell's policies

The north saw itself as under attack from a greedy Crown regime, and Cromwell became the 'evil genius' behind it all. The Treason Act, Royal Supremacy and heresy were all seen as clear examples of Cromwell's work. This scapegoating of Cromwell and his henchmen Richard Riche and Thomas Audley was particularly useful for the gentry and nobility engaging in court politics.

Aristocratic feud

Some historians, most notably G. R. Elton ('Politics and the Pilgrimage of Grace', in B. Malament (ed.), *After the Reformation*), have argued that the uprising was an orchestrated attempt by disaffected nobility to increase their power and influence at court. The nobles were angry and resentful at the position of Cromwell and Anne Boleyn.

ACTIVITY

Where would you place the Pilgrimage of Grace on the Richter scale of rebellions? Explain your choice.

1		Mild, isolated protests from peasants.
2		More vocal and sustained protests from various social groups in the lower orders. JPs order them to disperse.
3		Unrest begins to spread. Rebel leadership established. Meeting with local gentry and JPs.
4		Rebels produce a list of demands. Rebel camp is established. Numbers swelling. Suppression by local gentry attempted.
5		Rebel camp numbers thousands. Government intervention required. Pardon offered in return for rebels dispersing.
6		Rebels are advancing or have remained in place for at least four weeks. Meeting with regional nobility required. Government begins to prepare measures for suppression.
7		Troops raised. Suppression by regional nobleman attempted.
8		Rebellion requires full-scale military suppression.
9		Monarch's position severely threatened by the rebellion.
10	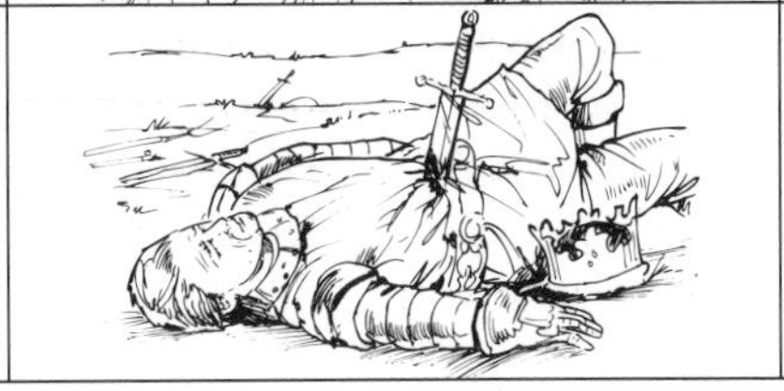	Rebellion succeeds in overthrowing the established dynasty.

■ **Learning trouble spot**

One of the most important and difficult skills to develop in Advanced History is that of being able to identify, understand and summarise the views of leading historians. The historiography (the writings and research of historians) of the Tudor century glitters with big name historians who have markedly different points to make about the people and events of the period.

To help develop your skill of understanding historiography, try the following:

1 Read the abstract on the back cover of books. This summarises the author's main points.
2 Read a section/chapter/book *just* looking for their opinion. They are unlikely to state 'My view on this is…', so look for the emphasis they place on different points.
3 Highlight where you think the author has stated their opinion. When you have finished making notes, look back to see if any common ideas or points stand out, which could be linked together to construct an argument.
4 Introductions and conclusions are often (though not always) places where the author will outline or restate their overall argument.
5 A useful exercise is to read an article or a chapter and then attempt to précis it in a small number of words (e.g. 100). This forces you to concentrate on the essential points of the text.
6 Once you have established what one historian thinks, try to compare and contrast it with the views of another.
7 Having established the historical arguments, it is vital that you form your own view and are prepared to challenge the opinions of established historians (and your teacher). History is about interpretation, and as long as you use evidence to back up your arguments, your view is as valid as anyone else's. Don't be overawed by the assertions of the professional historians. They, after all, often violently disagree with each other.

Historians and the Pilgrimage of Grace

Much has been written about the causes of the Pilgrimage of Grace and there remains much controversy about exactly why it began. The historians can be split into two broad groups: those who see the uprising as the work of a defeated court faction and those who see it as a genuinely popular expression of anger and dissatisfaction with Henrician rule. The two competing theses are summarised in Chart 10F.

■ 10F Interpretations of the Pilgrimage of Grace

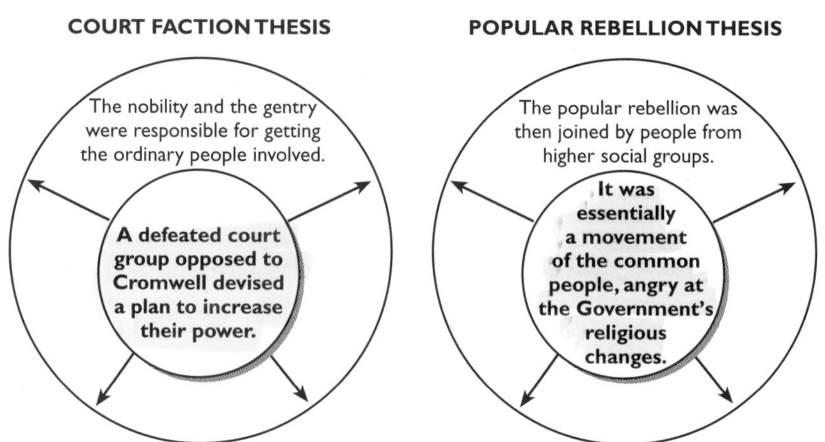

COURT FACTION THESIS
The nobility and the gentry were responsible for getting the ordinary people involved.
A defeated court group opposed to Cromwell devised a plan to increase their power.
POPULAR REBELLION THESIS
The popular rebellion was then joined by people from higher social groups.
It was essentially a movement of the common people, angry at the Government's religious changes.

The debates do not stop there, of course, as the historians within those two groups argue with each other over the relative importance of the different grievances – religious, political, economic and social.

ACTIVITY

Copy this table and complete it as you read through the historiography below.

	Court faction thesis	Popular rebellion thesis
Key people or groups involved		
Key evidence		
Historians who support the thesis		
Key quotations		

R. and M. Dodds, *The Pilgrimage of Grace and the Exeter Conspiracy* (1915)

One of the first accounts of the Pilgrimage of Grace was written by the Dodds sisters. Based on the meticulous use of the State Papers, it is still one of the most reliable narratives. They regarded the uprising 'as a truly popular movement which coerced the upper sort into compliance and promoted the restoration of the old church against the innovators'. The work is limited in its analysis, however, as the Dodds were too willing to accept the participants' own views of the events: Cromwell was always going to play up the importance of the agricultural causes of the conflict, as opposed to the religious ones of which he was the architect. Similarly, Aske was inevitably going to attempt to mitigate his own role in his confession by depicting himself as riding on the back of an unstoppable popular protest.

M. E. James, 'Obedience and dissent in Henrician England: the Lincolnshire Rebellion, 1536', in *Past and Present*, Vol. 48 (1970)

M. E. James' important interpretation of the causes of the Pilgrimage was based on his contention that all sectors of Lincolnshire society rose together in opposition to royal policy. He states, 'It seems then that the Lincolnshire movement originated less in tensions within the society than in fears of invasion without.' James believes that the county's fears and anger coalesced around the new interference of the Duke of Suffolk. He analyses the roles and motivation of each of the social groups, concluding that there was 'a powerful clerical initiative', a common people 'more easily roused by the prospect of plunder of parochial treasures than invasion by an alien religion' and, most contentiously, a gentry who rose together in opposition to royal policy.

G. R. Elton, 'Politics and the Pilgrimage of Grace', in B. Malament (ed.), *After the Reformation* (1983)

Elton famously argued that the Pilgrimage of Grace represented 'the effort of a defeated court faction to create a power base in the country for the purpose of achieving a political victory at court'. Elton denied the possibility of a spontaneous popular uprising and pointed to the evidence of prior planning and the key roles played by the Lords Darcy and Hussey. Elton's thesis is important in reminding us of the importance of the court connection (Darcy and Hussey were members of the Aragonese faction). However, he is surely too dismissive of the independent role played by the clergy and the lower orders.

S. Gunn, 'Peers, commons and gentry in the Lincolnshire Revolt of 1536', in *Past and Present*, Vol. 123 (1989)

This provided a detailed, well-researched rebuttal to the historians who regarded the Pilgrimage of Grace as the prime example of court politicians at the centre creating local disorder to further their own ends. His examination of the actions of the gentry undermined the idea of a planned, regional uprising, and he argued that Lord Hussey lacked the necessary political clout to have orchestrated such a rebellion. He concluded that the parish clergy played an important role, but 'more important still were the leaders of society in the villages and small towns, the richer yeomen and substantial tradesmen, who often acted as churchwardens, parish constables, and so on'.

M. L. Bush, *The Pilgrimage of Grace: A Study of Rebel Armies of October 1536* (1996)

Much of the recent research on the Pilgrimage has been done by Michael Bush. His research has revealed that the Pilgrimage was primarily a 'movement of the commons' with all nine host armies beginning as a 'protest of the people'. However, the ordinary people's belief in a 'society of orders' led them to insist on the gentry and noble families assuming leadership. He has pointed out that the original, contemporary term for the rising was 'pilgrimage for grace for the commonwealth'. This supports his argument that the rebels' aims were to protect the 'commonwealth' (by which they meant 'the commons' and 'the material good of the realm') from unfair and heavy taxation, from agrarian threats such as attacks on tenant rights and from the Government's onslaught on the wealth of the local churches.

TALKING POINT

What do you understand by the term 'Pilgrimage of Grace'? What could the rebels mean by 'pilgrimage'? What was the grace they were seeking and from whom – God or the King? What difference is made by calling it the 'pilgrimage for grace for the commonwealth' (see Bush's account) as opposed to the 'Pilgrimage of Grace'?

SOURCE 10.7 Christopher Haigh (ed.), *The English Reformation Revised*, 1987, p. 17

Because the Reformation came piecemeal, the significance of the pieces was not recognized, and this was the key to its success ... At any one time, there was not much Reformation to accept, and England accepted its Reformation because it didn't quite see what it was doing. The piecemeal Reformation was a peaceful Reformation.

C Why wasn't there more opposition to the Reformation?

The Pilgrimage of Grace had posed a significant threat to Henry's government and had been caused to a substantial degree by the changes of the Reformation. To understand why there were no other examples of major opposition, we must consider the following:

- people's reasons for *not* opposing the Reformation
- historians' views of the kind of Reformation that took place
- the Government's ability to prevent and suppress opposition (page 144).

Why did people *not* oppose the Reformation?

10G Reasons for lack of opposition to the Reformation

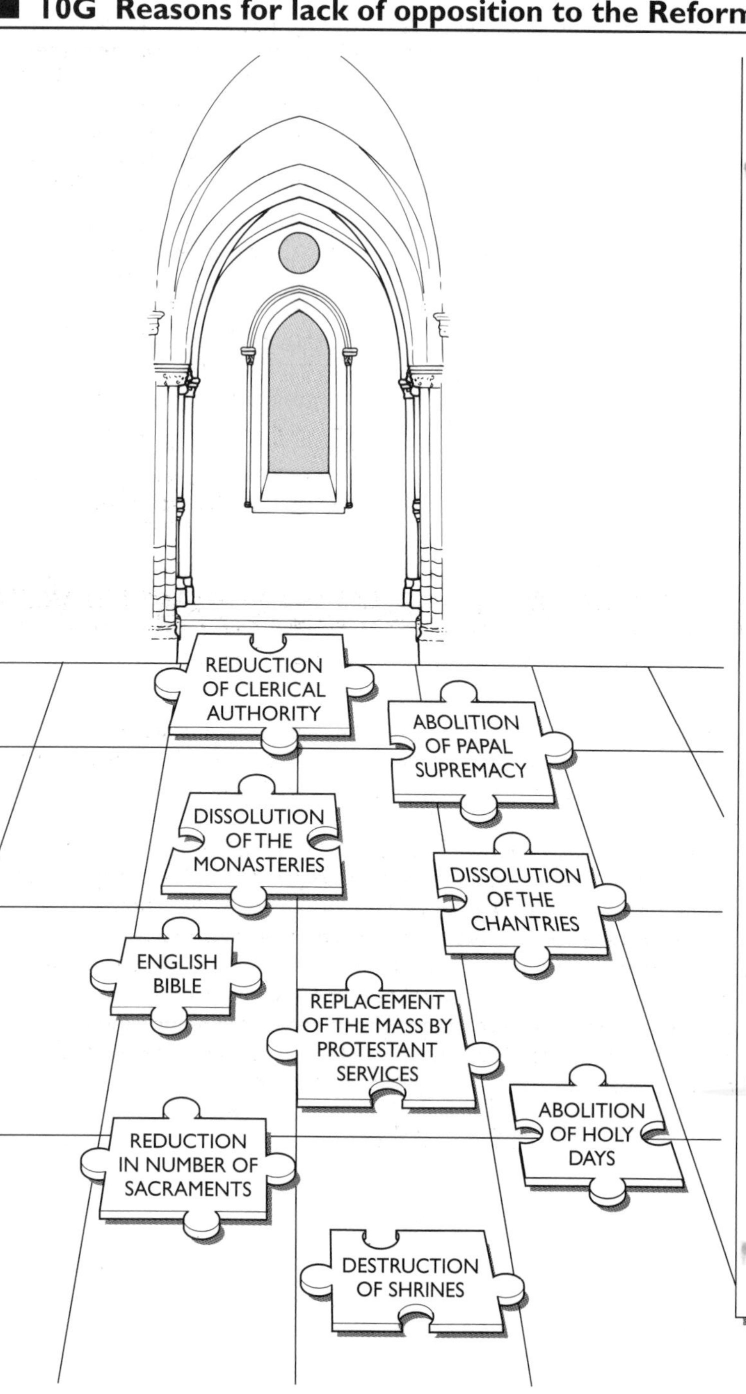

- **Fear.** Cromwell masterminded a machinery of enforcement that must have filled many with a terrified awe. We should not, therefore, assume that obedience and acceptance of the Reformation signified approval of Protestantism; it often more likely showed respect for the power and prestige of the Crown.
- **Many anticipated that the changes would not last.** 'Be you of good comfort, and be steadfast in your faith and be not wavering, and God shall reward us the more. For these things will not last long, I warrant you; you shall see the world change shortly' (a London priest, 1536).
- **Many expected Henry to remain Catholic.** 'For although the king hath conceived a little malice against the bishop of Rome because he would not agree to this marriage, yet I trust that the blessed king will wear harness on his own back to fight against ... heretics.'
- **Motivated by self-interest.** Many clergy went along with the Reformation because it offered them better career prospects. Many lay people gained substantially through the purchase of land and goods following the dissolution of the monasteries. In the video *Dissolution of the Monasteries*, J. J. Scarisbrick has called it the single greatest transfer of land in English history.
- **Concern for 'number one'.** Some put their own welfare and career before their beliefs. For example, the Vicar of Bray (who kept his living from the reign of Henry VIII to Elizabeth) was accused of repeatedly changing sides. He defended himself by saying, 'Not so for I always kept my principle, which is this, to live and die the vicar of Bray.'
- **Protestantism welcomed.** Some people, of course, welcomed the religious Reformation, both at court (in the shape of Cromwell, Anne Boleyn and Cranmer) and at the local level.
- **They did not notice the changes.** Many of the fundamental aspects of ordinary people's religious lives remained unchanged during the 1530s. They still went to the same church on Sunday and participated in the same Mass that they had known for generations.
- **The end result was far from clear.** It was far from obvious in the 1530s, even to those few who were closely in touch with the ebb and flow of events, that the changes would finally produce Protestantism. In *The English Reformation Revised*, historian Christopher Haigh argues that there was no pre-conceived Reformation agenda and no sudden breakthrough; it was in reality a piecemeal process that stretched over 30 years and so failed to stimulate mass opposition.

What can historiography tell us about why there was little opposition to the Reformation?

Any explanation of why the Reformation created little opposition will necessarily depend on what kind of Reformation you believe happened. Historians fiercely disagree about this.

■ 10H The historiography of the Reformation

Historical argument	Historians	Supporting argument
Rapid Reformation from above	G. R. Elton, *Reform and Reformation: England 1509–1558* (1977)	Elton regards the Reformation as a political process that was part of Cromwell's programme of reform; this included the nationalisation of the Church.
Rapid Reformation from below	A. G. Dickens, *The English Reformation* (1964)	Dickens stresses the religious roots of the Reformation and emphasises the springboard provided by Lollardy for the rapid advance of Protestantism. He argues that Catholicism was undermined by its own abuses and by anticlericalism.
Slow Reformation from above	P. Williams, *The Tudor Regime* (1979)	Williams argues that legal reforms did not change religion in the localities, but that popular Catholicism was broken by official preaching, printing and prosecution in Elizabeth's reign.
Slow Reformation from below	P. Collinson, *The Elizabethan Puritan Movement* (1990)	Collinson regards Elizabethan Puritanism as the evangelical era of English Protestantism. During Elizabeth I's reign, godly preachers took the new faith to the people.

ACTIVITY

Match the following explanations of why there was little opposition to the Reformation to the appropriate historical arguments in Chart 10H.

a) There was no significant opposition because the Reformation made little progress until the second half of the century. It took time for the Government to implement the apparatus required to produce a widespread, genuine change in beliefs.

b) People were forced and persuaded to accept the Reformation by a carefully organised campaign of preaching and printed propaganda. An effective system of enforcement at the centre and the localities prevented sizeable opposition.

c) No opposition materialised because Protestantism failed to take hold until a genuine conversion was performed by reformist priests in the key posts and until there was a strong supply of committed Protestant preachers.

d) There was no opposition because the people welcomed the Reformation. The Catholic clergy were too political and too uneducated to satisfy the spiritual needs of the people or to combat evangelical Protestantism.

Answers to this activity are given on page 323.

D What methods were used by the Government to prevent and suppress opposition?

ACTIVITY

What do the figures in Chart 10I reveal about the scale of opposition to the Reformation?

FOCUS ROUTE

Read pages 144–45 and complete your own copy of the following table, putting the methods of government control into rank order of effectiveness.

Method of control	Strengths	Weaknesses	Ranking
Pulpit	Large audience	Easily used by opponents	

10I Details of treason cases, 1532–49

Treason cases	No. of people
Total accusations of treason, 1532–40 Total executions for treason, 1532–40	883 308
Accusations of treason because of involvement in rebellion Executions for treason because of involvement in rebellion	287 178
No. of treason charges against noble opponents (from the Pole, Boleyn and Courtenay families, see Chart 10K) Executions of noble opponents for treason	34 20
Charges of other forms of treason Executions for other forms of treason	562 110
Total accusations of treason, 1540–49	96

10J Government methods of suppressing opposition

WHAT METHODS WERE USED BY THE GOVERNMENT TO PREVENT AND SUPPRESS OPPOSITION?

Law of Treason
The break with Rome brought the Government on to new and shaky ground with regard to the law of Treason. Under the existing law, the Government found itself unable to charge those who opposed the King in words only (such as the Holy Maid of Kent), so in 1534 the Treason Act was passed. The new Act made it treasonable:
- to attempt the death of the King, Queen or heir by act or malicious desire expressed in words or writing
- to call the King in words or writing a heretic, schismatic, tyrant, infidel or usurper
- to seize royal castles, ships, ordnance and munitions.

The core of the Act was that men could die for uttering words only; no plotting or other action was needed. For treason the punishment involved being drawn on a hurdle, hanged, cut down alive, disembowelled, castrated and finally beheaded.

The pulpit
The sixteenth-century equivalent of television, this was the most effective weapon for getting information across to the largest number of people. It was, of course, a platform as useful for those opposing as for those supporting the Government, and there is significant evidence of priests using the pulpit and the confessional to attack the innovations of the Reformation. To combat this, Cromwell introduced a nationwide scheme for licensing preachers and in January 1536 ordered bishops to take action against clergy who were dragging their feet over reform.

Injunctions
Injunctions (written religious orders) were normally issued by bishops in their dioceses. However, Cromwell began to by-pass the episcopacy and issue directives directly to the clergy. The First Royal Injunction for Clergy (August 1536) was used to enforce the Government's doctrinal and anti-papal position, raise the standards of the clergy, remove superstitious images and enforce the preaching of scripture. A second set of Injunctions in the autumn of 1538 required parishes to have an English Bible and to keep a register of all baptisms, marriages and burials.

Henry VIII
The character of Henry VIII stands like a colossus astride the massive changes of the 1530s. His utter conviction that he was the Supreme Head, his bitter intolerance of opposition and his terrifying ability to lash out at those around him ensured that there were few critics in and around the royal circle. His personal involvement in the burning of the Protestant John Lambert in 1538 revealed the lengths to which he would go to remove opposition and assert his authority. Lambert was burnt at a time when international hostility to Henry's reforms was at its height and the Truce of Nice between Charles V and Francis I made real the possibility of a joint invasion of England. To show the 'purity' of his Catholic faith, Henry, robed in white, watched pitilessly as Lambert was plunged repeatedly into the flames at the end of a lever.

Cromwell
Central to any examination of why the Reformation failed to provoke widespread opposition must be Thomas Cromwell, the King's vigilant, loyal, indefatigable and, where necessary, ruthless vice-gerent in spirituals. He worked ceaselessly, writing countless letters by hand, personally investigating many of the cases of treason, and making himself responsible for all matters of internal security. His enforcement does not appear, though, to have been indiscriminate, and he abided by the lawful methods of trial and investigation.

ACTIVITY

Construct a graph as shown.

Mark the events below along the horizontal axis. The point reached on the vertical axis will be determined by how serious you think the opposition created by these events was to Henry's regime. Connect the points together as a line graph.

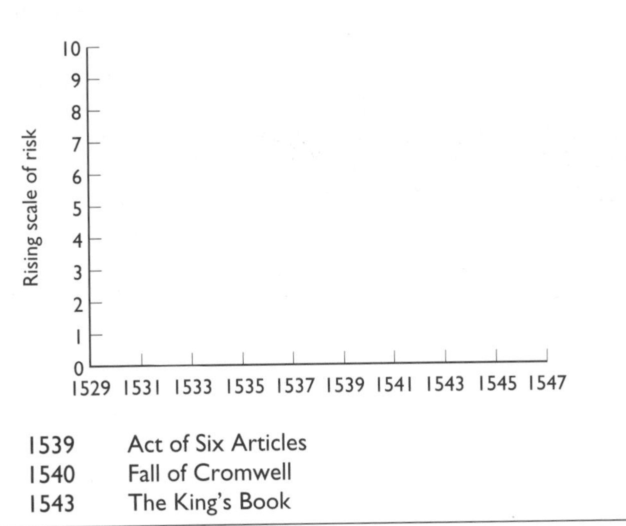

1529	Fall of Wolsey
1530	Clergy accused of *praemunire*
1532	Submission of the Clergy
1533	Marriage to Anne Boleyn
1533	Act in Restraint of Appeals
1534	Act of Supremacy
1534	Treason Act
1535	Execution of Bishop Fisher and Sir Thomas More
1536	Dissolution of the smaller monasteries
1536	Pilgrimage of Grace
1538	The Exeter conspiracy
1538–39	Threat of a foreign invasion
1539	Dissolution of the larger monasteries
1539	Act of Six Articles
1540	Fall of Cromwell
1543	The King's Book

■ 10K Other challenges to the Tudors' position during Henry VIII's reign

- May 1536: The Second Succession Act (made after Henry's marriage to Jane Seymour) declared both Mary and Elizabeth to be illegitimate. This could have created a very dangerous situation if Henry had died with no heir, so Parliament gave him unprecedented powers to choose his heir in his will.
- June 1538: Charles V and Francis I made peace in the Truce of Nice. There was now the serious possibility of a joint invasion and so massive defensive preparations were made.
- August 1538: Sir Geoffrey Pole, Henry Pole (Lord Montague), Margaret, Countess of Salisbury, Henry Courtenay (Marquis of Exeter) and Sir Edward Neville were arrested. Over the next three years all were executed, wiping out almost all the remaining Yorkists.

Printed propaganda

The government, according to Elton (*Policy and Police: The Enforcement of the Reformation in the Age of Thomas Cromwell*), undertook an intensive 'full-scale propaganda campaign' using the printing press. A host of pamphlets rolled off the presses of the King's printer, Thomas Berthelet. Much of this propaganda was written in an easily understandable form and its contents defended the King's position and denounced rebellion. In 1532, for example, *The Glass of Truth* was published in which Henry (partly with his own hand) gave a clear, lively and short version of the law in Leviticus that he argued required him to seek an annulment of his marriage to Catherine of Aragon. The Government also prefaced its new statutes with propagandist preambles before they were distributed throughout the country. However, it is very difficult to determine exactly how much propaganda was produced and impossible to judge the effects it had upon the people, the great majority of whom were, of course, illiterate.

Royal correspondence

Direct, authoritative and chillingly personal correspondence was 'Cromwell's ultimate weapon in the fight against disaffection' (Elton, *Policy and Police: The Enforcement of the Reformation in the Age of Thomas Cromwell*). Cromwell was skilful in using correspondence to generate fear and compliance. On 16 April 1535, for example, letters were sent to JPs ordering recipients to arrest those supporting the Pope. Letters flooded back to Cromwell reporting arrests and asking for 'further pleasure'. Cromwell was subtly creating an informal police force.

On 3 April 1535 he wrote to all bishops ordering them to ensure that all clergy preached the Royal Supremacy, and he enclosed model sermons for them to use. He then followed this up with a circular letter to county sheriffs commanding them to ensure that the bishops fulfilled their duties. In this way, he effectively made the sheriffs the watchdogs of the bishops.

Oaths

Oaths were used as a test of an individual's religious and political commitment. Cromwell and Henry turned the oath into a dramatic and devastating instrument of judgement of Sir Thomas More's loyalty. The oath for the First Act of Succession superficially required recognition of children born to Anne Boleyn and Henry. Although there was virtually no evidence of opposition at this early stage, the Government made an enormous effort to get all important men to swear. The oath for the Second Act of Succession (1536) and the Oath of Supremacy (1536) were less rigorously enforced.

Proclamations

These were public announcements of new laws or situations, made in the localities. Judges at the assize courts, for example, proclaimed the deaths of Fisher and More. Cromwell, however, rarely employed such proclamations, perhaps because he recognised that they could only inform, and not secure obedience.

Church visitations

In 1535 Cromwell arranged a whirlwind visitation of all church and monastic property, with the outward intention of assessing the wealth and condition of the Church. The product of these visitations, however, the *Valor Ecclesiasticus*, was used to justify the dissolution of the smaller monasteries (see p. 121). Through the dissolution Henry removed the last religious group that did not owe direct obedience to him.

FOCUS ROUTE

This chapter started with the hypothesis that 'The Reformation should have provoked more opposition than it did.'

Now that you have analysed the topic, write a response to this hypothesis either agreeing or disagreeing with its premise. Take into account the following issues:

- the extent to which people did oppose the Reformation (e.g. the Pilgrimage of Grace, martyrs)
- the reasons why people opposed the Reformation
- the methods and success of the Government in preventing and suppressing the Reformation
- the different ways in which people could and did oppose the Reformation
- the reasons why people did not oppose the changes (e.g. because they did not realise their significance)
- how close it came to an early Tudor crisis.

E Review: Why wasn't there an early Tudor crisis? How serious was opposition to the Reformation?

Perhaps the best indicator of how serious the opposition was and how near it came to causing a crisis is Henry's own reactions and state of mind. Outwardly, he reacted to all challengers with unshakeable, self-righteous indignation. He was never less than a monumental character and this must partly explain why he was able to weather the storm of the 1530s. Yet significant problems arose in the 1530s and in his reaction to them Henry's fear may be discerned:

- There was a major rebellion in the Pilgrimage of Grace, which Henry could not easily crush.
- Opposition to the religious changes led to Henry slamming on the policy brakes in the form of the Act of Six Articles (1539).
- The threat of a foreign invasion led to the largest fortification building programme in early modern history (1538–40).
- Henry's worry over the succession led him to wipe out a relatively inconsequential branch of the Yorkist family in the Exeter conspiracy (1538–40).

The Government's success in averting deeper trouble must also be attributed partly to the structural defences erected by Cromwell. Cromwell's astute management of the massive changes of the reign ensured that the Government was usually ready before opposition could mobilise and a tight net was drawn around those likely to resist. It is also true that many of the changes had as many supporters as opponents: the dissolution, for example, rocked the spiritual nation, but was welcomed by a large number of gentry who benefited financially from it. In terms of doctrinal reform, the piecemeal nature of the changes and the difficulty of enforcement meant that many would remain ignorant or unaffected by them. Opposition by inaction was a less threatening and more desirable option for most people.

Henry survived but a lesser monarch might well have been engulfed by the challenges. If Henry had attempted the reforms earlier in his reign or if circumstances had been different, the rarely spotted 'early Tudor crisis' might well have been more commonly seen in history textbooks.

KEY POINTS FROM CHAPTER 10: Why wasn't there an early Tudor crisis? How serious was opposition to the Reformation?

1. The most substantial and dangerous expression of opposition to aspects of the Reformation was the Pilgrimage of Grace, which dominated the north of England from October to December 1536.
2. The Pilgrimage of Grace was caused by a mixture of social and religious grievances, which made many localities in the north feel attacked and threatened by an uncaring, aggressive royal government.
3. The Pilgrimage was initially a popular movement, which grew to involve the gentry and the nobility.
4. Cromwell was responsible for the energetic enforcement of the Reformation.
5. The main methods that the Government used to enforce obedience were the new Treason Act, propaganda (via the pulpit and the printing press) and putting individuals under pressure (via oaths, letters and visitations).
6. Most of the opposition to the Reformation was provoked in the 1530s by the dissolution of the monasteries and changes to practices in worship, not by the Royal Supremacy.
7. Many people did not oppose the Reformation because they did not realise the long-term significance of the changes taking place, while others benefited from or agreed with the changes.
8. High-profile, dramatic cases of opposition, such as More's, are untypical. More common was evasion of government orders or outward compliance.

The third fiddle in Europe? How successful was Henry VIII's foreign policy?

CHAPTER OVERVIEW

The dawn of the sixteenth century looked unfavourable for the future Charles V, Francis I and Henry VIII, as none looked likely to ascend to his country's throne. Twists of fate, however, brought them to the ultimate positions of power, and each looked to make his mark on his contemporaries and on history through his actions in the field of foreign affairs. This chapter questions the significance of Henry and of England on the European stage, assessing what they achieved and whether they were powerful or important players.

The main issues that this chapter investigates are:

■ Learning trouble spot

It is vital to study the foreign policy of England from a *European* perspective. Only then will you be able to make a fair assessment of Henry's aims, achievements and failures. Henry himself was keenly interested in events on the Continent and would not make any decisions without being fully briefed on the state of play in the rest of Europe. If you do not view events in a similarly broad European context, you will not understand Henry's motives, the forces influencing him and the limitations on his actions. You may also fall into the trap of over-estimating the sway that England had over events in Europe.

To enable you to have a European context, this chapter has a number of timelines showing the main European events in *italics*. The chapter also adopts a comparative approach, allowing you to assess how much England was influenced by European events (e.g. the crucial battle of Pavia, see pages 158–60). You will be able to make up your own mind about whether Henry was really the 'third fiddle' in Europe.

A What was the situation in Europe like during Henry VIII's reign?

Before you study the details of Henry's foreign policy, it would be useful to:

- remind yourself of the strengths and weaknesses of the European powers by referring to Chart 4B on page 38.
- bear in mind the relative weakness of England as compared with its main European rivals – Valois France and the Habsburg Empire (see Chart 11A).
- reflect on the main concerns and priorities of the key European leaders by looking at Chart 11C on page 150.

■ Learning trouble spot

Students often find foreign policy difficult or intimidating because there are so many dates, events and changes of policy to remember. The third column in Chart 11B has been designed to help students get an easy 'handle' on the main issues, policies and events. Know this column and you have a workable outline of the whole reign.

■ 11A England's relative weakness in the 1520s

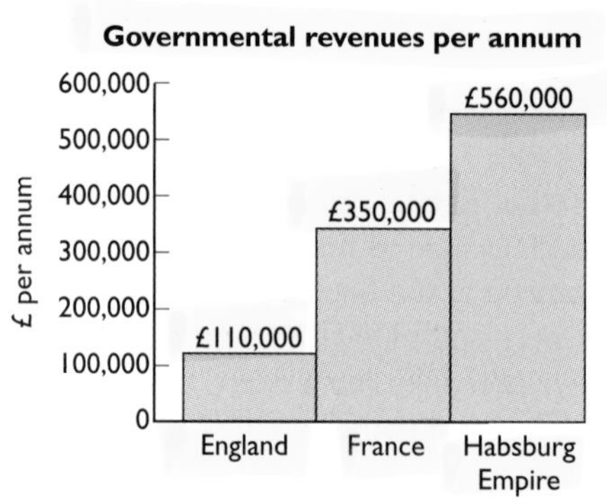

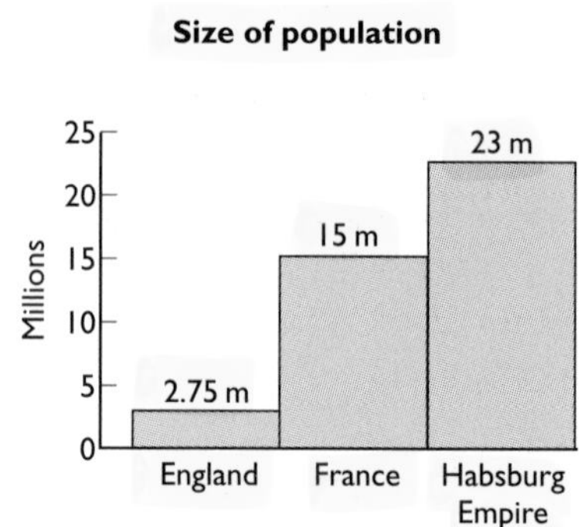

■ 11B Foreign affairs during the reign of Henry VIII

Year	English foreign policy	Events in Europe	Thrust of English policy
1509	Henry crowned Marriage to Catherine of Aragon	League of Cambrai	Anti-French
1511	Anglo-Spanish deal to attack France	Holy League against France	
1512			Start of First French War
1513	Capture of Therouanne Battle of the Spurs Defeat of the Scots at Flodden (death of James IV of Scotland) Capture of Tournai		
1514	Anglo-French peace treaty		End of First French War
1515		Francis I crowned and victorious at Marignano	
1516		Death of Ferdinand of Aragon Franco-Spanish Treaty of Noyon	
1517		Charles I crowned in Spain	
1518	Treaty of London		
1519		Death of Maximilian Charles elected Holy Roman Emperor	
1520	Henry met Charles V in England Field of Cloth of Gold Henry met Charles at Calais		
1521	Wolsey met Francis at Calais and Charles at Bruges Anglo-Imperial alliance	War between Charles V and Francis I Ottomans captured Belgrade	
1522			Start of Second French War
1525	Anglo-French Treaty of the More	Charles V victorious at Pavia Charles refused to partition France	End of Second French War

Year	English foreign policy	Events in Europe	Thrust of English policy
1526		League of Cognac against Charles V Ottomans victorious at Mohacs	
1527	Anglo-French Treaties of Westminster (April) and Amiens (August) Henry sought marriage annulment	Charles V's troops sacked Rome	Anglo-French entente began to develop Foreign policy geared to gaining a divorce
1528	Henry declared war on Charles over the Netherlands (war never actually took place)		
1529	Fall of Wolsey	Defeat of French by Charles V at Landriano (June) Peace of Cambrai (August) Ottomans at the gates of Vienna	
1532	Francis and Henry met at Calais Defensive alliance with French		
1533	Marriage to Anne Boleyn		
1534	Act of Supremacy	Ottomans captured Tunis	Break with Rome completed
1535	Negotiations with Schmalkaldic League	Charles V recaptured Tunis	Search for German Protestant alliance
1536	Execution of Anne Boleyn		
1537	Birth of Edward		
1538		Truce of Nice between Charles and Francis	Fear of invasion
1539	Invasion scare Act of Six Articles Cleves marriage negotiations		
1540	Cleves marriage and divorce Fall of Cromwell	War restarted between Charles and Francis	
1541	Planned meeting between James V and Henry at York Henry crowned King of Ireland		
1542	Scots defeated at Solway Moss James V died and his daughter Mary became Mary, Queen of Scots		Start of Third French War War against Scotland
1543	Treaties of Greenwich (July), repudiated by Scots		Anglo-Imperial alliance
1544	Hertford raided Scotland (May) France was invaded (June) Boulogne captured (September)	Treaty of Crépy ended war between Francis I and Charles V	End of Anglo-Imperial alliance
1545	Attempted invasion by the French French troops sent to Scotland		
1546	Anglo-French Peace of Ardres		End of Third French War
1547	Henry VIII died (January) French troops sent to Scotland	Francis I died Accession of Henry II (March) Charles V defeated German Protestants at Muhlberg	

ACTIVITY

Your aim is to learn the events of Henry's foreign policy using the format of the *Mastermind* quiz programme.

Prepare questions for the 'general' round using *only* the information in Chart 11B. Then select a major event from the list below and learn this in detail for your 'specialist' round. Each person must inform the others in advance of what their chosen specialist subject is so that the others can prepare questions.

Events

- First French War, 1512–14 (page 151)
- Treaty of London, 1518 (pages 152–53)
- Field of Cloth of Gold, 1520 (pages 154–55)
- Second French War, 1522–25 (page 158)
- Divorce proceedings, 1526–33 (pages 161–64)
- Wars with Scotland, 1513 and 1542–47 (pages 172–73)

When all the questions are ready, you can begin, taking it in turns to ask the questions first for the general round for everyone and then for the specialist round. Each round should last two minutes. You can play in pairs.

During questioning, players can pass, in which case you tell them the correct answer at the end. If they get it wrong, you should inform them of the correct answer straight away. The person with the highest number of marks over both rounds wins.

This would be a stimulating revision exercise.

■ 11C What were the main flashpoints in Europe, 1500–59?

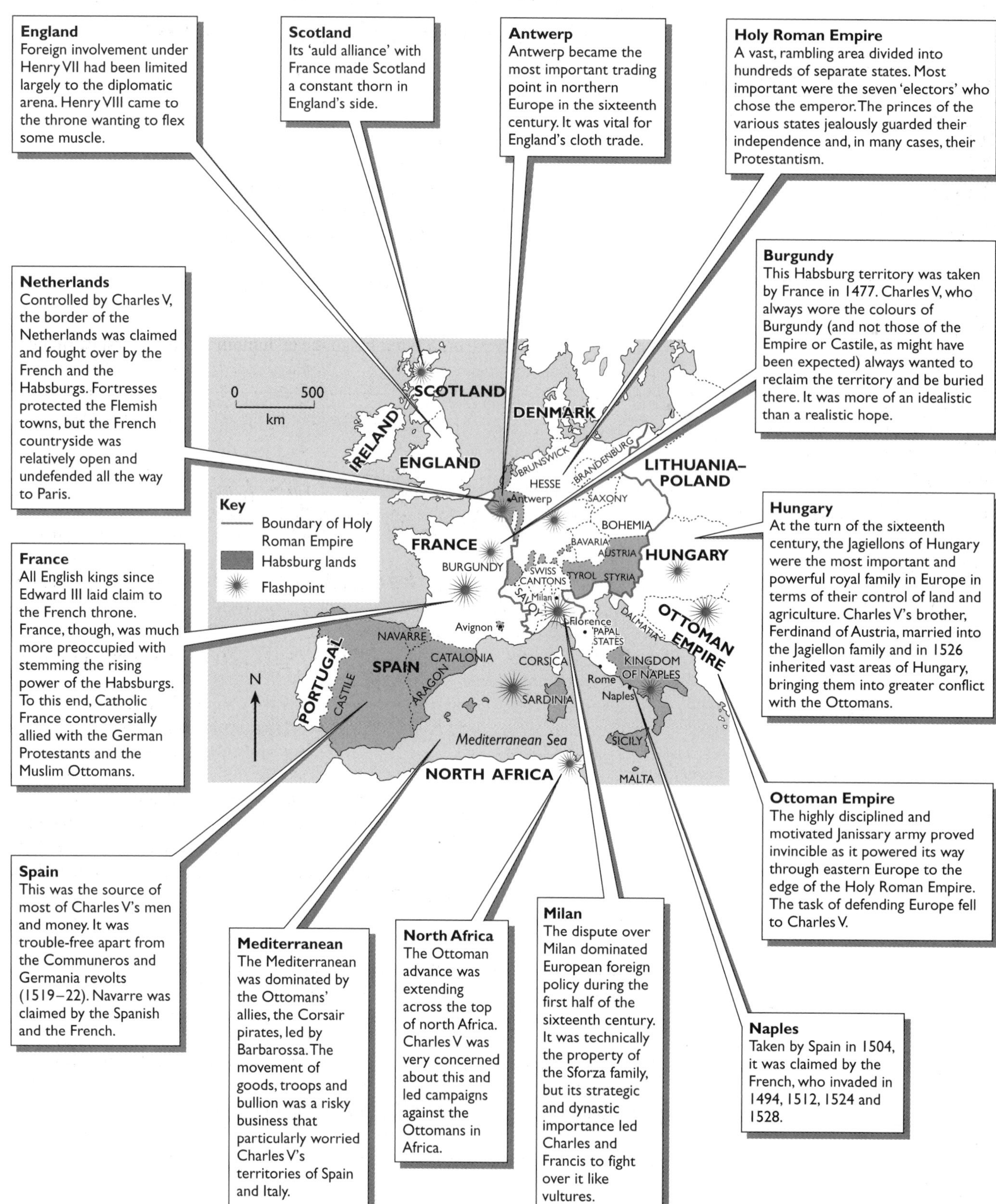

England
Foreign involvement under Henry VII had been limited largely to the diplomatic arena. Henry VIII came to the throne wanting to flex some muscle.
Scotland
Its 'auld alliance' with France made Scotland a constant thorn in England's side.
Antwerp
Antwerp became the most important trading point in northern Europe in the sixteenth century. It was vital for England's cloth trade.
Holy Roman Empire
A vast, rambling area divided into hundreds of separate states. Most important were the seven 'electors' who chose the emperor. The princes of the various states jealously guarded their independence and, in many cases, their Protestantism.
Netherlands
Controlled by Charles V, the border of the Netherlands was claimed and fought over by the French and the Habsburgs. Fortresses protected the Flemish towns, but the French countryside was relatively open and undefended all the way to Paris.
Burgundy
This Habsburg territory was taken by France in 1477. Charles V, who always wore the colours of Burgundy (and not those of the Empire or Castile, as might have been expected) always wanted to reclaim the territory and be buried there. It was more of an idealistic than a realistic hope.
France
All English kings since Edward III laid claim to the French throne. France, though, was much more preoccupied with stemming the rising power of the Habsburgs. To this end, Catholic France controversially allied with the German Protestants and the Muslim Ottomans.
Hungary
At the turn of the sixteenth century, the Jagiellons of Hungary were the most important and powerful royal family in Europe in terms of their control of land and agriculture. Charles V's brother, Ferdinand of Austria, married into the Jagiellon family and in 1526 inherited vast areas of Hungary, bringing them into greater conflict with the Ottomans.
0 500
km
Key
Boundary of Holy Roman Empire
Habsburg lands
Flashpoint
SCOTLAND
IRELAND
ENGLAND
DENMARK
BRUNSWICK
BRANDENBURG
HESSE
Antwerp
SAXONY
LITHUANIA–POLAND
BOHEMIA
BAVARIA
AUSTRIA
HUNGARY
FRANCE
BURGUNDY
SWISS CANTONS
TYROL
STYRIA
SAVOY
Milan
Avignon
Florence
PAPAL STATES
DALMATIA
OTTOMAN EMPIRE
NAVARRE
PORTUGAL
SPAIN
CASTILE
ARAGON
CATALONIA
CORSICA
SARDINIA
Rome
Naples
KINGDOM OF NAPLES
SICILY
MALTA
N
Mediterranean Sea
NORTH AFRICA
Spain
This was the source of most of Charles V's men and money. It was trouble-free apart from the Communeros and Germania revolts (1519–22). Navarre was claimed by the Spanish and the French.
Mediterranean
The Mediterranean was dominated by the Ottomans' allies, the Corsair pirates, led by Barbarossa. The movement of goods, troops and bullion was a risky business that particularly worried Charles V's territories of Spain and Italy.
North Africa
The Ottoman advance was extending across the top of north Africa. Charles V was very concerned about this and led campaigns against the Ottomans in Africa.
Milan
The dispute over Milan dominated European foreign policy during the first half of the sixteenth century. It was technically the property of the Sforza family, but its strategic and dynastic importance led Charles and Francis to fight over it like vultures.
Ottoman Empire
The highly disciplined and motivated Janissary army proved invincible as it powered its way through eastern Europe to the edge of the Holy Roman Empire. The task of defending Europe fell to Charles V.
Naples
Taken by Spain in 1504, it was claimed by the French, who invaded in 1494, 1512, 1524 and 1528.

ACTIVITY

1 Use Chart 11C to determine the three most important foreign policy concerns in rank order for Charles V, Francis I and Henry VIII.
2 Did Henry VIII share the same priorities as Francis I and Charles V?

B How successful was Henry in the First French War, 1512–14?

FOCUS ROUTE

Read pages 151–58 and make notes on the following questions.

1 What were the main successes and failures for England in the First French War?
2 What was the Treaty of London? What are the main reasons why it can be regarded as a success and a failure?
3 What was the Field of Cloth of Gold? How significant was this event?
4 During the years 1509–25, with whom did Henry ally and why?

1509 Henry VIII married Catherine of Aragon
1510 Anglo-French truce renewed
1511 Anglo-Spanish agreement to attack France
Holy League against France
1512 April: England declared war on France
June: Disastrous English campaign in the south west of France
1513 Army led by Henry departed for northern France
Siege and surrender of Therouanne and Tournai
August: Battle of the Spurs
September: Defeat of Scots at Flodden and death of James IV
1514 August: Anglo-French peace treaty

Although clothed in the dignifying language of 'honour', Henry's first campaign against the French was more reminiscent of a football hooligans' outing. Henry's desire for war was driven by xenophobia, a young man's need to 'prove' himself in fighting and the craving for conquest, victories and approval from his peers.

In his search for an active role in Europe against the French, Henry was drawn into the Holy League (Pope, Venetians, Swiss and Ferdinand of Aragon) in November 1511. Under the cover of the alliance, Henry agreed to attack south-west France with Ferdinand, with the intention of capturing Guienne (to which the English maintained a claim). The expedition in June 1512 was a catalogue of disasters and revealed Henry's naïveté in international diplomacy. Ferdinand had no intention of invading France and used the English troops in Guienne as a screen, behind which he seized Navarre, before withdrawing and making peace with the French. The English troops, meanwhile, returned home diseased and mutinous.

Allied to Ferdinand (ruler of Spain), Maximilian (ruler of the Holy Roman Emperor and the Netherlands) and the Pope, Henry personally led an army of 25,000 into northern France in 1513. His armies succeeded in seizing the towns of Therouanne and Tournai after sieges. His cavalry also won the much-hyped battle of the Spurs, when they chased after a detachment of French horse (who dug in their spurs to speed their escape) and captured some notable prisoners. Henry believed he had been draped in glory by the campaign, but a more sober assessment would suggest that he was again learning the cost of dealing with experienced international operators. The two captured towns were on the Burgundian/French border and it was Maximilian, not Henry, who gained strategically from their capture.

Maximilian and Ferdinand made peace with Louis XII of France, so Henry had to follow suit in August 1514. Under the agreement, Henry kept Therouanne and Tournai, was recognised as having a claim to the French throne and received pension arrears. His sister Mary married the toothless and lecherous Louis XII. One significant aspect of the First French War was the emergence of the brilliant new official, Thomas Wolsey, who had organised the campaign so effectively and had brokered the successful peace agreement in 1514. Although he may not have recognised it at the time, Henry had been convincingly shown that England was a third fiddle in Europe in terms of strategy.

C What were England's foreign policy objectives between 1515 and 1521?

1494–1516	*The dominant powers in Europe had been engaged in protracted and complicated war over lands in Italy*
1515	*Death of Louis XII and accession of Francis I and his victory at Marignano*
1516	*Death of Ferdinand of Aragon and accession of Charles I* August: *Franco-Spanish peace agreed at Treaty of Noyon*
1517	*Agreement between Francis and Maximilian, Holy Roman Emperor*
1518	September: Anglo-French peace treaty October: Treaty of London
1519	January: *Death of Maximilian and the beginning of the rivalry between Charles I and Francis I for the election of the next Holy Roman Emperor* June: *Election of Charles V as Holy Roman Emperor*
1520	May: Charles V visited England June: Field of Cloth of Gold July: Henry and Wolsey met Charles
1521	*Habsburg–Valois Wars broke out. They lasted until 1559* August: Calais conference; Wolsey met Charles V at Bruges Treaty of Bruges – an Anglo-Imperial agreement to attack France

In 1515 the new French king, Francis I, won a spectacular and unexpected victory over the Swiss at Marignano. His subsequent seizure of the hotly disputed Milan (see page 150) changed the complexion of Europe overnight. In response to this, Henry VIII ordered Wolsey to construct an anti-French coalition. Wolsey concluded an Anglo-Spanish treaty and made an agreement with Maximilian, but the subsequent events showed how much England's foreign policy was at the mercy of events on the Continent:

- Ferdinand of Aragon died and was replaced with Charles I. Charles made peace with Francis at Noyon which gave substantial territorial concessions to France.
- Maximilian, the Holy Roman Emperor, made peace with France.

England's anti-French policy was thus turned on its head, and Henry and Wolsey were forced to seek peace with France. This process led to the Treaty of London in 1518.

How important was the Treaty of London?

In October 1518 an Anglo-French peace treaty was signed. At the same time, Pope Leo X sent a representative to England to mobilise a campaign against the Ottomans. However, Wolsey hijacked the papal initiative and brilliantly extended it into an international treaty of universal peace and friendship – the Treaty of London. It was subscribed to by over twenty European rulers, including Francis I, Maximilian, Charles I and the Pope. It was hailed by contemporaries as a moral, political and diplomatic triumph. However, the Treaty of London is not even mentioned in general histories of sixteenth-century Europe. How significant was the treaty, if seen in the European context in which we must view all of England's actions and achievements?

SOURCE 11.1 P. S. Crowson, *Tudor Foreign Policy*, 1973, p.78

To Henry VIII, Wolsey offered the enormous prestige of leading Europe towards humanistic peace in place of the traditional prestige of European warfare (which, in any case, he could not finance for more than a few years at a stretch)... Wolsey shifted the emphasis from organising a European truce for the sake of a crusade [against the Ottomans] to organising all European nations into a self-sustaining truce for its own sake.

The treaty of London was not an empty gesture of self-advertisement. It contained detailed agreements which implied serious intent and it was given the sort of sequel which a continuing struggle for peace might be expected to require.

SOURCE 11.2 J. J. Scarisbrick, *Henry VIII*, 1997, pp. 104–5

This was to be the master-document, committing Europe to a new principle in her diplomatic life, namely that of collective security. Europe knew well the peace treaty between several powers, usually former combatants, but had never seen an attempt to create a treaty of universal peace by which all the powers, in advance, swore to punish any breach of the peace by any country...

There were flaws in the construction, certainly, and these showed clearly in the following years, but they are not in themselves evidence of dishonesty so much as of the extreme size of the problem. Nor does Wolsey's evident desire to parade himself, nor his use of dubious methods, prove that the whole project was fraudulent.

SOURCE 11.3 T. A. Morris, *Europe and England in the Sixteenth Century*, 1998, p. 160

This Treaty of London did not last, and thus it has often been dismissed as a mere exercise in egoism. It remains probable, however, that Wolsey was sincere, and he had temporarily outflanked the Pope in his role as European peacemaker. If the prominence and prestige of the crown were the primary aims of foreign policy, then that policy reached its highest point in the Treaty of London.

The Treaty of London, nevertheless, was wholly at the mercy of shifts in 'great power' politics over which England exercised no control. The momentous victory of Charles V in the imperial election (June 1519) caused the greatest of these shifts.

ACTIVITY

1. What, according to Crowson in Source 11.1, had Wolsey achieved in the creation of the Treaty of London?
2. What can we learn about the success of the treaty from the timeline on page 152, showing the broad European context in which it was signed?
3. What limitations in the treaty are revealed by Source 11.3 and by the fact that histories of Europe often omit the treaty?
4. Which of the following criteria should we use to judge whether the Treaty of London was a success?
   - whether it kept the peace
   - how long it lasted for
   - whether it brought prestige to Henry, Wolsey or England
   - how it was viewed by the rest of Europe
   - whether the negotiation itself was an achievement
   - how it has been viewed by historians of English history
   - how it has been viewed by historians of European history
5. Write your own assessment of the Treaty of London in not more than 100 words. Compare your view with those of others.

What was achieved at the Field of Cloth of Gold?

The Field of Cloth of Gold was a meeting that took place between Henry VIII and Francis I in June 1520 just outside Calais. It was the centrepiece of the series of intergovernmental meetings that Henry held in 1520 with Francis and Charles V. Both Francis and Charles wanted to secure Henry as an ally before the Habsburg–Valois war broke out. Henry was happy to be courted by the leading lights in Europe, as he and Wolsey vainly attempted to enforce the Treaty of London and also decide with whom they would ally if war did break out.

The Field of Cloth of Gold is normally remembered for its magnificence, but it should more properly be regarded as a fortnight-long jousting tournament. Henry and Francis I, diplomatically, did not fight each other.

Source 11.4 The Field of Cloth of Gold, painted by an unknown artist

Guisnes – the English outpost in the Calais Pale where Henry was lodged

Ceremonial dragon – this was fired before Wolsey sang Mass

The two kings meeting and embracing as a sign of their great friendship

Henry VIII arriving with Wolsey

ACTIVITY

A spin doctor in modern politics is a member of a political party who puts the best possible slant on events or decisions. Write a short presentation 'spinning' the Field of Cloth of Gold in a manner that would have been pleasing to Henry VIII.

Equally tactfully (or was it really skill?), Francis and Henry were the two most successful jousters. The mastermind behind the magnificent occasion was Wolsey, who organised a train of 6,000 people to follow and attend on the King. The elaborate event cost the equivalent of a year's revenue.

Was the event worthwhile? Certainly nothing of any diplomatic value was achieved. Nothing was decided at the meeting and the countries were at war with each other in less than two years. The weather too had turned against the event with high winds and freak dust storms forcing them to take down the ornate tents soon after they had been erected. Henry may well have been pleased, though, with the honour that he believed such a lavish event brought him.

The Field – the no-man's land where the kings met and the tournament took place

Ardres – the French border town where Francis I pitched his golden tents

Tree of Honour – a lavish, artificial construction decorated with hawthorns (the English symbol since Henry VII was said to have found the crown on a hawthorn bush after Bosworth) and raspberries (the French symbol)

The gallery – two kings and two queens watch the spectacle

The tiltyard – an arena about 275 m long and 100 m wide where the jousting took place

Prefabricated palace – this was much more sophisticated in design than anything Henry had yet built at home

Fountains that were flowing with wine

Triumphal arches built at the English and French ends

Diplomacy in Europe, 1520–21

The death of Maximilian just three months after the Treaty of London completely undermined the idea of peace, co-operation and friendship, as Charles and Francis (and for a time Henry) fought tooth and nail to secure their election to the post of Holy Roman Emperor. In June, Charles was elected, but it was clear now that a serious conflict was soon going to break out between Valois France and the Habsburg Empire of Charles V.

Francis and Charles jostled for advantage in the run-up to the opening of hostilities in the Habsburg–Valois War (which began in earnest in 1521). Henry, therefore, found himself in the pleasing position of being much in demand as an ally. In May 1520, Charles visited Henry in England, and in June, Henry went to meet Francis in France at the Field of Cloth of Gold (see pages 154–55).

Francis I declared war on Charles V in April 1521 when he invaded Luxembourg. The pretence that a peaceful outcome might still be found was maintained at a conference at Calais in August 1521. On the surface, it was a meeting at which Wolsey was supposed to broker a peace deal between representatives of Francis and Charles. In reality, all sides were playing for time and for allies before they made their next move.

SOURCE 11.5 *The Embarkation of Henry VIII*, by an unknown artist. The logistical nightmare of trips to France can be glimpsed in this painting of the King setting out to Calais in 1520. Henry is painted on the second ship from the right, although he actually left after the main fleet because of bad weather

Once the Habsburg–Valois War had started, Henry could act as no more than a linesman, for he lacked sufficient leverage to become an effective referee or arbiter of events. With the prestige that came from being a peacemaker gone, Henry looked to join in the fray. However, Henry and Wolsey had to decide with whom to ally – Francis or Charles?

ACTIVITY

It is August 1521 and war has broken out between Charles V and Francis I. Henry VIII must decide with whom he is going to ally. Use the timeline, the text so far and the table below to decide with whom you would ally. Discuss your decision.

Charles V	Francis I
• He has offered to marry Henry's daughter, Mary. • Charles controls the Netherlands, which is vital for trade. • He is the nephew of Catherine of Aragon.	• An Anglo-French alliance is the only way of stopping Habsburg dominance. • A deal with Charles could mean the French allying with Scotland. • Francis I is in a weak position, so he might make a better deal.

Two days after the arrival of the French representatives at the Calais conference, Wolsey headed off to Bruges to meet Charles V. Under the Treaty of Bruges, England and Charles agreed to declare war on France if Francis refused to make peace. The treaty was to be kept secret until November by which time Henry would have received the next instalment of his French pension (see page 175). Charles was to compensate Henry for the pensions he would have to forgo during the war, and Charles also became engaged to Mary, Henry VIII's young daughter.

Conclusion

The period 1515–21 was notable for the great meetings in London, the Field of Cloth of Gold, the Calais conference and Wolsey's meeting with Charles in Bruges. Henry was where he wanted to be: mixing it with the two great monarchs of Europe. Some historians have ascribed weighty motives to Wolsey's control of this period of foreign policy, such as humanistic peace (Scarisbrick, *Henry VIII*) or his desire to become Pope (Pollard, *Henry VIII*). What is more likely is that Wolsey was aiming to please his master by giving him status in Europe through hosting grand meetings with Charles and Francis, with the added extras of forming a peace treaty and acting as arbiter between them. England remained at the mercy of events in Europe, and when Francis and Charles decided on war, all Henry could do was to decide which one to follow.

D How successful was Henry in the Second French War, 1522–25?

1522 Declaration of war against France; English troops in Picardy
1523 English troops unsuccessful in march on Paris; Duke of Bourbon joined coalition against Francis
1525 February: Charles V's victory over Francis I at Pavia
March: Amicable Grant demanded
Charles V refused to partition France
August: Anglo-French Treaty of the More

England declared war on France in May 1522 but Wolsey's and Henry's fears that they would be abandoned by their Imperial ally were immediately borne out. Charles V was focusing his attention on northern Italy, recovering Milan in 1521 and winning the battle of La Bicocca in 1522. Imperial forces, therefore, provided no support for English troops who were making ineffective raids into Picardy. In 1523, however, the Duke of Bourbon, one of the greatest noblemen in France, took up arms against Francis. The possibility of a triple attack on Paris was now opened up and new agreements were hastily arranged. The Duke of Suffolk with 11,000 troops began to march on Paris in August. The direction of the march on Paris by the other allies was anything but straight. Bourbon failed to raise support and Charles's attacks from the Netherlands and Spain did not materialise. Suffolk's army returned in disarray. Henry had been abandoned by his allies again (as he had been in the First French War), but this time he had absolutely nothing to show for it. Wolsey secretly began looking for peace in 1524, until the bombshell of Pavia exploded.

E Why was the battle of Pavia the main turning point of the reign?

FOCUS ROUTE

Read pages 158–60 and take notes on the following:

1 How did the battle of Pavia alter the balance of power in Europe?
2 What were the consequences for England of the battle of Pavia?

On 24 February 1525 the army of Francis I was routed by Imperial forces at Pavia in northern Italy. Ten thousand French soldiers were killed and Francis himself was trapped under his horse and captured. This battle rocked the foundations of European policy, which had been based on the unstable balance of power that existed between Valois France and the Habsburg Empire.

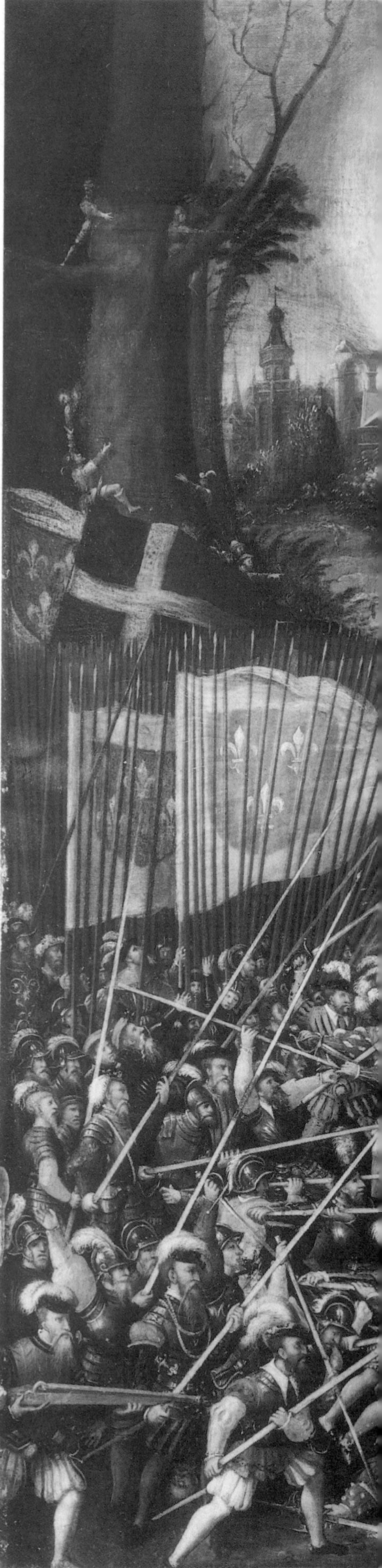

SOURCE 11.6 The battle of Pavia, painted by an unknown German artist, c.1530

ACTIVITY

The paintings on pages 154–59 could be valuable sources.

a) What might they tell us?
b) What questions do we need to ask before we can decide on their value?

328

SOURCE 11.7 The French confirmation of the Treaty of Amiens, 1527. This year saw more diplomatic activity with France than any other and the results have been described as a 'diplomatic revolution' (Starkey (ed.), *A European Court in England*). English policy towards France did a volte-face and England and France were now at peace until 1543. The Treaties of the More, Westminster and Amiens were marked with one of the most spectacular but least well-known celebrations of the reign at Greenwich

■ 11D Why was Pavia the main turning point of the reign?

1525 February: Charles enjoyed a crushing victory at Pavia.

SO ...

1525 Henry attempted to persuade Charles to make a decisive joint assault on France that would lead to Henry being crowned King of France and Charles becoming the monarch of all Christendom.

SO ...

1525 March: Wolsey gave orders to raise the Amicable Grant. This forced loan was needed to pay for Henry's proposed invasion of France. However, the Grant aroused serious opposition, which led to a rebellion, and the Grant was abandoned.

BUT ...

1525 Charles refused to attack France and annulled the proposed marriage between himself and Henry's daughter Mary.

SO ...

Having been rejected by Charles, England needed to make a fundamental change of policy towards France.

SO ...

1525 August: Anglo-French Treaty of the More – a friendship treaty.

1526 January: Charles V forced the Treaty of Madrid on Francis I.
Francis rejected the treaty immediately on his release and looked to form a coalition against Charles.

SO ...

1526 May: The League of Cognac was formed against the Holy Roman Empire. The League was made up of France, Venice, the Papacy, Florence and the exiled Duke of Milan.
England joined in September 1526 as a 'protector', but not as a member.

1527 April: Anglo-French Treaty of Westminster.
August: Treaty of Amiens – an Anglo-French agreement to attack Charles V.

SO ...

Pavia had forced England to end its old enmity with France. The new Anglo-French *entente* was cemented by the Treaties of the More, Westminster and Amiens. France and England did not go to war again until 1543.

F How did foreign affairs affect Henry's attempts to annul his marriage to Catherine of Aragon?

FOCUS ROUTE

Read pages 161–64 and make notes on the following:

1 What were the three main ways in which Wolsey sought to gain an annulment for Henry VIII?
2 What were the events in Europe that frustrated him in his efforts?

1527 Henry wanted to separate from Catherine of Aragon
May: *Sack of Rome by Charles' troops; Clement VII captured by Charles V*
1528 Declaration of war against Charles V in the Netherlands
French successfully invaded Italy down to Naples
1529 June: *French were defeated at the battle of Landriano*
Papal–Imperial Treaty of Barcelona
August: *Franco–Imperial Peace of Cambrai*
October: Fall of Wolsey
1532 Henry VIII and Anne Boleyn met Francis I at Calais; defensive alliance made
1533 Henry married Anne Boleyn

The year 1527 brought along with it the King's 'Great Matter' – the issue of securing an annulment of his marriage to Catherine of Aragon (see Chapter 9). This problem was more formidable than any Wolsey had yet faced. His future depended on finding a solution, but this could only be found overseas and Wolsey was tossed and turned on the tide of European politics as he attempted to get his master's divorce.

Europe in 1527

In May 1527, Charles V's mercenary troops sacked the city of Rome, shocking Europe with a week-long orgy of violence and brutality and the imprisonment of the Pope. The impact of this event is hard to over-estimate. If the victory at Pavia had left the states of Europe in the palm of Charles's hand, the sacking of Rome had added the Pope and the Catholic Church to his collection.

Finding a legal solution

In normal circumstances, a papal dispensation allowing the annulment of Henry's marriage to Catherine of Aragon would have been a relatively small matter. There were lots of precedents and the Pope would normally have been happy to oblige. However, the events of 1527 had put Charles in complete control of the Pope and as a consequence had sent Wolsey's policy into a spin. There was now little possibility of persuading the Pope to grant the annulment because Charles was the nephew of Catherine of Aragon and was utterly opposed to it.

Finding a military solution: war with the Netherlands

The events of 1527 meant that Wolsey needed to find a way of restoring the Pope's diplomatic independence. This would necessitate military action against Charles V, and Wolsey looked to the new-found alliance with the French for assistance, explaining Henry's predicament to Francis I. As France was already committed to invading Italy to recover Milan and Naples, they together declared war on Charles V in 1528. Under the Treaty of Amiens in 1527, England agreed to help pay for the French attack. Wolsey suspended trade with the Netherlands as a precursor to war and as a diplomatic tool to force the Habsburgs to further the annulment policy. But Wolsey and Henry soon found themselves having to back-pedal quickly. Henry was shocked by the public protests by English cloth workers who were dependent on the Antwerp markets, and a truce was made with the Netherlands in June 1528.

Europe in 1528–29

Francis I's troops were initially very successful in their invasion of Italy in 1528 and reached Naples in the south. Disease amongst their ranks forced them back, however, and at the battle of Landriano, in June 1529, Charles was once again victorious. The Pope made peace with Charles in the Treaty of Barcelona, and Francis followed suit in the Peace of Cambrai in August. Charles was now dominant, and Henry and Wolsey were left stranded. (*Continued on page 164.*)

What can the painting *The Ambassadors* show us about European attitudes to Henry's break with Rome?

The double portrait in Source 11.8 of the French ambassadors Jean de Dinteville (left) and Georges de Selve presents a dignified and calm façade to the world. The two men appear inscrutable and impassive, surrounded by objects that represent the advances of the Renaissance age with which they wish to be associated. Recent research and restoration have, however, revealed a complex and fascinating meaning to the picture. Once decoded, the painting becomes a ferocious criticism of Henry's break with Rome. Behind the calm façade, all hell is breaking loose.

The background

Jean de Dinteville had been sent by Francis I to represent him in England during 1533. In the previous year there had been tense negotiations as England, France and the Papacy struggled to find an acceptable solution to Henry's problems. Dinteville arrived too late and was too powerless to influence the events. He attended Anne Boleyn's coronation and observed, with evident disgust, that Anne was pregnant.

Georges de Selve, bishop of Lavaur, had made it his mission to heal the deep religious wounds opening in Europe. He had attended the Diet of Speyer in Germany in 1529, where the Protestants and Catholics attempted to settle their differences, and he had pleaded with the Protestants to return to the fold. He was in England on a similar mission, but it must have been clear that Henry had already made the decision to seek an annulment of his marriage to Catherine of Aragon.

The riddle

The Ambassadors, then, records the failed mission of two obscure diplomats. This raises the question: why was it painted? Why would Dinteville commission and pay so much money for such a major portrait when full-length portraits were normally reserved for royalty? Why are they surrounded by so many objects? And what is that bizarre grey slash across the bottom of the picture meant to signify?

The hidden meaning

In subtle, disguised ways, the painting portends a chaotic and destructive future because of Henry's split with Rome. The clues that support this conclusion are hidden so well that they are apparent only to those who have been told the painting's secrets. Recent restoration has amazingly revealed the central clue to the mystery of the meaning of the painting. It is the tiny silver crucifix, half-concealed behind the curtain in the top-left hand corner. The crucifix shows that the disappearance of the Catholic faith lies at the heart of the painting's message. That the issue under attack is specifically the break with Rome and not the Reformation in general is pinpointed by the date on the pillar dial: 11 April 1533 – the deadline set by Henry VIII for Pope Clement VII to agree to the annulment.

The most powerful message is contained in the striking grey mass at the bottom of the painting, which dramatically transforms into a perfectly proportioned skull. The skull represents death and in the context of the picture is probably pointing to the conflicts and deaths that it is believed will result from Henry's move to Protestantism. All of the objects on the table add, in discreet but irresistible ways, to the sense of chaos and division.

Dinteville must have felt himself at a momentous crossroads of history to want to commission such a painting. He presumably will have wanted to reveal to visitors to his château and to posterity his view of how catastrophic England's separation from the Papacy was going to be. Why else would he choose to have his expensive portrait dominated by a cunningly obscured skull?

SOURCE 11.8 Hans Holbein's *The Ambassadors*. A critical study of the painting and its cryptic symbolism reveals the sharp attack it is making on Henry's break with Rome. The objects in the painting are used to point to the impending chaos that will result from the break

The hidden silver cross.
The navigational and astronomical instruments are all misaligned to give a sense of earthly and celestial chaos.
The lute string is broken.
The anamorphosic skull – to see the transformation, look from the right-hand side of the picture with your eye level with the skull and very close to the page.
A pair of dividers.
The first word on the page of this ordinary maths book reads 'Dividiit' (let division be made).
The hymn book is open at the 'Veni Sanctus Spiritus', a hymn that was traditionally used to call for Church unification.

Finding a diplomatic solution

The Pope, Clement VII, did not rule out an annulment for Henry because keeping the possibility open was a useful bargaining tool in his struggle to free himself from Charles V's clutches. In June 1528 at the height of French power in Italy, he therefore commissioned Wolsey and Cardinal Campeggio to investigate the case in England. He also secretly gave Campeggio a dispensation making Henry's marriage to Catherine invalid. Clement was, however, playing for time and the court of investigation did not open until May 1529. A month later, after the battle of Landriano, Charles once again held sway and the Pope withdrew the court to Rome in July 1529. The last chance of an annulment being granted had gone. Wolsey had failed because of events on the Continent and he fell from power in October 1529.

ACTIVITY

This activity tests your understanding of the effects of foreign policy on Henry's search for an annulment. You need a chessboard and the chess pieces listed below. The pieces should be placed in their normal starting positions on the board (on either side).

You need three people: one person controls the black pieces, one controls the white pieces, and the third person asks the questions and checks that the answers given are correct. (Answers are on page 323.) Each player is asked a question (white first). If they answer correctly, they can move a piece according to normal chess rules. The aim of the game is to checkmate their opponent. The game is a draw if all the questions have been asked before checkmate is reached.

The pieces

Black

- King – Charles V, nephew of Catherine of Aragon, who strongly opposes the annulment
- Queen – Catherine of Aragon, who is utterly committed to maintaining the marriage with Henry VIII
- Bishop – Pope Clement VII who, because of the sack of Rome and Charles V's dominant position, is not in a position to grant an annulment
- Rook – Cardinal Campeggio, a wily, wary, gout-ridden old man whose purpose is to delay any decision being reached

White

- King – Henry VIII, a troubled man who is attracted to Anne Boleyn, desperate for an heir and believes that his marriage to Catherine offended God
- Queen (to be) – Anne Boleyn, who refuses to become Henry's mistress and has her eyes set on the big prize
- Bishop – Cardinal Wolsey, who needs to succeed in getting Henry a marriage annulment if he is to save his position and his neck
- Knight – Francis I, who is not a man of iron commitment to the Catholic faith and so is willing to give support to Henry if it helps to undermine his arch-rival, Charles V

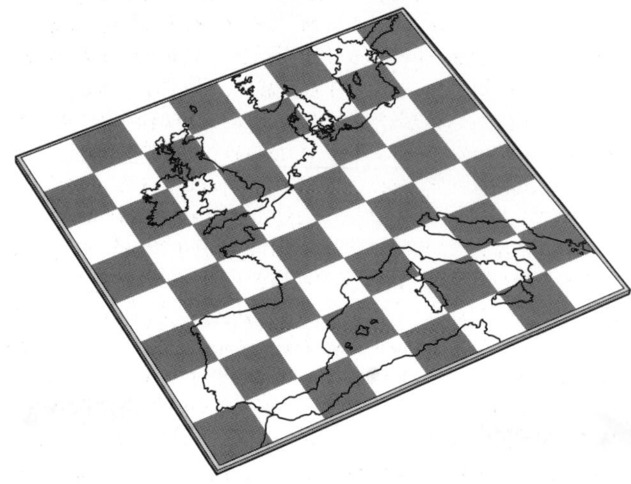

Stage 1: Proving that the marriage was void

1 What did the White King request from the Black Bishop?
2 How would the Black Bishop have normally felt about this move?
3 How did the White Queen force the White King into this situation?
4 What move by the Black King limited the freedom of the Black Bishop?
5 What did the White Bishop now consider?

Stage 2: Using military force to free up the Pope

6 What was the Black King's position in 1527?
7 Under what Anglo-French treaty of 1527 did the White Bishop provide money in 1528 for the White Knight?
8 What territories did the Black King control that the White Knight wanted?
9 What moves did the White Knight make in 1528?
10 What did the Black King do in June 1529?
11 What move did the White Bishop make in 1528 against the Black King?
12 What did the Black King and White Bishop agree in June 1528?
13 What agreement was made between the White Knight and the Black King in 1529?
14 What agreement was made between the Black Bishop and the Black King in 1529?
15 What effect did these agreements have on the White King?

Stage 3: Using diplomacy to get the annulment

16 Why did the Black Bishop not rule out an annulment?
17 What did the White Knight do in 1528 which allowed the Black Bishop more freedom of action?
18 What was the Black Rook sent to do?
19 Why was a settlement so important to the White Bishop?
20 What did the Black Bishop do in July 1529?
21 What happened to the White Bishop? When?
22 When was the marriage of the White Queen, which finally knocked the Black Queen off the board?
23 Which of the two pieces had been removed from power by 1533?

G Who ran England's foreign policy between 1514 and 1529 – Henry or Wolsey?

Why is this question difficult to answer?

Many of the interesting aspects of modern politics take place behind a veil of secrecy. The in-fighting, the struggles for power and the disputes often remain hidden from the glare of the media. However, it is fortunate for modern-day political analysts that many politicians have the convenient habit, after they have lost office, of spilling the beans in diaries, interviews and newspaper exclusives.

Unfortunately for historians of the Tudor period, there was no desire or financial incentive for Tudor politicians to 'dish the dirt'. We are therefore left to peer behind the many layers of façade that cloak their discussions and encounters. In the particular case of deciding who ran English foreign policy – Henry or Wolsey – we have a number of other difficulties to contend with:

- the complexity of Henry's character
- the resentment felt by Wolsey's rivals at the lofty position that this butcher's son was able to maintain for so long
- the lack of evidence of the personal relationship between the two men.

Who did contemporaries think was in control?

SOURCE 11.9 Wolsey's own account of his relationship with Henry, related to his gentleman usher, George Cavendish, in 1530, shortly before Wolsey's death

For I assure you I have often kneeled before him in his privy chamber on my knees the space of an hour or two to persuade him from his will and appetite; but I could never bring to pass to dissuade him therefrom. Thereafter, Master Kingston [another person in the room with them], if it chance hereafter you to be one of his privy council . . . I warn you to be well advised and be assured what matter ye put in his head; for ye shall never pull it out again.

SOURCE 11.10 A satirical poem written by John Skelton, a contemporary critic of Wolsey

Why come ye not to court
To which court?
To the King's court,
*Or to Hampton Court?**
Nay, to the King's court!
The King's court
Should have the excellence
But Hampton Court
Hath the pre-eminence.

* Hampton Court was the palace Wolsey built for himself.

SOURCE 11.11 Giustiniani, Venetian ambassador to England

This Cardinal is the person who rules both the King and the entire kingdom.

SOURCE 11.12 Polydore Vergil, contemporary historian of the Tudors

Wolsey carried on all business at his own will, since no one was of more value to the King.

Who do historians think was in control?

SOURCE 11.13 J. J. Scarisbrick, *Henry VIII*, 1997, pp.70–71

For much of his career as Chancellor, it was Wolsey who alone guided English affairs. His quick, strong hands grasped everything because Henry seemed unable, or unwilling, to make the smallest decision himself. Who shall attend upon the Princess Mary? What shall he reply to the regent of the Netherlands? . . . All these Wolsey had to decide for him, for they were problems which this apparently helpless man, for all his bluster and swagger, could not resolve. Wolsey must be servant and master, creature yet impresario; he must abase himself and yet dominate, playing a part which only a man of a superlative energy, self-confidence and loyalty could have endured. Yet the king who so often seemed to want nothing more than to dance and to hunt, and to have only the feeblest grip on royal duties, was also the man who, time and again, could show a detailed grasp of foreign affairs and hold his own with, if not outdo, foreign ambassadors; who could suddenly put off his supper until he had dealt with a stack of business; who could pounce on something Wolsey had missed, cut a proposal to ribbons with a few swift strokes, assess a situation exactly, confidently overrule his minister, correctly predict that a plan could not work, demand the recall of his ambassadors, order that undertaking. There is no doubt that, at times, Henry was furiously involved in public business and in commanding partnership with Wolsey, and that he could break into his minister's conduct of affairs with decisive results. There is no doubt that he had intense interest in certain things – in ships, in war, in what Francis I was doing, for example. That he was the true source of the really important events of his reign – the wars, the divorce, the breach with Rome – is scarcely disputable; and by the mid-1520s he seems to have acquired much more confidence and control (which he never wholly surrendered thereafter).

SOURCE 11.14 P. S. Crowson, *Tudor Foreign Policy*, 1973, p. 75

He [Henry] was like the creator and owner of a private business who has decided to retire to the Bahamas and leave his affairs to a salaried manager. Nevertheless, his mind is never wholly detached from his creation; three times a week he is on the trans-Atlantic telephone to be sure that his manager is pressing forward with the right policies; three times a year, whenever particularly urgent or brilliant opportunities seem to offer themselves, he flies into London unannounced to share with his manager the excitement of the moment, even erratically to take control himself. So it was with Henry between 1515 and 1529.

SOURCE 11.15 S. J. Gunn and P. G. Lindley (eds), *Cardinal Wolsey: Church, State and Art*, 1991, p. 157

The king took a more consistent and informed interest in foreign policy than in most other areas of government, and this both eased and complicated Wolsey's task. King and cardinal could work as a very effective double-act, using audiences with the king, 'simple and candid by nature', to encourage ambassadors frustrated by the cardinal's obstructiveness. Wolsey could use the king's disapproval as an excuse for refusing to contemplate concessions, or win goodwill from an ambassador by stressing the trouble he had had in persuading Henry to accept a proposal. Henry enjoyed lecturing envoys on such themes as the benefits of universal peace, but was equally happy to leave the grind of detailed negotiation to his minister. They regularly discussed important issues together, enabling Wolsey to conduct matters by his 'wisdom, discretion and intencion and mynde of his grace therein, by mowthe'. When they were apart, Wolsey took care to send on news from abroad as it reached him, keeping Henry in touch with the latest developments. At all times the most significant decisions, above all those of war and peace, rested with the king, and Wolsey never questioned the fact; indeed, he found it politic to refer to all the best ideas on policy, whatever their origin, as Henry's own.

Conclusion: who was in charge of foreign policy?

If a theatre analogy is used, Henry was the creator or the writer of foreign policy and Wolsey was the director who took charge of the details and by so doing imposed his own distinctive stamp on the proceedings. However, the ultimate say remained with the creator, Henry. It was his wilfulness that forced the *volte-face* in policy after the battle of Pavia; it was he who forced the destructive annulment proceedings; and it was he who wanted the wars against France. Wolsey gained prestige from the foreign policy he directed, but he always ultimately had to do his master's bidding.

ACTIVITY

1 Study Sources 11.9–11.12. What view did contemporaries have about the role that Wolsey played in government?
2 Summarise in the form of a newspaper headline the views of the historians in Sources 11.13–11.15.
3 How can you explain the differences between the views expressed by the contemporaries and the historians?
4 Who played a greater role in
   a) creating and
   b) directing the following policies and events:
      i) First French War (1512–14)
      ii) rivalry with Francis I (1515)
      iii) Treaty of London (September 1518)
      iv) Field of Cloth of Gold (1520)
      v) Treaty of Bruges (1521)
      vi) Second French War (1523–25)
      vii) the appeal to Charles to give France to England after Pavia (February 1525)
      viii) the annulment proceedings?

H How successful was Henry in the Third French War, 1543–46?

FOCUS ROUTE

In what ways was the Third French War a re-run of the First and Second French Wars and in what ways was it different? Copy and complete the following table:

	First French War, 1512–14	**Second French War, 1522–25**	**Third French War, 1543–46**
Allies	Ferdinand of Aragon and Maximilian, Holy Roman Emperor		
Causes	Hostility towards France		
Henry's aims	Glory		
Main events	Capture of Therouanne and Tournai Battle of Spurs		
Settlement	Kept Therouanne and Tournai Received a pension from France Henry's sister, Mary, married Louis XII		
Successful?	Henry duped by allies, but gained some glory		

1541 *June: Francis I and Charles V at war again*
1542 *French alliance with the Ottomans*
August: England declared war on Scotland
November: Decisive English victory over the Scots at Solway Moss
Death of James V of Scotland. Mary, Queen of Scots, becomes Queen
1543 February: Anglo-Imperial alliance against France
July: Treaty of Greenwich signed with Scotland
December: Treaty of Greenwich rejected by Scotland
1544 May: Earl of Hertford sacked Scottish towns
June: Army led by Henry departed for France
September: Boulogne captured
Franco-Imperial Peace of Crépy
1545 July: French attempted invasion of south-west England. French troops sent to Scotland
1546 June: Anglo-French Peace of Ardres

Just as the opening of the Habsburg-Valois War in 1521 created the conditions which led England to declare war on France in 1522, so the re-opening of the Habsburg-Valois War in 1541 again precipitated England's declaration of war against France in 1543. Again, Henry opted to ally with Emperor Charles V. Under the agreement both rulers pledged to invade France within two years. However, Henry was forced to delay invasion until 1544 because of an unexpected and dramatic turn of events in Scotland.

The collapse of the Scots at the battle of Solway Moss in 1542 and the subsequent and surprising death of James V had left an infant on the throne and a Scotland ripe for the taking (see pages 172–73).

By the middle of 1544 Henry's ambitions in Scotland had ground to a halt and he was able to focus his attention more fully on France. In June he sailed to Calais at the head of an army of 48,000 men. The agreed plan was for Henry and Charles to both march on Paris, but Henry very clearly had other ideas and split his forces: Norfolk attacked Montreuil and Henry besieged Boulogne. Recent research by Macmahon ('The English Campaign in France 1543–45') has suggested that, in his Third French War, Henry purposely decided to take revenge for being duped and abandoned earlier in his reign. In 1544 he invaded France with the deliberate policy of conquering for *himself* on *his* terms, and this time it was he who abandoned his ally.

Henry wanted Boulogne and he succeeded in acquiring it in September. Abandoning Charles did backfire somewhat, as Charles made a sudden and unexpected settlement with Francis at Crépy. Francis was now free to turn his desire for vengeance on England and vowed, 'to win as much as the Englishmen had on this side of the sea'. In this mood, Francis prepared to invade.

Conclusion

By September 1545 the invasion attempt had failed and both sides were ready to initiate peace talks. In June 1546 the Treaty of Ardres was signed and under its terms Henry was able to hold on to Boulogne. France also agreed to pay all outstanding pensions. The war had drained the English purse enormously. The Third French War and the conflict with France had cost £2 million. The wars were financed by:

- the dissolution of the monasteries
- debasment of the coinage
- large-scale borrowing on the Antwerp money market.

The consequence of this, according to Diarmaid MacCulloch in *The Reign of Henry VIII: Politics, Policy and Piety*, was that Henry had, 'engineered a mid-Tudor crisis even if fate had not stepped in with epidemics and wretched harvests in the Edwardian and Marian years'. Henry, though, would probably have regarded the capture of Boulogne as worth the expense. In the last of his French wars he had, at least, not been completely duped by his foreign allies.

SOURCE 11.16 Henry VIII lays siege to Boulogne in 1544

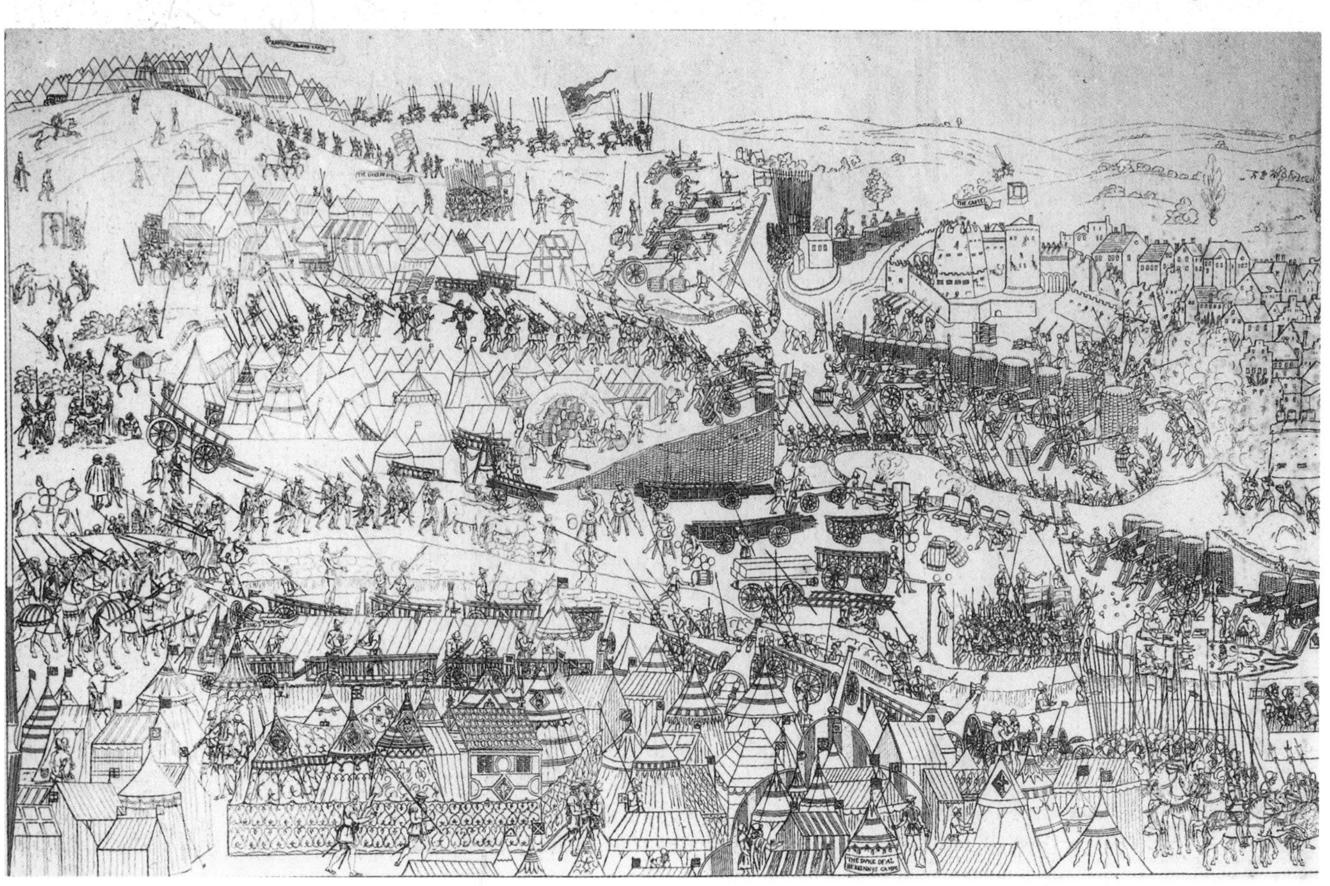

1 How did Henry fare in his rivalry with Charles V and Francis I?

The early part of the sixteenth century saw three young, ambitious monarchs ascend to their thrones. The natural competitiveness of each of these young men was brought out in an open and blatant rivalry that was closely observed by the court-watchers across Europe. Henry was acutely conscious of this rivalry and even had a conversation with a Venetian ambassador who had just passed through France about his physique as compared with that of Francis.

'Is he as tall as I am?'

'Yes, Your Grace, just about.'

'And as broad across the shoulders?'

'Not quite.'

'Ah! and his legs?'

'Rather thin, Your Majesty.'

'Look at mine!' And the King opened the folds of his tunic to reveal his thighs. 'And my calves too are every bit as beautiful!'

Comparing well with his fellow monarchs was probably one of the most important criteria of success for Henry. We shall try to assess how well he fared.

Henry VIII, painted in 1520 by an unknown artist

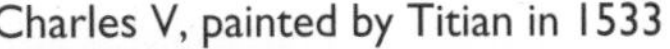

Charles V, painted by Titian in 1533

Francis I, painted by Jean Clouet

SOURCE 11.17 The young monarchs Henry VIII, Charles V and Francis I in their prime. All three were well respected for their prowess in jousting and in the arts of warfare

SOURCE 11.18 A description of Francis I towards the end of his reign, from L. B. Smith, *Henry VIII: The Mask of Royalty*, 1971, pp. 220–21

The big-nosed Valois King ... was visibly disintegrating in 1542, eaten up with what the Imperial Ambassador at varying times called a 'gathering under the lower parts', an 'ulcerated bladder', or chauvinistically the 'French disease'. [The disease was syphilis, which the French called the 'Italian disease'.] ... the Valois prince withered into an embarrassing and undignified roué [a lecherous man]. The once brilliantly articulate speaker fell victim to dental decay, mouthing his words between toothless gums; his face grew puffy and pustular; and men no longer laughed at the jest that the King's obsession for the hunt was so great that when old and sick he would be carried to the chase and when dead would go in his coffin.

SOURCE 11.19 A description of Emperor Charles V towards the end of his reign, from L. B. Smith, *Henry VIII: The Mask of Royalty*, 1971, p. 219

Methodically the Emperor Charles had kept a calendar of his gout – eleven attacks in sixteen years – but by 1544 anxiety and gluttony had made a travesty of the documentation; the pain had become so frequent that he gave up recording it ... Of the three sovereigns, the worn and unassuming Charles, who had lived as many years as the century and had perambulated the length and breadth of Europe – nine times to the Lowlands and Germany, seven times to Italy and Spain, four times to France and twice to England – had the toughest and most resilient personality.

SOURCE 11.20 A description of Henry VIII towards the end of his reign, from J. J. Scarisbrick, *Henry VIII*, 1968, p. 626

By now he was becoming a man of huge girth, eating and drinking prodigiously. His great weight must have exacerbated his condition no less than did his dauntless zeal for riding. In March 1544 – just as he was about to set out on his last campaign – the ulcer flared up once more and the fever returned. But in July of that year he crossed to Calais and rode a great courser to the siege of Boulogne. Though he was carried about indoors in a chair and hauled upstairs by machinery, he would still heave his vast, pain-racked body into the saddle to indulge his love of riding and to show himself to his people, driven by an inexorable will to cling to his ebbing life.

SOURCE 11.21 Henry VIII, c. 1542, by an unknown artist

■ 11E Military achievements: victories and conquests 1509–47

Charles V	Francis I	Henry VIII
Captured Milan Battle of Bicocca (1522)	Battle of Marignano (1515) made him dominant in Europe	Battle of the Spurs (1513) Captured Therouanne and Tournai (1513) Battle of Flodden (1513)
Battle of Pavia (1525) Francis I captured	Invaded Naples (1524), then driven back	Battle of Solway Moss (1542)
Battle of Landriano (1529) France gave up claims in Italy	Invaded Naples (1528), then driven back	Captured Boulogne (1544)
Recaptured Tunis from the Ottomans (1535)		
Came within about 30 kilometres of Paris, then decided to make peace (1544)		
Defeated German Protestants at battle of Muhlberg (1547)		

■ 11F Achievements in peace: the principal European treaties, 1509–47

Treaty	Charles V	Francis I	Henry VIII
Noyon (1516)	Forced to give territory to France	Gained territory for France	Excluded
Madrid (1526)	Gained all his territorial and political objectives	Forced to agree to all Charles' demands Renounced on release	Excluded
Cambrai (1529)	Gained all his territorial and political objectives	Forced to agree to all Charles' demands	Only aware of negotiations at later stages Wolsey made to stay in England
Nice (1538)	Territorial disputes shelved	Territorial disputes shelved	Vainly offered mediation
Crépy (1544)	Winning the war, but made peace to deal with German Protestants	Received promising marriage terms from Charles	Unaware of this secret deal Let down by his ally Charles

Conclusion: who was most successful?

There can be no doubt that Charles V achieved more in the field of foreign affairs than either Henry VIII or Francis I. But Charles' resources in terms of men and money dwarfed those of England. Henry's achievement in gaining a bloodless break with Rome has to be recognised. England came close to being attacked on two occasions, but Henry fulfilled the principal duty of a monarch and protected his country against outside aggression.

J How successful was Henry in his wars against Scotland, 1513 and 1542–47?

1513 Scots defeated at the Battle of Flodden; James IV killed
1542 August: England declared war on Scotland
November: Decisive English victory over the Scots at Solway Moss; death of James V and accession of Mary
1543 February: Anglo-Imperial alliance against France
July: Treaties of Greenwich with Scotland
December: Treaties of Greenwich rejected by the Scots
1544 May: Hertford sacked Scottish towns
June: Army led by Henry departed for France
1545 July: French attempted invasion in the south of England; French troops sent to Scotland
1546 June: Anglo-French Peace of Ardres

FOCUS ROUTE

Read pages 172–73 and make notes on the following:

1 What were the main events in Henry's dealings with Scotland? Were there any turning points?
2 What motivated Henry's policies towards Scotland in the 1540s?
3 Should Henry be considered successful in his policy towards Scotland?

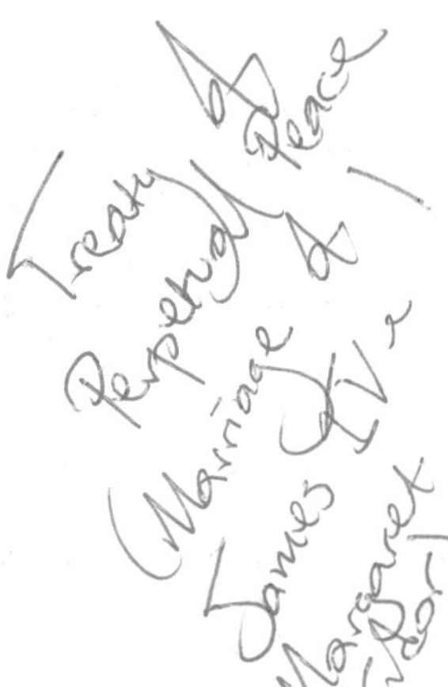

First Scottish War, 1513

In 1509, Henry VIII and James IV of Scotland renewed the 1502 Anglo-Scottish treaty, but relations soon deteriorated as the taut line of alliance maintained by France pulled them nearer to conflict. In 1513, as Henry was engaged in war with France, James launched a raid into England. The response organised by Catherine of Aragon was crushing. At the Battle of Flodden, the Scottish King and over 10,000 men were killed. This victory was not followed up and Henry's sister Margaret was left as regent for the infant heir James V.

Second Scottish War, 1542–47

In September 1541, Henry VIII, on his only trip to the north, had arranged to meet James V at York. Henry had been 'advising' his nephew in an overbearing way and, either out of mistrust or as a calculated insult, James failed to turn up. In his fury, Henry ordered a raid on Scotland that resulted in the defeat of the Scots at Solway Moss (November 1542). In the following month James V died, leaving his six-day-old baby as Mary, Queen of Scots. Henry was now faced with a number of options for dealing with Scotland:

- He could use the Scottish lords captured at Solway Moss to create a pro-English party in Scotland to promote his interests.
- He could launch a full-scale invasion of Scotland in order to seize the country for himself.
- He could arrange a marriage between his son Edward and Mary, Queen of Scots, to unite the two dynasties under the Tudors.
- He could ignore the Scots and concentrate on the coming war against the French.

ACTIVITY

Which of the options (or what combination) do you think Henry should choose? Justify your choice.

What happened after Solway Moss?

Henry adopted a combination of approaches towards Scotland after the victory over the Scots at Solway Moss. He chose not to launch an invasion and instead pushed hard for a marriage between Edward and Mary. He hosted the Scottish prisoners of Solway Moss at Christmas, before sending them back to Scotland to form a pro-English party for him and with the specific instruction to bring Mary to England. As a result of the pressure that Henry applied, the Treaties of Greenwich (July 1543) were signed. Under the agreements, peace was established and Edward and Mary were formally betrothed. The treaties did not, however, include a renunciation of the Franco-Scottish alliance, and by September the pro-French party was in control. In December, the Scottish Parliament rejected the Treaties of Greenwich and renewed all previous treaties with France. In fury, Henry ordered the Earl of Hertford to conduct a purely punitive raid to sack some Scottish cities. His Scottish policy in ruins, Henry turned his attention to France.

What was Henry's attitude towards Scotland?

SOURCE 11.22 J. Morrill, *The British Problem 1534–1707*, 1996, p.21

Henry VIII made no attempt to proclaim himself King of Scotland, even after the death of the son-less James V. He was not in the least interested in 'uniting' Britain. But as his adoption of new and distinctive ways of extending royal power throughout England, Ireland and Wales reached its crescendo, he did develop interventionist policies towards the Northern kingdom. If he did not claim immediate sovereignty over Scotland, he did claim suzerainty: that is, he did claim that Scotland had been for centuries a feudal dependency of England ... As a feudal lord, he could claim the right to supervise the arrangements for government during the minority [of Mary, Queen of Scots] and – even more important – to control the marriage of the heir to the throne. What made this so urgent was that the heir was a woman. In effect, whoever married Mary would bring Scotland into the ambit of his own family. Henry wanted both to acquire Scotland by a dynastic marriage between Mary and the Prince Edward, and perhaps even more to prevent her falling into the clutches of the royal house of France.

So Henry (and Cromwell) largely ignored Scotland throughout the 1530s, his concern being with the possibility of a Franco-Scottish (Catholic) pact. His relations with Scotland were essentially an aspect of his foreign policy.

ACTIVITY

1 What motivated Henry's policy towards Scotland in the 1540s? Indicate what the historian John Morrill's opinion is by marking the appropriate point on your own copy of the sliding scales below.

- extending his dynasty *Very important* ——→ *Not important*
- protecting against attack *Very important* ——→ *Not important*
- war against France *Very important* ——→ *Not important*
- plans for union *Very important* ——→ *Not important*
- hostility towards Scotland *Very important* ——→ *Not important*
- extending his power *Very important* ——→ *Not important*

2 Rank the six factors influencing Henry's foreign policy in order of importance. Explain your choices.

3 How successful had Henry been in his wars against Scotland?

K Review: The third fiddle in Europe? How successful was Henry VIII's foreign policy?

In assessing Henry VIII's success in foreign policy, we must take into account his aims, his achievements and an estimation of what was realistically possible.

FOCUS ROUTE

Read pages 174–77.

1 Complete your own copy of this table. Match each of Henry's conflicts or major foreign policy events to at least one of the numbered aims listed in this section.
2 Complete your own copy of the graph opposite to show the highs and lows of Henry's foreign policy. Mark on the main events (use those mentioned in the activity on page 176) at the correct date and put a cross at the height that you think reflects the success of the event for Henry. Then join up the points to make a line graph.
3 Write down the three main European events that influenced English foreign policy.
4 Answer the following essay question: To what extent can Henry VIII's foreign policy be considered a failure?

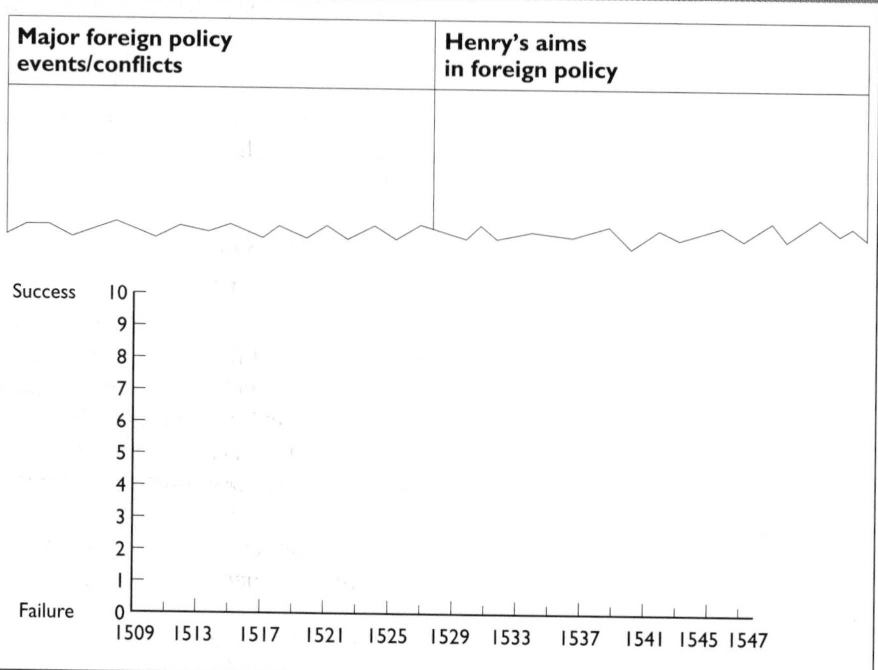

What were Henry's aims in foreign policy?

1 'The most goodliest prince that ever reigned'

Henry VIII was intensely concerned about his reputation and had the ambition to be regarded as 'the most goodliest prince that ever reigned over the realm of England'. Such an aspiration immediately threw him into historical competition with Henry V (1413–22). Henry V was remembered as the last true warrior-king, the 'flower and glory of all knighthood', because of his legendary against-the-odds victory over the French at Agincourt.

2 Pursuing an ambitious and aggressive policy towards the French

All English kings since Edward III had claimed the title of King of France and Henry made much of this in his rhetoric. Henry's impulses towards a French war were driven on by a xenophobia felt by aristocrats and common soldiers alike, who were keener to campaign in France than anywhere else. The enmity was maintained by the strategically damaging threat of the 'auld alliance' between France and Scotland.

3 Honour and glory

Henry and his peers had the mindset of a medieval nobility, psychologically geared to achieving 'honour' and 'glory' through war. Some historians (e.g. David Potter in 'Foreign policy' in D. MacCulloch (ed.), *The Reign of Henry VIII: Politics, Policy and Piety*) have questioned how much of this talk of 'honour' was mere rhetoric, but others (e.g. L. B. Smith in *Henry VIII: The Mask of Royalty*) are convinced that the quest for honour underpinned Henry's character. It is certain that honour was a driving factor behind his long, intense rivalry with Francis I and Charles V (see pages 169–71).

4 Maintaining links with the Netherlands

Strong links with the Netherlands were vital because the English cloth trade depended very heavily on the Antwerp cloth market. Moreover, the Netherlands was controlled by the Holy Roman Emperor, with whom Henry allied in all his wars against France.

5 Peacemaker of Europe

Under the guidance of Wolsey, Henry pursued the option of achieving honour through mediating peace. It could be argued that this policy was pursued because England was unable to achieve prestige through war. However, the Treaty of London (1518) was seen by English contemporaries as a glittering success.

6 Securing his dynasty

Securing the continuation of the dynasty was the foremost aim of all early modern monarchs. Henry was no exception and he tried, with miserable lack of success, to marry off members of his family. Examples are the engagements between his daughter Mary and Charles V, and his attempts to secure the marriage of his son Edward to the infant Mary, Queen of Scots, in the 1540s.

7 Collecting his pension

Recent research by David Potter ('Foreign policy' in D. MacCulloch (ed.), *The Reign of Henry VIII: Politics, Policy and Piety*) has suggested that, while Henry's claim to the French throne and his quest for honour proved to be decidedly flexible during his reign, Henry's demand for his pension was much more constant. The pension was the amount that France agreed to pay the English King every year to compensate him for the English lands lost in France. Demands for his pension were present in all of Henry's wars with France. However, the fact that the wars cost much more than Henry received in pension could not have been lost on him (see Charts 11G and 11H).

■ 11G The costs of war

1488–92	Henry VII's war against France	£108,000
1512–14	Henry VIII's First French War	£892,000
1522–25	Henry VIII's Second French War	£401,000
1542–46	Henry VIII's Third French War	£2,144,765
Total costs of these wars		£3,545,765

■ 11H Henry's French pension

1475 Pension started when Louis XI agreed to pay Edward IV £10,000
1492 Charles VIII agreed to pay Henry VII £10,000 per annum
1512 Pension stopped because of First French War
1518 Pension increased
1525 Pension increased
1527 Henry VIII to receive £21,316
1542 Pension arrears £205,379
Total paid by the French in Henry VIII's reign £730,379

■ Learning trouble spot

What were Wolsey's aims in foreign policy?

The amount that has been written on Wolsey's foreign policy aims must have severely depleted the rainforests. So, to save precious resources, here is the briefest of summaries of the aims attributed to Wolsey:

- humanistic peace (J. J. Scarisbrick, *Henry VIII*)
- become Pope (A. F. Pollard, *Henry VIII*)
- serve the King's interest (Peter Gwyn, *The King's Cardinal: The Rise and Fall of Thomas Wolsey*)
- avoid calling Parliament and raising taxation
- raise own profile
- become the arbiter of Europe, preserving the balance of power.

The Henry debate – a glorious hero or a failed dupe?

ACTIVITY

1 Sort the statements A–W below into the top five successes and the top five failures and then rank the top five in order of importance. Discuss or write an explanation of your selection.

A In the First French War (1512–14) Henry won the battle of the Spurs in 1513, captured territory (Therouanne and Tournai) from the French, and held it.

B The territory won in the First French War (1512–14) was of no tangible benefit to Henry. Therouanne and Tournai were targets suggested by Maximilian and were of no strategic advantage to Henry (Tournai is 160 kilometres from Calais).

C Tournai benefited Wolsey as he was granted the incomes that came from the bishopric he was awarded.

D The Treaty of London (September 1518) was 'a glittering success for Henry and Wolsey, whose fame as peacemakers spread throughout Europe' (Susan Doran, *England and Europe, 1485–1603*).

E The death of Maximilian, Holy Roman Emperor, in January 1519 sparked off the bitter race between Francis and Charles for the Imperial crown, thus destroying whatever fragile truce had been established by the Treaty of London.

F In organising the Treaty of London, Wolsey and Henry were able to upstage the Pope by forcing him to make Wolsey a papal legate and by sidelining the Pope's own ambitious plans to organise a truce so that Europe could launch a crusade against the Ottomans.

G In the Second French War (1523–25), the planned three-pronged attack by the Duke of Bourbon from the south of France, Charles V from the Netherlands and Henry from England did not materialise. Bourbon's offensive failed to get off the ground and Charles V was so busy with conflicts in Italy that he did almost nothing to assist England. Henry had been used by Charles to distract France and Henry was left to pick up the bill.

H After Charles V's stunning victory against Francis I at Pavia (February 1525), Henry wrote eagerly to Charles suggesting that they should together destroy the French monarchy and place the French crown on Henry's head. The rest, 'the whole monarchy of Christendom', would go to Charles. Charles rejected the suggestion.

I Henry did not make any significant foreign marriage alliances for himself or his family throughout the whole of his reign, despite trying to make marriage pacts with most of the major European royal families.

J Henry's break with Rome was a bold, daring and successful assertion of his Imperial ambitions.

K The break with Rome isolated England and, as should have been expected, made it a target for foreign aggression, especially after the Truce of Nice (1538).

L England came *very* close to being invaded twice during Henry's reign, in 1539 and 1545.

M Henry successfully preserved and protected the Tudor dynasty from any foreign or domestic threats.

N Henry's French invasions were motivated by a futile desire to 'prove' himself on the foreign stage, and failed to take into account England's inferior position.

O Henry's attacks on France, if seen in their appropriate historical context, were fulfilling the monarch's obligation to wage war to bring glory on himself and his country. In choosing France, Henry was making the popular choice of attacking England's traditional enemy.

P The Field of Cloth of Gold was a glorious spectacle that confirmed Henry's position as a central force in European power politics.

Q The elaborate and costly display at the Field of Cloth of Gold (it cost about one year of Henry's normal income) was a pretentious charade that achieved nothing of any lasting significance.

R Henry's capture of Boulogne (September 1544) was a major achievement, reminiscent of the victories in the Hundred Years War.

S Four days after the capture of Boulogne, Henry was again abandoned by his supposed ally as Francis and Charles signed the Peace of Crépy. This brought the war with France to an end.

T Despite Henry's two crushing victories over Scotland at Flodden (1513) and Solway Moss (1542) and the very favourable death of James V (1542), Henry gained nothing of long-term value from his conflict with his northern neighbour.

U Through his effective policy of integrating and strengthening his control over Wales and the outlying regions of England, Henry made his realm much more secure.

V Henry was successfully duped by Ferdinand of Aragon in 1512. Ferdinand and Henry had agreed to attack France together, but Ferdinand just used the English troops dispatched as a cover behind which he successfully acquired Navarre for himself. The English troops, diseased and mutinous, returned home shambolically four months later.

W The Scottish army were dealt a 'shattering defeat' (Scarisbrick, *Henry VIII*) at Flodden in 1513 and at Solway Moss in 1542. After Flodden, James IV was killed and most of the Scottish aristocracy were killed or taken prisoner; after Solway Moss, James V's death left Scotland vulnerable with only the six-day-old Mary as queen.

2 In pairs, discuss Henry's success in foreign policy. One of you must argue that he was a success, but on a signal from your partner, you must do a 180-degree turn and argue that he was, in fact, a failure. Then swap roles and have another go. You could limit your discussion to one of the wars or events listed above.

Conclusion

Whatever judgement you reach about Henry's success or failure in foreign policy, there is no denying his commitment, enthusiasm and effort in this field of government. Visiting foreign ambassadors, for example, always found him formidably well briefed and assertive. The list of significant successes is, though, pitifully short – the capture of Boulogne, Tournai and Therouanne, and the victories against the Scots at Flodden and Solway Moss. However, this has to be matched against England's limited resources.

- England was not a powerful country in Europe – only the third fiddle (and it is debatable if it was even that).
- England's geographical position at the edge of Europe made it irrelevant to most of the central issues that Europe was fighting over, such as Milan, the Ottomans in eastern Europe, and the Mediterranean.
- Shortage of money remained a constant ball and chain to Henry's conquering dreams. Only in the Third French War, when Henry had all the money from the dissolution of the monasteries, did England have the resources to compete on the same level as France and the Empire.

England was of third-fiddle status and its successes should be judged in this light.

KEY POINTS FROM CHAPTER 11: The third fiddle in Europe? How successful was Henry VIII's foreign policy?

1. England was neither a powerful nor an influential country and English foreign policy was often excluded from or at the mercy of the events on the Continent.
2. The central turning point of the reign in terms of foreign policy was the battle of Pavia (1525). Until Pavia, English policy was essentially anti-French; after Pavia, an Anglo-French *entente* was constructed in the Treaty of Amiens (1527) and the countries were at peace until the Third French War (1543).
3. The Truce of Nice (1538) was critical in ending the Habsburg–Valois war and focusing European Catholic antagonism on to England, leading to the fear of invasion in 1538–40.
4. Henry achieved notable victories against the Scots at Flodden (1513) and Solway Moss (1542).
5. His policies towards Scotland created hostility and deeper divisions, and failed to achieve his objectives.
6. Territorially, Henry's foreign policy achievements were very limited (Boulogne in 1544 being the only significant gain).
7. Henry felt that he achieved substantial 'honour' through some of his foreign policy exploits (e.g. the battle of the Spurs and the Field of Cloth of Gold).
8. Henry successfully defended England's independence after the break with Rome.
9. Although Henry's power was ultimately not seriously undermined, there were a number of potentially serious challenges (e.g. the French invasion attempt of 1545).
10. In the rivalry between Henry VIII, Francis I and Charles V, Charles was the most dominant and successful monarch.

12

Henry VIII – the verdict

CHAPTER OVERVIEW In this final chapter on Henry VIII, we are trying to evaluate his reign. We need to consider two important questions:

A Was Henry VIII reacting to, or leading, domestic events? (pp. 178–80)

B What were Henry's achievements? (pp. 181–83)

A Was Henry VIII reacting to, or leading, domestic events?

FOCUS ROUTE

Read the three case studies on pages 178–80. Make notes on each case under the following headings:

- what happened
- possible explanations
- what it tells us about Henry's involvement
- difficulties presented by the evidence in trying to reach a conclusion.

With Henry's oft-mentioned aversion to the mundane aspects of government, and the presence for the greater part of the reign of two very able 'chief ministers', Wolsey and Cromwell, it has been seductive to assume that Henry himself did not formulate policy decisions throughout his reign. Even in the 1540s he was, apparently, subjected to factional politics at court.

We are going to examine three case studies in the hope of shedding some light on this difficult question.

Case study 1: The expulsion of the minions, 1519

This case study is based on an article by Greg Walker in the *Historical Journal*, 1989.

What happened?

In September 1518, Henry created a new post in the royal household – Gentleman of the Privy Chamber, the latter being the place where he spent his most intimate moments. Those appointed to this prestigious post were his closest companions: Edward Neville, Nicholas Carew, Arthur Pole, Francis Bryan, Henry Norris and William Coffin. Not only did these men attend the King personally, but they were also sent on diplomatic missions and performed other tasks within the household. They made much of their new status.

However, within nine months, on 20 May 1519, four of them, Neville, Carew, Bryan and Coffin, along with some other courtiers, had been dismissed from their offices in disgrace. The reaction at court was one of astonishment. Sebastian Giustiniani, the Venetian ambassador, described the dismissals as being 'of as vital importance as any [event] that had taken place for many years'.

Possible explanations

Wolsey. It used to be thought that Wolsey moved against these intimates of the King because, for the first time, he was faced with the possibility of Henry's mind being turned against him by men beyond his direct control. Giustiniani wrote that 'the French ambassador . . . consider[s] that this [expulsion] took place either from suspicion about . . . France, or at the instigation of Wolsey'. This sounds feasible, until we start to examine the incident more thoroughly:

- If Wolsey felt threatened, why would he have expelled some of the men and not others?
- Why did he wait nine months?
- The men had been intimate companions of the King since at least 1515, so what difference did a formal title make?

- Immediately prior to the expulsions, Wolsey was suffering from one of his frequent bouts of illness – this time, dysentery. Dysentery is an extreme form of diarrhoea, which might have seriously affected Wolsey's capacity to orchestrate such events. He also may well have been absent from the Council meetings that preceded the episode.

The Council. The evidence that the minions were expelled at the Council's behest largely comes from the *Chronicle of Edward Hall.* Hall witnessed the whole of Henry's reign and his writings praise Henry's achievements. He wrote: 'yet the Kynges counsell thought it not mete to be suffred for the Kynges honor, and therefore thei altogether came to the King, beseching him al these enormites and lightnes to redresse'. In other words, the Council was concerned about the behaviour of the minions and wanted to limit their influence on the King, just as was argued in Wolsey's case.

The King. It has also been suggested that Henry himself, wanting to reform his lifestyle and his court, decided to expel the minions. The evidence for this explanation comes from reports of the Duke of Norfolk's view. Norfolk was the Lord Treasurer and often acted as the King's 'press secretary'. The fact that Giustiniani reported his view (see Source 12.1) suggests that this was the official line on the incident.

TALKING POINT

What are the advantages and disadvantages of ambassadorial accounts as evidence?

SOURCE 12.1 Report of Sebastian Giustiniani, Venetian ambassador

This stir was made because ... [the minions] had been the cause of [Henry's] ... incessant gambling, which has made him lose of late a treasure of gold and that on coming to himself, and resolving to a new life, he, of his own accord removed these companions of his excesses: this is the opinion of the Lord Treasurer.

ACTIVITY

1. Which version of events do you believe, and why?
2. What problems with the evidence itself make it more difficult for us to work out what really happened?
3. Even if Henry himself were *not* orchestrating the expulsion of the minions, would he have allowed it to happen had he disagreed with it?

Case study 2: The 'trial' of Cranmer, 1543

Thomas Cranmer was the Protestant Archbishop of Canterbury who had secretly married Henry VIII to Anne Boleyn in 1533. He had defended Cromwell's achievements, after the former had been arrested and charged with treason in 1540. During the 1540s, Cranmer was a victim of the factional struggles at court between the conservatives, such as Gardiner and Norfolk, and the reformers. In 1543, Cranmer was attacked by his conservative enemies. In Source 12.2, Scarisbrick describes what happened.

ACTIVITY

Which of the following explanations of Henry's actions in this incident do you agree with? (You can choose more than one.)

Henry supported Cranmer because:

- Cranmer enjoyed his esteem and affection
- Henry enjoyed the 'sport' of court politics and delighted in catching people out
- Henry wanted to show that, regardless of the factional struggles, he was in charge
- Henry was worried about unrest from the Protestants in Kent in support of Cranmer, at a time when England was at war with Scotland, and war with France was imminent.

SOURCE 12.2 J. J. Scarisbrick, *Henry VIII*, 1968, p. 481

Henry had been told that the archbishop was a heretic and had agreed that he should be seized at the Council table, like Cromwell, and taken to the Tower. But the same night he summoned Cranmer to Whitehall to warn him of the plot and explain that, once he was in prison, 'three or four false knaves will soon be procured to witness against you and condemn you'. Having thus revealed a true insight into the machinations of his servants, Henry gave Cranmer his ring and told him to produce it when he was arrested and appeal to be heard by the king himself. Next day, when the Council pounced, Cranmer did as the king had bidden and scattered his enemies, who, when they then repaired to the king, were savagely rebuked. Perhaps Henry had at least learned something from the fall of Cromwell about the ways of his servants, but because he took pleasure in intrigue or in confounding others, neither now nor later was he capable, apparently, of the simple and direct action of stamping out conspiracy when he first heard of it ... However, 'the greatest heretic in Kent', as Henry had jovially described Cranmer, survived...

Case study 3: Wriothesley's attempt to arrest Catherine Parr, 1546

Henry had married his sixth wife, Catherine Parr, in 1543. She was a reformer and one of the few people who could talk to Henry frankly about religious matters. In Source 12.3, Scarisbrick describes what happened after one of her meetings with the ailing king, at which Bishop Gardiner had been present.

SOURCE 12.3 J. J. Scarisbrick, *Henry VIII*, 1968, pp. 479–80

Henry turned to him and said, 'A good hearing it is, when women become such clerks; and a thing much to my comfort, to come in mine old days to be taught by my wife.' The bishop had long wanted to quash this dangerous woman and, having opined on the unseemliness of a woman presuming to impose her views on the Supreme Head 'so malapertly', went on to promise that, if the king gave him permission, he and others of the Council would lay before him such evidence of Catherine's treasonous heresy that 'his majesty would easily perceive how perilous a matter it is to cherish a serpent within his own bosom'. Henry at least pretended to be convinced by Gardiner's words and gave permission for 'certain articles' to be drawn up against the queen ... Even as her accusers closed in on her and drew up a bill of articles against her (which Henry signed), Catherine continued to visit Henry and plead with him to undertake further reformation of the Church. One evening, after she had been with him, Henry poured out complaints against her to his physician, one Dr Wendy, and told him the whole story of the plot against her, but bound him to secrecy. The bill of articles ... was immediately brought to the queen. When she read its contents and saw the king's signature she collapsed. Wendy ... broke the secrecy imposed on him and promised the queen that, if she humbly submitted to her husband, he would surely return her to favour ... Reverently and abjectly she threw herself on his mercy ... And when Catherine disowned so 'preposterous' a purpose as that she, a mere wife, should presume to instruct her husband ... Henry made the famous response: 'And is it even so, sweetheart, and tended your argument to no worse end? Then perfect friends we are now again as ever at any time heretofore.' ... Next day ... the lord chancellor arrived with some forty men to carry the victims off to the Tower. It was not Catherine who came to grief. Wriothesley knelt before the king to explain his coming ... Henry broke in with 'Knave! arrant knave! beast! and fool!' and sent him and his train away forthwith.

ACTIVITY

What is your explanation for Henry's behaviour on this occasion?

- At one point he wanted to throw Catherine to the wolves, then changed his mind.
- He only pretended to go along with Gardiner's conspiracy.
- He wanted to teach Gardiner and others a lesson.
- He wanted to frighten Catherine and/or teach her a lesson.
- He enjoyed being devious.
- He wanted to give a message to both the reformist and conservative factions that neither had the upper hand.

TALKING POINT

Can we make accurate deductions about whether Henry was reacting to or leading events, based on three case studies only?

Conclusion

All things considered, it seems likely that Henry did not have overall control of events, but that the final decision making was his. If you refer back to the sources on Henry's character and personality in Chapter 7, you will remember that Henry was someone who was used to being in the driving seat. However, Henry probably operated much like a modern-day prime minister, who would not always have been directly involved with carrying out policies and decisions on a day-to-day basis. Some final clarification on the matter is given by Steven Gunn in Source 12.4.

SOURCE 12.4 S. Gunn, *Early Tudor Government, 1485–1558*, 1995, pp. 37 and 54

The precise balance between the exercise of Henry VIII's will and the exercise of influence upon it in any individual decision is as hard to judge as the precise balance between leading ministers and personal servants amongst those seeking to influence the king. But it is clear that those around Henry – like those around his father or his children – thought it worthwhile to try to persuade him, and to enlist the support of his most intimate servants in doing so ...

However dramatic the rise of ministers, privy council and secretaries, Tudor government remained focused on the monarch. He or she took the final decisions in great matters of state: war and peace, dynastic alliances, religious policy. Whether or not susceptible to influence, he or she also took all the significant decisions in matters of patronage.

B What were Henry's achievements?

FOCUS ROUTE

Study Sources 12.5–12.7 on page 182.

1 List Henry's achievements in order of importance:
   a) to the King himself
   b) for the country
   c) as a legacy for his successor, Edward VI.
2 Make notes on how Henry's reign has been perceived by historians, giving examples.

ACTIVITY

What had Henry achieved by 1547? Look at the following list and identify the pluses and minuses:

- He had raised the status of the monarchy to near idolatry, and he had bolstered national pride.
- The succession was secure, albeit in a minor, which was not ideal.
- Religious reform saw the King as head of the Church in England, but it was not clear how many people were nominal Protestants and still Catholics at heart. Courtiers, bishops and people in general were divided over Protestant doctrine.
- He had been to war six times, but he had not made any territorial gains except for Boulogne.
- War made the dynasty financially vulnerable, and by 1547 Henry was in deep financial trouble. Having spent the revenue from the dissolution of the monasteries and DEBASED the coinage from 1544, Henry faced a serious deficit: his total expenses were £2,134,784, but subsidies and forced loans had raised only £656,245 and £270,000 respectively. The problem was further exacerbated by the serious inflation in England from 1545 onwards as a result of the debasement of the coinage.
- The Privy Chamber had established itself as the supreme executive body by the 1540s.
- The administration of government was more efficient than it had ever been.
- The legal system was more effective than before.
- There was less lawlessness, particularly in the Marcher lordships of Wales and in the north.
- The needs of the poor were not addressed from the revenues of the dissolution of the monasteries.
- Henry was a builder of great palaces, the like of which has not been seen since.
- Between 1532 and 1540, 883 people were convicted for treason, of whom 308 were executed.

DEBASE

To debase the coinage involved reducing the gold or silver content of coins so that they were still nominally of the same value, but the Government could profit from the gold or silver that had not been used. However, debasement led to high inflation and a loss of confidence in the currency.

Gold or silver coins are melted down.

Some gold or silver is removed for use by the Government.

New, less pure gold or silver coins are produced.

Debasement of the coinage results in inflation.

Historians' interpretations

SOURCE 12.5 J. J. Scarisbrick, *Henry VIII*, 1968, p.498

He had survived pretenders, excommunication, rebellion and threats of invasion, died in his bed and passed his throne peacefully to his heir. He had won a title, defender of the Faith, which English monarchs still boast, written a book which is still, occasionally, read, composed some music which is still sung. He had made war on England's ancient enemies and himself led two assaults on France. For nearly four decades he had cut an imposing figure in Europe, mattering to its [illegible] striding its high diplomacy as few of his predecessors, if any, had done. [illegible] fied pope and emperor, brought into being in England and Ireland a [illegible] Church subject to his authority, wiped about a thousand religious [illegible] the face of his native land, and of those areas of Ireland under his [illegible] and bestowed on English kingship a profound new dignity. He who [illegible] en the secular Church in England, hammered monks and friars, and, [illegible] laid his hand on the chantries, had brought the Scriptures in the [illegible] ur to his people, hesitantly and perhaps partly unwittingly, but none the [illegible] ively, allowed his country to be directed towards the Continental [illegible] ion into which it was to enter fully in his son's and second daughter's [illegible] nd given to his people a new sense of unity – the unity of 'entire [illegible] nen' rather than that of 'Englishmen papisticate' or of those who were [illegible] ur subjects'.

SOURCE 12.6 G. R. Elton, *England Under the Tudors*, 3rd edn, 1991, p.202

Fifty-seven years old, King Henry died on 27 January 1547, his hand in Cranmer's, convinced as he always had been of his own righteousness. The nation, informed three days later by Lord Chancellor Wriothesley (in tears), was stunned and frightened of the future. The follies of the last seven years made sure that the next reign would be burdened with an evil inheritance, but the earlier work of Henry VIII and his great ministers had not been done in vain.

SOURCE 12.7 D. Loades, *The Mid-Tudor Crisis, 1545–1565*, 1992, p.18

Henry VIII had spent the last twenty years of his reign trying to ensure the preservation of his own and his father's achievements, only to be succeeded by a minor and two women. In 1544, the thought that the first three provisions of his Succession Act would all become operative would have filled him with dread; and yet twenty years later the English state was, if anything, more secure than it was when he left it. One reason for this was that the lawful succession had been upheld, but another was the strength of the governmental machine itself.

ACTIVITY

1 It is 1547 and Henry VIII has just died. Write an account of his reign from the point of view of one of the following:

- a Protestant reformer
- a Catholic in England
- a prosperous gentleman who bought ex-monastic land
- a member of Queen Catherine of Aragon's household
- a foreign prince.

You will need to refer to Chapters 7–12 to do this. Read out the accounts in class, identifying the most and least supportive comments.

2 Who was more successful, Henry VII or Henry VIII? Look at both reigns and make comparisons of the problems and advantages that they each had.

EN EXPRESSA VIDES HENRICI REGIS IMAGO
QVÆ FVIT OCTAVI MVSIS HOC STRVXIT ASYLVM
MAGNIFICE CVM TER DENOS REGNASSET ET OCTO
ANNOS: QVIS MAIOR REGEM LABOR VLTIMVS ORNET
EX DONO ROBERTI BEAVMONT SACRE THEOLOGIE PROFESSORIS ET HVIVS COLLEGII MAGISTRI Aº1567

SOURCE 12.8 Henry VIII was an egotistical man who was desperately concerned about his image and how it reflected on his 'honour'. He wanted to be seen and remembered as a great king

KEY POINTS FROM CHAPTER 12: Henry VIII – the verdict

1 Henry fulfilled the main requirements of an early modern monarch – maintaining security and providing an heir – and much more besides. The establishment of the Royal Supremacy and the dissolution of the monasteries are events of huge significance in the history of England.
2 Overall, it is likely that even if Henry VIII was influenced by those around him, his will prevailed.
3 Historians are divided over Henry's achievements. Much of the criticism surrounds his personality and his treatment of those around him. Much of the praise surrounds the structural changes he made, to the government, the Church and the monarchy, which were of lasting importance.

Section 2 Review: Henry VIII

Henry VIII towards the end of his life, drawn by Cornelius Metsys. This portrait has been described by David Starkey as a 'Humpty Dumpty of nightmares' (*A European Court in England*)

The picture we see of Henry towards the end of his reign is a very different image from that with which this section started (see page 85). Gone is the picture of confidence and virility. Instead we see the bloated face of a man who had lived an extremely tempestuous life.

Ten years on from that original Holbein sketch, we might wonder how Henry VII would have judged the exploits of his son. How might the founder of the Tudor dynasty have viewed his successor? To come back to the key question of our introduction: was Henry VIII a successful king?

Let us examine the fundamental aspects of Henry VII's legacy and see how his son matched up:

- **Security.** Henry VIII did at least pass on his throne uncontested and therefore relatively secure. The fact that Edward VI was a minor can hardly be blamed on Henry VIII's lack of enthusiasm to produce a male heir!
- **Law and order.** Given the context of the period, England can be seen to have been largely at peace. The main threat of the Pilgrimage of Grace was fast fading into memory.
- **Finance.** Here Henry VII could have had serious cause for concern. The carefully maintained coffers of his reign had been thrown away by extravagant spending, largely on foreign wars. Nevertheless, thanks to the dissolution of the monasteries, income from Crown lands was higher in 1547 than in 1509.
- **Image.** Henry VIII had done his best to fulfil his role as warrior-king. The victory at Boulogne would live on in popular memory for the rest of the century. However, Henry had provoked real hostility in his personal life – his rejection of Catherine of Aragon and his series of new wives hardly matched his father's fidelity.
- **Religion.** Henry VII's deep religious commitment was followed by his son. But the state of ordinary people's beliefs would surely have set Henry VII spinning in his tomb! The certainty provided by the Catholic Church had been smashed and replaced with . . . Well, that was not entirely clear.

It is hard to see Henry VIII in a very positive light, both as man and as king. In a flippant moment we might see him as one of the flashier types of football manager, spending lots of money on foreign projects, but achieving little more than mid-table security. Henry talked a good game – his own church, warrior-like posing in foreign fields, monuments built to his own magnificence. But when asked the question 'What has Henry VIII ever done for you?', the peasant in the field might well have been lost for words.

ACTIVITY

Look again at the Holbein sketch of Henry VIII and his father on page 85. Write two speech bubbles for Henry VII – one for 1537, the other for 1547 – that reflect what he might have thought about the achievements of his son.

section

3

Edward VI

The Tudor propagandists were quick to create a bold, warrior-like image of Edward, as in this coin from 1551. But how much does this fit the reality?

J. Loach, 'Edward VI: a new look at the king and his reign', *History Review*, 1999

If we do not need to throw away entirely the image of Edward listening with such interest to a sermon, we do need to add to it the image of a boy boasting and showing off about his exploits on a horse, a boy who read books about greyhounds as well as the scriptures and the classics, a boy who copied out notes about Henry VI's military occupation of Normandy. And if Edward's commitment to the Protestant cause is seen together with his interest in military matters, perhaps what we have is not so much a godly imp as a 'guerrier de Dieu' (warrior of God), in the making.

Take your mind back to when you were nine years old. Imagine that your father, whom you have only dimly known, has just died (you never knew your mother). Your father had been on the throne for nearly 40 years and was a feared and powerful figure. You have been trained by your own private tutors, but still have only a vague awareness of what exactly it means to be king. How well do you think you would have coped?

What expectations could you have of someone in such a situation? That is the position that Edward faced in 1547.

Now cast your mind back to when you were fifteen years old (probably just about to take your GCSEs). Would you have been ready to take over control of the whole country? Do you feel confident about your grasp of finances and economics, your understanding of the role of Parliament and the Government, and your ability to keep the ambitious nobles around you in their place? What are your views on religion, England's position in Europe and what should happen if the people of the country are unhappy? Do you have answers for these questions? Then you realise you are about to die and you want to change the succession – what do you do? Edward was faced with these dilemmas in 1553.

In this section we will be examining how well Edward was equipped to cope with these challenges. We will examine how well foreign affairs, government and the economy were handled by him and his advisers.

Most of the historiography of Edward places him on the periphery of the reign. The histories are dominated by his two main councillors – Somerset and Northumberland. However, more recent works, such as Jennifer Loach's biography, *Edward VI*, have set out to reappraise this young monarch. The chapters in this section will place Edward right at the centre of the reign and interpret the events from his perspective.

Irrelevant Edward? How much influence did Edward VI have in government?

CHAPTER OVERVIEW

The knowledge that Edward died before he became an adult king can heavily distort our understanding of his power and influence as a young monarch. It is too easy to assume that, as he died still a child, he was always bound to be insignificant and (as some historians have mistakenly thought) too sickly to be of any consequence. If, however, we begin with the assumption that he *was* going to live to become the undisputed master, then our perspective on Edward and his relations with others changes decisively. Once he was crowned at the age of nine, he could not be ignored or contradicted. There was the very real expectation among all his councillors that Edward would very shortly be king in his own right.

There is a danger of taking this argument too far. He was, after all, only a child of nine when his father died. But when he died unexpectedly in 1553, he was only four months away from being king on his own. In such a position, the views of this highly intelligent, confident and opinionated young man suddenly become loaded with political significance. The historical judgement required now becomes chronological – the question is not *if*, but *when* he became relevant to the Government.

All the chapters in this section will examine the reign from the perspective that Edward's position on such issues as religion, government and foreign policy *could* have mattered. Therefore, we need to establish what Edward thought on each of these issues and then judge how much he influenced the Government and events of his reign. At the end of the section, we will need to make an evaluation of how relevant or irrelevant Edward actually was.

This first chapter will examine Edward's suitability for kingship and assess the amount of power he wielded.

A Was the reign of a minor necessarily a negative experience for a country?

SOURCE 13.1 A portrait of Edward VI, by an unknown artist, painted in 1542 when he was five years old

SOURCE 13.2 Hugh Latimer, quoting from the Book of Ecclesiastes in 1549

Woe to thee, O land, where the king is a child.

Hugh Latimer's quote in Source 13.2 is often used to highlight the crisis that historians and contemporaries thought that England was facing simply because a minor had ascended the throne. However, Latimer, a keen Protestant who delivered the quote in a sermon *in front of Edward*, would have been outraged by the way this sound-bite has been taken out of context. In the sermon, he very rapidly went on to extol the virtues of the current monarch. However, it is a valid question to ask if there are any problems inherent in having a child monarch. The evidence in Chart 13A will help you to reach an answer.

■ 13A Child monarchs prior to Edward

Child monarch	Age came to throne	Years of reign	Experience during the minority	Experience of reign once adult
Henry III	9	1216–72	Civil war was ended and the country was well ruled.	Henry's choice of Frenchmen at court provoked opposition.
Richard II	10	1377–99	At 14 he quelled a hostile mob during the Peasants' Revolt, but the Hundred Years War went badly.	Richard alienated many because of his arrogant attitude. He was deposed and later murdered.
Henry VI	9 months	1422–71	Factions developed, but the country remained peaceful and the Hundred Years War went well initially.	He was a weak leader; England experienced the worst of the Wars of the Roses during his reign.
Edward V	12	1483	Murdered, probably on the orders of his uncle Richard III	

ACTIVITY

1 Can any general points be made about the experience of having a boy-king?
2 Can any general points be made about the adult years of kings who had ascended the throne as minors? Can you provide any explanation for your conclusions?
3 What might be assumed to be the dangers of having a minor on the throne?

B What was Edward like and how well was he prepared for kingship?

SOURCE 13.3 A modern drawing of Edward's coronation, which took place on 20 February 1547 in Westminster Abbey. A phoenix, representing Jane Seymour, descends from Heaven to mate with a crowned lion, representing Henry VIII. Then a younger lion (Edward himself) steps forward to be crowned as his 'parents' withdraw.

Edward was presented with three swords symbolising his three kingdoms – England, Ireland and France – and a fourth symbolising 'the spirit' (Bible). The pageantry and elaborate symbolism of Tudor ceremonials were very important for establishing the continuity and continuing authority of the dynasty. Edward's contemporary biographer says that Edward demanded the fourth sword. This is an early example of Edward asserting his Protestantism and his authority

■ Learning trouble spot

The main historical source on the character and opinions of Edward is his Chronicle. The Chronicle was a diary that he started at the age of twelve and completed almost daily until just after his fifteenth birthday. It shows him to be an able young monarch who was remarkably well informed about the minutiae of Government business. The Chronicle was initially produced for the scrutiny of his tutors, but after May 1551 he was more clearly using his own initiative and pursuing his own objectives. The entries are all terse, impersonal and factual, but they show real objectivity in his view of people and events.

The problem with drawing conclusions about Edward's character and views from the Chronicle is that we cannot be entirely clear about why he was writing it and who the audience was meant to be. Edward was probably not writing for himself alone and therefore may well have been careful about what he said about others and what he revealed about himself.

A page from Edward's Chronicle is illustrated on page 204 (Source 14.3).

His upbringing

So desperately wished for, but so long in the coming, Henry's first (and, as it proved, only surviving) male child was inevitably going to be given a most protected and cosseted upbringing. No expense or care was spared, but nor was Edward going to emerge from such a childhood unaffected.

SOURCE 13.4 Margaret Giggs, Edward's nurse, painted by Hans Holbein the Younger

- **Love and affection.** Until he was six years old, Edward, as he himself recorded in his Chronicle, was 'among the women', being cared for by his nurse Mother Jack (see Source 13.4). His own mother, Jane Seymour, died shortly after his birth and Henry's subsequent wives – Anne of Cleves and Catherine Howard – had little to do with him. Henry's final wife, Catherine Parr (married 1543), offered the only maternal affection that Edward had known and he was soon calling her mother. Henry's relationship with his son was very traditional: Henry saw Edward very infrequently and the reports written by Edward's carers and tutors were sent to Henry's ministers, not to Henry himself.
- **Attendants.** Edward had an army of personal servants, including three physicians, six surgeons, two apothecaries, a French cook, a stone engraver, an organ maker, three court painters, a French tutor (Jean Belmain, a Calvinist), five scholars, only five musicians (as Edward didn't like music) and four principal gentlemen for the 'singular care' of his person.

- **Protection.** Three gentlemen and five grooms were always present, with one being in the bedchamber at night. Edward was hardly ever alone. He was never allowed to incur the dangers of contact sports such as jousting. The walls and floors of his apartment were washed three times a day and great care was taken over the cleanliness and quality of his food.

His character

It might be a useful starting point to consider what kind of character could have developed out of such a tightly disciplined and pressured upbringing and education. The cold family relations, his lofty status and his drilled training would have made Edward stiff and aloof even if these had not been traits in his character.

- **Interests.** Some of Edward's favourite pastimes are akin to modern-day trainspotting: when studying the Hundred Years War, for example, he was fascinated by the sources of revenue for the campaign, the different kinds of troops, how they were paid and the final treaty articles. He seems to have been naturally studious, intelligent and devout (for example, Edward scribbled notes in Greek as he listened to long and difficult sermons). But he also enjoyed hunting, rackets, archery, jousting (as an observer) and horse riding.
- **Personality.** Edward was a serious child. One of the few known examples of Edward laughing was when he saw a tight-rope walker slide down a rope on his chest from the battlements in St Paul's churchyard to the ground. The King 'laughed right heartily' and refused to go on with his coronation procession. A natural childish excitement was also shown when he met the French representative Marshal St André, who bestowed on Edward the Order of St Michael. Except on these occasions, he was always self-disciplined.
- **Relations with others.** There are plenty of examples of Edward's coldness towards others. In his Chronicle there is no reference to the death of his grandmother, there are only two mentions of his sister Elizabeth, and the entry on the death of his uncle (Somerset) is terse and functional. He was also distrustful and could be vindictive. The only warmth he displayed was towards his aristocratic friend Barnaby Fitzpatrick.
- **Health.** The early death of Edward appears to have led to the myth that he was always a weak and sickly child. This is certainly *not* the case. He had a fever when he was four, and measles and smallpox when he was fourteen, but otherwise he was in good health, until he was struck down by a chest infection in February 1553 which developed into a fatal septicaemia.

His education

Edward's formal education began in 1543 and probably ended when he was fourteen in June 1552. His two principal teachers were Richard Coxe and Sir John Cheke. The significance of this is that both were prominent humanists and Coxe was a Protestant. To keep Edward company, an exclusive palace school with fourteen high-born boys was established. The pupils included his cousin Henry Brandon, Duke of Suffolk; Henry, Lord Hastings; and Robert Dudley, the son of John Dudley, Viscount Lisle. Edward's best friend, Barnaby Fitzpatrick, became the royal whipping boy (literally taking Edward's beatings) after Edward had become king and could no longer be punished.

Edward was devoted to his studies, spending several hours a day reading Roman and Greek classics, the scriptures, history and geography, and learning six foreign languages. Coxe was a progressive teacher and believed that learning should be enjoyed rather than driven in through constant beatings. As a consequence, Edward was able to develop his interests in logic, natural philosophy and astronomy. Nor was his training as a gentleman neglected; he was groomed in good manners, fencing, horsemanship and the rules of hunting. More important for his future role were his lessons in statecraft and government. William Thomas (Clerk to the King's Council) wrote 'Discourses' for Edward on different topics such as religion and the economy. Edward also gained an encyclopaedic knowledge of the nobility and the main gentry, including their religious beliefs.

SOURCE 13.5 An abbreviated version of a memorandum prepared by Edward for the Privy Council, April 1551

A SUMMARY OF MATTERS TO BE CONCLUDED
10. Bringing the Augmentation Court into the Exchequer, and likewise the Court of First Fruits and Tenths, and saving all those fees that may be spared.
13. Gathering and coining of the church plate.
14. Sale of certain lands of chantries.
18. The sale of bell metal.

FOR RELIGION
1. A catechism to be set forth to be taught in all grammar schools.
2. An uniformity of doctrine to which all preachers should set their hands to.
3. Commissions to be granted to those bishops that be grave, learned, wise, sober, and of good religion, for the executing of discipline.
4. To find fault with the slothfulness of pastors and to deliver [to] them articles of visitation, willing and commanding them to be more diligent in their office and to keep more preachers.

FOR THE STRENGTH AND WEALTH OF THE REALM
1. The fortifying of Portsmouth.
7. Repairing of Dover castle and haven.
12. The making of more great ordnance of the copper in the Tower and the bell metal.

■ Learning trouble spot

Historians have often been quick to dismiss Edward as an insignificant and weak pawn in his reign. In *England Under the Tudors* Geoffrey Elton said of him: 'easily swayed by cunning men, he exercised such little influence'. His biographer W. K. Jordan, who wrote a major study of his reign and edited his Chronicle for publication, has presented him as a sickly child who, although very talented, was destined not to make it through to become an adult king (*The Chronicle and Political Papers of King Edward VI*). It is an interesting question why such views have been so prevalent.

There is, of course, the danger of hindsight; of knowing he would die young and so writing his role in history from this perspective. Historians also appear to have been taken in by Foxe's startlingly successful Protestant propagandist work, *The Book of Martyrs*, which celebrated the brief role that Edward played in establishing Protestantism in England before passing on to a better place. Historians seem to have become locked into thinking that they are studying a *boy*-king and have narrowed the scope of their investigation accordingly. Recent works on Edward, such as Jennifer Loach's study (*Edward VI*), have attempted to establish a more balanced assessment of his character and achievements.

ACTIVITY

Listed below are the kinds of task that Edward was given up to the age of fourteen. Attempt them individually or divide them among a group.

1 On a map of Europe, label the following main ports in the correct places: Deal, Dover, Leith, Calais, Antwerp, Le Havre, Boulogne.
(Edward also knew the trades, tides and kinds of vessels that used these ports.)
2 Identify the moral lessons that can be learnt from the following proverbs:

He who tills his land has enough to eat,
but to follow idle pursuits is foolishness.
The stronghold of the wicked crumbles like clay,
but the righteous take lasting root.
The wicked man is trapped by his own falsehoods,
but the righteous comes safe through trouble. (Proverbs 12:11)

(Edward read Solomon's Proverbs every day and was taught 'to beware of strange and wanton women'.)
3 Write a brief letter to a friend in Latin, French, Greek, German, Spanish or Italian.
(Edward was not fluent in all of these languages, but at the age of seven he was proficient in conjugating Latin verbs and had written 'forty or fifty Latin verses'.)
4 Write a discourse (speech) on the failings and abuses within society today and what remedies are necessary. Limit your speech to 60 words.
(Edward wrote seventeen political and state papers running to many thousands of words. Source 13.5 is a sample.)
5 Write a pro and contra list (the advantages and disadvantages) for making Southampton into a trading centre capable of challenging Antwerp.
(Edward liked for/against lists and was particularly interested in economic affairs. His proposals for establishing a trading centre in England (9 March 1552) covered six pages and ran to 46 separate points.)
6 Write a summary of the current state of your finances. This should include:

- debts you owe
- debts owing to you
- subsidies (money from your parents!)
- bullion (savings in the bank)
- treasure (value of goods owned by you)
- land (income you earn).

(Finance was Edward's greatest political interest and he said he wanted to secure 'a mass of money' totalling £300,000 to pay off debts.)

■ 13B A summary of some of Edward's ideas

Topic	What Edward wrote	What it shows about how Edward *might* have acted if he had reached his majority
Reform of the government	He produced a memo recommending the reorganisation of the Privy Council and the limiting of its functions.	He might have introduced significant reforms to the administration and the legislative system.
Financial and economic problems	He wrote about the problems of the economic system, particularly inflation.	He might have overhauled England's economic and financial structure.
Foreign affairs	His diary entries reveal his great interest in the details of the Habsburg–Valois Wars.	He might have led a foreign expedition like his father.
Religion	He wrote about the need to promote good preaching and the disciplining of clergy (particularly bishops).	He might have given a very high priority to the promotion of the Protestant religion. He might have removed the episcopal structure.
Social problems	He wrote about the country being like a body in which every group must fulfil its duties and be in proper proportion for the 'whole' to work and be healthy.	He might have introduced measures to increase social justice, such as limits on the amount people could earn or own, and put an end to enclosure.

ACTIVITY

1 Judging from Source 13.5 and Chart 13B, how ready was Edward to take over the reins of government?
2 Is it likely that the Protector or other Privy Councillors would have seen Edward as being irrelevant to the Government or its decisions?

C What was Edward's role in the Government, 1547–53?

Edward's assumption of power

1537 12 October: Birth of Prince Edward
1547 28 January: Accession of Edward at the age of nine years and three months
31 January: Edward Seymour made Lord Protector
20 February: Coronation of Edward VI
21 March: Somerset made Protector until Edward was *eighteen*
1549 20 March: Thomas Seymour, Lord Sudeley, Somerset's brother, executed
31 October: Somerset's Protectorate dissolved
1550 21 February: Northumberland appointed Lord President of the Council
1551 August: Edward began to attend Privy Council meetings aged fourteen
1552 21 January: Somerset executed
Spring: Privy Council agreed Edward should become king in October 1553 (when he was *sixteen*, two years earlier than had been planned)
Summer: Edward conducted a progress through the south of England
1553 February: Edward seriously ill with pulmonary tuberculosis
21 May: Lady Jane Grey married the Duke of Northumberland's son, Guildford Dudley
12 June: Edward VI changed his will to name Lady Jane Grey as the successor
6 July: Death of Edward from septicaemia

■ **Learning trouble spot**

Seymour → Hertford → Somerset

- Edward Seymour (uncle of Prince Edward) was made Earl of Hertford in October 1537.
- He made himself Duke of Somerset on 16 February 1547.
- From 31 January 1547 until 31 October 1549, Somerset ruled as Lord Protector.

Dudley → Warwick → Northumberland

- John Dudley was made Earl of Warwick in February 1547.
- He made himself Duke of Northumberland on 11 October 1551.
- On 21 February 1550, Northumberland was appointed Lord President of the Council. He ruled until Mary's accession.

To avoid confusion, they will be referred to as Somerset and Northumberland.

FOCUS ROUTE

As you read pages 193–94 on Edward's influence in government, look for examples that show you how influential he was. Using your own copy of the following table, rate his influence on the following scale:

6 he was the most important power
5 he had a large degree of control
4 he had significant influence
3 he could not be ignored
2 he had little influence
1 he was irrelevant.

Time	Power rating	Supporting example
On his accession		
At Somerset's fall		
Early under Northumberland (1550–51)		
Later under Northumberland (1552–53)		
At the end of his reign		

Edward and the Government, 1547–49

Within days of Henry VIII's death, the Duke of Somerset had ignored Henry's intentions that the country should be ruled by a regency council and had himself made Lord Protector by the Council. Somerset was very strict with his nephew; he reduced the number of servants in Edward's household and kept Edward under the close control of his brother-in-law, Sir Michael Stanhope. More importantly for the government of the realm, Somerset ruled by using the dry stamp (see page 96) and proclamations, and he was based not at the court but at his expensive new residence, Somerset House. He had, in effect, assumed autocratic control of the Government and was alienating the other members of the court.

Edward, who on Somerset's fall from power was still only twelve, complained of the lack of pocket money he received from his uncle. At this stage, Edward had virtually no *direct* involvement in politics and much of his time was taken up with his education. Edward was, in the words of historian Penry Williams, 'a cypher in politics' (*The Later Tudors: England 1547–1603*).

However, even in this context his influence was considerable. In the autumn of 1549, Somerset was losing his grip on power and retreated to Windsor Castle, crucially taking the young king with him. However, Edward ostentatiously 'fell' poorly with a chill and complained of the cold surroundings: 'Methinks I am a prisoner here.' Edward's public support at this stage could have saved Somerset, but the young king's abandonment of him was fatal. Edward further condemned his uncle by saying that Somerset had threatened to create riots in the streets if he were overthrown. Somerset's denial was worthless; he could not contradict the King. His fall from power was swift and unstoppable. Somerset had reaped the bitter rewards of his failure to cultivate a relationship with his nephew.

Edward and the Government, 1550–53

Somerset's fall, the change in the personnel at the top of government and Edward's growing maturity all led to Edward gradually assuming a much more significant role in the Government after 1549.

By August 1551 Edward was attending some Privy Council meetings and by November 1552 he was attending them regularly and was setting some agendas. He was taking the lead in some business and had his own clearly thought-out views on some of the most pressing matters of the day (see the memorandum in Source 13.5 on page 190). In recognition of his advanced performance, the Council announced in spring 1552 that Edward would reach his majority at age sixteen rather than eighteen. By mid-1552 Edward was learning his craft in practice rather than through lessons. He was quickly developing effective political skills. His entries on foreign events in the Chronicle show that he was using sources beyond the normal flow of information available to the Council. He was already cultivating links with foreign ambassadors and making independent use of his secretaries, Cecil and Petre.

Northumberland, learning from Somerset's mistakes or just recognising the increasing power of the rapidly maturing king, was careful to ensure that Edward was consulted and involved much more in government. Even Northumberland's title – Lord President of the Council – showed recognition of the diminished role of the Regent.

The argument should not be taken too far. Northumberland was still in overall control and placed limits on what aspects of government Edward could be involved in – foreign policy, for example, was out of bounds. Northumberland also manipulated where he could, by placing his own men around the King and by packing the Privy Council with his own supporters. But as with Somerset, Northumberland was circumscribed by Edward's known views. It may well be the case that Northumberland's pursuit of Protestantism was chiefly motivated by Edward's fierce commitment to it (see Chapter 15). The final and potentially most serious act to which Edward was party was the attempt made to change the succession in favour of Lady Jane Grey (see Chapter 18 for analysis of Edward's involvement).

D Review: How much influence did Edward VI have in government?

The maxim most often applied to the reign of minors is that whoever had 'control of the King's person' held the reins of power. To this extent, historians rightly study the relations of Somerset and Northumberland with the young king. However, what we may also need to add to this historical equation is the extent to which Edward gained 'control of his own person' as the reign progressed. The serious nine-year-old who was cowed by Somerset in January 1547 was not the same person as the self-confident and assertive nearly sixteen-year-old who worked with Northumberland on changing the succession. Historians must be careful to acknowledge the changes that had taken place in Edward during these six years.

His upbringing, character, education and training meant, in the words of one of Edward's biographers, that 'Few monarchs in history have been as well equipped for their task as was Edward VI' (W. K. Jordan (ed.), *The Chronicle and Political Papers of King Edward VI*). Edward was certainly not irrelevant to the Government during his reign, and the fall of Somerset seems to have afforded Edward an opportunity to decisively increase his involvement. The usually impartial Venetian ambassador also remarked that 'there is perhaps no instance on record of any other King of that age being more beloved, or who gave greater'. The potential for the reign of the adult Edward was great indeed.

ACTIVITY

Based on what you have learned so far about Edward, make a prediction as to what kind of monarch Edward would have been if he had reached adulthood. You should consider the following:

- How good would he have been (compared with his father and grandfather)? What would have been his strengths and weaknesses?
- What would have been his policies with regard to religion, foreign policy and government?
- How might Edward's upbringing and position have affected the development of his relationships?

TALKING POINT

Is your experience of growing from nine to sixteen years old of use in understanding Edward's changing role in government?

KEY POINTS FROM CHAPTER 13: Irrelevant Edward? How much influence did Edward VI have in government?

1. Edward was a highly intelligent, serious-minded and hard-working person.
2. He showed few emotions and did not form close relationships.
3. In temperament, aptitudes and approach to government, he was more like his grandfather, Henry VII, than his father.
4. He received a very effective education and training for kingship.
5. His Chronicle and political writings reveal him to be very well informed and to have a detailed understanding of a full range of governmental issues.
6. During his reign, day-to-day decisions were made by Somerset or Northumberland and the Council.
7. Lord Protector Somerset (1547–October 1549) excluded Edward from government, but Northumberland (1550–53) included Edward in decisions and policy making.
8. Edward's most significant power came from his position as king; everyone had to take heed of his views.
9. He was a person of very strong opinions, the most important and strongly held of which was his Protestantism.
10. Edward's support or lack of it was a significant force in his reign: for example, in Somerset's fall from power.

How successfully was England governed during Edward's reign?

CHAPTER OVERVIEW

Edward's Government was dominated by two major ministers: first by the Duke of Somerset, who ruled almost as a king from Henry VIII's death in January 1547 until he was forced from power in October 1549; then by the Duke of Northumberland, who emerged as the new leader of the Government in January 1550. Northumberland was finally brought down by his enemies as a result of his attempt to alter the succession in July 1553. The distinctive characters and approaches of Northumberland and Somerset have fascinated historians through the years.

This chapter will examine the careers of Somerset and Northumberland, focusing on their social and economic policies and on the nature of their rule. The fact that two men headed a minority for the same length of time offers us an irresistible comparison, and this chapter will reach an assessment of which of the two was more successful in fulfilling his roles.

A How well suited were Somerset and Northumberland to government? (pp. 195–97)

B How did Somerset and Northumberland gain power? (pp. 198–99)

C What social and economic policies did the Government follow during Edward's reign? (pp. 200–204)

D How did Somerset's and Northumberland's approaches differ? (p. 205)

E Who was more successful at governing, Somerset or Northumberland? (pp. 206–207)

F Review: How successfully was England governed during Edward's reign? (p. 208)

How well suited were Somerset and Northumberland to government?

ACTIVITY

Based on what you have already learned about Northumberland and Somerset and their relationship with Edward, what preconceptions have you formed about the likely quality of their government?

FOCUS ROUTE

As you read through this chapter, complete your own copy of the following table to build up a picture of the qualities of the two most significant individuals in the Government.

	Strengths	Example	Weaknesses	Example
Somerset				
Northumberland				

■ 14A What was Somerset like?

SOURCE 14.1
Edward Seymour, the Duke of Somerset

- Stubbornly committed to particular policies
- A man of action
- Obsessed by the problem of Scotland
- An obsessive gambler (he won 35 shillings at the Archbishop of Canterbury's palace)
- A mildly radical Protestant
- An autocratic ruler – arrogant, rude and difficult to work with
- Accumulated wealth and jewels
- Not a well-educated or bookish person
- Spent lavishly – built Somerset House at the cost of £10,000 (significantly more than any subject had ever paid for a house)

Somerset's rise to power

- He was born Edward Seymour in about 1506.
- The brother of Jane Seymour, his political rise dates from her marriage to Henry VIII in 1536.
- In March 1537 he became a member of the Privy Council; he became the Earl of Hertford after the birth of Edward.
- During the 1540s he had experience of diplomacy and the battlefield in Scotland and France.
- On 31 January 1547, after Henry VIII's death, the Privy Council elected Somerset as Protector and he ruled with virtual royal authority.
- On 4 February 1547 Edward and thirteen executors signed a document giving Somerset sovereign authority until Edward was eighteen.
- On 16 February 1547 he became the Duke of Somerset.
- In October 1549 he was dismissed from his offices and imprisoned.
- In April 1550 he was released and returned to the Privy Council.
- In January 1552 he was tried and executed.

ACTIVITY

Physiognomy is the art of judging character from someone's appearance. It is not a particularly historical skill, but everyone inevitably uses it! Study the portraits of Somerset and Northumberland in Sources 14.1 and 14.2. What conclusions would you draw about their personality from their appearance?

SOURCE 14.2
John Dudley, the Duke of Northumberland

- A skilled politician
- Not a pious man
- Suffered from illness and depression
- Effective at delegating responsibility
- A soldier
- Ambitious for power
- An opportunist

Northumberland's rise to power

- He was born John Dudley in 1504, son of Edmund Dudley (who was executed by Henry VIII as a scapegoat for Henry VII's financial policy).
- He was brought up by Sir Edward Guildford, who married Dudley to his daughter and treated him as his son.
- He received various court posts under Henry VIII, including Master of the Horse for Anne of Cleves – probably a job he did not want!
- In March 1542 he became Viscount Lisle on the death of his stepfather.
- In the 1540s he earned his military reputation in land and sea battles against the Scots and French.
- In February 1547, on Henry VIII's death, he became the Earl of Warwick and Lord Great Chamberlain.
- In August 1549 he crushed Kett's rebellion (see page 233).
- In October 1549 he planned Somerset's removal.
- In January 1550 he became Lord President of the Council.
- In October 1551 he became Duke of Northumberland.
- In July 1553 he attempted to change the succession to his own advantage.
- In August 1553 he was tried and executed. He died on 22 August.

ACTIVITY

1. What similarities and main differences are there in the personalities and careers of Somerset and Northumberland?
2. Which of them seems better equipped to lead the Government? Give reasons.

B How did Somerset and Northumberland gain power?

How did Somerset come to power?

Henry VIII had intended to create a balanced Privy Council in his will – sixteen members all governing together with equal powers until Edward reached eighteen. Before his death, however, Henry's plans had gone awry when Gardiner's expulsion from the Council and Norfolk's arrest unbalanced the Privy Council in favour of the Protestants. Henry's plan to have his will obeyed was never likely to succeed. The Privy Council was designed to function with a chief executive, and Norfolk's fall from power had left Somerset as the dominant figure.

Somerset's assumption of power was an entirely natural outcome. Henry's will had allowed for a majority to 'devise and ordain' whatever they thought best for government and this led to Somerset becoming Protector. Despite personal shortcomings, he was the obvious choice because he was the King's uncle, had a strong military reputation and had been in favour during the last part of Henry's reign. The transfer of power was smoothly achieved because Somerset kept the King's death secret until he had possession of Edward. He already had custody of the will and the dry stamp, and the highly effective William, Lord Paget acted on his behalf. New titles and land grants helped to win over any opposition:

- Edward Seymour himself became Duke of Somerset.
- John Dudley became Earl of Warwick.
- Thomas Seymour became Lord Seymour.
- William Parr became Marquis of Northampton.
- Thomas Wriothesley became Earl of Southampton.

Why did Somerset fall from power and how did Northumberland gain power?

ACTIVITY

1 Is there any indication from Chart 14C that Northumberland led the coup and intended to oust Somerset from power?
2 Does Northumberland seem to have been attempting to gain power for himself?
3 Why was Somerset's general summons on 5 October and the subsequent support of the ordinary peasants likely to prove fatal to his cause?
4 Produce a two-minute radio broadcast which explains why and how Somerset was replaced by Northumberland at the head of the Government.
5 Which individual played the most significant role in the events between November 1549 and February 1550 – Northumberland, Arundel, Southampton, Lord St John, or Lord Russell? Explain your choice.
6 'Not a carefully planned coup but a piece of brilliant opportunism.' Do you agree with this view of Northumberland's role in the coup of 1549–50?
7 Was Northumberland right to judge that the benefits of rehabilitating Somerset outweighed the risks?
8 'Northumberland and Somerset came to power because they happened to be the right people in the right place at the right time. It was not because of anything that they did.' Do you agree with this statement?

■ Learning trouble spot

The underhand and secret dealings of politicians as they jockey for position obviously present a problem for the historian. The exact nature and reasons for the changes in the Privy Council in late autumn 1549 remain unclear. We can only speculate on the basis of the outcome and the rise and fall of the various people in each faction.

■ 14C How did Northumberland gain power?

1 THE PLAYERS
all members of the Privy Council

Duke of Somerset	Lord Protector
Earl of Arundel Earl of Southampton Lord Russell Lord St John	Conservatives in religion
Lord Paget	Neutral
Earl of Warwick (becomes Duke of Northumberland in 1551; see Learning trouble spot on page 192) Archbishop Cranmer	Protestant reformers

2 THE GRIEVANCES
the reasons why people were opposed to Somerset

- **Poor leadership.** Somerset had alienated many people through his high-handed management. He was reluctant to delegate, often by-passed the Council and (in the words of the Imperial ambassador) ruled from 'the Protector's palace'.
- **Mishandling of foreign policy.** The failed campaign in Scotland and the declaration of war by France in August 1549 disappointed a Council who saw foreign affairs as a very important issue.
- **Favouritism.** Somerset packed the key positions with his own men and thereby controlled the King (e.g. Sir Michael Stanhope was made Groom of the Stool in August 1547, Chief Gentleman of the Privy Chamber in 1548).
- **Money making and extravagance.** He built lavishly, was able to accumulate fees, salaries, offices and chantry lands, and added £5,000 to an already substantial income.
- **Social policy.** His views on social justice alienated the aristocracy and were seen to be bearing terrifying fruit in the Western rebellion and Kett's rebellion in the summer of 1549.
- **Religious policy.** Many leading Catholics, such as the Earls of Arundel and Southampton, were opposed to the religious reforms.

3 THE COUP, 1549
the removal of Somerset

August	Northumberland suppressed Kett's rebellion.
15 September	Somerset's plan for the creation of a 'new council' was opposed by the Earls of Arundel, Southampton and Northumberland.
September	Steady mobilisation of troops (about 2,500) for the conservatives. Somerset made an unsuccessful appeal for the support of Lord Russell's army, still together after the suppression of the Western rebellion.
30 September	Somerset ordered all soldiers to leave the City of London.
5 October	Somerset and the King moved to Hampton Court (he had about 400 troops). Somerset made a general summons to all the King's loyal subjects to defend the King at Hampton Court. They were joined by hundreds of poorly armed peasants.
6 October	Somerset took Edward to Windsor Castle.
7 October	Conservative lords accused Somerset of rousing the commons and of kidnapping the King.
8 October	Somerset appealed to Northumberland for help as a friend.
10 October	Somerset surrendered.
14 October	Somerset was imprisoned.

4 THE MANOEUVRING
the balance changes in the Council

17 October	The Council had a majority of religious conservatives.
Late October	Sir Edward Peckham, a conservative, was removed from the Council.
6 November	Thomas Goodrich, bishop of Ely (a Protestant and a friend of Cranmer), was sworn on to the Council.
29 November	The Marquis of Dorset, a Protestant and ally of Northumberland, was appointed to the Council.
2 December	The Council had a Protestant majority.

5 THE STING, 1549–50
Northumberland takes power

Early December	Lord St John warned Northumberland that the Catholics Arundel and Southampton were planning to use the case against Somerset to overthrow Northumberland, as he had been a friend of Somerset.
13 December	Northumberland declared to the Council that anyone who sought Somerset's blood also sought his own. The conservatives had been wrong-footed and outmanned in the Privy Council. Lords St John and Russell changed sides and were rewarded by Northumberland, who made them Earls of Wiltshire and Bedford respectively.
End of January	The Earls of Arundel and Southampton were dismissed from the Council. Northumberland had secured control of the Privy Council and made himself its Lord President. By this time, Northumberland's friends and relations had been placed around the King, who must have acquiesced to their presence, presumably on the basis of approving of their leaning towards Protestantism.

6 THE AFTERMATH
What happened to Somerset after the coup?

Northumberland made a determined effort at reconciliation with Somerset. By mid-1550 Somerset had returned to court, his goods had been restored and his daughter had married Northumberland's son. Somerset, however, continued plotting and Northumberland fabricated details in order to get Somerset executed in January 1552.

What social and economic policies did the Government follow during Edward's reign?

What were the Government's policy considerations?

ACTIVITY

You are a sixteenth-century business consultancy (think of a name for yourselves), which has been asked to advise the Government on what policies it should follow in 1547 (when Somerset was in charge) and then in 1550 (when Northumberland was in charge). You need to analyse the areas of policy and the possible solutions (see Charts 14D and 14E). You must then produce a flip-chart action plan with your recommendations and your reasons for these choices. Your presentation should be as convincing and flashy as possible. You will be presenting to the Privy Council, which includes Somerset (in 1547), Northumberland and Edward.

■ 14D Policy considerations in 1547

Policy area	Considerations
Foreign policy *How should the Government handle relations with Scotland?* Options: • Wage war against Scotland with different tactics • Bring the war against Scotland to an end	Somerset was bound by Henry's wish for Edward to marry Mary, Queen of Scots, and by the need to retain the support of the war-like nobility. The policy of periodic invasions of Scotland had failed to achieve the overall objectives and war was extremely expensive. Somerset had been the leader of successful attacks in the 1540s and now had a plan to save money on invasions by garrisoning the Scottish lowlands. Pursuing the war would require large sums of money to be raised. Ending the war would be highly unpopular.
Economy and finance *How should England raise money and improve the* ECONOMY *and government* FINANCES*?* Options: • Debasement – continue or end? • Sale of Crown lands – continue or end? • Borrowing – continue or end? • Sale of chantry lands – continue or end?	This was a high priority because the country was bankrupt and inflation was extremely high. However, effective reform would be unpopular and would require difficult decisions. Debasement (started by Henry VIII), while being an easy way of raising money, was a cause of inflation and economic instability. The sale of Crown lands raised large sums, but meant the Government raised less from rents every year. If the Government borrowed money, it could be charged high rates of interest. The sale of chantry lands would raise money and continue Henry VIII's policy.
Religion *What policy should the Government adopt towards the Reformation?* Options: • Push strongly towards Protestantism • Retain the fairly neutral position left at the end of Henry VIII's reign • Move back towards Catholicism	The Catholic Act of Six Articles (1539) was still in force, but the pressure from the reformers was pushing the country towards Protestantism. Edward, Cranmer and Somerset all had Protestant views. Somerset needed to keep the reformers on board, but there was a danger of provoking the Catholics into rebellion. Edward's Catholic sister Mary posed a particularly difficult problem, as she remained resolutely determined to retain her faith and was supported by some of the leading figures at court and by the Holy Roman Emperor, Charles V. Moves towards Catholicism would therefore ease the foreign situation. Remaining neutral would dissatisfy the radicals on both sides.
Social order *How should the Government deal with the problems of enclosure and vagrancy?* Options: • Order commissions to investigate enclosures • Act against vagrants	There was growing concern about poverty because of social injustice and because it was seen as a threat to order. Particular anger was felt over enclosure. Enclosure was blamed for many economic problems, but a commission would raise expectations among the people that action would be taken against enclosure. Fear of the poor was increasing, so clamping down on vagrants would show the Government to be acting against the poor who were not looking for work.

ECONOMY AND FINANCE
The *economy* refers to the economic health and structure of the whole country, such as the wool trade and harvests. *Finance* refers to the system of money and credit employed by the Government, such as taxation, revenues and expenditure.

■ 14E Policy considerations in 1550

Policy area	Considerations
Foreign policy *How should the Government handle relations with Scotland and France?* Options: • Continue to wage war against Scotland and France • Bring the wars to an end	Somerset's policy of establishing garrisons had been a costly failure. The aristocracy still looked to warfare as a way of achieving status and prestige. Holding on to Boulogne (captured by Henry VIII) had become an important symbol of maintaining Henry's legacy. Pursuing the wars would require large sums of money to be raised. Ending the wars would ease the financial situation.
Economy and finance *How should England raise money and improve the economy and government finances?* Options: • Debasement – continue or end? • Sale of Crown lands – continue or end? • Borrowing – continue or renegotiate? • Reform the Government's financial situation • Raise taxation	The war against Scotland had been expensive and debasement was known to cause damage to the economy. Debasement, while being an easy way of raising money, was a cause of inflation and economic instability. The sale of Crown lands raised large sums, but meant the Government raised less from rents every year. If the Government borrowed money, it could be charged high rates of interest. Somerset had not attempted any economic reforms. Reforms would require unpopular cuts in expenditure and changes to the structure and efficiency of the Crown's finances, which would arouse opposition. Raising taxation might cause social unrest and would be hard to justify if the country were not at war.
Religion *What policy should the Government adopt towards the Reformation?* Options: • Push strongly towards Protestantism • Maintain the mildly Protestant position left by Somerset • Move back towards Catholicism	The First Book of Common Prayer (1549) had established a moderate Protestant position, but had provoked rebellion in various parts of the country. The pressure from the reformers (including Edward, Cranmer and Northumberland) was increasing. Radical Protestants were gaining influence in London and various parts of the country. Keeping the current religious position would dissatisfy the radicals on both sides. A return to Catholicism would be supported by Mary and some leading figures at court and would ease the foreign situation in relation to Charles V.
Social order *How should the Government deal with enclosure, vagrancy and other threats to public order?* Options: • Continue Somerset's policies against enclosures • Continue to act against vagrants • Take action to relieve the hunger of the poor	The widespread and dangerous rebellions in the summer of 1549 had raised great fears among the ruling elites. Northumberland had played a central role in crushing Kett's rebellion. Somerset's anti-enclosure policy had been seen as a cause of the rebellions in1549. Expectations were raised among the people that action would be taken against enclosure. Somerset's policy against vagrants had been seen as too harsh, but the problem of large numbers of poor and the belief that this led to disorder remained. The harvest of 1549 had been poor, but the harvest of 1550 was even worse.

FOCUS ROUTE

As you read through the remainder of this chapter and the other chapters in this section, identify the policy choices that Somerset and Northumberland made and complete your own copy of the following table.

Policy area	Somerset	Northumberland
Foreign policy		
Economy and finance		
Religion		
Social order		

What social policies were followed during Edward's reign?

FOCUS ROUTE

Study Chart 14F and make notes on the following questions:

1 What were the main social problems facing the Government?
2 How effective were the solutions that Somerset and Northumberland attempted?
3 What were the consequences of Somerset's social policy?

COPYHOLDER
Tenant of land held 'according to the custom of the manor'.

■ 14F Social policy under Somerset and Northumberland

SOMERSET'S POLICY 1547–49

Vagrancy Act

The number of poor in sixteenth-century England was undoubtedly increasing, and they were becoming more mobile in response to the rapid expansion of key towns such as London. It was traditional for governments to clamp down on the poor because of the heightened fear of disorder that large numbers of poor created. The Vagrancy Act (known as the 'Slavery Act'), introduced in 1547, was an unpopular law that involved 'a savage attack on vagrants looking for work' (Heard, *Edward VI and Mary: A Mid-Tudor Crisis?*). Under the law, able-bodied persons who had been out of work for three days were to be branded with a V and sold into slavery for two years. Further offences were to be punished by permanent slavery. Children of vagrants were to be taken from their parents and made to work as apprentices. None of these provisions was ever put into effect, and they can perhaps be best seen as a knee-jerk reaction by the Government to alleviate the concerns of the landed classes.

The Act did, however, take the Government a step further towards the poor relief provision that evolved during the late sixteenth century. It ordered local officials to provide housing and collections for all 'idle, impotent, maimed, and aged persons' who were not vagabonds.

Enclosure

Somerset, influenced by the Commonwealth group of churchmen and intellectuals, was a keen supporter of anti-enclosure measures. Enclosure, especially where it involved the decline of tillage (land used to grow arable crops), was seen as a cause of many economic problems and the Government acted forcefully against it. A commission to investigate enclosure in the Midlands was established under John Hales (although it failed to bring any cases against enclosers) and in June 1548 proclamations were issued enforcing all statutes against enclosure for grazing. Somerset passed an Act protecting COPYHOLDERS on his own estates. In March 1549 a 5 per cent tax on personal property and a special tax on sheep (regarded as the principal reason for enclosure and so a threat to tillage) were passed against stiff opposition.

According to M.L. Bush in *The Government Policy of Protector Somerset*, Somerset's social programme was not particularly advanced and 'was in keeping with the age'. However, the policy had disastrous political consequences for Somerset. It raised hopes of effective government action among ordinary people and generated fears of unrest among the landed classes. The Western rebellion and Kett's rebellion in 1549, although not directly caused by enclosure, were too coincidental for comfort. Somerset had established a reputation for being a poor man's friend that he could not shake off.

NORTHUMBERLAND'S POLICY 1550–53

Northumberland did not continue Somerset's anti-enclosure measures; commissioners were withdrawn, the unpopular sheep tax was repealed in 1550 and existing enclosure legislation was enforced. The unpopular 1547 Vagrancy Act was repealed, although its provisions for the care of the disabled were retained. By 1551 Northumberland's government had taken action to control stocks of grain to relieve the crisis caused by the harvest failures. Northumberland kept order by traditional means to prevent the kind of widespread disorder that had occurred in 1549. He introduced new Treason Laws in 1550 and used Lords Lieutenant and the retainers of trusted nobles to keep order.

How effectively were the financial and economic problems dealt with in Edward's reign?

FOCUS ROUTE

Study Chart 14G and make notes on the following questions:

1 What were the main pressures on the Government's finances and the economy?
2 How effective were the solutions that
   a) Northumberland **b)** Somerset
   attempted?

■ 14G Economic and financial policy under Somerset and Northumberland

Henry VIII's financial legacy
Henry had left his son in deep financial trouble. There were three main problems:

- **Debasement.** In 1544 Henry VIII had begun large-scale debasement of the coinage. Debasement was a tempting, but short-sighted way for a government to raise money. It was tempting because it raised large sums (£363,000 in Henry's reign and £1,270,684 by the end of 1551). However, it was short-sighted because at home it led to inflation (running at extremely high levels), a loss of confidence in the currency and economic disruption. Abroad, the loss of confidence in the English currency disrupted trade, caused the exchange rate to fall and made it more difficult for the Government to obtain credit.
- **Heavy expenditure.** Henry had spent in a lavish way and the ordinary income would not meet the expenditure required. The huge sum raised by the dissolution of the monasteries had been eaten away by the greater cost of war against France and Scotland in the 1540s. By 1547 almost half of the land had been sold, and so it would no longer supplement ordinary income.
- **Debt.** Henry had borrowed heavily at home and abroad: by the end of his reign, for example, he owed £100,000 to the Antwerp money market.

↓

Somerset – problems and solutions
Somerset's overriding concern with the Scottish war led him to continue the heavy military expenditure. The campaigns in Scotland between 1547 and 1549 cost £580,393 and Boulogne continued to be fortified. The policy of debasement was continued at full speed. Somerset attempted no reforms of the Government's finances.

↓

Northumberland – problems and solutions
Northumberland showed a determination to get the Crown finances back on course. The talented William Paulet, Marquis of Winchester, was appointed Lord Treasurer in February 1550 with the task of reforming the finances. The Government's plans, outlined in June 1551, were threefold:

- to end debasement
- to reduce expenditure so that it matched income and allowed the King to 'live of his own'
- 'to have His Majesty out of debt'

↓

End to debasement
Proclamations were issued to reduce the value of the coinage in 1550, but the decision to end debasement was not taken until April 1551. Even then, Northumberland did not dare call in the debased coinage and replace it with coins containing the correct amount of precious metal (this was done in 1560). Northumberland was therefore only telling people to lower prices and trust the coinage without giving them a concrete reason to do so. The collapse of the Antwerp market in 1551–52 caused further economic problems, especially for the cloth trade.

Reduction in expenditure
Drastic reductions were ordered in military and household expenditure. Boulogne was returned to France for £133,333 and the garrisons were withdrawn from Scotland, although expenditure on the navy and on fortifications continued. Commissions were established to inquire into the state of the finances and Winchester enforced stricter methods of accounting. An emergency household fund – a privy coffer – was established. Northumberland faced the difficulty of needing to keep a tight grip on the finances at the same time as rewarding his supporters with grants and advantageous sales of land, and ordinary income was not increased. Although expenditure was pruned, it was not realistic in the mid-sixteenth century for a king to 'live of his own'.

Debts
The debts, at their worst in 1550, at £300,000, had been reduced by 1553 to £180,000. To achieve this, it had been necessary to continue the sale of Crown and chantry lands (raising £100,000 and £110,486 respectively). Once sold, however, the lands no longer contributed to the Crown's ordinary income. Parliamentary taxes (raising £336,000), debasement up to 1551 (raising £537,000) and the clawing back of debts owed to the Government (£16,667) were also necessary.

Sir Thomas Gresham was authorised to pay off royal debts on the Antwerp market. He showed great energy and ingenuity, crossing the Channel 40 times in a few months and manipulating the exchange so as to improve the worth of sterling. He was so successful that he paid off all of the Government's Antwerp debts in two years and renegotiated the loans at 12 per cent interest, whereas the Emperor was borrowing at 16 per cent.

↓

How successful was Northumberland in dealing with the financial and economic problems?
Northumberland had inherited a dire financial situation and in only two and half years had managed to improve the Government's position significantly and go a long way towards achieving his three initial objectives. He can be credited with grasping half of the nettle. He ended debasement, but did not take the measures needed to restore full confidence in the currency. He substantially reduced the Government's expenditure, but was forced by political necessity to compromise in order to reward his supporters. Finally, he markedly reduced the debt, but weakened the Government's long-term financial position in the process.

SOURCE 14.3 Edward was taught Italianate handwriting. What would a graphologist make of this piece of writing from the later pages of his Chronicle? What does it suggest about his intelligence and emotions?

The gouuernaunce of this realme is deuided into tow parties, on ecclesiasticall, the other temporell.

Th'ecclesiasticall consisteth, in settingforth the worde of god, The settingfurth of the worde of god consisteth, in the good discreet doctrine and example of the teachours and spirituall officers. For as the good husbandmane maketh his ground good and plentifull, so doth the true preachour, w^t doctrine and example print and grafe in the peples mind the word of god that they at length become plentifull. Prayers to god also must be made continually of the peple and officers of the church to assist them w^t his grace. And thos prayers, must first with good consideracion be setfurth, and fautes therin be amendid, next being setfurth the peple must continually be allured to heire them. For discipline it were uery good that it wentfurth, and that those that did notablye offend in swearing rioting neglecting of gods word, or such like uices were duely punished so that thos that shuld be thexecutours of this discipline, were men of tried honesty wisdom and iudgment. But bicause thos bishops who shuld execute, some for papistrye, some for ignoraunce some for age, some for their ill name some for al theis, ar men unable to execute discipline, it is therefor a thing unmete for thies men. wherefore it were necessary that those that were apointed to be bishops or preachours, were honest in life and lerned in their doctrine, that by rewarding of such men other might be allured to folow their good life.

D How did Somerset's and Northumberland's approaches differ?

FOCUS ROUTE

Study Chart 14H and make notes on Somerset's and Northumberland's:

a) style of government
b) use of the Privy Council.

■ 14H Government under Somerset and Northumberland

	Somerset	**Northumberland**
Style of government	Somerset was granted quasi-royal powers by Letters Patent in March 1547. As his authority had not been granted by Parliament, he was more independent of that body. Somerset used more proclamations than any other Tudor ruler (over 70 in less than three years), which meant that he was creating laws without using Parliament. Historians have accused him of ruling autocratically, although his contemporaries at his trial did not accuse him of misusing proclamations. He obtained sole custody of the dry stamp, which had been left under the control of four councillors, and he tried to insist that the King's true signature was not valid without his own counter-signature. He also used his own household servants – Sir Thomas Smith, Sir Michael Stanhope, William Cecil, Sir John Thynne and William Grey – as government officials. His methods aroused intense opposition and at his downfall nineteen of the Council accused him of 'malice and evil government . . . pride, covetousness and extreme ambition'.	Northumberland's style of government was geared closely to his personal political objectives. His role in the downfall of Somerset and his subsequent elevation to power seems to have been motivated by his instinct for survival (see pages 198–99). Once in power he organised the Government and the Council to secure his position. He staffed the household with his men, who could then control access to Edward. For example, Sir John Gates as Vice Chamberlain commanded the King's guard, held the dry stamp and reported to Northumberland all the comings and goings of the King. The astute and capable William Cecil made the switch from Somerset's camp to act as Northumberland's deputy.
Use of the Privy Council	Somerset effectively by-passed the Privy Council. The Council that he called frequently convened at Somerset House and his group of household servants were nicknamed the 'new council'.	Northumberland extended the use and importance of the Privy Council. His political 'genius' (D. Hoak, 'Rehabilitating the Duke of Northumberland: politics and political control, 1549–53' in R. Tittler and J. Loach (eds), *The Mid-Tudor Polity c. 1540–1560*) was to see that his political survival (during the coup of 1549–50) and his continued political dominance (after he had achieved power in January 1550: see page 199) depended on his control of the Council. He made himself Lord President of the Council so that he had the power to fix agendas and meetings and to bar councillors (which he did to Catholics on the first day). He also assumed the King's power to create new councillors. Northumberland's reform of Privy Council procedures marked the 'revival' of government by the Council (D. Hoak, *op.cit.*).
Use of Parliament	The practice of frequent parliaments (established under Henry VIII in the 1530s) continued under Edward VI. There were two parliaments in six years and 1551 was the only year without a session. Parliament was used to pass religious laws. Parliament was not, however, used to establish or destroy the Protectorate, or to pass the Act of Succession.	

ACTIVITY

1 Does the evidence of Somerset's style of government justify the claim that he 'acted more in the manner of a king'?
2 What lessons had Northumberland learned from Somerset's style of leadership? What changes did he make?

E Who was more successful at governing, Somerset or Northumberland?

In traditional historiography, Somerset and Northumberland have generated the most extreme of passions. Judgements of them have been forced to the opposite ends of the spectrum, Somerset being presented as the 'Good Duke' and Northumberland as the 'Evil Duke'. Figures from history rarely match up to such eternally 'good' or 'evil' images. This section will allow you to examine the traditional views of Somerset and Northumberland, to compare these with the more recent revised opinions, and then to reach your own decision about their effectiveness in government.

Traditional historiography: 'Good Duke' versus 'Evil Duke'

The 'Good Duke'

- He established a court of requests in his London house in order that he might hear the cases of poor people.
- He refused to allow anyone to be tortured or burned.
- He had a progressive social policy, wanting to fix rents and abolish enclosures.
- He criticised wealthy, self-seeking men.

The 'Evil Duke'

- He masterminded the coup in 1549 that gave him control of the Privy Council. He then purged the people who had helped him in the coup.
- He arbitrarily ordered Somerset's arrest and then manufactured the evidence in the trial (December 1551) that led to his execution.
- He was two-faced on religion. For the coup, he posed as a Catholic, after which he became a radical Protestant. On the scaffold before his execution, he announced his conversion back to Catholicism.
- He attempted to change the succession so that he could retain his grip on power.

SOURCE 14.4 W. K. Jordan, who wrote in 1968, quoted in J. Loach, *Protector Somerset: A Reassessment*, 1994, p. 9

[Somerset was] a very great man whose magnanimity and high idealism were never to be forgotten as Englishmen spoke in quiet corners, in the fields and on the sea of the age of the 'Good Duke'.

SOURCE 14.6 W. G. Hoskins, *The Age of Plunder: The England of Henry VIII*, 1976, p. 223

[Northumberland was in] the most unprincipled gang of political adventurers and predators that England had seen for many centuries.

TALKING POINT

Alison Weir (Source 14.7) is a historian whose books are aimed at the general reader, not at an academic or school audience. Her book was published in 1996, long after historians had reassessed Northumberland's role. What does this suggest about this book?

SOURCE 14.5 A. F. Pollard, who wrote in 1902, quoted in J. Loach, *Protector Somerset: A Reassessment*, 1994, p. 9

Ambitious he certainly was, yet his was an ambition animated by no mean or selfish motives, but by the desire to achieve aims that were essentially noble.

SOURCE 14.7 A. Weir, *Children of England: The Heirs of King Henry VIII*, 1996, p. 92

John Dudley was arguably the most evil statesman to govern England during the sixteenth century. He was greedy and rapacious, corrupt, cruel and unscrupulous.

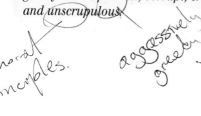

Revised interpretations

Revised views of Somerset and Northumberland have focused more on their abilities as leaders than on judgements on the morality of their rule.

Somerset

14.8 - Somerset legitimately overthrown.
14.9 - Scottish war underpinned Somerset's policies.
14.10 - Political skill yet to be fully explored - appreciated
[illegible].11 - Politically astute, survival instinct key to rise & consolidation.

SOURCE [illegible] 14.8 J. Loach, *Protector Somerset: A Reassessment*, 1994, p.42

[illegible]ould appear that the London [illegible]rges against the Protector [illegible]derable justice: he had, [illegible]iled in Scotland and France, [illegible]ishandled his colleagues and [illegible] of 1549, and he was both [illegible]nd greedy. There is no need, [illegible]ee his overthrow as the [illegible] of reaction'. Indeed, few of the [illegible]aid against Somerset related [illegible] matters; other than the [illegible]elating to the enclosure [illegible]ion, the only charge made [illegible] Somerset which might be held up as the London lords' harshness towards the lower orders relates to the court of requests which the duke held in his own house.

SOURCE 14.9 M. L. Bush, *The Government Policy of Protector Somerset*, 1975, p. 161

Underlying the policy of the Somerset regime was the Scottish war. Because of the war, the course it took and the pressures it exerted, the government's policy as a whole acquired much of its character. The war determined the nature of the regime's domestic as well as its foreign concerns. It strongly influenced the evolution of the government's social programme, largely by preventing the government from proceeding against inflation with a monetary solution; it determined the government's treatment of peasant rebellion in 1549 when the tactics employed against the rebels owed much to Somerset's initial wish not to be diverted from his Scottish plans. It made a decisive effect upon the religious settlement since the Scottish war made it essential not to antagonize Emperor Charles V, and thus Somerset had to proceed with caution and ambiguity rather than in accordance with his religious beliefs.

Northumberland

SOURCE 14.10 D. Loades, *John Dudley, Duke of Northumberland*, 1996, p. 81

He was both more honest and skilful than he has often been given credit for, and in power he was an effective chief executive. The extent of his achievement, however, beyond the building of his own career, remains problematical. He was probably most successful as Lord Admiral . . . However it must also be remembered that he held the minority government of Edward VI together from 1550 to 1553, and enabled it to survive a period of acute financial and social stress which could have inflicted much greater damage than it did.

SOURCE 14.11 D. Hoak, 'Rehabilitating the Duke of Northumberland: politics and political control, 1549–53', in R. Tittler and J. Loach (eds), *The Mid-Tudor Polity c. 1540–1560*, 1980, p. 33

Politically, the future lay with the Council, a Council whose members would in reality share the authority to govern England during the remainder of Edward's minority. It was Northumberland's genius to see that his political ambition depended on procedural control of such a Council. However, the fact that he achieved this administrative control by February 1550 was the accidental result of the fiercest struggle for the powers of the Crown since the Wars of the Roses. In this struggle (October 1549 to February 1550) Northumberland simply aimed to avoid political destruction . . . Indeed, given the circumstances which he inherited in 1549, the duke of Northumberland appears to have been one of the most remarkably able governors of any European state during the sixteenth century.

TALKING POINT

What reasons can you suggest for historians' changing interpretations on this topic?

ACTIVITY

1 Read Sources 14.8–14.11. For each source, produce a list of the main points that the historians make about Somerset and Northumberland.
2 Compare the traditional and revised historical views on
   a) Somerset
   b) Northumberland.
   Which do you find the most persuasive? Explain why.
3 Who governed England more effectively, Somerset or Northumberland? Base your answer on the opinions in Sources 14.4–14.11 and on your own assessment of their performances.

Review: How successfully was England governed during Edward's reign?

Somerset and Northumberland were both traditional sixteenth-century aristocrats, military men who had succeeded in politics owing to their ambition and to their astute handling of the circumstances in which they found themselves.

Somerset was more ideologically motivated, allowing his genuinely held social and religious beliefs to influence government policy. But both these areas of policy took a back seat to his stubbornly held desire to subdue the Scots. Somerset overstretched himself through the war with Scotland and his anti-enclosure policies. He alienated too many powerful nobles with his domineering and aloof attitude. When the rebellions broke out in 1549, he found that he had burnt all his bridges, including the one to Edward, who was only too happy to watch his uncle's fall.

Northumberland was more pragmatic and was driven first and foremost by his personal ambition. He gave the reorganisation of the Privy Council and the Government's finances a high priority, as both would make his position more secure. He was careful to cultivate a close relationship with Edward and pursued policies that would guarantee to keep him in royal favour when Edward became king in his own right (such as the move towards Protestantism: see Chapter 15). In the end, Northumberland's instinct for survival, which had served him so well in his career, led to his downfall.

The success of Somerset and Northumberland may be judged by their legacies. Somerset's was a financial débâcle, social unrest and unachievable social and foreign policies. Northumberland left healthy finances, a stable domestic and foreign situation, and a strong religious position, which would have greatly pleased his master had he lived.

KEY POINTS FROM CHAPTER 14: How successfully was England governed during Edward's reign?

1. Somerset ruled as Lord Protector with almost royal powers from January 1547 to October 1549, making little use of the Privy Council or Edward.
2. Northumberland ruled from January 1550 to July 1553 through the Privy Council (as its Lord President) and cultivated a strong relationship with Edward.
3. Somerset came to power with the support of the Privy Council on Henry VIII's death (January 1547).
4. Northumberland, after struggling for several months for dominance in the Privy Council, was able to seize power after the Catholic faction unsuccessfully tried to remove him (January 1550).
5. Somerset was forced from office by the majority of the Privy Council because his arrogant and autocratic method of governing and his social and foreign policies had made him highly unpopular.
6. Northumberland was forced from power after his attempt to alter the succession failed (see Chapter 18).
7. Somerset's main policies were war against Scotland, anti-enclosure measures and a careful move towards Protestantism.
8. Northumberland's main policies were reform of the Privy Council and of the Government's finances, ending foreign conflicts and introducing radical Protestantism.
9. The main financial problems of debasement, heavy expenditure and debt were effectively tackled by Northumberland's administration.
10. Northumberland's historical reputation has undergone a revival among historians such as David Loades and Dale Hoak, who recognise his skilful management of government.
11. Somerset's historical reputation has been lowered by historians such as M. L. Bush, who have pointed out the shortcomings in his blinkered approach to government, as in his obsession with the war against Scotland.

The pendulum swings decisively – what drove the move towards Protestantism during Edward VI's reign?

CHAPTER OVERVIEW

Henry VIII had lurched between moderate Protestantism and traditional Catholicism and had, as a consequence, left an inconsistent patchwork of religious laws and beliefs. The reign of his son, however, witnessed a decisive shift towards Protestantism. Historians have sought to explain this marked change towards Protestantism by examining the beliefs and actions of a number of key individuals during Edward's reign. This chapter will pursue this approach by assessing the contribution made by such powerful individuals as Protector Somerset, the Duke of Northumberland, Archbishop Cranmer and other domestic and international reformers. However, in keeping with the other chapters in this section on Edward, it will also attempt to evaluate the significance of the views and decisions of the young monarch himself. He was certainly a committed Protestant and was displaying the cool and determined political skills demonstrated by his grandfather.

We will be examining the following issues:

FOCUS ROUTE

Make your own copy of the table below, showing changes in religious beliefs and practices. Fill in the first two columns by referring back to Chapter 9, then fill in the remaining two columns as you work through this chapter.

	1529	1547	1550	1553
Eucharist (transubstantiation/ consubstantiation?)	Mass unchallenged	Act of Six Articles (1539) re-established transubstantiation		
Communion (one or both kinds?)				
Sacraments (how many?)				
Clerical celibacy				
Bible (language? who is allowed to read it?)				
Worship of images and saints (allowed?)				
Monasteries				
Chantries				
Services (in Latin?)				
Salvation (how is it to be achieved?)				
Priestly vestments (to be worn?)				
Prayers for the dead (allowed?)				

A What were Edward's religious beliefs?

The expectation that Edward would advance the cause of Protestantism was established from the very beginning of his reign. At his coronation, Archbishop Cranmer compared Edward with the biblical child-king, Josiah (see Source 15.1). The Josiah analogy was a perfect model for Protestant reformers. Josiah had come to the throne aged eight, after a father who had worshipped idols. Josiah embarked on ICONOCLASM and reinstated the book of Law (i.e. the Bible for Edward's contemporaries). Edward was clearly being heavily steered in a Protestant direction. Or was he driving the change himself? This section on the young monarch is trying to unravel the mystery of exactly where power and influence lay during Edward's reign. How much evidence is there that Edward himself supported and indeed led the purposeful move towards Protestantism?

IDOLATRY AND ICONOCLASM
Idolatry is the worship of idols and images; iconoclasm is the destruction of idols and images.

SOURCE 15.1 Archbishop Cranmer, speaking at Edward VI's coronation

... to see, with your predecessor Josiah, God truly worshipped, and IDOLATRY destroyed, the tyranny of the bishops of Rome banished from your subjects, and images removed. These acts be signs of a second Josiah...

A description of Maister Latimer, preaching before Kyng Edward the syxt, in the preachyng place at Westminster.
K.Edward.
M.Latimer.

SOURCE 15.2 Bishop Latimer, one of the leading reformers, preaching before the King

ACTIVITY

1 Identify three of the pieces of evidence in Chart 15A which are most effective in showing us whether Edward was a committed Protestant.
2 Can we determine from the evidence whether Edward chose to be Protestant, or whether Protestantism was imposed on him by those around him?

■ 15A Evidence regarding the King's religion

- Miles Coverdale, translator of the vernacular Great Bible, became bishop of Exeter (1551) and was chaplain to the King.
- Only 5 per cent of Edward's Chronicle is devoted to the subject of religion. His main religious concern in the Chronicle is not doctrine (there is no mention of the prayer book), but the control and structure of the episcopacy (see Source 14.3 on page 204).
- Edward liked long, complicated sermons and scribbled Greek notes as he listened.
- Of the 22 known royal preachers, 20 were reforming bishops or evangelical preachers.
- In April 1550, the Spanish ambassador reported that all those around the King were advanced Protestants and that the King delighted in supporting their beliefs.
- At Easter 1547, the Compline was sung *in English* at the Chapel Royal to show Edward's support of Protestantism.
- Many of the people close to the King were Protestant, including Catherine Parr, Archbishop Cranmer, his tutor Sir Richard Coxe and two of his advisers, Sir William Cecil and John Hales.
- Edward was held in very high esteem by the leading reformers. Martin Bucer, for example, described him as godly 'to a marvel'.

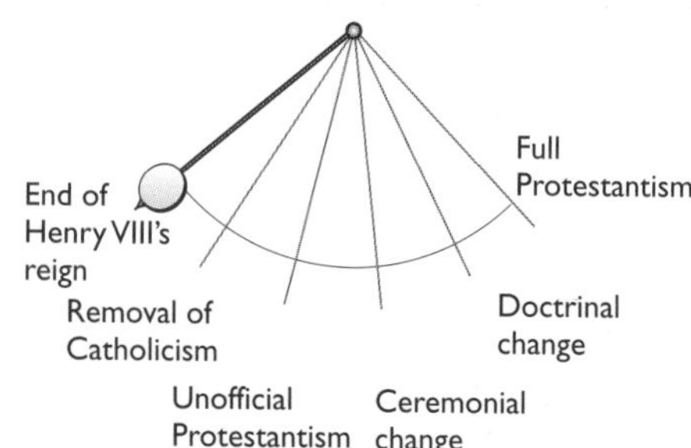

B How did religion change during the reign of Edward VI?

Religious change in England during Edward's reign followed neither a pre-planned nor a natural course of development. It followed a stop–start approach as the Government struggled to find its way and to appease both radicals and traditionalists. Reformation from the moderate Catholic position at the end of Henry's reign to a radical Protestant stance could not be achieved overnight. A number of phases first had to be passed through.

■ 15B The phases of the Edwardian Reformation

PHASE 1: DESTRUCTIVE
During 1547 Catholicism came under attack.

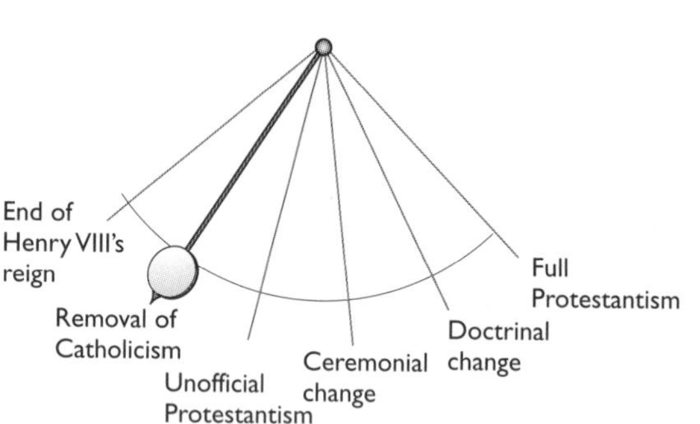

Date	Change	Explanation	Comment
1547	Royal visitation	Commissioners were sent to all bishoprics to examine the state of the clergy, and the doctrine and practices of the Church.	Episcopal authority was suspended until the visitation had been completed in the autumn.
July 1547	Book of Homilies and Paraphrases	It was ordered that the Book of Homilies (a collection of model sermons to be read out by clergy who were unable to preach themselves) and Erasmus' Paraphrases (summaries of the New Testament) should be placed in every church.	The Book of Homilies contained some Protestant sermons written by Cranmer, including one supporting the Lutheran belief of justification by faith alone. Gardiner and Bonner objected and were imprisoned. The Homilies and Paraphrases were established in almost all parish churches by the end of 1549.
July 1547	Royal Injunctions	Orders were given for all clergy to preach in English, and have an English Bible and Protestant literature in every parish church. Superstitious images were to be removed.	
4 November–24 December 1547 Parliament	Chantries Act	This Act of Dissolution was revived from Henry's last Parliament (1545), but contained a crucial new preamble condemning all prayers for the dead (see Chart 15C).	'In fact the Chantries Act was more significant as a gesture of reform than it was as an act of plunder' (D. Loades, *The Mid-Tudor Crisis, 1545–1565*)
4 November–24 December 1547 Parliament	Act of Six Articles repealed	The Act of Six Articles (passed in 1539) had re-established the key Catholic doctrines.	The repeal of this Act left the Church effectively without an official doctrine.
4 November–24 December 1547 Parliament	Treason Act repealed	This Act removed the old heresy, treason, censorship and proclamation laws. This allowed people to discuss religion freely without fear of arrest or imprisonment, and to print and publish freely.	Radicals leapt on this opportunity to spread their views and in some cases destroy Catholic images and altars. The Government had stripped itself of the powers needed to curb these outbursts. Protestant pamphlets bitterly attacked the Mass and Catholics in general.

PHASE 2: STATE OF LIMBO
The Acts of the previous Parliament had left the Church without an official doctrinal position and the lifting of the treason and heresy laws had unleashed a surge of radical Protestant activity which the Government struggled to control through 1548.

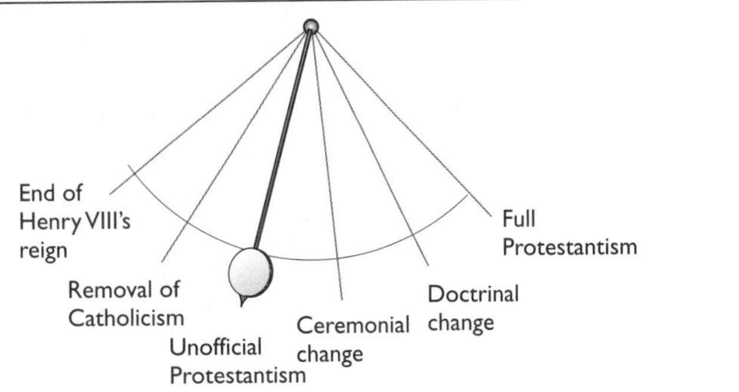

Date	Change	Explanation	Comment
January–March 1548	Series of proclamations issued to dampen Protestant unrest	The Privy Council felt the need to assert that transubstantiation was still technically in force and that Catholic rites still needed to be adhered to.	The Government was trying to achieve order and was playing for time while Cranmer produced the new Prayer Book.
11 February 1548	All images to be removed from churches		This was achieved with remarkably little opposition.
24 April 1548	Proclamation stating only authorised clergy to preach		The Government felt this was necessary because of the flood of unauthorised Protestant preachers that had followed the repeal of the treason and heresy laws.
23 September 1548	Proclamation stating no preaching until new liturgy introduced	A liturgy is the instructions setting out how a church service must be performed.	This is a clear sign that the Government felt that the situation was slipping out of control.

PHASE 3: FORMATIVE
A Protestant form of worship and belief was established during the years 1549–53.
Up to January 1552 a number of ceremonial changes were made.

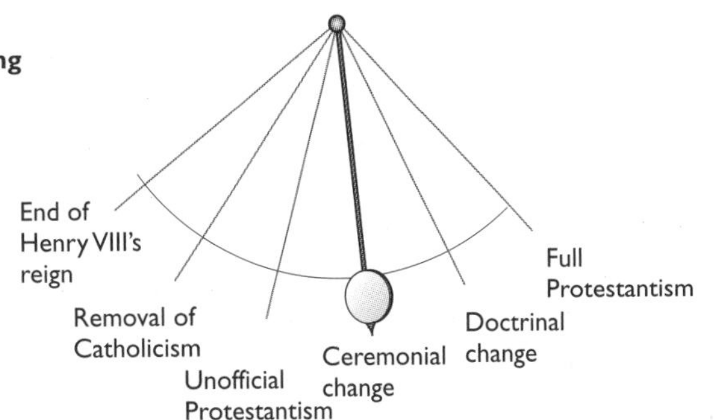

Date	Change	Explanation	Comment
December 1548	First Prayer Book	This was a manual written by Cranmer outlining the liturgy (the form of worship) to be followed in services.	See page 215.
January 1549	Act of Uniformity	This made the Book of Common Prayer the official liturgy.	It was very effectively enforced, despite pockets of resistance. Most notable of these was the Western rebellion (1549) (see Chapter 16).
November 1549	Parliament removed all laws against clerical marriage. All ecclesiastical courts were in the King's name		
25 December 1549	Proclamation issued (confirmed in Parliament) which ordered the destruction of remainder of images		
January 1550	New reformed Ordinal	The Ordinal detailed the ceremony to be followed when clergy were ordained.	The radical Protestant Hooper was outraged by the swearing of an oath to saints and by the need to wear a white surplice. A controversy raged between Hooper and Ridley, until Hooper was forced to back down (see page 221).

(Continues on page 214)

November 1550	Removal of stone altars and replacement by wooden ones		
January 1552	New Treason Act	This made it an offence to question the Royal Supremacy or any articles of faith in the Church.	

PHASE 4: COMPLETION
From January 1552, further reforms saw the establishment of full Protestantism.

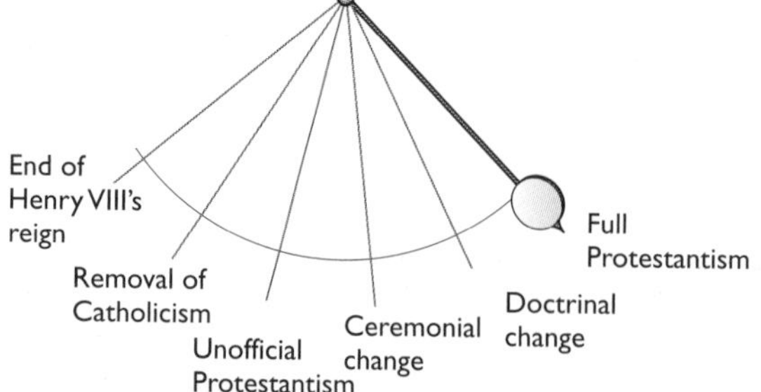

Date	Change	Explanation	Comment
January 1552	Second Book of Common Prayer	This was a highly Protestant document (produced by Cranmer with advice from Bucer), as it removed all traces of Catholicism and clearly established a Eucharist ceremony in line with Calvin's belief in a 'spiritual presence'. Prayers for the dead and the wearing of vestments were removed.	'With the advent of the second Prayer Book the worship of the English Church could be described as fully reformed' (D. Loades, *The Mid-Tudor Crisis, 1545–1565*). Despite its radical Protestant views, it was still opposed by some reformers, who resented being expected to kneel during Communion (see 'Black Rubric' below).
April 1552	Second Act of Uniformity	This enforced the Second Book of Common Prayer. It became an offence for both clergy and laity not to attend Church of England services.	'The new service was introduced in every parish in the sample [study based on churchwardens' accounts] within the prescribed period in 1552–3' (R. Hutton, 'The local impact of the Tudor Reformations', in C. Haigh (ed.) *The English Reformation Revised*).
November 1552	'Black Rubric' Proclamation	This explained that kneeling to receive the Communion was for the sake of good order, not out of idolatry.	Edward personally intervened in this debate.
24 November 1552	42 Articles submitted	They were issued by the Government on 9 June 1553, but never became parliamentary law. They were based on Cranmer's ideas.	The articles were strongly Protestant, being based on the doctrine of justification by faith alone and, loosely, on Calvin's belief in predestination. The 42 Articles became the basis for the 39 Articles in Elizabeth I's reign.
1553	Short catechism was produced (without Parliamentary approval)	A catechism was a manual for teaching the main beliefs of the Church. It was written in a question-and-answer format (e.g. Q: What will ensure you go to heaven after you die? A: My faith in God alone will ensure that I will go to heaven).	Luther and Calvin had produced catechisms.

■ 15C Why was the ending of prayers for the dead so important?

Prayers for the dead
The preamble added to the Chantries Act, ending the prayers for the dead, has been described as 'probably the most shattering and irreversible action of the reformation in England' (W. K. Jordan, *Edward VI: The Threshold of Power – the Dominance of the Duke of Northumberland*). Catholics believed that prayers after they had died would help their souls in purgatory: chantries, colleges, land endowments for Masses, confraternities and monasteries had all been established to pray for the dead. Without prayers, a Catholic's soul and salvation were in peril. So the sudden dismissal of this crucial Catholic belief had a significant impact on the people who had depended upon it.

Chantries
Since the chantries played an integral role in the lives of many local communities, the attack upon them affected the parishes in a way that the destruction of the monasteries had not. Edward's commissioners visited every county and dissolved 3,000 chantries, along with 90 colleges, 110 hospitals and thousands of confraternities, and they confiscated thousands of minor parish endowments (gifts for the poor). Some chantries were turned into schools or the money from their dissolution was redirected into the parishes, but these were the exceptions.

Confraternities
A confraternity was a group or guild of lay men (and, in some cases, women), formed under the patronage of a particular saint. It provided its members with prayers for them when they died – a kind of poor man's chantry. Remaining records of the confraternities are very sparse, so it is almost impossible to judge the numbers of confraternities or the size of their membership. But there were certainly thousands of them (over 100 existed in Northamptonshire alone) and some of them were very influential and grand. When the prayers for the dead were ended, the death knell sounded for the confraternities. Their demise did not greatly concern the Government, which had nothing financially to gain, and it has not overly bothered historians who, apart from Scarisbrick (*The Reformation and the English People*), have largely overlooked them, but they would have been missed by the thousands of people who had played such an active part in them.

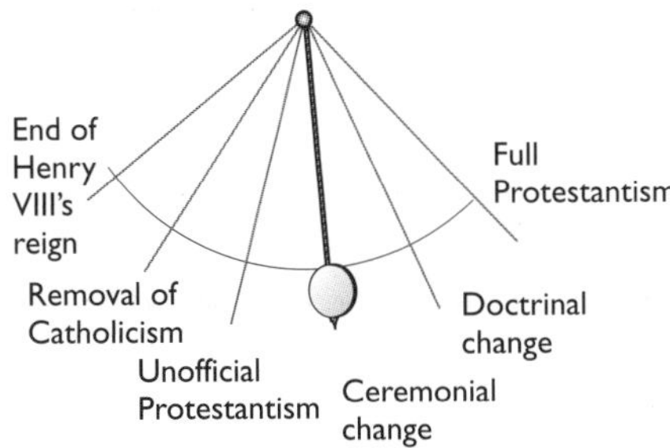

How far did the pendulum swing with the First Book of Common Prayer?

Cranmer's First Book of Common Prayer was unveiled in December 1548 and became law under the Act of Uniformity in 1549. The Prayer Book was essentially a fudge – it was a document in which Cranmer was outlining what he thought would be politically acceptable rather than what he himself believed. As a consequence, it satisfied few people: the Catholics saw it as implicitly Protestant; and for the Protestants it smacked of popery.

The Prayer Book outlined the liturgy to be used in church services. It included the following:

- services in English
- sacraments – Eucharist, baptism, last rites, confirmation, marriage
- Communion in both kinds
- clerical marriage allowed
- purgatory – still unclear
- no prayers for the dead
- worship of saints discouraged (not banned)
- traditional robes in church
- transubstantiation
- fast and holy days remained.

ACTIVITY

1 Henry's VIII's Reformation was piecemeal. Was Edward's piecemeal or can we discern a plan in his Reformation?
2 Make a Short Catechism to teach younger children the religious position of the Church in 1550 and/or 1553.

How far did the pendulum swing with the Second Book of Common Prayer?

The Second Book of Common Prayer undoubtedly represents the furthermost limit of the swing of the pendulum towards Protestantism. It broke radically with the past and satisfied radical reformers. The changes were thorough and Cranmer was probably satisfied with his work:

- It clearly established a Eucharist ceremony in line with Calvin's belief in a 'spiritual presence'.
- The Eucharist was now called the Lord's Supper; communicants were to kneel (see 'Black Rubric' in Chart B, page 214).
- Traditional robes were not to be worn.
- Altars were replaced by communion tables (for eating not sacrificing).
- In confirmation, the sign of the cross was abolished.

Under the Second Act of Uniformity it became an offence for both clergy and laity not to attend Church of England services (punishable by fines and imprisonment).

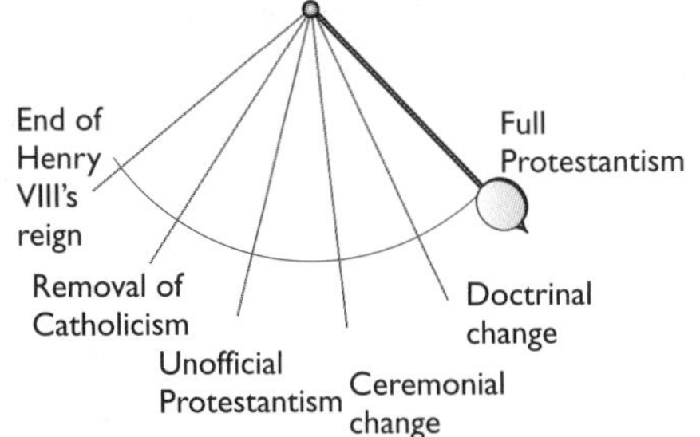

ACTIVITY

1 For both Books of Common Prayer:
a Identify and list the *doctrinal* and the *ceremonial* changes.
b Which of the items in the list would radical Protestants find unacceptable?
2 How significantly did the *doctrine* of the Church change between the Act of Six Articles in 1547 and the Second Prayer Book in 1552?

SOURCE 15.3 Edward VI and the Pope, or an allegory of the Reformation under Edward VI. This painting, by an unknown artist *c.* 1570, includes portraits of all the key people involved in the religious changes during Edward's reign. Like many Tudor paintings, it is loaded with meaning. As the audience, you are meant to discover its message from the clues provided. See if you can decode this painting on the religious situation in Edward's reign

ACTIVITY

1. What do the words on the book and on and around the Pope suggest about the religious views of the artist?
2. What is Henry's hand pointing at? What is his message? (There are at least three options.)
3. What is impossible about the dais on which Edward's throne is resting?
4. What are the monks doing? What meaning is being conveyed by this?
5. What is happening to the Pope? What is this a reference to?
6. What are the men in the inset in the painting doing? Why?
7. The building in the inset probably represented the Tower of Babel built by Noah's descendants to reach up to God. God, however, sent many languages to hinder the builders. Babel was also often associated with Babylon, which God destroyed. What might the collapsed building behind the men represent in Tudor England?
8. The painting was designed to have a horizontal divide across the middle of the painting. What is being separated (look at the people)?
9. What is the overall message of the painting? Refer to: the monks pulling the chains, the destruction of the pillared statue of Mary and Jesus, the position of the Pope, the words on the painting and Henry's pointing finger.
10. The four blank spaces in the painting were intended to be filled with text. This was a common practice in Tudor paintings, in which words imparted most of the message. Infrared reflectology has shown that the framed spaces were an integral feature in the original design but unfortunately it has revealed no trace of the original words. Design short statements to put in each blank to give the meaning of this painting.

Answers to this activity are given on page 323.

Pope Paul III. The Pope had a triple cross and a triple crown to represent his unique triple lordship over earth, heaven and purgatory, and his position as king, prince and emperor.

Protector Somerset
Thomas Seymour, Lord Sudeley **or** the Duke of Northumberland (if it was painted after Seymour's execution on 20 March 1549)
Thomas Cranmer, Archbishop of Canterbury. Cranmer can be seen with stubble. He only started to grow a beard some time after the death of Henry VIII.
Lord Russell, Keeper of the Privy Seal
Sir William Paget, Chief Secretary of State
Thomas Wriothesley, Earl of Southampton, Lord Chancellor
Cuthbert Tunstall, bishop of Durham
William Paulet, Lord St John, Great Master of the King's Household

C Where was the driving force behind the religious change in Edward's reign?

SOURCE 15.4 Edward VI writing in April 1551

As for the prayers and the divine service [the First Book of Common Prayer], it were meet [that] the faults were drawn out, as it were appointed, by learned men, and so the book to be established, and all men willed to come thereunto, to hear the service, as I have put in remembrances in articles touching the statutes of this Parliament.

FOCUS ROUTE

Go back through the phases of the Edwardian Reformation in Chart 15B. Identify the main changes and the people mainly responsible for them and complete your own copy of the following table. Indicate the overall significance of each change by using a scale of 1 (not very important) to 5 (very important).

Change	Person/factor mainly responsible for change and/or in charge of Government	Difference it made to church services for ordinary people	Overall significance of change
Book of Homilies			
Repeal of Act of Six Articles			
First Book of Common Prayer			
Second Act of Uniformity			
42 Articles			

Edward VI

As a minor, Edward was not going to be able to play as prominent a role in the religious change of his reign as if he had been an adult monarch. However, this should not lead historians to think that he did not make a significant contribution through his own actions and words, and through the recognition and deference that others paid to his well-known Protestant beliefs. Edward was a religious force to be reckoned with. At the age of thirteen, he was deeply embroiled in the most important religious change of his reign, the Second Prayer Book. Source 15.4 shows that Edward was clearly:

- not satisfied by the moderate First Book of Common Prayer
- aware of the details of the debate surrounding the writing of the Second Book of Common Prayer
- involved in the parliamentary legislation behind the Second Act of Uniformity
- determined to make everybody attend Protestant services.

In addition:

- Edward was the driving force behind the persecution of his Catholic sister Mary and was involved in the attempt to prevent her succession (see Chapter 18).
- The decisive shift in policy came in 1550–51 when he had become a teenager and when Northumberland, as Lord President, was taking noticeably more interest in Edward's views.
- He attended Privy Council meetings at which the important religious changes of his reign were discussed.
- He favoured and encouraged the radical reformers, who held him in high esteem.
- Northumberland knew that Edward would soon become monarch in his own right and so pursued a radical religious policy that would be to the liking of his future king.
- Edward actively promoted preaching as 'the true preacher with doctrine and example print and engrave in the people's mind the word of God'.

Edward VI, painted by William Scrots, in 1546

Protector Somerset

Somerset was undoubtedly an advanced Protestant, but the governmental problems of maintaining uniformity and order led him to pursue a wavering path towards religious change. Under his Protectorship the Catholic Act of Six Articles and the Treason Laws were repealed, images were destroyed and Communion in both kinds (in which the congregation was allowed to partake of both the bread and the wine) was encouraged. By 1549 the moderately Protestant First Prayer Book (enforced by the Act of Uniformity) had completed a significant shift in the *rituals* of the Church. *Doctrinally*, however, Somerset had been forced by domestic and foreign policy constraints to tread water. He was restrained by fear of Charles V, by the rebellions of 1549 and by his concern over the war against Scotland.

He initially associated with the leading reformers (e.g. Hooper and Bucer) and Calvin even regarded him as a co-religionist. However, his moderate enforcement of Protestantism (few conservative bishops were removed and *nobody* was persecuted for heretical beliefs during his three years in office) soon lost him the approval of the radical Protestants (John Knox attacked Somerset by saying that he preferred to visit the masons building his new house on Sunday than to hear the Scriptures). Somerset is best described as an Erastian Protestant (Erastianism was the belief that the state should have authority over the Church), who struggled to reconcile the demands of government with the religious changes he wanted to introduce. He would only introduce religious changes when the political situation made it possible.

The Duke of Northumberland

Northumberland's religious position has been described as an 'enigma' (J. Guy, *Tudor England*). At several crucial moments in his life he declared himself a Catholic (at his death and in the coup to seize power from Somerset), yet while he was the head of the Government (1550–53) the religious pendulum swung most decisively towards Protestantism (the enforcement of the Second Prayer book and the 42 Articles). The answer to the enigma is perhaps that Northumberland was above all a politician; for him religion took second place to the search for power. Northumberland would have enjoyed a number of significant political benefits from moving towards Protestantism:

- He would have increased the bond of affection with and the influence he had over Edward VI and his undoubtedly strong Protestantism.
- He judged that the religious future lay with the evangelical Protestants and supported this by appointing radicals (e.g. John Hooper became the bishop of Gloucester).
- Power and money lay with further stripping of the Catholic Church.
- John Guy in *Tudor England* argues that Northumberland may have been influenced by 'public order considerations', as Protestantism more naturally lent itself to social control (e.g. through the limiting of holy days and the control of alehouse keeping).

Archbishop Cranmer

Cranmer, with great reluctance and much ponderous thought, became the towering spiritual figure in the English Reformation. It was his pen that drafted the Prayer Books and the 42 Articles, and it was he who judged what position the Church should take on the key issues. His significance, according to David Loades, was 'not because he was a saint, or a great theologian (he was neither of those things), but because he was able to take the unique ecclesiastical polity devised in England between 1530 and 1540, to develop it, and to make it work' (*The Mid-Tudor Crisis, 1545–1565*).

During Henry VIII's reign, he had remained his master's loyal servant and had confined his thinking to what he knew the King would find acceptable. When Edward ascended the throne, Cranmer was able to edge towards his own theological position. In his Homilies (1547) he asserted the Lutheran belief of justification by faith alone (the Catholic belief was in salvation by faith and good works) and in the Second Prayer Book he achieved a fully Protestant position. However, it is important to note that recent research emphasises the role played by the European reformers (all invited to England by Cranmer), and especially Bucer, in shaping the documents that Cranmer finally produced. Cranmer's guiding light was his unshakeable belief in Royal Supremacy, and he always recognised that the head of the Church was the monarch, whose wishes had to be respected.

The clergy

The central importance of the Bible within Protestantism meant that the quality and quantity of good preachers was always going to be an essential tool if the Reformation was to spread widely. Pockets of Protestantism were fostered by effective preachers in London, East Anglia and some large towns such as Newcastle and Exeter. Ports were often a particular hotbed of Protestantism, too. However, on the whole the lack of preachers was probably the greatest problem faced by the nationwide Reformation. The Prayer Book and Homilies helped evangelicalism, but they were no replacement for educated and committed Protestants.

Under Somerset the balance of bishops favoured Catholicism: eight were undecided, nine were reformers and ten were Catholics. However, under Northumberland active reformers were appointed to the sees of London, Gloucester, Rochester, Chichester, Norwich, Exeter, Worcester and Durham. The radical Bishop Hooper was to find, however, that Protestant bishops were no guarantee of effective clergy. In a highly depressing visitation of his own diocese, he discovered that out of 311 clergy, ten could not recite the Lord's Prayer and 171 could not repeat the Ten Commandments.

SOURCE 15.5 Hugh Latimer, bishop of Worcester, painted in 1555 by an unknown artist

John Hooper

John Hooper was the belligerent leader of the EVANGELICAL Protestants. His aim was to sweep away all remaining aspects of Catholicism and vigorously to enforce a radical and pure form of Protestantism throughout the country. He was a man of enormous energy and commitment. Every day, he allowed four poor people to share his table after instruction in the Creed, the Lord's Prayer and the Ten Commandments; and, as a bishop, he conducted 'the most searching and efficient' visitations of his diocese.

His significance for the Reformation was that he spearheaded the push towards radical Protestantism and gained the favour of Edward and Northumberland (he was made bishop of Gloucester in 1550). His uncompromising nature brought him into conflict with other Protestants. Most notable was his clash with Cranmer and Ridley over whether bishops should wear ceremonial garments when they were ordained. He was imprisoned before finally giving in.

EVANGELICALS

Evangelicals are ardent Protestants who place greatest importance on the Bible and believe that their faith should be vigorously spread to others.

SOURCE 15.6 Nicholas Ridley, bishop of Rochester and then London, painted in 1555 by an unknown artist

European reformers

Between 1547 and 1553, 40 of Europe's reformers came to reside in England, most of them at the invitation of Archbishop Cranmer. The main contribution of the foreign reformers was to provide ideas and preaching talents to the Reformation in England. They are also increasingly recognised as having influenced the direction of the religious change by putting pressure on for a move towards Protestantism and particularly for the abandonment of the Mass. Cranmer's Second Book of Common Prayer was, for example, heavily influenced by Bucer's criticisms of the First. Cranmer was also in close correspondence with Melanchthon, the leader of Lutheranism after Luther's death. Calvin also kept a critical eye on developments in England. Edward warmly welcomed the reformers and was well regarded by them. On Edward's death, Calvin wrote 'I consider that, by the death of one youth, the whole nation has been bereaved of the best of fathers.'

The principal reformers who came to England were:

- Martin Bucer, who arrived in March 1549 and was made Regius Professor of Divinity at Cambridge. His impact was electric and his lectures were regularly packed.
- Peter Martyr, who arrived in December 1547 and became Regius Professor of Divinity at Oxford. He asserted that transubstantiation had to go.
- Bernard Ochino arrived with Martyr in December 1547 and was appointed to a prebend at Canterbury.

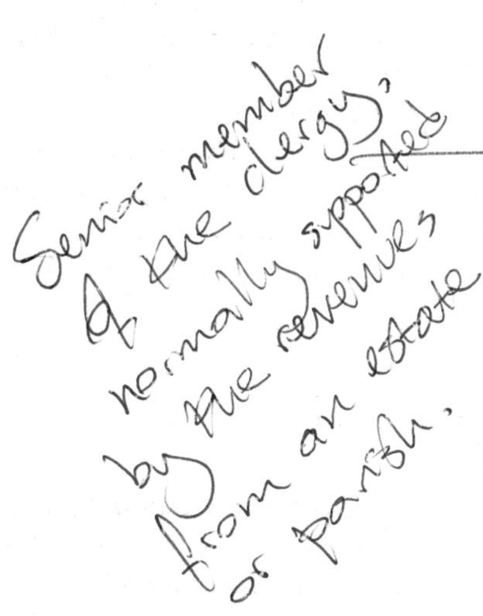

Senior member of the clergy, normally supported by the revenues from an estate or parish.

Lack of opposition

The period of the Reformation under Edward VI is notable for its lack of opposition and the virtual absence of persecution, particularly of the lower clergy. Although this should not be assumed to mean that there was positive enthusiasm for the reforms, it did make the Government's job of enforcement easier.

The only serious organised resistance, the Western rebellion (see Chapter 16), was successfully suppressed in 1549. The only two high-profile opponents of the Edwardian Reformation were Stephen Gardiner (bishop of Winchester) and Edmund Bonner (bishop of London). Gardiner was opposed to the services in English, toleration of image breaking and any doctrinal change of the Church. He expressed his views publicly in 1548 and was sent to the Tower, where he remained until Mary's accession. Bonner was less confrontational than Gardiner and only began to oppose publicly when the Privy Council instructed him to preach about Holy Communion. His response was to preach at St Paul's about transubstantiation, for which offence he was put in prison. Both were deprived of their bishoprics and were replaced by reformers.

Greed

During the last three years of Edward's reign, Government attention was turned towards extracting the remaining wealth of the Church. In 1552 a survey of the bishops and all clergy worth more than £50 per year discovered that the total untapped wealth of the Church was £1,087,978 (bishoprics were worth £606,511; other ecclesiastical offices £481,467). In 1553 Northumberland began to attack these vast resources, which were worth half of all the monastic wealth and much more than the chantries.

The doctrinal shift away from transubstantiation had made the plate, vestments and other objects associated with the Mass redundant. Northumberland ordered their expropriation in 1553, but there was not enough time to complete the collection and to sell or melt down the metals before Edward's death brought a halt to the activity. The acquisition of the bishops' wealth was to be achieved by a reallocation of resources on the appointment of a new bishop. For example, when Bishop Tunstall of Durham was imprisoned in the Tower in October 1552, it was proposed that Durham was to be allocated £1,320, the new see of Newcastle was to be given £665 and the surplus of £2,000 was to go to the Crown. This was again not put into effect because of the death of Edward.

ACTIVITY

1. Examine each of the personalities and factors in turn and produce a short statement summarising how each influenced the move towards Protestantism:
   a) Edward VI
   b) Duke of Northumberland
   c) Protector Somerset
   d) Archbishop Cranmer
   e) John Hooper
   f) The clergy
   g) European reformers
   h) Lack of opposition
   i) Greed.
2. If we say that the reform of the Edwardian Church equals 42, give each of the personalities and factors a weighting according to how significant you think each was in leading to the reform. The total for the nine factors must equal 42. Compare your weightings with others in your class and justify your decisions.

D How successful was the Edwardian Reformation?

SOURCE 15.7 Lord Paget writing to Protector Somerset in 1549

Look well whether you have law or religion at home, and I fear you shall find neither. The use of the old religion is forbidden by a law, and the use of the new is not yet printed in the stomachs of the eleven of twelve parts of the realm.

SOURCE 15.8 John Foxe, *Acts and Monuments*, 1563

Amongst the whole number of popish sort, of whom some privily did steal out of the realm, many were crafty dissemblers, some were open and manifest adversaries; yet, of all that multitude, there was not one man that lost his life. In sum, during the whole time of the six years of this king, much tranquillity, and, as it were, a breathing time, was granted to the whole Church of England.

TALKING POINT

What do you need to know about the authors of Sources 15.7 and 15.8 to enable you to judge their usefulness as sources?

SOURCE 15.9 E. Duffy, *The Stripping of the Altars*, 1992, pp. 502–3

There were parishes where the reform was embraced with ardour, at least by those with most influence, and where a new solidarity began to emerge on the basis of the new faith.

Even in the communities where this was not so, the passage of time and the relentless push of Conciliar policy had its effect. The men and women of Tudor England were, by and large, pragmatists. Grumbling, they sold off as much of their Catholic past as they could not hide or keep, and called in the carpenters to set boards on trestles and fix the forms round the communion tables. Used to obedience, many of them accepted the changes, however unwelcome, as unavoidable . . . Four years of exposure to the matchless and memorable dignity of Cranmer's English services could not be without effect. As we shall see, even men of profoundly Catholic convictions found themselves drawing on the rhythms of Bible and prayer-book when they came to express their convictions. Even for the traditionalists nothing would ever be the same again. But when all that is said, the experience of Morebath [the case study in Duffy's book] almost certainly offers us a more accurate insight into what the locust years of Edward had meant to the average Englishman than the embryo godly communities which had begun to emerge in parts of Essex, Suffolk, or Kent, and which historians, dazzled by hindsight, have too easily seen as the inevitable future of Tudor England. In the majority of English villages, as in Morebath, men breathed easier for the accession of a Catholic queen.

SOURCE 15.10 R. Hutton, 'The local impact of the Tudor Reformations', in C. Haigh (ed.), *The English Reformation Revised*, 1987, p. 120

The regime of Protector Somerset has been regarded by Protestants at the time, and historians since, as relatively moderate and willing to compromise in the work of reform. Yet its impact was devastating: the great majority of the decorations and rites employed in and around English churches in early 1547 had gone by late 1549. As far as the churchwardens' accounts tell the story, all that the succeeding 'radical' administration of Northumberland had to do was to 'mop up' by revising the Prayer Book, replacing the altars with communion tables and confiscating the obsolete church goods. The new service was introduced in every parish in the sample [study based on churchwardens' accounts] within the prescribed period in 1552–3, and the other reforms were just as thoroughly carried out, although over a longer period...

To conclude: the evidence of the churchwardens' accounts bears out the assertions of Dr Haigh and Professor Scarisbrick, that the great majority of the English and Welsh peoples did not want the Reformations of Henry, Edward and Elizabeth. Catholic practices retained their vitality in the parishes until the moment they were proscribed, and there were few anticipations of official instructions. Indeed, accounts suggest that Tudor parishioners were reluctant to implement any religious changes. If it be asked then why they got them, the answer is that they were forced to conform. The machinery of coercion and supervision deployed by the government was so effective that for most parishes passive resistance was simply not an option . . . In essence, churchwardens' accounts suggest that the English Reformation has been treated too much as a confessional struggle and not sufficiently as an episode in the history of the secular British polity.

15.9 - Catholic beliefs remained but Protestant practice became accepted.
15.10 - Somerset drove (fast-paced) Reformation despite reluctance of population.
15.11 - Gradual change led to success.
15.12 - Artificial changes which disappeared for most upon accession of Mary.

SOURCE 15.11 W. K. Jordan, *Edward VI: The Threshold of Power – the Dominance of the Duke of Northumberland*, 1970, p. 241

The ultimate and probably the irrevocable success of the government in the making of England into a Protestant nation was probably gained by the gradual winning over of the inert mass of men to spiritual acceptance by the very gradual, moderate, and in some ways almost insensible change in the order and spiritual of worship.

SOURCE 15.12 D. Loades, *The Mid-Tudor Crisis, 1545–1565*, 1992, p. 178

...stantism of Edward VI's reign was not a natural growth, it was highly ...and imposed by authority; nevertheless it was successfully imposed. ...vestments, images and liturgical books were often taken away and ...nformity was effectively enforced upon the parish churches. Not only ...cclesiastical authorities surprisingly energetic in this respect, they were ...ed up by the secular magistrates ... Mary's policies provided the acid ...e Edwardian achievement, and it soon became apparent that the ...t preachers had accomplished rather more than their despair in the ...f 1553 would suggest. The prevailing emotion was certainly one of ... willingness to return to the old ways. But there were now congregations which were Protestant in more than a conformist sense.

ACTIVITY

Use a scale of high/medium/low and brief comments to complete your own copy of this table.

What the sources tell us about:	Source 15.7	Source 15.8	Source 15.9	Source 15.10	Source 15.11	Source 15.12
The level of acceptance of Protestantism among the people						
The success of governmental enforcement						
The level of opposition to Protestantism						
The reasons why people were/were not accepting Protestantism						
The overall success of the Edwardian Reformation						

Review: The pendulum swings decisively – what drove the move towards Protestantism during Edward VI's reign?

During Edward's reign the pendulum had swung as far as it could towards Protestantism. While Somerset was Protector, the last vestiges of Catholicism had been swept away and the ceremonial and ritual aspects of Protestantism had begun to be established. As Lord President, Northumberland had overseen the creation of the doctrine of a fully reformed Church. Behind all these changes two people remain constant figures – Cranmer and Edward. Cranmer was undoubtedly the craftsman behind the religious changes – the Prayer Books, the Homilies and the 42 Articles. But was he perhaps too hesitant to be the major motivating force? Edward (in the second half of his reign) might have been that engine of change. An exercise in counterfactual history may help us to assess if he was.

Counterfactual conclusion

Counterfactual history is when you speculate about what might have happened under different circumstances. It is not a precise science, but it is useful in determining the significant factors that made history turn out as it did.

If Edward had been a moderate Catholic in the mould of his father...

- would religion have changed during his reign?
- would an astute and ambitious politician like Northumberland have pursued such an extreme Protestant policy, knowing that he would lose everything once Edward reached his majority?
- would the radical reformers have achieved such prominence and influence without such obvious royal favour?
- would Cranmer, whose touchstone was always Royal Supremacy, have created a religious policy that was so out-of-step with that of his monarch?
- would the Protestants have been allowed to preach from such important pulpits as St Paul's Cross and the royal chapel?

This is not to suggest that Edward was *the* most important factor behind the religious change, but his role certainly merits more recognition than historians have normally granted him. Edward was, remember, only four months away from becoming king in his own right when he died.

KEY POINTS FROM CHAPTER 15: The pendulum swings decisively – what drove the move towards Protestantism during Edward VI's reign?

1. Cranmer wrote the two Books of Common Prayer (1549 and 1552) which gave the Church a Protestant service.
2. Edward was a radical Protestant and was very involved in the religious changes of his reign.
3. The main opponents of the reforms were Stephen Gardiner and Edmund Bonner.
4. The main radical reformers were John Hooper and European reformers like Martin Bucer.
5. The Edwardian Reformation took place in phases: first, Catholicism was swept away; then Protestant ceremonial changes were made; and finally a reformed doctrine was introduced.
6. Protector Somerset was a committed Protestant, but he was constrained in the introduction of Protestantism by domestic and foreign problems.
7. The Duke of Northumberland advanced the cause of Protestantism while he was in charge of the Government (1550–53), although his own religious leanings are difficult to pinpoint.
8. The spread of Protestantism was made more difficult by the lack of good preachers.
9. Although the Government had changed the doctrine and ceremonies of the Church, they had not necessarily changed the fundamental beliefs of the people.

16

The year of the many-headed monster – how dangerous were the rebellions of 1549 for Edward VI's government?

CHAPTER OVERVIEW

Disorder and demonstrations are not confined to distant history. The Tudor period was one, however, which experienced high levels of disorder. Even a formidable monarch such as Henry VIII found himself defeated by one rebellion (the Amicable Grant uprising in 1525) and seriously struggling against another (the Pilgrimage of Grace in 1536, which was the largest co-ordinated revolt in English history).

In 1549 large swathes of the country were shaken by rebellion. The huge geographic extent of the rebellions of 1549 made them the most serious, widespread movements of disorder since the Peasants' Revolt of 1381. About 10,000 people died in the unrest, which as a proportion of the total population equates to around 165,000 people in twenty-first-century terms (this is similar to the death toll per year in the First World War).

It was the Western rebellion in Devon and Cornwall and Kett's rebellion in Norfolk that particularly rocked the administration of Protector Somerset and were the largest factors in leading to his downfall. This chapter will focus on the causes and impact of these two rebellions.

However, historians are left with a paradox: the rebellions were significant and frightening for those in authority, yet the demands and actions of the rebels made it clear that they were *not* intending to threaten the established order. They did not march on London, nor did they put forward an alternative candidate to the infant-king, nor did they call for equality for all classes. In order to understand this apparent contradiction between the perception and the reality, this chapter will examine the nature of disorder in early modern England and assess the danger the rebels posed to Edward VI's government. We will look at the following issues:

■ 16A The rebellions of 1549

A long hot summer! The Western rebellion and Kett's rebellion in Norfolk justifiably dominate the historiography, however in 1549 England was splashed with minor uprisings (23 counties were affected). All of them were successfully dealt with by the authorities, but the geographic extent of the rebellions of 1549 made the situation very serious for the Government.

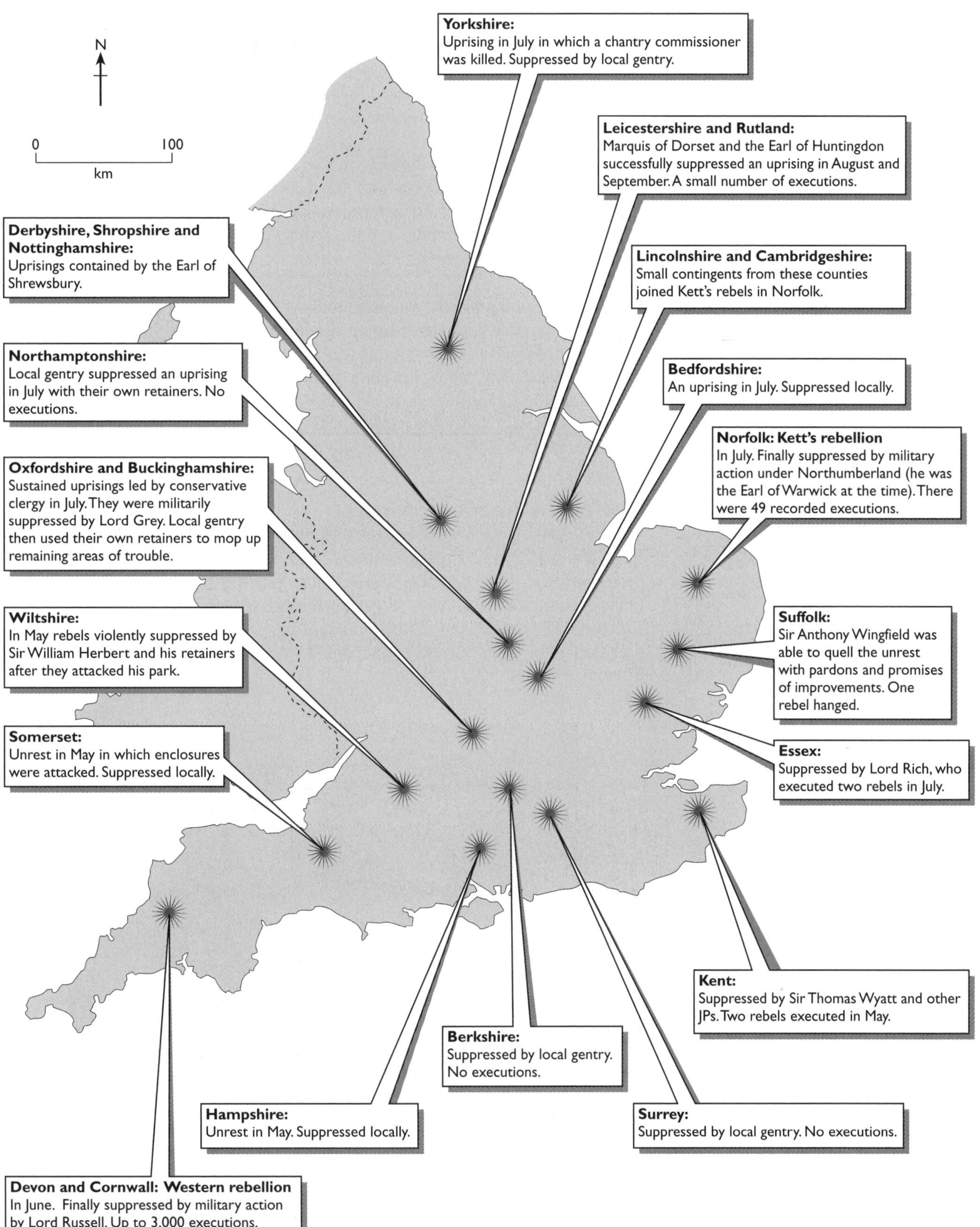

N
0
100
km
Yorkshire:
Uprising in July in which a chantry commissioner was killed. Suppressed by local gentry.
Leicestershire and Rutland:
Marquis of Dorset and the Earl of Huntingdon successfully suppressed an uprising in August and September. A small number of executions.
Derbyshire, Shropshire and Nottinghamshire:
Uprisings contained by the Earl of Shrewsbury.
Lincolnshire and Cambridgeshire:
Small contingents from these counties joined Kett's rebels in Norfolk.
Northamptonshire:
Local gentry suppressed an uprising in July with their own retainers. No executions.
Bedfordshire:
An uprising in July. Suppressed locally.
Norfolk: Kett's rebellion
In July. Finally suppressed by military action under Northumberland (he was the Earl of Warwick at the time). There were 49 recorded executions.
Oxfordshire and Buckinghamshire:
Sustained uprisings led by conservative clergy in July. They were militarily suppressed by Lord Grey. Local gentry then used their own retainers to mop up remaining areas of trouble.
Wiltshire:
In May rebels violently suppressed by Sir William Herbert and his retainers after they attacked his park.
Suffolk:
Sir Anthony Wingfield was able to quell the unrest with pardons and promises of improvements. One rebel hanged.
Somerset:
Unrest in May in which enclosures were attacked. Suppressed locally.
Essex:
Suppressed by Lord Rich, who executed two rebels in July.
Kent:
Suppressed by Sir Thomas Wyatt and other JPs. Two rebels executed in May.
Berkshire:
Suppressed by local gentry. No executions.
Hampshire:
Unrest in May. Suppressed locally.
Surrey:
Suppressed by local gentry. No executions.
Devon and Cornwall: Western rebellion
In June. Finally suppressed by military action by Lord Russell. Up to 3,000 executions.

16B The Great Chain of Being

The theoretical defence that protected the existing social order was the Great Chain of Being. Under this theory, all classes of society were interdependent and subordinate to another (see Source 16.1).

SOURCE 16.1 William Gouge, a contemporary, explaining the Great Chain of Being

They that are superiors to some are inferiors to others . . . Yea, God hath so disposed every one's several place, as there is not any one, but in some respect is under another, and all under the king. The king himself is under God.

A How should we view protest and disorder in Tudor England?

■ **Learning trouble spot**

Most of us have preconceived ideas about protesters and those whose job it is to control them; we may see large crowds as threatening and potentially violent, while the authorities are perceived as being the respectable upholders of law and order. Historians must learn to be aware of and to counter these kinds of preconception if they are to arrive at a balanced and accurate analysis of an event.

The sources relating to disorder in the sixteenth century inevitably come mainly from those in authority and they betray a natural fear and distrust of the protesters. However, the historian must look closely at the aims (often revealed in a list of demands) and the actions of the rebels in order to assess what threat they really posed and to whom.

The fabric of Tudor society was essentially very weak. Only the thin threads of duty and deference kept the common people in order. The ruling authorities had no police force and no standing army to suppress rebellion if it broke out. This deep insecurity, felt by the gentry and nobility in the counties and by the Government in London, helps to explain why they viewed social unrest with such fear and why they often reacted with such savage punishments (for example, at least 3,000 people were killed after the Western rebellion was crushed).

The many-headed monster

The educated, ruling orders saw the vast mass of common people as a 'many-headed monster'; a body that was essentially irrational, stupid and fickle. This perception was created by fear and by the authorities' failure to recognise that the commoners were allowed few opportunities to voice their political concerns. The people, therefore, in attempting to bring their grievances to the attention of the Government, could often do so only through violent or disruptive action.

The authorities failed to acknowledge that many of the rebellions were remarkably peaceful and passive. Violence, when it came, was very specifically targeted at the objects of the rebels' anger (e.g. the enclosure fences and hedges in the case of Kett's rebellion), and only rarely were people from the higher orders murdered. Widespread physical violence was almost invariably a consequence of Government suppression. Nevertheless, the propaganda about the 'many-headed monster' continued to proliferate.

Customs and traditions

The ordinary people accepted the fact that they were subordinate and were not, in their rebellions, attempting to overturn the order established by the Great Chain of Being. They had, however, a clear sense of what rights and privileges they could expect within the existing social framework. This idea of their rights came from age-old customs and traditions, and the rebels saw themselves as acting to *defend* their positions (see the wording of Articles 4, 5, 6 and 10 of Kett's demands in Source 16.7 on page 237). The rebellions, therefore, should be seen as cries for help from the people to their monarch, and the Government's response would do much to determine how dangerous the uprising became. The authorities at local, regional and national levels recognised this and their first response to a rebellion was always to negotiate. However, rebellions were, as all parties would have recognised, tense and frightening events.

B What happened in the Western rebellion and Kett's rebellion?

FOCUS ROUTE

As you study this section on the events of the rebellions, complete your own copy of the following table.

Details	Western rebellion	Kett's rebellion
County		
Date started		
Leader/s		
Trigger causes		
Articles (list of complaints) produced? (yes/no)		
Main base		
Local gentry reaction		
Government reaction		
Negotiation? (yes/no)		
Suppression (who by? how? when?)		
Punishments		

■ 16C Events of the Western rebellion

Background

Cornwall, with its own language and its geographical location at the edge of the country, was 'a land apart' (J. Cornwall, *Revolt of the Peasantry, 1549*). The largest town was Bodmin with only 1,000 inhabitants and the county relied heavily on the meagre profits that were made from tin mining. Poverty and a vigorous sense of regional identity had triggered the rebellion of 1497 against Henry VII's tax request and had led 3,000 Cornish people to join Perkin Warbeck's attempt to claim the throne later in the same year. Devon shared much of its neighbour's natural conservatism with regard to matters social and religious, and the common people of the county were, according to David Loades in *The Mid-Tudor Crisis, 1545–1565*, more hostile towards their gentry than in most other parts of England.

WESTERN REBELLION

Trigger causes

The Western rebellion had two principal triggers:

- In Cornwall, resentment sprang from the activities of the much-hated figure of William Body, a commissioner investigating church property in the county in 1547. His arrogance and the investigation into the chantries created a swirl of rumours and fears about the confiscation of church goods. The destruction of church images by Body the following year led a group in Helston to set upon and murder him. Devon gentlemen quickly dealt with the uprising, but the deep-seated antagonism remained. The final straw was the introduction of the new Prayer Book on 10 June (Whitsunday) 1549.
- In Devon, in the tiny village of Sampford Courtenay, the people were also provoked into rebellion by their priest's use of the new Prayer Book on Whitsunday, 1549.

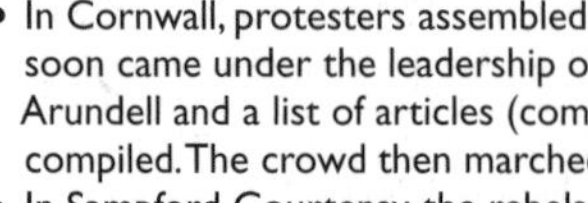

The rebellion takes hold

- In Cornwall, protesters assembled in Bodmin. They soon came under the leadership of Humphrey Arundell and a list of articles (complaints) was compiled. The crowd then marched on to Devon.
- In Sampford Courtenay, the rebels persuaded the priest to deliver a traditional Catholic Mass and then moved on to join the forces from Cornwall at Crediton on 20 June.

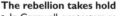

Local reaction

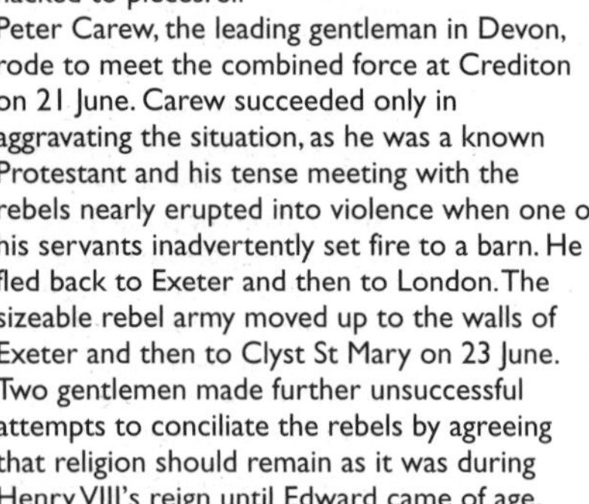

Very quickly the gentry lost their grip on the counties. A gentleman called Hellier, who attempted to calm the rebels in Devon, was hacked to pieces. Sir Peter Carew, the leading gentleman in Devon, rode to meet the combined force at Crediton on 21 June. Carew succeeded only in aggravating the situation, as he was a known Protestant and his tense meeting with the rebels nearly erupted into violence when one of his servants inadvertently set fire to a barn. He fled back to Exeter and then to London. The sizeable rebel army moved up to the walls of Exeter and then to Clyst St Mary on 23 June. Two gentlemen made further unsuccessful attempts to conciliate the rebels by agreeing that religion should remain as it was during Henry VIII's reign until Edward came of age.

■ 16D The Government's response to the Western rebellion

First Government response
Somerset was acting on inadequate information and had only limited resources at his disposal. On 29 June he urged Lord Russell, a Catholic member of the Council, to find a peaceful settlement and wrote a conciliatory response to the rebel demands. At the time, Somerset was struggling to suppress enclosure riots in the Midlands, maintain adequate forces on the Scottish border and watch for any French aggression. He could therefore provide the cautious Russell with only a small army. Russell, knowing the weakness of his position, avoided confronting the enemy.

The descent into bloodshed
Loyalty to the Crown led the citizens of Exeter to defend their city staunchly against the rebel attack for six weeks. Russell still prevaricated and on 8 July he made his last attempt to reach a settlement with the rebels. On 12 July reinforcements under Lord Grey were delayed by another uprising in Oxfordshire (see Chart 16A on page 227). On 28 July, in response to pressure from Somerset, Russell began his advance against the rebels. He was aided by the much-needed arrival of the forces of Lord Grey on 3 August.

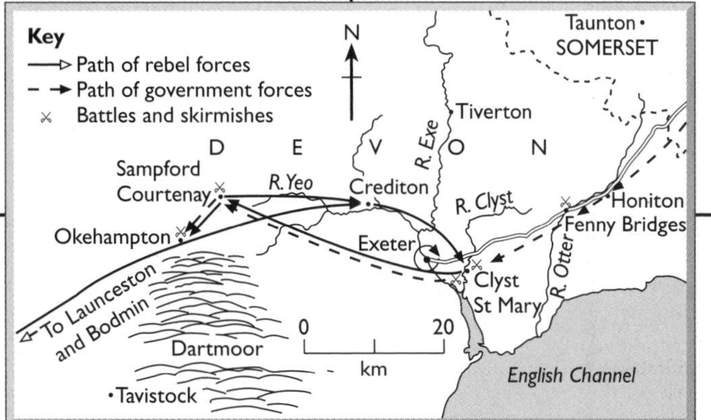

Government suppression
Confrontations between the rebels and the Government forces under Russell took place at Fenny Bridges, Clyst St Mary and Clyst Heath, and each time the rebels were pushed further back. On 6 August, Russell relieved Exeter and Government reinforcements under Sir William Herbert arrived. Time was running out for the rebels. Somerset heaped yet more pressure on to Russell to finish the job, as the French had declared war on England on 8 August. Finally, on 16 August, Russell advanced on and defeated the rebel forces at Sampford Courtenay.

Aftermath
The resilience and commitment of the rebels remained strong to the end and, even after the victory on the battlefield, Russell had to deal with rearguard action and pockets of resistance until an estimated 3,000 people had been killed. Robert Welsh, the vicar of the church of St Thomas and probably the leader of the rebellion, was hanged on gallows erected on his church tower, in his vestments and with a 'holy-water bucket, a sprinkle, a sacring bell, a pair of beeds and such other like popish trash hanged about him'. The Government operation further deepened hostility as Government forces had acted illegally, executing without trials and confiscating and redistributing property.

ACTIVITY

1 Why did the rebels not march on London, as they had in 1497?
2 The rebels carried the banner of the Five Wounds of Christ in front of them. Which previous rebellion used this banner and what is its significance?

■ 16E Events of Kett's rebellion

Background

East Anglia was the most densely populated and highly industrialised part of the country. After London, Norwich was the second biggest city in the country (16,000 people) and had become a major textile centre. A collapse in the textile industry had, however, thrown large numbers of cloth workers out of work, and many independent, small farmers were being badly affected by the enclosure of wooded pastoral areas by gentry and yeoman farmers.

KETT'S REBELLION

Trigger causes

Between 6 and 8 July the entire community around Wymondham gathered to enjoy a play and a drunken feast. Anger and high spirits overflowed and the crowds broke down some enclosure fences and hedges, including those of a local lawyer, John Flowerdew. Flowerdew was unpopular because he was in dispute with local people over a local abbey he had bought and was pulling down. The townspeople believed that it was they who had bought the abbey for the parish and were incensed by Flowerdew's actions.

The rebellion takes hold

Flowerdew encouraged the crowds to attack the hedges of a local tanner and landowner, Robert Kett. Kett, however, welcomed their action and immediately assumed leadership of the movement. The other leading figures in the uprising were all yeomen farmers. The absence of clergy, gentry and nobility was very significant. The motives that fuelled Kett's involvement in the rebellion remain unclear. He might have been motivated by a genuine feeling of guilt about the effect of the enclosures, or the revolt might have been an outlet for the frustrated social ambition of a man just at the fringes of the gentry.

By 10 July the rebels had reached Norwich and by 12 July they had encamped on Mousehold Heath, with a crowd that had swelled to 16,000. Kett then produced their list of articles (demands) and sat in wait for the favourable Government response that he fully expected.

Local reaction

The size and speed of the movement paralysed the authorities of the county. Norwich found itself uneasily attempting to keep peaceful relations with its new mighty neighbour camped on Mousehold Heath. The sheriff was nearly arrested when he attempted to disperse the rebels and the rest of the gentry were powerless against this well-established force.

■ 16F The Government's response to Kett's rebellion

First Government response
On 21 July the York Herald arrived to offer a full pardon to all those who dispersed. The tone of the offer was conciliatory, promising to prohibit landlords from acting as farmers or clothiers, to reduce the price of wool by a third, and to appoint commissioners to reform abuses. Many of the crowd wanted to accept it, but Kett rejected it, saying that they had committed no crime. The herald ordered his swordbearer to arrest Kett, but the mood grew ugly and the herald was forced to retreat.

The descent into bloodshed
The rebels, the city of Norwich and the Government now prepared for conflict. It was clear that the moment for a negotiated settlement had gone. The rebels fetched cannon from coastal defences and attacked Norwich after the herald's departure. By the end of the evening of 22 July, the rebels had taken Norwich and the herald had fled back to London.

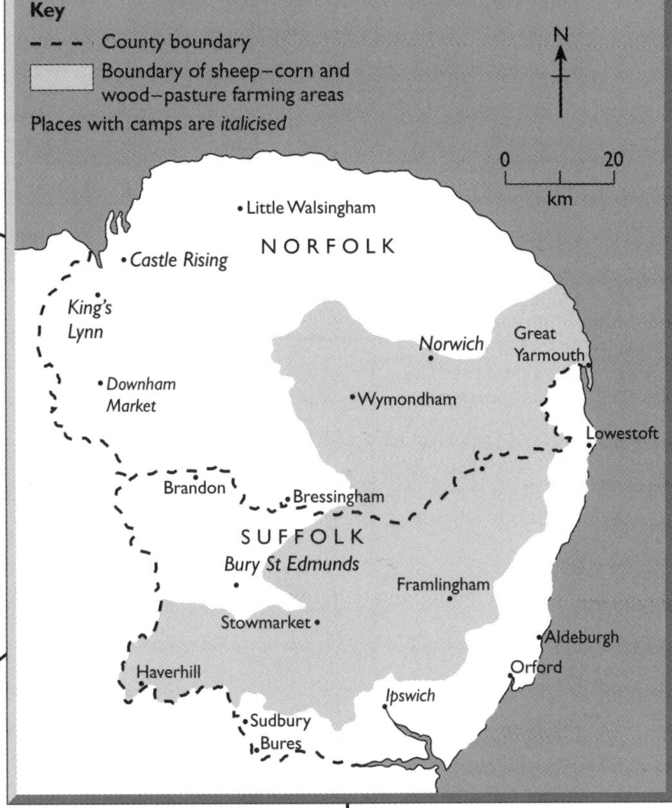

The Government's first attempt at suppression
Somerset sent a small army of about 1,800 under the command of William Parr, Marquis of Northampton, to Norwich with orders to negotiate and cut off the rebels' supply lines. Northampton arrived on 30 July and occupied Norwich. He offered a full pardon to any who dispersed, but the minds of the rebels were set firm and only twenty responded. This was the first time the rebels had faced a senior member of the nobility, but Northampton crucially did not wield the weight of his authority in negotiations with Kett. Kett was left with no option but to attack and his army succeeded in recapturing Norwich. Northampton 'had succeeded in turning a vast popular demonstration into a full-scale rebellion, when everywhere else the commotions had been defused' (Fletcher and MacCulloch, *Tudor Rebellions*).

Full-scale rebellion
Northampton retreated in disgrace to London. His inept handling of the situation had created a crisis for the Government and the county. Commissions were issued for the militias to be raised in all the counties around Norfolk, troops were taken from the garrisons on the border with Scotland and mercenaries were employed. Northumberland (or the Earl of Warwick as he was at the time), at the head of this force of 12,000 men, arrived outside Norwich on 23 August.

Government suppression
On the arrival of the royal herald at the rebel camp, the men 'put of theyr caps and cryed God Save King Edward', but Northumberland's offer of a pardon was refused. Over the next three days Northumberland's professional army ground down the resistance of the grimly determined rebels and on 26 August Kett made the fatal decision to abandon their fortified position on the top of Mousehold Heath and take up hastily constructed defences in the vale of Dussindale. Northumberland's army was bolstered by another 1,000 foreign mercenaries and the scene on 27 August was one of carnage. Three thousand rebels were slaughtered and Kett was arrested.

Aftermath
Kett was tried for treason and was hanged on 26 November. Northumberland resisted the bloodthirsty impulses of the Norfolk gentry and ensured that the rebels were dealt with strictly in accordance with the letter of the law. He appears to have dealt leniently with the rebels, as MacCulloch (*The Tudor Rebellions*) has found clear evidence of only 49 executions.

ACTIVITY

In pairs, write a dialogue of the confrontation between York Herald and Kett, which you will then act out in front of the class. You will need to study the demands of the rebels (see Sources 16.6 and 16.7) and the expected relationship between the people and the authorities (see the theory of the Great Chain of Being and the fear of the many-headed monster, pages 228–29).

ACTIVITY

1 Compare Kett's rebellion and the Western rebellion. Did the fact that both rebellions occurred at the same time affect the Government's ability to handle them?
2 What may explain the harsher treatment that the Western rebels received?
3 Which of the two rebellions was more threatening to the Government? Explain your answer.

C What caused the rebellions?

FOCUS ROUTE

Read through pages 234–35 and complete your own copy of the following table to show the main causes of the two revolts.

Types of cause	Western rebellion	Kett's revolt
Somerset's policies Enclosure Rents Bad local government Religion Personality clashes		

What do you think was the main cause of each of the two rebellions?

16G Causes of the Western rebellion

Religious grievances
In contrast to Kett's rebellion, religion was unquestionably the central issue that sparked the Western rebels. The list of articles resolutely demanded the reintroduction of Catholicism (see Source 16.6). This was to be achieved through the reinstatement of Henry VIII's Act of Six Articles, the use of Latin, Communion in one kind (the congregation receiving the bread only), prayers for the dead and Mass every Sunday. The widespread response of the ordinary people was perhaps provoked as much by the unfamiliarity of the new practices as by the doctrinal and political issues behind them. The removal of the images and the introduction of the new Prayer Book service (described in the articles as a 'Christmas game') would have left all the community in no doubt as to how significantly religion under Protector Somerset had changed.

Economic factors
Although the articles produced by the rebels were dominated by the religious grievances, Anthony Fletcher believes that 'to interpret the rebellion as solely religious would be a vast simplification' (*Tudor Rebellions*). In the early stages of the rebellion, economic grievances figured more highly. Complaints about taxes on sheep and cloth generated rumours about further taxes on other animals. The list of demands reproduced in Source 16.6 was in fact a second list that superseded the first. In the initial list there were complaints about taxes and food prices, which probably reflect more accurately the fears of the rank and file members of the crowd. By the time the second list was compiled, a small group of clergy led by Robert Welsh had hijacked control of the movement and their theological concerns are heavily reflected in the articles.

SOURCE 16.2 J. Loach, *Protector Somerset: A Reassessment*, 1994, p. 26

None of this adds up to an overall economic and social explanation of the rising: religion was, clearly, the main driving force of the risings in the south-west and the Thames Valley.

Personality clashes
In Devon, the government agent William Body intensified the antagonism felt towards the religious changes with his heavy-handed investigation into church property (see Chart 16C).

16H Causes of Kett's rebellion

Enclosure (see page 138)
The rebels' attacks on fences and hedges show that they were opposed to enclosure in wooded pasture areas (not in sheep/corn districts). The first article of their demands opposed any future enclosure (but did protect the enclosure of expensive saffron fields). Over the preceding half-century more enclosures had been created because there was more money in the sale of wool and other animal products than in cereal crops. In response to this, some farmers had begun to specialise in sheep farming and had built enclosed sheep runs. It was the attack on Flowerdew's enclosure that triggered the whole rebellion. The list of demands does, however, contain complaints on a whole range of local farming issues, not just enclosure.

Government action against enclosure

May 1548	The royal deer park at Hampton Court was disparked (they removed the fences that had been erected to enclose the land and create deer parks).
1 June 1548	Commission of inquiry established under John Hales to investigate the extent to which existing legislation on enclosure was being enforced in the Midlands.
June 1548	Proclamation issued against men being 'driven to extreme poverty and compelled to leave the places they were born' because of enclosure.
Summer 1548	An unusually large number of rural riots broke out, including in Buckinghamshire where Hales was investigating.
Summer 1548	The Council voiced opposition to Somerset's policy and accused Hales of stirring up trouble.
Summer 1549	In the face of mounting opposition and with the populace increasingly restless, Hales began the work of his commission again, but his work was a miserable failure and he did not manage to bring proceedings against any enclosers.

Rents
The rebels also complained strongly about the increase in rents. These complaints came in a period of rapid inflation, which worsened the economic situation for ordinary people. Rack-renting (extortionately high rent charges) was seen as a way in which unscrupulous landlords passed on the increased costs to the peasantry.

Somerset's policies

Somerset's reputation as the 'Good Duke' was largely built on his social policy. Somerset's perceived sympathy with the plight of the poor and the social and agrarian problems they faced was believed by contemporaries and some historians to have encouraged the common people to riot. If some of the rebels were confident of the Protector's support, it gave them an extra incentive to express their grievances. The evidence for Somerset's sympathy is as follows:

- He gave support to the 'Commonwealth men' – a group of Christian reformers who campaigned against the exploitation of the poor.
- He appointed John Hales to lead a commission into enclosure (one of the most fiercely resented of the agrarian problems that the common people faced).
- He attacked landlords' greed, saying: 'Maugre [in spite of] the Devil, private profit, self-love, money and such like the Devil's instruments, it [anti-enclosure] shall go forward.'
- He passed an Act protecting the rights of copyhold tenants on his own estates.
- He created a special tax on sheep with a higher rate for flocks on enclosed land.

SOURCE 16.3 D. Loades, *The Mid-Tudor Crisis, 1545–1565*, 1992, p. 2

The riots and risings of 1549 were not a cry of despair from a hopeless and exploited peasantry, but the anger of men who felt that what they held by law and custom was being eroded, and who thought that they had been given promises of adequate protection ... The main responsibility for that lay not with an acquisitive and unprincipled aristocracy, who seem to have been no worse and no better than in most generations, but with those idealists who believed that they could transform human behaviour by appeals to conscience and Christian principles. Somerset for his own reasons accepted many of their arguments at face value, and in so doing turned a harmless moral and literary fashion into a potentially explosive ideology. The blood of Dussindale, of Sampford Courtenay and of Oxfordshire was the price – a price which the Protector also eventually paid himself.

Protest against bad government in East Anglia

Kett's rebels picked out the gentry and JPs in their county for the most vehement attack both in their articles and in their actions. Kett's tactics seem to have been to appeal over the heads of the local gentry directly to the central Government. This appeal fits in with the traditional belief that the Government would respond to valid grievances and work on behalf of the ordinary people to redress them. Kett must have been devastated when on 21 June the herald rejected this position.

To prove that the quality of the governance of the county was one of their major concerns, the rebels ran Mousehold Heath camp fairly and effectively, setting up their own court and sending out searches for food with commissions in the King's name. There was no gentry involvement in the rebellion and it was led throughout by those just outside governing classes, who may have been ambitious for power themselves.

SOURCE 16.4 A. Fletcher and D. MacCulloch, *Tudor Rebellions*, 1997, p.74

The events at Norwich in July and August 1549 indicate a breakdown of trust between the governing class and the people who normally sustained local government that has no parallel in the Tudor period.

Religion and the clergy

The articles relating to religion are thoughtful calls for more competent and involved clergy, rather than controversial doctrinal statements. There was clearly concern with the poor quality of priests and their failure to fulfil their duties. One article requests that they do more to educate the poor and another states that the clergy should be priests for the whole community and not just chaplains for the gentry. The rebels' inclination towards Protestantism is shown by their demand for congregations to choose their own clergy and by their use of the new Prayer Book at Mousehold Heath camp.

SOURCE 16.5 J. Cornwall, *Revolt of the Peasantry, 1549*, 1977, p. 236

In Norfolk religion was not at issue; complaints about the Church were confined to the shortcomings of its ministers. Protestantism was firmly established among the rebels; it never occurred to them to enlist the sympathy of Mary even though she was living not far away, under house arrest at Kenninghall in Suffolk.

Personality clashes

In both rebellions, hatred of particular individuals helped tip the counties over into rebellion. In Norfolk the first fences and hedges to be uprooted were those of John Flowerdew, who had outraged the village of Wymondham with his rapacity (see chart 16E).

TALKING POINT

Why would rumours be such powerful factors in a rebellion?

D What can be learned from the rebels' demands?

Compiling a list of articles was a normal means in a rebellion by which the rebels articulated their demands and grievances. The Western rebellion produced several versions of their articles. Part of the final and most complete copy is reproduced in Source 16.6. The exclusion of the local and economic issues that appeared in the earlier versions may have been because the clergymen who assumed leadership asserted their thinking and priorities on the document. The demands of Kett's rebellion (see Source 16.7) appear to have been the work of their eponymous leader. The contents of both documents provide a fascinating historical insight into the minds of the rebels. The articles have been placed after the explanation of the causes so that you can now relate the rebels' demands to the general causes and make your own decision as to how important the causes were for each uprising.

FOCUS ROUTE

1 Read the demands from the Western rebellion and Kett's rebellion in Sources 16.6 and 16.7. Sort the articles into categories in your own copy of the following table, by putting the number of the article in the appropriate box.

Type of demand	Western rebellion	Kett's rebellion
Religious beliefs		
Enclosure		
Rent		
Role and competence of priests		
Agrarian issues		
Local rights issues		
Quality of local government		
Others		

2 What does the completed table tell you about the main complaints of the rebels?

SOURCE 16.6 Selected articles of the Western rebels, 1549

1 *First we will have the general counsel and holy decree of our forefathers observed, kept and performed, and who so ever shall speak against them, we hold them as heretics.*
2 *We will have the Laws of our Sovereign Lord King Henry the VIII concerning the Six Articles, to be used as they were in his time.*
3 *We will have the mass in Latin, as was before, and celebrated by the priest without any man or woman communicating with him.*
4 *We will have the Sacrament hung over the high altar, and there to be worshipped as it used to be, and they which will not thereunto consent, we will have them die like heretics against the holy Catholic faith.*
5 *We will have the sacrament of the altar but at Easter delivered to the people, and then but in one kind.*
6 *We will that our curates shall minister the sacrament of baptism at all times, as well on the week days as on the holy days.*
7 *We will have holy bread and holy water made every Sunday, palms and ashes at the time accustomed, images to be set up again in every church, and all other ancient old Ceremonies used as heretofore, by our mother the holy church.*
8 *We will not receive the new service because it is but like a Christmas game. We will have our old service of matins, Mass and evensong and procession as it was before; and we utterly refuse the new English.*
9 *We will have every preacher in his sermon, and every priest at the Mass pray, especially by name, for the souls in purgatory as our forefathers did.*
10 *We will have the whole Bible and all books of scripture in English to be called in again, for we be informed that otherwise the clergy shall not of long time confound the heretics.*

SOURCE 16.7 Selected articles from 'Kett's Demands being in Rebellion', 1549

1 *We pray your grace that where it is enacted for enclosing [legislation against enclosure] that it be not hurtful to such as enclosed saffron grounds for they be greatly chargeable to them, and that henceforth no man shall enclose any more.*

2 *We certify your grace that where as the lords of the manors have been charged with certain free rent, the same lords have sought means to charge the freeholders to pay the same rent, contrary to right.*

3 *We pray your grace that no lord of no manor shall common upon the Commons.*

4 *We pray that priests from henceforth shall purchase no lands neither free or bondage [under this peasants were not free and were required to work for their landlord in return for land], and the lands that they have in possession may be letters to temporal men, as they were in the first year of the reign of King Henry VII.*

5 *We pray that Redeground [grassland] and meadow grounds may be at such price as they were in the first year of King Henry VII.*

6 *We pray that all marsh that are held by the Kings majesty be free rent or of any other, may be again at the price that they were in the first year of King Henry VII.*

7 *We pray that all Bushels within your realm be of one size, that is to say, to be in measure viii gallons.*

8 *We pray that priests or vicars that be not able to preach and set forth the word of God to his parishioners may be thereby put from his benefice [a living from a Church office], and the parishioners there to choose another or else the patron or lord of the town.*

9 *We pray that the payments of castillward rent [an old feudal payment], and blanche ferme [payments in money rather than goods], and office lands [rents raised on advice from government officials], which have been accustomed to be gathered of the tenements [land holdings], whereas we suppose the lords ought to pay the same to their bailiffs for the rents gathering, and not the tenants.*

10 *We pray that no man under the degree of a knight or a squire keep a dove house, except that it has been an old and ancient custom.*

11 *We pray that all freeholders and copyholders [whose land and property were rented] may take the profits of all commons, and there to common, and the lords not to common nor take profits from the same.*

ACTIVITY

1 What do the articles of both Kett's rebellion and the Western rebellion reveal about their views of the past? How do they use the past (see Western articles 2, 4, 7, 8, 9 and Kett's demands 4, 5, 6, 10)?

2 What differences are there in the nature of the religious demands of the two rebellions?

3 Which of the two sets of demands do you think most clearly reflects the grievances of the rank-and-file members of the crowd?

4 Do the rebels' demands support the conclusions drawn by historians about the causes of the rebellions (see Charts 16G and 16H)?

E Review: The year of the many-headed monster – how dangerous were the rebellions of 1549 for Edward VI's government?

16I The extent of the threat

Reasons why the rebellions did not pose a threat to the Government	Reasons why the rebellions were a problem
• There was virtually no attempt at co-operation or synchronisation between the isolated uprisings. There was some uniting of forces within regions: for example, Devon and Cornwall joined forces and Kett's rebels were joined by small contingents from Lincolnshire and Cambridgeshire. However, there was no attempt at cross-regional co-operation, which could have been extremely dangerous for the Government.	• In some cases, most notably Norfolk and Devon and Cornwall, the local gentry failed to deal with the uprisings and the central Government had to intervene.
• The rebellions were not directed at the Government or the monarch. There was no attempt to march on London, as there had been in 1381, 1450 and 1497.	• Raising troops was difficult and expensive. The normal method of raising troops was through the local militia, but the Government was understandably reluctant to ask the rebellious peasantry for support. Russell in the south-west had to raise troops from distant counties, while the Government employed foreign mercenaries.
• The Government was always in control of its forces and was never in danger.	• Against his will, Somerset had to bring troops back from Scotland to assist in the crisis. This marked the end of his policy of garrisoning the northern border.
• There was a noticeable and significant lack of aristocratic and gentry leadership.	

ACTIVITY

1. What does Source 16.8 reveal about how the gentry reacted to the rebellion?
2. What does Edward's Chronicle entry (Source 16.9) reveal about his views on the danger posed by the rebels in the spring and early summer?
3. What does Edward's entry show about how the rebellions were normally suppressed?
4. Study Source 16.11. Do the military preparations instigated by Somerset necessarily prove that the rebellions were dangerous?
5. What evidence is there to support David Loades' statement in Source 16.11 that 'it looked as though the whole of southern England was on the point of social and economic disintegration'?
6. Do the sources support or contradict the idea of rebellion given in the rebels'-eye view (see Chart 16J) that rebellion was a basic type of communication between the elites and the common people?

SOURCE 16.8 Nicholas Sotherton, *The Commotion in Norfolk*, 1549

For they cryid out of the Gentlemen as well for that they would not pull downe theyr enclosid growndis, as allsoe understood they by letters fownd emonge theyr sarvants how they sowt by all weyes to suppres them, and whatsoever was sayde they would down with them soe that within a ii or iii wekes they had so pursuyd the Gentlemen from all parts that in noe place durst one Gentleman keepe his house but were faine to spoile themselves of theyr apparrell and lye and keepe in woods and lownde placis where no resorte was: and some fledd owte of the countrye and gladd they were in theyr howses for saving of the rest of theyr goods and cattell to provide for them daiely bred mete drinke and all other viands and to carry the same at their charge even home to the rebellis campe, and that for the savinge theyr wyves, and chydren and sarvants.

SOURCE 16.9 Edward VI's Chronicle on the events in May and June 1549

The people began to rise in Wiltshire, where Sir William Herbert did put them down, overrun and slay them. Then they rose in Sussex, Hampshire, Kent, Gloucestershire, Suffolk, Warwickshire, Essex, Hertfordshire, a piece of Leicestershire, Worcestershire and Rutlandshire, where by fair persuasions, partly of honest men among themselves and partly by gentle men they were often appeased.

SOURCE 16.10 M. L. Bush, *The Government Policy of Protector Somerset*, 1975, p. 85

The bulk of the stirs tended to embarrass the government by seeking to implement rather than resist its policy. The government at no point fought for its life. No rising in 1549 threatened the government physically in the manner of those of 1381, 1450 and 1497 with a sustained march on London. Nor did the rebels plan to release the king from the grip of evil ministers. If anything, the aim was to aid the government against the aristocracy, or to make it change its religious policy. Also to the government's relief, the 1549 risings stand out for their lack of aristocratic participation and leadership.

SOURCE 16.11 D. Loades, *The Mid-Tudor Crisis, 1545–1565*, 1992, p. 114

In 1548 the situation had been contained without too much difficulty, which may have induced a sense of false security, but as the summer of 1549 advanced, it looked as though the whole of southern England was on the point of social and economic disintegration. By July the foreign mercenaries, recruited for the war in Scotland, were being deployed against English rebels; and London was garrisoned and protected with artillery.

ACTIVITY

Sort the Western rebellion and Kett's rebellion into types A and B and decide where to place them on the Richter scale of unrest according to how dangerous they were.

- Type A: Attempts by political leaders to seize the throne.
- Type B: Mass demonstrations to draw attention to grievances and to force changes.

1	Mild, isolated protests from peasants.
2	More vocal and sustained protests from various social groups in the lower orders. JPs order them to disperse.
3	Unrest begins to spread. Rebel leadership established. Meeting with local gentry and JPs.
4	Rebels produce a list of demands. Rebel camp is established. Numbers swelling. Suppression by local gentry attempted.
5	Rebel camp numbers thousands. Government intervention required. Pardon offered in return for rebels dispersing.
6	Rebels are advancing or have remained in place for at least four weeks. Meeting with regional nobility required. Government begins to prepare measures for suppression.
7	Troops raised. Suppression by regional nobleman attempted.
8	Rebellion requires full-scale military suppression.
9	Monarch's position severely threatened by the rebellion.
10	Rebellion succeeds in overthrowing the established dynasty.

■ 16J What can we learn about how dangerous Kett's rebellion was by examining it from the rebels' perspective?

1 Tradition

The word 'rebellion' conjures up images of violence, destruction and uncontrollable anger. The rebels of 1549 were certainly angry and determined, but to understand the rebellion from the ordinary rebels' point of view you need to understand the importance of order and tradition, as well as violence. Traditional beliefs, practices and customs affected every aspect of Kett's rebellion. The rebellion began on a traditional festival day – a feast to celebrate Saint Thomas Becket's relics. It was often the case that unrest began on special days because they were times when crowds naturally assembled. There was, however, no element of pre-planning and no prior intention to attack Flowerdew's enclosures. Although there are no records of the rebels' thoughts on that first day, it can be imagined that their discussions and anger at the festival, enhanced by the drink and the feeling of strength that comes from being in a crowd, turned their minds to resolving the problems that so embittered them.

Tradition also dictated the articles that the rebels compiled and the places where the camps were set up throughout East Anglia. The sites were normally market centres or assize areas (courts) because they acted as focal points and helped the spread of news. Mousehold Heath, the site of the main rebellion under Kett, was traditionally used as an assembly point in disturbances. In their demands they appealed for the re-establishment of relations and conditions as they had been under Henry VII. They seemed to be looking to recreate a lost golden past when rents were reasonable, grassland was cheap and local officials were honest and effective. By pulling down the hedges and fences around enclosures, they saw themselves to be restoring the old structure of the landed economy and re-establishing rights of way and common grazing rights. They viewed the enclosers and not themselves as the culprits and they were supported in this by government proclamations. These government statements, which blamed enclosure for the country's economic ills, and the enclosure inquiry under John Hales in the Midlands only helped to legitimise and encourage the rebels.

2 Discipline and order

The rebels' actions during the uprising were almost always disciplined. There is little evidence of wanton violence being meted out and even John Flowerdew seems to have remained unmolested. The rebels seem to have been guided by a desire to maintain order and to demonstrate the legitimacy of their position. The Mousehold Heath camp was effectively organised and run by Kett. A pseudo-county council was created – two representatives were elected from each of the 22 hundreds (administrative areas) in Norfolk and one from Suffolk – and proper legal procedures were always followed. They had their own open-air court under a tree that they called the Oak of Reformation with the assembled people acting as the jury. The court was established so that the rebels could 'be admonished to beware of their robbings and spoiling and other their evil demeanours and that account they had to make'. Even those searching for food went armed with a commission in the King's name. Diarmaid MacCulloch has concluded that 'The 1549 camps were probably more like a rough and ready garden fête or assize meeting than the savage centres of misrule which the government later tried to picture'. (Fletcher and MacCulloch, *Tudor Rebellions*).

3 Communication

Rebellion itself was seen as a drastic but acceptable form of communication with superiors. The ordinary people had few other ways of expressing their dissent or complaints. It can perhaps be best compared to a game of medieval football, with the rebels on one side and the authorities on the other. The rules were loose and poorly understood, but by invading the other side's space you forced them to take notice and *always* provoked a response. Violence and physical destruction were highly likely, but the intention at the outset was *not* to cause maximum harm. Tactics in the rebellion were naïve and underdeveloped. The rebels were, above all, rebelling to make the authorities aware of their grievances. The aim was to force a response from them, not to overturn them. This is why the rebels *camped* rather than marched – they were waiting until they were given satisfaction and they realised that only their continued presence could pressurise their superiors into conceding their demands. If the rebels had been the mindless and uncontrollably destructive monster of sixteenth-century propaganda, the violence would have been more widespread and indiscriminate, the list of demands would not have been as considered and detailed, and the rebellion would have been more aggressive. In fact, the only gentlemen and noblemen who were killed died in active combat and gentry were normally humiliated rather than attacked. Only two instances of personal molestation were recorded in Norfolk. One was against Mr Wharton, who was forced to run the gauntlet from the camp to the city gate while being stabbed with spears and knives. Derision was one of the principal tools of the rebels: they approached Norwich 'bear arssyde' and 'most shamefully turned up their bare tayles agenst those which did shoote, whych soe dysmayed the archers that it tooke theyr hart from them'.

4 The response of the authorities

Both sides recognised the need to bridge the gulf and reach an understanding. There is a set pattern to how the authorities dealt with unrest. Their first action was always to seek meetings at a local level. In these they would attempt to begin a dialogue with the rebels and try to establish understanding and trust. If this failed and suppression by local gentry was not possible, the next step would be a meeting with the principal regional nobleman. Again the magnate would try to *negotiate* and reach a compromise. At this stage, if not before, the Government would intervene and would take the rebels and their demands seriously. Failing this and the offer of a royal pardon, troops were raised. But even when the army arrived, they would initially offer a pardon to all but the ringleaders. Most of the 1549 risings were ended by the return of senior court figures to their localities to talk to the rebels and, if need be, offer money and pardons. In Suffolk, for example, Sir Anthony Wingfield was able to quell the unrest with pardons and promises of improvements. In Sussex, the Earl of Arundel invited the leading rebels to his house for dinner. The rebels, perhaps cowed by the sheer weight of his status and authority, reached agreement. The rebellions in Norfolk and the south-west were perhaps not suppressed because there was no one to do the job. The senior noble families in the south-west (the Courtenays) and in East Anglia (the Howards) had been removed in Henry VIII's reign.

What were the consequences of the rebellions of 1549?

- Most historians agree that the coup which removed Protector Somerset was made directly possible by the rebellions and by Somerset's handling of them. Somerset's support of the anti-enclosure measures had disastrously earned him the widespread reputation of being a friend of the commons. His failure to quickly crush the rebellions sealed his fate (see page 199).
- Northumberland's successful military suppression of Kett's rebellion added to his own political credibility and status. He was able to use this to gain extra support when he made his bid to become ruler in January 1550 (see page 199).

ACTIVITY

1 Write an account of Kett's rebellion from the perspective of the Government and gentry. Show how they would have seen the rebellion and explain why they would have regarded it as dangerous.
2 Produce an essay on the following subject: How dangerous were the rebellions of 1549 to the Government of Edward VI?

- The military demands of suppressing the uprisings of 1549 helped to produce a turning point in England's foreign policy strategy. The desperate need for troops required Somerset drastically to scale down his favoured policy of garrisoning the border with Scotland. The French also took advantage of England's internal domestic turmoil by declaring war and besieging Boulogne in the summer of 1549. Northumberland went on to bring both conflicts with Scotland and France to a natural end in 1551 (see Chapter 17, pages 252–54).

Conclusion

By any estimation, the uprisings of 1549 were serious. They eventually resulted in the overthrow of the well-established ruler, Protector Somerset, they mobilised tens of thousands of angry commoners across the country and they took the Government's resources near to breaking point. The loss of life (so easily forgotten in the analysis of history) was very significant, as around 10,000 are known to have died. The rebellions of 1549 were not, however, threatening in an overtly political way. Their purpose was not to overthrow any member of the Government or ruling family.

It is important to assess the danger each posed separately. In the case of Kett's rebellion, the rebels saw themselves as appealing to the national government against a local government that had failed in its duty to implement existing laws. They appealed to tradition and custom, not to a radical agenda, and they remained disciplined and clear-sighted about their objectives. In the Western rebellion, the rebels did have a more challenging religious agenda that openly rejected the Government's Protestant changes. Their articles were written more assertively and they did not display the kind of deference expected in the sixteenth century. In the midst of such mass protest, it was difficult, if not impossible, for a hierarchy conditioned to fear the spectre of popular unrest to respond in any other way than they did. The frightened eyes of the authorities saw only the ugly, rearing head of the many-headed monster in the rebellions of 1549.

KEY POINTS FROM CHAPTER 16: The year of the many-headed monster – how dangerous were the rebellions of 1549 for Edward VI's government?

1 There were many minor rebellions in 1549, but the two major uprisings were Kett's rebellion in East Anglia and the Western rebellion in Devon and Cornwall.
2 The rebellions were caused by a mixture of economic, religious and local issues.
3 In Kett's rebellion, the major issues were agrarian grievances (including enclosure) and dissatisfaction with local government.
4 The Western rebellion was mainly provoked by anger at the introduction of Protestantism (particularly the First Prayer Book), although there were some economic complaints (including a new tax on sheep).
5 The Government's first response was to attempt to appease the rebels with promises of pardons and the redress of some of their grievances.
6 The rebellions in East Anglia and the south-west eventually had to be suppressed by military force.
7 The rebellions of 1549 never posed a direct threat to the Government and the Tudor dynasty.
8 The rebellions had important knock-on consequences, the most important of which was the fall of Protector Somerset, who was associated in many people's minds with the outbreak and poor handling of the rebellions.
9 The rebellions were not as dangerous as they could have been because of the absence of gentry and aristocratic involvement.
10 The authorities in the sixteenth century saw mass protest as an irrational and frightening event and the crowd as a many-headed monster.

17

On the sidelines of Europe? How successful was foreign policy during Edward VI's reign?

CHAPTER OVERVIEW

A month after his sixth birthday, Edward witnessed his father's celebrations following the emphatic English victory over the Scots at Solway Moss. Just before Edward's eighth birthday, his father returned from France celebrating the greatest foreign policy achievement of his reign – the capture of Boulogne. The young prince must have been affected by his father's ambitions. But did Edward inherit his father's aggressive ambitions and, in his short reign, how much influence could the young king bring to bear on foreign policy?

The legacy of Henry's foreign policy for his son was substantial – an unfinished war against Scotland; Edward's engagement to Mary, Queen of Scots; continuing tension with France (especially over Boulogne) – and the reign of Edward VI was to be dominated by these issues. The personnel was also much the same in both reigns. Somerset and Northumberland, Henry's most successful generals, became the overall commanders of military and foreign policy for Edward VI. During Edward's reign, Somerset continued the war against Scotland, adopting the strategy of garrisoning the northern border. On Somerset's fall, Northumberland brought the wars against France and Scotland to an end by surrendering Boulogne, effectively ending the active foreign policy of Edward's reign.

This chapter will evaluate the success of English foreign policy during the years 1547–53 by examining the following questions:

A What was Henry VIII's foreign policy legacy to his son?

FOCUS ROUTE

1 Make your own copy of the following table. Fill in the column for Henry VIII using Chapter 11, then fill in the final column as you read through this chapter.

Aim	Henry VII	Henry VIII	Edward VI
Honour and glory	War in France in 1492		
Defeat the French	France won Brittany; peace at Etaples (1492)		
Maintain trade with the Netherlands	Lost temporarily; restored by *Intercursus Magnus* (1496)		
Increase control over Scotland	Marriage of Margaret to James IV		
Protect England	Achieved		
Preserve the Tudor dynasty	Achieved with difficulty		
Keep the peace	Yes – in last part of reign		
Conserve the finances	Yes – left a surplus		

2 Using the completed Henry VIII column, make notes on whether the achievements and failures of Henry's foreign policy made the situation more difficult for Edward.

ACTIVITY

As you read the chapter, use the Focus Route table on this page to decide which were the top three foreign policy objectives for:

a) Somerset
b) Northumberland
c) Edward.

■ 17A The legacy of Henry VIII

Henry VIII
Henry VIII was always going to be a hard act to follow. His egotism had given England ambitions beyond its means and his unshakeable self-belief had made these implausible objectives seem possible. He had also left his son a legacy of debasement and debt, in spite of raising huge sums from the dissolution of the monasteries. His reign had been dominated by the quest for honour and the defeat of the traditional enemy France, led by his great rival, Francis I. Henry believed that he had achieved both of these objectives spectacularly by the capture of Boulogne in 1544. He had sought to increase control over the Scots and had celebrated his victory over them at Solway Moss (1542). In his wars against France, Henry had allied with the Emperor Charles V and this had enabled him to maintain links with the Netherlands (controlled by the Emperor). Was Edward going to continue in this shadow, or try to break free?

A chance for a fresh start?
The accession of a minor gave England's foreign policy a breathing space, as there was no immediate need for the new monarch to prove himself in war. Henry VIII's relations with others had been shaped by his personality, so his death gave an opportunity for England to follow new, less personal policies. The rest of Europe watched closely for new policy initiatives, particularly in respect of religion. Europe itself had been transformed in 1547 by the deaths of Henry and Francis I and also by Charles V's decisive victory over the German Protestants (see pages 000-00), and the new patterns of diplomacy had not yet emerged.

Trapped in the old king's ways?
It was difficult to withdraw from the shadow of such a major monarch as Henry VIII. Sharp turns in policy were in any case against the instincts of sixteenth-century politicians, and the continuity in personnel (Somerset and Northumberland had been Henry's leading generals) increased the likelihood of a continuity of policy. Henry had also committed England in concrete ways. The Treaty of Greenwich (1543) had arranged for the marriage of Edward VI and Mary, Queen of Scots, and this betrothal had been confirmed in Henry's will. The Treaty of Ardres (1546) had left Boulogne in English hands until 1554 when it would be bought back by the French. The campaign against the Scots had been conducted by Somerset, who now took over as Protector and was likely to continue with the aggressive approach. The 'auld alliance' between the Scots and the French remained, and English fears would continue to be dominated by the prospect of facing war on two fronts.

ACTIVITY

'A chance for a fresh start' or 'Trapped in the old king's ways'. Which of these statements more accurately describes the position of Edward's foreign policy at his accession?

SOURCE 17.1 This portrait, by an unknown artist, portrays Edward as the juvenile version of the 'great' Henry VIII; the boy challenging all-comers with his posture and expression, ready to follow in his father's footsteps. Compare this with Holbein's portrait of Henry VIII on page 85

■ **Learning trouble spot**

What counted as success in foreign policy?

A king's basic responsibilities were to keep the peace at home, to ensure that the rule of law was respected and that the country was guarded against foreign invasion. However, these were primarily domestic objectives and whenever monarchs ventured into foreign affairs the waters of success and failure become murkier. A king could certainly achieve glory by winning victories and territories abroad, and this would please the warlike tendencies of his nobles at home. However, ignominious defeat, massive financial demands and insecurity were more often the accompaniments of foreign adventures. Aggression was, though, the most natural line for a monarch to follow. It would take a strong-minded leader like Henry VII to see peace and financial probity as a more reasonable policy to adopt.

In Edward VI's reign, Somerset regarded foreign policy through the same prism as his warlike old master, Henry VIII. Northumberland, once he was ruling, forgot his days as a general and adopted the more peaceful, pragmatic approach of Henry VII. What Edward would have done had he ruled as an adult and what he would have perceived as being success or failure in foreign affairs is difficult to call. Historians judging what counted for success in foreign policy must avoid being anachronistic by regarding peace as being fundamentally more desirable than war. The fairest way of assessing success or failure is to judge the achievements of the rulers in the light of the aims they set themselves, the resources they had at their disposal and the problems they faced.

B What role did Edward VI play in foreign policy?

His interest

It is clear that Edward was very excited by chivalry and war. His Chronicle reveals his fascination with jousts (although he was not permitted to participate in them), guns, battles and fortifications. One of the papers he produced revealed his fascination with the past days of the Hundred Years War (see Source 17.2). In keeping with his character, his interest was more academic than warlike. He noted the various sources of revenue for the campaign, the different kinds of troops and how they were paid, and the final treaty articles.

The heroic potential of foreign affairs did lead him to drop momentarily his normally cold and impenetrable façade. Uncharacteristically, he displayed a boyish enthusiasm on his meeting with the Marshal St André of France, who awarded him the Order of St Michael. In his Chronicle he also looked forward to the prospect of his glorious entry on to the European stage.

SOURCE 17.2 Edward VI's 'Notes on the English occupation of France in the reign of Henry VI', undated

The revenue of the county of Maine and city of Maine was 56,200 francs, which is English £6,244 and 4 francs odd, the year of Our Lord God 1434. Out of which [was] paid to 121 lances on horseback, 34 lances afoot, and 510 archers in 4 garrisons, of which one was kept but seven months, and had in one lance on horseback two on foot, and 30 archers, the sum of 55,362 francs, which is English £6,151 6s 8d.

His knowledge

Edward was certainly very well informed about foreign affairs and was able to draw on sources of information (foreign ambassadors, for example) beyond those that normally went to the Privy Council. The subjects of defensive fortifications, marriage policy and foreign affairs are all covered in his Chronicle. Between May and June 1552, for example, he recorded in detail the clashes of Maurice of Saxony, Henry II and Charles V in the Habsburg–Valois Wars. He was also present at Privy Council meetings at which these issues were discussed.

His influence

The evidence is not as clear, however, on the level of influence Edward wielded in foreign policy. The conduct of war was regarded as the special preserve of the adult male aristocracy. It is difficult to conceive of the teenaged Edward holding much, if any, sway over the foreign affairs decisions of the hardened veteran Somerset. Although Northumberland did allow Edward 'a great deal of freedom' (as the Imperial ambassador observed), there is no definite evidence that Edward dictated policy. Indeed, there would have been less opportunity to influence foreign policy under Northumberland's regency, as the signing of the Treaty of Boulogne in March 1550 effectively brought to an end the active foreign affairs of Edward's reign.

TALKING POINT

Does the evidence suggest that Edward, had he lived, would have emulated his father and led his own expeditions on to the Continent? Or does it suggest that he was just 'an anorak', interested only in the technical details of warfare?

C What were the main events in Europe during Edward's reign?

For over 30 years the European scene had been dominated by the larger-than-life figures of Henry VIII, Francis I and Charles V. The year 1547 was a critical one for all three of them: Henry and Francis both died, worn out and physically wrecked, while Charles reached the zenith of his power. However, the years 1547–53 saw the most decisive conflicts of the Habsburg–Valois Wars (1519–59), during which Charles' position of dominance was abruptly overturned. He was forced to flee the Holy Roman Empire and shortly afterwards to abdicate.

■ 17B The dominance and decline of Charles V, 1547–55

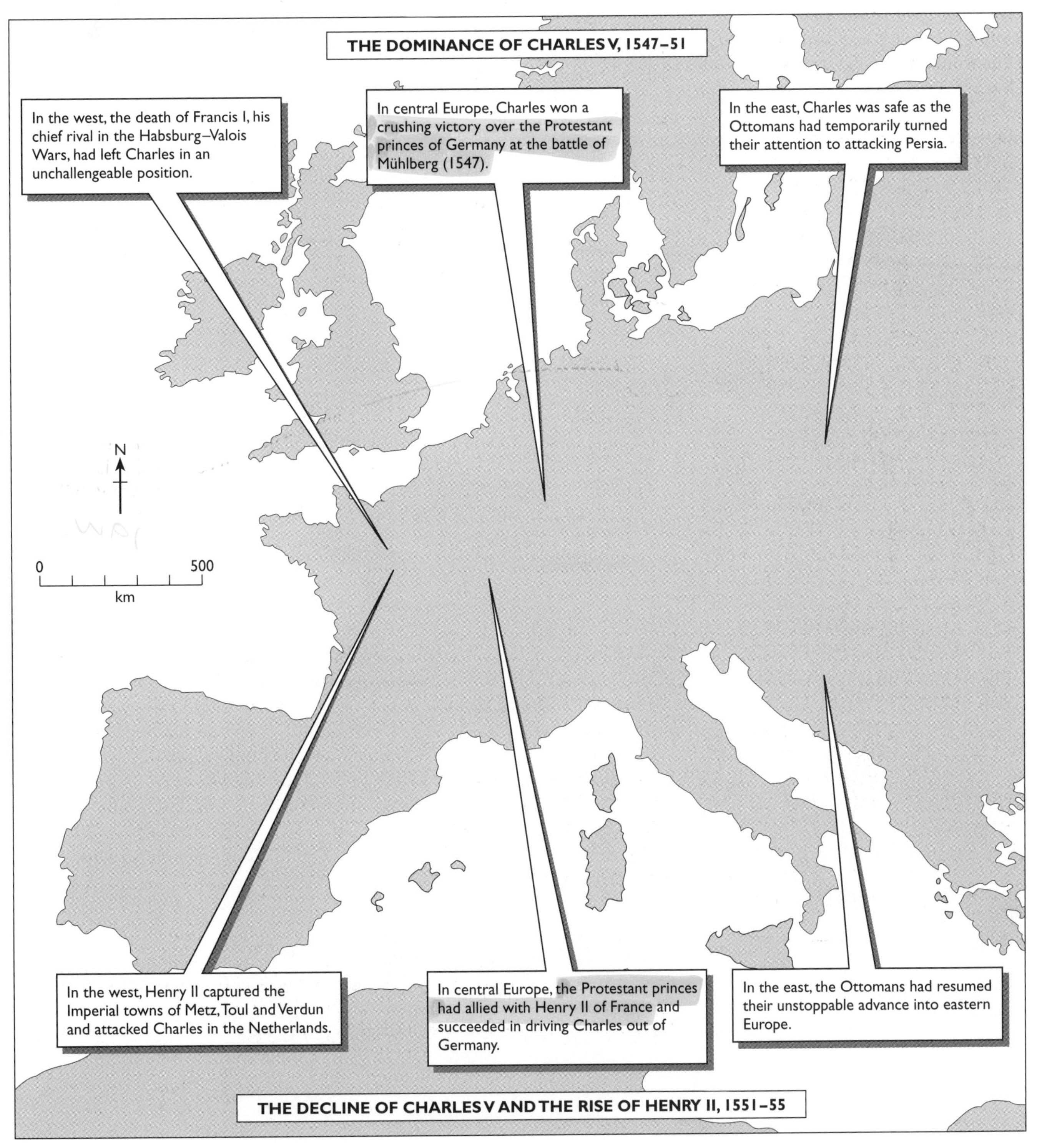

THE DOMINANCE OF CHARLES V, 1547–51
In the west, the death of Francis I, his chief rival in the Habsburg–Valois Wars, had left Charles in an unchallengeable position.
In central Europe, Charles won a crushing victory over the Protestant princes of Germany at the battle of Mühlberg (1547).
In the east, Charles was safe as the Ottomans had temporarily turned their attention to attacking Persia.
N
0
500
km
In the west, Henry II captured the Imperial towns of Metz, Toul and Verdun and attacked Charles in the Netherlands.
In central Europe, the Protestant princes had allied with Henry II of France and succeeded in driving Charles out of Germany.
In the east, the Ottomans had resumed their unstoppable advance into eastern Europe.
THE DECLINE OF CHARLES V AND THE RISE OF HENRY II, 1551–55

Why did Charles V matter so much for English foreign policy?

Charles V mattered to England because:

- The fear of an invasion by Charles to restore Catholicism remained strong. In 1547, for example, Charles was in such a formidable position that William Thomas, Clerk of the Council, declared, 'Where shall he end this fury but against us?'
- In conflict against France and Scotland, England needed an alliance with Charles V. In June 1549, Somerset ratified the Anglo-Imperial Treaty of 1544, which gave no active support, but showed friendship in spite of the Reformation.
- In the event of war against France, England would have to rely on Charles V for mercenaries and supplies from the Netherlands.
- Edward was personally fascinated by the events in Europe surrounding Charles V. During the period from May to June 1552, Edward's Chronicle is dominated by details of the Habsburg–Valois Wars, which had reached a critical stage for Charles.
- Charles' territories in the Netherlands were by far England's most important trading partner.

England mattered to Charles because:

- Charles remained concerned about the fate of his cousin, Mary Tudor. In 1551 the Imperial ambassador, Schevyfe, 'came with a short message of war if I [Edward] would not suffer his [Charles V's] cousin the Princess to use her Mass'.
- As a devout Catholic, he was disturbed by the thrust towards Protestantism under Edward.
- In his conflict with the Valois kings of France, an English alliance could be very useful.

SOURCE 17.3
Portrait of Charles V at the battle of Mühlberg, painted by Titian

Why did Henry II matter so much for English foreign policy?

TALKING POINT

How significant would the policies and actions of Charles V and Henry II be in changing English foreign policy? What would the main impact be?

Henry II was an unremarkable character; he was melancholy, dominated by his mistress, Diane de Poitiers, and neither sharp nor witty. He did, however, have a love of war and he was to have a decisive influence on the European scene.

SOURCE 17.4 Portrait of Henry II of France, by François Clouet

He mattered because:

- He came to the throne at the age of 28 determined to make an impact. When he was a child he had been held prisoner for four years by Charles V, so he was partly motivated by a desire for revenge.
- He saw the opportunity to manipulate the 'auld alliance' with Scotland to England's detriment. One of his first acts was to send French troops into England and remove Mary, Queen of Scots, to France in 1548. This pulled the rug from under England's plans to marry her to Edward. His dispatch of large numbers of troops to Scotland (1547–49) ruined Somerset's policy of garrisoning.
- His search for revenge on Charles V made him willing to sign the Treaty of Boulogne in 1550 to keep England out of the frame.
- His alliance with the German princes (Treaty of Chambord, 1552) reversed Charles V's dominance and made Henry II the major figure in Europe.

How successful was Somerset's policy towards Scotland?

FOCUS ROUTE

Make notes on the following questions as you read the remainder of the chapter.

1 What were the principal problems and benefits of using garrisons in Scotland?
2 Was Somerset a failure in Scotland? Explain your view.
3 Should the Treaty of Boulogne be regarded as a success or a failure? List the points that support both views.
4 How effectively did Northumberland manage foreign policy?

■ 17C Main events in foreign policy, 1547–53

In the following list, *italic* type is used for European events.

1547	March: *Henry II became King of France. French troops were sent to Scotland.*
1547	April: *Charles V defeated the German princes at the battle of Mühlberg.*
1547	September: England defeated Scotland at the battle of Pinkie.
1547–49	English garrisons were established in Scotland.
1548	June: *10,000 French troops arrived in Scotland.*
1548	July: *Mary, Queen of Scots, was removed to France.*
1549	Summer: Western rebellion and Kett's rebellion.
1549	August: *France declared war on England.*
1550	March: Treaty of Boulogne established peace between France and England.
1551	July: The Treaty of Angers was signed – Edward VI became engaged to Elizabeth of France.
1552	*Henry II captured Metz, Toul and Verdun from Charles V.*

Somerset's aims

Somerset had a distinguished military record under Henry VIII. He was Lord Admiral (1542–43), spearheaded the attacks on the Scots (May 1544 and September 1545) and saw military service in France (1545 and 1546, being made Lieutenant of the Kingdom of France in 1546). It was more than likely, then, that he would seek a military solution to England's foreign policy problems when he became Protector. His aims were as follows:

- The main priority of Somerset's foreign policy was Scotland. He hoped to achieve the marriage of Edward and Mary, Queen of Scots, which had been arranged under the Treaty of Greenwich (1543) and had been stipulated in Henry VIII's will. Such a marriage would result in the political union of the crowns of England and Scotland.
- He wanted to complete the unfinished business of conquering Scotland that he had started as military commander for Henry VIII. Every year since 1541 there had been some kind of attack upon the Scots, and it would have appeared only natural to Somerset that he should continue these.
- He wanted to avoid war with France. He therefore tolerated provocations such as their military support of Scotland.
- He aimed to prevent another revival of the dangerous alliance of the Scots and the French.

English victory over the Scots

In June 1547 the aggressive new French monarch, Henry II, had sent a fleet with 4,000 soldiers to Scotland. In September 1547, Somerset launched a naval and land invasion of Scotland. A decisive victory was very quickly achieved at the memorably named battle of Pinkie. Somerset entered Edinburgh and captured all of the main border strongholds. Pressing domestic concerns forced him to return to London before the end of the month, leaving garrisons behind to maintain control. In January 1548 he made an appeal to the Scots to agree to marry Edward and Mary so that the countries would become like 'two brethren of one island of Great Britain'.

The policy of garrisoning

Somerset was well aware of the deficiencies of Henry VIII's policy of invading Scotland when the need arose. It was expensive, ineffective at rooting out the Scottish aggressors (who always melted back into the Highlands on the approach of an English army) and did not maintain a consistent pressure on the Scots. Somerset was determined to find an alternative strategy and he settled on garrisons. Garrisoning formed the central thrust of Somerset's military policy in Scotland between 1547 and 1549. Twenty-five garrisons were established and a further fourteen were planned.

French attacks in Scotland

The logistical difficulties of sustaining garrisons were already proving a real headache for the English when the arrival of 10,000 French troops in June 1548 made the garrison system unworkable. The poorly defended garrisons were no match for the might of the French. A treaty was rapidly signed between the French and the Scots, under which the marriage of Mary to Henry II's son was agreed and the Scots placed themselves under the control of the French King. In July, Mary was taken away to France, removing the most important reason for the English presence in Scotland. The English garrisons had stood by helplessly.

The French then turned their attention to the English garrisons and began to besiege Haddington. Somerset was caught in a dilemma: if he risked sending troops to relieve Haddington, the French might use the opportunity to retake Boulogne, which they had been harassing. Troops led by the Earl of Shrewsbury were sent to Scotland and temporarily succeeded in relieving the garrison. Somerset's problems multiplied in 1549 when the rebellions in England broke out (see Chapter 16). He delayed bringing troops back from Scotland, only finally giving the order in August. He had been forced to abandon Haddington, but coincidentally the French had withdrawn from Scotland, drained by the cost of the campaign and intent on recovering Boulogne.

■ 17D The main English garrisons in Scotland

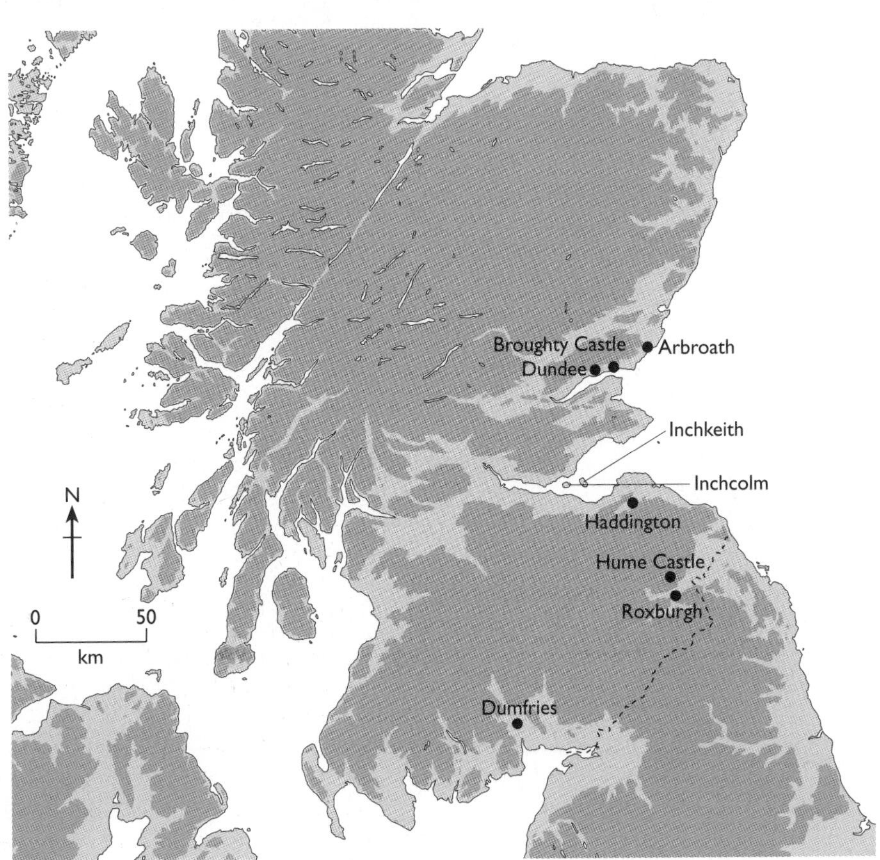

■ 17E The pros and cons of garrisoning

Pros	Cons
Garrisons would enable the English to launch rapid reprisal raids after Scottish attacks.	Only two of the garrisons were substantial fortresses. The rest were simply camps with improvised ramparts on the sites of old castles.
Garrisoning was expected to be a long-term solution to the Scottish policy of hit-and-run guerrilla warfare, which major invasions could do nothing about.	Contrary to Somerset's expectations, garrisoning proved more expensive than Henry's raids: Somerset spent £351,521 on wages to Henry VIII's £235,383.
Henry VIII's policy of raids was seen to have been an expensive failure.	The English found they had substantial problems in provisioning the garrisons. When supplies ran out, the soldiers took them from the locals, thereby worsening relations between them.
Garrisons would help to protect the 'assured' Scots – those who looked favourably upon English intervention.	Most of the garrisons had only a few hundred troops, so they could hold a Scottish attack at bay, but could not drive the attackers off or defeat them.
A permanent English presence would, it was hoped, help to secure acceptance of the marriage of Edward VI and Mary Stuart.	The Government found it difficult to recruit English soldiers and was forced to use mercenaries from Albania, Hungary, Italy and Spain. However, by 1549 even they refused to serve in Scotland.
In an effort to avoid antagonising the Scottish populace, the English did not take taxes, supplies or rents from the locals living near the garrisons.	Control of the troops was very difficult; soldiers rebelled against or ran away from the awful conditions, especially the outbreaks of the plague.

ACTIVITY

Produce a Committee of Inquiry report into the policy of garrisoning in Scotland. Your report should include:

a) an explanation of what the garrisoning policy was

b) an assessment of how effectively the garrisoning policy supported Somerset's policy in Scotland.

E How successfully was war with France and Scotland brought to a close?

■ 17F French Channel ports

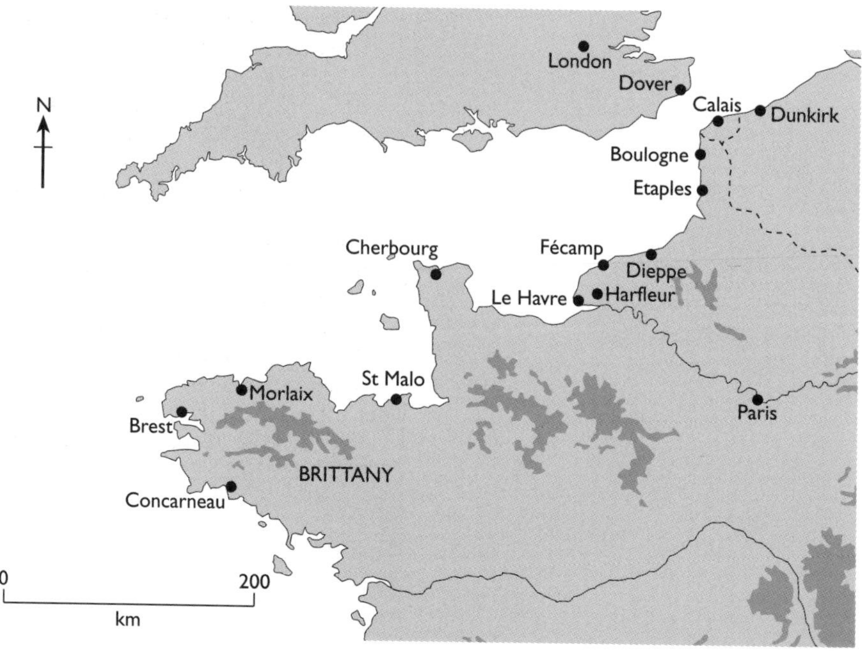

Somerset fell from power in October 1549. In January 1550, Northumberland established himself as Lord President of the Council and was ruling the country and directing foreign policy.

The French had not been slow in taking advantage of England's domestic difficulties (the Western rebellion and Kett's rebellion: see Chapter 16). In August 1549, while the English countryside was in open rebellion, Henry II had attacked Boulogne. The French succeeded in cutting the supply lines between Calais and Boulogne, but an English victory at sea meant that the English navy retained control of the Channel. Northumberland was faced with an unenviable position:

- England was bankrupt, so it was not able to raise an army to relieve the siege of Boulogne.
- Attempts to get support from Emperor Charles V had failed.
- Henry II was, however, concerned that Charles V might still intervene on England's side in the dispute.
- An abandonment of Boulogne could be highly unpopular.
- Northumberland was still attempting to secure a strong power-base at court, so he needed all the support he could get.
- Under the Treaty of Ardres, the French were to buy back Boulogne for 2 million crowns in 1554.

In January 1550, Lord Russell and Lord Paget were sent to France to negotiate a settlement with a French team who were clearly in a much stronger bargaining position.

ACTIVITY

1 You are to play the role of the English ambassadors negotiating the peace settlement with France. Draw up a proposed settlement using the list of issues to be decided below. Your settlement should be favourable to England's interests, but it must be one that the French would be likely to accept.

- Should a marriage be arranged between Edward and Mary, Queen of Scots, or Elizabeth, a French princess? Should a dowry be involved?
- Should the English withdraw from Boulogne?
- If Boulogne is given up, should England be compensated? Financially or territorially?
- Should the English withdraw completely from Scotland? Or, should the English maintain that Scotland is a totally separate issue?
- Should England and France sign an alliance? Should they support each other if either of them goes to war against Charles V?
- Should Calais be given up to the French?
- Should any promises or guarantees be extracted from the French? If so, what?
- Should any promises be given to the French about English involvement in European affairs?
- Should the English Crown give up its claim to the French throne?
- Should the French continue to pay the English a pension? Should the English receive backpay for pensions owed (see Chapter 11, page 175)?
- Should the fortress at Boulogne be destroyed?

2 Discuss your proposed settlement with the rest of the group, raising the following issues: Which would have been the most important issues for the English and French governments? Would the French have agreed to the settlement that you propose? How would the other court politicians have viewed your deal? How does your settlement affect England's strength/position in Europe? What would be realistic proposals?

3 Now compare your settlement with the actual terms of the Treaty of Boulogne (page 254). Was the treaty a good one for England?

Terms of the Treaty of Boulogne (28 March 1550)

1 England gave up control of Boulogne in return for 400,000 crowns (more than Henry II wanted to pay, but much less than was promised to Henry VIII).
2 Marriage was arranged between Edward VI and Elizabeth, daughter of Henry II, with Elizabeth bringing a dowry of 200,000 crowns. (The marriage was agreed at the Treaty of Angers (1551), but never took place.)
3 England agreed to pull all its troops out of Scotland and not to declare war unless provoked.
4 England and France made a defensive alliance and England agreed to remain neutral in continental wars.
5 The fortress at Boulogne was passed intact to the French and all the English artillery and stores remained there.
6 The English claim to the French throne was not abandoned.
7 The King of France was no longer to pay a pension to the King of England.

Assessment

The town of Boulogne was militarily and strategically useless, but its loss was very significant. It was a humiliating abandonment of Henry VIII's most glorious foreign adventure. England had been shown to be completely helpless in the face of the French and had to submit to almost all of their demands, even ones relating to Scotland. However, Northumberland was recognising the realities of the situation. England could no longer sustain its control of the port and its resources were hopelessly overstretched. With the French dominant in Scotland and the English armed forces depleted, there was little choice but for England to make peace with Henry II.

F How successfully did Northumberland handle foreign policy between 1550 and 1553?

■ 17G English foreign policy under Northumberland

Relations with Scotland
Soon after the Treaty of Boulogne, hostilities with the Scots were brought to a close, but the antagonisms and root causes of the conflict remained unresolved. In April 1550, Northumberland undertook a complete reorganisation of Scottish border policy. He made himself General Warden of the North and inspected the borders in person. After lengthy negotiations and pressure from the French, the boundary was finally restored in March 1552 to the line it held before Henry VIII's Scottish campaigns.

Trade with the Netherlands
The cloth trade with the Netherlands was a vital pillar of the English economy and had been protected by the *Intercursus Magnus* since 1496. A breakdown in normal trading relations with the Netherlands occurred because of Charles V's implacable opposition to Protestantism. In April 1550, Charles issued an edict allowing the Inquisition to arrest any heretics in the Netherlands (although foreigners were excluded). This damaged trade (as many of the Netherlands' traders were Protestants) and helped to bring about a disastrous collapse in the Antwerp cloth market. Charles' hostility to the Reformation in England and the ill-treatment of Mary Tudor led him to consider an invasion of England in the autumn of 1551. In response, England put a temporary embargo on the sale of cloth to the Netherlands. Economic pressures and Charles' need for support led to an improvement in trading relations by June 1552.

Relations with France
When he became king in 1547, Henry II declared his intention of recovering Boulogne and Calais. By 1550 he had achieved the first objective, but by the summer of 1551 there was a show of peace as Edward became engaged to Elizabeth, daughter of Henry II, and the Marshal St André enchanted the young king with a chivalric charm offensive. England's relations with France remained tense, however, as it was feared that it would only be a matter of time before Henry attacked Calais. When war broke out between France and the Holy Roman Empire in spring 1552, the garrison at Calais was reinforced.

Relations with Charles V
Alliances with England had been helpful to Charles V in his long struggle with the Valois kings of France, so he was dismayed by the Anglo-French agreements reached at Boulogne and Angers. He was angered by the sharp swing towards Protestantism under Northumberland's government and by the harassment of his cousin, Mary Tudor, because of her Catholic faith. He was further upset by England's tactless ambassador at the Imperial court, Sir Richard Morison, who lectured Charles and demanded the right to hold Protestant services at his residence. Northumberland resisted the pressures exerted on him by Charles, doggedly pursued a policy of neutrality and refused to be dragged into the Habsburg–Valois Wars.

G Review: On the sidelines of Europe? How successful was foreign policy during Edward's reign?

Edward himself, despite his knowledge of and interest in foreign affairs, does not appear to have played any substantial role in determining policy. An assessment of foreign policy during his reign must therefore focus on the two main architects, Protector Somerset and the Duke of Northumberland.

Somerset assumed control of foreign policy at a very difficult time. He was bound to uphold the unsuccessful policy bequeathed by Henry VIII. Yet, England was in a weak military and diplomatic position. The French held all the aces, especially after they had gained control of Mary, Queen of Scots. Somerset's room for manoeuvre was further reduced by the fact that England was more vulnerable because its monarch was a minor.

Despite these problems, however, Somerset can be fairly criticised for not capitalising on his achievements and for not seeing the long-term consequences of his actions. He defeated the Scots at Pinkie (as decisive a victory as Solway Moss in 1542 or Flodden in 1513), but his decision to garrison the border was a costly mistake (approximately £200,000 a year was spent on Scotland). The decisiveness that had made him so successful as a general made him a blinkered commander-in-chief. Somerset's policy in Scotland undoubtedly failed and his obsession with the conduct of the Scottish campaign had a detrimental effect on many other areas of policy.

- The rebellions of 1549 mushroomed out of control because Somerset only agreed to release troops from Scotland to suppress the rebellions at the last moment.
- While he was so committed in Scotland, Somerset needed friendly relations with Charles V to help to deter a French attack. In order to secure these better Anglo-Imperial relations, he was forced to adopt a slower and more ambiguous development of religious policy than he would otherwise have wished for.
- The financial situation was disastrous, with heavy debts, high inflation, a badly debased coinage and a poor exchange rate.

Northumberland is increasingly being seen by historians as a pragmatic and successful practitioner of foreign policy. His recognition of England's financial and military weakness meant that the surrender of Boulogne was the only realistic option available. Nothing further could be gained by dragging out the conflict against the Scots or by becoming embroiled in European affairs. He skilfully guided England through three difficult years as the Habsburg–Valois Wars reached their peak on mainland Europe. By cutting England's losses he was able to turn his attention to reforming finances and pursuing a more vigorous religious policy at home.

SOURCE 17.5 D. Loades, *John Dudley, Duke of Northumberland*, 1996, p. 53

Warwick [Northumberland] was above all concerned to avoid any further war, and in that he was completely successful. This was not pusillanimity but common sense.

On balance, the foreign policy of Edward's reign is perhaps most significant for its effects on domestic policy – its negative effect on finances and its impact on religion. The years of Edward's reign coincided with the moments of greatest triumph (1547) and defeat (1552) of Europe's central figure, Charles V, and England wisely remained in a partly self-imposed obscurity on the sidelines.

TALKING POINT

What were the similarities and differences between Northumberland's policies abroad and those of Henry VII? Why was Northumberland in particular well placed to appreciate Henry VII's policies?

ACTIVITY

'Foreign policy in Edward's reign was an ignominious failure.' Sort the points below into your own copy of the table, expanding on them in order to assess this judgement.

- Mary, Queen of Scots
- French military strength
- Trade with the Netherlands
- Pragmatism
- Somerset's policy towards Scotland
- Garrisoning
- Treaty of Boulogne
- Shift towards Protestantism in England
- Neutrality
- Financial resources
- Habsburg–Valois Wars
- Legacy of Henry VIII
- Northumberland's realistic policy of peace
- Edward's involvement in foreign policy

Failure	Neutral	Success
Edward's engagement to Mary, Queen of Scots, was central to England's policy to gain greater control over Scotland. Her removal to France completely undermined this policy.		

ACTIVITY

A panel of Edward's contemporaries has been brought together to evaluate the success of foreign policy during his reign. Each member of the panel must be prepared to answer any questions asked by the audience on foreign affairs during Edward's reign, but particularly those on their own specialist subject.

Panel

Garrison commander in Scotland: You were commander of the Haddington garrison from its establishment in 1547 until its closure in September 1549. You need to be familiar with the purpose of the policy of garrisoning and its practical difficulties.

Protector Somerset: As an experienced military commander under Henry VIII and as the main military strategist under Edward, you need to be able to defend the aims of your foreign policy and defend your tactics (such as avoiding war with France and garrisoning).

Duke of Northumberland: You assumed control of foreign policy in January 1550. Your main action was to sign the Treaty of Boulogne, surrendering the port and ending the wars with France and Scotland. You should be able to defend this treaty and the subsequent policy of non-involvement in foreign affairs.

Charles V, Holy Roman Emperor: As an enemy of France, a devout Catholic and a cousin of Mary Tudor, you are extremely interested in the direction of English foreign policy. You are vastly experienced in European matters and are pragmatic in your approach. You should be ready to comment on how English foreign policy fits into the wider European picture.

Other roles

Interviewer: You must chair the debate and ensure that it runs smoothly. Your duties involve choosing people to ask questions, adding supplementary questions of your own, and ensuring that all the panel get the opportunity to answer questions.

Audience: As a member of the audience, you must prepare questions on any aspects of foreign policy during Edward's reign. Your questions should be geared towards evaluating the success of the policies rather than towards extracting factual information.

KEY POINTS FROM CHAPTER 17: On the sidelines of Europe? How successful was foreign policy during Edward VI's reign?

1. Edward VI was engaged to Mary, Queen of Scots (Treaty of Greenwich, July 1543), and then to Elizabeth, daughter of King Henry II of France (Treaty of Angers, July 1551).
2. Protector Somerset invaded Scotland, winning a decisive victory at the battle of Pinkie (September 1547). He then initiated an unsuccessful policy of establishing garrisons in Scotland.
3. Somerset's aim in Scotland was to force the Scots to agree to the marriage between Edward VI and Mary, Queen of Scots, and so create a union between the countries. The policy failed and Mary was sent to France.
4. The Treaty of Boulogne (March 1550) successfully brought the conflicts with Scotland and France to an end. Under the treaty, Boulogne was bought back by the French.
5. Edward VI was very interested in foreign affairs, but he does not appear to have exercised much influence over the formation of policy.
6. England's foreign policy was influenced by the Habsburg–Valois Wars in Europe, which came to a head during the reign of Edward VI, leaving Henry II dominant over a declining Charles V.
7. Northumberland effectively prevented English involvement in the Habsburg–Valois conflict.
8. Foreign policy affected English domestic policy during Somerset's rule, slowing down the spread of religious change and making the financial situation worse.

18

The chain is broken – how was the succession altered on Edward's death?

CHAPTER OVERVIEW

After invasions from abroad, surreptitious internal plots and struggles to create heirs, arguably the greatest threat to the Tudor dynasty throughout its entire time as England's royal family was Edward's stipulation that on his death he should be succeeded by Lady Jane Grey or one of her sons. It was Northumberland who put this plan into full effect on Edward's death, and he was foiled only by the determined and skilful actions of the strictly legal heir, Mary.

This chapter will explore where responsibility for the attempt to change the succession lay and how close it came to succeeding.

FOCUS ROUTE

As you read pages 257–63, make notes on the following questions:

1 What attempt was made to alter the succession?
2 How did Mary secure the throne?

A Whose will was done – Edward's or Northumberland's?

Edward's illness

Edward's decline was neither swift nor an obvious and immediate threat to the succession. He had been a healthy child, but then he fell ill in late January 1553 with a chest infection or tuberculosis. Physicians warned the Privy Council that it was serious; however, by April there were some signs of improvement. Edward went out into the park at Westminster and took a barge journey to his favourite palace at Greenwich. By May his physicians predicted a full recovery.

Suddenly, however, in late May he suffered a serious relapse, probably contracting septicaemia. His condition now was extremely serious. He could only sleep with opiates and he was producing 'sputum' which was 'livid, black, fetid, and full of carbon' and smelled 'beyond measure'. Death was now predicted. He survived through June, but on the evening of 6 July he died. His last words were 'I am faint; Lord have mercy upon me, and take my spirit.'

The chronology of Edward's illness is important to know because it was only when his condition deteriorated significantly that the succession became a 'live' issue. Those wanting to avoid a Marian succession, therefore, only had June in which to achieve their objective. This makes it unlikely that there was any long-term planning.

■ 18A Claimants to the English throne

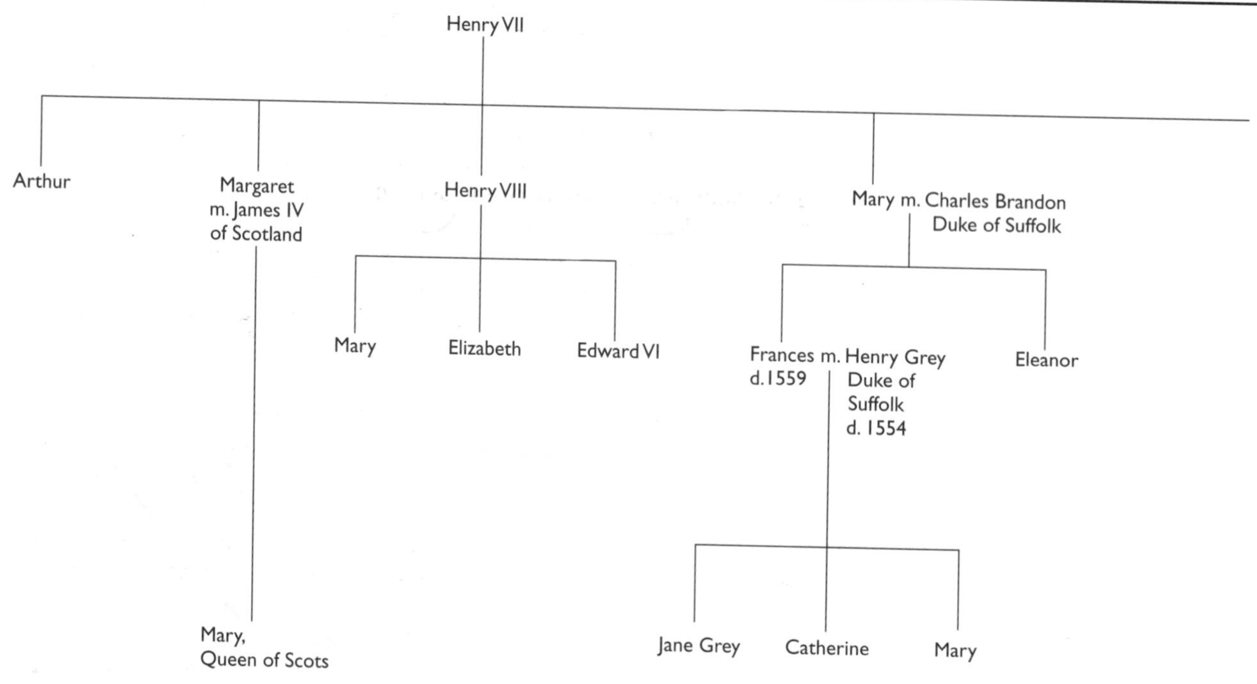

Lady Jane Grey

Born in the same month and year as Edward (October 1537), Jane Grey probably had no realisation that she was to share the same position until days (possibly even hours) before she was proclaimed queen. Famous as the monarch who ruled for just nine days, this talented but unfortunate woman was little more than a pawn in the hands of her ambitious parents, Henry Grey, Marquis of Dorset, later Duke of Suffolk, and Frances Brandon, Henry VIII's niece (daughter of Henry VIII's sister, Mary Tudor). She was tiny, intelligent and plain in her tastes, preferring black and white clothes to the ostentation of her peers.

The Duke of Northumberland and the Duke of Suffolk presenting the Crown of England to Lady Jane Grey (eighteenth-century painting by Giovanni Battista Cipriani)

How was the will changed?

It is not possible to be absolutely clear about whether the significant parts of the 'Devise' to change the succession originated with Edward or Northumberland, as both appear to have been involved at key moments. Original notes on the succession were jotted down in January in Edward's own hand. He obviously intended first and foremost to bar Mary's succession on the grounds that she was a Catholic. The attempt to steer the succession to the advantage of Northumberland was a secondary and later inclusion.

Edward initially suggested that the Crown should go to 'Lady Jane's heirs male'. Jane Grey was chosen because she was a Protestant and had sufficient royal blood to make her claim plausible (she was Henry VIII's great-niece). Her marriage to Northumberland's son Guildford Dudley in May 1553 does not appear to have been directly related to the succession because Edward was recovering at this time.

The crunch came when Edward suffered his serious relapse in late May. On 12 June he was visited by Northumberland and his law officers and the order was given for a new will to be drawn up incorporating Edward's Devise. This now stipulated that the throne would pass to 'the Lady Jane and her heirs male' – there was no time for Jane to have any children, since Edward was obviously dying.

The lawyers must have squirmed as they heard what was being asked of them. As a minor, Edward was not able to make a will or override a parliamentary statute, and the legitimate claim clearly lay with Mary. The air must have crackled with tension as the Lord Chief Justice, Montague, refused to make the will 'for the danger of treason'. Northumberland exploded, falling 'into a great anger and rage, and called me [the Lord Chief Justice] traitor before all the Council, and said that in the quarrel of that matter he would fight in his shirt with any man living' (quoted in D. Loades, *John Dudley, Duke of Northumberland*). Montague reluctantly agreed to draft the will as Letters Patent, but warned that it was not legal. On 21 June anyone who was of any importance was found to sign the will and to swear to the Devise in front of the dying king. Signatories included Cranmer, the Lord Chancellor, Privy Councillors, 22 peers, judges, household officers and the Lord Mayor of London.

Edward's death before Parliament could confirm the Devise left the succession in dangerous limbo. Henry's Third Succession Act, naming Mary next, was still valid and stood in opposition to Edward's express, but not strictly legal, last wish. Northumberland and Mary now had to decide their next moves.

Whose will was done?

SOURCE 18.1 Edward VI, Letters Patent for the Limitation of the Crown, 21 June 1553

And forasmuch as the said limitation of the imperial crown of this realm, being limited by the authority of Parliament as is aforesaid to the said Lady Mary and Lady Elizabeth, being illegitimate and not lawfully begotten, forasmuch as the marriage between our said late father and the Lady Catherine . . . and the Lady Anne, was clearly and lawfully undone . . . which said several divorcements have been severally ratified and confirmed by authority of divers acts of Parliament remaining in their full force . . . Whereby as well the said Lady Mary as also the said Lady Elizabeth to all intent and purposes are and be clearly disabled to ask, claim, or challenge for the said imperial crown . . . that if the said Lady Mary or Lady Elizabeth should hereafter have and enjoy the said imperial crown of this realm, and should happen to marry with any stranger born out of this realm, that then the same would rather adhere and practice to have the laws and customs of his or their own native country or countries to be practised or put to use within this realm . . . which would tend to the utter subversion of the commonwealth of this our realm . . . We therefore declare [the order of succession] to be 1. sons of Lady Frances, if born in our lifetime, and their heirs male; 2. Lady Jane and her heirs male.

SOURCE 18.2 W. K. Jordan, *Edward VI: The Threshold of Power – The Dominance of the Duke of Northumberland*, 1970, p. 494

But it was the King, not Northumberland, who was in fact exerting continuous and irresistible pressure. On June 15th the judges were again called before him, and with 'sharp words and angry countenance' the King commanded Montague to obey on his allegiance, which several Lords standing near by declared it manifest treason to refuse.

SOURCE 18.3 D. Hoak, 'Rehabilitating the Duke of Northumberland: politics and political control, 1549–53', in R. Tittler and J. Loach (eds), *The Mid-Tudor Polity c. 1540–1560*, 1980, p. 49

Contrary to what had been thought, the scheme to alter the succession originated in Northumberland's camp and not in King Edward's brain, but although Northumberland rightly accepted responsibility for it . . . barring Mary from the succession was a cause in which the young King believed. The chronology of the whole episode leaves one with the impression that the original object of the 'Devise' was not to make Northumberland the manipulator of a puppet queen, but simply to ensure the rule of any one of a number of Protestants, all of whom were to be male. Indeed, it was not originally apparent (by the terms of the first draft) that either Northumberland or his family would benefit by the 'Devise', for at the time of his son's marriage Lady Jane Grey had not been named as an heir to the throne. Only when it was realised that Edward VI really was dying and had not willed the throne to anyone alive did Gates [Sir John Gates, Vice-Chamberlain] persuade the boy to revise the draft in favour of Jane.

ACTIVITY

1. After analysing the formation of Edward's will, which of the historians' opinions in Sources 18.2 and 18.3 do you agree with as regards who was principally behind the Devise?
2. What reasons does the Devise give for ruling out the accession of Mary and Elizabeth? How valid are the reasons?

SOURCE 18.4 A woodcut showing the execution of Lady Jane Grey – queen for nine days as a result of the efforts of Edward VI and Northumberland to alter the succession

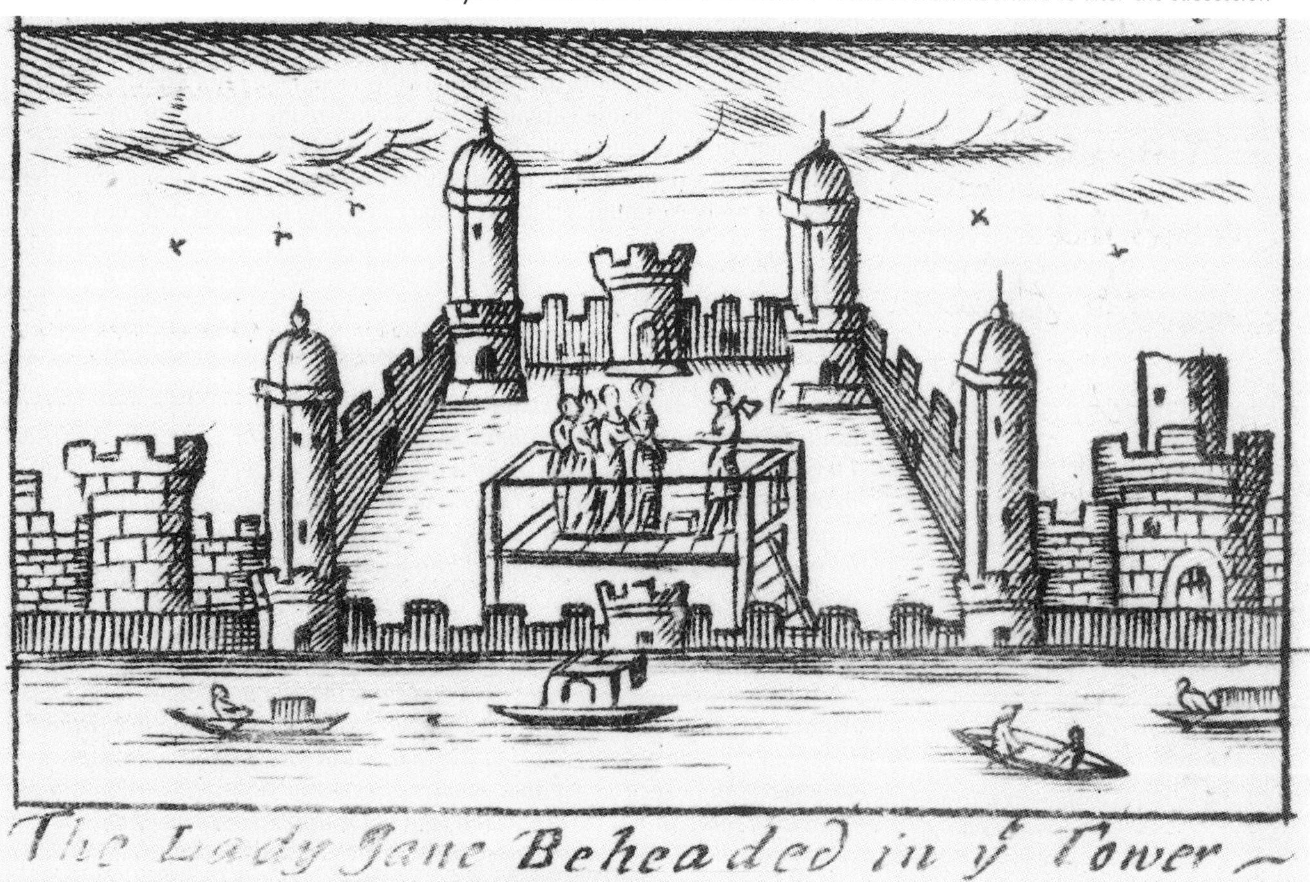
The Lady Jane Beheaded in ye Tower

How close did the Tudor dynasty come to being toppled for good?

■ 18B Key events in Mary's succession

Date	Events concerning Northumberland's position	Events concerning Mary's position
6 July 1553	Edward died. His death was kept secret for two days.	
8 July	The Lord Mayor of London, aldermen and representatives of the Merchant Adventurers were summoned to Greenwich to be informed of Edward's death. They were forced to sign the Devise for the new succession. The Council ordered sheriffs and justices of nearby counties to raise forces.	
9 July	Lady Jane Grey was taken to Northumberland's house in Chelsea. She probably did not know the full details of the Devise.	
10 July	Lady Jane Grey was taken by river to the Tower, where she was, against her wishes, proclaimed queen.	News arrived that Mary had proclaimed herself queen in East Anglia. She had appealed to the Emperor Charles V for assistance and it was clear that she was not trying to escape by sea. Proclamations and letters of summons (which had already been drawn up by Mary) were issued. The Council rejected her claim and she began mustering troops. Scheyfve, the Emperor's ambassador, feared that nothing could be done to prevent Jane's succession because none of the senior nobles or Privy Councillors had declared for Mary. He also thought that Northumberland must have had assurances of French support.
11 July	London was quiet. Northumberland decided to go to Norfolk to restore order. His sons had unsuccessfully attempted, with a small force, to intercept Mary.	
12 July		Reports arrived from East Anglia of people (including senior gentry and noble families and some Protestants) supporting Mary.
13 July	Northumberland reckoned that he had enough strength to defeat Mary, but he was afraid to leave the Privy Council in London, as he feared the Catholic noblemen Arundel and Winchester. However, there was no one else he could trust to send, so he set out with only 2,000 troops of limited reliability.	
15 July	The Privy Council were all in the Tower for protection. They were disquieted by the turn of events and did not send the reinforcements that Northumberland requested.	Mary had moved to Framlingham Castle with large numbers of supporters declaring for her.
16 July	Northumberland had reached Cambridge.	
17 July	Northumberland's forces started to desert and refused to go beyond Bury St Edmunds because of rumours that Mary had 30,000 in her camp. Northumberland retreated to Cambridge.	
19 July		Mary's forces numbered 20,000 and had been bolstered by the arrival of the Earl of Oxford. In London almost all the Council left the Tower and said they had fallen into error. People in the streets of the capital celebrated the accession of Mary. The Duke of Suffolk announced to his daughter that she was no longer queen. Mary was proclaimed queen in London.
20 July	Arundel arrested Northumberland in Cambridge.	
3 August		Mary entered London to great celebrations.
22 August		Northumberland was executed.

Jane executed 12/02/1554. – Due to paranoia/suspected involvement in Wyatt's Rebellion.

ACTIVITY

At the moment of Edward's death, Northumberland had to decide how he was going to act. He had a number of options:

- ignore the Devise and proclaim Mary queen
- uphold Edward's Devise
- proclaim himself ruler.

1 What were the advantages and disadvantages of each option?
2 Which option would you have recommended to Northumberland?

SOURCE 18.5 D. Loades, *John Dudley, Duke of Northumberland*, 1996, p. 75

From a historical distance it looks as though Mary had an easy victory, but contemporary outsiders were flabbergasted, and in fact it had been a close call. If the radical Protestants had not been alienated by his 'worldliness', if he had stayed in London after 13th July, or if he had had a couple of thousand reliable men, the outcome might have been different. It is misleading to speak simply of the 'legitimism' of the English, or their religious conservatism, or even of Northumberland's unpopularity as being the main causes of Mary's success. The actual outcome was determined by human courage and human error. Northumberland's most serious error had been to rely on offices and money rather than men. Apart from his own family, there was hardly anyone who was prepared to stand with him in adversity and no 'country' for him to retreat into or appeal to once he had lost his grip over the crown and the machinery of central government.

ACTIVITY

1 Why had Mary succeeded and Northumberland failed? Consider the following in your answer – support, tactics and claims to the throne.
2 In a post-match briefing, what criticisms would football pundits have made of the way in which Northumberland had acted?
3 What, according to Loades in Source 18.5, were the reasons why Northumberland was unsuccessful?
4 What is the 'legitimism of the English' that Source 18.5 refers to?

What can be learned from Northumberland's final actions?

After his trial, Northumberland made frenetic last efforts.

- He announced his conversion to Catholicism and publicly said that he had 'erred from the faith these sixteen years'.
- He tried to convince the Privy Council that they needed him.
- He spoke to the leading Catholic, Stephen Gardiner (whom he had imprisoned for several years), and he wrote a letter to the Earl of Arundel begging him to plead on his behalf (see Source 18.6).

SOURCE 18.6 Letter from Northumberland to the Earl of Arundel, 12 August 1553

Alas my good lord, is my crime so heynous as no redemption but my blood can wash away the spots thereof? . . . And if my life be lengthened by your medication and my good Lord Chancellors . . . I will vow it to be spent at your honourable feet.

TALKING POINT

How should we interpret Northumberland's final actions? Choose from the following options:

- an expression of his genuinely held views
- the operation of his political survival instincts
- the desperate attempt of a doomed man to save himself by any means.

C Review: The chain is broken – how was the succession altered on Edward's death?

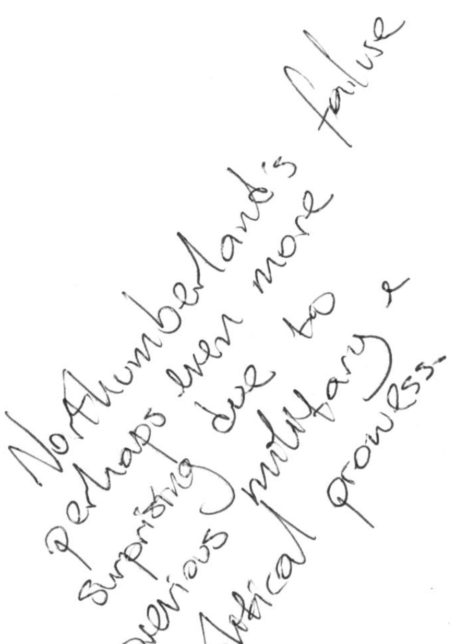

The significance of the events of July 1553 is hard to over-estimate. Edward undoubtedly supported a change in the succession – *an end to the Tudors.* A successful coup by Northumberland could have risked returning the country to the civil conflict of the Wars of the Roses. It could have denied history the reigns of Mary and Elizabeth.

However, Mary was successful because she acted without hesitation and she had the legitimate claim, which attracted an impressively committed and broad spectrum of support. Northumberland failed because he did not mobilise the full military forces at his disposal (the household troops, the garrison of the Tower of London, the fleet and the retainers of his allies) and he did not act decisively. Had he responded forcefully to the threat that Mary posed, by rallying his forces, distributing propaganda and locking in the support of the Council behind him, he could relatively easily have succeeded.

The Tudor dynastic chain *was* broken and the fact that it was only for such a short time was principally the result of Northumberland's failure at the critical moment. His political and military skills seem almost to have been frozen by the momentousness of what he was attempting. The Tudors survived and Mary, after 37 years in the wings, was about to stamp the country with her own distinctive style of Tudorism. But how close did the Tudors come to being toppled? Well, too close for any self-respecting bookmaker to risk taking any bets if he had been there at the time.

KEY POINTS FROM CHAPTER 18: The chain is broken – how was the succession altered on Edward's death?

1 Edward VI and the Duke of Northumberland collaborated on a plan to divert the succession from Mary to Lady Jane Grey.
2 Lady Jane Grey was proclaimed queen and the Tudor dynasty had effectively been ended.
3 Mary's decisive actions on Edward's death helped to secure her the throne.

Edward VI – the verdict

CHAPTER OVERVIEW

In April 1551 London was struck by its worst-ever outbreak of sweating sickness. Shops were closed for twenty days, up to 2,000 people died (2.5 per cent of the city's population), and fear and tension reached epidemic proportions. In the same year, the harvest failed, inflation reached new heights and the Antwerp market, on which the English cloth trade depended, collapsed. It is against the background of these economic and natural disasters that historians have pictured a mid-Tudor crisis.

The task of reassessing this gloomy picture is well under way. In this section we have already asserted the importance of the role of Edward in his reign. The Duke of Somerset has been placed in a proper sixteenth-century context as a traditional but flawed statesman. The Duke of Northumberland has undergone rehabilitation as a reforming and able administrator. To make a wider assessment of whether a crisis did occur, this chapter will bring all the elements together by asking the following questions:

A Did Somerset's government lead to a crisis? (pp. 265–66)

B Was there a mid-Tudor crisis in Edward's reign? (pp. 267–68)

FOCUS ROUTE

By reflecting on what you have learned in this section and by making notes as you proceed through this chapter, complete your own copy of the following table. Use examples, historians' views and your own ideas.

	Crisis?	**Not a crisis?**
Government		
Religion		
Economy and finance		
Law and order		
Foreign policy		

A Did Somerset's government lead to a crisis?

As Chapter 14 showed, the reputation of Somerset and his government has undergone considerable revision. Rather than being held up as a shining example of progressive government – the 'Good Duke' – a critical searchlight is now being put upon the policies he followed and the way in which he ruled.

ACTIVITY

This role-play is designed to allow you to assess the issues and policies of Somerset's time in power. On page 266 you will find role cards to help you to play your part.

You will each write a speech from the point of view of your character and the meeting will be run formally according to the agenda. The meeting will focus on whether Somerset should continue as Protector. You should discuss whether his policies have led to a crisis for England. A vote at the end of the meeting will determine whether Somerset should continue as Protector.

Privy Council meeting, 14 October 1549
This was the date of a real Privy Council meeting to which Somerset was summoned. The following people were present on that day. The agenda below is not historically accurate, but these issues were probably raised at the actual meeting.

Present
Protector Somerset, Earl of Warwick (to become Duke of Northumberland), Lord Grey, Lord St John, the Archbishop of Canterbury, Sir William Paget, Sir William Herbert, the Earl of Southampton, the Earl of Arundel, Lord Russell, the Earl of Shrewsbury and the Marquis of Northampton.

Agenda
'Has everything gone wrong because of the ill-government of the Lord Protector?'

Item – The rebellions in the south-west and in Norfolk.
Reports from Lord Russell and Sir William Herbert on the Western rebellion, and from the Earl of Warwick and the Marquis of Northampton on Kett's rebellion.
Item – The religious changes under Protector Somerset.
Protestant opinion from the Archbishop of Canterbury; Catholic opinion from the Earl of Arundel.
Item – The parlous state of the economy.
Expert opinion will be sought from Lord St John and Sir William Paget.
Item – Somerset's handling of the war against Scotland.
Update from Lord Grey and the Earl of Shrewsbury.
Item – Does Protector Somerset retain the confidence of this Council?
Speech against by Earl of Southampton;
Protector Somerset in his own defence.

Role cards

Lord St John (William Paulet)

- You are an able administrator with particular expertise in finance. You are appalled by Somerset's financial policy and in the meeting you will attack it. You will give a description of the country's current financial state. You must also suggest remedies, such as the ending of debasement to balance the value of the currency, the ending of the costly wars against Scotland (particularly the garrisoning policy) and France, and taking measures to end depopulation and inflation.
- You hope for promotion if Somerset is toppled.

Marquis of Northampton (William Parr)

- You fared well under Henry VIII (your sister was Catherine Parr, his last wife) and you were rewarded for supporting Somerset's seizure of power in 1547. However, you are increasingly concerned about the way Somerset has been governing the country. Your main worry is the increasing unrest of the people. You blame Somerset's sympathetic attitude to the poor – in particular, the Commissions of Inquiry into enclosure and aspects of the Vagrancy Act (1547).
- In your speech you should describe Kett's rebellion and attack Somerset's humanitarian policy as a failure. In the meeting, you should work with Cranmer in defending the Protestant religion.

Sir William Herbert

- You are a soldier by profession. You helped Lord Russell put down the Western rebellion in 1549. You blame Somerset and his policies for the uprising.
- You support Somerset's religious policy.
- You hope that you may get further favour under the Earl of Warwick.
- You keep your cards close to your chest in the meeting and are reluctant to voice strong support for Somerset. In your speech you must (with Lord Russell) give a report on the Western rebellion.

Lord Russell

- You had the job, along with Sir William Herbert, of crushing the Western rebellion. You had great difficulty in suppressing the uprising and you are angry at Somerset. You blame Somerset's religious policy and his sympathetic attitude to the poor.
- In the meeting you must say what happened in the Western rebellion. You must attack Somerset's policies. However, you do have some sympathy for Somerset and you helped to bring him to power in 1547.

Thomas Cranmer, Archbishop of Canterbury

- You are the leader of the Protestant Reformation. You are responsible for the First Prayer Book which (under the First Act of Uniformity) became the legal form of worship. You skilfully ensured that it would appeal to a wide range of people. Somerset has been generally supportive of the religious changes, but you would now like to move the reforms on faster, and he may oppose this on political grounds.
- You are outraged by the Catholic demands of the Western rebels and by the insubordinate attitude of Kett's rebels. For this reason, you are losing patience with Somerset.
- Your principal role in the meeting is to defend the Protestant reforms against the Catholics in the Council. You do not want to commit yourself to supporting Somerset.

Earl of Warwick (you become the Duke of Northumberland)

- You are a soldier by profession and you gained a good military reputation in the French and Scottish wars in the 1540s. You are extremely ambitious and some see you as being greedy and arrogant. You are a very able politician.
- You have just (June 1549) put down Kett's rebellion in Norfolk. You are appalled by Somerset's sympathetic policy to the poor, which you believe has led to this uprising and the Western rebellion.
- You have an army of 12,000 in the field and you see this as an opportunity to oust Somerset. In the meeting, you must attack Somerset and look for supporters. Although you have Protestant views, you could ally with the Catholics.

Sir William Paget

- You are a very able and well-respected administrator. You were Henry VIII's secretary and were instrumental in ensuring that Somerset became Protector. You are still loyal to Somerset, but you are having doubts about his handling of the Western rebellion and Kett's rebellion. You have been constantly urging Somerset not to push forward on so many policies at once.
- You must work to defend Somerset in the meeting. If he falls from power, you may too. You must defend his financial policy in particular.

Earl of Arundel

- You work closely with the conservative Catholic faction in the Council.
- You have been appalled by the Protestant reforms initiated by Somerset and Cranmer. Your principal objections are:
  - the repeal of the Six Articles
  - the removal of Catholic bishops
  - the dissolution of the chantries
  - the Prayer Book and the Act of Uniformity.
- You must attack Somerset, Cranmer and their Protestant policies, particularly the Prayer Book. You must champion Catholicism and the Catholic Acts passed during Henry VIII's reign.

Earl of Southampton

- You are the leader of the conservative Catholic faction.
- You have been dismayed by the Protestant reforms under Somerset. In particular, you oppose the repeal of the Act of Six Articles, the immigration of Protestant radicals and the imprisonment of Gardiner and Bonner.
- You are in contact with Edward's sister, Mary, and greatly respect her strong defence of Catholicism.
- The Earl of Warwick, who wants to topple Somerset, has started negotiations with you. Although he has been Protestant in the past, are you prepared to work with him to remove Somerset? If so, on what terms?
- You must attack Somerset, Cranmer and their Protestant policies. Your close ally is the Earl of Arundel.

Duke of Somerset

- You are the King's uncle and a soldier by profession. You quickly established yourself as the Protector after Henry VIII's death with the help of the able administrator William Paget.
- You are proud, even arrogant, and you spend money lavishly to display your power and wealth.
- You have come under attack for being aloof and for avoiding the Privy Council. Your handling of the Western rebellion and Kett's rebellion has been heavily criticised. Most of the nobility are very uneasy about your social policies, which they believe encourage disobedience among the poor.
- Your religious reforms are said to be half-hearted and you have done little to improve the economy.
- Your enemies are closing in and you must be prepared to defend yourself at the meeting.

Earl of Shrewsbury

- You are a soldier by profession and you led the campaign in Scotland in 1548 to relieve the garrisons. You were not impressed by Somerset's policy of establishing garrisons, preferring periodic invasions (as followed by Henry VIII). You believe that garrisoning has been very expensive and strategically useless (leaving the garrisons very exposed), and that it has not achieved its objectives.
- In the meeting you should report on the problems in the Scottish war and how Somerset's policies have been responsible for them. At the time of this meeting, England is also at war with France and will face considerable difficulties in defending Boulogne, which was such a hard-fought-for prize for Henry VIII.

Lord Grey

- You are a soldier by profession and you recently led the campaign in Scotland. You are aware of the difficulties of devising a policy that will allow England to subdue Scotland. Somerset's policy of establishing garrisons may not have worked, but neither did Henry VIII's strategy of periodic invasions. There is not at the moment any clear alternative.
- In the meeting you should report on the problems in the Scottish war and the difficulties any commander would face. You can emphasise how circumstances (e.g. the 1549 rebellions and the French declaration of war) have made life very difficult for Somerset.

B Was there a mid-Tudor crisis in Edward's reign?

ACTIVITY

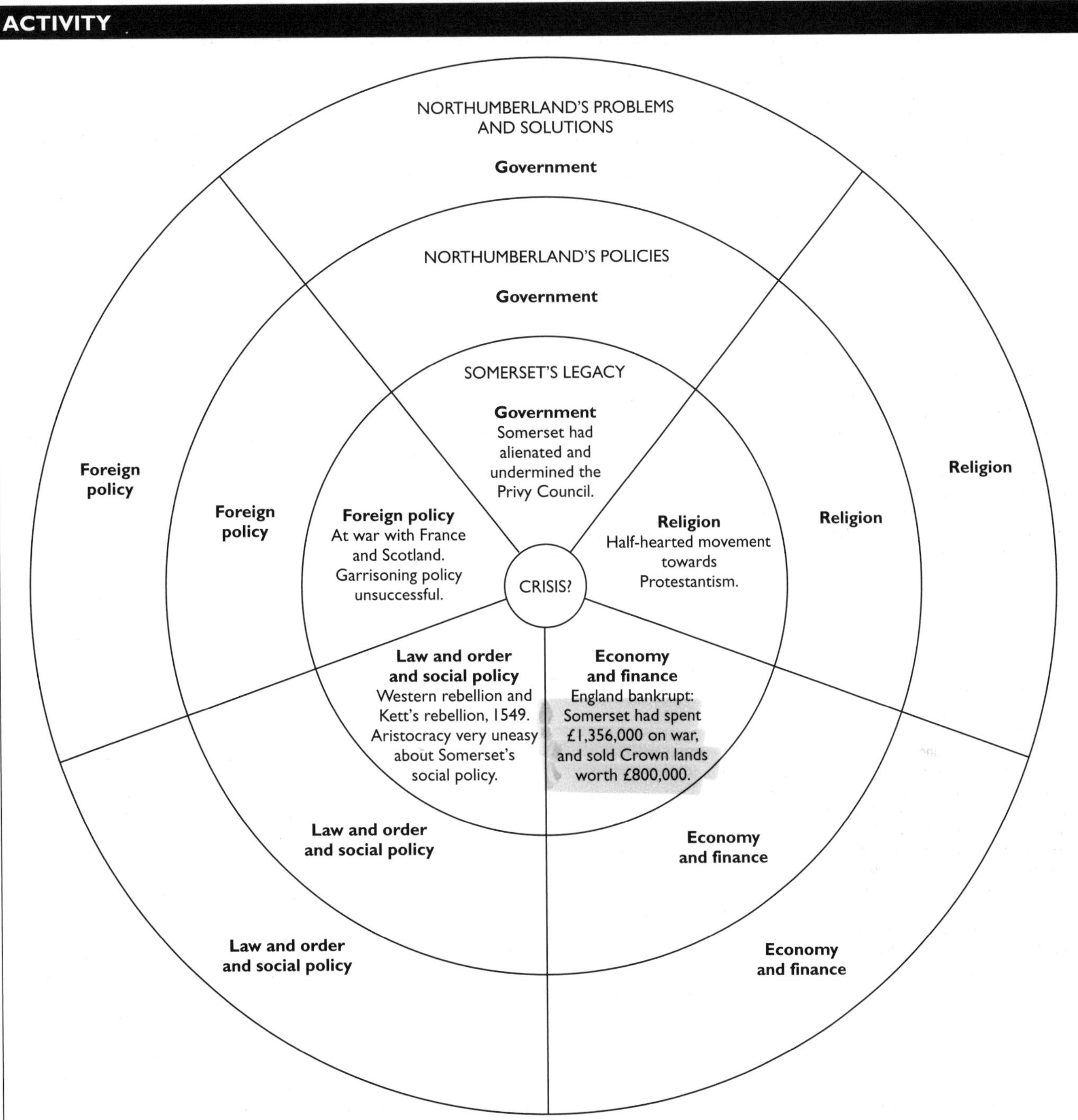
NORTHUMBERLAND'S PROBLEMS AND SOLUTIONS
Government
NORTHUMBERLAND'S POLICIES
Government
SOMERSET'S LEGACY
Government
Somerset had alienated and undermined the Privy Council.
Foreign policy
Foreign policy
Foreign policy
At war with France and Scotland. Garrisoning policy unsuccessful.
CRISIS?
Religion
Half-hearted movement towards Protestantism.
Religion
Religion
Law and order and social policy
Western rebellion and Kett's rebellion, 1549. Aristocracy very uneasy about Somerset's social policy.
Economy and finance
England bankrupt: Somerset had spent £1,356,000 on war, and sold Crown lands worth £800,000.
Law and order and social policy
Economy and finance
Law and order and social policy
Economy and finance

The pie chart shows the main policy areas that you need to examine in any reign. They can easily be remembered by the mnemonic GRELF (taking the first letter from each policy area).

1 Copy the pie chart, adding in note form the main policies and problems of Northumberland's government. Adjust the size of each pie section to show how great a problem you think it was (i.e. the bigger the problem, the bigger the section).
2 Did Northumberland's government solve or create more problems for Edward's reign?

ACTIVITY

To help you to decide if Edward's reign experienced a crisis, it is useful to speculate about what might have happened if events had not turned out as they did. In groups, each person should take a different 'What if' and suggest how history might have been changed. Do the changes heighten or reduce the sense of crisis?

What if…

- there had been an aristocratic rebellion against Somerset?
- Edward had not died?
- Southampton, not Northumberland, had taken control of the Government in 1550?
- Charles V had invaded in defence of Mary's position?
- Mary's plan to flee in 1550 had succeeded?
- Lady Jane Grey had remained on the throne?
- Edward had attempted to keep Somerset as his Lord Protector in 1549?

Conclusion

The idea of there being a mid-Tudor crisis continues to find its way on to exam papers and into textbooks; proof that, once labelled, a topic in history has great difficulty in shaking off its reputation. The concept that there was a crisis in Edward's reign is, though, difficult to sustain. The major element of the 'crisis' thesis – that the accession of a minor led to instability and weak government – can easily be dismissed. Edward was utterly secure on the throne; no one in England or Europe questioned his right to rule and there were no claimants to challenge his authoritative position. The accusation of weak government is seriously undermined by the changes imposed on the Church in the six years of his reign; they amounted to the most radical doctrinal shift during the whole of the century. These religious changes were also accomplished with little opposition, which historians are now recognising was a consequence of the mass of the population's tendency to be generally content with the decisions of the ruling regime, be it Catholic or Protestant.

Some elements of a crisis can be identified. (For further discussion of the mid-Tudor crisis, see Chapter 24.) The problems of the poor and the sick were intensified and their lives became even more a crisis of survival. Edward's surprisingly early death and the attempt to alter the succession did create the most serious crisis of his reign because it threatened the continuity of the Tudor dynasty. However, in its central features England was untroubled during Edward's reign. There was no danger of invasion, society remained essentially stable (in spite of the turmoil of 1549) and the authority of the monarchy was undiminished. Edward and his contemporaries might well have asked, 'Crisis? What crisis?'

ACTIVITY

Answer the following essay question: To what extent and for what reasons can the reign of Edward VI be seen as representing a crisis in Tudor society?

KEY POINTS FROM CHAPTER 19: Edward VI – the verdict

1. Many of the economic and social problems of Edward's reign, such as inflation, had been building up for a number of years and were not confined to the middle part of the century.
2. The natural disasters (e.g. sweating sickness and harvest failure) were no worse than many other such incidents in early modern England.
3. There are no elements of a 'crisis' which can be linked to the fact that a minor was on the throne.
4. The religious changes that took place under Edward were the most radical acts of his government, but they did not provoke any serious opposition (apart from the isolated Western rebellion).
5. The greatest threat to the Tudor dynasty was the attempt to alter the succession in favour of Lady Jane Grey (see Chapter 18).

Section 3 Review: Edward VI

At the beginning of this section we aimed to establish what degree of involvement Edward had in policy making and the government of the country. We also aimed to establish how successfully England had been run during the years 1547–53. Edward's reign has, of course, been traditionally identified as marking the start of the mid-Tudor crisis (to which we will return in Section 4 and the Conclusion). You should by now be formulating your own views on these issues. The activities below and overleaf are designed to help you to consolidate them.

ACTIVITY

Complete your own copy of the following table.

Policy	**Level of Edward's involvement** (high/medium/low)	**Supporting example**	**Success of policy area** (high/medium/low)	**Supporting example**
Government				
Religion				
Economy and finance				
Law and order				
Foreign policy				

This contemporary woodcut depicts the main events of Edward's reign: the coronation, the restoration of Protestantism and the execution of Somerset in 1552

ACTIVITY

The woodcut shows a sixteenth-century view of what the main events of Edward's reign were. What do you consider were the main features of Edward's legacy to his sister? Identify the three main benefits and drawbacks for Mary as she ascended the throne after a 37-year wait.

The Coronation of King Edward the sixt
Popery banished True Religion Restord
The D. of Somerset L. Protector Beheade

section 4

Mary I

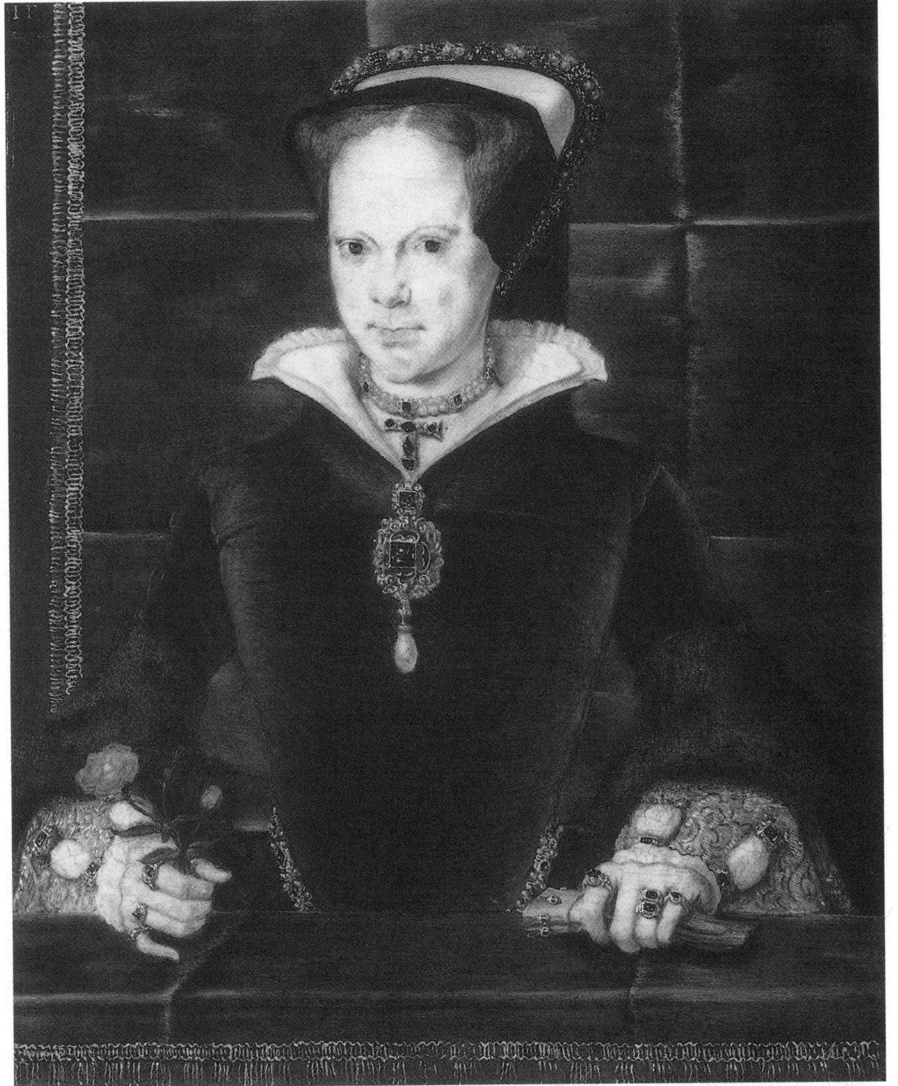

Mary I, painted in the year after her accession by Hans Eworth

Mary became queen at the age of 37 in July 1553. For her father, Henry VIII, it would have been the nightmare scenario: a queen and, moreover, a queen who followed a minor. For Mary, it was the recognition of her legitimacy as Henry's heir and Catherine of Aragon's daughter that mattered. The royal princess who had been bastardised and periodically ostracised from court by her father, who was forbidden to see her mother in the years before her death, and who yet was the focus of Catholic expectation, was now queen. She had been restored to the succession by Henry VIII and had overcome the plot to subvert the succession on her half-brother Edward's death.

What would Mary make of the monarchy? Would she undermine or reinforce the Tudor dynasty? Would a woman be able to rule the country in the sixteenth century? You will be able to reach conclusions about all these issues.

20

The chain restored – did Mary have what it took to continue the Tudor dynasty?

CHAPTER OVERVIEW Following the abortive attempt by Northumberland and Edward to put Lady Jane Grey on the throne, Mary finally entered London on 3 August 1553. The Tudor succession had prevailed, but with a woman at the helm – a woman who had initially been excluded from the succession by being bastardised by her father, Henry VIII. What sort of monarch would Mary prove to be? Would she be able to build on the work of her predecessors and further secure the Crown, or would the authority of the Crown be undermined by her? Mary's five-year reign has aroused a historical controversy that is inversely proportional to the reign's length. In this chapter, therefore, we will be examining these questions:

A How was Mary received in 1553?

FOCUS ROUTE

1 Compare the circumstances of Mary's accession to those of her brother, father and grandfather (you will need to revisit Chapters 2, 7 and 13). Complete your own copy of the following table.

	Public opinion at the time	**Preparation for and attitude towards being a monarch**	**Aims and ambitions**
Henry VII			
Henry VIII			
Edward VI			
Mary I			

2 Was Mary in a worse situation than her three immediate predecessors? Explain your answer.

Mary, accompanied by an entourage including her half-sister Elizabeth and other leading people of the realm, rode through London on 3 August 1553. The streets were decorated with banners and streamers, trumpets sounded and citizens cheered on every side. But it would be wrong to view this as rejoicing for Mary's accession *per se*. What, precisely, was being celebrated by these ordinary London folk? An endorsement of Mary herself or the Tudor dynasty that she now represented, or the restoration of more conservative religion? Mary was queen as the result of her father's will. She was the legitimate heir, and this was partly why Northumberland's and Edward's plotting had failed.

Mary Tudor was England's first crowned queen. True, there had been a woman ruler in the twelfth century – Matilda, the daughter of Henry I. But she was never crowned queen, and she did not use the title *cwen* (Anglo-Saxon for queen), because it meant 'wife', which implied that she did not hold the throne in her own right. Matilda had been unable to hold on to her throne. How far either Mary herself, or the public, were aware of this by the sixteenth century is by no means certain.

What we do know is that Henry VIII had spent the greater part of his reign trying to avoid leaving a female heir. The warrior-king could not countenance a woman leading troops into battle – the battlefield being 'unmeet for women's imbecilities', as he once commented. Hence neither of his daughters was trained to rule, although they were well educated.

TALKING POINT

What is your instinctive reaction to Mary at this stage? Successful/unsuccessful queen? Positive/negative attributes? Popular/unpopular? For/against her?

1 As a class draw a large continuum like this:

Anti ◄—— Neutral ——► Pro

2 Write your name (in red) at the place on the continuum that best illustrates your view of Mary.
3 Repeat the exercise at the end of the chapter (in blue) and of the section (in black).
4 Have your views changed? Explain why/why not.

SOURCE 20.1 Henry VIII was not the only man to doubt whether a woman could rule the country. Such views were even more strongly expressed by John Knox, a radical Protestant, in *The First Blast of the Trumpet Against the Monstrous Regiment of Women*, 1558

To promote a woman to bear rule, superiority, dominion or empire above any realm, nation or city is repugnant to nature; contumely to God, a thing most contrary to his revealed will and approved ordinance; and finally, it is the subversion of good order, or all equity and justice.

We should therefore not be surprised that Parliament found it necessary to pass an Act 'declaring that the Royal power of this realm is in the Queen's Majesty as fully and absolutely as ever it was in any of her most notable progenitors, kings of this Realm'. However, Mary's gender may prove less important than her character and attitude when we try to assess her achievements.

Radical Protestantism influenced views.

Act of Parliament surprising but it validated/legitimised Mary's position.

B How has Mary been received by historians?

Just as politicians suffer by comparison to their more illustrious contemporaries – John Major to Margaret Thatcher, for instance – Mary has suffered the same fate, being adversely compared to her half-sister, Elizabeth I. We should not be too surprised by this, as the propaganda that poured out of Elizabeth's sycophants was designed to detract from prior events or achievements and was pro-Protestant or pro-Puritan.

Sources 20.2–20.5 should enable you to get a flavour of the trends in interpreting Mary's reign.

ACTIVITY

Read Sources 20.2–20.5.

1 Identify the criticisms of Mary that have been made by historians.
2 Does the historiography change between the time that Elton was writing (1974) and the time that Williams was writing (1995)? Explain your answer.
3 Account for the change in attitude towards Mary.
4 Having read the sources, what questions about Mary's reign now come into your mind? Do this as a class and then make a collective list.

SOURCE 20.2 G. R. Elton, *England Under the Tudors*, 1974, pp.214–15

The reign of Mary Tudor lasted only five years, but it left an indelible impression. Positive achievements there were none: Pollard declared that sterility was its conclusive note, and this is a verdict with which the dispassionate observer must agree . . . all her good qualities went for nought because she lacked the essentials. Two things dominated her mind – her religion and her Spanish descent. In the place of the Tudor secular temper, cool political sense, and firm identification with England and the English, she put a passionate devotion to the catholic religion and to Rome, absence of political guile, and pride in being Spanish. The result cannot surprise . . . she died only five years later execrated by nearly all. Her life was one of almost unrelieved tragedy, but the pity which this naturally excites must not obscure the obstinate wrong-headedness of her rule.

SOURCE 20.3 C. Erickson, *Bloody Mary*, 1978, pp.vii–viii

Mary Tudor has no monument in England. In her will she had asked that a memorial be raised to herself and her mother, 'for a decent memory of us', but her request was ignored. The day of her death, November 17 – the day of Elizabeth's accession – was a national holiday for two hundred years . . . Succeeding generations called her Bloody Mary, and saw her reign through the pictures in Foxe's Book of Martyrs *– pictures of Protestant prisoners fettered with leg irons, being beaten by their Catholic tormentors, praying as they awaited execution, their faces already touched with the ecstatic vision of heaven . . . Mary Tudor bore an extraordinary burden, yet she ruled with a full measure of the Tudor majesty, and met the challenges of severe economic crises, rebellion and religious upheaval capably and with courage. Her resiliency impressed itself on the men around her. In describing her character several of them hit on the same metaphor. She was a single candle, they wrote, which shone on even when battered about by great winds, and seemed to burn more resplendently in the midst of the storm.*

SOURCE 20.4 R. Tittler, *The Reign of Mary I*, 2nd edn, 1991, p.79

For a number of reasons, it is more difficult to arrive at informed judgements on Mary's reign than on most in the Tudor period. Chief among them is the brevity of the reign, and the proportionately high time and energy spent in establishing the regime and organising its followers. Because they broke sharply with their predecessors in foreign and religious affairs, Mary and her government faced a larger than usual task of political transition. Not only did they have to reward their followers and deal with their initial opponents, but they had substantially to reweave the whole political fabric of the nation: to stitch carefully together those personal links which attached the centre to the periphery and animated the administrative processes of shire, hundred and borough.

SOURCE 20.5 P. Williams, *The Later Tudors: England 1547–1603*, 1995, p.113

For centuries Mary's reputation has suffered from a bombardment of hostile propaganda, its intensity determined from the beginning by John Foxe. In Protestant and Elizabethan tradition she is displayed as the arch opponent of true religion and as the friend of England's enemy, Spain. Her contribution to English history has been scorned as a legacy of hatred both for her faith and for the country of her husband. 'Sterility', in Pollard's cruel judgement, 'was the conclusive note of Mary's reign.' However, within the last decade several historians have modified, even in some respects reversed, that verdict.

C Was Mary fit to rule?

It may seem strange to pose this question of Mary, when we have not posed it of her predecessors – the grandfather who was a usurper, the father who became king at the tender age of seventeen, and the half-brother who was a minor. However, in the light of the contemporary concerns about her gender, and historians' sometimes damning verdicts, it is one that we should investigate.

■ 20A Fit to rule?

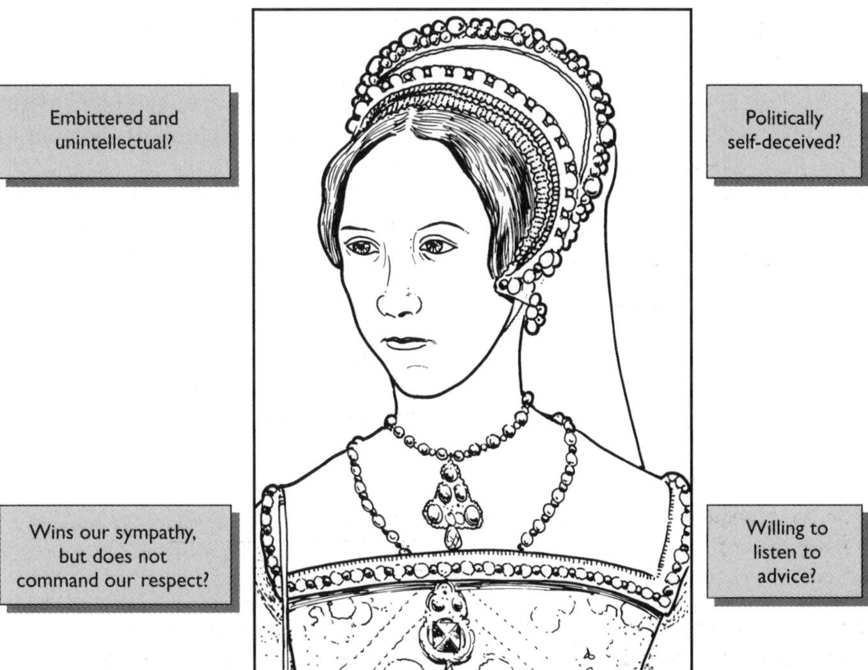

Embittered and unintellectual?
Politically self-deceived?
Wins our sympathy, but does not command our respect?
Willing to listen to advice?

Mary's background

How did Mary's background affect her outlook when she became queen? Born in 1516, she had her own household three years later. This meant that she had her own servants and expenses, separate from those of her mother and father. She was sent to Ludlow in 1525, although not as Princess of Wales. She saw her parents only occasionally for the next three years, and was recalled to the home counties in 1528 with a reduced household. When Henry repudiated Catherine of Aragon as his wife in 1531, Mary, who had once been betrothed to the Emperor Charles V, became increasingly dependent on Charles for advice about her circumstances. Needless to say, Charles was furious with Henry for having divorced his aunt, Catherine of Aragon, and for renouncing Mary as his heir in favour of Princess Elizabeth.

In 1533, Mary refused to accept that she had been made illegitimate as a result of the marriage between Henry and Anne Boleyn, and was forced to live as part of her half-sister Elizabeth's household. Her movements were restricted and she was denied access to her mother, although she did receive visits from Chapuys, the Emperor's ambassador in England. She resisted taking the Oath of Supremacy (the sworn declaration that Henry VIII was Supreme Head of the Church in England) until after the death of her mother and only took it then because of the threat of execution for high treason hanging over her in 1536. Unsurprisingly, during this time her health was a constant source of anxiety.

Restored to favour somewhat after this capitulation, Mary appeared at court more frequently. But she lamented her father's inaction in finding her a husband, which made her 'only the Lady Mary, and the most unhappy lady in Christendom'. In 1543 her place in the succession was settled – she would become queen in the event of Edward being childless.

Mary during the reign of Edward

As the reign of Edward progressed, an increasingly Protestant programme was advanced by Somerset and Cranmer, and Mary had to tread carefully. In 1549 she flouted the introduction of the new Prayer Book and the prohibition of the Mass by celebrating Mass in her chapel at Kenninghall – publicly too. When there were fears for her safety in 1550, Van der Delft, the Emperor's ambassador in England, set up an escape for her. This came to nothing owing to an eleventh-hour panic on Mary's part.

In 1553, a 'Devise' for the succession was drawn up that excluded both Mary and Elizabeth on the grounds of their illegitimacy. As Edward's health deteriorated further, the Devise was changed so that Lady Jane Grey was to succeed on the death of Edward. In the event, Mary proclaimed herself queen in Norfolk on 10 July 1553, and she demanded and secured the allegiance of the Council. This resulted in an end to the plot and Northumberland's arrest. These events are covered in more detail in Chapter 18.

Mary's appearance and character

Mary's appearance, character and personality are described in contemporary accounts and these provide entertaining reading. An example is given in Source 20.6.

SOURCE 20.6 Giovanni Michiel, the Venetian ambassador, 13 May 1557

She is of low rather than middling stature, but, although short, she has no personal defect in her limbs, nor is any part of her body deformed. She is of spare and delicate frame, quite unlike her father, who was tall and stout, nor does she resemble her mother, who, if not tall, was nevertheless bulky . . . When younger, she was considered, not merely handsome, but of beauty exceeding mediocrity . . . Her voice is rough and loud, almost like a man's, so that when she speaks, she is always heard a long way off.

ACTIVITY

1. How important is a person's background to their ability to do a job in later life?
2. What effect did Mary's upbringing and circumstances have on her ability to be queen?
3. Compare her early life with those of Henry VII, Henry VIII and Edward VI. Was she any better or worse off than they had been in terms of preparation for the monarchy?

TALKING POINTS

1. Does it matter if a monarch is very different from their predecessor(s)? Can this be a positive thing?
2. Is our opinion of Mary likely to be affected by contemporary descriptions of her? Were we so concerned with Henry VII's appearance?
3. How accurate do you think Source 20.6 is likely to be, given the nationality and religion of the author?

D What was Mary's agenda?

FOCUS ROUTE

1. Study Chart 20B. Divide your page into two columns and identify the priorities for Mary personally and the priorities for the survival of the Tudor dynasty.
2. Were the two considerations necessarily the same? Write down your reasons.
3. What problems does this identify for the rest of the reign?

Our starting point in history is often at the end rather than the beginning. We know now that Mary's reign would only last for five years. But she didn't. Mary had a number of actions that she wanted to take, and policies that she wanted to pursue. Chart 20B shows what they were.

■ 20B Mary's policy agenda

Convince the old Privy Chamber of her right to be queen
Restore the Catholic religion
Marry
Have children
Choose Privy Councillors
Decide how to deal with Northumberland and his supporters
Defend Calais and Guisnes – the only territory in France still held by the English
Look after her health
Bolster her security
Restore her legitimacy – she and her half-sister Elizabeth had been declared illegitimate by royal patent on 21 June 1553

As you studied Chart 20B, you will have quickly realised that these issues were not of equal importance; indeed, some were merely a means to an end. We can identify three priorities that were most vital as far as Mary was concerned:

- **The restoration of the Catholic religion.** As we shall see in Chapter 23, Mary was a pious Catholic who saw it as her God-given duty to save the souls of the English people, who had been hijacked by Protestantism. Mary was determined to bring England back to the papal fold, by restoring the Pope as head of the Church, rather than the monarch.
- **The succession.** As we have seen with Henry VII, and Henry VIII in particular, ensuring a smooth uncontroversial succession from one monarch to the next, preferably by having a son, was essential. For Mary, the necessity of achieving this by having her own children was given added importance by her desire to consolidate the Catholic revival after her death.
- **War with France.** In Chapter 22, we will discover why Mary became embroiled in a war against England's traditional enemy when she did not really need to.

E Was Mary likely to be successful?

FOCUS ROUTE

Read pages 278–80.

1 Complete your own copy of the following table by identifying the factors that were likely to make Mary successful (pluses) and those that were not (minuses).
2 Does this information suggest that Mary was likely to strengthen the Tudor dynasty or not? Write down the reasons for your answer.

	Pluses	Minuses
Background		
Character		
Gender		
Factors outside Mary's control		

There are several factors to take into consideration here. With hindsight, we know that Mary's reign lasted a mere five years, the same amount of time as a British government today is allowed to be in power before a general election must be called. When we are talking about success, we must define precisely what that means in terms of Mary's objectives. The continuance of the Tudor monarchy was obviously one important objective, as were the policies outlined in Chart 20B. But remember also that, as with any other monarch or leader, things happened to Mary that were outside her control.

Was Mary's gender likely to affect her chances of being successful? In the sixteenth century, the status and role of women was, of course, very different from nowadays. Whether we like it or not, women in Britain only got the vote in the twentieth century. Certainly Mary's authority as queen was acknowledged by the Council, even if its members did not always agree with her actions. A leader's character, personality and judgement are often essential to their success, and Mary was no exception in this respect.

A particularly important factor in whether Mary was likely to be successful is her religious policy. If England was still fundamentally Catholic on Mary's accession, as she seems to have believed, then her religious policy would not appear to be so ambitious. If, on the other hand, Protestantism had tightened its grip on the people, then the restoration of papal authority and the Catholic rite in the Mass, together with the added complication of what to do with the lay landowners of ex-Church lands, was likely to cause Mary serious problems.

■ 20C Overview of Mary's reign

Date	Marriage and succession	Religion	Society and economy	Rebellion	Foreign policy
1553					
6 July	Edward VI died at Greenwich.				
10 July	Lady Jane Grey proclaimed queen at the Tower.				
3 August	Mary acclaimed queen in London. Lady Jane Grey imprisoned in Tower.				
22 August	Northumberland executed for treason.				
14 September		Cranmer arrested.			
1 October	Mary's coronation.				
16 November	Mary informed Commons that she would marry Philip of Spain.				
5 December	Mary dissolved Parliament after it passed an Act restoring her.	Mary relinquished title 'Supreme Head of the English Church'.			
1554					
January	Publication of royal marriage treaty.			Wyatt's rebellion.	
7 February				Wyatt arrested.	
12 February	Lady Jane Grey executed. Princess Elizabeth imprisoned in the Tower.				
6 March	Mary formally betrothed to Philip.				
11 April				Wyatt executed.	
22 May	Elizabeth freed.				
25 July	Mary married Philip.				
28 November		Cardinal Pole reunited the English and Roman Catholic Churches.			
1555					
September	Philip became ruler of the Netherlands and left England.		Harvest failure.		
16 October		Bishops Latimer and Ridley burned at the stake in Oxford.			
November		Death of Stephen Gardiner, bishop of Winchester.			
13 November		Cranmer deprived of Archbishopric.			
December		Cardinal Pole made Archbishop of Canterbury.			*Continued overleaf*

Date	Marriage and succession	Religion	Society and economy	Rebellion	Foreign policy
1556					
16 January					Charles V abdicated. Philip became King of Spain and the Netherlands.
18 March				Sir Henry Dudley arrested after plot to place Elizabeth on throne.	
21 March		Cranmer burned at the stake in Oxford.			
22 March		Pole consecrated Archbishop.			
September			Worst harvest of the century.		
1557					
20 March	Philip returned to England (departed again in July).				
June		Cardinal Pole recalled to Rome to face heresy charges; Mary refused to let him go.			
July			Widespread dearth and sickness in England.		
1558					
7 January					Calais surrendered to the French.
30 March	Mary altered her will to exclude all but her own children from the succession.				
September			Dearth widespread and severe sickness and influenza epidemic.		
17 November	Death of Mary and Cardinal Pole.				
14 December	Burial of Mary at Westminster.				

TALKING POINTS

1. What does Chart 20C reveal about the degree to which Mary was successful in her aims?
2. Can you identify any events that account for the negative portrayal of Mary's reign?

KEY POINTS FROM CHAPTER 20: The chain restored – did Mary have what it took to continue the Tudor dynasty?

1. Mary was England's first crowned queen in her own right.
2. Mary's reign has been viewed more negatively than positively, both by contemporaries and by historians.
3. Contemporaries recognised that Mary, not Lady Jane Grey, was the legitimate heir on the death of Edward VI, which says a lot about the strength of the Tudor dynasty by this time.
4. Mary had three main priorities: the restoration of Catholicism; marriage and children to secure the succession; and war with France.

21

A marriage of inconvenience – how beneficial was Mary's marriage to Philip?

CHAPTER OVERVIEW

Nowadays, people have various views on marriage, but many believe that romance should feature in the relationship. Four hundred or so years ago, marriage for royalty was a matter less of romance and more of diplomatic gain. For instance, a marriage could secure an alliance between two rival families, as we saw with Henry VII and Elizabeth of York in 1486.

More often, marriage was used to cement alliances between two countries, as in the cases of Henry VIII, who was married to Catherine of Aragon in 1509, and Henry's brother, Prince Arthur, who had married Catherine before him in 1501. Other examples of diplomatic marriages are those of Henry VIII's sister, Margaret Tudor, who married James IV of Scotland, and the Emperor Charles V, who married Isabella of Portugal.

The marriages were arranged by monarchs, often when the wedded couple were still in infancy, and they were more like business deals. The participants of such unions might have craved some romance from them, but generally, if husband and wife were actually in the same place, it was a bonus. As we saw in Chapter 20, Mary had wanted her father to arrange a marriage for her, but it had not happened. On her accession in 1553, at the age of 37, prospects for Mary the woman looked grim. She was, after all, sadly lacking in physical appeal. However, the hand of Mary the Queen offered an altogether brighter outlook for a would-be suitor.

This chapter will investigate the following issues:

ACTIVITY

You are Mary and have decided to marry Philip of Spain. However, you are conscious that there will be concerns about English interests becoming subservient to those of Spain. What will be in your marriage treaty? Think about the following issues:

- Will your husband be called King of England?
- Where will he live? In England or Spain?
- What powers will he have in government? Will he be able to use Spanish advisers?
- Where will your children be brought up?
- What will happen if you die before him?
- What will your heirs inherit? Will the countries remain together or will they be divided? Will the inheritance be the same for either a boy or a girl?

A Was Mary's a marriage of equals?

FOCUS ROUTE

Write an account to identify and explain the ways in which Philip's power in England was to be curtailed, according to the terms of the marriage treaty.

As with all monarchs, it was Mary's duty to provide an heir, and this was especially important for Mary because a son or daughter would be more likely to perpetuate the Catholic faith that she sought to restore. Despite her age and certain gynaecological problems, Mary was determined to bear children, and to do that she needed a husband.

The two principal contenders for Mary's hand were Philip of Spain and Sir Edward Courtenay. Whatever the merits of each suitor, it seems that Mary had already set her sights on Philip. Marriage to him would enhance her half-Spanish inheritance from her mother, Catherine of Aragon, and, since Philip already had a son from his first marriage, he was a proven breeder. Philip was eleven years younger than Mary, but his father, Charles V, thought he would be an ideal husband for her. At 53, Charles was weary of ruling and was dividing his territories between his son, Philip, and his brother, Ferdinand. With Philip taking over Spain and the Netherlands, it would be very useful for the Habsburgs to have a strong bond with England in opposition to France. Philip himself was not especially enthusiastic about marrying Mary, but his dynastic interests superseded his personal ones, especially if he could get some credit for returning England to the papal fold.

The marriage treaty

Charles' ambassador, Simon Renard, presented an official proposal of marriage to Mary on 10 October 1553. The Council consented to the terms of the treaty on 7 December 1553, and it was approved by Parliament in April 1554. Philip himself had no direct part in the negotiations, but his father did agree to the majority of the terms, which were very favourable to England.

■ 21A Terms of Mary and Philip's marriage treaty

1 A son of the marriage would inherit England and the Low Countries, but not Spain.

2 If the only surviving child were to be a daughter, the same provisions would apply.

3 If there were no heirs, or if Mary were to die before Philip, neither he nor his heirs would have any claim to the English throne.

4 Philip was to receive the title 'King' and rule as joint sovereign, but he could not possess any sovereign authority in his own right.

5 He could not promote foreigners to hold office in England.

6 He had to uphold the laws of England.

7 He was not allowed to take the Queen or any children they might have out of the country, without the permission of the nobility.

8 England was to uphold the treaties of 1543 and 1546 with the Netherlands, which stated that the former should come to the aid of the latter with 6,000 men if the provinces were invaded by the French.

TALKING POINTS

1 How beneficial was the marriage – and to whom?
2 Can you foresee any problems?

B Marriage – a revolting issue?

FOCUS ROUTE

Read pages 283–86 and write your answers to the following questions:

1. List all the factors that caused difficulties for the marriage initially.
2. Explain how the marriage was perceived by:
   a) Mary
   b) Philip
   c) England at large.
3. To what extent was Mary's marriage to Philip the cause of Wyatt's revolt in 1554?
4. How serious a threat to the Crown was Wyatt's revolt?

In looking at Mary's marriage, we are interested in two different aspects:

- the state of the marriage
- did it lead to revolt in the country?

The state of the marriage

Mary and Philip did not have a courtship prior to marriage; indeed, they hardly knew each other. They met for the first time on 23 July 1554, two days before their wedding took place in Winchester Cathedral. Even the ring that Mary had received on their betrothal had come not from Philip, but from the Emperor. The union was further complicated by language barriers, as Philip could only speak a few words of English, and Mary's Spanish had no doubt become rusty since her childhood conversations with her mother, Catherine of Aragon. Mary and Philip's common language was French, which she could speak and he could understand. Communication was probably further thwarted by Philip's lack of social skills: according to the Venetian ambassador, here was someone for whom 'Being by himself is his greatest pleasure.' That said, by all accounts he made an effort to treat Mary with warm affection.

SOURCE 21.1 A portrait of Mary and Philip in 1558, attributed to Hans Eworth

Mary believed herself to be pregnant on two occasions, the first towards the end of 1554, and the second at the beginning of 1558. It is probable that she was never really pregnant at all, although she was desperate to believe that she was.

Philip did set out to ingratiate himself at court. He drank beer and gave out pensions and gifts from his own private resources, as he did not have access to any English patronage. But tensions were ever present. He had to form a joint household of his Spanish entourage and the English personnel appointed to him, which caused friction between the two nationalities as there were too many people to discharge the required duties. Some of his followers were disgusted by the lack of deference shown to him, commenting for instance that at the wedding the Queen's throne had been higher and more ornate than his.

There was considerable anti-Spanish feeling in London – so much so, that disturbances were reported in the summer of 1555. One took place at the end of May, involving about 500 men and five or six deaths. Another occurred on 13 June when a mob attacked a church in which a number of Spaniards were worshipping. Anti-English sentiments were also evident in Spain, where there was a belief that all the English were heretics and savages.

What of the actual marriage itself? Contemporary correspondence affords us tantalising glimpses. Although both Mary and Philip knew their marriage was for mutually beneficial diplomatic reasons, they nevertheless had different perceptions of it, as we might have predicted (see Sources 21.2 and 21.3).

SOURCE 21.2 In a letter to the Emperor on 15 August 1554, Mary expressed high hopes of her then three-week-old marriage

[It] renders me happier than I can say, as I daily discover in the King, my husband and your son, so many virtues and perfections that I constantly pray God to grant me grace to please him and behave in all things as befits one who is so deeply embounden to him.

SOURCE 21.3 Philip had a rather different view of the marriage, as shown in this letter to his father on 17 August 1554

This match will have been a fine business if the Queen does not have a child, and I am sure she will not.

It became ever likelier that the marriage would be childless because of Philip's prolonged absences throughout the reign, with which Mary was clearly not happy, according to Source 21.4.

SOURCE 21.4 A letter from Cardinal Pole to King Philip

A fact well known to His Majesty, is the Queen's earnest desire for his presence, which is the more just, she herself being conscious that, as clearly manifest, she thus does not so much indulge her love for her consort as that for the kingdom common to both of them, and which, being her first love, and thinking chiefly of its welfare and safety, induced her to select such and so great a prince, able and willing to uphold religion and justice, then persecuted in the realm.

In fairness to Philip, he preserved an outward appearance of being satisfied with the terms of the marriage contract, but he was not necessarily happy with the union for other reasons, as summed up by David Loades in Source 21.5.

SOURCE 21.5 D. Loades, *The Reign of Mary Tudor: Politics, Government and Religion in England, 1553–58*, 2nd edn, 1991, p. 75

The marriage was as unpopular in Spain as it was in England. The prince's courtiers and servants had no desire to follow him to a chilly land of barbarous heretics and his other subjects had no desire to see him go. Those who knew the terms of the treaty felt that Philip's honour had been disparaged and it is quite probable that he shared that view, although he never said so openly.

Did Mary's marriage lead to revolt in the country?

The causes of Wyatt's rebellion

SOURCE 21.6 Sir Thomas Wyatt, after whom the rebellion of 1554 was named

Tudor rebellions usually had more than one cause, and often the motives of those participating were different from each other. In this case Wyatt's revolt, in the spring of 1554, followed hot on the heels of the announcement of Mary's marriage treaty to Philip in January 1554. The rebels, led by Sir Thomas Wyatt, did not want Mary to marry a foreigner. Wyatt probably feared that the Government would be taken over by a foreigner, and that English interests would become subservient to those of Spain. There is evidence, too, of more widespread xenophobia in a contemporary chronicle, *The Chronicle of Queen Jane and Queen Mary*, which noted that when the Spanish negotiators arrived in England to discuss the terms of the marriage treaty, 'the people, nothing rejoicing, held down their heads sorrowfully'. Curiously, similar scenes did not appear to accompany the news that Catherine of Aragon, a foreign princess, was to marry Prince Arthur and, later, Henry VIII. Perhaps there was a different perception when the monarch was a woman, because there was a real danger that the interests of the queen's country would be subordinated to the interests of the king's country.

Undoubtedly, some of the rebels were taking part in the rebellion for religious reasons: that is, they did not wish to see a Catholic restoration. But the significance of religious motives should probably not be overplayed, even though they were identified as the cause of the revolt in a contemporary book about the rising, written by John Proctor in 1554: *The Historie of Wyates Rebellion*. This work was commissioned by the Government, which thought that if religious grievances were portrayed as the mainstay of the trouble, it would divert attention from opposition to the marriage.

It is no coincidence that in Kent, where the rebellion started, there had been a decline in the cloth industry over a long period, and economic hardship tends to make people less tolerant of change and more likely to air their grievances. There was also local political instability in Kent caused by a shake-up in office holding, and some of the younger gentry feared that Philip's presence at court might adversely affect their career opportunities.

■ 21B Events of Wyatt's rebellion

1553	
Autumn	Some gentry at court, some of whom were MPs but not councillors, began to discuss the possibility of engineering a Protestant succession. Mary would be deposed and Edward Courtenay, the Earl of Devon, would marry Princess Elizabeth, who would become queen.
December	Plans were concluded for co-ordinated risings in Kent, Herefordshire, Devon and Leicestershire on 18 March 1554.
27 December	The Emperor's commissioners arrived in England to begin negotiations on the marriage treaty.
1554	
14 January	The terms of the marriage treaty were announced by proclamation. This provoked earlier action than the rebels had planned.
Mid-January	Renard got wind of the plot, and Courtenay was made to confess all he knew. Three out of the four locations did not raise supporters, but in Kent Sir Thomas Wyatt, from a prominent shire family, raised 2,500 armed men.
29 January	The Duke of Norfolk, whom the Government had chosen to stop Wyatt's men, was forced to return to court when his troops were persuaded to join those of Wyatt.
3 February	Wyatt eventually reached the Thames at Southwark.
12 February	Wyatt led his troops about 20 kilometres west to Kingston, before eventually being stopped at Ludgate, half a kilometre from the Queen at the Tower. Wyatt and his supporters were forced to surrender and ask for mercy.

Reaction to the rebellion

Ninety rebels were executed, including Wyatt himself. He became something of a martyr, as people dipped their handkerchiefs in his blood following his execution. Lady Jane Grey and her husband were executed although they were innocent. Princess Elizabeth's life was spared because she had not been involved in Wyatt's plans.

■ **Learning trouble spot**

How serious were rebellions in the Tudor period?

When trying to work out how serious a rebellion was for Tudor monarchs, it is important to find out the motives of the rebels themselves. It would be wrong to think that all rebellions were aimed at the overthrow of the monarch, for instance. Sometimes, disaffected people wanted merely to petition the monarch with their grievances and to seek a solution.

What did those involved in the Wyatt rebellion want to achieve? Events can be misleading. Rebels with a grievance needed to bring it to the attention of the Queen. Such persons would not stay in their local area (in this case, Kent) because the Queen was not based there: they would attempt to reach London. Just because Wyatt's supporters marched on London and came within half a kilometre of the Queen herself before they were stopped does not necessarily mean that they wanted to overthrow her. However, we can be sceptical of Wyatt's defence that he did not want a change of monarch. When asked, 'Sir, is your quarrel only to defend us from overrunning by Strangers [i.e. Philip] and not against the Queen?', he replied: 'We mind nothing less than anywise to touch her Grace.'

Remember that, faced with the prospect of execution for treason, many scared rebels would lie. Also, while the motives of the chief conspirators might have been to topple Mary, many of the lesser mortals taking part probably wanted simply to make a protest against her marriage. After all, it was only six months since she had foiled Northumberland's plot, largely due to popular support and the belief in her legitimate right to the throne.

A study of Tudor rebellions shows that rebels often had various grievances and that Tudor governments were both effective and lucky in dealing with them successfully.

ACTIVITY

1 Below is some additional information about Wyatt's rebellion.

- Courtenay was weak and confessed his involvement easily.
- The French, having been in touch with the conspirators through Noailles, their ambassador, did not seize the opportunity to invade.
- Events moved too fast for the conspirators, whose planned rising had to be moved forward by two months.
- Mary gave a rousing speech to Londoners at the Guildhall on 1 February 1554, in which she professed 'as a mother doth love a child' to stand firm in her cause.
- Orthodox Protestant leadership did not want to get involved in the revolt – so much so that some imprisoned ministers refused to be liberated by the rebels.
- Opposition to the marriage was strong, but not as strong as the feeling had been to put Mary on the throne.
- The vigilance of Renard and Paget took the sting out of the rebels' plans.
- The elderly Duke of Norfolk failed to stop the rebels *en route* to London from Rochester.
- Wyatt was able to raise a force of nearly 3,000 men, while Mary's Council could not agree on what to do.
- Mary decided against the help of Imperial troops, which would have fuelled the rebels' xenophobia.
- Mary decided to wait for the rebels in London, rather than sending forces to meet them in Kent.

Use this information to complete your own copy of the following table.

Rebellion dangerous	Rebellion not dangerous

ACTIVITY

1 In Chapters 3, 8 and 10 we looked at the Cornish rebellion of 1497, the Amicable Grant rising in 1525, and the Pilgrimage of Grace in 1536. Using the information about these three rebellions and Wyatt's revolt, complete your own copy of the following table.

	Cornish rebellion	Amicable Grant	Pilgrimage of Grace	Wyatt's rebellion
Causes				
Location				
Type of people involved				
Strength/nature of Government reaction				
How dangerous to the stability of the Crown?				

2 What is your overall conclusion about how dangerous Wyatt's rebellion was? Decide where you would place it on the Richter scale of unrest.

1		Mild, isolated protests from peasants.
2		More vocal and sustained protests from various social groups in the lower orders. JPs order them to disperse.
3		Unrest begins to spread. Rebel leadership established. Meeting with local gentry and JPs.
4		Rebels produce a list of demands. Rebel camp is established. Numbers swelling. Suppression by local gentry attempted.
5		Rebel camp numbers thousands. Rebels are led by gentry. Government intervention required. Pardon offered in return for rebels dispersing.
6		Rebels are advancing or have remained in place for at least four weeks. Meeting with regional nobility required. Government begins to prepare measures for suppression.
7		Rebels are led by nobles. Troops raised. Suppression by regional nobleman attempted.
8		Rebellion requires full-scale military suppression.
9		Monarch's position severely threatened by the rebellion.
10	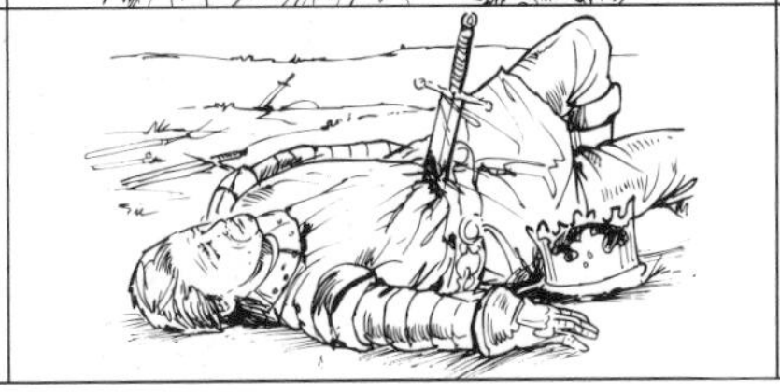	Rebellion succeeds in overthrowing the established dynasty.

C Review: A marriage of inconvenience – how beneficial was Mary's marriage to Philip?

FOCUS ROUTE

Read this page and make notes on the following:

1 What impact did Philip have on English affairs between 1553 and 1558?
2 Compare Philip's actions to the terms of the marriage treaty in Chart 21A on page 282. Comment on whether or not the treaty was adhered to.

As historians, what we are really interested in is whether or not Mary's marriage to Philip benefited the country, rather than Mary herself. When considering any impact that Philip might have had on domestic and foreign policy in England between 1553 and 1558, remember that the marriage itself did not take place until July 1554, almost twelve months into the reign, and that even after the ceremony itself, Philip spent more time abroad than in England. Any discussion of his impact must be seen in this context.

First and most obvious, despite Mary's pregnancies, real and imagined, no children resulted from Mary's union with Philip. Mary's fragile health, added to Philip's absences, hardly made successful conception likely. No direct heirs meant no guarantee of a Catholic legacy after Mary's death. However, much as Mary did not wish it, her half-sister, Elizabeth, succeeded to the throne in 1558. She was the legitimate heir according to the will of Henry VIII, and ultimately of Mary on her death bed. So the Tudor dynasty was secure, and Elizabeth's right to be queen was uncontested.

Second, following Philip's request to Mary for naval supplies, funds and English naval support in the Channel, England was eventually drawn into war alongside Spain against France in 1557 (see Chapter 22). It is hardly surprising that it was Philip who encouraged the English navy to build six new ships and to repair others. However, this did lead to the regular allocation of peacetime funds for the navy after 1557, something from which Elizabeth would derive the benefit.

What impact did Philip have in domestic affairs? True, the marriage treaty did limit Philip's power in government, but he could still exert some influence. For instance, it was he who helped to negotiate Cardinal Pole's return to England as papal legate in 1554. Pole was to mediate with the Pope so that England would be able to return to papal authority and Catholicism (see Chapter 23). Does this suggest that Philip was involved in day-to-day government? He did set out to establish a working relationship with as many councillors as possible, and his name was included in all official documents. According to David Loades in *The Mid-Tudor Crisis, 1545–1565*, it seems as though Philip 'involved himself actively, but discreetly, in English internal affairs, working mainly through those councillors in whom he had confidence' – notably, Paget, Pembroke and Arundel.

At best, the marriage to Philip provided Mary with an intermittent and distant confidant. At worst, it embroiled England in a war with France at a very inopportune time given the severe social and economic problems at the end of the reign. How much blame for this is Mary's rather than Philip's is debatable – after all, she *was* the Queen, and he the King in name only.

KEY POINTS FROM CHAPTER 21: A marriage of inconvenience – how beneficial was Mary's marriage to Philip?

1 Mary, like any other Tudor monarch, had to marry to secure the succession.
2 She chose Philip of Spain as her husband, much to the dislike of the Council, the country and Parliament.
3 The marriage treaty restricted Philip's powers in England.
4 The marriage sparked rebellion with Wyatt's revolt in 1554. Although the rebels reached London, it was successfully suppressed.
5 Philip was out of the country for most of Mary's reign, but he influenced the government through key advisers who remained in England.
6 Mary had no children as a result of the marriage.
7 War with France was an unfortunate by-product of Philip taking advantage of his marriage to Mary.

22

A Spanish pawn? Did England benefit from being a close ally of Spain, 1553–58?

CHAPTER OVERVIEW

Mary's foreign policy has rightly been inseparably connected to the loss of Calais in 1558. This was the last of the French land that had been held by England during the Middle Ages, so its loss was of great symbolic importance. The French capture of Calais was seen as being a direct result of Mary's pro-Spanish diplomacy. However, Calais was only captured in the last year of Mary's reign and it is important not to skew an assessment of her foreign policy with an over-emphasis upon its loss. Mary's foreign policy had two aims:

- to re-establish ties with Rome
- to ally England to the Spanish Habsburgs through the friendship with the Emperor Charles V and the marriage to Philip II of Spain.

It is upon Mary's success in achieving these objectives that her foreign policy may be more fairly judged.

In this chapter we will be looking at the following issues:

FOCUS ROUTE

As you read pages 291–97, complete your own copy of the following table to show the English reaction to the main foreign policy events in Mary's reign.

Date	Event	Effect on England
1554		
January	Marriage of Mary and Philip arranged	What internal unrest occurred? How were relations between the Habsburg Empire and England now perceived by most English people?
1555–1556		
October–January	Abdication of Charles V and splitting of his Empire between Philip II and Ferdinand	What effect did this have on Philip's opinion of the importance of England?
1556		
February	Treaty of Vaucelles established peace between France and Spain	Who had been attempting in 1555 to act as a peacemaker?
July	Alliance between France and the Papacy reopened the Habsburg–Valois War	What effect did this have on Anglo-Papal relations?
1557		
January	England sent troops to the Netherlands	Why was the Netherlands considered worth defending?
March	Philip returned to England to press for support in the war	Was Philip successful?
April	Landing of Thomas Stafford at Scarborough	Who supported this invasion and protected exiled Protestants?
June	England declared war on France	Why did England finally declare war on France?
August	Victory for Philip II over Henry II at St Quentin	How significant was the English contribution to this battle?
1558		
January	Capture of Calais Pale by the French	How significant was the loss of Calais?
1559		
April	Treaty of Cateau-Cambrésis	Did Philip push for the return of Calais in the negotiations?

A How did the break-up of Charles V's Empire affect England?

■ 22A Europe during the reign of Mary I

ACTIVITY

Did the break-up of the Holy Roman Empire and changes in Europe make Mary's aims easier or harder to achieve?

Scotland
Scotland remained the traditional enemy of England and had become more important since 1542 when Mary, Queen of Scots, had become the sole heir and was betrothed in 1548 to the dauphin of France.

Holy Roman Empire
At the start of Mary's reign, Europe was still dominated by the Habsburg–Valois War in the Netherlands and Germany. Charles V's failure against the combined forces of the French and the German princes led to the Peace of Augsburg (1555), and to Charles' abdication in October 1555. Charles' brother, Ferdinand, became the Holy Roman Emperor with control only of Germany; the other territories went to Philip (see Philip II's Habsburg Empire below).

England
During Edward's reign traditional English foreign policy had been turned on its head by Northumberland's peace deal with France (Treaty of Boulogne), and by his arm's-length relations with the Habsburgs (because of Charles V's support for Mary). On Mary's accession, Charles now looked for a positively pro-Habsburg policy from England; this was particularly the case after the marriage of his son Philip to Mary in July 1554.

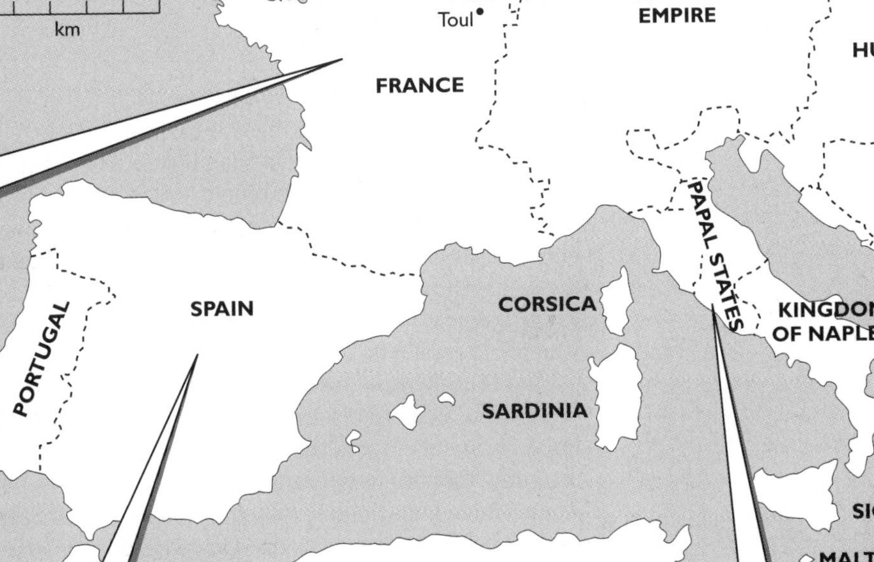

France
Henry II's victories in 1552 (his capture of Metz, Toul and Verdun) shifted the main focus of the Habsburg–Valois War away from Italy towards Germany and the Netherlands, thereby bringing England and the English Channel more directly into the major European arena of conflict.

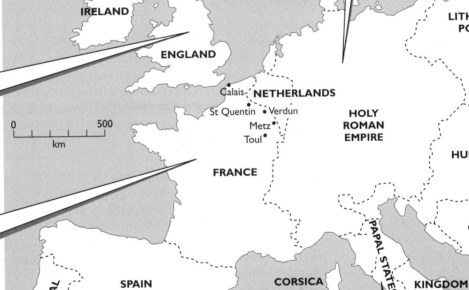

Philip II's Habsburg Empire
In January 1556, on his father's abdication, Philip became the ruler of Spain, Spanish America, Naples and the Netherlands. This massive inheritance and the realisation in mid-1555 that Mary would not provide him with an heir meant that Philip now had little time for England.

The Habsburg–Valois War was briefly brought to a halt by the Truce of Vaucelles (February 1556), but the formation of a Franco-Papal alliance reopened the war (July 1556). Philip now demanded help from England, and Mary had to decide how she was going to respond (see pages 292–93).

Papacy
In 1555 the hard-line Paul IV became Pope. A Neapolitan, he wanted to fight the Habsburgs over their control of Naples. To achieve this, the Pope allied with France and Mary found herself brought into conflict with the Papacy that she had struggled for so long to rejoin.

B Why did England go to war with France?

■ 22B Main events in foreign policy, 1555–59

In the following list, *italic* type is used for European events.

1555 *September: Philip left England.*
October–January 1556: Abdication of Charles V and splitting of his Empire between Philip II and Ferdinand.

1556 *February: Treaty of Vaucelles – peace between France and Spain.*
July: Alliance between France and the Papacy reopened the Habsburg–Valois War.

1557 January: England sent troops to the Netherlands.
March: Philip returned to England to press for support in the war.
April: Landing of Thomas Stafford at Scarborough.
June: England declared war on France.
July: Scottish raids on England began.
August: Victory for Philip II at St Quentin.

1558 January: Capture of Calais Pale by the French.

1559 *April: Treaty of Cateau-Cambrésis.*

1553–55

Situation in Europe

When Mary came to the throne, her long-standing supporter in Europe, her cousin Charles V, was in the last desperate struggle of his part in the Habsburg–Valois War, the conflict that had dominated European foreign policy for more than 30 years. By 1555 he had abdicated; his son Philip had taken over in the west and Charles' brother Ferdinand had taken over in the east of the Habsburg Empire.

Situation in England

In the eyes of many of her subjects, Mary's marriage to Philip made England little more than a submissive satellite in orbit around the massive Habsburg power. Wyatt's rebellion is the most obvious manifestation of this fear. However, although the notion that England was merely a pawn of the Habsburgs has much validity, historians must exercise caution before reaching a final conclusion.

It is clear that Mary showed a genuine desire to remain at peace, even acting as mediator between France and the Habsburgs at Gravelines in the spring of 1555. By the summer, physical and emotional distance had been put between Philip and Mary when it became evident that she was not going to have any children, and so he left England.

1556–57

Situation in Europe

The truce brokered between France and the Habsburgs at the Treaty of Vaucelles (February 1556) was ended in September 1556 when Philip attacked the fiercely anti-Spanish Pope Paul IV, who was allied to the French. Henry II of France countered and England immediately came under pressure to join the war on Spain's side.

Situation in England

The ridiculousness of making war against the Papacy that she had so earnestly wished to rejoin cannot have been lost on Mary; nor can she have been unaware of the strong opposition to a war against France. Philip, however, demanded English support and returned to the country in March to press his claim for funds, naval support and troops. Six thousand troops had been sent to the Netherlands in January 1557 to help this trade-sensitive region resist the French attack; however, Philip was not able to persuade Mary to support him. It was the French who clumsily provoked England into joining the war.

The French were openly tolerating exiled English Protestants and rumours were circulating that Henry II planned to recapture Calais. French support for the invasion attempt of the Protestant exile Thomas Stafford in April 1557 was the straw that broke the camel's back. The hapless and hopeless Stafford sailed from France with French weapons and landed in Scarborough, but he was arrested within three days. No one could now oppose war with France.

On 7 June 1557, England declared war on France. The navy proceeded to clear the Channel and patrol in the Atlantic. Garrisons in Scotland were strengthened in anticipation of a pincer attack by the 'auld alliance', and raids by the Scottish duly came in July 1557. Troops were put on stand-by in the Calais Pale and 7,000 soldiers were sent to aid the 70,000 Spanish and Imperial troops fighting the French. At the battle of St Quentin, Philip defeated Henry II with minimal support from the English.

1558

Situation in England

The French, facing certain defeat, sought an easy compensation and the obvious target was Calais. They launched a surprise attack in mid-winter across the frozen marshes. The 2,000 English troops had not received winter reinforcements and stood no chance against the 27,000 French, who captured the Calais fortress and the whole of the Calais Pale within three weeks. In response, the English Government raised an army of 7,000 and a fleet of 140 ships to attack Brest, but succeeded only in capturing Le Conquet.

Situation in Europe

Philip II's success in 1557 and financial exhaustion made him look to bring the forty-year Habsburg–Valois conflict to an end. Peace negotiations finally began in October 1558 at Cateau-Cambrésis and were completed in April 1559. Philip did not attempt to recover Calais for England.

SOURCE 22.1
The battle of St Quentin, 1557

C How significant was the loss of Calais?

SOURCE 22.2 The port of Calais and the Calais Pale

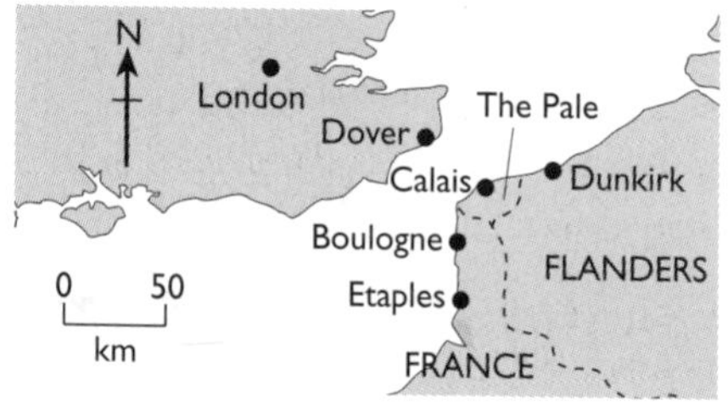

SOURCE 22.3 The fall of Calais: an engraving by Moulet

Economically

In *Tudor Foreign Policy*, the historian P. S. Crowson describes the loss of Calais as an economically 'crippling blow' because of the loss of trade that came through the port. However, in *The Reign of Mary I*, Robert Tittler argues that this is a vast exaggeration as the importance of the STAPLE merchants in Calais had been brought to an end by the long-term decline in the traditional markets.

Image and morale

The kings of England had claimed this land since 1347 and its final surrender could then only be seen as a humiliating abandonment of sovereign English territory. The Protestant propagandists of Elizabeth's reign were not slow to put forward the equation:

Spanish marriage + Catholic policy = Loss of Calais

Morale was shaken by the loss, but without the efforts of the propagandists the sense of national humiliation would not have lasted for so long.

Territorially

Calais was the last territory on the French mainland controlled by England, so it gained importance from this status. However, little could be achieved by maintaining it, and it was only going to be a question of time before the French took the trouble to take it back.

Militarily

The Calais Pale had been used as a springboard to launch Henry VIII's attacks in the 1520s and 1540s, but it had become something of a strategic irrelevance. It was difficult and expensive to maintain a permanent garrison there and it had become a burden as it was yet another frontier that had to be defended.

Diplomatically

The loss of Calais has often been seen as a result of the failed Anglo-Habsburg alliance. Mary's dependence on Spanish advisers and her slavish pursuit of Spanish Habsburg policy were seen as betraying England's interest. Philip certainly abandoned England by allowing France to keep Calais under the Treaty of Cateau-Cambrésis, but this was made easier by the death of Mary in November before the treaty had been signed.

STAPLE
The staple was the place which acted as the main trading centre for particular products in Europe.

ACTIVITY

The significance of England's loss of Calais has been hotly debated since its capture and there are a number of different levels on which it can be analysed.

Make a copy of the table below and, for each of the categories, assess the loss of Calais using the information in this section. Rate the significance of the loss on a scale from 0 (unimportant) to 5 (very significant).

Category	Significance of loss	Main example
Economically		
Image and morale		
Territorially		
Militarily		
Diplomatically		

Review: A Spanish pawn? Did England benefit from being a close ally of Spain, 1553–58?

■ 22C Pros and cons of the alliance with Spain

Why did Mary ally with Spain?
Mary pursued a foreign policy closely aligned to that of the Spanish Habsburgs for very personal and understandable reasons. She was herself half-Spanish, the most consistent and most supportive figure in her life had been her cousin, the Emperor Charles V, and she saw herself surrounded at home (even in her Council) by heretics whom she felt she could not trust. Mary quickly learned to trust and act on the advice of Simon Renard, the shrewd Imperial ambassador. The Habsburg alliance, apart from being personally important to Mary, also represented the traditional orientation of English foreign policy.

What were the negative aspects of the Spanish alliance?

Mary's marriage to Philip and her pursuit of pro-Spanish policies were unpopular and distanced her from her people. Protecting England and English interests did not appear to be a significant priority, and English subjects felt that their country was being used as a Spanish pawn. The Spanish-led foreign policy resulted in England becoming a new battleground in the Habsburg–Valois War; it led to the loss of Calais and to Spain eventually replacing France as the principal enemy of England in Elizabeth's reign.

What were the positive aspects of the Spanish alliance?

Criticisms of Mary's foreign policy should be based upon the intentions and strategies behind it and not on the unforeseeable consequences of the events themselves. The loss of Calais was neither an obvious nor a predictable result of England's involvement in the Habsburg–Valois War. Mary had resisted involvement as long as she could and the contribution finally made was modest (about 7,000 troops) and non-committal. The French attack in winter across the frozen marshes was unexpected and, although the English garrison should have been resupplied and reinforced, an impossibly large number of troops would have been needed to withstand such a large French attack.

Military developments

During Mary's reign, the armed forces were substantially strengthened. With the encouragement of Philip, the navy was reorganised and improved: a Naval Treasurer was appointed and the number of ships available for active duty increased from three in 1555 to 21 in 1557. The navy during Mary's reign was said to have been better managed than ever before in its history.

Equally significant improvements took place in army recruitment. The inefficient old system of getting individual lords and gentlemen to raise troops was replaced with that of the militia, under which Lords Lieutenant and JPs in each county were now given responsibility to raise troops. This system of the militia, which had been evolving through the 1540s and 1550s, was finally pulled together in 1558 and was to last for 300 years.

Conclusion

Mary failed to gain any tangible benefits from the alliance with the Spanish Habsburgs, and the return to Rome has been described as 'an unconditional surrender' (Crowson, *Tudor Foreign Policy*). It is difficult, however, to conceive of an alternative policy that Mary could have followed. She could not have allied with the traditional enemy, France, and an alliance with the Habsburgs was both strategically advantageous and a natural consequence of Mary's religion and her alienation from her own population. Although she did follow a policy led by Spain's involvement in the Habsburg–Valois War from 1557, Mary had followed her own priorities until then. The loss of Calais was significant, but her reign should not be condemned just because of this one event.

TALKING POINTS

1 How different was Mary's foreign policy from that of her father and grandfather?
2 Was avoidance of war a key principle of Mary's foreign policy, as it had been of Henry VII's?
3 Was her Habsburg alliance at odds with the policy of her father?
4 Did Mary rate foreign policy as such a high priority as Henry VIII had?

KEY POINTS FROM CHAPTER 22: A Spanish pawn? Did England benefit from being a close ally of Spain, 1553–58?

1 Mary's foreign policy was linked, from the start of her reign, to the interests of the Spanish Habsburgs – the Emperor Charles V and Philip II.
2 The final stages of the Habsburg–Valois War were fought out between 1552 and 1559, and Philip II continually pressed England to support him in this conflict.
3 Mary avoided joining the Spanish war against France until 1557 when French support of Stafford's attempted invasion provoked her into taking action.
4 England was at war with France from June 1557 to the end of Mary's reign.
5 The French capture of Calais (the last English territory on the French mainland) in January 1558 was the most significant event in Mary's reign.
6 Mary's foreign policy has received a mainly negative press from contemporaries and historians.

23

The pendulum swings back again – how Catholic was England by 1558?

CHAPTER OVERVIEW

You will recall from Chapter 9 that Henry VIII started a religious reformation by a series of laws during the 1530s. By the end of his reign in 1547, England was to some extent a Protestant country. In Chapter 15 you learned about the measures undertaken by Edward VI's government which supposedly resulted in England becoming even more closely identified with Protestantism, although after less than twenty years of haphazard reformation, it would be wrong to believe that Catholic beliefs and practices had died out completely by 1553. But Mary held the Catholic faith dear, and we have already seen that one of her priorities would be to return her kingdom to the Catholic fold officially, by reinstating the Pope as head of the Church in England. In this chapter, we will be investigating Mary's religious policies by asking the following questions:

A What was Mary's personal piety? (pp. 299–300)

B What was Mary's religious policy? (pp. 300–303)

C How did Mary use persuasion and persecution to promote her religious aims? (pp. 304–308)

D Review: The pendulum swings back again – how Catholic was England by 1558? (pp. 309–311)

■ Learning trouble spot

Who's who in religion in Mary's reign?

Here are the names and brief details of the key figures who influenced Mary's religious policy throughout her reign.

Stephen Gardiner	Bishop of Winchester and Lord Chancellor. He had been imprisoned during Edward VI's reign.
Simon Renard	The Imperial ambassador from Charles V.
Reginald Pole	A cousin of Mary's. He became papal legate with a brief to restore papal authority in England.
Philip II of Spain	Son of Charles V and husband of Mary.
Charles V	Mary's cousin, and Holy Roman Emperor. Mary maintained a regular correspondence with him throughout her reign, regarding him as something of a father-figure.
Julius III	Pope when Mary acceded to the throne in 1553. He wanted all ex-Church lands to be returned to the Church before England could be reconciled to Rome.
Paul IV	Pope from 1555. He was fiercely anti-Habsburg and this brought England into conflict with the Papacy.

A What was Mary's personal piety?

FOCUS ROUTE

Read pages 299–300 and write answers to the following questions:

1 Explain how Mary viewed her religious commitment to
 a) herself
 b) the country.
2 What options did Mary have as far as restoring Catholicism in England was concerned?
3 What problems was Mary likely to face in doing so?

That Mary would restore Catholicism was never in doubt. She was devout in her personal worship, hearing Mass at least once a day and saying prayers in her chapel every night. She had not given up her Catholic faith while a princess, and had only accepted the Royal Supremacy of her father in 1536 under duress. Cardinal Pole compared her to Jesus's mother, Mary, encouraging her to view her life in terms of a divine purpose – to bring England back to what she termed the true faith. Furthermore, Mary interpreted her initial popularity more as an endorsement of the Catholic faith than as a reaction to the unpopularity of Northumberland, or indeed her own legitimacy as rightful queen.

Unfortunately for her, Mary's quest to restore Catholicism was rooted more in religious conviction – the need to rescue England from 'mortal sin' – than in political astuteness. On 13 August 1553, the Lord Mayor and Aldermen of London had been told that Mary 'meaneth graciously not to compel or constrain other men's consciences', but she proclaimed on 18 August that she hoped that others would follow her religion. There was, indeed, evidence that some of her subjects were only too eager to restore the old faith. At Oxford, chalices were brought out and the Mass was celebrated. On 23 August, an altar and a cross were set up at St Nicholas Cole Abbey in London, and Mass was said. The next day, six more London churches followed suit, 'not by commandment but of the people's devotion'.

Instances such as these confirmed Mary's misguided assessment that the majority of her subjects were 'still fundamentally Roman Catholic and had been led astray by a minority which had previously enjoyed government support' (Tittler, *The Reign of Mary I*). To Mary, Protestant reformers were heretics, 'the devil's agents, who ensnared the souls of the innocent and ignorant and confused the faithful with a babble of false and conflicting doctrines' (Loades, *The Mid-Tudor Crisis, 1545–1565*).

How far was Mary prepared to go in restoring Catholicism? Would she revert to the situation in 1547, or to the situation in 1529, with the Pope again being recognised as head of the Church? If the latter, what would happen to all the former Church lands, now in lay hands as a result of the dissolution of the 1530s? Surely the new owners would not be prepared to give them up.

ACTIVITY

1 Should Mary revert England to the religious situation of 1529 or 1547, or make no change? Complete your own copy of the table below by adding the possible consequences of each option in the correct column.

No change: Full Protestantism	1529: Full Catholicism	1547: Moderate Catholicism

- All the ex-monastic land would have to be given back to the Church.
- The Pope would have to forgive England for making the monarch head of the Church.
- The Protestant reformers would be very angry, and probably cause a lot of trouble for Mary, perhaps even rebellion.
- Princess Elizabeth might become the focus of Protestant discontent.
- Changing the religion back to how it was pre-Reformation might not do much for Mary's credibility.
- Mary would annoy Charles V and Philip of Spain, not to mention the Pope.
- The Catholics would be very angry because they would have been anticipating more.
- Those who owned ex-monastic lands would not support Mary's quest to have the Pope back as head of the Church.

2 Which option would be the most problematic for Mary in terms of her security as queen?

Mary's advisers

If Mary was slow, unable and/or unwilling to see the political implications of restoring Catholicism, others were not. Gardiner, Mary's most trusted English adviser, was unenthusiastic about a return to Papal Supremacy. Renard was worried about the property concerns. Charles V and Pope Julius III urged caution, for they feared that moving too quickly might cause unrest, thereby jeopardising Mary's throne itself. Cardinal Pole, appointed as papal legate with a brief to restore Papal Supremacy, did not arrive in England until a year after the start of Mary's reign, perhaps because Charles wanted to keep him in the Netherlands until the marriage between Mary and Philip had been agreed. As for Philip himself, reconciliation with Rome became his top priority in his first year of marriage to Mary – he wished to gain the credit for helping to bring about ecclesiastical change in England.

FOCUS ROUTE

Write answers to the following questions:

1 Look at Chart 23A. Identify the problems and obstacles that Mary had to overcome in order to make the religious changes that she wanted.
2 Study Chart 23B on page 301. What does it show about:
   a) Catholicism under Mary
   b) methods used to achieve it
   c) obstacles that Mary faced
   d) Mary's contingency plans?
3 Read the text on page 302. How was England brought back under papal authority?

B What was Mary's religious policy?

We have established that Mary wanted to make England a Catholic country again. Actually achieving this would, however, be quite difficult, as Chart 23A shows. Before we go into the detail of what Mary did, you might find it helpful to study Chart 23B to get an overview of key religious events in the reign.

■ 23A Dilemmas for Mary

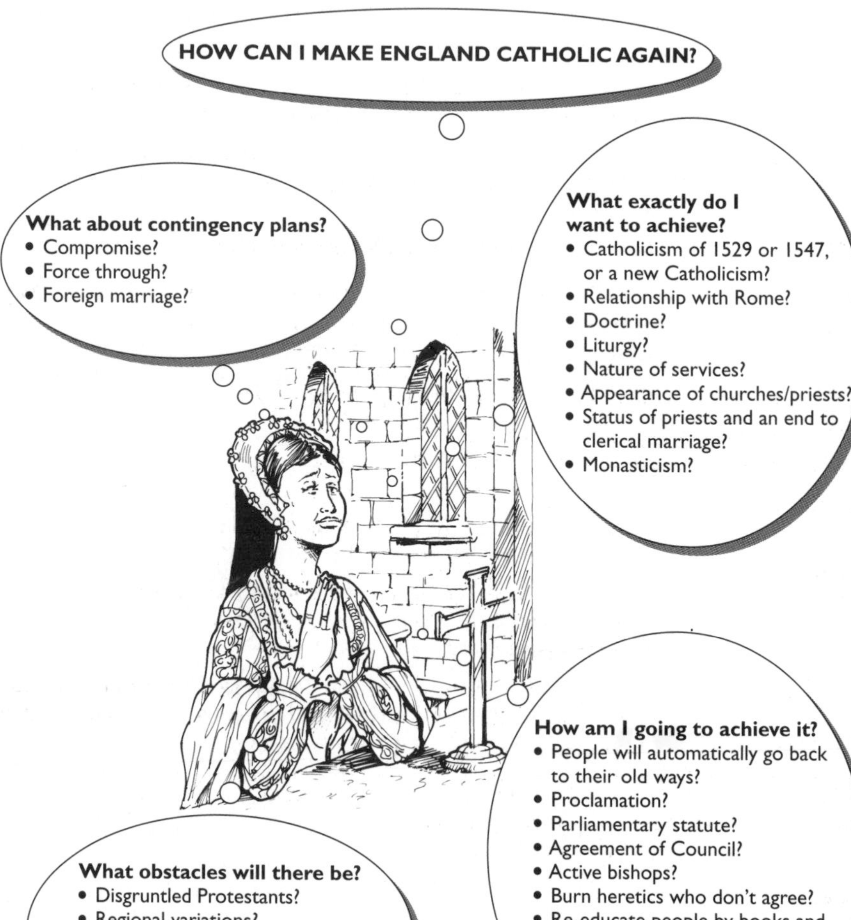

HOW CAN I MAKE ENGLAND CATHOLIC AGAIN?
What about contingency plans?
• Compromise?
• Force through?
• Foreign marriage?
What exactly do I want to achieve?
• Catholicism of 1529 or 1547, or a new Catholicism?
• Relationship with Rome?
• Doctrine?
• Liturgy?
• Nature of services?
• Appearance of churches/priests?
• Status of priests and an end to clerical marriage?
• Monasticism?
How am I going to achieve it?
• People will automatically go back to their old ways?
• Proclamation?
• Parliamentary statute?
• Agreement of Council?
• Active bishops?
• Burn heretics who don't agree?
• Re-educate people by books and
• Catholic teaching?
• Have children to secure long-term future?
What obstacles will there be?
• Disgruntled Protestants?
• Regional variations?
• Passive resistance?
• Financial implications?
• Rebellion?

To what extent Mary herself thought through all these issues, as systematically as Chart 23A suggests, is not certain. Chart 23B outlines the actions that Mary took during her reign.

■ 23B Key religious developments during Mary's reign

Date	Event
1553	
August	Proclamation that Mary 'mindeth not to compel any her said subjects thereunto [i.e. religious conformity] until such time as further order by common assent may be taken therein'. Many prominent Protestant clergy were deprived of their livings.
September	Archbishop Cranmer was arrested. Hugh Latimer, John Hooper, Nicholas Ridley, John Rogers and others were imprisoned.
Autumn	Parliament met and refused to repeal the Act of Supremacy. Parliament did pass an Act of Repeal which undid all of the Edwardian Reformation, revived the Mass, ritual worship and clerical celibacy, and implicitly reaffirmed the traditional doctrine of the Lord's Supper (i.e. the Catholic belief in transubstantiation). This restored the Church to what it had been in 1547 under the Act of Six Articles.
December	Mary gave up the title of Supreme Head of the Church.
1554	
January	Mass exodus of Protestants to Germany and Switzerland, estimated to have been some 800 in all.
March	The Royal Injunctions were issued, which ordered bishops to suppress heresy, remove married clergy, re-ordain clergy who had been ordained under the English Ordinal, and restore Holy Days, processions and ceremonies. Bishop Gardiner began to deprive married priests of their livings. In the diocese of Norwich, 243 priests lost their posts, 90 in Bath and Wells. Eventually 10–25 per cent of clergy were deprived for having married, although some were reinstated when they conformed. Gardiner also deprived the Protestant bishops of Gloucester, Hereford, Lincoln and Rochester, and the Archbishop of York, of their sees. They were all replaced by committed Catholics.
April	Parliament initially rejected the reintroduction of the heresy laws, but agreed when promised that former monastic lands would not be restored to Church ownership.
November	Cardinal Pole returned to England; the sentence of excommunication was lifted from England. Parliament passed the Second Act of Repeal, which undid all anti-papal legislation since 1529 and the Henrician Reformation.
1555	Publication of Bishop Bonner's Book of Homilies.
January	Mary appointed a commission to consider refounding some of the religious houses.
February	John Rogers, a biblical translator, became the first Protestant martyr of the reign, when he was burned under the restored heresy laws.
16 October	Bishops Ridley and Latimer were burned for heresy in Oxford.
12 November	Stephen Gardiner died.
13 November	Cranmer was deprived of the see of Canterbury.
December	Reginald Pole was named as Archbishop of Canterbury. The London Synod met under Pole (until February 1556).
1556	
February	Synod issued Twelve Decrees on clerical discipline, against abuses such as absenteeism, pluralism, simony and heresy. Refoundation of the Benedictine House at Westminster. Many more Protestants were burned for heresy.
21 March	Cranmer recanted all retractions and was burned at the stake in Oxford. Cardinal Pole argued with Pope Paul IV and was deprived of his position as legate.
22 March	Pole was consecrated Archbishop of Canterbury.
1557	Refoundation of some small religious houses.
June	Pole was recalled to Rome to answer charges of heresy. Mary refused him permission to go and rejected his replacement as legate.
1558	
10 November	Five Protestants were burned at the stake in Canterbury. In all, about 300 people were executed during Mary's reign. Thomas Bentham, a returned exile, was ministering to the Protestants of London.
17 November	Mary and Pole died.

As Chart 23B shows, Mary was eager to restore the Papal Supremacy in England, herself renouncing the title Supreme Head of the Church in December 1553. But this did not automatically mean that the Pope resumed his pre-1534 role. There were many stumbling blocks to overcome before England could be accepted once again into the papal see. Cardinal Pole, appointed papal legate by Pope Julius III in August 1553 with a brief to effect the reconciliation, was adamant that former Church lands would have to be restored if England was to return to the authority of the Pope. But this was not a simple matter. According to Renard, the Catholics held more former Church land than the Protestants. By the end of June 1554, the Pope realised that concessions would have to be made over secularised lands, or reconciliation itself might never happen.

It was Philip who made a positive and crucial contribution to the negotiations. Following his marriage to Mary in July 1554, he gave the matter top priority, saying that he did not wish to rule over a country of either heretics or schismatics (people who had rejected Papal authority). Eventually, on 30 November 1554, Pole granted absolution to the whole realm and welcomed 'the return of the lost sheep' in the Pope's name. The issue of land ownership was still unresolved, but by January 1555 Pole, supported by Mary, who apparently even threatened to abdicate over the issue, had to concede that Church lands redistributed after the dissolution of the monasteries and chantries would remain in lay hands. The great Act of Repeal, which reunited England with Rome, went through Parliament and received royal assent on 16 January 1555.

ACTIVITY

In Chapter 15 you found out how the religious pendulum swung towards full Protestantism in stages. Use Chart 23C to examine how the pendulum swung back to Catholicism under Mary I.

1 On your own copy of the pendulum in Chart 23C, mark when and how the changes were made. Use Chart 23B to help you.
2 What does your completed diagram tell you about:
   a) the speed of change
   b) how opposition to the changes were dealt with
   c) the success of the changes?

■ 23C Religious change under Mary I

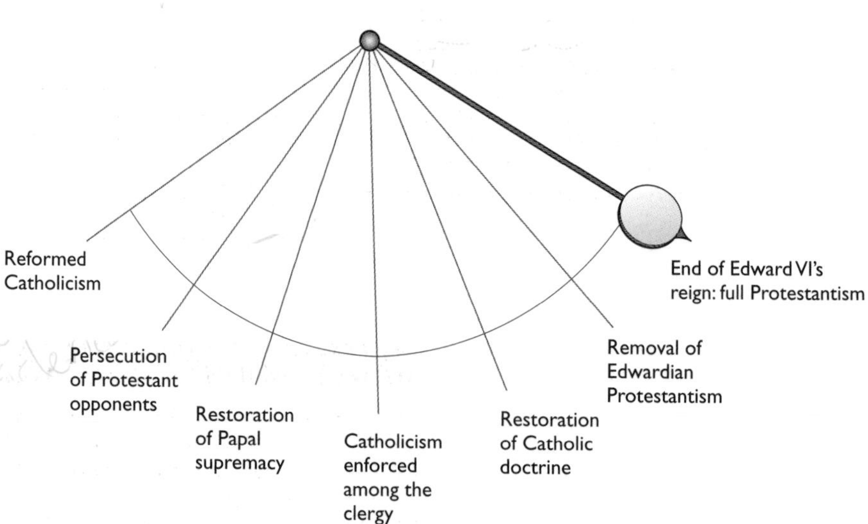

■ 23D Factors hindering Catholic restoration in Mary's reign

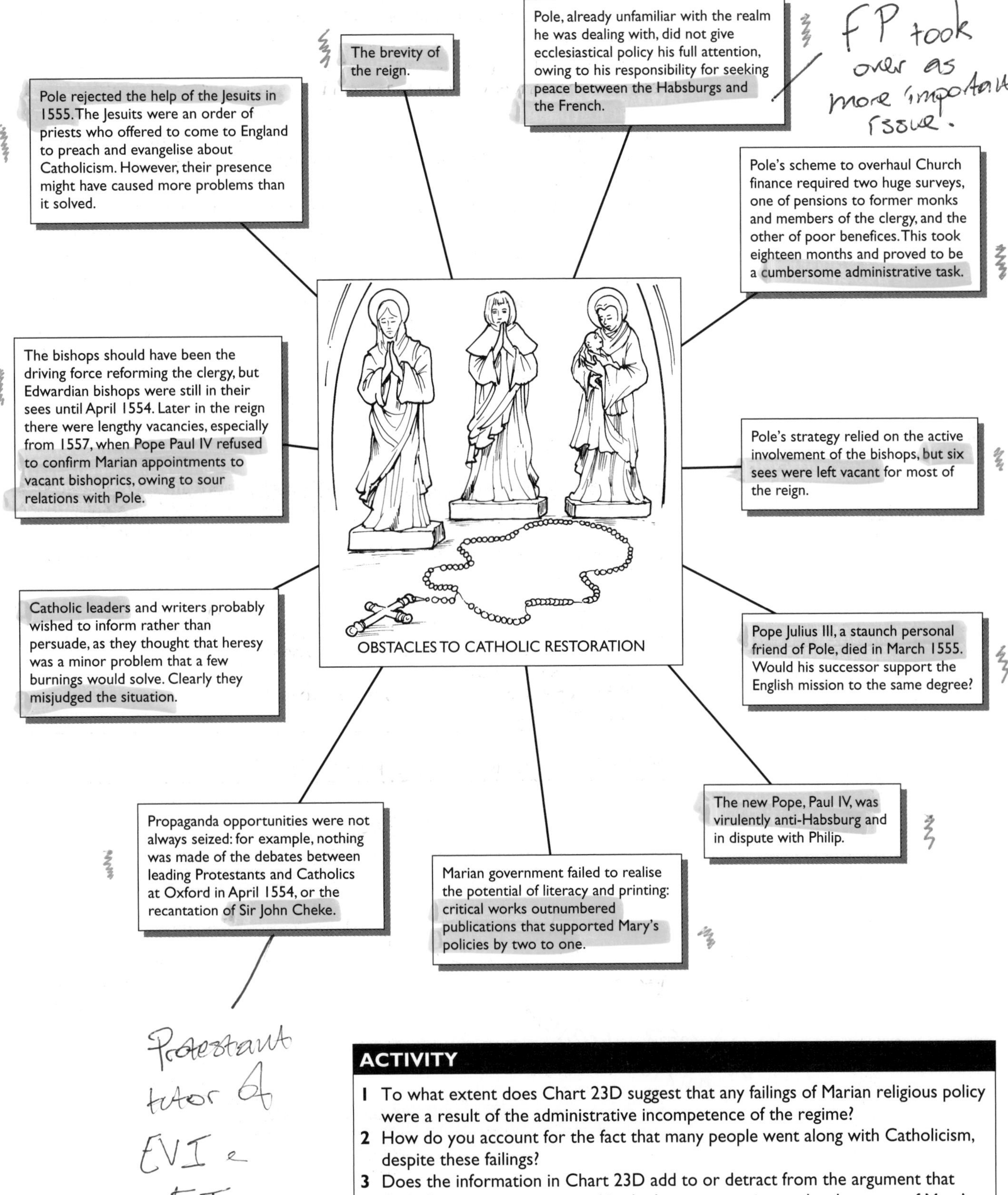

The brevity of the reign.
Pole, already unfamiliar with the realm he was dealing with, did not give ecclesiastical policy his full attention, owing to his responsibility for seeking peace between the Habsburgs and the French.
FP took over as more important issue.
Pole rejected the help of the Jesuits in 1555. The Jesuits were an order of priests who offered to come to England to preach and evangelise about Catholicism. However, their presence might have caused more problems than it solved.
Pole's scheme to overhaul Church finance required two huge surveys, one of pensions to former monks and members of the clergy, and the other of poor benefices. This took eighteen months and proved to be a cumbersome administrative task.
The bishops should have been the driving force reforming the clergy, but Edwardian bishops were still in their sees until April 1554. Later in the reign there were lengthy vacancies, especially from 1557, when Pope Paul IV refused to confirm Marian appointments to vacant bishoprics, owing to sour relations with Pole.
Pole's strategy relied on the active involvement of the bishops, but six sees were left vacant for most of the reign.
Catholic leaders and writers probably wished to inform rather than persuade, as they thought that heresy was a minor problem that a few burnings would solve. Clearly they misjudged the situation.
OBSTACLES TO CATHOLIC RESTORATION
Pope Julius III, a staunch personal friend of Pole, died in March 1555. Would his successor support the English mission to the same degree?
Propaganda opportunities were not always seized: for example, nothing was made of the debates between leading Protestants and Catholics at Oxford in April 1554, or the recantation of Sir John Cheke.
The new Pope, Paul IV, was virulently anti-Habsburg and in dispute with Philip.
Marian government failed to realise the potential of literacy and printing: critical works outnumbered publications that supported Mary's policies by two to one.
Protestant tutor of EVI & EI.

ACTIVITY

1. To what extent does Chart 23D suggest that any failings of Marian religious policy were a result of the administrative incompetence of the regime?
2. How do you account for the fact that many people went along with Catholicism, despite these failings?
3. Does the information in Chart 23D add to or detract from the argument that Catholicism was not restored in the long term owing to the shortness of Mary's reign?

– Fixable

– Insurmountable

C How did Mary use persuasion and persecution to promote her religious aims?

> **FOCUS ROUTE**
>
> Read pages 304–308 and write answers to the following questions:
>
> 1 List the positive ('carrot') and negative ('stick') methods that Mary's government used to promote Catholicism.
> 2 Which approach had the greater effect?
> 3 Why was Mary's 'war of words' not effective?
> 4 Were the burnings of Protestants counterproductive?
> 5 What were the main reasons why the Catholic restoration was not as successful as Mary would have hoped?

England was officially Catholic again by late 1553, but it took longer to ensure the people of England worshipped in a Catholic way. How was this to happen? Mary believed that the vast majority of the population would do so anyway, but what should be done with the stubborn few who refused to worship in a Catholic way?

The idea of monarchs using a 'carrot and stick' approach to achieve their aims is something we encountered earlier when we looked at the ways in which Mary's grandfather, Henry VII, tried to control the nobility. Mary also adopted this kind of dual approach to ensure that Catholicism was restored and Protestant influence eradicated – persuasion and persecution were to be the order of the day.

Persuasion

Perhaps it would be more accurate to say that Mary used a combination of persuading and informing as two aspects of a more positive approach to gathering the 'lost sheep' back into the Catholic fold. Mary and Pole believed that errant Protestants merely needed to have the error of their ways pointed out to them. Pole, having the blessing of both Mary and Philip, instituted a number of measures that sought to improve the quality of the Church itself.

■ 23E Pole's 'top-down' strategy for the restoration of Catholicism

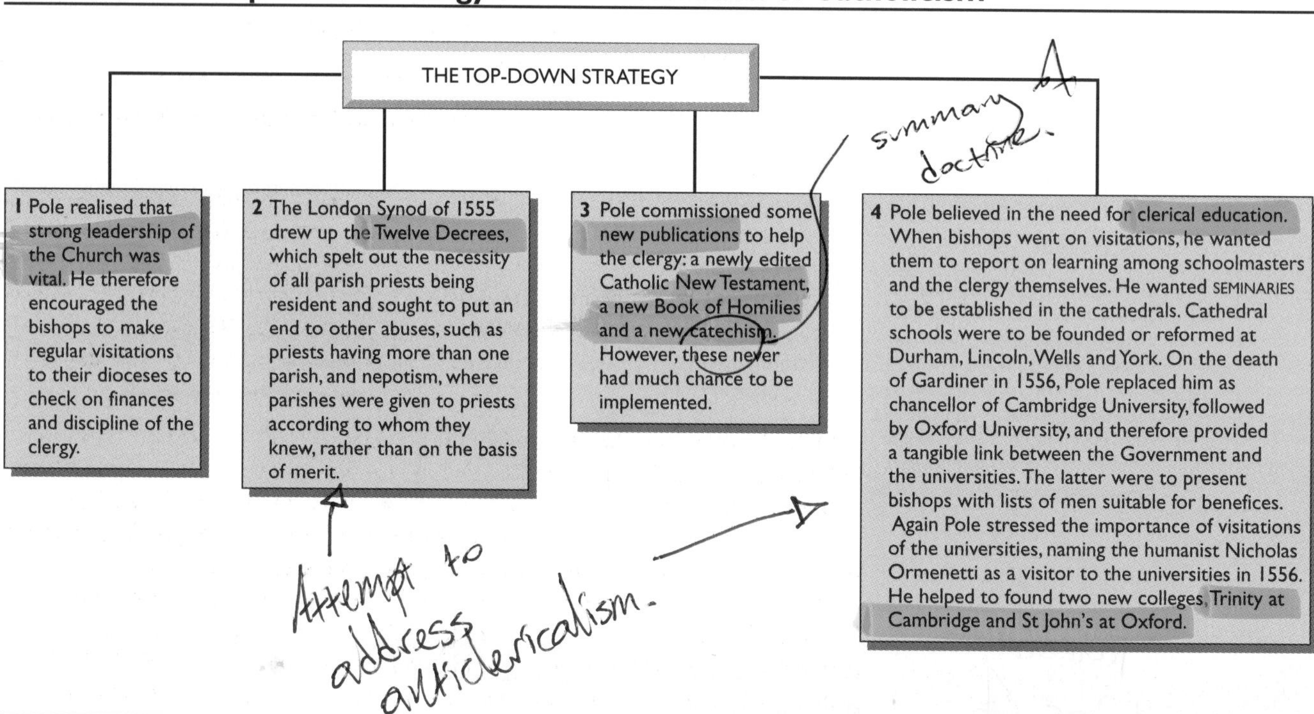

THE TOP-DOWN STRATEGY
1 Pole realised that strong leadership of the Church was vital. He therefore encouraged the bishops to make regular visitations to their dioceses to check on finances and discipline of the clergy.
2 The London Synod of 1555 drew up the Twelve Decrees, which spelt out the necessity of all parish priests being resident and sought to put an end to other abuses, such as priests having more than one parish, and nepotism, where parishes were given to priests according to whom they knew, rather than on the basis of merit.
3 Pole commissioned some new publications to help the clergy: a newly edited Catholic New Testament, a new Book of Homilies and a new catechism. However, these never had much chance to be implemented.
4 Pole believed in the need for clerical education. When bishops went on visitations, he wanted them to report on learning among schoolmasters and the clergy themselves. He wanted SEMINARIES to be established in the cathedrals. Cathedral schools were to be founded or reformed at Durham, Lincoln, Wells and York. On the death of Gardiner in 1556, Pole replaced him as chancellor of Cambridge University, followed by Oxford University, and therefore provided a tangible link between the Government and the universities. The latter were to present bishops with lists of men suitable for benefices. Again Pole stressed the importance of visitations of the universities, naming the humanist Nicholas Ormenetti as a visitor to the universities in 1556. He helped to found two new colleges, Trinity at Cambridge and St John's at Oxford.

> **SEMINARY**
> A training college for priests.

> **ACTIVITY**
>
> 1 What weaknesses can you identify in Pole's actions in terms of bringing about religious change?
> 2 What impact do you think these measures had on 'ordinary' churchgoers?

The war of words

Henry VIII and Thomas Cromwell used public relations as a means of promoting their message and securing the compliance of the people. Would Marian government manage to manipulate people as successfully?

There was a policy of censorship throughout Mary's reign. Two of her earliest proclamations forbade the printing of seditious rumours (28 July 1553) and the 'playing of interludes and printing of false fond books, ballads, rhymes and other lewd treatises ... concerning doctrine in matters now in question' (18 August 1553). There was an index of proscribed writers (i.e. those banned by the Government) and towards the end of the reign it was declared that the possession of treasonable books would result in the death penalty. Several Acts of Parliament made slander of Mary or Philip punishable as treason, and commissions were created 'to enquire concerning all heresies, heretical and seditious books, with power to seize all books and writings and to enquire into all enormities'.

The second aspect of controlling information was concerned with suppressing Protestant words. It has been estimated that around 19,000 copies of the 1552 Prayer Book were in circulation – plenty to sustain a Protestant underground. A lack of consistency hampered efforts to control literature. Prosecutions of 'seditious' writers did take place, and some attempt was made to prevent the smuggling of books. On the other hand, Latimer and Ridley, imprisoned Protestant leaders in Oxford, were able to write pamphlets and letters from inside gaol, which were then circulated outside. Most Protestant writings were published abroad and they outweighed the Marian ones significantly.

ACTIVITY

1 Why did Mary's government need to control religious writing?
2 Why was it not likely to be successful in this?

Marian government did try to be proactive as well as repressive in the war of words:

- A number of sermons were sponsored at St Paul's Cross in London. This was the most prestigious pulpit in the country. For instance, Gardiner announced the reconciliation with Rome from there in early December 1554.
- Pro-government writers such as Miles Hogarde, a London hosier, published tracts in defence of the regime. His main tract was *The Displaying of the Protestants* in 1556, which incurred the rancour of the Protestants whom he attacked in it.

Ultimately, however, the attempts of the Government to win the war of words failed. Mary herself failed to cultivate the awe of monarchy in the way that her father had done; nor did she inspire the intellectuals of her day. Few of her advisers had studied abroad, and they were therefore handicapped by a narrow intellect and a lack of debating skills. English Protestants in exile were more heavyweight than the Marian supporters. The Government was also hampered by a practical problem – it is probable that there were only half as many printers in Mary's reign as before. This was because a number of Protestant printers left England on her accession. Given that Pole's priority was for the clergy to have all the publications they needed (missals, hymnals, etc.), printers struggled to keep up with the demand, and they were less able to produce and sell other works for limited readership as a result.

TALKING POINT

Why do you think that Mary failed to maximise propaganda opportunities? Would it have made any difference if she had?

Persecution

The fact that more draconian measures were taken against those who refused either to acknowledge the Catholic view of the Eucharist (i.e. the belief in transubstantiation) or to conform to the restored Catholic rite does not in itself mean that attempts to persuade were unsuccessful – merely that they would take time. A dual strategy was required. In December 1554, therefore, the heresy laws were restored, and trials and executions began of those who refused to accept Catholic belief and practice.

SOURCE 23.1 The execution of Latimer and Ridley in 1555, from John Foxe's *Book of Martyrs*

SOURCE 23.2 An account of the burning of John Hooper on 9 February 1555, from C. Erickson, *Bloody Mary*, 1978, pp. 401–2. Hooper, the bishop of Worcester, was critical of Catholics who believed in transubstantiation. The words in quotation marks have been taken from Foxe's *Book of Martyrs*

He stood on a high stool and looked out over the crowd that gathered to watch him, and 'in every corner there was nothing to be seen but weeping and sorrowful people'. He prayed for a time, until interrupted by a man asking his forgiveness. Hooper said he knew of nothing to forgive. 'O sir!' the man said, 'I am appointed to make the fire.' 'Therein thou dost nothing offend me,' said Hooper. 'God forgive thee thy sins, and do thine office, I pray thee.'

Two small loads of green faggots were laid about the stool and reeds laid on top of them reaching up to the victim's legs. Hooper took two bundles of reeds in his hands and hugged them to him, kissing them, and putting one under his arms he showed the man who was building the fire where the rest were needed to make the circle complete. The torch was then put to the faggots, but because they were green they were slow to kindle, and the reeds took even longer to catch fire. After a time the flame reached Hooper's legs, 'but the wind having full strength in that place, it blew the flame from him,' and the fire only teased at his feet and ankles. More faggots were brought – there were no more reeds – and a new fire kindled, but because of the wind and the heavy overcast it did no more than burn his hair and scorch his skin a little. 'O Jesus, the Son of David,' he prayed, 'have mercy upon me, and receive my soul!' By this time, Hooper's legs were being consumed, but the fire was going out, leaving his upper body unharmed. 'For God's love, good people,' he was heard to say, 'let me have more fire!'

ACTIVITY

Foxe was an exiled Protestant, highly critical of Mary. Does this mean that Sources 23.1 and 23.3 are of no value to historians?

SOURCE 23.3 The martyrdom of Cranmer in 1556, from Foxe's *Book of Martyrs*

Published from Switzerland. (Basel)

A third time kindling was brought and embedded in the smoking ashes, and this time the flames were strong enough to reach the two bladders of gunpowder which had been tied between the sufferer's legs. But instead of exploding upward and killing him as they were meant to do, to spare him the excruciating pain of having his torso burned away while he remained conscious, the wind blew them out away from him so that they exploded in the air, and 'did him small good'. He was now heard to repeat, 'with a somewhat loud voice', 'Lord Jesus have mercy upon me; Lord Jesus have mercy upon me: Lord Jesus, receive my spirit!' His lips continued to move after his throat was so scorched he could make no sound, not even a scream, and onlookers noticed that even 'when he was black in the mouth, and his tongue swollen, that he could not speak, yet his lips went till they were shrunk to the gums.' In the end he could move nothing but his arms, yet he knocked them against his breast in the gesture of contrition until one of them fell off and the other, with 'fat, water, and blood' dropping out at his fingers' ends, stuck fast to the remains of his chest. In this position he bowed his head forward and died. Hooper had been burning alive for nearly three quarters of an hour.

ACTIVITY

1 Look at Sources 23.1 and 23.3. In what ways do they show that the burnings were counterproductive in terms of having the desired impact on religious change?
2 Identify the ways in which Hooper, in Source 23.2, used his impending death as a propaganda opportunity against Mary's government.

How effective were the burnings?

Burnings were often public spectacles. The execution of Christopher Wade in Dartford in July 1555 attracted large crowds, much to the delight of the fruiterers who brought loads of cherries to sell to the spectators. The impact that the martyrdoms had on the public is far from clear.

By what process, then, was a person condemned to death in this way? The Crown issued heresy commissions and the bishops conducted visitations in an effort to identify individuals who were deemed to be heretics. On being accused of heresy, they would be imprisoned, then tried by bishops. If they recanted and admitted the error of their ways by asking for forgiveness and embracing Catholicism once again, their life would be spared. However, if they obstinately stuck to their Protestantism, a writ was issued by the Lord Chancellor condemning them to be consumed by the flames.

In the case of prominent Protestants, as the first victims were, the process could be very lengthy. For instance, after conviction in Newgate prison, Hooper was visited by Bonner and several chaplains in an effort to get him to conform. Sometimes lesser victims were released, then rearrested when they were found not to be conforming, as in the case of Alice Benden in Kent.

Did the burnings work? In other words, were Protestant sympathies stamped out? Certainly the process did not always run smoothly. There were administrative disruptions and delays, such as in Essex, Kent, Suffolk, Staffordshire, Rochester and Colchester in July 1557, when the Council contacted the responsible authorities to ask why certain executions had not been carried out. The probable cause was the declaration of war against France in June, rather than any concern to ease up on heretics.

Unsurprisingly, given his Protestant sympathies, Foxe gives the impression that the martyrs in London were supported by the crowds who watched them die; there is some evidence to support his case. When Rowland Taylor died at Hadleigh, the streets were lined with crowds. The cry 'Ah! good Lord! there goeth our good shepherd from us, that so faithfully hath taught us, so fatherly hath cared for us, and so godly hath governed us' was heard. Other Protestant writers noted that the fortitude with which the 'heretics' died showed that they gave their lives in a good cause.

On the other hand, apart from in London, there is no evidence that there was a strong reaction against the burnings. Moreover, Mary's government was able to recruit laymen such as the Earl of Derby in Lancashire and Sir John Tyrell in Suffolk to hunt heretics.

SOURCE 23.4 P. Williams, *The Later Tudors: England 1547–1603*, 1995, p. 116

Persecution did not eliminate heresy; and scattered congregations of Protestants met in many places. London was the safest haven for them in spite of the presence of central government, and reformers assembled there on board ship, in taverns, in the fields, in prisons, and in private houses . . . But the Protestant clergy, the leaders of their Church, were either executed or exiled; the faithful in England were often led by laymen; and there seems to have been no missionary movement organised by the exiled Protestants.

TALKING POINTS

1. Is there any evidence that the pro-Marians realised that the burnings would not ultimately persuade committed Protestants to recant?
2. Did the burnings backfire?
3. In Britain, the last time that the death penalty was invoked was in the early 1960s, so can we say objectively whether the burnings justified the sobriquet 'Bloody Mary'?

■ 23F The burnings – some facts and figures

- 280 people were burned to death in 46 months.
- Five were bishops.
- Fifty-one were women.
- Alice Downs, a 60-year-old widow, was burned with five other people outside Colchester on 2 August 1557.
- The burnings were mainly in the south-east, nearly half of them in London, Canterbury and Colchester.
- In the sixteenth century, thousands of people were slaughtered throughout Europe, including Scotland, in the name of some version of the 'true faith'.

Review: The pendulum swings back again – how Catholic was England by 1558?

■ Learning trouble spot

What problems do historians have in trying to assess how successful Mary's religious policies were?

Remember that Mary has been labelled 'Bloody Mary' not only because of the burnings, but also because of the extremely bad press given to her by the exiled contemporary Protestant, John Foxe. He attacked her both for the persecutions of her reign and for the fact that she was a woman. Try to base your judgement of her actions on what she was trying to achieve, and on the circumstances of the sixteenth century rather than those of the twenty-first.

FOCUS ROUTE

Read pages 309–10 and write your answers to these questions:

1 Explain why John Foxe's writings have made subsequent objective judgements about Mary's religious policies very difficult.
2 According to Sources 23.5–23.11, what evidence is there about the extent to which Catholicism had retaken root by 1558?

As a Protestant, John Foxe was on the winning side in the long term, and people like him wrote the 'received' version of events in the reign of Elizabeth. As you can imagine, she was only too pleased for this to happen. This has had a knock-on effect, though, for historians, as Robert Tittler explains in Source 23.6.

SOURCE 23.5 John Foxe, *Book of Martyrs*, 1563

We shall never find any reign of any prince in this land or any other which did ever show in it so many great arguments of God's wrath and displeasure as were to be seen in the reign of this Queen Mary, whether we behold the shortness of her time or the unfortunate event of all her purposes.

SOURCE 23.6 R. Tittler, *The Reign of Mary I*, 2nd edn, 1991, p.34

Though some historians no longer attribute quite as much significance to Foxe's Acts and Monuments *– more commonly known as the* Book of Martyrs *and first published in 1563 – as they used to do, Foxe's detailed and carefully compiled account of nearly all the executions still evokes strong images and heightened emotions. It cannot be insignificant that the work enjoyed at least five editions in its first quarter century, and that it came to be one of the most frequently printed works in the English language.*

As you might expect, historians disagree about the extent of Mary's success in restoring Catholicism. To a large degree, analysis depends on how you view the strength of Catholicism in England at the beginning of the reign. In *English Reformations: Religion, Politics and Society Under the Tudors,* Christopher Haigh has argued that it is wrong to view Mary's reign as an aberration in the process of the Protestant Reformation. Rather, he argues, it was Edward's reign that was out of place in a process of Catholic restoration that was begun in 1539 by Henry VIII, and which continued under Mary. Read Sources 23.7–23.11 on page 310 and decide which interpretation you agree with.

SOURCE 23.7 D. Loades, *The Reign of Mary Tudor: Politics, Government and Religion in England, 1553–58*, 2nd edn, 1991, p. 396

Not only did Mary and her bishops give traditional doctrines and practices a new lease of life, they also made considerable progress in restoring the material fabric of the church ... Also, in spite of Pole's failure to generate a spiritual revival and make catholicism a measurable political force amongst the lay aristocracy, he did help to produce a new generation of learned and devout catholic scholars. At the same time, ironically, Protestantism gained much more than it lost by being subjected to persecution.

SOURCE 23.8 N. Heard, *Edward VI and Mary: A Mid-Tudor Crisis?*, 2nd edn, 2000, p. 99

In general it appears that by 1558 the majority of people in England were still undecided about religion. Among the elites there was strong support for royal supremacy, but they were willing to follow the religion of the legitimate monarch. The mass of the population do not appear to have had strong formalised convictions, and in most cases they were prepared to follow the lead of their social superiors. Although there were small minorities of committed Protestants and Catholics, neither religion seems to have had a strong hold in England when Mary I died. When Elizabeth I came to the throne the country was willing to return to a form of moderate Protestantism. However, during her reign deeper religious divisions began to appear and the unity of the Church of England ended.

SOURCE 23.9 D. Loades, *The Mid-Tudor Crisis, 1545–1565*, 1992, p. 180

Under Mary the Protestant settlement turned out to be much stronger at the grass roots than it was at the level of political action. The great majority of ordinary people followed the example of their betters and conformed, but the Marian Church was actually less effective in imposing conformity upon the reluctant than the Edwardian Church had been. This was partly, of course, because the catholic restoration cost money. Altars had to be rebuilt, images restored, new vestments purchased ... There was often uncertainty, particularly after 1555, as to how long the Restoration was going to last ... The restored religious communities were elderly, and attracted few new vocations. By 1558 traditional piety had not even recovered the level of 1546, let alone that of 1530.

SOURCE 23.10 C. Haigh, (ed.). *English Reformations: Religion, Politics and Society Under the Tudors*, 1993, p. 236

The Marian reconstruction of Catholicism was a success. It was not a total success, for the Protestants could not all be crushed and the indifferent could not all be made enthusiasts – at least, not in five years. But the evidence from the parishes is of considerable and continuing support for traditional services and celebrations ... In Mary's last year recruitment to the priesthood was better than it had been for thirty years, and the laity's giving to parish religion was probably greater than for twenty. In England, religious division may have been easing; the persecution had slackened, as determination among both heretics and hunters apparently declined.

SOURCE 23.11 P. Williams, *The Later Tudors: England 1547–1603*, 1995, pp. 118–19

There can be little doubt that on Mary's death England was still largely Catholic. When Elizabeth succeeded, the returning Protestant exiles found it a country of popish darkness: at Oxford there were 'few gospellers ... and many papists'. In many sees the new bishops had to struggle against the old faith: Bishop Horne described Winchester in 1562 as 'nursled in superstition and popery'. Undoubtedly religious attitudes varied dramatically from one region to another. Lancashire was loyal to Catholicism; Protestants were stronger in London, Essex, and Kent...

However ... the health of the Church could please neither active papists nor rigorous Protestants. Both groups identified some of the same weaknesses: the revenues of the Church had been despoiled and were too small to maintain episcopacy or parish clergy; many parishes had no incumbent; many priests were ... ignorant of the central truths of Christianity, their parishioners still more so.

ACTIVITY

1 What does Loades mean in Source 23.7 by saying 'Protestantism gained much more than it lost by being subjected to persecution'?
2 Uses Sources 23.7–23.11 to complete your own copy of the following table:

Historian	Ways in which Catholic revival was attempted	How Catholic was England by 1558?	How convincing are historians' arguments?

FOCUS ROUTE

Answer the following essay question: To what extent was Mary I successful in her quest to restore Catholicism in England?

■ 23E Religious changes in the sixteenth century

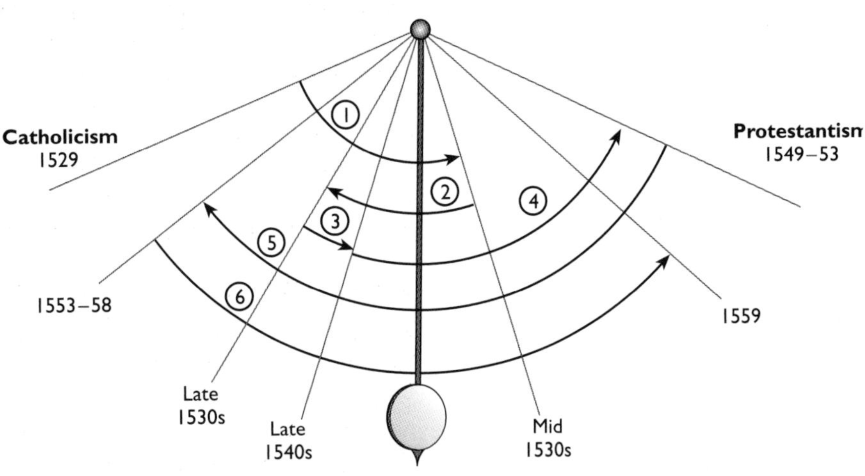

The numbers represent the order in which developments happened.

KEY POINTS FROM CHAPTER 23: The pendulum swings back again – how Catholic was England by 1558?

1 Mary succeeded in returning the English Church to Rome in an organisational sense, but Protestant beliefs still existed in England.
2 Mary was helped chiefly by Cardinal Pole, but her actions had the support of the Council.
3 A combination of proactive and reactive tactics were used to restore Catholicism.
4 Mary successfully used Parliament to restore Catholicism in England, but she had to bow to pressure and recognise that monastic land could not be returned to the Church.
5 Emphasis was placed on reforming the Catholic Church by improving the quality of the clergy, through training and removing abuses, etc.
6 Marian government did not maximise propaganda opportunities.
7 Nearly 300 Protestants were burned as heretics during Mary's reign, but the effectiveness of the burnings in converting people back to Catholicism was probably limited.
8 Mary's reputation as 'bloody Mary' has largely been the result of work by ardent Protestant contemporaries such as John Foxe and the subsequent propaganda of Elizabeth I's reign.
9 Ultimately, the restoration of Catholicism would not last because Mary did not have any children, and Elizabeth would not countenance it.

Catholic succession crucial to — long-term change.

24

Mary I – the verdict

CHAPTER OVERVIEW

We saw in Chapter 23 how easy it is for our judgement of Mary to be clouded by adverse contemporary accounts, such as John Foxe's, among others. The burnings, Mary's marriage to a Spaniard, dearth, an epidemic of influenza that killed thousands of people and the loss of Calais were all interpreted by Protestant contemporaries as God's judgement on a regime that they sought to discredit.

Robert Tittler has suggested in *The Reign of Mary I* that it is difficult to make informed judgements about Mary's reign because Mary and her government 'faced a larger than usual task of political transition' as a result of breaking sharply with their predecessors in foreign and religious affairs.

In this chapter, we will be focusing on the following for judging Mary's success:

A Was Mary responsible for a social and economic crisis during her reign?

How effectively did Mary use finance?

For Mary, all other policy areas were secondary to religion. 'She was always prone to put her conscience before her purse' (D. Loades, *The Mid-Tudor Crisis, 1545–1565*). However, she had the gifted William Paulet, Marquis of Winchester, as her Lord Treasurer. Under his direction, the Exchequer expanded to incorporate the Court of Augmentations and the Court of First Fruits and to handle 75 per cent of Crown income, which was in the region of £265,000 per annum. Chart 28A shows the measures taken to increase income during Mary's reign.

■ 28A Methods used to increase income during Mary's reign

- Rents on Crown lands were re-evaluated and raised. It has been estimated that this raised £40,000 per annum.
- The Exchequer successfully pursued Crown debtors, some of whom had debts that had been outstanding for over 40 years. Sir Thomas Egerton, for example, owed £7497 and probably repaid the money in full after a spell in the Tower. However, not everyone paid up, especially those in political favour, such as Pembroke or Lord Williams.
- A new Book of Rates, which fixed the level of duty to be paid on certain products, was introduced in 1558. It was badly needed because the levels were last fixed in 1507 and hundreds of commodities were untaxed or taxed well below the level of inflation. The new rates were on average 100 per cent higher. As a result, customs revenues rose from £29,315 in 1556–57 to £82,797 in 1558–59, but too late for Mary to feel the benefit.
- The cost of garrisoning Calais was removed.
- Plans were made to reissue the coinage, after the debasements made during the reigns of Henry VIII and Edward VI. This did not actually take place until Elizabeth's reign.

Mary's financial record was, if not outstanding, at least 'adequate' (P. Williams, *The Later Tudors: England 1547–1603*). Mary had begun her reign with debts of £185,000 but by her death this had increased to only £300,000, which David Loades regards as a 'considerable achievement' (*The Mid-Tudor Crisis, 1545–1565*). The situation would have been considerably better had she not been involved in war with France for the last eighteen months of her reign.

The social and economic problems of Mary's reign

Unfortunately for Mary's reputation, social and economic problems occurred during her reign over which she had no control.

- In 1555 and 1556 heavy rain caused the worst harvest failures of the century (apart from 1596), which resulted in unprecedented rises in the price of grain and widespread famine.
- In 1556–58 typhus epidemics were followed by an outbreak of influenza, which killed one in ten people. This was the only time since records began that the death rate was twice as high as normal. The population, which up until this point had been gradully rising, fell and may have dropped by as much as five per cent between 1556 and 1561.
- By 1559 the purchasing power of an agricultural worker's wages had dropped to 59 per cent of what it had been fifty years earlier, as a result of inflation.

There is no question that the ordinary people of England suffered extremes of hardship and illness during the mid-sixteenth century. However, Mary should bear little responsibility for these crises and her government's policies were as effective and responsive as any contemporary regime could have been.

TALKING POINT

If there were such social and economic problems today, the Government would be heavily critiscised. Why was Mary's Government not held responsible for these crises?

B Were Edward and Mary responsible for a mid-Tudor crisis?

One of the most damning criticisms of the Tudors is that they were responsible for a mid-Tudor crisis (see Chapter 19). The case for regarding the mid-Tudor years as being ones of crisis has been easy to make. There was the reign of a sickly minor who was dominated by an arrogant Protector. The Protector's policies were believed to have encouraged social disorder and as a consequence he was toppled by his peers. He was replaced by a greedy and ruthless duke, who precipitated a constitutional crisis through his attempts to alter the succession. This crisis was followed by the accession of the country's first female monarch, whose rule was made ineffectual by her obsession with Catholicism and Philip II.

Although this notion of a mid-Tudor crisis has had a long currency, it is now being effectively revised by historians.

SOURCE 24.1 N. Heard, *Edward VI and Mary: A Mid-Tudor Crisis?*, 1990, p. 143

The concept of a mid-sixteenth-century crisis in England is now considered to be difficult to maintain. This is certainly true if by 'crisis' it is implied that the whole country, and all of the people, were experiencing a crisis continuously between 1547 and 1558. Indeed, it is only really possible to say that the country as a whole and some sections of society underwent very short-lived crises at times between these dates. If this is the case, most historians would consider that this was normal for any country at any time. Mid-Tudor England faced a variety of problems. Many of these arose from the political, social and economic consequences of the feudal crisis. Others, like the reactions to the English Reformation, can be seen as more short term. A few, such as the succession crisis of 1553, were responses to immediate events. At no time, even in 1549, was the country in danger of collapse, and for most people life went on as normal.

SOURCE 24.2 D. Loades, *The Mid-Tudor Crisis, 1545–1565*, 1992, p.4

Historians, in short, have become rather too fond of inventing crises, and are in danger of devaluing the word. The reason for this is simple and pragmatic. A crisis is something easy to identify, and to catch the readers' attention. It can be studied, analysed and discussed when neither time nor energy permit a more comprehensive approach. 'Crisis spotting' is not only a good way to focus a study, it is also a good way of bringing the historian's name to the attention of his interested audience. A crisis is something interesting and exciting, when mere change and development (or, worse still, continuity) are not . . . The true significance of the reigns of Edward VI and Mary lies less in what happened than in what did not happen.

ACTIVITY

1. Why does Nigel Heard in Source 24.1 reject the idea of a mid-Tudor crisis?
2. Why, according to David Loades in Source 24.2, have historians used the label 'crisis'?
3. Write an essay to answer the following question: To what extent can the reigns of Edward and Mary be regarded as forming a mid-Tudor crisis?

FOCUS ROUTE

By reflecting on what you have learned in this section, complete your own copy of the following table. Use examples, historians' views and your own ideas.

	Crisis?	Not a crisis?
Government		
Religion		
Economy and finance		
Law and order		
Foreign policy		

ACTIVITY

How persuaded are you by Loades' views on each of the issues in the diagram?

The following diagram gives a selection of David Loades' views on the key issues. The extracts are from Loades' book, *The Mid-Tudor Crisis, 1545–1565*, pages 2–5.

TYPES OF CRISIS

Conclusion
'In fact the years from 1545 to 1565 should be seen in a very positive light, not as years of crisis, but as years of achievement. The sovereignty of parliament was consolidated, the Anglican Church created, and the foundations laid of the great national myth which was to sustain the most unlikely and successful empire of modern times.'

Economic
'Serious inflation dates from about 1545, and was largely the result of Henry VIII's policy of debasement, but the disruption to trade was short-lived, and no worse than that caused at other times by war or political embargo. The social and agrarian problems which certainly existed had nothing to do with the particular circumstances of the mid-century; they had been building up for half a century, and continued for another two generations. Inflation continued to rise and fall, until at least the end of the century.'

Dynastic security
'Both Edward VI's premature death and the failure of Mary's pregnancy in 1555 were dynastic crises which altered subsequent history, but they were no more serious in their implications than the death of Arthur in 1502, the death of young Prince Henry in 1511, or Elizabeth's attack of smallpox in 1562.'

Law and order
'The rebellions of 1549 and 1554 were pyrotechnic but relatively harmless. Edward's government would not have been destroyed had the battles of Sampford Courtenay or Dussindale gone the other way. The rebels had no alternative claimant to the throne, no leaders of substance and no policy beyond the immediate redress of their grievances.'

Government
'In fact Edward's government was not ineffective, and the problems of 1549 were caused rather by over-ambitious policies and confused ideology than by any weakness in the council. Contrary to what is sometimes supposed, the insurgents were not taking advantage of a regime which lacked adequate leadership so much as exploiting ambiguities in the Protector's thinking.'

Religion
'Exposed to dramatic change by the creation of the Royal Supremacy, it was forced through a protestant revolution between 1547 and 1549, only to be forcibly re-catholicised by Mary, and then returned to the Edwardian settlement by Elizabeth. This was undoubtedly a crisis of a sort, but it was the intervention of Mary which caused the main confusion.'

Succession
'The sharpest, and potentially the most far reaching [crisis], was that caused by the Duke of Northumberland's attempt to divert the succession in July 1553.'

C What have historians said about Mary's reign?

FOCUS ROUTE

Read this page and answer the following question:
What were the strengths and weaknesses of Mary's reign?

Mary's reign can be considered to have been barren in the sense that she had no children, but are there other reasons why it can be viewed as such? Let's turn to historians' comments to find out.

SOURCE 24.3 J. Guy, *Tudor England*, 1988, pp. 226–27

Despite the efforts of modern historiography to boost her reputation, Mary I will never appear creative. This has little to do with her campaign of persecution: in a European context her 'inquisition' was small scale: we must be aware of the bias of John Foxe and other Protestants writing in Elizabeth's reign who prefer us to believe that Mary did nothing but persecute. It has more to do with her financial and government 'reforms', which, although recently thought to have 'revitalized' exchequer and common law in innovative style, were in fact inspired by near-ideological conservatism. Even her reunion with Rome, it can be argued, lacked the fire of true Counter-Reformation.

SOURCE 24.4 D. Loades, *The Reign of Mary Tudor: Politics, Government and Religion in England, 1553–58*, 2nd edn, 1991, p. 394

Mary's government was not weak in any general sense of being unable to enforce its will. All the evidence suggests that the council was throughout assiduous in the discharge of its administrative duties and that it made its will known and obeyed at least as successfully as that of Elizabeth during most of her much longer reign. Moreover, in spite of arousing considerable opposition and in spite of having to endure the misfortunes of harvest failure and exceptional mortality, Mary survived. She succeeded in enforcing her will over three major matters: her marriage, the return to Rome and the declaration of war.

SOURCE 24.5 P. Williams, *The Later Tudors: England 1547–1603*, 1995, pp. 122–23

No one could pretend that the policies of Mary Tudor were popular. Her foreign marriage bred fears of Spanish domination and the return to Rome alarmed many, especially the holders of Church lands. Anxiety on both these scores was only partially allayed. Nevertheless Mary secured her main objectives: the restoration of the Mass, the return to Roman jurisdiction, the marriage to Philip, and entry into her husband's war with France. She was denied only the bill for confiscating the lands of exiles and authorization for the coronation of Philip. Within the limits set upon government action at this time she was reasonably, even remarkably, successful . . . But there was of course one great failure: the lack of a male heir.

ACTIVITY

1 According to Sources 24.3–24.5, what were the weaknesses of Mary's reign?
2 Which of the historians are the least and most sympathetic to Mary? Identify possible reasons for this.
3 Which view do you most agree with, and why?
4 Write a paragraph that sums up your views of Mary's reign.

D Review: Mary I – the verdict

On first consideration, it would be easy to identify aspects of Mary's reign which suggest that her policies did cause problems. We saw in Chapter 21 that Wyatt's rebellion was mainly instigated in response to Mary's marriage to Philip of Spain. The campaign to restore Catholicism was more punitive than constructive, with some 300 people being burned at the stake and many others imprisoned. The Marian Council was a divided one, and not helped by Mary's determination to take advice more widely from her husband and father-in-law and the papal legate. And if all this were not enough, a country that suffered the scourge of harvest failure and the worst influenza outbreak of the century was also dragged into war against France, thanks to the manoeuvres of Philip.

However, was Mary's reign unique in such events? Rebellion was endemic throughout the Tudor period, and Wyatt's attempt to unseat Mary failed, as had those of Simnel and Warbeck with Henry VII. Neither Henry VII nor Henry VIII balked at putting their opponents to death, so why should Mary be called 'bloody'? Divided councils were something that each of the Tudor monarchs had to deal with, and this was not necessarily a bad thing. Mary could hardly be blamed for the natural disasters of the reign, and as far as the war with France was concerned, it was certainly ill-advised, but couldn't that criticism be levelled against almost all the forays into Europe since 1485?

Mary's reign certainly had its problems, but this feature was not unique to her reign. Remember that when Mary died in 1558, Elizabeth succeeded as she should have done. Another Tudor sat on the throne. In this, and in her efforts to restore Catholicism in the long term, Mary had not achieved what she wanted, but the dynasty did continue.

KEY POINTS FROM CHAPTER 24: Mary I – the verdict

1. England suffered from terrible harvests (1555 and 1556) and a devastating epidemic (1558) during Mary's reign.
2. Although Mary left a legacy of debt, her finances were well managed.
3. The Tudor succession in 1558 was as it should have been – Elizabeth was the legitimate heir, which even Mary recognised.
4. Traditionally, Mary's reign has been heavily criticised by historians, but recent work, by Loades (*The Mid-Tudor Crisis, 1545–1565*) and Williams (*The Later Tudors: England 1547–1603*) for example, has started to portray her in a more positive light.
5. The notion of a mid-Tudor crisis has recently been revised by historians.

Section 4 Review: Mary I

ACTIVITY

We have seen that Mary has been subject to many and changing views among historians. Here is a reminder of what has been said about her:

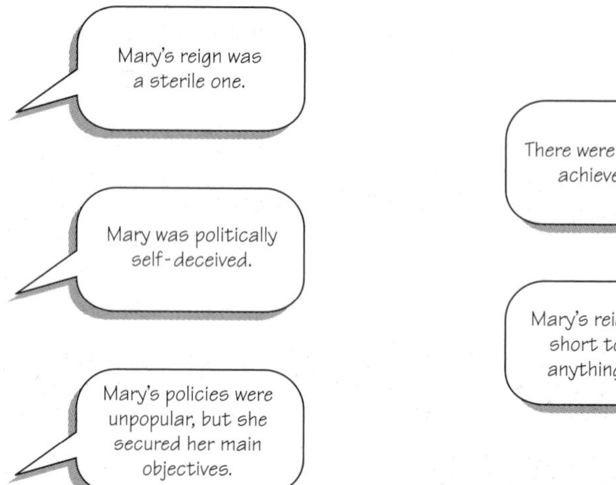

Mary's reign was a sterile one.
There were no positive achievements.
Mary was politically self-deceived.
Mary's reign was too short to achieve anything lasting.
Mary's policies were unpopular, but she secured her main objectives.

1 Use the information in Chapters 20–24 to find evidence supporting each of these views.
2 Which of the views is most fully supported by the evidence?
3 In your opinion, which of the views above combine together, and why?
4 As a class, devise your own selection of soundbites that you think best describe Mary's reign.

FOCUS ROUTE

Answer the following essay question: To what extent did Mary's reign undermine the Tudor dynasty?

■ Learning trouble spot

By now, you should have had a lot of practice at essay writing, but here are some points that might help to answer the Focus Route question.

- **Don't** fall into the trap of finding evidence that **only** supports the argument that Mary undermined the Tudor dynasty.
- **Do** ensure that your essay contains paragraphs on:
  - the succession issue
  - religious policy
  - other domestic policies
  - foreign policy
  - other issues.
- **Do** make some comparisons with the reigns of Henry VIII and Edward VI, especially on matters such as rebellions.
- **Do** draw on the opinions of a range of historians.

Conclusion: How successful were the Tudors?

Panorama of the Thames, by Visscher. This is what London would have looked like at the time of Mary's funeral. London had a population of about 100,000 out of a national population of roughly 3 million people

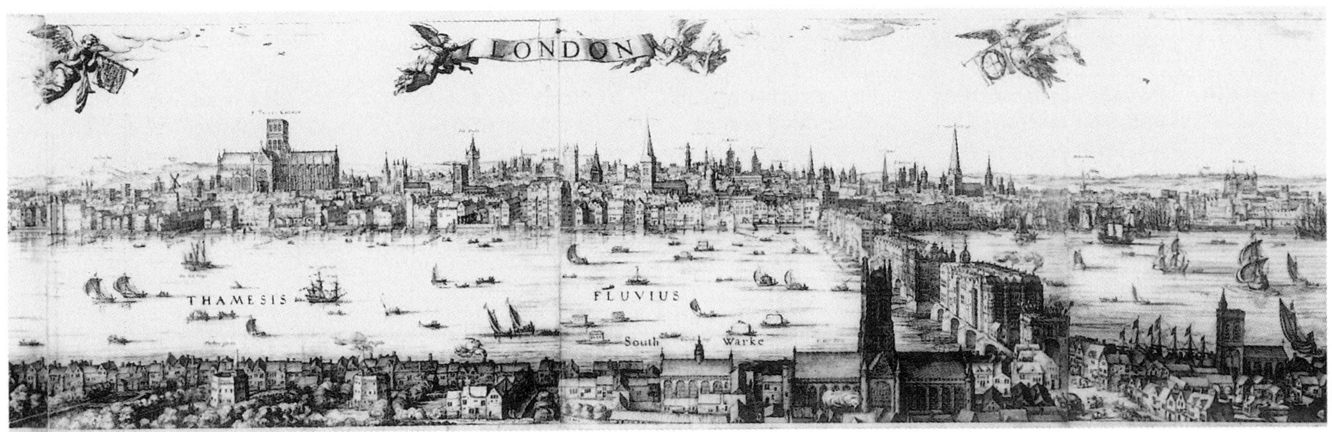

ACTIVITY

1 Sort the following crises into rank order with the greatest crisis for the Tudors first.
   - Establishment of Royal Supremacy, 1532–34
   - Dissolution of the monasteries, 1536–40
   - The pretenders Simnel and Warbeck threatening Henry VII
   - Cornish rebellion, 1497
   - Invasion scares, 1538–39 and 1545
   - Accession of a woman, 1553
   - Terrible harvest, 1551
   - Wyatt's rebellion, 1554
   - Attempt to alter the succession, 1553
   - Accession of a minor, 1547
   - Sweating sickness, 1551–52
   - Marriage to a Spaniard, 1554
   - Edward VI's shift towards Protestantism, 1547–53
   - Henry's failure to produce a male heir until 1537

2 Does your list tell you anything about:
   a) how under threat the Tudor dynasty was
   b) whether one reign was more successful than another?

A Thames boatman born on 22 August 1485 might have lived to see all four of the early Tudors come and go. What would he have remembered about them?

- **Rebellions** There had been rebellions in each of the monarchs' reigns: the Cornish rebellion (1497), the rebellion against the Amicable Grant (1525) and Wyatt's rebellion (1554) all briefly threatened London, and the boatman would have heard of the Pilgrimage of Grace (1536), the Western rebellion and Kett's rebellion (1549).
- **Religion** Major changes would have taken place in the church that the boatman visited. There had been repeated changes in church decorations, the role of the priest, and the beliefs that the boatman was supposed to hold. All of the country's monasteries and chantries had been closed.
- **Disasters** Influenza would have killed at least one member of the boatman's close family (1557–9), and food would have been short during the bad harvests of 1549–51 and 1555–56.
- **Economy and finance** The prices of all goods would have gone up and the boatman would have been repeatedly asked for tax by a Parliament on which the monarch was increasingly dependent.
- **Laws and punishments** These had stayed the same as before Henry VII, although JPs in the countryside had become much more important.
- **Wars** As before, there had been wars against France and Scotland, with some notable victories. But, after the loss of Calais, England no longer owned any land in France.
- **Society** The social hierarchy remained the same. It was still the rich nobles and gentlemen who ruled.
- **Jobs** People still had the same jobs, and farming practices were also the same.
- **Rulers** The boatman would have been ruled by two men, a child and a woman, all of whom bore the name 'Tudor' (which no one would have heard of before the boatman was born). And there was one 'Grey' woman, whom the boatman saw being taken down the river to the Tower. But at the end of his life, the Tudors were still on the throne.

How successful were the Tudors?

The table below summarises briefly some of the conclusions that the authors of this book have reached. You may well disagree with some or all of these conclusions. Such is the beauty of history and the myriad conclusions that can be drawn from the evidence.

Monarch	Security	Foreign policy	Image	Overall success
Henry VII	A constant struggle – he only just made it.	Used as a tool – largely successfully – to make himself more secure.	Started the deliberate and widespread use of imagery to identify his family with the Crown.	He had far more to battle against than any of his offspring. He must take credit for establishing the dynasty.
Henry VIII	Perhaps not as secure as historians have often assumed. He didn't get a male heir until 1537. Why also did he kill all the Courtenays and fear invasion between 1538 and 1545?	Henry's achievements never came near to matching his grandiose expectations.	Henry was a complex character who is very difficult to understand fully. His ministers were important but Henry always had the last say.	The break with Rome and the dissolution of the monasteries were unique achievements. His reign was otherwise a bit of a hotchpotch.
Edward VI	He was never really threatened, but the Devise, created with Northumberland before his death, ended the Tudor dynasty.	Somerset led a disastrous Scottish campaign. Northumberland sealed a realistic peace.	Edward's role and importance to the reign require reassessment. He mattered a lot to the reign – particularly his religious views.	A decisive and rapid move towards Protestantism was achieved.
Mary I	Her failure to produce an heir was a personal disaster.	Contrary to a commonly held view, England was not at the beck and call of Spain.	Most things in Mary's reign were subservient to her religious ambitions.	Mary and Pole achieved a switch back towards Catholicism.

The main aims of a monarch were to defend his or her subjects against foreign invasion, to keep the peace at home and to see that the law was respected and operated. The Tudors certainly scored well in these areas (with some obvious exceptions) and they were above all fascinating and memorable people to study. So, from the point of view of the historian, they were a success!

Answers to activities

Section 1

Chapter 2

Page 17

1 Edward, the Black Prince – RICHARD II
Lionel, Duke of Clarence – EDWARD IV and V, RICHARD III
John of Gaunt – Henry IV, V, VI and VII
Edmund, Duke of York – EDWARD IV and V.

2 Henry VII's royal blood came from John of Gaunt through two lines: on his mother's side, from the Beaufort line (disputed because John of Gaunt and Catherine Swynford were not married when John Beaufort was born); and from his paternal grandmother, Catherine of France, who had been married to Henry V.

3 Because the death of Henry VI's only son, Edward, left Henry Tudor as the principal 'Lancastrian' claimant to the throne.

4 The marriage would bring together the Houses of York and Lancaster. Henry needed to marry Elizabeth to:

- attempt to reconcile the divisions of the Wars of the Roses
- prevent anyone else from marrying her and gaining a claim to the throne;
- fulfil his pledge to marry her, made during his exile in Brittany.

(Henry was careful not to marry her until after he had been crowned, so that it did not appear that he was using her claim to bolster his own.)

5 His claim was very distant and weak. He was not regarded as a significant claimant at the time and he was not the strongest legitimate claimant. The order would have been:

1 Elizabeth of York (as the only surviving child of a monarch)
2 Edward, Earl of Warwick
3 John de la Pole, Earl of Lincoln
4 Henry Tudor.

Chapter 4

Page 40

Dilemma 1: Henry chose option c. He allowed limited unofficial aid to Brittany (500 men under Lord Scales) and then issued an apology to the French to ensure he remained on good terms with them.

Page 41

Dilemma 2: During the winter of 1488–89, Henry came to diplomatic agreements (option a) with Brittany, Spain and Burgundy to create an anti-French alliance.

Page 42

Dilemma 3: Henry actually did a combination of a and b. He prepared an invasion fleet, but did not set sail until mid-September 1492. He remained in his garrison at Calais for over a month before setting out to besiege Boulogne. The oncoming winter would guarantee a short campaign, since fighting did not take place beyond the autumn. The French seem to have been keen for a quick negotiated settlement and only twelve men were wounded or killed. Two days later, peace terms were agreed at Etaples and Henry returned home portraying himself as a conquering hero.

Page 42

Dilemma 4: Henry was pressured by Ferdinand into joining the Holy League as a nominal member in 1496, but Henry made it clear that he would not declare war on France (options a and c). Henry was careful to maintain the favourable relations with France established at Etaples in 1492. In 1497 Henry signed a trade treaty with France, and in 1498 he renewed the Treaty of Etaples with the new king, Louis XII.

Page 43

Dilemma 5: Henry realised that Philip (option b) was the safe bet and began to extricate England from a Spanish alliance and Prince Henry from the marriage to Catherine of Aragon.

Page 43

Dilemma 6: Henry chose both options b and c. A second trade treaty (*Intercursus Malus*) was signed which was so favourable to English interests that it aroused fierce opposition in Burgundy and was never implemented. In March 1506, the Earl of Suffolk was handed over to Henry, on the condition that his life would be spared (he was executed by Henry VIII in 1513). Possible marriage plans were outlined: Henry VII to Margaret of Austria (Philip's sister); Prince Henry to Eleanor (Philip's daughter); and Mary (Henry VII's daughter) to Charles (Philip's son and heir). None of the marriages ever took place. Henry agreed to recognise Philip and Joanna as monarchs of Castile and funded their venture to the tune of £138,000 by cancelling loans.

Page 43

Dilemma 7: By the end of his reign, Henry had been forced to settle for option c. Of the marriages to France and Burgundy that had been discussed, only the plans for the prestigious match between Mary and Charles were finalised (December 1507), although the marriage was later called off.

Henry vigorously pushed for a marriage between himself and Joanna, but Ferdinand was not prepared to allow her claim to the Castilian throne to settle in foreign hands. Henry's attempts to restore the match between Prince Henry and Catherine of Aragon were not successful in his lifetime, but Henry VIII confirmed the marriage within days of becoming king.

Page 44

Dilemma 8: Henry settled on option b. In 1486 the Scots recaptured Dunbar. Henry turned a blind eye to this and a three-year truce was signed in July 1486, under which the dispute over Berwick would be resolved by commissioners and the possibility of a marriage alliance would be explored.

Page 44

Dilemma 9: Henry's solution was a mixture of a and c. He gave support to the Scottish rebel lords in the spring of 1489, but his commitment was limited because of the Brittany war and a Yorkshire tax rebellion in the north of England. He continually pushed the proposal for his daughter Margaret's marriage to James IV, but with limited success.

Page 45

Dilemma 10: Henry was bent on full-scale war (option a). He extracted 'the heaviest taxation of the century' to create 'the largest military force of his reign' (Gunn, 'Henry VII (1457–1509),' in *New Dictionary of National Biography*). He received consent for a forced loan of £50,000 and Parliament granted two-fifteenths and tenths (see page 69) and a subsidy, together worth £120,000. He used this to fund two royal armies, a fleet to carry 5,000 men and substantial artillery support.

Chapter 5

Page 63

The following are verbatim extracts from the article by Dominic Luckett in *Historical Research* (October 1996).

1 'In the following year [1473] he was among those sent to capture the Lancastrian rebel John, earl of Oxford, suggesting that the government was confident that he had not inherited his family's Lancastrian leanings . . . Although Robert may have been seen primarily as a soldier, Edward IV increasingly turned to him for assistance in the civil administration of the south-west, particularly in the later years on the throne. Most propitious were his appointments as sheriff of Cornwall in 1478 and of Devon in 1480, seemingly confirming his position as a leading light of the south-west establishment.'

2 'It may . . . be that like many of the rebels Robert felt a deep sense of loyalty towards Edward IV and outrage at the treatment of his sons by the usurper Richard. It is, however, difficult to see why Robert should have felt great attachment to King Edward and his heir. For whilst Edward had employed him in the south-west, this had not been recognized by any tangible reward. Equally, it is difficult to see why Robert should have felt any particular warmth towards the Lancastrians. He did, of course, come from a pro-Lancastrian family, but his own treatment during the readoption, when he received neither employment nor patronage, can hardly have inspired within him any great enthusiasm for Lancastrianism. It seems unlikely therefore that Robert's decision to rebel had much to do with dynastic loyalties. More important may have been the pressure brought to bear by close friends, neighbours and associates who had themselves decided to join the revolt. Alternatively, Robert may simply have been frustrated at the modest speed of his advancement: his participation in what he hoped would be a successful revolt may thus have been an attempt to kick-start his career.'

3 'The first indication of just how much trust the new king placed in Robert came as soon as the fighting at Bosworth had ended, when Henry sent him north to Sheriff Hutton to take the earl of Warwick into custody. That he was entrusted with this important and delicate duty suggests that, during the time the two had spent together in exile, Henry had been particularly impressed by Robert's loyalty and ability. This impression is confirmed by the marks of favour which Robert acquired in the first months of the reign.'

4 'Like most of Henry's supporters, Willoughby received little in the way of land, owing largely to the relatively low number of Ricardian magnates who were attainted and the king's need to use much of the land which was forfeit to provide endowments for members of his own family . . .

The treatment which Robert received after Henry's victory in 1485 is eloquent testimony to the degree of royal trust and even affection which he enjoyed. Yet he never seems to have gained admission to that inner circle, consisting of men such as Reginald Bray, Giles Daubeney and Lord Oxford, upon which the king relied for advice on the formulation of high-level policy. This is perhaps best seen in his position in the council where, despite having been sworn in early in the reign, he attended only infrequently. This apparently reflects the fact that Henry intended Robert to have an executive rather than a policy-making role. He was valued as a loyal servant who could be trusted to put the king's decisions into effect, rather than as a man of imagination and intellect capable of helping to make those decisions.'

5 'Robert died on 28 September 1502. His career exemplifies the possibility for advancement which the turmoil of the late fifteenth century opened up to those with an eye for the main chance.'

Page 64

5 'Thus within less than four decades the prospects of Willoughby greatness which seemed so impressive on the morrow of Bosworth had come to nought. For the historian of late fifteenth- and early sixteenth-century England, there are several important lessons to be drawn from this tale of the transience of earthly glory. For one thing, the ascent of Robert the elder shows the opportunities for advancement offered by the turmoil of the late fifteenth century. Robert's promotion was almost wholly the result of rebellion and war. In the relatively peaceful years up to 1483, he had made little headway in carving out a career of note. Only his involvement in the 1483 rebellion allowed him to come to the attention of Tudor, and only victory at Bosworth allowed this notice to be translated into tangible promotion and reward. Yet, if the father's career shows that advancement could come easily, that of the son suggests that it was far more difficult to maintain that position in the more tranquil conditions of the sixteenth century. It also highlights the importance of personal links in determining political relationships. The key factor in Robert I's promotion was the personal relationship which he had struck up with the king in exile. Robert II enjoyed no such bond with Henry, and hence his career failed to progress. Because Henry did not really know Robert II, he had no particular reason to trust him and thus no cause to promote him. That said, it is clear that the king did not wish entirely to destroy Willoughby influence in the south-west after the death of Robert I. As the new head of a family with important local ties and connections, Robert II could be extremely useful to the government. The Crown was, however, careful to limit and direct the use to which that local influence was put. This it did by a clear and deliberate policy of forcing Robert II into an increasingly awkward financial position. Having got the young peer at its mercy, the Crown was then able to direct his actions whenever it saw fit.'

Page 65

John de La Pole, Earl of Lincoln

- Early on, he made his peace with Henry. Henry left him alone. However, Henry may have regretted this decision as de la Pole supported and possibly organised Lambert Simnel's rebellion. De la Pole died in the battle of Stoke.

Thomas Grey, Marquis of Dorset

- In order to have his attainder reversed, Dorset had to renounce all grants that Edward IV had given to him. He also had to reject all rights to wardship, marriage and custody of Edward, Earl of Warwick.

- In 1487 Henry imprisoned Dorset in the Tower because he was suspected of being involved in the Simnel rebellion.
- Henry freed him after the battle of Stoke and he remained loyal thereafter. (See page 61 for further details.)

Henry Percy, Earl of Northumberland
- Henry imprisoned him immediately after Bosworth.
- He was soon freed and rewarded with the office of Warden of the East and Middle Marches (in the north). This was because Henry recognised Percy's influence in the north.
- Percy was murdered by rioters in Yorkshire on 28 April 1489.

Francis, Viscount Lovell
- He was attainted by Henry in 1485.
- He took sanctuary in Colchester immediately after Bosworth.
- He attempted an uprising that failed in April 1486 and fled to Flanders.
- He joined Simnel in 1487 and either was killed or fled. In any case, he disappeared for ever.

Edward Plantagenet, Earl of Warwick
- Henry sent Robert Willoughby de Broke to Yorkshire to arrest Edward.
- Edward was kept in the Tower of London and then executed in 1499 after he and Warbeck tried to escape.

Thomas Howard, Earl of Surrey
- He was attainted by Henry and then imprisoned in the Tower.
- Henry released him in 1489 after he had taken an oath of allegiance (see the section on Acts of Attainder on page 61 for further details on Surrey).

Edward Stafford, Duke of Buckingham
- Henry reversed the Act of Attainder that had been passed against his father.
- Nevertheless, Henry kept all of Buckingham's lands under Crown control while he was a minor. This land was to be governed partly by Margaret Beaufort and partly by Reginald Bray (as steward and surveyor).

John de Vere, Earl of Oxford
- Henry appointed him as his Lord Great Chamberlain and Admiral.
- He became one of Henry's most trusted councillors.
- Henry rewarded his loyalty by making him the major landowner in East Anglia.

Section 2
Chapter 9
Page 112
Robert Whiting concludes: 'The evidence surveyed would suggest that, on the eve of the Henrician Reformation, traditional religion continued to attract a substantial and often impressive degree of popular support. This support, however, was markedly higher for some components (like parish churches) than for others (like monasteries). In general . . . it seems also to have been higher in the north and west than in the south-east.'

Chapter 10
Page 143
a) Williams
b) Elton
c) Collinson
d) Dickens

Chapter 11
Page 164
1. An annulment of the marriage.
2. All right – there were precedents.
3. By refusing to become his mistress.
4. Charles V captured Rome and took the Pope prisoner.
5. Wolsey considered war against Charles V.
6. He was the dominant force in Europe.
7. Treaty of Amiens.
8. Milan, Naples and Navarre.
9. Francis I invaded Italy.
10. Charles V won a crushing victory over Francis I at Landriano.
11. He ended trade with the Netherlands in preparation for war.
12. A truce.
13. Peace of Cambrai.
14. Treaty of Barcelona.
15. He was left diplomatically stranded with little means of forcing an annulment.
16. It was a useful bargaining tool against Charles V.
17. Francis I had successfully invaded Italy.
18. Cardinal Campeggio was sent to investigate the case for an annulment.
19. His career and survival depended upon an annulment.
20. The Pope withdrew the case to Rome.
21. He fell from power in October 1529.
22. 1533.
23. White Bishop (Wolsey) and Black Queen (Catherine of Aragon).

Section 3
Chapter 15
Page 216
1. In modern English, 'The Word of the Lord endureth for ever', 'Idolatry', 'Superstition', 'Feigned holiness' and 'All flesh is grass'. These words clearly establish the painter as a reformer, as he is attacking the Pope and promoting the scriptures.
2. Possible answers (exact answer is unknown): Edward (meaning Edward should continue Henry's religious changes), Somerset (he should lead the changes) or the iconoclasm (Henry approves of it).
3. It is floating!
4. They are pulling the chains attached to Edward's dais in an attempt to remove him from power.
5. He is collapsing under the dais. This is a reference to the Royal Supremacy.
6. They are pulling down religious statues because worship of images is seen as idolatry.
7. The building might represent Papal Supremacy, which had been destroyed under Henry VIII.
8. The divide separates the Catholics at the bottom of the painting from the Protestants at the top.
9. The painting is showing how the religious changes, begun under Henry VIII, have been furthered by his son and his Protestant advisers (on his left). The painting is attacking the Catholic worship of images (such as Mary and Jesus), the position of the Pope and attempts being made to restore England to the see of Rome (the monks pulling the dais).
10. Various answers possible.

Bibliography and Selected Reading

Ackroyd P., *The Life of Thomas More*, Chatto and Windus, 1998
Anglo S., *Images of Tudor Kingship*, Seaby, 1992
Archer R.E. (ed.), *Crown, Government and People in the Fifteenth Century*, Alan Sutton, 1995

Bennett M., *Lambert Simnel and the Battle of Stoke*, Sutton Publishing Ltd, 1987
Bennett M., *The Battle of Bosworth*, Sutton Publishing Ltd, 1985
Bush M. L., *The Government Policy of Protector Somerset*, Edward Arnold, 1975
Bruce M. L., *The Making of Henry VIII*, Collins, 1977
Bush M. L., *The Pilgrimage of Grace: A Study of Rebel Armies of October 1536*, Manchester University Press, 1996

Carpenter C., 'Henry VIII and the English polity', in Thompson B. (ed.), *The Reign of Henry VIII*, Standford University Press, 1995
Carpenter C., *The Wars of the Roses: Politics and the Constitution in England c. 1437–1509*, Cambridge University Press, 1997
Chrimes S. B., *Henry VII*, Methuen, 1972
Coleman C. and Starkey D., *Revolution Reassessed*, Clarendon Press, 1986
Collinson P., *The Elizabethan Puritan Movement*, Clarendon Press, 1990
Condon M. M., 'Ruling elites in the reign of Henry VII', in Ross C. (ed.), *Patronage, Pedigree and Power*, Sutton Publishing Ltd, 1979
Cornwall J., *Revolt of the Peasantry, 1549*, Routledge & Kegan Paul, 1977
Crowson P. S., *Tudor Foreign Policy*, A. & C. Black (Publishers) Ltd, 1973

Davies C. S. L., *Peace, Print and Protestantism*, Fontana Press, 1995
Dawson I., *The Tudor Century, 1485–1603*, Thomas Nelson & Sons, 1993
Dickens A. G., *The English Reformation*, B. T. Batsford Ltd, 1964
Dickens A. G., *The English Reformation* (2nd edn), B. T. Batsford Ltd, 1989
Dickens A. G., 'The Reformation in England', in Hurstfield J. (ed.), *The Reformation Crisis*, Edward Arnold, 1965
Dodds R. and Dodds M., *The Pilgrimage of Grace and the Exeter Conspiracy*, Cambridge University Press, 1915
Doran S., *England and Europe, 1485–1603*, Longman, 1996
Duffy E., *The Stripping of the Altars*, Yale University Press, 1992

Elliot J. H., *Imperial Spain*, Edward Arnold, 1963
Elton G. R., *England Under the Tudors*, Routledge, 1955
Elton G. R., *England Under the Tudors*, 2nd edn, Routledge, 1974
Elton G. R., *England Under the Tudors*, 3rd edn, Routledge, 1991
Elton G. R., *Policy and Police: The Enforcement of the Reformation in the Age of Thomas Cromwell*, Cambridge University Press, 1972
Elton G. R., *Reform and Reformation: England 1509–1558*, Hodder & Stoughton, 1977
Elton G. R., 'Politics and the Pilgrimage of Grace', in Malament B. (ed.), *After the Reformation*, Manchester University Press, 1980
Elton G. R., *The Tudor Revolution in Government*, Cambridge University Press, 1953
Erickson C., *Bloody Mary*, J. M. Dent, 1978

Fletcher A. and MacCulloch D., *Tudor Rebellions*, Longman, 1997

Grant A., *Henry VII*, Metheun, 1985
Griffiths R. A. and Thomas R. S., *The Making of the Tudor Dynasty*, Gloucester, 1985
Gunn S., 'Peers, commons and gentry in the Lincolnshire Revolt of 1536', in *Past and Present*, Vol. 123, 1989
Gunn S., 'The structures of politics in Early Tudor England', *Transactions of the Royal Historical Society*, No. 65, 1995
Gunn S. J. and Lindley P. G. (eds), *Cardinal Wolsey: Church, State and Art*, Cambridge University Press, 1991
Gunn S. J., 'The Courtiers of Henry VII', *English History Review*, No. 426, January 1993
Gunn S. J., *Early Tudor Government, 1485–1558*, Macmillan, 1995
Guy J., *Tudor England*, Oxford University Press, 1988
Guy J. (ed.), *The Tudor Monarchy*, Edward Arnold, 1997
Guy J., ' Wolsey, Cromwell and the reform of the government', in MacCulloch D. (ed.), *The Reign of Henry VIII: Politics, Policy and Piety*, Macmillan, 1995
Gwyn P., *The King's Cardinal: The Rise and Fall of Thomas Wolsey*, Pimlico, 1990

Haigh C. (ed.), *English Reformations: Religion, Politics and Society Under the Tudors*, Oxford University Press, 1993
Haigh C. (ed.), *The English Reformation Revised*, Cambridge University Press, 1987
Haigh C., 'Revisionism, the Reformation and the history of English Catholicism', *Journal of Ecclesiastical History*, No. 36, 1985
Heard N., *Edward VI and Mary: A Mid-Tudor Crisis?*, 1990; 2nd edn, Hodder & Stoughton, 2000
Hoak D., 'Rehabilitating the Duke of Northumberland: politics and political control, 1549–53', in Tittler R. and Loach J. (eds), *The Mid-Tudor Polity c. 1540–1560*, Macmillan, 1980
Hoskins W. G., *The Age of Plunder: The England of Henry VIII*, Longman, 1976
Hoyle R., 'War and public finance', in MacCulloch D. (ed.), *The Reign of Henry VIII: Politics, Policy and Piety*, Macmillan, 1995
Hunt J. and Towle C., *Henry VII*, Longman, 1998
Hurstfield J. (ed.), *The Reformation Crisis*, Edward Arnold, 1965
Hutton R., 'The local impact of the Tudor Reformations', in Haigh C. (ed.), *The English Reformation Revised*, Cambridge University Press, 1987

Ives E., *Anne Boleyn*, Basil Blackwell, 1986
Ives E. W., *Faction in Tudor England*, 2nd edn, Historical Association, 1986
Ives E. W., 'Henry VIII: the political perspective', in MacCulloch D. (ed.), *The Reign of Henry VIII: Politics, Policy and Piety*, Macmillan, 1995
Ives E. W., 'Patronage at the Court of Henry VIII: the case of Sir Ralph Egerton of Ridley', *Bulletin of the John Rylands Library*, Vol 52, No. 2, Spring 1970

James M. E., 'Obedience and dissent in Henrician England: the Lincolnshire Rebellion, 1536', *Past and Present*, Vol. 48

Jones M. and Underwood M., *The King's Mother, Lady Margaret Beaufort*, Cambridge University Press, 1992

Jordan W. K. (ed.), *The Chronicle and Political Papers of King Edward VI*, Ithaca Press, 1966

Jordan W. K., *Edward VI: The Threshold of Power – the Dominance of the Duke of Northumberland*, George Allen & Unwin Publishers Ltd, 1970

Jordan W. K., *Edward VI: the Young King and the Protectorship of the Duke of Somerset*, George Allen & Unwin Publishers Ltd, 1968

Lander J. R., *Government and Community*, Edward Arnold, 1980

Lloyd C. and Thurley S., *Henry VIII: Images of a Tudor King*, Phaidon Press Ltd, 1990

Loach J., 'Edward VI: a new look at the king and his reign', *History Review*, December, 1999

Loach J., *Edward VI*, Yale University Press, 1999

Loach J., *Parliament Under the Tudors*, Clarendon, 1991

Loach J., *Protector Somerset: A Reassessment*, Headstart History, 1994

Loades D., *Henry VIII and his Queens*, Sutton Publishing Ltd, 1994

Loades D., *John Dudley, Duke of Northumberland*, Headstart History, 1996

Loades D., *Politics and the Nation*, B. T. Batsford Ltd, 1964

Loades D., *The Mid-Tudor Crisis, 1545–1565*, Macmillan, 1992

Loades D., *The Reign of Mary Tudor: Politics, Government and Religion in England, 1553–58*, 2nd edn, Macmillan, 1991

Loades D., *The Tudor Court*, Historical Association, 1989

Lockyer R. and O'Sullivan D., *Tudor Britain, 1485–1603*, Collins, 1999

Lockyer R. and Thrush R., *Henry VII*, Longman, 1983

Lotherington J. (ed.), *The Tudor Years*, Hodder & Stoughton, 1994

Luckett D., 'Patronage, violence and revolt in the reign of Henry VIII', in Archer R. E. (ed.), *Crown, Government and People in the Fifteenth Century*, Allan Sutton, 1995

Luckett D., 'The rise and fall of a noble dynasty: Henry VII and the Lords Willoughby de Broke', *Historical Research*, October 1996

MacCulloch D. (ed.), *The Reign of Henry VIII: Politics, Policy and Piety*, Macmillan, 1995

MacCulloch D., *Thomas Cranmer*, Yale University Press, 1996

McFarlane K. B., *The Nobility of Later Medieval England*, Clarendon Press, 1973

McGurk J., *The Tudor Monarchies, 1485–1603*, Cambridge University Press, 1999

Mackie J. D., *The Earlier Tudors, 1485–1558*, Oxford University Press, 1994

Macmahon L., 'The English Campaign in France, 1543–45', unpublished MA thesis, University of Warwick, 1993

Mattingly G., *Renaissance Diplomacy*, Jonathan Cape, 1955

Morrill J., *The British Problem 1534–1707*, Macmillan, 1996

Morris, T.A., *Europe and England in the Sixteenth Century*, Routlege, 1998

Murphy V., 'The Literature and Propaganda of Henry VIII's First Divorce', in MacCulloch D. (ed.), *The Reign of Henry VIII: Politics, Policy and Piety*, Macmillan, 1995

O'Day R., *The Debate on the English Reformation*, Methuen, 1986

O'Day R., *The Longman Companion to the Tudor Age*, Longman, 1995

Palmer M. D., *Henry VIII*, Longman, 1983

Pogson R. H., 'Reginald Pole and the priorities of Government in Mary Tudor's Church', *Historical Journal*, No. 18, 1975

Pollard A. F., *Henry VIII*, Groupil & Co, 1902

Pollard A. J., *Wars of the Roses*, Macmillan, 1988

Potter D., 'Foreign policy', in MacCulloch D. (ed.), *The Reign of Henry VIII: Politics, Policy and Piety*, Macmillan, 1995

Randell K., *Henry VIII and the Government of England*, Hodder & Stoughton, 1991

Redworth G., 'A study in the formulation of policy: the genesis and evolution of the Act of Six Articles', *Journal of Ecclesiastical History*, No. 37, 1986

Rogers C., *Henry VII*, Hodder and Stoughton, 1991

Ross C. (ed.), *Patronage, Pedigree and Power*, Sutton Publishing, 1979

Scarisbrick J. J., *The Dissolution of the Monasteries*, University of Warwick Video

Scarisbrick J. J., *Henry VIII*, Yale University Press, 1968; 1997

Scarisbrick J. J., *The Reformation and the English People*, Blackwell, 1984

Smith L. B., *Henry VIII: The Mask of Royalty*, Panther, 1971

Starkey D. (ed.), *A European Court in England*, Collins and Brown, 1991

Starkey D., 'Court and government', in Guy, J. (ed.), *The Tudor Monarchy*, Edward Arnold, 1997

Starkey D., *The Reign of Henry VIII: Personalities and Politics*, Collins & Brown, 1985

Storey R. L., *The Reign of Henry VII*, Blandford Press, 1968

Thompson B. (ed.), *The Reign of Henry VII*, Stanford University Press, 1995

Tittler R. and Loach J. (eds), T*he Mid-Tudor Polity c. 1540–1560*, Macmillan, 1980

Tittler R., *The Reign of Mary I*, 2nd edn, Longman, 1991

Turvey R. and Steinberg C., *Henry VII*, 2nd edn, Hodder & Stoughton, 2000

Van Cleave Alexander M., *The First of the Tudors: A Study of Henry VII and His Reign*, Croom Helm, 1981

Walker G., 'The expulsion of the minions of 1519 reconsidered', *Historical Journal*, No. 32, 1989

Walker G., 'Henry VIII and the invention of the Royal Court', *History Today*, February 1997

Walker G., *Persuasive Fictions: Faction, Faith and Political Culture in the Reign of Henry VIII*, Scolar Press, 1996

Weir A., *Children of England: The Heirs of King Henry VIII*, Pimlico, 1996

Wernham R. B., *Before the Armada*, W.W. Norton, 1966

Williams P., *The Later Tudors: England 1547–1603*, Oxford University Press, 1995

Williams P., *The Tudor Regime*, Clarendon Press, 1979

Youings J., *The Dissolution of the Monasteries*, Allen & Unwin, 1971

Text acknowledgements

p.8 source 1.1 J. Guy, *Tudor England*, 1988, by permission of Oxford University Press; **p.13** source 2.1 A. J. Pollard, *Wars of the Roses*, 1988, Macmillan; **p.21** source 2H, adapted from A. J. Pollard, *Wars of the Roses*, 1988, Macmillan; **p.29** source 3.4 C. Carpenter, *The Wars of the Roses: Politics and the Constitution in England c.1437–1509*, 1997, Cambridge University Press; **p.30** source 3C, adapted from Ian Dawson, *The Tudor Century 1485–1603*, 1993, Nelson Thornes; **p.39** *source 4.1 R. B. Wernham, *Before the Armada*, 1966, Harcourt Brace; *source 4.2 G. Mattingly, *Renaissance Diplomacy*, 1955, Jonathan Cape/Random House; **p.55** *source 4.4 B. Thompson (ed.), *The Reign of Henry VII*, 1995, Stamford; *source 4.5 G. Mattingly, *Renaissance Diplomacy*, 1955, Jonathan Cape/Random House; **pp.63–64** *case study adapted from Dominic Luckett, 'The rise and fall of a noble dynasty: Henry VII and the Lords Willoughby de Broke' in *Historical Research*, October 1996; **p.66** *source 5.2 C. S. L. Davies, *Peace, Print and Protestantism*, 1977, A. P. Watt; source 5.4 J. R. Lander, *Government and Community*, 1980, reprinted by permission of Edward Arnold Publishers; *source 5.5 C. Carpenter, 'Henry VII and the English polity' in B. Thompson (ed.), *The Reign of Henry VII*, 1995, Paul Watkins Publishers; **p.74** *source 5.10 R. L. Storey, *The Reign of Henry VII*, 1968, Cassell and Co.; source 5.11 G. R. Elton, *England Under the Tudors*, 2nd edition, 1974, Routledge; source 5.12 R. Lockyer and R. Thrush, *Henry VII*, 1983, Pearson Education Ltd; *source 5.15 C. Carpenter, 'Henry VII and the English polity' in B. Thompson, (ed.), *The Reign of Henry VII*, 1995, Paul Watkins Publishers; **p.76** source 5.17 S. B. Chrimes, *Henry VII*, 1972, Yale University Press; **p.77** source 5.19 C. Carpenter, *The Wars of the Roses: Politics and the Constitution in England c.1437–1509*, 1997, Cambridge University Press; **p.81** *source 6.1 R. L. Storey, *The Reign of Henry VII*, 1968, Cassell and Co.; source 6.3 S. B. Chrimes, *Henry VII*, 1972, Yale University Press; source 6.4 J. Guy, *Tudor England*, 1988, by permission of Oxford University Press; *source 6.5 C. Carpenter, 'Henry VII and the English polity' in B. Thompson, (ed.), *The Reign of Henry VII*, 1995, Paul Watkins Publishers; **p.89** source 7.8 L. B. Smith, *Henry VIII: The Mask of Royalty*, 1971, Academy Chicago Press; **p.90** *source 7.9 J. J. Scarisbrick, *Henry VIII*, 1968, University of California Press/Routledge; source 7.10 J. Guy, *Tudor England*, 1988, by permission of Oxford University Press; **p.99** source 8.4 S. J. Gunn and P. G. Lindley (eds), *Cardinal Wolsey: Church, State and Art*, 1991, Cambridge University Press; **p.100** source 8.7 J. Guy, 'Wolsey, Cromwell and the reform of government' in D. MacCulloch (ed.), *The Reign of Henry VIII: Politics, Policy and Piety*, 1995, Macmillan; **p.101** source 8.8 E. Ives, 'Henry VIII: the political perspective' in D. MacCulloch (ed.), *The Reign of Henry VIII: Politics, Policy and Piety*, 1995, Macmillan; **p.107** source 9.1 E. Ives, *Anne Boleyn*, 1986, Blackwell Ltd/Polity Press; *source 9.2 J. J. Scarisbrick, *Henry VIII*, 1968, University of California Press/Routledge; **p.109** source 9.3 V. Murphy, 'The literature and propaganda of Henry VIII's first divorce' in D. MacCulloch (ed.), *The Reign of Henry VIII: Politics, Policy and Piety*, 1995, Macmillan; source 9.4 E. Ives, *Anne Boleyn*, 1986, Blackwell Ltd/Polity Press; source 9.5 L. B. Smith, *Henry VIII: The Mask of Royalty*, 1971, Academy Chicago Press; source 9.6 Extract from *The King's Cardinal: The Rise and Fall of Thomas Wolsey* by P. Gwyn published by Barrie and Jenkins. Used by permission of The Random House Group Limited; **p.112** source 9D adapted from R. Whiting in D. MacCulloch (ed.), *The Reign of Henry VIII: Politics, Policy and Piety*, 1995, Macmillan; **p.113** *source 9.10 A. G. Dickens, 'The Reformation in England' in J. Hurstfield (ed.), *The Reformation Crisis*, 1965, HarperCollins; *source 9.11 J. J. Scarisbrick, *Henry VIII*, 1968, University of California Press/Routledge; source 9.12 G. R. Elton, *Reform and Reformation: England 1509–1558*, 1977, by permission of Edward Arnold Publishers; source 9.13 C. Haigh, 'The continuity of Catholicism in the English Reformation' in C. Haigh (ed.), *The English Reformation Revised*, 1987, Cambridge University Press; source 9.14 E. Duffy, *The Stripping of the Altars*, 1992, Yale University Press; **p.130** source 10.1 G. R. Elton, *Policy and Police: The Enforcement of the Reformation in the Age of Thomas Cromwell*, 1972, Cambridge University Press; *source 10.2 P. Ackroyd, *The Life of Thomas More*, 1988, Random House; **p.142** source 10.7 C. Haigh (ed.), in *The English Reformation Revised*, 1987, Cambridge University Press; **p.153** source 11.1 P. S. Crowson, *Tudor Foreign Policy*, 1973, A&C Black (Publishers) Ltd; *source 11.2 J. J. Scarisbrick, *Henry VIII*, 1997, University of California Press/ Routledge; source 11.3 T. A. Morris, *Europe and England in the Sixteenth Century*, 1988, Routledge; **p.165** *source 11.13 J. J. Scarisbrick, *Henry VIII*, 1997, University of California Press/Routledge; **p.166** source 11.14 P. S Crowson, *Tudor Foreign Policy*, 1973, A&C Black (Publishers) Ltd; source 11.15 S. Gunn, *Cardinal Wolsey: Church, State and Art*, 1991, Cambridge University Press; **p.170** source 11.18 L. B. Smith, *Henry VIII: The Mask of Royalty*, 1971, Academy Chicago Press; source 11.19 L. B. Smith, *Henry VIII: The Mask of Royalty*, 1971, Academy Chicago Press; *source 11.20 J. J. Scarisbrick, *Henry VIII*, 1968, University of California Press/Routledge; **p.173** source 11.22 J. Morrill, *The British Problem 1534–1707*, 1996, Macmillan; **p.179** *source 12.2 J. J. Scarisbrick, *Henry VIII*, 1968, University of California Press/Routledge; **p.180** *source 12.3 J. J. Scarisbrick, *Henry VIII*, 1968, University of California/Routledge; source 12.4 S. Gunn, *Early Tudor Government 1485–1558*, 1995, Macmillan; **p.182** *source 12.5 J. J. Scarisbrick, *Henry VIII*, 1968, University of California Press/Routledge; source 12.6 G. R. Elton, *England Under the Tudors*, 3rd edition, 1991, Routledge; source 12.7 D. Loades, *The Mid-Tudor Crisis, 1545–1565*, 1992, Macmillan; **p.207** *source 14.8 J. Loach, *Protector Somerset: A Reassessment*, 1994, Plantagenet Press Ltd; source 14.9 M. L. Bush, *The Government Policy of Protector Somerset*, 1975, by permission of Edward Arnold Publishers; source 14.10 D. Loades, *John Dudley, Duke of Northumberland*, 1996, by permission of Oxford University Press; source 14.11 D. Hoak, 'Rehabilitating the Duke of Northumberland: politics and political control, 1549–1553' in R. Tittler and J. Loach (eds), *The Mid-Tudor Polity c.1540–1560*, 1980, Macmillan; **p.223** source 15.9 E. Duffy, *The Stripping of the Altars*, 1992, Yale University Press; source 15.10 R. Hutton, 'The local impact of the Tudor Reformations' in C. Haigh (ed.), *The English Reformation Revised*, 1987, Cambridge University Press; **p.224** source 15.11 W. K. Jordan, *Edward VI: The Threshold of Power – The Dominance of the Duke of Northumberland*, 1970, Routledge; source 15.12 D. Loades, *The Mid-Tudor Crisis 1545–1565*, 1992, Macmillan; **p.231** source 16D adapted from A. J. Fletcher and D. MacCulloch, 1997, *Tudor Rebellions*. Reprinted by permission of Pearson Education Ltd; **p.233** source 16F adapted from A. J. Fletcher and D. MacCulloch, 1997, *Tudor Rebellions*. Reprinted by permission of Pearson Education Ltd; **p.235** source 16.3 D. Loades, *The Mid-Tudor Crisis 1545–1565*, 1992, Macmillan; **p.239** source 16.10 M. L. Bush, *The Government Policy of Protector Somerset*, 1975, by permission of Edward Arnold Publishers; source 16.11 D. Loades, *The Mid-Tudor Crisis 1545–1565*, 1992, Macmillan; **p.260** source 18.2 W. K. Jordan, *Edward VI: The Threshold of Power – The Dominance of the Duke of Northumberland*, 1970, Routledge; source 18.3 D. Hoak, 'Rehabilitating the Duke of Northumberland: politics and political control 1549–1553' in R. Tittler and J. Loach (eds), *The Mid-Tudor Polity c.1540–1560*, 1980, Macmillan; **p.262** source 18.5 D. Loades, *John Dudley, Duke of Northumberland*, 1996, by permission of Oxford University Press; **p.274** source 20.2 G. R. Elton, *England Under the Tudors*, 1974, Routledge; *source 20.3 C. Erickson, *Bloody Mary*, 1978, Fraser and Dunlop Ltd; source 20.4 R. Tittler, *The Reign of Mary I*, 2nd edition, 1991, Longman Group UK Ltd 1983, 1991. Reprinted by permission of Pearson Education Ltd; source 20.5 P. Williams, *The Later Tudors: England 1547–1603*, 1995, by permission of Oxford University Press; **p.284** source 21.5 D. Loades, *The Reign of Mary Tudor: Politics, Government and Religion in England 1553–1558*, 2nd edition, 1991, Pearson Education Ltd; **pp.306–7** *source 23.2 C. Erickson, *Bloody Mary*, 1978, Fraser and Dunlop Ltd; **p.308** source 23.4 P. Williams, *The Later Tudors: England 1547–1603*, 1995, by permission of Oxford University Press; **p.309** source 23.6 R. Tittler, *The Reign of Mary I*, 2nd edition, 1991, Longman Group UK Ltd, 1983, 1991. Reprinted by permission of Pearson Education Ltd; **p.310** source 23.7 D. Loades, *The Reign of Mary Tudor: Politics, Government and Religion in England*, 2nd edition, Pearson Education Ltd; source 23.8 N. Heard, *Edward VI and Mary: A Mid-Tudor Crisis?*, 2nd edition, 2000, by permission of Edward Arnold Publishers; source 23.9 D. Loades, *The Mid-Tudor Crisis 1545–1565*, 1992, Macmillan; source 23.10, C. Haigh (ed.), *English Reformations: Religion, Politics and Society Under the Tudors*, 1993, by permission of Oxford University Press; source 23.11 P. Williams, *The Later Tudors: England 1547–1603*, 1995, by permission of Oxford University Press; **p.314** source 24.1 N. Heard, *Edward VI and Mary: A Mid-Tudor Crisis?*, 1990, by permission of Edward Arnold Publishers; source 24.2 D. Loades, *The Mid-Tudor Crisis 1545–1565*, 1992, Macmillan; **p.315** diagram from D. Loades, *The Mid-Tudor Crisis, 1545–1565*, 1992, Macmillan; **p.316** source 24.3 J. Guy, *Tudor England*, 1988, by permission of Oxford University Press; source 24.4 D. Loades, *The Reign of Mary Tudor: Politics, Government and Religion in England, 1553–1558*, 2nd edition, 1991, Pearson Education Ltd; source 24.5 P. Williams, *The Later Tudors: England 1547–1603*, 1995, by permission of Oxford University Press; **p.322** *Dominic Luckett, 'The rise and fall of a noble dynasty: Henry VII and the Lords Willoughby de Broke', *Historical Research*, October 1996.

*Every effort has been made to contact copyright holders, and the publishers apologise for any omissions which they will be pleased to rectify at the earliest opportunity.

Index

Note: Entries in **bold** refer to the historical terms explained in the glossary boxes and the pages on which those glossary boxes occur.